THE PRINCETON REVIEW

THE BEST

L A W

SCHOOLS

1998 EDITION

THE PRINCETON REVIEW

THE BEST

LAW

SCHOOLS

1998 EDITION

DAVID ADAM HOLLANDER, ESQ.
AND ROB TALLIA

Random House, Inc.
New York 1997

http://www.randomhouse.com

Princeton Review Publishing, L.L.C.
2315 Broadway
New York, NY 10024
E-mail: info@review.com

Graph, "Paying for Law School," *USA Today*, Friday, January 10, 1997, p. 1A.
Graph, "Comparison of First-Year Law School Experiences of Women and Men," Law School Admissions Council, Inc., 1996.
Various charts, *Employment Report and Salary Survey*, National Association for Law Placement, 1996.
Every effort has been made to trace and acknowledge copyright material. The authors and publisher would welcome any information from those who believe they own copyright material in this book.

ISBN: 0-679-77781-4

Editor: Amy Zavatto
Production Editor: James Petrozzello
Production Manager: Chee Pae
Designer: Meher Khambata

Manufactured in the United States of America on partially recycled paper.

9 8 7 6 5 4 3 2 1

DEDICATION

To my Mom and Dad, Mr. P. and the whole gang at
TD&H. And to John Maloney—the greatest law student
I ever saw.

CONTENTS

Dedication vii

Acknowledgments xi

Introduction xiii

Chapter 1 The Law School Education 1

Chapter 2 Law School Admissions 17

Chapter 3 The LSAT and the Decay of Civilization 29

Chapter 4 Interview with a Maverick: Dean Lawrence Velvel 47

Chapter 5 Diversity in Law School: A Progress Check 57

Chapter 6 Women in Law School: An Update 73

Chapter 7 Career Outlook 89

Chapter 8 Money Matters 99

Chapter 9 The Law Schools 113

Chapter 10 The Law Schools Ranked by Category 125

Chapter 11 How to Use This Book 139

ABA–Approved Law School Profiles 146

The CBA Schools: An Introduction 489

CBA Law School Profiles 496

School Indexes

Alphabetical 510

State 512

Bibliography 515

Upcoming Reading 517

About the Authors 519

ACKNOWLEDGMENTS

Sibyl Goldman, Frank Tirnady, John McCaghren, Professor Kendall Thomas, Jackson Leeds, Evan Schnittman, Christine Chung, Jay Rosner, Eric Owens, Greta Englert, Professor Mary Becker, and Professor Linda Hirshman.

Special thanks to Chee Pae, James Petrozzello, Amy Bryant, Bruno Blumenfeld, Patricia Acero, Greta Englert, Muammar Hermanstyne, Josh Lewis, Robert McCormack, John Pak, Evelin Sanchez-O'Hara, and Meher Khambata.

Our very, very special thanks to Amy Zavatto for her patience, guidance, and open mind.

INTRODUCTION

You're gonna love this book! *The Princeton Review: The Best Law Schools* has been a bestseller since it came out on the market five years ago. It remains the only guide to American law schools that actually surveys the student's opinions about each school. More than just a reprint of a given law school's admissions booklet, our guide pulls from a number of different sources, giving you the most complete and accurate data on student/faculty ratios, pass rates, ethnic and gender percentages, bar exam pass rates, tuition expenses, and more. But we're not resting on our laurels—no sir.

This year's edition contains the most updated information of any book of its kind on the state of legal education in America. The first eight chapters in the book are all new articles dealing with cutting-edge issues: women in law school, diversity and affirmative action, admissions trends, alternative careers in law, and an exclusive interview with a wily law school dean who is revolutionizing the business of legal education. This year we surveyed more law students than ever before. Plus, we now specially profile California law schools, including fourteen that are not ABA accredited! In short, *The Best Law Schools* is a comprehensive review of almost 200 U.S. law schools, and deals with the hottest issues confronting today's law school applicants.

Most of all we want you to have fun with this book. The process of applying to law school and becoming a lawyer can be a terrific journey. When you choose to become a lawyer, you are making a commitment in your life to take on a tremendous intellectual challenge. You'll be joining a rich and varied profession that has attracted people as diverse as Tony LaRussa, Mahatma Gandhi, Ruth Bader Ginsburg, and Thurgood Marshall. We think there's a lot worse ways you can spend your time (unless of course you're litigating for the cigarette companies). So revel in the process. And let this book serve to illuminate the incredible range of choices you have in demarcating your legal career.

CHAPTER 1
THE LAW SCHOOL EDUCATION

You teach yourself the law. I teach you how to think.

—PROFESSOR KINGSFIELD, *THE PAPER CHASE*

Regrettably, a great many students arrive at law school not really knowing what it's all about. Law school is mind training. You will not walk out of law school fully equipped to practice law. In fact, it is possible to graduate from an ABA-approved law school without ever having seen a courtroom, written a contract, filed a motion, conducted a deposition, or done most other actual tasks performed by lawyers in the profession. What you *get* from law school is a reshaping of your analytical skills—reading, writing, and thinking—using the academic study of law as a pedagogic vehicle. But you will be provided with a phenomenally powerful and versatile education. You will graduate from law school with not only new intellectual tools directly relating to the practice of law but also an education that broadly translates into success in almost any other profession.

LEARNING THE LAW

As you read about the various law schools in this book, you may ask yourself: At which one of these schools will I learn the most law? Which school will teach me the law better than the others? Right now, you might have this vision of yourself in the future, emerging from law school as a veritable walking legal encyclopedia, able to rattle off, on request, the governing rules of law that apply in any given situation. That's not what you learn in law school. Your law school professors will not be handing out a twenty-three-volume bound set listing numerous rules or be referring to some ancient stone tablets that represent what is the law. Rather, you will discover that the law is a constantly evolving system of principles struggling to define its meaning through case-by-case application. These principles are sometimes clear, oftentimes ambiguous. Nonetheless, half of every student's challenge is the same in every law school: To comprehend, synthesize, and coherently articulate these often complex principles to a professor's satisfaction on a three-hour exam at the end of each semester.

Hence, the real question you need to ask is: How motivated am I to teach myself?

In no other educational endeavor could the adage "You get out what you put in" be more true than in law school. In terms of getting a premium legal education, no matter what law school you select, the onus is on the student. In many important respects your first-year experience will depend very little on which school you attend. Every law school gives you access to virtually the same material. The same textbooks, hornbooks, commercial outlines, and various other study aides can be found in every law school bookstore. Each law school library contains the great majority of, if not all, reported federal and state cases in book form as well as statutes, regulations, and law reviews. All have access to the amazing comprehensive computer research services of WESTLAW and LEXIS-NEXIS. Professors in some schools may be better or worse lecturers, but the content they deliver is virtually the same everywhere. The definition of a contract tested on exams at Harvard is the same one tested in Hawaii.

The only real variable in law school is you. It is on the shoulders of each student to draw from the vast resources available as much knowledge and depth of understanding of the subject matter as he or she can. In law school, you must teach yourself the information that you are required to know. This is not an atmosphere where the teacher gives pop quizzes to make sure you're up to speed. Nor is it a coddling environment where you receive a lot of feedback—positive or negative. The law student spends a great deal of time alone, either at home at a desk or in a library carrel, in the company of several large books, toiling in a vast nebula of seemingly incomprehensible material. It is in that time of solitary study where each student accepts or rejects the self-imposed obligation demanded by law school. That is, she will teach herself what she needs to know no matter how difficult the material and no matter how long it takes to learn it. The student who survives (and often succeeds) in law school is the one who refuses to merely *kind* of understand a concept.

The law student spends a great deal of time alone, either home at a desk or in a library carrel, in the company of several large books, toiling in a vast nebula of seemingly incomprehensible material.

1L HELL AND BEYOND

First year they scare you to death,
second year they work you to death,
and third year they bore you to death.

OLD LAW SCHOOL ADAGE

The first semester of law school has the well-deserved reputation of being among the greatest challenges to the intellect and stamina that one may ever face. It is not the material itself that explains the challenge. Though complex and difficult, the subject matter in first-year law school courses is probably no more inherently difficult than what is taught in other graduate or professional schools. What grinds down most 1Ls is the sheer volume of work required night in and night out combined with the foreign nature of the material. With good reason, high stress and anxiety levels among 1Ls is ubiquitous and real.

Along with a certain instructional style (the Socratic method and the casebook), a fairly uniform course of study in the first year has traditionally defined the law school experience. The first-year curriculum in the law school you attend will almost certainly be composed of a combination of the following courses:

TORTS
From the Middle French for "injury," torts are wrongful acts, excluding breaches of contract, that are actionable under civil law. Students of torts might not be surprised to hear that the Latin root of the word means "twisted." Torts can range from the predictable to the bizarre, from Dog Bites Man to Man Bites Dog and everything in between. It is the study of civil court cases with the goal of understanding the changeable legal rationale behind decisions pertaining to the extent of, and limits on, the civil liability of one party for harm done to another.

CONTRACTS
Fairly self-explanatory, it seems. Sign on the dotted line and—presto!—you've got a contract. Well, not exactly. (Remember The Devil and Daniel Webster?) Contractual relationships are a far sight more varied and complicated

than that, as two semesters of your Contracts course will teach you. Again, through the study of past court cases, you will follow the largely unwritten law governing the system of conditions and obligations a contract represents, as well as the legal remedies available when contracts are breached.

CIVIL PROCEDURE

If Contracts and Torts teach you what lawyers do in civil court, then Civil Procedure teaches you how they do it. "Civ. Pro.," as it is generally referred to, is the study of the often dizzyingly complex rules that govern not only who can sue whom, but also how, when, and where they can do it. This is not merely a study of legal protocol, for issues of process have a significant indirect effect on the substance of the law. To understand the importance of this subject, consider not only the complexities of trial procedure, but also the fact that such a small proportion of cases ever go to trial. Rules of Civil Procedure govern the conduct of both the courtroom trial and the steps that might precede it: discovery, pleading, pretrial motions, etc.

PROPERTY

Like so much U.S. law, the laws governing the purchase, possession, and sale of property in the United States often date back hundreds of years to English common law (for instance, "Possession is nine-tenths of the law"). The broad rights of property ownership are a defining element of the society in which we live. You may never own a piece of land, but your life will inevitably and constantly be affected by the laws of property. Not that weeks and weeks spent dwelling on the difference between "real" and "personal" property are going to be very inspiring, but anyone interested in achieving an understanding of broader policy issues will appreciate the significance of this material. Many property courses will emphasize, to varying degrees, economic analysis of Property law, particularly as more and more law professors of the Law and Economics School (originally associated with the University of Chicago) take their places on law school faculties.

CRIMINAL LAW

This is where you learn that the answer to the question "What is a crime?" is no less fuzzy than the answer to the question "What is a sin?" Even if you become a criminal prosecutor or defender, you will probably never prosecute or defend someone charged with the crimes you will be exposed to here. Can a man who shoots the dead body of someone he believes to be alive be charged with attempted murder? What if someone else was forcing him to do so at gunpoint? What if they were both on drugs? What if they both had really rough childhoods? Nowhere will the Socratic dialogue be taken to such extremes as in your Crim. class, and criminal-law professors are notorious for their ridiculously convoluted exam questions.

CONSTITUTIONAL LAW

Often a second-year requirement or even an elective now, Constitutional Law is still a part of the first-year program at many schools. As close to a history class as you will take in your first year, Con. Law will fill in the blanks between such Jeopardy! standards as Marbury, Plessy, Brown, and Roe. Most courses will emphasize issues of government structure (e.g., federalism and separation of powers) and individual rights (e.g., personal liberties, freedom of expression, and property protection). Nearly every law school now offers advanced Con. Law courses that focus on special areas like civil rights or affirmative action.

LEGAL METHODS

One of the few twentieth-century improvements on the traditional first-year curriculum that has taken hold nearly everywhere, this course travels under various aliases, such as Legal Research and Writing or Elements of the Law. In recent years, increased recognition of the importance of legal writing skills has led over half of the U.S. law schools to require or offer a writing course after the first year. This will surely be your smallest class and possibly your only refuge from the Socratic method. Methods courses are often taught by junior faculty or even by second- or third-year students, and are designed to help the first-year student acquire fundamental skills in legal research, analysis, and writing. The Methods course may be the least frightening a 1L faces, but it can easily consume an enor-

Can a man who shoots the dead body of someone he believes to be alive be charged with attempted murder?

mous amount of time. This is a common lament, particularly at schools where very few credits are awarded for the Methods course. So, a typical first-year law student's schedule might look like this:

Fall	Spring
Torts	Property
Contracts	Legal Writing
Civil Procedure	Civil Procedure
Legal Methods	Constitutional or Criminal Law, possibly an elective course

In addition to these course requirements, many law schools require 1Ls to participate in a moot-court exercise. As part of this exercise, students—sometimes working in pairs or even small groups—must prepare briefs and oral arguments for a mock trial (usually appellate). This requirement is often tied in with the Methods course so that those briefs and oral arguments will be well researched—and graded.

BEYOND 1L HELL: FIGHTING THE MALAISE

After you survive your first year and recover some semblance of the free will you surrendered upon arrival at law school, you will have near-total freedom to choose your course of study. Though this sounds marvelous, critics of the law school curriculum have called the second and third years of law school unfocused and even useless. An informal survey of recent law graduates you may know would probably reveal the widely held opinion that, by third year, law school often degenerates into an exercise in clock-watching. (That time may be best spent looking for a job!) The third year does, however, afford law students the opportunity to take more niche law courses, including environmental, family, or tax law.

> An informal survey of recent law graduates you may know would probably reveal the widely held opinion that, by third year, law school often degenerates into an exercise in clock-watching.

SKILLS TRAINING AND CLINICAL LEGAL EDUCATION

The most significant curricular development in American legal education in the last thirty years is an ironic one.

Though the modern law school came into being when certain legal scholars deemed academic training alone sufficient preparation for the practice of law, the latest so-called innovation in legal education is very much a return to the old way, to an emphasis on practical experience as a beneficial component in the training of future lawyers. Hands-on training in the practical skills of lawyering now travels under the name "clinical legal education."

Clinics work in various ways, and the term encompasses a broad range of meanings. Generally, a clinical course is one that focuses on the development of practical lawyering skills rather than on the development of lawyerly thinking or the communication of a body of legal knowledge. In some cases, the word "clinic" means exactly what an outsider would take it to mean: a working law office that serves actual human beings. In these clinics, second- and third-year law students counsel real clients under the supervision of a staff attorney. (A very limited number of law schools allow first-year students to participate in legal clinics.) In those states that grant upper-level law students a limited right to represent clients in court, student participants in a law school's clinic might actually follow cases through to their resolution in court. At some schools, there is a single on-site clinic, which operates something like a general law practice, dealing with cases ranging from petty crime to landlord-tenant disputes. At those schools that have dedicated the most resources to their clinical programs, numerous specialized clinics deal with narrowly defined areas of law, such as employment discrimination. Relatively speaking, however, the opportunities to participate in such live-action programs are limited. Because clinical legal education is so much more expensive than traditional classroom instruction, few law schools can accommodate more than a small percentage of their students in their clinical programs.

More widely available are external clinical placements and simulated clinical courses. In a clinical externship, a student might work with a real firm or public agency several hours a week and meet with a faculty adviser only occasionally. Students who participate in such programs are unpaid, and placements are generally chosen quite carefully to ensure that students stay students rather than becoming mere slaves.

In simulated clinical courses, students might perform all of the duties that a student in a live-action clinic would, but the clients would be imaginary, and their work might be recorded on video for later review with a clinical instructor.

JUDICIAL INTERNSHIPS

Whether your law school offers internships as part of the curriculum or just provides you with leads, these unpaid external placements provide invaluable practical experience and are highly encouraged. Unless you opt (or, depending on your perspective, are lucky enough to be selected) for a judicial clerkship post-law school, this may be the only time you get to work closely with a judge. Judicial interns not only research and draft opinions but observe trials, settlement conferences, and other activities "in chambers." In many internships, the judge will indulge interns, openly discussing his or her decision-making process. Judicial internships are available on both the state and federal levels.

Whether your law school offers internships as part of the curriculum or just provides you with leads, these unpaid external placements provide invaluable practical experience and are highly encouraged.

SPECIALIZATION

A great number of schools now officially sanction special programs of study akin to undergraduate majors. At certain schools, you may receive your J.D. with an official emphasis, such as taxation. The argument in favor of offering such opportunities is easily understood. As in medicine, specialization has become a watchword in the legal profession. General practitioners in the law are becoming less and less common, so it appears to make sense to let future lawyers begin to specialize while still in school. In some cases, however, "special programs" seem to do nothing more than add a few words to your diploma. But a good number of schools take specialization quite seriously, offering active guidance and near-immersion in a particular field of study after a traditional first year. It has been said that this is the trend of the future, particularly for those smaller or newer schools whose graduates cannot simply get by on their school's established reputation of excellence.

A majority of law schools still do not offer formal programs of specialized study. By no means, however, should you regard such a school as resistant to specialization. It is simply that most schools prefer to keep specialization informal.

JOINT DEGREE PROGRAMS

In addition to offering specialized areas of study, many law schools have instituted formal dual-degree programs. These schools, nearly all of which are directly affiliated with a parent institution, offer students the opportunity to pursue a J.D. while also working toward a master's degree. Although the J.D./M.B.A. combination is the most popular joint degree sought, many universities offer a J.D. program combined with masters' degrees in public policy, public administration, and social work, among others. Amid an increasingly competitive legal market, dual degrees may make some students more marketable for certain positions come job time. Dual-degree programs, however, should not be entered into lightly; they are indeed a lot of work.

LEARNING TO THINK LIKE A LAWYER

You may have seen the movie *Hoosiers*—the true story of a small-town Indiana high school basketball team that won the state championship in the 1950s under the guidance of a coach who stressed discipline and fundamentals. Gene Hackman plays the highly principled coach whose new methods of preparing his players are misunderstood, making the new coach quite unpopular with the provincial townfolk. At the first practice, the coach enters the gym announcing to his players that for their first two weeks together most drills will not require a basketball. Baffled, the players ask the coach how they're supposed to get ready to play basketball games without using a basketball. The coach firmly responds, "You're not ready to touch a basketball yet."

Many students lament that law school doesn't prepare them to practice law because it doesn't teach the practical skills you need to be a lawyer in the real world. They are missing the point. Law school is basketball practice without the basketball. It is the footwork and coordination that precedes the full performance. The Socratic method/case method instruction style is intended to train your mind fundamentally in a particular way of thinking. It breaks down old habits of reading, writing, and analyzing you brought with you and replaces those habits with an entirely new set of instincts, perspectives, and expression. Law school is not a vocational school. It is cerebral boot

Law school is not a vocational school. It is cerebral boot camp.

camp. At law school you will undergo a near-total restructuring of your analytical thought process beginning with an acceptance of your own ignorance and a willingness to start at ground zero learning the most basic skills for the first time. Then, after you have learned to think like a lawyer you can get out there and act like one.

THE CASE METHOD

Look at it simply in the light of human nature. Does not a man remember a concrete instance more vividly than a general principle?

—OLIVER WENDELL HOLMES, 1886

In the majority of your law school courses the primary text (and sometimes the only text) will be casebooks—collections of written judicial decisions in actual court cases. On one educational level, each case you read represents a principle or doctrine in the distinct subject (Contracts, Torts, Criminal Law, etc.) of law that you are studying. On an exam you will never be asked to name cases—but you will be asked to apply the legal principles that you gleaned from them to hypothetical cases that your professor presents. On another educational level, you are learning how to analyze cases by studying arguments put forth by the lawyers and the reasoning used by the judge. This is the way you build your own arsenal of arguments to present in class and on exams. This process of absorbing hundreds and hundreds of cases not only exposes you to numerous legal principles that comprise a given topic in the law but, more importantly, it schools you in numerous reasoning tactics that can be used to resolve legal conflicts.

In practical terms, the case method works like this: For every class meeting (including your very first), you will be assigned a number of cases to read. The cases you read are the written judicial opinions rendered in court cases that were decided at the appellate level. (The reason for reading cases from courts of appeals or supreme courts is that such cases turn on issues of law, not of fact. If you are charged, tried, and convicted of murder and wish to appeal your case, you do not simply get a whole new trial at a higher level. You must argue that your conviction was improper, not that it was inaccurate.) Your casebook will contain neither instructions nor explanations. Your assignments simply will be to read the cases and be in a position to answer questions based on them. There will be no written homework assignments, just cases, cases, and more cases.

You will write, for your own benefit, briefs of the cases you are assigned. In a brief, you attempt to summarize the issues and laws around which a particular case revolves and to make sense of a court's findings in terms of similar cases. (The exercise of briefing cases also serves the underlying purpose of getting you to think fundamentally like a lawyer.) Over the course of a semester, you will try to integrate the content of your case briefs and your notes from in-class lectures, discussions, or dialogues into some kind of cohesive whole, which you will call your "outline." Your outline will serve as a basis for the rote memorization of legal rules and rationales you must do to prepare for an exam.

The first time you try to read a case it will be incredibly slow going. You might spend almost an hour on one page. You'll find yourself highlighting every sentence you read. Eventually, though, it will become second nature. The process will be a reflex, occurring when you are reading not only cases but also op-ed pieces, movie reviews, and the backs of cereal boxes. As you read more and more cases, you will quickly be able to distinguish between the important and the unimportant. Your mind will instinctively store and recall multiple sets of complex facts for multiple purposes. You will become a super-active reader, speeding through cases while absorbing five times the level of detail that you were able to before you learned how to brief. After law school, the way you read and analyze will be changed forever. The end product will be a mind that thinks like a lawyer.

THE SOCRATIC METHOD AND HOW TO KEEP IT IN PERSPECTIVE

The use of the Socratic method in the classroom generally follows the same form: directed questioning and limited lecturing. A student is invited by the Socratic professor to attempt a cogent summary of a case assigned for that day's class. Regardless of the accuracy or thoroughness of the student's initial response, he or she is then grilled on the details overlooked or the issues unresolved. A professor will often manipulate the facts of the actual case at hand into a hypothetical case that may or may not have demanded a different decision by the court. This approach forces a reasonably well prepared student to go beyond the immediate issues in a given case to consider its broader implications. The dialogue between the effective Socratic instructor and his victim-of-the-moment will also force non-participating students to question their underlying assumptions of the case under discussion. Is this really a good way to learn?

Many people disagree about the pedagogic value of the Socratic method in law school. Some educators believe that it simply heightens anxiety among students, often unnecessarily humiliating them and creating an unhealthy adversarial relationship between an instructor and his class. Economists point out that the Socratic method is a money-making innovation because it allows a single professor engaged in dialogue with one other student to effectively teach a class of over a hundred students. Social critics complain that the Socratic method is churning out practicing lawyers who are being taught to "argue anything" without concern for the moral implications of their position. What is widely accepted is that the Socratic method is the single aspect of law school that prospective law students fear the most.

Fear not. There is an enlightened perspective on the value of the Socratic method in law school: The method serves as an academic exercise that intrinsically prepares you to think like a lawyer. The Socratic method does not simply teach you how to "argue anything." It conditions your mind to be able to quickly marshal facts and construct an argument based on little, some, or extensive advanced preparation. Real lawyers must do this all the time—not just in a courtroom, but every day when the phone rings at their desks or in the midst of spontaneous negotiations. A lawyer who has benefited from Socratic training becomes a far more powerful advocate for whatever cause he or she decides to champion. If your skills as an advocate are no stronger after law school than before you enrolled, then you didn't get your money's worth.

PREPARATION, PREPARATION, PREPARATION

The anxiety students feel about their inevitable confrontation with the Socratic demon is actually a healthy one. The antidote to that anxiety is another fundamental skill you acquire from a law school education that is of paramount importance: Preparation. The key to both law school success and success as a lawyer is preparation, preparation, and more preparation.

Preparation is a skill you learn by doing. The more prepared you are, the less you will dread being called on in class and the more confident you will be when it actually happens. This important habit of continual preparation translates directly into the actual practice of law. Just as the law student must be prepared daily to handle whatever queries a professor might throw out, the practicing attorney must be prepared to fence with an opposing counsel who suddenly wants to negotiate or to run to court and argue motions on a routine basis. The object lesson of the Socratic Method of instruction is not whether you got the best of your instructor or your instructor got the best of you. The value of the Socratic drill is that it will get you in the lawyerly habit of being "on call."

Through the Socratic method, you are forced to develop an internal mechanism to instantly retain and recall facts, draw distinctions between principles, and argue your position. That instinct, combined with thorough preparation, is the essence of being a lawyer. If fear of humiliation motivates you to prepare, so be it. A better perspective for the law student is to use the Socratic method as the personal daily test of how well you have prepared. The habit of constant, ongoing diligent preparation is a fundamental skill you should carry away with you from a law school education. Plus, if you do the daily preparation you will find yourself in much better shape when it comes time to organize yourself for final exams.

By the way, with very few exceptions, your in-class performance has nothing to do with your final grade. Classroom participation rarely counts in law school. Your entire grade usually rides on one exam given at the end of the semester. So relax and don't worry if you look completely stupid in front of your peers. It won't affect your grade. You may find it helpful to participate in class because it challenges you to verbally articulate the difficult concepts with which you are grappling. But please keep it in perspective: The only thing that counts toward your grade is your final exam.

SOCRATES IS MY FRIEND

It is important for a law student to realize that Socratic training probably propels you to think like a lawyer more so than any other single component of the law school education. If you take nothing else away from your law school education it should be this: The greatest skill a lawyer can have is *not* the ability to find the right answers, but the ability to ask the right questions. Although law students get frustrated when professors annoyingly answer questions with more questions, the professor is, by example, instructing the student how to continuously test the validity of his or her own arguments, the validity of an opponent's argument, and the validity of the court's reasoning. Law students must understand that the pompous, intimidating jerk in front of the class is demonstrating, for the student's own good, the type of constant self-questioning a lawyer must engage in all the time. (You might say that the Socratic method is law school's version of tough love.) Especially on law school exams, professors are far more impressed with your ability to raise issues and argue all sides than with your ability to regurgitate memorized rules of law.

In the best tradition of The Princeton Review, we offer some advice. Fear the Socratic method and you will waste a lot of needed energy being frustrated and angry at your professor. Master the Socratic method and your law school education will be a source of intellectual empowerment.

The greatest skill a lawyer can have is not the ability to find the right answers, but the ability to ask the right questions.

CHAPTER 2
LAW SCHOOL ADMISSIONS

LSAC, LSAT, LSDAS

The Law School Admission Council (LSAC), headquartered in Newtown, Pennsylvania, is the governing body that oversees the creation, testing, and administration of the LSAT (Law School Admission Test). The LSAC also runs the Law School Data Assembly Service (LSDAS), which provides information (in a standard format) on law school applicants to the schools themselves. All American Bar Association (ABA) approved law schools are members of LSAC. Fascinating.

INTRODUCTION

The process of applying to law school, while simple enough in theory, is viewed by many to be about as painful as a root canal. The best way to avoid the pain is to start early. If you're reading this in December, and hope to get into a law school for the following year and haven't done anything about it, you're in big trouble. If you've got an LSAT score that you're happy with, you're in less trouble. However, your applications will get to the law schools after the optimum time and the applications themselves, even with the most cursory glance by an admissions officer, may appear rushed. The best way to think about applying is to start early in the year, take care of one thing at a time, and be totally finished by December.

This chapter will be mainly a nuts-and-bolts manual on what to do when applying to law school and when to do it. There will be a checklist, information about Law School Forums, fee waivers, the Law School Data Assembly Service (LSDAS), and several admissions calendars, which will show you when you need to take which step.

TRENDS

Currently, law schools are experiencing a drop in the number of students that are considered "ABA applicants." At the same time, LSAC is experiencing a drop in the number of students who take the LSAT.

Testing Year	1st Year Enrollment	Total LSAT Administrations	Est. ABA Applicants	% of Takers Applying
1981-82	42,521	119,291	72,912	61%
1982-83	42,034	112,125	71,755	64%
1983-84	41,159	105,076	63,801	61%
1984-85	40,747	95,563	60,338	63%
1985-86	40,796	91,848	61,304	67%
1986-87	40,195	101,235	65,145	64%
1987-88	41,055	115,988	74,938	65%
1988-89	42,860	137,088	82,741	60%
1989-90	43,826	138,865	88,303	64%
1990-91	44,104	152,685	94,026	62%
1991-92	44,050	145,567	91,954	63%
1992-93	42,793	140,054	86,104	61%
1993-94	43,644	132,028	84,574	64%
1994-95	44,298	128,553	78,821	61%
1995-96	44,000	119,186	70,899	59%
1996-97	44,000	105,315	63,500	60%

While there is some talk about certain schools cutting back on the number of seats, there are also fewer people who are applying overall (even though the number of first-year law students has remained much more constant than either the number of LSAT takers or the number of ABA applicants). What does this mean? It might mean that there is slightly less competition for those 1L seats, even though the percentage of students who are applying to schools after they've taken the LSAT has remained fairly constant.

WHEN TO APPLY
Consider these application deadlines for fall admission: Yale Law School, on or about January 10; New York University Law School, on or about February 1; Loyola University Chicago School of Law, on or about April 1. While some of this information may make starting the application process in December seem like a viable option, remember that law schools don't wait until they've received every application to start selecting students. In fact, the longer you wait to apply to a school, the worse your

Law School Forums
Law School Forums are an excellent way to talk with representatives from and gather information on almost every law school in the country simultaneously. Over 150 schools send admissions officers to these forums, which take place around the country between July and November. If possible, GO:

Atlanta, GA   9/12–9/13
Omni Hotel at CNN Center, 100 CNN Center

New York, NY   9/19–9/20
New York Marriott World Trade Center, Three World Trade Center

Houston, TX   10/17–10/18
JW Marriot, 5150 Westheimer

Chicago, IL   10/24–10/25
Chicago Hilton & Towers, 720 S. Michigan Ave.

Boston, MA   10/31–11/1
Marriot Copley Place, 110 Huntington Ave.

Los Angeles, CA   11/14–11/15
Wyndham Hotel at LAX, 6225 West Century Blvd.

chances are of getting into that school. Maybe your chances will go only from 90 percent to 85 percent, but you shouldn't risk it if you don't have to.

Additionally, some schools have "early admissions decisions" options, so that you may know by December if you've been accepted (for instance, NYU's early admission deadline is on or about October 15th). This option is good for a few reasons: It can give you an indication of what your chances are at other schools; it can relieve the stress of waiting until April to see where you're going to school; and, if you're waitlisted the first time around, you might be accepted a bit later on in the process—i.e., when everyone else is hearing from law schools for the first time. However, not every school has an early admission option, and not every school's option is the same, so check with your prospective institutions' policies before you write any deadlines on your calendar.

Let's take a look at the major steps in the application process:

Take the LSAT. All ABA-approved and most non-ABA-approved law schools in the United States and Canada require an LSAT score from each applicant. The LSAT is given in February, June, October (occasionally very late September), and December of each year.

Register for LSDAS. You can register for the Law School Data Assembly Service at the same time you register to take the LSAT—both forms are contained in the *LSAT & LSDAS Registration Information Book* (hence the name).

Select at least seven schools. After you've selected your schools, you'll be able to see which schools want what types of things on their applications—though almost all of them will want three basic things: a personal statement, recommendations, and a resume. Why seven schools? Better safe than sorry. Each applicant should be thinking about putting law schools into three categories: (1) "reach" schools, (2) schools where you've got a good chance of being accepted, and (3) "safety" schools. As a minimum, each applicant should apply to two to three schools in each category. (Most admissions experts will say either 2-2-3 or 2-3-2; to play it safe, apply to three in each category.) It is not uncommon for those with extremely low grades or low LSAT scores (or both) to apply to fifteen or twenty schools.

Write your personal statement(s). It may be that you'll only need to write one personal statement (many schools will ask that your personal statement be about why you want to obtain a law degree), but you may need to write several—which is why you need to select your schools fairly early.

Obtain two or three recommendations. Some schools will ask for two recommendations, both of which must be academic. Others want more than two recommendations and want at least one of your recommenders to be someone who knows you outside traditional academic circles.

Update/create a resume. Most law school applications ask that you submit a resume. Make sure yours is up to date and suitable for submission to an academic situation.

Get your academic transcripts sent to LSDAS. A minor administrative detail, seemingly, but then again, if you forget to do this, LSDAS will not send your information to the law schools. LSDAS helps the law schools by acting as a clearinghouse for information—LSDAS, not you, sends the law schools your undergraduate and graduate school transcripts, your LSAT score(s), and an undergraduate academic summary.

Those are the major steps in applying to law school. From reading this chapter, or from reading the *LSAT & LSDAS Registration Information Book*, you might discover that there are other steps you need to take—such as preparing an addendum to your application, asking for application fee waivers, applying for a special administration of the LSAT, etc. If you sense that you might need to do anything special, start your application process even earlier than what is recommended in the *LSAT & LSDAS Registration Information Book*, which is unquestionably the most useful tool in applying to law school. This information book not only contains the forms to apply for the LSAT and LSDAS, but also has a sample LSAT, admissions information, the Law School Forum schedule, and two sample application schedules. These schedules are very useful. For instance, one sample schedule recommends taking the June 1997 LSAT for fall admission. This schedule allows you to focus on the LSAT in the spring and early summer and then start the rest of your application process rolling. That's good advice—as mentioned in the LSAT chapter in this book, the

Law Schools that Look at Highest LSAT Scores First

Baylor University
Benjamin Cordozo School of Law
Cleveland State University
University of Colorado
University of Denver
Golden Gate University
Gonzaga University
Hamline University
University of Illinois
University of Indiana—Indianapolis
University of Kansas
University of Kentucky
Lewis and Clark College
Louisiana State University
Loyola University—New Orleans
Marquette University
Mississippi College
University of Missouri—Kansas City
University of North Carolina
Northwestern University
University of Notre Dame
University of Pittsburgh
Quinnipiac College
University of Richmond
Roger Williams University School of Law
St. Louis University
University of San Diego
Santa Clara University
Seattle University
St. John's University
Suffolk University
Texas Southern University
Thomas M. Cooley Law School
Tulane University
Wake Forest University
Washburn University
Whittier Law School
Willamette University
William Mitchell College of Law
University of Wyoming

LSAT is the most important factor in getting into the best law school possible.

The sample schedule also indicates that you should research schools in late July/early August. While you are doing this, go ahead and subscribe to LSDAS and send your transcript request forms to your undergraduate and any other educational institutions—there's no reason to wait until September to do this (you should pay LSDAS for nine law school applications, unless you're positive you want to apply to only a few schools). Why do this? Because undergraduate institutions can and will screw up and delay the transcript process—even when you go there personally and pay them to provide your records. This is essential if you're applying for early decision at some law schools—the transcript process can be a nightmare. Your undergraduate institution already has all your money; why should they care about administrative matters like transcripts?

Finally, you should be sending your applications to law schools between late September and early November. Naturally, if you bombed the LSAT the first time around, you're still in good shape to take the test again in October. Another good piece of news on that front is that more and more law schools are now just simply taking the highest LSAT score that each applicant has, rather than averaging multiple scores. If you've got to take the LSAT again, this is good news—but with proper preparation (see the LSAT chapter) you can avoid having to spend too much quality time with the LSAT.

A SIMPLE CHECKLIST

The following is a simple checklist for the major steps of the application process. Each shaded box indicates the recommended month during which you should complete that action.

	Jan.	Feb.	Mar.	Apr.	May	June	July	Aug.	Sept.	Oct.	Nov.	Dec.
Take practice LSAT*	■											
Research LSAT prep companies*		■										
Obtain *Registration Information Book***			■									
Register for June LSAT				■								
Take LSAT prep course				■	■							
Take LSAT						■						
Register for LSDAS							■					
Research law schools							■					
Obtain law school applications								■				
Get transcripts sent to LSDAS								■				
Write personal statement(s)									■			
Update/create resume									■			
Get recommendations									■			
Send early decision applications										■		
Finish sending all applications											■	
Chill												■

*See LSAT chapter.

**The *LSAT & LSDAS Registration Information Book* is traditionally published in March of each year. Call them at (215) 968-1001 to order your materials.

HELPFUL HINTS ON PERSONAL STATEMENTS, RECOMMENDATIONS, RESUMES, AND ADDENDA

While your LSAT score is the most important factor in the admissions process, you should still present a professional resume, get excellent recommendations, and hone your personal statement when preparing your law school applications.

Many law schools still employ the "three-pile" system in the application process:

Pile 1 contains applicants with high enough LSAT scores and GPAs to admit them pretty much automatically.

Pile 2 contains applicants who are "borderline"—decent enough LSAT scores and GPAs for that school, but not high enough for automatic admission. Admissions officers look at these applications thoroughly to sort out the best candidates.

Pile 3 contains applicants with "substandard" LSAT scores and GPAs for that school. These applicants are usually rejected without much further ado. There are circumstances in which admissions officers will look through pile 3 for any extraordinary applications, but it doesn't happen very often.

What does this mean? Well, if you're lucky, you are in pile 2 (and not pile 3!) for at least one of your "reach" schools. And if you are, there's a good possibility that your application will be thoroughly scrutinized by the admissions committee. Consequently, make sure the following four elements of your application are as strong as you can possibly make them:

PERSONAL STATEMENT

Ideally, your personal statement should be two pages long. Often, law schools will ask you to identify exactly why you want to go to law school and obtain a law degree. "I love L.A. Law reruns" is not the answer to this question. There should be some moment in your life, some experience that you had, or some intellectual slant that you are interested in that is directing you to law school. Identify that, write about it, and make it compelling. Then you should have three or four people read your personal statement and critique it. You should select people whom you respect intellectually, not people who will merely say, "Gee, that looks cool." Also, your personal statement is not the place to make excuses, get on your soapbox, or try your hand at alliterative verse. Make it intelligent, persuasive, short, and powerful—those are the writing and analytical qualities law schools are looking for.

RECOMMENDATIONS

Most law schools ask for two or three recommendations. Typically, the longer it has been since you've graduated, the tougher it is to obtain academic recommendations. However, if you've kept your papers and if your professors

Make it intelligent, persuasive, short, and powerful—those are the writing and analytical qualities law schools are looking for.

were tenured, chances are you'll still be able to find them and obtain good recommendations—just present your selected prof with your personal statement and a decent paper you did in their course. That way, the recommender has something tangible to work from. And that's the simple secret to great recommendations—if the people you're asking for recommendations don't know anything specific about you, how can the recommendation possibly be compelling? Getting the mayor of your town or a state senator to write a recommendation only helps if you have a personal and professional connection to them in some way. That way, the recommender will be able to present to the admissions committee actual qualities and accomplishments you have demonstrated. If you've been out of school for some time and are having trouble finding academic recommendations, choose people from your workplace, from the community, or from any other area of your life that is important to you. You should respect the people you choose—you should view them as quality individuals that have in some way shaped your life. If they're half as good as you think they are, they will know, at least intuitively, that they in some way were responsible for part of your development or education, and they will then be able to talk intelligently about it. Simply put, these people should know who you are, where you live, what your background is, and what your desires and motivations are—otherwise, your recommendations will not distinguish you from the ten-foot-high pile that's on the admissions committee desk.

RESUMES

Resumes are a fairly simple part of your application, but make sure yours is updated and proofed correctly. Errors on your resume (and, indeed, anywhere on your application) will make you look as if you don't really care too much about going to law school. Just remember that this should be a more academically-oriented resume, since you are applying to an academic institution. Put your academic credentials and experiences first—no matter what they are.

ADDENDA

If your personal and academic life has run fairly smoothly, you shouldn't need to include any addenda with your application. Addenda are brief explanatory letters written to explain or support a "deficient" portion of your application. Some legitimate addenda topics are: academic probation, low/discrepant GPA, low/discrepant LSAT score, arrests/convictions, DUI/DWI suspensions, a leave of absence or other "time gap," etc. The addenda is not the place to go off on polemics about standardized testing–if you've taken the LSAT two or three times and simply did not do very well, after spending time preparing with a test prep company or private tutor, merely tell the admissions committee that that's what you've done–you worked as hard as you could to achieve a high score and explored all possibilities to help you achieve that goal. Then let them draw their own conclusions. Additionally, addenda should be brief and balanced–do not go into detailed descriptions of things. Explain the problem and state what you did about it. Simply put, do not whine.

GATHERING INFORMATION AND MAKING DECISIONS

There are some key questions that you should ask before randomly selecting law schools around the country or submitting your application to someone or other's list of the "top ten" law schools and saying, "If I don't get in to one of these schools, I'll go to B-school instead." Here are some questions to think about:

WHERE WOULD YOU LIKE TO PRACTICE LAW?

For instance, if you were born and bred in the state of Nebraska, care deeply about it, wish to practice law there, and want to someday be governor, then it might be a better move to go to the University of Nebraska School of Law than, say, University of Virginia, even though UVA is considered a "top ten" law school. A law school's reputation is usually greater on its home turf than anywhere else (except for Harvard and Yale). Apply to the schools in the geographic area where you wish to practice law. You'll be integrated into the community, you may gain some experience in the region doing clinics during law school, and it should be easier for you to get more interviews and position yourself as someone who already knows, for instance, Nebraska.

Fee Waivers

Even though the cost of taking the LSAT, subscribing to LSDAS, paying for LSAT prep materials, and paying application fees will probably be one-hundredth of your total law school outlay, it's still not just a drop in the bucket. The LSAT is $84, LSDAS is $85, and, if you're applying to nine schools, LSDAS charges you another $56. And law school applications themselves are typically around $50 each. As a result, LSAC, as well as most law schools, offers a fee waiver program. If you're accepted into the LSAC program, you get one free LSAT per year, one LSDAS subscription, three LSDAS law school reports, and one TriplePrep Plus (which contains three previously administered LSATs). With proper documentation, you can also waive a good portion of your law school application fees. You can request a fee waiver packet from Law Services at (215) 968-1001, or write to them at Law Services, Attn: Fee Waiver Packet, Box 2000, 661 Penn Street, Newtown, PA, 18940-0998.

WHAT TYPE OF LAW WOULD YOU LIKE TO PRACTICE?

Law schools *do* have specialties. For instance, if you are very interested in environmental law, it might be better to go to the University of Vermont School of Law than to go to New York University. The University of Vermont is one of the most highly regarded schools in the country when it comes to environmental law. So look at what you want to do in addition to where you want to do it.

CAN YOU GET IN?

Many, many people apply to Harvard. Very, very few get in. Go right ahead and apply, if you wish, but unless you've got killer scores and/or have done some very outstanding things in your life (it's okay if you haven't; really it is) your chances are, well, *slim*. Apply to a few reach schools, but make sure they are schools you really want to go to.

DID YOU LIKE THE SCHOOL WHEN YOU WENT THERE?

What if you decided to go to Stanford, got in, went to Palo Alto, California, and decided that you hated it? The weather was horrible! The architecture was mundane! There's nothing to do nearby! Well, maybe Stanford wasn't the best example—but you get the point. Go to the school and check it out. Talk to students and faculty. Walk around. Kick the tires. *Then* make a decision.

CONCLUSION

The application process is pretty darned simple. It's a lot easier than taking the extremely stressful LSAT, which in turn will be a lot easier than your first year of law school—no matter where you go. However, you've still got to want to go to law school. Otherwise, your applications will be sloppy and late, and you won't get accepted by the schools that you really want to go to. If all this administrative stuff seems overwhelming (i.e., you're the type of person who dreads filling out a deposit slip), the major test-prep companies have designed law school application courses that force you to think about where you want to go and make sure you've got all your recommendations, resumes, personal statements, addenda, and everything else together.

Whatever your level of administrative facility, the choice of where you want to go to school is yours. You'll probably

Applying On Computer

Almost all law schools want their applications typed. While this is not exactly an insurmountable hurdle, there are two services that can help you simplify the process. One, Law Multi-App, has more than sixty applications on computer. The other, the LSACD, will be released in September 1997 and will be on display at the fall 1997 Law Forums. The LSACD will have almost all the schools on CD-ROM, and will also contain a searchable database to help you find the best schools for you. You can reach Law Multi-App at (800) 525-2927 or (610) 544-7197, and you can order the LSAC CD-ROM from the LSAT & LSDAS Registration Information Book or from the Law Services website at www.lsac.org.

be paying a lot of money to go, so you should really make sure you go to the place that's best for you. Take the time to do research on the schools, because you'll be paying for law school for a long, long time.

CHAPTER 3
THE LSAT AND
THE DECAY OF CIVILIZATION

We have not used the LSAT so responsibly...we have relied too heavily on LSAT scores and undergraduate grade averages, attaching significance to small differences that statisticians tell us are entitled to no significance.

—PHILIP D. SHELTON, PRESIDENT AND
EXECUTIVE DIRECTOR, LSAC

The Law School Admissions Test (LSAT) is a three-and-a-half-hour multiple-choice examination that is required by every single ABA-accredited law school in the country. So if you have deep antipathy for this form of educational totalitarianism but you want to go to law school, you've got very few options.[1] Therefore, just suck it up (for the moment) and move on. In 1996, the LSAT was administered to 106,000 people, all of whom ostensibly had some desire to go to law school. However, only 65,000 of those people subsequently chose to submit applications to law schools. So when you're filling in your bubbles during the test and looking at all the other people around you, don't worry–chances are, only 60 percent will wind up applying to a school.

Currently, the LSAT is used, in conjunction with one's undergraduate grade-point average, to help law schools (a) differentiate among the vast pool of applicants and (b) "predict" one's first-year law school performance. In theory, it is not an intelligence test, it does not predict how good a lawyer you can be, and it does not test your knowledge of the law in any way, shape, or form. The Medical College Admissions Test (MCAT), by contrast, does test knowledge of physical and biological sciences (to some degree), so medical schools, at least on a surface level, have a way to test knowledge of something that is "useful" in medical school. The LSAT, on the other hand, "only" professes to evaluate one's reading and critical thinking skills and one's ability to logically organize and manage information. Gee, that's not too much to ask of a 101-question, time-compressed, multiple-choice test, is it? But then, the pretensions of standardized testing advocates have never been very modest, have they?

[1] See the CBA-school section in this book...but remember, most of those schools are trying for ABA accreditation. See also the interview with Massachusetts School of Law Dean Lawrence Velvel (chapter 5).

WHY THE LSAT IS SO IMPORTANT

The pretensions of the LSAT folks would be tolerable if the LSAT weren't the *single most important factor in law school admissions*. It is more important than your undergraduate grade-point average, your academic credentials, the reputation of your undergraduate institution, your work experience, your references, and the quality of your application essays. The fact that performance on a 101-question multiple-choice test is more important in evaluating an applicant than their entire undergraduate body of work is among the most intellectually idiotic beliefs in all of higher education. It is also indicative of colossal laziness on the part of the ABA and the law schools themselves. If one's undergraduate performance isn't enough of a predictor of law school performance, then let's design an undergraduate course of study or, at least, some sort of research project required for admission that is enough of a predictor. There are way too many variables to take into account on a standardized test (the testing conditions, for instance, or the specific vocabulary that the LSAT uses) for it to be such an important factor. Yet it is, nonetheless. Of course, if the application process were actually intellectually challenging and required more evaluation time on the part of the law schools, as well as a greater commitment on the part of the applicants, fewer students would actually apply to law schools; and when they did, they would apply to fewer schools. While this sounds great, law schools would no longer generate the massive cashflow they obtain every year through the submission of thousands of applications, and additionally they would then have to spend more money per applicant in evaluating that student's worthiness. And who wants that?

So what should one do about this situation? Get mad, learn absolutely everything there is to know about the LSAT, and get the absolute best possible score—and then go and burn every last scrap of LSAT preparatory material you've purchased.

Bias and Standardized Testing

Not even the SAT is required at all four-year colleges and universities. In fact, more and more undergraduate institutions are not using the SAT as part of their admission requirements. Why? Well, there is almost definitely both an ethnic and a gender bias on the SAT. And, since there is a correlation between the SAT and the LSAT, one can make the fairly valid assumption that there may be both an ethnic and a gender bias on the LSAT as well (for a separate discussion on women and minorities in law school, see chapters 4 and 5).

THE SCORING AND CONTENT OF THE LSAT

The LSAT consists of 101 scored multiple-choice questions, an unscored experimental multiple-choice section, and a writing sample. It is scored on a scale of 120–180, so there are 61 possible scores. Here is the format of a sample LSAT:

Section #	Length	Type of Section	Description
1	35 minutes	Logical Reasoning	Small, "argument-style" paragraphs— between 24 and 26 of them
2	35 minutes	Logical Reasoning— Experimental Section	35 minutes of unpaid work you do for the testing company
3	35 minutes	Reading Comprehension	4 incredibly dull passages, with 5-8 questions each, for a total of 27 questions
Break	10 minutes		A 600-second interval in which the students have time to contemplate their doubt, fear, and exhaustion.
4	35 minutes	Analytical Reasoning	4 "logic" games, with 5-7 questions each, for a total of 24 questions
5	35 minutes	Logical Reasoning	Another group of "argument-style" paragraphs, again with 24-26 questions
6	30 minutes	Essay	An essay that has a very small chance of ever being read by anybody

Remember that the above chart is merely a sample LSAT— the actual test could be in a slightly different order. Some things remain fixed, however—the essay is always last, for instance, and the 10-minute break is always after section 3 (except when you have the occasional test proctor with the brainpower of a school of guppies). Furthermore, the experimental section is typically among the first three sections of the test—though theoretically it could be section 5.[2] Finally, it's rare to get three Argument sections in a row (i.e., two scored and one unscored)—though that can happen.

One good thing about the LSAT (which differentiates it from the SAT and the GMAT, for instance) is that there is no penalty for guessing. But since there are five answer choices for each question, random guessing will get you only about twenty correct answers, which translates to the very low score of 124. Nevertheless, you can still pick up a few extra points by going slower on the test, skipping questions that look like they will bog you down, and then going back later on and merely randomly guessing on those questions.

Since its inception in 1947, the LSAT's content and scale have changed at various times. The LSAT was first scored on a 200–800 scale, and then up to 1991, it was scored on a 10–48 scale. In 1991, however, the scale changed to 120–180. Why did the scale change? Well, too many people began scoring too highly (the high 40s) on the test in the late 1980s and early 1990s. There were only 39 possible scores in the pre-1991 scale, but there are 61 now—which helps the testers to spread out the curve and better "differentiate" among test takers. In turn, this scale change helped admissions officers out. On the old scale many applicants were scoring very highly on the LSAT and it was more difficult to tell how worthy a student was. Admissions folks were overworked since they had to use rating tools besides the LSAT, so the scale changed. The two graphs on the following page show how the LSAT curve spread out and steepened significantly in 1991:

LSAT Score Conversion Scale

This conversion scale is based on the reported percentile equivalencies for versions of the LSAT given between 1988 and 1991. The exact percentile of a given score will vary with each test form, but only slightly. For purposes of estimating your chances of admission to a particular law school, such and approximation is more than close enough.

LSAT Score	%-ile
180	99.9
179	99.9
178	99.9
177	99.8
176	99.8
175	99.7
174	99.6
173	99.4
172	99.1
171	98.8
170	98.4
169	97.8
168	97.2
167	96.4
166	95.2
165	94.1
164	92.5
163	91.1
162	88.9
161	86.5
160	83.9
159	81.3
158	78.3
157	74.5
156	70.4
155	66.5
154	63.3
153	58.7
152	54.8
151	50.5
150	45.9
149	41.4
148	37.9
147	33.6
146	29.4
145	26.5
144	23.8
143	20.4
142	17.4
141	15.4
140	13.2
139	10.7
138	9.7
137	7.7
136	6.9
135	5.4
134	4.5
133	3.9
132	3.0
131	2.5
130	2.0
129	1.6
128	1.3
127	1.0
126	0.9
125	0.8
124	0.6
123	0.5
122	0.4
121	0.4

[2]Naturally the testing folks don't want their precious "equating" section to be at the end of the exam, when you're tired and pretty much at the end of your emotional rope. They'd rather administer this section early, when you're still thinking and acting relatively human. This gives them better data for question testing. Some questions you see on experimental sections will be used on later LSATs. Of all the obnoxious things about standardized testing, the experimental section, where you do unpaid work for the testing company, is the most obnoxious thing of all.

The LSAT Curve Steepens

A comparison of the old LSAT scoring distribution
with the new anti-score inflation curve

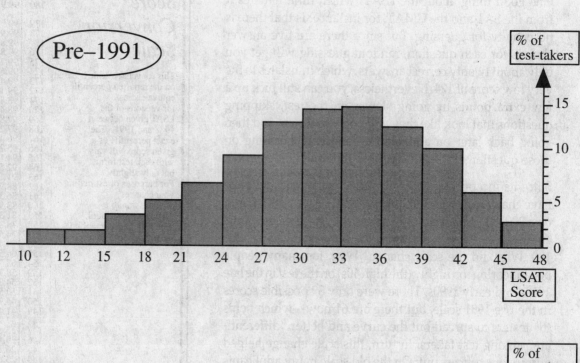

Pre–1991

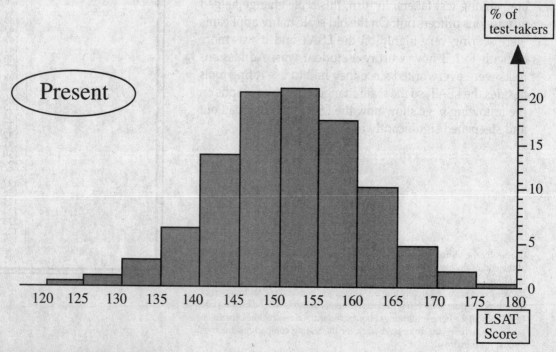

Present

What this scoring change did is obvious—first, it bunched more people in the middle (i.e., between 140 and 160) of the curve. This helped the top-end law schools to weed out a bunch of people who would not have scored within that margin before 1991. Additionally:

> The middle of the curve is packed tight, and very few people score at the extremes. Perhaps more important, there are now twenty-one scoring slots for the top 15 percent of the country (from 160 to 180), more than twice what there were under the 10 to 48 scale. Furthermore, a perfect score of 180 in the current format corresponds to a percentile of 99.9+, into which perhaps a few dozen test takers will fall annually. In 1991, perfect LSAT scorers could have filled Harvard's first-year class; now they would have a hard time fielding a softball team.[3]

Clearly, the pre-1991 LSAT was not a good enough diagnostic tool for the law schools, and so presto! Change the curve (a much cheaper solution than paying more admissions officers to actually read and evaluate all application essays and recommendations) and all the law schools are happy again. (Well, the top law schools are. Now, all the rest of the law schools get to muddle around in that 140–160 range, where they probably have a bit tougher time differentiating among the students.)

However, that's not all the schools are happy about. Not only has the LSAT scoring curve gotten tougher, so has the content of the LSAT. When the LSAT was first administered, there was math on the test. But by the mid-1980s, the content of the LSAT was Arguments, Logic Games, Reading Comprehension, and a section called Facts and Rules. In Facts and Rules, the tester was given a set of facts and then two rules in which to evaluate those facts. The answer choices were standard, i.e., one choice was that there was enough information to "rule" on the facts, another was that there wasn't, etc. Seems at least remotely lawyerly, doesn't it?

Well, be that as it may, Facts and Rules was eminently coachable. Consequently, the major test preparation companies were having a ball helping their students through this section. If this was a lawyerly-type section, and many

---

[3]From the 1997 edition of *The Princeton Review's Best Law Schools*, Ian Van Tuyl, p. 79.

students could be coached into doing very well on it, what was the implication of that? Clearly, the fact that many people could learn lawyerly-type things. So after the test prep companies had pretty much cracked this section in the 1980s, goodbye Facts and Rules. Then the test was changed to three equal (in terms of time allotted) sections of Arguments, Logic Games, and Reading Comprehension. But still too many people were scoring too highly on the exam—since Logic Games is another eminently coachable section.

So, in that watershed year of 1991, the LSAT changed to its current format—two sections of Arguments, one of Reading Comprehension, and one of Logic Games. Arguments, ostensibly the toughest section on the LSAT, comprises 50 out of 101 questions; Reading Comprehension is 27 questions; and Logic Games is merely 24 questions. So it has been for the past six years, and there is no indication that the format will change anytime soon. In today's testing racket, this is actually an eerily long time for a standardized test to be running without a format change. Furthermore, the GMAT and the GRE now offer computer-adaptive versions of their exams. The LSAT is merely at the research stage of computer-adaptive testing. The LSAC (Law School Admission Council, the folks who bring you the LSAT) has embarked on a research study that will end in approximately the year 2000. Only then will LSAC make a decision to either go computer-adaptive or stick with the pencil-and-paper version of the LSAT.

Thus, in the history of the LSAT, this is probably the worst time to be taking it. But don't despair.

BE ALL YOU CAN BE
The LSAT, in case you blotted this out of your mind, is the single most important factor in the entire law school application process. In many cases, your LSAT score can and will determine where you are going to go to law school. At the very least, it will probably determine whether or not you're going to go to a top-20 school, a first-quartile school, or a second-quartile school, etc. Therefore, you've got to prepare. There's no way around it.

Currently, many people take the LSAT "to see how they'd do," "to see if they really want to go to law school," or "to see if they've got what it takes to be a lawyer." As we have seen, the LSAT is nothing more than a hurdle that you have to jump over and, in terms of the correlation between your score and your success with the law itself, may as well be testing you on the agricultural history of Patagonia. Any test preparation instructor worth his salt will tell you: *Standardized tests basically test how well you do on that particular standardized test.* Additionally, there is no current course of study in college that specifically teaches you the skill of performing well on standardized tests. However, even though the LSAT is a load of crap, it is a very difficult test. Taking it cold is NOT the way to go.

First of all, you should only be taking the LSAT if you've already made up your mind that you really, really, really want to go to law school. "Seeing what you might get" on the LSAT should not be a component of your application strategy. People who are properly motivated to prepare for the LSAT and who really want to go to law school will do better on the test than those people who are taking it for exploratory purposes. If you need help in deciding whether or not you should go to law school, there are several options for you: Work as a paralegal, intern in a law firm or similar place, attend a law camp, read books about the law school experience, etc. You will not do as well on the LSAT if you're merely taking it cold.

Why is that? Simply, the LSAT is the toughest of all the standardized tests. Only 24 out of 101 questions have a "correct" answer (Logic Games), as opposed to Arguments and Reading Comprehension, where you are asked to choose the "best" answer. The GMAT and the SAT are each half math; the GRE is one-third math and has Logic Games; and the MCAT is part science. Only the LSAT tests almost no specific knowledge of anything—which turns out to be the toughest type of standardized test. Therefore, the only proven course of study for the LSAT is to study the LSAT itself.

Naturally, as writing and administering the LSAT is, for LSAC, a multi-million-dollar business, so is the teaching of the test by private test preparation companies. However, teaching people how to drive or how to speak a foreign

Law Camp

The National Institute for Legal Education (NILE) is a great law camp that gives potential future lawyers a real taste of life in law school. Students go for either one or two weeks and are put into mock law school classes taught by actual law professors. Such an experience is much more valuable in terms of the decision-making process than a three-and-a-half-hour standardized test, which relates to nothing except itself.

language is a money making endeavor. And while you might think that paying a test-preparation company $900 is highway robbery, especially compared to paying a driving school $500 for a much more useful skill, consider the fact that law school itself will probably cost you $75,000, at least. Suddenly that $900 doesn't look so bad, or, at least, that $75,000 looks totally obscene. Either way you slice it, you're going to be spending so much money once you get to law school that the amount of money you spend on test preparation and application fees will look like chump change.

That doesn't mean that you should simply go out and start writing big checks. There's a very simple first step: Order a recent LSAT from LSAC (you can call them at (215) 968-1001, or go to their website at www.lsac.org) and take it. Do not, however, take it casually over the course of a few weeks—instead, buy a friend a six-pack of beer and have him or her come over and administer the test to you under strict timed conditions. You should follow the test booklet instructions exactly and do it right—simulate an actual testing experience as much as possible. Don't do this in the middle of a party or on the beach or some such nonsense and then give yourself a few extra points at the end because "you'll do better on test day." Then, have your friend score it. Once you've got a score, you've got a baseline for making a test preparation decision.

What's a good score on the LSAT? It's the score you need to get you into the law school you want to go to. Remember that a large part of the admissions game is the formula of your UGPA (undergraduate grade-point average) times your LSAT score. Chances are you're at a point where your UGPA is pretty much fixed (if you're reading this early in your college career, start getting very good grades immediately), so the only piece of the formula you can have an impact on is your LSAT score. Look at the Law Schools section of this book and consult the UGPA/LSAT medians.

If your practice LSAT score is already at a point where you've got a very high percentage chance of getting accepted to the law school of your choice, chances are you don't need very much test preparation. You should order half a dozen or so more real tests from LSAC (always order the most recent exams) and work through them over the course of a few months, checking your progress and making sure you understand why you are making specific mistakes. If your college or university offers a free or very cheap prep course, take it to get more tips on the test. Many of these courses are taught by pre law advisors who can speak very intelligently about the test and are committed to helping you get the best score you can. Also, you can buy LSAT preparation books at the bookstore (such as The Princeton Review's *Cracking the LSAT*). Then go and take the real test and never worry about it again.

However, chances are you may not be at the score you need for the school that you want to go to. Many students are surprised at how poorly they do the first time they take a dry run on the LSAT. But it's better to be surprised sitting at home than actually taking the test for real. The fact that you got all As in college and made academic honors or that you've got a Ph.D. in archaeology or discovered a new solar system or something does not mean that you'll do well on this test. Many academically strong candidates make the mistake of assuming that the LSAT is no more difficult than their college courses and go in cold. It's a big mistake.

So you've taken your practice LSAT under timed conditions, and you're, say, ten or fifteen points below where you wish to be. You can still take the course of action outlined in the previous paragraphs, but at this point you probably should go to an expert. Test preparation companies actually spend quite a lot of money analyzing the tests and measuring the improvements of their students. You should talk to other people who have scored well on the test to find out which company or companies they were successful with. And you should also do a significant amount of research about these companies yourself. For instance, you should ask questions such as: How many hours of instruction do they give? Do they use real, previously released LSATs in their courses? How many tests can you take under actual conditions? When you tell them what you scored on your practice test, see what kind of response you get from them. If you're going to spend the money on a private course, you should do enough research so that you know you're getting the most bang for your buck.

> *The fact that you got all "A"s in college and made academic honors or that you've got a Ph.D. in archaeology or discovered a new solar system or something does not mean that you'll do well on this test.*

However, once you've paid the money to the test prep company, you won't simply be getting a magic pill from them that allows you to kick ass on the LSAT. The first thing any reputable company will tell you is this: Your score will go up exponentially in relation to the amount of work you put into the course. If you don't do all the homework that these companies' instructors assign and follow their instructions, you've flushed a whole bunch of money down the toilet. You don't go to a foreign language class and then start conjugating verbs differently than your teacher does—what's the point of going at all? So if you're going to spend the money on the course, be as committed to that course as you plan to be in the courses you will take in law school itself—because the LSAT, like law school, is no cakewalk.

A FEW BASIC TIPS

The first basic tip to doing well on the LSAT is to *slow down*. Any function you perform, from basic motor skills to complex intellectual problems, will be affected by the rate at which you perform that function. Generally, the slower you go, the better you'll do. This goes for everything from cleaning fish to taking the LSAT. On the next page you'll find a sample scoring grid:

```
              CONVERSION CHART
   For Converting Raw Scores to the 120-180 LSAT
                  Scaled Score

Reported Score                  Raw Score
                    Lowest              Highest
    180               99                  101
    179               —*                  —*
    178               98                  98
    177               97                  97
    176               96                  96
    175               95                  95
    174               94                  94
    173               93                  93
    172               92                  92
    171               91                  91
    170               90                  90
    169               89                  89
    168               88                  88
    167               86                  87
    166               85                  85
    165               84                  84
    164               82                  83
    163               81                  81
    162               79                  80
    161               77                  78
    160               76                  76
    159               74                  75
    158               72                  73
    157               71                  71
    156               69                  70
    155               67                  68
    154               65                  66
    153               63                  64
    152               61                  62
    151               59                  60
    150               58                  58
    149               56                  57
    148               54                  55
    147               52                  53
    146               50                  51
    145               48                  49
    144               46                  47
    143               44                  45
    142               43                  43
    141               41                  42
    140               39                  40
    139               37                  38
    138               36                  36
    137               34                  35
    136               32                  33
    135               30                  31
    134               29                  29
    133               27                  28
    132               26                  26
    131               24                  25
    130               23                  23
    129               22                  22
    128               20                  21
    127               19                  19
    126               18                  18
    125               17                  17
    124               16                  16
    123               15                  15
    122               14                  14
    121               13                  13
    120                0                  12
```

*There is no raw score that will produce this scaled score for this form.

As you can see, you can still get twenty-five questions wrong and receive a score of 160, which is a very good score (it's in the 84th percentile). That means that you can get at least six questions wrong per section—or, even better, you can IGNORE the two or three toughest, most convoluted questions per section, STILL get three or four others wrong, and get an excellent overall score. And if you're at a lower score level at the beginning of your LSAT practice curve, you can ignore even more questions per section until your accuracy increases. Your goal here is to find your particular working speed at which you will get the highest number of questions correct without sacrificing a significant degree of accuracy.

Second, *remember that there is no guessing penalty*. This means that if you don't have time to finish the exam, you've got to leave yourself at least 30 seconds at the end of each section in which to go back and bubble in random answers to any questions you didn't have time to get to. Be careful with waiting until the last possible second to do this, because proctors occasionally cheat students out of anywhere from 15 seconds to 2 minutes per section. By guessing, you can pick up anywhere from two to four points per section, even on the questions you didn't have time to do or didn't like the look of, depending on the total number of questions you skipped originally. Your goal here is to remember to fill in every little bubble before time is called. Pick a letter, any letter, and use it to fill in the questions you left blank.

A third basic tip is to employ *Process of Elimination* at all times. On three-quarters of the LSAT, you're not looking for the *right* answer, only the *best* answer. Eliminating even one answer choice will increase your chances of getting the question right from 20 to 25 percent. Process of Elimination dictates that you should look at not only each answer choice's worth as compared to the question, but also each answer choice as compared to every other answer choice. If you can narrow the range of choices down to two or even three, you've taken a step in the right direction. Very few things will look exactly right on the LSAT—more often than not, you'll be picking the lesser of five evils. Therefore, don't get discouraged when an answer does not leap out at you from the choices given—decide what is wrong with each answer choice and then pick the answer that you can criticize the least. Your goal here is to remember to measure the comparative worth of each answer choice against all the other answer choices, and to constantly look for reasons why a particular answer choice is bad, so you can eliminate it, thereby increasing the chances of getting the correct answer.

Fourth, *attack the test at all times*. Read the test with an antagonistic, critical eye. Read it like it's a contract you're about to sign with the devil—look for holes and gaps in the reasoning of the specific arguments you will encounter. Many LSAT questions revolve in some way around what is WRONG with the stated line of reasoning—the more you can identify what is wrong with a problem before going to the answer choices, the more successful you will be.

Additionally, *write all over your test booklet*. Actively engage the exam and put your thoughts on paper. Circle words, cross out all answer choices you've eliminated, draw diagrams, and connect the dots. In the instructions for Logic Games, the LSAT says that "it may be helpful to draw a rough diagram." Actually, the more exact and complete your diagram is, the more helpful it will be. Drawing detailed diagrams is not what the LSAT writers expect you to do—so do it.

Furthermore, do the questions *in the order you wish to do them*. Just because Logic Game 1 is presented first, it doesn't mean that it's the game you have to start with. There is no order of difficulty on the LSAT[4], so you should go and hunt down those types of questions that you are best at. If a Reading Comprehension passage looks inscrutable, skip it. If you read the first sentence of an argument and you don't know what the hell it's saying, move on—the second sentence won't clarify matters for you. If you cannot picture or diagram a Logic Game in any way, go find one that you can diagram.

Remember, the LSAT is designed to keep you OUT of law school—not facilitate your entrance into it. Therefore, fight

---

[4]This is decidedly different than the SAT, and GRE and GMAT math, where there is indeed an order of difficulty. On those exams, it behooves you to spend more time on the earlier, easier questions—you've got a greater percentage chance of getting those questions correct. Not so on the LSAT.

against the test every step of the way, up until time is called for section 5—don't lose steam or get discouraged, even if you think you did poorly on a particular section. That section may have been (and probably was) the experimental section.

Finally, *do not get overly stressed about this exam*. Many students have done well in practice test situations and then freaked out on the real exam. One test prep teacher remembers a student who had a very vivid dream: She went in to take the LSAT, and each bubble was about six feet high. She kept trying to fill in the first gigantic bubble and didn't even get to answer a second question. While this *Alice in Wonderland*-like experience may never happen to you (while you're sober, at least), it's a cautionary tale against how stressed one can become. Don't try to kid yourself into not being stressed, because some stress is natural. But if you feel as if your stress level will damage your performance, do whatever is necessary to keep it under control—yoga, relaxation exercises, etc. A good test prep company will have some material about test anxiety in their course—it can't hurt to check it out. It would be a waste to study so hard for the LSAT only to get so tense that every answer looks right or that your proctor seems to have rabbit ears.

Here's a recap of the tips mentioned above:

- **Slow down**—do fewer questions, and do them more effectively.

- **Bubble everything in**—remember there is no guessing penalty on the LSAT.

- **Use Process of Elimination**—look for the least bad answer out of all the choices.

- **Attack the Exam**—read everything super-critically.

- **Use that pencil**—write all over your test booklet.

- **Make your own order**—do questions in the order you want to do them.

- **Don't let a "bad" section throw you off**—don't get discouraged if you think you didn't do too well on a particular section. It may very well have been the experimental section.

- **Watch your stress level**—some stress is good, even desirable. Just don't freak.

Please remember that the LSAT is only a test and only one hurdle of many that you will encounter throughout your life and your legal career. Treat the LSAT with respect, since it is a very difficult test, but also recognize that it's a scam on the part of higher education to create a pseudoscientific, anti-intellectual method of distinguishing some applicants from other applicants. Use this knowledge in any way you need to so that you are able to get the best possible score on this exam. Then let it fade to black, like all nightmares eventually do.

CHAPTER 4
INTERVIEW WITH A MAVERICK:
DEAN LAWRENCE VELVEL,
MASSACHUSETTS SCHOOL OF LAW

Dean Lawrence Velvel

"End the secrecy so that people know what is going on and can comment intelligently on what is going on."

By David Adam Hollander, Esq.

I first met Dean Lawrence Velvel fifteen years ago in my freshman dorm room. He had just finished playing a game of one-on-one basketball with his son, my roommate. Wearing gym shorts, high-top sneakers, and a faded University of Michigan T-shirt, he sat on my roommate's single bed, pouring over the Sunday New York Times. Then a practicing Washington, D.C., attorney, Mr. Velvel raced through each headline and column alerting me to the various injustices of the day that enraged him. His intensity was self-evident. Little did I know that he had just begun to fight.

In the late 1980s, Velvel headed to New England to pursue a career in academia. Fed up with the widespread inadequacy he observed in the field of legal education, Velvel decided to prepare law students his way. In 1988, he co-founded Massachusetts School of Law at Andover (MSL), where he created a curriculum that emphasized practical lawyering skills. Instead of hiring law professors who spent their professional lives doing research, Velvel recruited judges and seasoned practitioners to teach his classes. At MSL students not only take the traditional subjects like Contracts and Criminal Law, but also take courses like Writing for Lawyers, Motions and Litigation Practice, The Legal Profession, Factual Investigation, Asset and Protection Planning, and Accounting for Lawyers.

Perhaps even more ambitious are Velvel's innovations in MSL's admission policy. Rejecting the American Bar Association (ABA) standard, MSL does not require an LSAT score from its applicants. Instead, MSL gives a mandatory personal interview to all those seeking admission. And, while the median first-year tuition to law school has skyrocketed up around $20,000, MSL charges only $9,000 a year.

After MSL was denied provisional accreditation by the ABA in 1993, Dean Velvel sued the ABA, the Law School Admissions Council (LSAC), and about two dozen others alleging that the defendants acted as a "cartel" to eliminate competition in the field of legal education. Clearly, he was on to something because shortly after his suit was filed in 1995, the Justice Department began prosecuting the ABA for antitrust violations in its accreditation process. Essentially, the ABA threw up their hands and entered into a settlement with the Justice Department, agreeing to change a number of its accreditation standards. Those changes were not enough for Dean Velvel. He continues his legal battle with the ABA, claiming, among other things, that his law school should not have to require the LSAT from its applicants and that the ABA's student-faculty ratios unnecessarily drive up the already exorbitant costs of law school tuition. On February 28, 1997, a United States Circuit Court of Appeals affirmed a lower court's dismissal of Massachusetts Law School's suit against the ABA. Not surprised, Velvel has called the decision an obvious display of "judicial bias." He has another suit pending in state court against the ABA as well.

When I caught up with him in the spring of 1997, I wanted to see if the father of my old college roommate was becoming a little battle-weary. Needless to say, the gloves are still off.

TPR: Does the ABA hold a "monopoly" on legal education?

VELVEL: Pretty much—yes. There are only a handful of states in this country that will permit graduates of a law school to take their bar examinations and practice law if the school is not ABA-approved. That would include schools in California, Tennessee, Alabama, Georgia, and Massachusetts. So, right from the get-go there is an advantage of a school attaining ABA accreditation. When you get right down to it, there are forty-six jurisdictions in which a school would not be able to survive without ABA accreditation because its students would not be able to take the bar examination in the state where the school is located. In reality, when you get past, let's say, twenty to twenty-five schools, most schools are largely in-state student bodies.

Now, the extent to which the monopoly is not a perfect monopoly is reflected by the following: There are a large number of states—eighteen or twenty—that permit persons to take their bar examinations after a period of practice in another state. So for example, if a person graduates from a school in California that is not ABA-accredited and passes the California bar exam, then after three or five years of practice in California, sometimes longer, those eighteen to twenty states will let that person sit for their bar exam. Now, some people don't mind waiting those three years; others don't care to wait. Massachusetts School of

Law (MSL) has been making inroads on the monopoly because the states of Maine, New Hampshire, California, and West Virginia permit our students to take their bar as soon as they pass the Massachusetts bar exam. Vermont actually permits our students to take the bar even before they pass the Massachusetts state bar. We are attempting to make further inroads. Right now, we have petitions pending in Rhode Island and Connecticut.

TPR: What role does the LSAC have in this monopoly?

VELVEL: Well, it's a little known fact that without the LSAC and what it has done, the ABA either would not have the monopoly or, far more likely, it would have a monopoly but would have been unable to do most of the things it has done. It would have been unable to force upon law schools the tremendous high-cost requirements, which create high-cost tuition.

Here's a little history for you. The LSAC decided in the early 1970s as did the American Association of Law Schools (AALS) that it wanted to be a big player in legal education and ABA accreditation. Both of these organizations began to infiltrate the ABA's Section of Legal Education to the point where the leadership of all three organizations is approximately the same leadership. The same people hold high positions in all three organizations. And it's fair to say that there is somewhere between thirty to forty people in legal education—a field that has about 6,000 professors—who control all of legal education. These people have been called the "administrative ruling class" of legal education.

In the late 1970s–early 1980s, the LSAC was looking around for some way to use the huge sums of money that it was making and retaining because all applicants were forced to take the LSAT. Being forced to take the LSAT, of course, is a consequence of both the desire of law schools (a) to be elitist and (b) to simplify the jobs of their professors and administrators by creating an admission process that is by the numbers and requires no judgment—and the LSAT is a result of that basic fact that the ABA had forced it upon all law schools. So the LSAC was making these huge gobs of money, and it was looking around for something to do with the money in its "surplus." (Remember they're a non-profit organization or we'd call it "profit.") So the LSAC decided to use this surplus as seed money to create Law

> *"Well, it's a little known fact that without the LSAC and what it has done, the ABA either would not have the monopoly or, far more likely, it would have a monopoly but would have been unable to do most of the things it has done."*

Access in order to provide and arrange for loans to law students with which they could pay their tuition. Law Access became the major player in the field of law school loans. You must always remember, the ABA accreditors really are, in part, the very same people who run the LSAC. The people who run LSAC make up a large portion of the ABA accreditation group called the Section of Legal Education and Admission to the Bar.

TPR: That sounds like a far cry from the Department of Education regulation that requires the ABA and LSAC to be "separate and independent"?

VELVEL: You can't even mention that regulation and those organizations on the same planet.

But it was those loans from Law Access that enabled the ABA to impose upon law schools the requirements that drove tuitions through the roof, because without those loans students would have no way of paying the high tuitions. It is now widely accepted that the liberal provision of loans has been one of the major engines in the inflation of tuition for all of higher education. But the law schools outstripped them all, raising tuition three times over the rate of inflation in the past twenty years.

Therefore, the LSAC is responsible for enabling the ABA not just to continue as a monopolist, but as a monopolist to impose upon all law schools the requirements that are causing law students to pay up to $24,000 a year in tuition. This is not just irresponsible. It is irresponsibility in the service of economic selfishness.

There's one point I really want to make. In this interview we will keep referring to the "ABA." There is a very realistic sense in which it is hardly the "ABA" at all. It is really the ABA's Section of Legal Education headed by its "council." The way the ABA works, each section has extensive power to do whatever it wants. The ABA is such a political organization, with the people in the central governing groups being hell-bent to become president, that they wish to offend nobody. The ABA Board of Governors, which is their central body, has for years permitted the Section of Legal Education to run wild. The Department of Justice said in their lawsuit against the ABA that the Board of Governors did not even know what the Section of Legal

> *"This is not just irresponsible. It is irresponsibility in the service of economic selfishness."*

Education was doing. Now that they do know what the Section of Legal Education has done they are continuing *not* to control it because everyone on the Board of Governors is only concerned about political advancement.

TPR: Did the Department of Justice (DOJ) go far enough in its prosecution of the ABA for antitrust violations?

VELVEL: In no way did it go far enough. The DOJ left in place most of the machinery and many of the rules by which the Section of Legal Education has caused educational quality in the law schools to be far below what it should be. This is essentially because the law schools follow an education model that stresses law taught in the abstract by professors who have no practical experience. Instead we should follow the educational model used for the past ninety years by medical schools, which mixes tremendous amounts of practical experience and practical teaching along with academic knowledge.

TPR: Should there be more emphasis on practical lawyering skills in legal education today?

VELVEL: The Section of Legal Education has made only the slightest inroad insofar as requiring schools to give practical education. Most schools still don't give and fewer students are able to take the courses that could be considered practical education courses. This is a terrible situation in which the professors remain research-oriented and the schools are not going to be able to afford to give practical education. They can't afford it because they are required by the ABA to create a research-oriented institution comprised of people who have virtually no experience in practice. The average law professor has about two years' practical experience. And that experience consists generally of working as a glorified law clerk in a big firm after serving as a clerk for a judge for a year. That person has no practical experience whatsoever.

TPR: For the first time ever, the ABA published bar pass rates for its schools. That's a good thing. What other important consumer information is still being withheld?

VELVEL: What should be made available is the entire accreditation record on each school, which would consist of each school's self-study, answers to the ABA questionnaire, the ABA's site evaluation reports, the responses by the schools to the site evaluation reports, the ABA's action letters, the schools' responses to the action letters, and any transcripts or documents upon appeal before the accreditation committee to the council (to the Section of Legal Education) and from the council to the House of Delegates.

What would people learn from this? Number one, if all of this material were available, even though it would be beyond the reading power of any given applicant, you may rest assured that an industry would spring up to advise us what schools, on the basis of these records, appear to be good schools doing good things, and what schools appear to be not such hot schools and why they are not so hot. Just like we now have an industry of college advisers, we would have a sophisticated industry of law school advisers. No doubt The Princeton Review and other such companies would be in the forefront of such a industry.

What would applicants find out from these documents that the prevailing secrecy still does not allow them to know? What the schools are claiming in response to the alleged deficiencies and what the accreditors are saying in response to those responses. [With this knowledge] one is in a far better position to evaluate if the Section of Legal Education is giving you a lot of hooey designed to promote its own interests, that is, the interests of the law professorate. Only then one can determine whether there is something valid in what the Section on Legal Education is saying.

> "[With this knowledge] one is in a far better position to evaluate if the Section of Legal Education is giving you a lot of hooey designed to promote its own interests, that is, the interests of the law professorate."

Legal education should be no different than anything else in our society. Wherever people are given access to information they learn a lot more of value to them than if access is denied. That is why we have corporate disclosure laws for securities regulations. That is why we have sunshine laws in states. That is why we have a Freedom of Information Act. That is why Congress is up in arms today about giving money for political campaign contributions. What I'm saying is no different than what has been true in this country for scores of years and was encapsulated by Justice Brandies when he said, "Sunlight is the best disinfectant."

TPR: Why don't you require the LSAT for admission to your law school?

VELVEL: The LSAT is a socially pernicious test. I need not go into all the reasons as you guys know more about this than I do. We decided, and it is well known, that the test disadvantages mid-life people, minority people, working-class people, people who don't read particularly fast even though they may be very thoughtful and intelligent, and people who, for whatever reasons in the past, have not learned the techniques that are desirable on multiple-choice tests. Such techniques are not necessarily desirable and in fact may be quite undesirable in both law school and the legal profession. These are techniques that favor speediness and facility rather than thought. We decided that if we accepted standardized test scores but said we wouldn't use them nobody would believe us. Then we might lose a lot of very fine people.

So we decided to use an admissions process that is—I hate to use the word because it has become such hackneyed jargon—"holistic." We do not admit anybody by the numbers. I don't have to tell TPR how many law schools divide applicants up strictly by the numbers: "What's your GPA and what's your LSAT." I literally know cases where people had Ph.D.s but didn't get into law school. They don't care whether you are diligent. They don't care whether you have experience in life, which counts for a great deal in law school and beyond that in the legal field. All they do is establish numbers equating to "presumptive admits" and "presumptive denials." They don't have their professors deal with any of this. They just turned it over to a bunch of administrators.

We simply concluded that the LSAT is a bad deal for the kinds of people we wish to attract to our law school, which are people who have had less advantage in life due to their economic background or because of their educational background, or, sad to say they don't do particularly well on multiple-choice standardized objective tests even though they're very intelligent and get good grades in school and do very well in life thereafter. So we said, "The hell with the LSAT."

We also give our own test, which we laughingly call the MSLAT. Invariably, there are two questions we ask: (1) What are the reasons this person should be admitted to MSL? and (2) What are the reasons this person should be

> "So we said, 'The hell with the LSAT.'"

denied admission to MSL? They have an unlimited amount of time to complete the test. The "tests" are graded by our admission committee, which is made up only of professors.

TPR: Given that standardized multiple-choice tests don't really tell us much about how someone will perform in law school or as a lawyer, do you think states should require a bar exam?

VELVEL: That's a good question. If we are going to give a bar examination surely it should be the kind of examination used extensively in other fields such as medicine. This is coming into greater prominence in the legal field, as states like California are using a performance test. I think that I have no objections to a performance-based bar exam.

I have enormous objections to the bar exams we have today, because those tests are simply a repeat of the kinds of tests people took to get into law school in the first place. The same people are disadvantaged by those tests that were disadvantaged getting into law school. And one of the worst things is that the government has permitted the ABA to continue its ban on for-credit or required bar review courses. This means that the Section of Legal Education precludes law schools from giving their students the type of training that would enable their students to pass the bar examination in its current, unsatisfactory form. If the ABA thinks that students are going to rush in droves to take a course that requires extensive work for no credit, then they're crazy.

One reason MSL was not accredited was that we give our students a required, for-credit bar review course. We do this because we know that many of our students scored poorly on the LSAT. But we've seen those same students pass the bar exam first time out of the box.

So I believe the bar exam in its current form is a bad idea. Bottom line, they need to change the whole bar exam into a performance-based examination.

TPR: You're still suing the ABA. What will it take to satisfy you?

VELVEL: What will it take to satisfy us? If one wishes to create a decent, honest, and legitimate system truly dedicated to improving legal education there are several things that are required. First is an open system. End the secrecy so that people know what is going on and can comment intelligently on what is going on. Secondly, put onto the committee and in positions of power people who are dedicated to improving legal education instead of the crowd that for thirty years has been dedicated to improving the economics of the law professors. And thirdly, get rid of these preposterously educationally pernicious rules that abound in ABA accreditation and create a whole new series of standards that replicate the kinds of standards that are used by almost all other accrediting bodies in the United States—that is to say, standards that talk about producing high-quality, not hollow-quantitative, objectives.

CHAPTER 5
DIVERSITY IN LAW SCHOOL:
A PROGRESS CHECK

In 1950, the Supreme Court of the United States ordered the admission of James Sweatt, a black student, to an all-white University of Texas Law School.[1] Sweatt had previously been denied admission on the grounds that the state's black law school was a substantially equal facility. The Supreme Court disagreed. *Sweatt v. Painter* signified the beginning of the end for "separate but equal."[2] Ironically, the battleground was law school admissions.

Today, the fight for ethnic diversity in law school classrooms has grown increasingly tense. Although the past twenty-five years of aggressive diversity initiatives by law schools has produced steady growth in admissions for African Americans as well as other minorities, recent developments in courtrooms and political spheres threaten to slow the rising numbers. The battle, however, isn't confined to the student population. Representation by minorities among law school faculty—particularly tenured faculty—still falls way short of the changing law school student body. Some feel that the lack of minority law school professors creates a learning environment where nonwhite students are marginalized, which may account for underperformance by those students. An entire movement of legal scholarship known as "Critical Race Theory" argues that the very fundamentals of American jurisprudence are so removed from racial and cultural reality that it is no wonder that students outside the dominant culture find the study of law unduly frustrating and completely foreign.

So, the questions remain: Will recent legal and political trends negatively impact law school admissions policies that aim for ethnic diversity? Once accepted, are minority students finding themselves in an academic environment that allows them to excel? Are minorities underrepresented on law school faculties and, if so, do minority students

[1] See generally *Sweatt v. Painter*, 339 U.S. 629 (1950).

[2] The legal doctrine of "separate but equal" by the U.S. Supreme Court in *Plessy v. Ferguson*, 163 U.S. 537 (1896), where the Court upheld a Louisiana law calling for separate-but-equal accommodations for white and black railroad passengers. Plessy's validation of "separate but equal" remained the law until 1954. However, in a series of pre-1954 cases involving graduate school education, the Court found that facilities available to blacks were not in fact "equal" to those given to whites. Finally, in *Brown v. Board of Education*, 347 U.S. 483 (1954), the court explicitly rejected the "separate but equal" doctrine, at least as far as public education was concerned.

suffer academically because of it? Finally, what is Critical Race Theory and what is its significance for minorities and the study of law?

ADMISSIONS: SO FAR, SO GOOD

Figures published by the American Bar Association's Committee on Legal Education[3] tell us that back in 1978, 92 percent of the roughly 118,000 law students in 163 ABA-approved law schools were white. The last twenty years have seen the number of nonwhites enrolled in law school nearly double, from 9.8 percent to 18.7 percent of 134,949 law students attending 179 ABA-approved law schools. (Figures have tripled since 1972, when minority enrollment was only 5.9 percent!) The graph below indicates that the faces in law school classrooms today are beginning to bear a closer resemblance to the ethnic composition of the community at large. For sure, we have come a long way since *Sweatt v. Painter*.

Diversity in the Law Schools

Comparative diversity of law-school graduates, college graduates, and Americans in general.

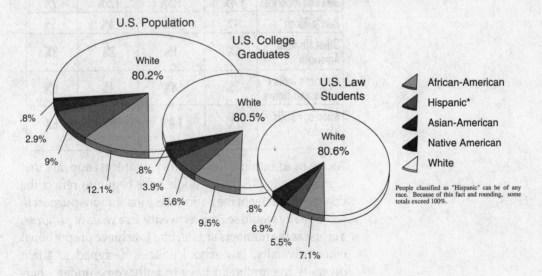

Sources: U.S. Census, Journal of Education Statistics and ABA Review of Legal Education in the United States, 1992, 1995, 1998

[3]Statistics taken from *A Review Legal Education in the United States*, p. 67–70, American Bar Association Section of Legal Education and Admissions to the Bar, Fall 1995 and *ABA Approved Law Schools: Statistical Information on American Bar Association Approved Law Schools*, Rick L. Morgan and Kurt Snyder, Esq., Editors, MacMillan, New York (1998).

The ABA divides minority enrollment into six ethnic subgroups: African American, Mexican American, Puerto Rican, other Hispanic American, American Indian or Alaskan Native, and Asian or Pacific Islander. Currently, African Americans are the greatest-represented minority group in law schools, at about 7.1 percent of total law school enrollment. In the table below, you can see how the percentage of representation for each subgroup has steadily increased over the last twenty years. Note that the Asian/Pacific Islander subgroup has enjoyed the most dramatic rise in enrollment, jumping from 1 percent of total enrollment in 1978 to 6 percent in 1996. Whereas most other minority groups have approximately doubled their total number of enrolled students in the last twenty years, there are more than seven times the number of Asian and Pacific Islander students in law school today than there were in 1978,[4] making that group second only to African Americans in terms of enrollment figures and proportionality.

Rising Percentages of Minority Enrollment in U.S. Law Schools				
	1978–79	1985–86	1990–91	1996–97
African American	4.5%	5%	6%	7.1%
Mexican American	1.4%	1.3%	1.5%	2%
Puerto Rican	.4%	.3%	.4%	.5%
Other Hispanic American	6%	1%	2%	3%
American Indian or Alaskan Native	.3%	.4%	.4%	8%
Asian or Pacific Islander	1%	1.8%	3%	6%

As we head into the next century, it at least appears that admissions to U.S. law schools have begun to reflect the diverse character of the nation these institutions purport to serve. Many would see this as twenty-five years of progress. Yet just as the numbers are starting to achieve proportional ethnic diversity, law school policies designed to attain diversity in enrollment have recently come under a barrage of serious legal and political attacks. No question about it: The gloves are off in the fight for diversity in law school admissions, again.

[4]In 1978–79 there were 1,424 Asian/Pacific Islander law students. In 1995–1996 there were a reported 7,719. *ABA Review of Legal Education*, p.69, Fall 1995.

THE IMPACT OF HOPWOOD ON AFFIRMATIVE ACTION

Most people do not object to achieving diversity on a law school campus. How to go about it is where the debate becomes heated. At this point, *affirmative action* has become one of those phrases with so many proffered definitions that, although at one time you may have understood its meaning, now the mere mention of it cannot be disassociated from the indecipherable media haze that necessarily follows.

Here's our best shot at clearing it up: Affirmative action, as it applies to law schools, means that schools assume a duty to affirmatively erase the vestiges of their past discriminatory practices through new admission and employment practices specifically aimed at remedying the effects of their past discrimination. (Whew!!) That sounds fair enough. However, critics of affirmative action complain that these programs wrongly focus on an applicant's gender or ethnicity rather than on his or her "qualifications."

The legal tension inherent in affirmative action programs is this: Giving special consideration to any ethnic group seemingly runs counter to the neutrality principle embedded in the Equal Protection Clause of the Fourteenth Amendment, which, among other things, seeks to eliminate the purposeful discrimination of all individuals on the basis of race. So, affirmative action draws most of its strength from one legal forum: The United States Supreme Court.

BAKKE: THE LEGAL FOUNDATION FOR AFFIRMATIVE ACTION ADMISSIONS POLICIES

In 1978 the Supreme Court decided *Regents of the University of California v. Bakke*, the most highly publicized and perhaps the most important court case ever dealing with affirmative action. Alan P. Bakke, a white applicant, had been denied admission to the medical school at the University of California at Davis. The UC-Davis Medical School practiced a form of affirmative action whereby they used numerical admissions quotas based on race. Bakke claimed that the university's admissions policy was tantamount to "reverse discrimination." The Supreme Court ruled that because race was the sole factor in the university's decision to reject Bakke, this particular affirmative action policy ran

But That's the Whole Point. . .

Law school applicants' "qualifications" are weighted heavily by their LSAT scores. Yet consider the following admission by Philip D. Shelton, President and Executive Director of LSAC, made in his June 1997 newsletter:

"We have not used the LSAT so responsibly in the process we apply to nonminority applicants. We have relied too heavily on LSAT scores and undergraduate grade averages, attaching significance to small differences that statisticians tell us are entitled to no significance."

If the maker of the exam tells you that the LSAT is a limited vehicle for measuring an applicant's merit, then why do law schools continue to make the LSAT such an important factor in the admission process?[1]

Even the Supreme Court has weighed in on the matter. As stated by Justice William O. Douglas: "Insofar as the LSAT test reflects the dimensions and orientation of the Organization Man they do a disservice to minorities. I personally know that admissions tests were once used to eliminate Jews. How many other minorities they claim I do not know. My reaction is that the presence of an LSAT test is sufficient warrant for a school to put racial minorities into a separate class in order to better probe their capacities and potentials."[2] See chapter 3 in this book for a full discussion of the value (uselessness) of the LSAT as a measure of anybody's qualifications for anything, including law school.

[1] *Hmmm, good question. It's such a good question that the United States Department of Education announced on June 15, 1997 that they will be investigating whether the LSAT, as it is being used in the law school admissions process, violates the Civil Rights Act of 1964. Stay tuned.*
[2] *DeFunis v. Odegaard. 416 U.S. 312, 342 (1974).*

afoul of the Fourteenth Amendment. The Court ordered that Bakke be admitted to the UC-Davis Medical School.

The Court, however, *did not invalidate* all affirmative action admissions policies. The Court's opinion, announced by Justice Lewis E. Powell, laid the groundwork for recognizing diversity as a compelling state interest in higher education. Justice Powell approved the consideration of ethnicity in the admissions process as "one element in a range of factors a university properly may consider in attaining the goal of a heterogeneous student body."[5] Justice Powell speculated that a program in which "race or ethnic background may be deemed 'a plus' in a particular file, yet does not insulate the individual from comparison with all the other candidates for the available seats," might pass constitutional muster.[6]

A problem with this decision that would loom larger over time was that six justices filed opinions, none of which garnered more than four votes. Nonetheless, *Bakke* effectively legalized those race-based admissions policies that stopped short of quotas and used race as a factor—not the *sole* factor—in evaluating candidates.

RUMBLINGS

The post-*Bakke* era of admissions saw many law schools adopt progressive affirmative action admissions policies and employ aggressive minority recruitment efforts. Minority representation in law school enrollment after the landmark case jumped roughly from 10 to 20 percent. The necessary flip side to these numbers, of course, is the 10 percent decrease in the representation among white law students. And law students just love a good argument . . .

Spring 1991: Georgetown law student Timothy Maguire published an article in the law school newspaper entitled "Admissions Apartheid." In the article, Maguire, a white student, made public confidential records regarding incoming students that he was privy to in his capacity as a work-study student employed in the admissions office. Maguire revealed that the LSAT scores and undergraduate GPAs of white law students were higher than those of their African American counterparts.

[5]*Regents of the University of California v. Bakke*, 438 U.S. 265, 314 (1978).
[6]Id. at 317.

Laughably, Maguire pretended to champion the interests of his African American classmates. His "apartheid" reference implied that Georgetown's two-tier admissions policy, intended to help African Americans, was in fact doing them harm. Maguire argued that accepting less qualified candidates in such a competitive atmosphere as Georgetown Law Center would place these students in over their heads. "They," he maintained, would be better off attending a less demanding institution where they could more fairly compete for honors and grades.

Calls for Maguire's dismissal focused primarily on the impropriety of his using confidential information. Maguire cast himself as a victim of "political correctness." His case received considerable notoriety, especially in the D.C. press. Under protest, he was allowed to graduate with his class.

Fall 1995: Hundreds of stolen academic records from the University of Miami Law School admissions office, mostly of minority students, came into the possession of David Scott, a second-year law student and a vocal opponent of affirmative action at the law school. Scott, a reporter for the school newspaper, announced to the student body that he would write an article publishing information contained in the stolen, confidential records that demonstrated "outrageous" disparities between the academic credentials of admitted minority and admitted nonminority students.[7]

Infuriated, minority students at the University of Miami Law School protested to the administration, claiming their privacy had been invaded. The entire law school was immersed in debate over affirmative action. Facing expulsion, Scott returned the records and did not run the story. Scott insists that his virulent opposition to affirmative action stems from his desire for "educational excellence."

February 1996: Under pressure from Governor Pete Wilson, the University of California Board of Regents voted to end the use of ethnic and gender preferences in admitting students and in hiring and contracting workers. Although some voiced praise for the regents' plans, protests erupted throughout the state. At UCLA, thirty-one students were arrested after refusing to disperse at a major Los Angeles intersection.

[7]See generally "Diversity Dilemma" by Christine Riedel, *The National Jurist*, p.14, April/May 1996.

Ironically, the university system that paved the way for affirmative action in Bakke—one of the largest state university systems in the country—is among the first to eliminate its affirmative action policies.

Ironically, the university system that paved the way for affirmative action in *Bakke*—one of the largest state university systems in the country—is among the first to eliminate its affirmative action policies. The vote called for new, nonracially based admissions policies to be instituted, beginning with the fall 1997 semester for graduate students and the spring 1998 semester for undergraduates.

March 1996: A federal circuit court of appeals reversed a district court ruling by finding the affirmative action admissions policy of the University of Texas School of Law unconstitutional under the Equal Protection Clause of the Fourteenth Amendment.

HOPWOOD V. TEXAS: CHIPPING AWAY AT *BAKKE*

The University of Texas School of Law gave ethnic preferences to African American and Mexican American applicants in its admissions process. Cheryl Hopwood and three other white plaintiffs who had been denied admission to the law school sued, claiming that less qualified applicants had been unfairly (illegally) admitted on the basis of race.

The admissions process was as follows. The University of Texas School of Law based their admissions decisions largely on what the school called the "Texas Index" (TI). The TI was a numerical ranking derived from a formulaic combination of an applicant's LSAT score and undergraduate GPA. According to TI, applicants were sorted into three piles: "presumptive admit," "presumptive deny," and "discretionary zone."[8] The TI sorting for African Americans and Mexican Americans was different. The TI ranges that were used to place nonminority students into the three admissions categories were lowered to allow the law school to consider and admit more minorities.[9]

[8] The *Hopwood* case gave all of us a rare inside look into what actually takes place behind the closed doors of one law school's admission process. Having read this far, it should be obvious how incredibly important the LSAT score is in just getting in the door of a given law school (you'll read plenty about this in Chapter 3 in this book). For another revealing look at the law school admissions process, track down "Affirmative Action: New Spin on an Old Trick" by Professor Monroe Freedman, *New Jersey Law Journal*, July 1991. Professor Freedman, Dean of Hofstra University Law School 1973–77, candidly describes how he exercised his own personal version of affirmative action giving preferences to cops, those with strong community service records, and minorities. Professor Freedman defends his admission practices because he claims the objective criteria of LSAT scores and grade point averages are of minimal usefulness in predicting performance in the first year of law school—and virtually useless in predicting success in practice. He should know. He helped develop and write the LSAT and served for years on Law School Admissions Test Council for years.

The court focused on the admissions process at the University of Texas School of Law for 1992 to illustrate the disparity between its treatment of minorities and nonminorities. In that year, the presumptive denial score for nonminorities was a TI of 192 or lower, and a presumptive admit for minorities was 189 or higher. Thus, minority candidates with TIs of 189 or above would almost certainly be admitted, even though their scores were considerably below the level at which white candidates would almost certainly be rejected. The court observed that "out of the pool of resident applicants who fell within this range (189-192 inclusive), 100 percent of blacks and 90 percent of Mexican Americans, but only 6 percent of whites, were offered admission."

The court quickly confronted the precedent in *Bakke*. Writing the opinion on behalf of the Fifth Circuit, Judge Jerry Smith seized on the fact that *Bakke* was not truly a majority decision. He concluded that *Bakke* was not a binding precedent and that Justice Powell's view on using race as a factor in the admissions process was nothing more than a "lonely opinion."

Consequently, Judge Smith employed the highest constitutional test of "strict scrutiny" in examining whether the racial preferences used by the law school were "narrowly tailored" to serve a "compelling state interest." The law school offered two compelling state interests: achieving diversity and remedying the present effects of past discrimination.

Judge Smith rejected diversity as a compelling interest. He reasoned that "[the principle of diversity] treats minorities as a group, rather than as individuals. It may further remedial purposes but, just as likely, may promote improper racial stereotypes, thus fueling racial hostility." Judge Smith elaborated on the logical disconnection between ethical preferences and obtaining diversity: "The use of race . . . simply achieves a student body that looks different. Such a criterion is no more rational on its own terms than would be choices based on physical size or

> "The use of race . . . simply achieves a student body that looks different. Such a criterion is no more rational on its own terms than would be choices based on physical size or blood type of applicants."
>
> —Judge Jerry Smith, Hopwood v. Texas

[9]It is necessary to keep in mind that the group of applicants considered minorities receiving preferential treatment was extremely limited. For example, the law school decided that a black citizen from Nigeria would not get preferential treatment but a resident alien from Mexico, who resided in Texas, would. Likewise, Asians, American Indians, Americans from El Salvador and Cuba and many others did not receive a preference.

The Aftermath of Hopwood

Hopwood could potentially impact almost every law school. Most private schools receive state funding, bringing them under the umbrella of Fourteenth Amendment "strict scrutiny."[1] What would be the result if affirmative action was banned everywhere and law schools simply admitted people by the numbers?

A recent study of 1990–91 law school applicants by Professor Linda F. Wightman published in the New York University Law Review analyzed the consequences of law schools removing ethnicity as a factor in admissions.[2] Professor Wightman noted that if UGPA and LSAT scores had been the sole criteria for admission, among the 3,435 African American applicants who were admitted by at least one of the schools to which they applied, only 687 would have been accepted. Professor Wightman also examined whether there would be any difference, within any ethnic group, in bar passage rates and graduation rates between students who would not have been admitted under the strict UGPA/LSAT criteria and those who would have. The study concluded that there was no significant difference.[3]

The devastating effects of banning affirmative action in Texas and California are already being felt. Boalt Hall, the law school at University at California at Berkeley announced that that none of the 14 black students admitted for the fall 1997 term would be enrolling, and that Hispanic enrollment would drop to 18, from 28 last year. No African-American students will be enrolling in University of Texas' Law School for the fall 1997 first year class. These numbers have prompted a number of voices in legal education to

blood type of applicants." Instead, Judge Smith pointed to plaintiff Cheryl Hopwood—a thirty-two-year-old member of the Armed Forces who was married and raising a severely handicapped child—as an excellent example of someone who would lend diversity to a law school.

The court also rejected the law school's argument that there was a compelling interest to remedy the present effects of past discrimination. The court acknowledged that there may have been past discrimination in regard to African Americans but ruled that any identifiable present effects of such discrimination, specifically by the law school, had not been shown.

Judge Smith firmly concluded that the University of Texas School of Law could no longer use race as a factor to achieve diversity, to combat the perceived effect of a hostile environment at the law school, to better the reputation of the law school with the minority community, or to eliminate present effects of past discrimination by entities other than the law school.

Although the Fifth Circuit really only has authority in the states of Texas, Louisiana, and Mississippi, many fear this case could be sounding the death knell for affirmative action in higher education. For now, the widespread legal implications of Hopwood beyond the Fifth Circuit remain to be seen.

DIVERSITY AMONG FACULTY?

In April 1990, Harvard Law Professor Derrick Bell, an African American and a nationally recognized legal scholar, took a leave of absence without pay in protest over Harvard's failure to grant tenure to the law school's only African American female law professor. Two years later, after taking a number of visiting professorships at various schools, he was teaching some courses at New York University Law School. That year, Harvard demanded that Bell return or lose his post. Resolute, Professor Bell pointed out that the law school had still not granted his African American female colleague tenure. Bell remained at NYU and continues to teach there today.

The episode of Derrick Bell brought widespread publicity

to a condition in law school of which minority law students are acutely aware: Minority law school professors are scarce. While minority law students comprise almost 20 percent of the law student population, only 12.8 percent of the nation's teaching/faculty positions are occupied by nonwhites. The numbers for tenure and tenure-track positions for minorities are less than that.

In this book we rank individual law schools by percentage of minority professors on the faculty. The table below, provided by the American Association of Law Schools (AALS), is a five-year study of numbers and percentages of minority faculty. It's easy to do the math in these columns as the increases have been at best modest.

5-year Comparison: Full-Time Minority Law Faculty in the Directory of Law Teachers	Academic Year				
	1991–92 #/%	1992–93 #/%	1993–94 #/%	1994–95 #/%	1995–96 #/%
Dean	14/8.0	15/8.7	17/9.7	16/9.0	17/9
Assc. Dean/No Prf	11/11.8	10/10.5	12/12.4	11/11.5	10/9
Assc. Dean/w/ Prf	22/11.1	19/9.0	18/8.9	16/7.8	18.8
Asst. Dean/No Prf	38/19.0	42/19.7	46/20.6	49/19.9	56/20
Asst. Dean/w/Prf	3/14.3	3/16.7	3/20.0	4/25.0	5/29
Head Librarian	16/9.9	15/9.1	15/9.2	16/10.1	13/7
Professor	213/6.3	246/7.0	268/7.5	287/7.8	322/8
Assc. Prf	206/20.3	206/20.2	213/20.9	244/22.4	275/24
Asst. Prf	154/23.2	179/26.8	179/27.4	178/28.7	178/28
Vis. Prof/any rank	21/19.1	21/15.3	22/16.3	28/18.2	22/14
Lecturer/Instr.	20/6.8	26/8.3	47/13.9	43/11.7	44/11
Dean/Prof. Emer.	17/3.4	19/3.6	20/3.6	21/3.5	25/4
ALL MINORITY FACULTY	735/10.8	801/11.4	860/12.0	913/12.3	985/12

When Derrick Bell left Harvard he cited his inability to continue being a "role model" for African American men and women working in a place that resisted diversity. Is the issue simply one of proportional representation among faculty? Or, is there a causal connection between the lack of minorities teaching in law schools and the academic performance of minority law students?

discuss creative ways to achieve diversity without race-based affirmative action policies.

Some law school administrators suggest using "economic disadvantage" as a factor in admissions, which might help a greater number of minorities gain admission. However, most studies indicate that as long as UGPA and LSAT scores remain the primary factors for admission, ethnic minorities will still be at a disadvantage. Lani Guinier, professor of law at University of Pennsylvania, recently suggested drastically minimizing the importance of the LSAT in the admissions process.[4] Under Professor Guinier's admissions model, law schools would pre-set an acceptable minimum test score and then hold a lottery among the applicants who meet the minimum standard.

On the other hand, there's brazen Harvard Law Professor and constitutional scholar Laurence H. Tribe, who discourages schools even within the Fifth Circuit from prematurely trashing their affirmative action programs. Tribe, who assisted in the Texas law school's appeal, advises that "[if] they use the Fifth Circuit dictum as an excuse to completely eliminate all uses of race, even as a factor, they will certainly be doing so as a matter of choice rather than compulsion."[5]

[1] Even the ABA is affected. They may have to re-write their admission Standard 212, which expressly calls for "special concern" to "qualified members of groups" (notably racial and ethnic minorities) which have been victims of discrimination in various forms.
[2] Wightman, Linda, The Threat to Diversity in Legal Education: An Empirical Analysis of the Consequences of Abandoning Race as a Factor in Law School Admission Decisions, 72 NYU L. Rev. 1 (April 1997).
[3] So the LSAT adversely impacts ethnic minorities and it is not a good predictor of law school success. Do you see a civil rights problem here?
[4] "The Real Bias in Higher Education", Lani Guinier, (Op-Ed), The New York Times, June 24, 1997.
[5] "High Court Refuses to Hear Appeal of Ruling That Barred Considering Race in Admissions," Douglas Lederman and Stephen Burd, Chronicle of Higher Education, July 12, 1996.

MINORITY STUDENTS IN THE CLASSROOM

In 1996, Linda Wightman published a study for the Law School Admission Council comparing the performance and experiences of men and women in law school.[10] Professor Wightman's study is remarkable in its depth and detail. Although her analysis revolves around gender comparisons, most statistics are broken down by racial subgroups within gender classification.

Throughout her analysis of how well each gender performed in law school compared with how well they were predicted to perform, Wightman could not help but notice the statistically significant disparity regarding underperformance by minorities within gender classifications, particularly with respect to African American women.[11] Professor Wightman observed that the most statistically significant data in the study of underperformance in gender emerged when she added ethnicity to the analyses.

Is it that minorities find the material more difficult or perhaps that the academic environment in law school somehow discourages the minority student? The graph on the following page from the Wightman study speaks volumes to the latter.

[10]*Women in Legal Education: A Comparison of Law School Performance and Law School Experiences of Men and Women*, Linda F. Wrightman, LSAC Research Report Series, Chapter 3, Law School Admission Council, 1996.

[11] For a full discussion on the experiences of women in law school , see chapter 6 in this book.

WHAT A DIFFERENCE A YEAR MAKES

A survey of law students asked to assess their own abilities.

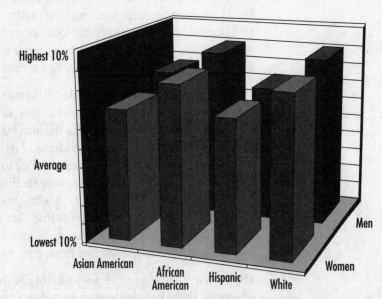

Ratings of academic ability compared with their first-year classmates prior to the first year of law school

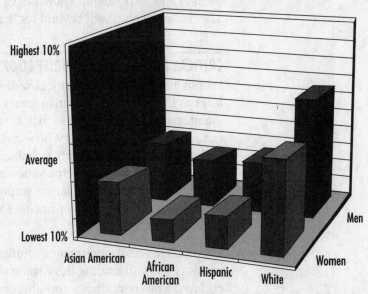

Ratings of academic ability compared with their first-year classmates after the first year of law school

Wow! We all know that the first year of law school is one of the greatest ego deflations of all time, but what makes it so much worse for nonwhite students? Certainly, the small number of minority law professors does not help. Lorraine Dusky, in her portrait of academic inequality in law school, *Still Unequal: The Shameful Truth About Women and Justice in America*, cites one theorist's common sense explanation as to why minorities underperform. She writes:

> Critical race scholar Kimberle Williams Crenshaw argues that because minority students' experiences and beliefs clash not only with those of teachers, but also with those of most students, law school is especially disorienting. Asked to relate to rules and arguments and not asked to evaluate them in light of the worldview they reflect—a white middle-class worldview—minority students find that they must disassociate themselves and somehow assume an intellectual stance divorced from their existence.[12]

The growing belief that there is something intrinsic to legal education that alienates minority students has manifested itself in numerous writings and lectures, creating a movement in legal scholarship known as Critical Race Theory. The challenge goes well beyond legal academia.

CRITICAL RACE THEORY: A BRIEF LOOK

Within the last ten years, Critical Race Theory (CRT)[13] has leapt to the forefront of contemporary legal debate. CRT maintains that conventional legal principles used in American jurisprudence have very little to do with the social, economic, and political reality for minorities. According to CRT, not only do legal principles such as "equality," "neutrality," and "objectivity" fail in empowering disenfranchised minorities but these principles work toward their continued exclusion.

The problem is that much of the evolution of legal discourse in this country (including the writing of the Constitution) occurred when minorities were either enslaved, segregated,

[12]*Still Unequal: The Shameful Truth About Women and Justice in America*, Lorraine Dusky, p.41, Crown Publishers, 1996, New York, NY.

[13]For an excellent review of Critical Race Theory read *Critical Race Theory: The Key Writings that Formed the Movement*, edited by Kimberle Crenshaw, et al., The New Press, New York, NY 1995.

or otherwise discriminated against in various aspects of American life. The evolution of legal and social reality for minorities in this country has produced a very different perspective. Critical Race theorist Professor Charles R. Lawrence III, explains the difference: "What we see and feel today, our own perspectives and perceptions, appear distorted and unreal when they appear against the background of a history that excludes the voices of those who have seen the world from positions most like our own."[14] CRT warns that once minorities engage in speaking the language of the "dominant legal discourse" they enter a tradition of storytelling that disregards their own stories, their own histories. For the minority law student, the study of law will actually be the study of someone else's contrasting reality— he or she will feel alienated and marginalized.

CRT argues that as long as dominant legal discourse "is premised upon the claim to knowledge of objective truths and the existence of neutral principles"[15] then the subjective truth for minorities, communicated through their own "word," will continue to be ignored. Sociological data will likewise be ignored. Therefore, the social, political, and economic power disparity will continue.

CRT warns of the danger in Supreme Court decisions that falsely claim to contribute to a "color-blind society." In other words, all these "color-blind" decisions do is allow society to pretend everything is okay because the Supreme Court said so. The practical consequence will be that people of color will continue to suffer from real discrimination and the dominant culture will continue to view the discrimination as an acceptable, judicially sanctioned status quo.

In short, CRT sees the legal tradition in America and the legal condition of minorities as two totally different narrative voices informing our legal discourse. The former babbles in a world of abstract ideals; the latter shouts up from the cold floor of realism, heard only by itself. Until there is true social equality, CRT insists that equality under the law will be illusory.

> "What we see and feel today, our own perspectives and perceptions, appear distorted and unreal when they appear against the background of a history that excludes the voices of those who have seen the world from positions most like our own."
> —Professor Charles R. Lawrence, III

[14]*The Word and the River: Pedagogy as Scholarship as Struggle*, Charles R. Lawrence, III, reprinted with permission in *Critical Race Theory: The Writings that Formed the Movement*, Edited by Kimberle Crenshaw, Neil Gotonda, Gary Peller, Kendall Thomas; p. 339, The New Press, New York, NY, 1995.

[15]Ibid, p. 338.

CHAPTER 6
WOMEN IN LAW SCHOOL: AN UPDATE

In 1994, Professor Lani Guinier and four colleagues from the University of Pennsylvania Law School published an article entitled "Becoming Gentlemen: Women's Experiences at One Ivy League Law School." Simply put, it is a seminal work of research and evaluation about how one law school (University of Pennsylvania) and its women students coexist with each other. "Becoming Gentlemen" also makes a disturbing and discouragingly strong case that in at least one institution (U Penn Law School), women are underperforming in law school.

Naturally, this is not necessarily the case at every law school, nor at every top-20 law school. However, it sent a powerful message to the law school establishment, since it seems that anything written about women in law school since November 1994 has referenced Professor Guinier's work.

The work's findings are clear. Women at U Penn Law School with credentials (undergraduate GPAs, LSAT scores, undergraduate honors) identical to those of their male counterparts underperform in the areas of grades, leadership positions, and academic honors, and this pattern is established *by the end of the first year of law school*.[1] This pattern continues throughout law school and even affects women's chances for obtaining the "prestigious and/or desirable jobs after graduation."[2] But it is right in the beginning, as 1Ls, that women begin to underperform. As Professor Guinier writes:

> For many women, therefore, the first year of law school is experienced as the construction of the law school hierarchy; for them it is the most emotionally draining and intellectually debilitating year.[3]

Professor Guinier's study is far from the only documentation of women underperforming, and of women having an "emotionally draining and intellectually debilitating" law school experience. Six years earlier, in 1988, Catherine Weiss and Louise Melling published an equally powerful essay entitled "The Legal Education of Twenty Women" in the *Stanford Law Review*. Weiss and Melling had just com-

[1]See Guinier, Lani, et al, "Becoming Gentlemen: Women's Experiences At One Ivy League Law School", *University of Pennsylvania Law Review*, November 1994, p. 3.
[2]Ibid, p. 5.
[3]Ibid, p. 67.

pleted their studies at Yale Law School, and had documented their own and fellow women's experiences there. During the course of their studies (1984–1987), they formed a focus group of approximately twenty women, and their essay is a powerful account of how the women in the focus group experienced law school. Weiss and Melling's study illustrates how this emotional drain led to their alienation in law school:

> Two premises underlie our study. First, men and women experience law school differently. From the moment the group organized, we identified our alienation as a women's issue. Our second premise is that women's alienation in law school matters. We are angry about our exclusion and want to feel engaged. Our alienation also impoverishes the intellectual and emotional life of the law school. The drowning of women's speech in a flood of men's voices squelches the diversity of ideas and styles that ought to sustain institutions of learning.[4]

Both studies show that women are running into roadblocks once they get to law school. However, there is other data that is quite positive—data that makes the existence of those roadblocks even harder to believe.

SOME GOOD NEWS

Basics on Women in the Legal Profession	
Roles	Percent
Women entering Law School	44%
Women in Law School Faculty and Administrative Positions	28%
Women Tenured Law School Professors	16%
Women Law School Deans	8%
Women in the Legal Profession	24%
Women Partners in Law Firms	12.9%

There is, indeed, plenty of good news for women who want to pursue a career in the legal profession. As an American Bar Association Commission on Women in the Profession

[4]See Weiss and Melling, "The Legal Education of Twenty Women", *Stanford Law Review*, May 1988, pp. 1300-1302.

Feminist Jurisprudence: A Brief Look

Feminist Jurisprudence is not a single theory—it is comprised of various critical approaches that current scholars apply to legal issues. Two major critical approaches are "formal equality" and "dominance theory." Formal equality attempts to erase gender differences in the law in an attempt to treat both genders equally. This is Supreme Court Justice Ruth Bader Ginsburg's approach. While a practicing lawyer, she "challenged sex-based classifications that discriminated against men as well as those that discriminated against women."[1] Dominance theory (sometimes referred to as "nonsubordination theory"), however, looks at the power relationship between men and women. Dominance theory's creator is Catharine MacKinnon, one of the most highly regarded legal scholars of the twentieth century, especially in areas of feminism. Dominance theory "focuses on power inequities and demands legal rules that increase women's power relative to men."[2]

There are other strains of Feminist Jurisprudence—hedonic feminism, pragmatic feminism, different voice theory, and postmodern feminism, but formal equality and dominance theory are the two main legal tools for reevaluating the laws of the United States with a feminist/equal-gender perspective. For additional reading on feminist jurisprudence, see the three articles listed in the footnotes below.[3]

[1]See Katherine T. Bartlett, Gender Law, The Duke Journal of Gender, Law, & Policy 1, 1994, p. 2.
[2]See Mary Becker, Strength in Diversity: Feminist Theoretical Approaches to Child Custody and Same-sex Relationships, Stetson Law Review, 23, Summer 1994, p. 702.
[3]See the abovementioned two articles for excellent capsule summaries of these varying approaches. See also Chicago-Kent Law Review, 69, No. 2, 1993, Symposium: Is the Law Male?. This issue is dedicated entirely to feminist legal viewpoints and is edited by Linda Hirshman.

publication called *Unfinished Business: Overcoming the Sisyphus Factor* reports,

> During the past decade, the number of women lawyers has escalated rapidly. Women undeniably have become more visible at the top: Two women sit on the U.S. Supreme Court, two women head the U.S. Department of Justice, and two women lead the ABA. More than 11% of all law firm partners are women, and more than one quarter of all firms have female partners. To date, women comprise 31% of President Clinton's federal judicial appointments.[5]

Additionally, nearly 25 percent of all lawyers in private practice are women[6] and, for the 1993–1994 academic year, 44 percent of first-year law students were women.[7]

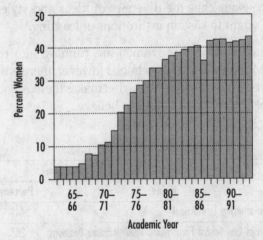

Percent Women in First-Year Law School Class
for Academic Years 1963–1964 to 1993–1994

[Source: *A Review of Legal Education in the United States* (Fall 1993),
Julia D. Hanrahan, ed.(Chicago: American Bar Association,
Section of Legal Education and Admissions to the Bar, 1994)]

There are also some law schools that have done studies similar to that of Guinier's, with markedly different results. One such school was the University of Iowa College of Law, where Professor Jean Love's results showed that

[5]*Unfinished Business: Overcoming the Sisyphus Factor*, American Bar Association Commission on Women in the Profession, 1995, p. 3.

[6]See Dusky, Lorraine, *Still Unequal: The Shameful Truth About Women and Justice in America*, 1996, p 1. Dusky begins her book with the same bright news from The Sisyphus Factor. However, both Dusky's book and The Sisyphus Factor go on to tell quite different stories.

[7]See *Women in the Law: A Look at the Numbers*, American Bar Association Commission on Women in the Profession, December 1995, p. 6.

men were not outperforming women, and that "the number of women who achieved [high grades, academic honors, and leadership positions] was in proportion with their enrollment figures."[8] And at CUNY Law School in Queens, New York (one of the best public-policy law schools in the country), 59 percent of the faculty are women.[9]

Consequently, there *are* law schools where female students will see a representative number of women (based on the percentage of women in the general population) on faculty, and have a positive, equally (as compared to men) successful law school experience. But at many law schools, and, more worrisome, at a preponderance of the top-20 law schools, women in general seem to be having grave difficulties achieving equal success.

WOMEN AT A DISADVANTAGE: THE NUMBERS

In September 1995, Professor Linda R. Hirshman of Chicago-Kent College of Law published a revised ranking of *U.S. News & World Report*'s annual law school rankings in a rather unlikely place—Glamour magazine. Hirshman looks at two key statistics: the percentage of women on law review versus the percentage of women in that law school class, and the percentage of female tenure or tenure-track faculty members. Yale, ranked number one, dropped to tenth place; Harvard, tied for second place, dropped to fourteenth place. Duke went from eighth place to first place, because it actually had a higher percentage of women on law review (48 percent) than were in second- and third-year classes (40 percent), and 21 percent of their tenure or tenure-track faculty were women.[10]

Right on the heels of this article came a *National Jurist*[11] ranking in October 1995. The *Jurist*'s ranking was based on the percentage of students at the school that were women, the percentage of female faculty, an "equal treatment"

[8]See Latham, Shanie, Iowa Study Defies Trend, as quoted in "Is Law School Still a Man's World?" *The National Jurist*, Oct/Nov 1995, p. 28.

[9]Ibid. According to *The National Jurist*'s figures, which in turn are based on the ABA's *Review of Legal Education in the United States* (Fall 1994), this is the highest percentage of female faculty of any ABA-approved law school.

[10]If this number sounds low, consider the fact that only two schools on Hirshman's list had 25 percent or more female representation in their faculty: Georgetown (25 percent), and University of Minnesota (28 percent). CUNY's, if you remember, was 59 percent, compared to (for instance) University of Chicago (13 percent).

[11]*The National Jurist* is a free, bi-monthly magazine about the law and the law school experience, and is distributed on most (if not all) law school campuses.

category that was based on The Princeton Review's survey data, and a "leadership score" that was based on women's participation on law reviews and in student bar associations. All of this data was combined to rerank 168 ABA-approved law schools. In this ranking, the only top-20 school in the top *thirty-five schools* in the *Jurist*'s rankings was Stanford (at twenty-sixth place). Duke was 135th, Yale was 145th, and Harvard was 167th (out of 168!). While some may have doubts about Hirshman's and especially the *Jurist*'s methodology,[12] the data, at the very least, is suggestive of a major problem at the top of the law school food chain. Here's a comparison chart based on the three methodologies:

Law School	U.S. News Rank	Glamour Rank	Jurist Rank
Yale	1	10	145
Harvard	2	14	167
Stanford	2	3	26
University of Chicago	4	19	166
Columbia	5	6	118
New York University	6	4	90
University of Virginia	7	18	162
Duke	8	1	135
University of California, Berkeley	8	13	71
University of Michigan at Ann Arbor	8	16	136
University of Pennsylvania	11	9	139
Northwestern	11	15	155
Georgetown	13	17	60
Cornell	14	7	157
University of Southern California	15	20	102
Vanderbilt	16	11	143
University of Texas at Austin	17	12	137
University of Minnesota at Twin Cities	18	5	87
University of Iowa	19	2	70
University of Illinois at Urbana-Champaign	20	8	127

[12]Needless to say, plenty of people have problems with U. S. News' ranking methodology as well—just go to any Pre-Law Advisor or AALS or ABA Conference and listen for 15 minutes. The topic is sure to come up. Unfortunately, you'll hear a lot fewer people calling into question the methodologies behind the acceptance of standardized testing as a predictor of law school performance—an equally off-base but supposedly "objective" measurement standard. Hence: the law schools hate being ranked by U.S. News, but yet rely heavily on standardized testing and undergraduate rank when looking at potential applicants.

Great caution should be used when looking at school vs. school-type data; much more trustworthy is the overall data that is being collected on law schools, such as the data provided by Linda Wightman of the Law School Admission Council (LSAC). Here is where we see disturbing patterns emerging—first, the fact that women have higher UGPAs than men, even (actually, *especially*) when you look at specific majors such as humanities, business, or social science, but they have lower LSAT scores and lower First-Year Averages (FYAs) in law school; and second, that this pattern is *not* the case in business school, medical school, and certain other graduate programs.[13]

What does this indicate? That something is occurring in law school (very early on, according to the U Penn study), that results in the underperformance of women. That there is indeed a gender bias in law school. And that this gender bias may even be mirrored by a gender bias on the LSAT (see sidebar on Standardized Testing).

As Wightman states, "The patterns of academic performance [in law school] are not consistent with the patterns of academic performance of women compared with men in high school, undergraduate school, or graduate school."[14]

The LSAC report has even more disturbing data to reveal. Later in the study, we see that women seem to have a self-esteem problem as 1Ls—they rated themselves lower than men in terms of competitiveness, public speaking ability, and self-confidence in academic situations.[15] Furthermore, approximately one-third of women in law school (again, across all major ethnicities) report discrimination based on gender. And finally, while white women make up 66 percent of the total number of women who performed "better than expected" in law school, black women make up almost 60 percent of the total number of women who performed "worse than predicted."[16]

[13]See Wightman, Linda F., *Women In Legal Education: A Comparison of the Law School Performance* and *Law School Experiences of Women and Men; LSAC Research Report Series*, The Law School Admission Council, 1996, chapter 3.

[14]Wightman, Women in Legal Education, p. 15.

[15]Ibid, p. 54. This data even took race into account—Asian American, Black, Hispanic, and White women all rated themselves lower than men did in these categories. The LSAC report is scrupulous in accounting for race in most matters—an important delineation.

[16]Ibid, p. 81. For a good discussion of how Black women's experiences as 1Ls are particularly disturbing, see *Women in Legal Education*, p. 81, and the chapter in this book on "Minorities and Law School."

Problems with Standardized Testing? (Gasp!)

Imagine. An ethnic or gender bias on a standardized test. What the Law School Admission Council's data reveals is that women outperform men in high school, in college, and in most graduate schools. The areas where they don't outperform men are on the SAT, on the LSAT, and in law school. There's been plenty of documentation about a correlation between the SAT and the LSAT (see a study done by Pre-Law Advisor David Mann in at the College of Charleston in 1992, or go to the Educational Testing Service's own library in New Jersey), so if one test is gender-biased, why not the other? In the undergraduate arena, women are able to overcome the barrier to admission due to lower SAT scores. MIT, for instance, reportedly adds sixty points to every woman's SAT score during their admissions process. However, since the LSAT counts for so much of the law school admissions process, women (a) may not be getting into the law school of the quality they deserve, and (b) law school itself mirrors (in either the same or in different ways) the gender bias that is on the SAT and the LSAT. Naturally, someone writing for LSAC would not be able to draw those conclusions for obvious reasons. For more documentation of gender bias in standardized testing, check out various suits by the nonprofit organization FairTest, especially the New York regents case from 1989. There is a lot of correlation research and gender-bias research that needs to be done before any conclusions can be made. However, in the meantime, all one needs to ask is: Why do women perform well in medical school but not in law school?

Guinier's study tells us things about the University of Pennsylvania in particular that are even more disturbing than the LSAC report. According to "Becoming Gentlemen," men at U Penn Law School "are three times more likely than women to be in the top 10 percent of their law school class."[17] Finally, Guinier reveals that "women were five times more likely to seek professional help (i.e., some type of therapy) for law-school concerns, with rates of 15.5 percent for the women, compared with 3.6 percent for the men."[18]

WOMEN AT A DISADVANTAGE: "QUALITATIVE DATA"

Men were called upon much more frequently than women. Someone argued that this is a bonus for women, but in classes where grades are based in part on classroom participation, women [find themselves] at a disadvantage. In one class, I held up my hand for 45 minutes but I was not called on. When I approached the professor afterwards and asked why, I was told to "get used to it, you're a woman."[19]

With all the quantitative data just mentioned, there is plenty of statistical evidence that women in general have more of a struggle than their male peers, particularly at the top schools. But if the numbers aren't convincing enough, there is a plethora of anecdotal accounts as well. Interviews that Weiss and Melling, Guinier, Dusky, the ABA Commission on Women in the Profession, and others have conducted illustrate what these numbers mean on a personal level: increased hostility of male students toward female students; sexual harassment; subtle classroom issues (such as snickering when women answer questions and professors ignoring women's answers); one-sided (i.e., the defendant's perspective only), insensitive, and woefully inadequate coverage of rape and sexual harassment issues in criminal law classes; feelings of alienation on the part of

[17]Guinier, *Becoming Gentlemen*, p. 3.

[18]*Ibid*, p. 44. Clearly, this is something that should be closely examined by ALL law schools.

[19]See *Elusive Equality: The Experiences of Women in Legal Education*, ABA Commission on Women In the Profession, 1996, p. 16. *Elusive Equality* is a brief, excellent overview of the entire situation—the experiences of women law students, male bias in the law itself, faculty issues, the glass ceiling in the legal profession, and 25 pages of recommendations.

female students; etc. The following are a few of these powerful anecdotes.

On entering law school:

[My friend] and I took this U-Haul across [the] country....I couldn't move into my apartment till the next day so I was going to stay in the law school. So I drive the U-Haul up to the front steps of the law school. I had my pink tennis shoes on and this bright pink shirt and I think I had a Walkman on...and I kind of bop up and say, "Hi. Where's the housing office?"...[T]here...were these three law students just kind of sitting on the stairs. And they looked at me and said, "This is Yale." And I said, "I know. Where's the housing office?" And they said, "This is Yale Law School."...They all looked me up and down and just like, "Oh God, someone on the admissions committee made a mistake."[20]

On being ignored in the classroom:

I had a professor who ignored the women in his classes—except to have them give quick, short answers to questions such as "Do you know the rule of law?" The guys would complain that the women had it easier, because he would have the men in the class standing for 20 minutes while they briefed a case. How could any woman expect to do well in a class like that? He simply wouldn't call on women. I would raise my hand for 5 minutes and he wouldn't call on me, so if I had a question that I wasn't sure someone else could explain to me, I would lean over to a guy and ask him to ask it. They were good about that. The guy would be called on and I would write the answer down.[21]

This last example is one of the most prevalent comments seen in even a cursory review of the current literature. Women are simply being ignored in many classrooms to a much greater degree than men are (most law students of both genders have had their comments ignored at some point during law school—no professor is perfect), and this in turn can affect their grades, the types of academic pursuits and honors they choose to focus on, and their overall feelings of alienation.

[20]Weiss and Melling, *The Legal Education of Twenty Women*, p. 1322.
[21]Dusky, *Still Unequal*, p. 24.

On the attitudes of male students:

If you are assertive, people label you a "bitch" and assume you are difficult to deal with. Sometimes when a woman brings up a point of law where the law is obviously wrong regarding women, you will hear comments in the class expressing impatience with her—"There goes that woman going PC again." They roll their eyes, they groan, they turn around and stare at the person. I am pretty reticent in class. I rarely volunteer.[22]

I have a real problem with the male students not being reined in here. Some male student asked me if I were sleeping with [Professor A] when he found out I was researching for him. He did it to intimidate me. Men don't want the competition.[23]

As we've also seen from the quantitative data, the result of all the kinds of gender-based discrimination illustrated above is the alienation and underperformance of women in law school. And the following anecdote shows how this underperformance is not only sensed by women in law school, but also by men:

Bartow, then a student at [U Penn], reported that some of her male colleagues chose their upper-level law school classes based on the number of women enrolled in each class. Women were perceived as "Q-absorbing" buffers, with Q ("Qualified") being the lowest passing grade on formal and informal grading curves. These men assumed that their own chances of receiving a grade higher than Qualified increased as the number of women enrolled in the class increased because the women would absorb a disproportionate number of the Qualified grades. They sarcastically referred to large groups of women in a class as the "Q quotient."…What she did not articulate, but her male colleagues perhaps intuitively realized, was that our findings about women's performance were already known on some level within the law school community.[24]

[22]Dusky, *Still Unequal*, p. 38.

[23]Weiss and Melling, *The Legal Education of Twenty Women*, p. 1325.

[24]Guinier, Lani, et al, *Becoming Gentlemen*, pg. 31–32.

FIXING A HOLE

There's no question that women will very likely encounter *some* amount of gender-based discrimination in law school. The main issue is: What can be done to fix this problem? *Elusive Equality* (see footnote #19) contains many suggestions—diverse teaching methods,[25] unbiased testing methods, blind grading of exams,[26] better classroom dynamics, faculty support, multicultural and intellectually diverse hiring practices, continuous surveying, support groups, security, and gender and ethnic bias and harassment awareness training of staff and students. It's clear what can happen when some of these practices are followed:

> In one class, I have a black woman professor. The number of minority students that speak in that class is a thousand to one [as compared with] other classes. It has something to do with the fact that she is a black woman and a role model.[27]

Weiss and Melling's article contains many of these recommendations, and it claims that if law schools concentrated more on basic lawyering skills (i.e., "nuts and bolts" training), this might be a better forum than the Socratic method in which women can assert themselves and affect change. Lorraine Dusky calls for a serious revamping of how rape and sexual harassment is taught in law school. As usual, however, Professor Guinier has the last (and most powerful) words:

> Changing the number of women faculty, ensuring a critical mass of women students, or even institutionalizing gender-neutral language may help some women achieve their true potential as productive lawyers. But it is not enough just to add women and stir. These data plead instead for a reinvention of law school, and a fundamental change in its teaching practices, institutional policies, and social organization.[28]

[25]There is some good data that women as a group do not respond as "well" as men to strict Socratic teaching methods. See the chapter on the Law School Curriculum for a discussion of the Socratic method, and see Weiss and Melling, Guinier, and *Elusive Equality* for discussions of gender bias within the Socratic method.

[26]There's plenty of anecdotal data that professors can easily identify the gender of the student on handwritten exams, and that this may affect equal grading of men and women.

[27]*Elusive Equality: The Experiences of Women in Legal Education*, p. 16.

[28]Guinier, Lani, et al, *Becoming Gentlemen*, p. 100.

THE CASE OF MARY BECKER

Mary Becker is a full professor of law at the University of Chicago School of Law. She is the liaison from the AALS to the ABA Commission on Women in the Legal Profession. She has published law review articles on feminist jurisprudence. She is one of the most intelligent, outspoken, knowledgeable, and well-respected professors in the area of women and law school. Yet, despite Professor Becker's successes, she is only one of two tenured female professors at the University of Chicago, the fourth-ranked law school in the nation.[29]

And as Mary Becker sits in her cluttered office overlooking the University of Chicago, she is continually involved in Gender Committee studies for her law school, she writes articles on how to do gender studies, she dispenses advice for prospective male and female law students, and the situation at her law school...*worsens*. There are fewer tenured and tenure-track female professors now at U Chicago than there were four years ago. All of the senior female staff members have left to take prestigious appointments elsewhere, except for Becker.[30] And Linda Hirshman places the University of Chicago Law School nineteenth (out of twenty) on her list of female-friendly top law schools. As a result, the University of Chicago is another example—like Yale and U Penn—of a highly respected law school that needs to examine its gender issues.[31]

Mary Becker does not show any signs of slowing up, however. She still collects voluminous amounts of material on women in law school and consults with her colleagues around the nation on the studies they are doing. But one can't help but feel that she is the proverbial female professor who has yet to come in from the cold, that as she documents and tracks the progress of women in law school around the country, the walls are falling in all around her.

[29]The other tenured female professor (who is not a J.D.) shares an appointment with a divinity school in the Chicago area. Interestingly, however, Catharine MacKinnon has just accepted a position as a visiting professor. She'll mainly teach in the spring (she'll still be at Michigan in the fall, presumably) for the next 5 years.

[30]Dusky, *Still Unequal*, p. 86.

[31]There is an oft-repeated anecdote (which is printed in Dusky's book) about how, at a University of Chicago alumnae dinner, a speaker (the dean at the time, perhaps?) stated that women could now take courses from 14 (Dusky's book said 23) women at the law school. Hissing immediately broke out, since apparently at least some people in the audience already knew of Chicago's pathetic percentage of tenure and tenure-track female professors.

Mary Becker's case is by no means singular—all you need to do is look at Linda Hirshman's *Glamour* article for the low percentages of female tenured or tenure-track professors (Harvard and U Chicago are at 13 percent, Northwestern[32] is at 15 percent). And while the percentage of female tenured and tenure-track professors is not the only statistic that reveals a law school's "friendliness" toward women, it is a key statistic. Mary Becker states that if you're going to look at one statistic, the "proportion of women on law review is the best measure of how women perform at that law school," and that "the size of the school, the size of the classes, and the political culture of the law school" are all important empirical data. Finally, she states that there has been a slowdown in the hiring of women tenure-track professors in the past few years. It's no surprise that *Elusive Equality* backs her up:

> Particularly disturbing is the slowdown in the increase of tenured women in an era (from 1987 to 1994) when the percentage of women in the profession is increasing. Some tenured faculty report that tenured women faculty are only tokens at their school.[33]

Unfair (or, at least, unequal) hiring practices are by no means limited to law schools, however. A full third of Dusky's book is reserved for the hiring and conditions of women in the legal profession. There is plenty of documentation of unequal pay scales, unfair treatment, and sexual harassment.[34] Unfortunately, the gender bias does not stop at the law school level.[35]

[32]Linda Hirshman flatly states that Northwestern "has few women on faculty and is a bad place for women in general."

[33]*Elusive Equality*, p. 29.

[34]See Dusky, *Still Unequal: The Shameful Truth About Women and Justice in America*. One interesting statistic is in the *National Association for Law Placement (NALP)'s Class of 1995: Employment Report and Salary Survey*. Women who are over the age of 46 and are seeking their first job after graduation are receiving a mean salary of $41,910, while men in the exact same situation are receiving $51,307. It has been suggested that this almost $10,000 discrepancy may have to do with the fact that these women are being hired by male associates and partners who are 10–20 years younger than the women are, and that the men are either consciously or unconsciously offering lower starting salaries to women to protect their male dominance. Or they are just being flat out gender-biased.

[35]The final third of Dusky's book is about the unequal justice women receive in U.S. courtrooms.

A PRACTICAL GUIDE TO CHOOSING A LAW SCHOOL[36]

If you're applying to law school, whether you're a man or a woman (but especially if you're a woman), there are some simple things that you should do before you decide where to go to learn the law. The first is of course to read both "Becoming Gentlemen" and "The Legal Education of Twenty Women." These two essays should be required reading for anyone who wants to apply to law school. Why? Because a natural assumption would be that the "higher" the level of education, the lower the levels of unprofessional behavior, inappropriate comments, sexual harassment, and unfair practices. However, these two studies blow that assumption out of the water. In certain law schools, women are shocked at how badly they are being treated—and it shows in how they are performing.

The second thing you can do is to check certain statistics on the law schools you are interested in, such as the percentage of women on law review and the percentage of female tenure and tenure-track professors. Your third step should be to go to each law school and talk with female students and female professors about how women are treated at that law school. And finally, see if the school has published any gender studies about itself; then obtain and read those studies. If ignorance of the law is not a reasonable defense for a defendant, than ignorance of your prospective law school's policies and practices shouldn't be the one factor that ruins your chances at a decent education. When narrowing down your law school choices, you should do your own informal gender study of the schools in which you are interested as part of your general research. While this may seem like a lot of work, it will seem like nothing compared to the amount of work that you'll be expected to complete while in law school. The point here is this: If you're going to commit three years of your life and anywhere from $50,000 to $150,000 (which you'll probably be borrowing), you should have enough respect for your own well-being to find a law school that you'll be happy with—or at least a law school that you won't regret having gone to.

There are clearly many law schools in existence that will not make you regret your choice—your mission, should you choose to accept it, is to find that place...just don't

[36]Mary Becker has written a (so far) unpublished 18-page article on "Questions Women (and Men) Should Ask When Selecting a Law School."

assume that it will be the "best" or most highly ranked law school out there. Because until law schools as a whole free themselves from their medieval rigor mortis with regard to their perception and treatment of women (and their twentieth-century rigor mortis with regard to their reliance on standardized testing to evaluate applicants), one can't assume that every institution of higher learning will necessarily be a place where *both* genders can excel.

CHAPTER 7
CAREER OUTLOOK

CONSIDER THE ALTERNATIVES[1]

Naturally, after law school, you'll begin a promising career as an urchin diver. Or you'll run your own snowboarding business. Train thoroughbred horses? Run a state prison? Become an interior designer?

You think we're kidding?

The most recent study shows that more than 3,000 law school graduates chose employment in nonlegal fields.[2] The study, conducted by the National Association for Law Placement (NALP), surveyed the graduating law school class of 1995. The jobs mentioned in the first paragraph were just a few of the alternative careers actually reported as sources of full-time employment by 1995 law school graduates. In the twenty-two years that NALP has been doing this study, the 1995 report yielded a record number of respondents, accounting for the employment status of 83 percent of all graduates. The study shows that 86.7 percent of law school grads were employed within six months after graduation. The number is a 2 percent increase over the previous year, making 1995 the first time since 1987 that the rate measurably increased.

Before you get too excited, understand that this number should be contrasted with the 89–92 percent employment rate reported for the classes of 1983 to 1990. Clearly employment prospects for law school graduates are not what they were in the glory days of the 1980s, but things are beginning to turn around.

Yet, as you can see from the NALP survey, the increase in employment is coming not from the law firms but from career opportunities outside the legal field. More and more law school graduates are finding their legal degrees to be very attractive to employers in the business sector. The trend in nonlegal employment has been steadily increasing since 1990 and now accounts for over 10 percent of employment for law school graduates. Check out the following graphs from the NALP report, which break down full-time and part-time legal and nonlegal positions as well as the type of employer within both legal and nonlegal fields.

[1]For a thorough look at non-legal careers, check out The Princeton Review's Alternative Careers for Lawyers, by Hillary Mantis, Director of the Career Planning Center at Fordham University School of Law.

[2]All data taken from Class of 1995 Employment Report and Salary Survey, National Association for Law Employment (NALP), Washington, DC, 1996. NALP conducts these surveys annually.

WHERE ARE THEY NOW?

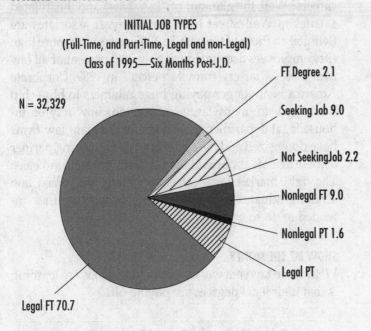

INITIAL JOB TYPES
(Full-Time, and Part-Time, Legal and non-Legal)
Class of 1995—Six Months Post-J.D.

N = 32,329

FT Degree 2.1

Seeking Job 9.0

Not SeekingJob 2.2

Nonlegal FT 9.0

Nonlegal PT 1.6

Legal PT

Legal FT 70.7

Note: N represents 89.3 of survey respondents and excludes 49 employed
graduates for whom job type, e.g., legal non-legal, was not reported

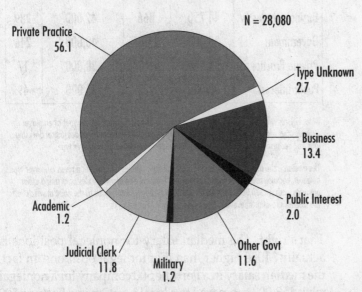

INITIAL EMPLOYMENT BY TYPE OF EMPLOYER
Class of 1995 — Six Months Post-J.D.

Private Practice
56.1

N = 28,080

Type Unknown
2.7

Business
13.4

Public Interest
2.0

Academic
1.2

Judicial Clerk
11.8

Military
1.2

Other Govt
11.6

This chart includes all job types—both legal and non-legal, full-time and part-time—but omits
graduates studyingfull-time for an advanced degree. Note: N represents 77.6% of respondents.

Why are more and more law students seeking alternative careers? Well, the glamour of "L.A. Law" and the inflated salaries in Wall Street firms for first-year associates are definitely a thing of the past. In 1995, firms with more than fifty employees accounted for only 28.6 percent of all law firm jobs—a far cry from 44 percent in 1989. Corporate America is no longer paying huge retainers to blue-chip firms. Instead, many large corporations now rely on in-house legal departments. As a result, the giant law firms have downsized and the opportunities for making partner at these firms is about as likely as winning at keno in Vegas. The tight market for legal employment has forced law school graduates to enter other fields whether they intended to do so or not.

SHOW ME THE MONEY
What these lawyers working at nonlegal jobs are learning is that their legal degrees are paying off.

Salary Medians by General Employer Type Legal and Non-Legal Jobs				
Employer Type	Legal Jobs	N	Non-Legal Jobs	N
All Types	$39,000	15,543	$40,000	1,424
Academic	**36,750**	**34**	**35,000**	**98**
Business/Industry	44,750	866	42,000	989
Government	33,000	2,067	40,000	246
Private Practice	50,000	9,757	30,000	17
Public Interest	30,000	225	35,000	49

Note: Figures reflect full-time jobs only. The number of jobs reported for all types of employer exceeds the sum of the individual employer types because the former includes judical clerkship jobs and because not all job data with a salary reported included an employer type.

The median is the mid-point in a ranking of *all* full-time salaries reported for a given employer type. however, because so many reported salaries are identical and especially cluster at round dollar amounts, such as $30,000, the median should generally be interpreted as the point at which half the salaries are at or above that figure and half are at or below it.

That's right. The median salary for nonlegal positions is actually $1000 higher than that for legal positions. In fact, the median salary in a Fortune 500 company for a nonlegal job is $53,000 compared to a legal position in a Fortune 500 company, where the median salary is $51,750. It appears that the business sector values a legal degree more than the legal profession does. Of course, median starting salaries in private practice are the highest of any specific job type, at $50,000. However, salaries of more than $70,000 accounted for just 11.2 percent of all salaries reported. With less jobs available at huge law firms, smaller firms of twenty-five lawyers or less now provide 50 percent of all legal employment.

Even those students who passionately insist that money is not their primary motivation for becoming a lawyer should be forewarned. These altruistic souls may want to know that the starting median salary reported for legal public interest jobs was $30,000 and the starting median salary for nonlegal public interest jobs was $35,000. (Where's the justice in that?)

The changing landscape of legal employment should not discourage you from planning to pursue exactly the type of job, legal or nonlegal, that you're dreaming of as you fill out your law school applications. All we suggest is that you keep your career options open and remember that a law school education is a versatile training for which many employers in various professional and entrepreneurial fields will gladly pay a premium.

GEOGRAPHICS
It's no surprise that for the last five years, New York and California have been number one and two, respectively, for states where the most law graduates have found jobs. The highest median salary for any full-time job was in New York at $55,000; the lowest was in Montana, where you can cash in your law degree for a starting median salary of $28,000. And as for individual cities, in Palo Alto, California, you can enjoy the beautiful northern California weather and garner a median starting salary of $71,000. Still, nothing beats the Big Apple, where law school graduates from all over the country take up city living and vie for Manhattan's top median starting salaries at $83,000. A quick word of advice: Unless you're attending a top-ten law school, it is always much easier to find a job in the state in which you went to law school. Below is a table listing the top-ten states for the last five years, ranked by number of

---

They're Lawyers?

How will you explain to your friends and family that after three years of law school you've decided that you don't want to practice law? The last thing you want to hear at a family gathering is Uncle So-and-So rhetorically snarling at you, "Now don't you feel like all that education is wasted?" Feel free to pull out this list of other people who "wasted" their legal educations:

LITERATI
John Grisham, author
Scott Turow, author
Steve Martini, author
Mortimer Zuckerman, editor
Franz Kafka, writer
Jules Verne, writer
Henry James, writer
Wallace Stevens, poet
Robert Louis Stevenson, writer and poet
Honore de Balzac, writer

MEDIA
Geraldo Rivera, talk-show host
Jeff Greenfield, political commentator
Catherine Crier, anchor

SPORTS
Paul Tagliabue, NFL Commissioner
David Stern, NBA Commissioner
Tony La Russa, manager, St. Louis Cardinals
Howard Cosell, sportscaster
Steve Young, quarterback, San Francisco 49ers

ENTREPRENEURS
Jerry Levin, CEO of Time/Warner
Larry Rosenfeld and Rick Flax, co-founders of California Pizza Kitchen
Tim and Nina Zagat, publishers of Zagat's restaurant and hotel guides

ARTISTS
Otto Preminger, filmmaker
Cole Porter, musician
Paul Cezanne, artist
Igor Stravinsky, musician

POLITICAL LEADERS
Bill Clinton, U.S. President
Mahatma Gandhi, leader of India

jobs taken by law school grads. We've also provided a listing of the median starting salaries of law school graduates in all fifty states for the class of 1995 .

	States with Largest Number of Jobs Taken From 1990 – 1995					
	1990	1991	1992	1993	1994	1995
1.	New York	New York	New York	New York	New York	New York
2.	California	California	California	California	California	California
3.	Washington, DC	Illinois	Pennsylvania	Texas	Texas	Texas
4.	Illinois	Washington, DC	Illinois	Illinois	Illinois	Illinois
5.	Texas	Pennsylvania	Washington, DC	Pennsylvania	Washington, DC	Washington, DC
6.	Pennsylvania	Texas	Texas	Washington, DC	Florida	Florida
7.	Florida	New Jersey	Massachusetts	Florida	Pennsylvania	Pennsylvania
8.	Massachusetts	Massachusetts	Florida	New Jersey	New Jersey	New Jersey
9.	New Jersey	Florida	New Jersey	Massachusetts	Massachusetts	Massachusetts
10.	Ohio	Ohio	Ohio	Ohio	Ohio	Ohio

Starting Salaries—All Full-PartTime Jobs—States Ranked by Median Salaries

Start of Job	Median	Start of Job	Median
NY	55,000	WA	35,450
CA	52,000	MO	35,000
DC	50,500	NC	35,000
TX	48,000	KY	35,000
GA	44,500	CO	35,000
MA	42,000	NM	35,000
IL	40,000	MS	34,128
HI	40,000	FL	34,000
NV	39,500	NH	33,750
MI	38,523	MD	33,500
OH	38,000	OR	33,500
VA	38,000	NJ	33,000
CT	37,500	KS	33,000
IN	37,000	NE	33,000
AK	36,672	OK	33,000
PA	36,442	ND	32,000
WI	36,000	SC	32,000
MN	36,000	RI	31,000
WV	36,000	ME	30,000
TN	36,000	VT	30,000
LA	36,000	IA	30,000
AZ	36,000	AR	30,000
DE	35,578	ID	30,000
AL	35,500	SD	29,500
UT	35,500	WY	29,500
		MT	29,500

DEMOGRAPHICS

Employment patterns have emerged along ethnic and gender lines. For example, the 1995 NALP survey showed that almost one-third of employed women took government, public interest, and judicial clerkship positions compared to one-quarter of employed men.

INITIAL EMPLOYER TYPES—MEN AND WOMEN
Full-Time Jobs Only

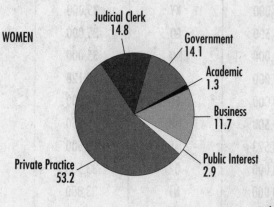

WOMEN

Judicial Clerk
14.8

Government
14.1

Academic
1.3

Business
11.7

Public Interest
2.9

Private Practice
53.2

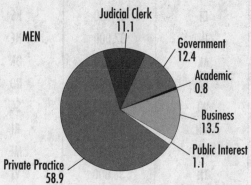

MEN

Judicial Clerk
11.1

Government
12.4

Academic
0.8

Business
13.5

Public Interest
1.1

Private Practice
58.9

Note: To enhance clarity the unknown category is not shown on the chart.

Thirty-four percent of minority graduates took public service positions compared to 27 percent of nonminority graduates. It is notable that government jobs accounted for more than one-fifth of jobs taken by African Americans, a number twice that for white graduates. African Americans and Native Americans were the least likely to take jobs in private practice. However, the NALP study does indicate that minorities obtained 14.2 percent of all law firm jobs in 1995. That figure is an increase from 12 percent in 1994 and a significant increase ("statistically significant" at least) from the 9-10 percent reported in the three previous years. Asian and Pacific Islander and white law school graduates were least likely to accept public interest positions, both groups coming in at less than 2 percent. Regardless of what jobs each ethnic group is gravitating toward, the number of job opportunities means very little if the compensation isn't fair. Judging by the table below, it may be better to be in the minority.

Full-Time Salaries by Race/Ethnicity									
	Percent of Salaries Which Were:								
Race/Ethnicity	$25,000 or less	$25,001– $35,000	$35,001– $45,000	$45,001– $55,000	More than $55,000	Median	Mean	Most Frequently Reported Salaries	Number Reported
All Races	8.0	30.1	23.3	12.2	26.4	$40,000	$45,000	$30,000 (7.4)/$35,000 (5.1)	16,967
Caucasion	8.4	31.3	23.3	12.2	24.8	38,000	44,888	30,000 (7.7)/35,000 (5.4)	13,845
African or African American	7.6	29.1	21.9	11.7	29.6	40,000	46,711	30,000 (6.9)/70,000 (4.9)	894
Native American	11.5	25.3	23.0	10.3	29.9	41,600	46,599	30,000 (8.0)/36,000 (8.0)	87
Hispanic	6.4	28.0	27.0	12.5	26.1	40,000	45,878	30,000 (7.6)/40,000 (6.1)	656
Asian/Pacific Islander	4.9	19.7	24.5	11.0	39.9	48,000	51,874	70,000 (5.9)/83,000 (5.9)	833

Note: Figures reflect full-time jobs only. The number of jobs reported for all racial/ethnic groups exceeds the sum of the individual groups because not all job data with a salary reported included information on race/ethnicity. Figures in parentheses in the column labelled "Most Frequently Reported Salaries" indicate the percentage as salaries reported at that level.

FINDING A JOB WHILE IN LAW SCHOOL

On graduation day from law school, less than half of the graduates have job offers. The truth is that meeting the demands of law school and at the same time doing a coordinated job search in a highly competitive job market is more than most people can handle. To ease the burden, just about every law school has a career services department. These departments have all kinds of resources, including job listings, employer directories, self-help books, resume workshops, interview techniques, and sometimes a shoulder to cry on.

A particularly obnoxious service that law school career centers provide for their students is "on-campus interviews." The big-name firms come to campus to interview the lucky few (usually only the students on law review) whose resumes passed the smell test. These firms will probably give offers to two people even though they only have one position available. Students who do not receive interviews feel left out and discouraged. Their lives would be much easier if employers continually came to campus rather than each student having to seek out his or her own interviews.

What the NALP survey reveals is that "self-initiated contact" was just as successful in creating pregraduation employment as were the on-campus interviews. In fact, self-initiated contact was far and away the most effective way to get a job after graduating law school. The table below should give you a good idea of what works and what doesn't when law students are looking for jobs. Hopefully, when the time comes, you will combine "what you know" with "who you know" and create a network of contacts who will effectively become your self-created executive search firm.

CHAPTER 8
MONEY MATTERS

The following chapter is not meant to discourage you. It is meant to inform, empower, and enable you. Legal education is expensive—what we aim to do in the next few pages is offer some perspective on how expensive it really is, which schools are willing to help ease the costs, and what financial aid exists for law school applicants.

THE REALITY CHECK

Let's face it: In the last ten years more people have been graduating from law school, but fewer law school graduates have been able to find jobs. The law schools themselves have only exacerbated the situation with median tuition among ABA-accredited schools rising 127 percent in the same ten-year period (there's been a 570 percent increase in the last twenty years!!). Consequently, over 70 percent of these law school graduates enter a difficult job hunt carrying tens of thousands of dollars in loan debt. The result: a lot of law school loan default.

YOU DO THE MATH

Clicking through New York University School of Law's web site, you'll come across the following information:

Tuition	$23,450
Health/Registration	$741
Housing	$6,975
Living Expenses/Food	$6,074
Course Expenses	$650
Federal Loan Origination Fees	$740
Health Insurance	$575
Total	**$39,205**

Now take that $39,205 and multiply by three. You should get $117,615. Correct for inflation (NYU certainly will), add things like computers and all other miscellany, and you can easily imagine spending $125,000 by the time you're through. $125,000! Now use the table on the next page (handily provided by, you guessed it, NYU) to look at what that means for monthly payments after you graduate:

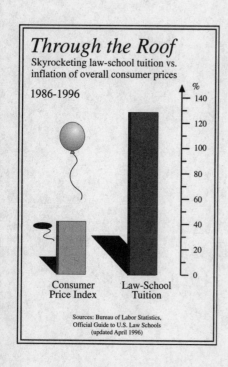

Through the Roof
Skyrocketing law-school tuition vs. inflation of overall consumer prices

1986-1996

Consumer Price Index

Law-School Tuition

Sources: Bureau of Labor Statistics, Official Guide to U.S. Law Schools (updated April 1996)

# of Years	5	10	15	20	25	30
5%		.01061				
8%	.02028	.01214	.00956	00.837	.00772	.00734
8.25%	.0204	.01227	.0097	.00852	.00789	.00751
8.5%	.02052	.0124	.00985	.00868	.00806	.00769
9%	.02076	.01267	.01015	.009	.0084	.00805
9.5%	.021	.01294	.01044	.00932	.00874	.00841
10%	.02125	.01322	.01075	.00965	.00909	.00878
10.5%	.0215	.0135	.01106	.00999	.00945	.00915
11%	.02175	.01378	.01137	.01033	.00981	.00953
11.5%	.022	.01406	.01169	.01067	.01017	.00991
12%	.02225	.01435	.01201	.01102	.01054	.01029

Take that $125,000 and assume you had to borrow every penny of it. Multiply it by, let's say, 8 percent at ten years (a common assumption by law school applicants is that they will be able to pay all their debt back in ten years or less). You get monthly payments (that's what the table above is calculating) of $1,517.50. No problem, right? You'll be making $2 million a year as a partner at Skadden, Arps by then, so why worry? Take a look at the chart below:

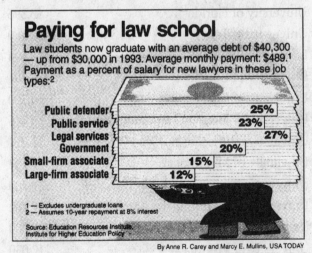

Paying for law school

Law students now graduate with an average debt of $40,300 — up from $30,000 in 1993. Average monthly payment: $489.[1] Payment as a percent of salary for new lawyers in these job types:[2]

Public defender	25%
Public service	23%
Legal services	27%
Government	20%
Small-firm associate	15%
Large-firm associate	12%

1 — Excludes undergraduate loans
2 — Assumes 10-year repayment at 8% interest

Source: Education Resources Institute, Institute for Higher Education Policy

By Anne R. Carey and Marcy E. Mullins, USA TODAY

Since you'll be paying three times as much as the folks in the chart above do, multiply those percentages by 3. And let's say that halfway through law school, you decided that you really didn't want that big partnership at Skadden, and that you wanted to be a public defender. Well, the good news is that you've still got 25 percent of your salary left in which to feed, clothe, and house yourself.

Consequently, it's no wonder that 56 percent of first-year law students are "very concerned" about the level of their educational debt.[1] Of course, there are many, many mitigating factors. The average debt for NYU students is slightly over $50,000; the average graduate earns almost $70,000 as a starting salary. Running those numbers through the calculation process, again at 8 percent for ten years, gets you to a point where your loans are only 9.6 percent of your monthly gross salary (the monthly payment is $607). Additionally, New York University is one of many schools that has a very progressive, very appealing Loan Repayment Assistance Program (see the section in this chapter entitled "Post-Graduation Assistance Programs"). So chances are that it will not be as bad as the first situation, but that first situation is far from fantasy.

LOW-COST LAW SCHOOL OPTIONS

What are other options for law students, then? Well, here's a random sampling of in-state tuition figures for some very, very good schools (remember, NYU's tuition was $23,450):

Law School	In-State Tuition
University of Florida	$3,396
University of Texas	$3,780
University of Arizona	$3,894
University of Colorado	$4,394
University of Washington	$4,500
University of Iowa	$5,166
University of Wisconsin	$5,211
University of Minnesota	$7,524
University of Connecticut	$10,300
University of California, Los Angeles	$10,782
University of California, Berkeley	$10,800
University of Virginia	$12,030

[1]Wightman, Linda F., *Legal Education at the Close of the Twentieth Century: Descriptions and Analyses of Students, Financing, and Professional Expectations and Attitudes*, The Law School Admission Council, Newtown, PA, 1995, p. 56.

Six of the schools listed above are commonly in the "top 25" of various rankings—Texas, Iowa, Minnesota, UCLA, Berkeley, and Virginia. For any of these schools, if you stay in the state and practice law there after school is over, you'll have very little debt and at the same time a great chance of landing a good job, since all of the schools listed above are even more highly respected in their state than they are nationally.

Our advice, therefore, is to *take a year and establish residency in one of these states!* There's no reason to come out of law school saddled with $60,000 worth of debt if you can possibly help it. And having little debt will free you up to practice whatever type of law you wish and not force you to go work for a huge firm to pay back your loans. It's worth the extra year of living in a cool place like Minneapolis or Seattle or Berkeley or Austin or Boulder. Go to those places, wait tables, hang out, listen to music, walk the earth, and then follow your dream of studying law.

POSTGRADUATION ASSISTANCE PROGRAMS

> *[You'll get] a base salary of eighty thousand the first year, plus bonuses. Eighty-five for the second year, plus bonuses. A low interest mortgage so you can buy a house. Two country club memberships. And a new BMW. You pick the color of course. All of our partners are millionaires by the age of forty-five.*
>
> —THE FIRM, JOHN GRISHAM

If you happen to land a job like the one taken by the protagonist in the thriller *The Firm*, you'll probably be able to write your loan repayment checks while teeing off on the back nine. The most recent report from the National Association of Law Placement shows, however, that only about 11 percent of law school grads receive starting salaries of $70,000 or above. So how will the other 89 percent pay back loans and eat something other than spaghetti and butter for dinner? The Bible says: "Seek forgiveness"—in this case, loan forgiveness.

There are a growing number of sources that are willing to pay your loans for you ("loan forgiveness"; it's as if you've sinned by taking out loans). In return, you must commit to employment in public interest law. These programs are generally called Loan Repayment Assistance Programs (LRAP). At last check, fifty law schools have instituted LRAPs. That number is increasing every year.

The way most LRAPs work is like this: A law student commits himself or herself to working for a public service or public interest job as defined by their his or her school's LRAP. The criterion for what qualifies as "public service" is usually quite liberal. As long as the graduate's gross income does not exceed the prevailing public service salary[2] for an attorney who is an equivalent number of years out of law school, then all your "eligible" loans will be paid in full for up to ten years. Eligible loans are typically any educational debt that is financed through the law school office (we list them all at the end of this chapter) which only really excludes loan sharks, anonymous benefactors, and Beelzebub.

The state bar associations are chipping in as well. Currently in Arizona, Maryland, Minnesota, North Carolina, and Tennessee you can apply for excellent LRAPs through local bar associations. Additionally, a number of legal service programs in cities all over the country provide some type of loan deferral or loan forgiveness to qualifying employees. There are likely to be many more such programs by the time you graduate from law school.

LRAPs are great programs. Some of you may feel that doing a tour of duty in public service law may put off your dream of working in a big firm or becoming the next Gerry Spence. The other way to look at it is that a program that covers your monthly $489 debt payment turns your median starting public interest salary of $30,000 into $36,000. Plus, you get major frontline experience which, after a couple of years, makes you extremely attractive to private firms that will pay you the big money.

For a comprehensive listing of all the LRAPs and other loan forgiveness information, contact an outstanding organization called The National Association for Public Interest Law in Washington, D.C., which can be reached by phone at (202) 466-3686, on the Internet at http://www.napil.org, or via E-mail at napil@napil.org.

[2]Even if your salary does exceed the "prevailing public service salary" most LRAP programs will pay a good percentage of your debt service. Nice, huh?

BEG, BORROW, OR STEAL—TYPES OF LOANS

The most common sources of financial aid to law students are loan programs, several of which we will describe briefly. Not all schools have access to all of these funds, and some offer additional sources of aid not listed here. To get a general idea of availability of aid at a given institution, check its catalog. If you are serious about attending a particular school, we recommend contacting its financial office directly for reliable information on just how much aid you stand to receive.

A simple but oft-forgotten piece of advice: If you don't ask, you don't get. Be pushy. Demand that the school give you more. Exercise those skills of advocacy that you are seeking to hone. Most schools have reserves of cash that go unused unless a student chirps up and threatens to transfer if the school doesn't provide more financial aid. (The better your grades, of course, the more apt they are to crack open their safe of financial goodies for you.)

PARENTAL CONTRIBUTION

If you have never applied for financial aid in the past and are operating under the assumption that, as a tax-paying grown-up x number of years out of school, you will be recognized as the self-supporting adult that you are, well, you're in for a surprise. Veterans of financial-aid battles will not be surprised to hear that financial-aid offices have a difficult time recognizing when apron strings have legitimately been cut. Some schools will consider your parents' income in determining your eligibility for financial aid, regardless of your age or tax status. Policies vary widely, so be sure to ask the schools you consider exactly what their policies are regarding financial independence for the purposes of financial aid.

THE PERKINS LOAN

This need-based, federally funded loan is about as close as it gets to free money for law students. It is awarded by an individual school on the basis of the Federal Methodology for need assessment described earlier.

- Rate: 5 percent
- Amount Available: $5,000 per year cumulative $30,000 maximum, including any residual undergraduate Perkins debt

If you have never applied for financial aid in the past and are operating under the assumption that, as a tax-paying grown-up x number of years out of school, you will be recognized as the self-supporting adult that you are, well, you're in for a surprise.

- Term: Ten years maximum after repayment begins

- Standard Deferment: Interest begins to accrue upon beginning repayment

- Grace Period: Granted upon application, nine months post-graduation

- Minimum Payment: $30–40/month

- Sources: You will apply for the Perkins directly with the school you choose to attend. Perkins funds are limited everywhere and nonexistent in some places. Each individual school has control over the size and number of the Perkins loans it awards

OTHER LOAN PROGRAMS

Currently, the Stafford, Supplemental Loan, and Law Access Loan programs are the source of most law students' loans, but the program is being phased out in favor of the William D. Ford Federal Direct Loan program, which will eliminate banks entirely from the lending process. Beginning in 1995, the Stafford was merged with the Supplemental Student Loan, and the details of the new loan's terms closely resemble the previous terms of the combined loans. Due to all of these changes, each school may have its own lending process, but you can expect to find these basic parameters.

THE STAFFORD LOAN

The Stafford Loan is more widely available than the Perkins. Stafford Loans are either subsidized or unsubsidized. A subsidized loan is awarded on the basis of financial need. The federal government pays interest on the loan until you begin repayment. An unsubsidized loan is not awarded on the basis of need. You'll be charged interest from the time the loan is disbursed until it is paid in full. You can receive a subsidized loan and an unsubsidized loan for the same enrollment period. The amount available is greater than under the Perkins program, but the interest rate is nearly twice as high. Before Ronald Reagan got to it, the Stafford was the Guaranteed Student Loan (GSL), and almost anybody could get one. But a lot of people decided not to pay it back, *60 Minutes* did an exposé, and the rest is history. The loan is now made by an outside lender (like your regular bank), but it is guaranteed by an independent agency and insured by the federal government.

- Rates: New Loans—variable interest rate with a 9% cap (if you already carry Stafford or GSL debt at 7, 8, or 9 percent, any additional Stafford loan will be made at that rate)

- Additional Fees: They stick it to you here on the Stafford. The lender may charge an "origination fee" of up to 5 percent and an "Insurance Premium" of up to 3 percent. These amounts are deducted automatically from the amount you receive but not from the amount you owe

- Amount Available: Maximum $18,500 per year; maximum subsidized $8,500 per year. Cumulative maximum (including any residual Stafford or GSL debt): $138,500 (no more than $65,500 of this amount may be in subsidized loans)

- Term: Ten years maximum after repayment of principal begins

- Standard Deferment: Interest starts to accrue upon beginning repayment for subsidized loans and on disbursement for unsubsidized loans

- Grace Period: By application, generally six months postgraduation

- Minimum Payment: $50/month

- Sources: You can apply for the Stafford Loan through a bank, a credit union, or possibly through the school you attend, but the easiest way to apply is through the Access Group (next page)

THE SUPPLEMENTAL STUDENT LOAN (SLS)

Quite a bit closer to the real world, the SLS is guaranteed by the feds but issued by a private lender at a variable rate. Eligibility for the SLS, which is often used by students to cover the estimated Parental Contribution (PC) discussed earlier, is not based on need. In almost every respect, however, its terms are significantly less favorable than those of either the Perkins or the Stafford.

- Rate: 52-week T-Bill rate on June 1st plus 3.25 percent, capped at 12 percent (in 1991, the rate was 11.49 percent)

- Additional Fees: No origination fee, but a possible insurance fee of up to 3 percent to be deducted from the loan's proceeds but (of course) not from the amount owed

- Amount Available: Maximum $4,000 per year. Cumulative $20,000 maximum (including any residual undergraduate SLS debt)

- Term: Ten years postgraduation maximum

- Standard Deferment: Interest begins to accrue with the origination of the loan. Furthermore, only payments on the principal can be deferred until after graduation. This means that you may have to make payments while still in school. An exception to this rule is SLS loans taken through the Access Group, which in some cases will allow interest payments to be postponed until repayment of the principal begins. In any case, interest continues to accrue

- Grace Period: None, though recipients of the SLS through Law Access may apply for a six-month grace period

- Minimum Payment: $50/month

- Sources: Banks, savings and loans, credit unions, Law Access

THE LAW ACCESS LOAN (LAL)

The Law Access Loan is administered by the Access Group, the largest provider of private law school loans in the country, offering graduate and professional student loan financing to those in all disciplines. The LAL itself is very similar to the SLS; it is not need-based and its rate varies with the Treasury Bill rate. Applicants for the LAL are expected, however, to have clean credit histories and to apply for the Stafford and SLS first. Conveniently, LAL applicants can apply for the Stafford and the SLS through the Access Group itself, which can supply you with a handy packet containing all three applications.

- Rate: Varies quarterly. Ninety-one-day T-Bill rate plus 3.25 percent with no cap. The average rate has recently hovered around 11 percent

- Additional Fees: Deducted from the proceeds of the loan are a guaranty fee of 11 percent [!] (7 percent at disbursement and an additional 4 percent upon repayment). These fees do not affect the amount owed

- Amount: Maximum $120,000 for most schools

- Term: Twenty years maximum

- Standard Deferment: Interest begins to accrue with the loan's origination, and payments on it can be deferred only under "limited circumstances"

- Grace Period: Principal repayment begins nine months after graduation

- Minimum Payment: $50/month

- Source: The Access Group

In addition to these major sources of loan funds, there are any number of commercial lenders that have student-loan programs, though the terms of the loans they offer will almost surely be less attractive than those of the loans described above. Also, some individual schools have loan programs specifically for their students. Such information will be made available to you when you apply for aid through a school's financial-aid office.

LAWLOANS

The LAWLOANS program allows students to apply for both Federal Stafford loans and Private Law Student Loans at the same time, making the application process easier and faster. The LAWLOANS program is a cooperative effort by HEMAR Insurance Corporation of America (a subsidiary of SallieMae), SallieMae, Northstar Guarantee Inc., and Norwest Bank South Dakota, N.A.

ELIGIBILITY:

The borrower must be a U.S. citizen, U.S. national, or permanent resident. Permanent resident borrowers are required to obtain credit-worthy U.S. citizen cosigners.

Borrowers must be full-time or part-time graduate students in ABA-approved law schools.

The borrower must meet lender's credit criteria.

Borrowers must first apply for a Federal Stafford loan. (However, if the borrower's school participates in the FDSLP, the borrower is not required to apply for the Stafford loan to qualify for this program.)

ANNUAL LOAN LIMITS

Minimum for a first-time borrower: $1,000. For a continuing borrower: $500.

Maximum without a cosigner: $75,000. With a cosigner: $100,000.

Aggregate lifetime loan limits from all sources (includes Stafford loans, Private Law Student Loans, and Bar Study Loans):

Without a cosigner on private loans: $125,000.

With a cosigner on private loans: $150,000.

INTEREST RATE:

Interim: Varies quarterly. Based on 91-day T-bill + 3.25%.

Repayment: Varies quarterly. Based on 91-day T-bill + 3.50%.

Interest capitalization: At beginning of repayment.

Repayment term: Up to 15 years.

Repayment options: Level or graduated repayment. Borrowers also have access to Sallie Mae's money-saving Law Rewards and Direct Repay benefits. Stafford loans received through the LAWLOANS program qualify for the same repayment options and borrower benefits as any other Stafford loans serviced by Sallie Mae's Loan Servicing Centers.

Minimum payment: $50 per month per loan.

Repayment begins: Following a nine-month grace period after leaving school, or four years after disbursement, whichever comes first.

Total origination or insurance fees: 6.5 percent at disbursement, and 5.25 percent at repayment if borrower does not have a cosigner; 6.5 percent at disbursement only for cosigned loans.

MAKING UP YOUR MIND

During law school, many, many students change their minds about what they wish to practice and where they wish to practice it. And it's understandable that financial concerns play a part in that decision—remember, 56 percent of first-year law students are very concerned about their amount of debt. Law school should be an intellectually challenging experience—don't go to a school that's so expensive that the only thing you worry about while you're there is how you're going to pay for it after you leave. Only eleven percent of salaries for first-year graduates are $70,000 or above. Be smart—research schools that are both good and relatively inexpensive, apply to schools with Loan Repayment Assistance Programs, establish residency before attending a state school, and choose the best possible array of loans—by doing all this, law school will be the enjoyable and intellectually challenging experience it's supposed to be.

CHAPTER 9
THE LAW SCHOOLS

BY REGION

With 170 ABA accredited schools in the country and only a relative handful of them enjoying broad name recognition, you might find it helpful to see how many law schools there actually are in your part of the country. On the following pages you will find a listing of all the ABA-approved U.S. law schools profiled in this book, arranged by geographic region. This handy reference should make it easy to come up with a tentative list of law schools for further consideration.

The geographic regions as we have drawn them correspond roughly with those of the United States Census Bureau. As we have designated them, those regions are:

The Mid-Atlantic:	New Jersey, New York, and Pennsylvania
The South Atlantic:	Delaware, The District of Columbia, Florida, Georgia, Maryland, North Carolina, South Carolina, Virginia, and West Virginia
The South:	Alabama, Kentucky, Mississippi, Tennessee, Arkansas, Louisiana, Oklahoma and Texas
The Pacific Coast:	Hawaii, Washington, Oregon, and California.
The Heartland:	Iowa, Kansas, Minnesota, Missouri, Nebraska, North Dakota, South Dakota, Wyoming, Montana, Idaho, Colorado, Utah, New Mexico and Arizona
The Midwest:	Illinois, Indiana, Michigan, Ohio, and Wisconsin
New England:	Connecticut, Maine, Massachusetts, New Hampshire, and Vermont

THE MID-ATLANTIC

The Mid-Atlantic region is one of the most law school rich in the nation. New Jersey, New York and Pennsylvania are home to twenty-six law schools all told, many of them among the most highly respected in the country. Columbia, NYU, Cornell, and Penn, for instance, are perennial members of everybody's top twenty. The region is also home to several excellent public law schools, including both Rutgers schools and the State University of New York at Buffalo, as well as the nation's leading producer of public-interest lawyers—the City University of New York School of Law at Queens College. Overall, the Mid-Atlantic region is the second-largest producer of law graduates, yet demand for young lawyers in this region significantly outstrips supply. (This is particularly true in New Jersey, where there are nearly twice as many jobs as graduates.) Fully 85 percent of all the Mid Atlantic's 7,500 graduates remain in the region, and nearly 2,500 others move in. This is hardly surprising, of course, when one considers that the region is home to the capital of the American legal profession: New York. Indeed, the legal community of New York City alone accounts for nearly ten percent of all the law jobs in the nation and nearly half of all jobs in this region.

New York	CUNY School of Law at Queens College
	SUNY at Buffalo
	Brooklyn Law School
	Columbia University
	Cornell University
	Fordham University
	Hofstra University
	New York Law School
	New York University
	Pace University
	St. John's University
	Syracuse University
	Touro College
	Union University, Albany Law School
	Yeshiva University, Benjamin N. Cardozo School of Law
New Jersey	Rutgers University

	Camden Rutgers University
	Newark Seton Hall University
Pennsylvania	University of Pittsburgh
	Temple University
	Dickinson School of Law
	Duquesne University
	University of Pennsylvania
	Villanova University
	Widener University

THE SOUTH ATLANTIC

The states of the South Atlantic region are packed with excellent law schools. Several of the region's twenty-nine schools are among the most highly respected in the nation; the law schools at Georgetown, the University of Virginia, Duke University and the University of North Carolina, for instance, are perennial members of everybody's top twenty, and those at George Washington and Emory aren't very far behind. Happily for the bargain hunter, neither quality nor value drops off much the farther one goes down the list of the region's schools. The law schools at George Mason, William and Mary, the University of Georgia, and the University of Florida are all among the finest public schools in the nation. All told, the South Atlantic law schools produce fully one fifth of all U.S. lawyers, and the region's legal communities employ a nearly identical proportion. The South Atlantic's largest job market, Washington, D.C., is the second-largest in the nation, accounting for more than six percent of all jobs nationally. The volume and prestige of these jobs means that the nation's capital imports highly qualified grads from all over the country, many of them from the top schools in nearby North Carolina and Virginia, states that produce far more law grads than they employ.

Maryland	University of Baltimore
	University of Maryland
Delaware	Widener University
District of Columbia	American University
	Catholic University
	George Washington University
	Georgetown University
	Howard University

Virginia	William and Mary
	George Mason University
	University of Virginia
	University of Richmond
	Washington and Lee University
West Virginia	West Virginia University
North Carolina	University of North Carolina
	North Carolina Central
	Campbell University
	Duke University
	Wake Forest University
South Carolina	University of South Carolina
Georgia	University of Georgia
	Georgia State University
	Emory University
	Mercer University
Florida	University of Florida
	Florida State University
	University of Miami
	Nova University
	Stetson University

THE SOUTH

Outside of Texas, the South—as we have aligned it—is a region that is sparsely populated with law schools. Happily for the bargain hunter, however, the majority of the region's law schools are public institutions, many of them among the least expensive in the nation. One of these public schools, the University of Texas School of Law, is also a perennial member of everybody's top twenty, as is Tennessee's Vanderbilt University Law School. These two schools, along with SMU and Tulane, are the most highly regarded schools in a region dominated by regional schools. The public and private law schools in Alabama, Arkansas, Kentucky and Mississippi draw the vast majority of their students from within their home states. Due to relatively limited job opportunities, however, a significant proportion of law grads from those states seek employment elsewhere. Indeed, Texas is the only state in this region that employs more recent law grads than it produces. More than one quarter of the law jobs in this region are to be found in Texas, the nation's fifth-largest and second-highest-paying legal job market.

Louisiana	Louisiana State University
	Southern University
	Loyola University, New Orleans
	Tulane University
Texas	University of Houston
	University of Texas
	Texas Southern University
	Texas Tech
	Baylor University
	Southern Methodist University
	St. Mary's University
	South Texas College of Law
Mississippi	University of Mississippi
	Mississippi College
Alabama	University of Alabama
	Samford University,
	Cumberland School of Law
Tennessee	Memphis State University
	University of Tennessee
	Vanderbilt University
Oklahoma	University of Oklahoma
	Oklahoma City University
	University of Tulsa
Kentucky	University of Kentucky
	University of Louisville
	Northern Kentucky University
Arkansas	University of Arkansas, Little Rock
	University of Arkansas, Fayetteville

THE PACIFIC COAST

The Pacific Coast is more densely packed with fantastic law schools than perhaps any other region in the country. The West's most highly esteemed schools—Stanford, Berkeley, Hastings, UCLA, and USC—are to be found in California, but quality and value are to be found throughout the region. The University of Washington School of Law, like the four schools in the University of California system, is one of the most highly regarded public law schools in the nation. The law schools at Lewis and Clark, the University of Oregon, and the University of Hawaii are also highly popular and well-respected institutions. Many of these schools draw thousands of applications from non-Westerners, relatively few of whom (fewer than 15 percent) elect to leave the region after completing their degrees. The reason for this is simple: The twenty-four law schools in this region do not produce as many law grads as the Western legal communities can consume. California alone accounts for roughly 11 percent of all U.S. law jobs, thanks largely to Los Angeles and San Francisco, respectively the fourth- and eighth-largest job markets in the nation. The high salaries commanded by recent law grads in these markets also make California the highest-paying state in the nation for young attorneys.

California	University of California, Berkeley
	University of California, Davis
	University of California, Hastings
	University of California, Los Angeles
	California Western
	Loyola Marymount University
	Pepperdine University
	Southwestern University
	University of San Diego
	University of San Francisco
	Santa Clara University
	University of Southern California
	University of the Pacific, McGeorge School of Law
	Stanford University
	Thomas Jefferson School of Law
	Whittier College
	Golden Gate University
Oregon	University of Oregon
	Lewis and Clark College
	Willamette University

Washington	University of Washington
	Gonzaga University
	University of Puget Sound
Hawaii	University of Hawaii

THE HEARTLAND

It may be ridiculous to group such states as Arizona and Minnesota in the same region, but these thirteen states between the Pacific and the Mississippi share at least one characteristic: they are all relatively sparsely populated—with law schools as with people. Whatever the Heartland may lack in volume, however, it more than makes up for in quality and value; Residents of this region do not go wanting for lack of opportunity to pursue a legal education in a fine, inexpensive institution. Two of the public law schools in this region—those at the University of Iowa and the University of Minnesota—are perennial members of most top-twenty-five lists, and many of the others aren't far behind. The law schools of the University of Utah, the University of Colorado, and the University of Arizona, for instance, are easily among the finest public law schools in the country. Only slightly higher up the price scale, there is the BYU law school, the most highly respected private law school in the region after Missouri's Washington University School of Law. Though this region is home to sizable legal job markets in Denver, Minneapolis, and Pheonix, the Heartland accounts for only 10 percent of all jobs for recent law school graduates. This imbalance is greatest in Iowa and Utah, both of which produce nearly twice as many law grads as they employ.

North Dakota	University of North Dakota
South Dakota	University of South Dakota
Iowa	University of Iowa
	Drake University
Kansas	University of Kansas
	Washburn University
Minnesota	University of Minnesota
	Hamline University
	William Mitchell College of Law

Missouri	University of Missouri, Columbia
	University of Missouri, Kansas City
	Saint Louis University
	Washington University
Wyoming	University of Wyoming
Montana	University of Montana
Nebraska	University of Nebraska
	Creighton University
Idaho	University of Idaho
Colorado	University of Colorado
	University of Denver
Utah	University of Utah
	Brigham Young University
Arizona	University of Arizona
	Arizona State University
New Mexico	University of New Mexico

THE MIDWEST

The top-twenty law schools at the University of Chicago, the University of Michigan, Northwestern, and Notre Dame are the most highly prestigious in a region that produces more than 6,000 young lawyers annually. Well behind these giants in terms of national prestige, but highly respected in and around the Midwest, is a group of schools whose quality and value represent a great resource to residents of this region. Indiana University, Bloomington; the University of Illinois; Ohio State University; the University of Cincinnati; and the University of Wisconsin are all among the finest public law schools in the nation. There is, however, a downside to the ready accessibility of a quality legal education in most of these states: The volume of law grads churned out by the twenty law schools in Indiana, Michigan, Ohio, and Wisconsin comfortably exceeds demand for young attorneys in the legal communities of those four states. Illinois does its part to absorb much of this excess, but a healthy proportion of all graduates of midwestern law schools begin their careers outside the region. Though Chicago is the country's third-largest job market for recent law school graduates, even its big shoulders can support only so many lawyers.

Illinois	University of Illinois
	Northern Illinois University
	Southern Illinois University
	University of Chicago
	DePaul University
	Illinois Institute of Technology, Chicago-Kent College of Law
	John Marshall School of Law
	Loyola University
	Northwestern University
Ohio	University of Akron
	University of Cincinnati
	Cleveland-Marshall School of Law
	Ohio State University
	University of Toledo
	Capital University
	Case Western Reserve University
	University of Dayton
	Ohio Northern University
Wisconsin	University of Wisconsin
	Marquette University
Michigan	University of Michigan
	Wayne State University
	University of Detroit, Mercy School of Law
	Detroit College of Law
	Thomas M. Cooley Law School
Indiana	Indiana University, Bloomington
	Indiana University, Indianapolis
	University of Notre Dame
	Valparaiso University

NEW ENGLAND

Though not the dominant region in legal education that it is in undergraduate education, New England is home to several of the best law schools in the nation, including the twin titans Harvard and Yale. It is also home to some of the largest schools in the nation—the average enrollment of the six schools in and around Boston is nearly 1,300. (By comparison, the national average is slightly more than 700.) The sheer volume of law students in these schools accounts for the fact that of all regions in the United States, New England is the most over-supplied with law school graduates. Many future lawyers earn their degrees in New England, but fewer spend their careers here. The ratio of law graduates to legal jobs here is roughly 6 to 5, and only 65% of all graduates remain in New England. Of those who do, one in three works in Boston, the nation's sixth-largest legal job market. As large as many of New England's law schools are, few are inexpensive. In a region dominated by private institutions, there are fewer options for the bargain hunter than anywhere in the rest of the country. The law schools at the Universities of Maine and Connecticut are the only public law schools in the region, and both have very limited enrollments.

Connecticut	University of Connecticut
	Bridgeport School of Law at
	Quinnipiac College
	Yale University
	New England School of Law
	Suffolk University
Maine	University of Maine
New Hampshire	Franklin Pierce Law Center
Massachusetts	Boston College
	Boston University
	Harvard University
	New England School of Law
	Suffolk University
	Northeastern University
	Western New England College
Vermont	Vermont Law School

CHAPTER 10
THE LAW SCHOOLS
RANKED BY CATEGORY

On the following pages, you will find a number of lists of law schools ranked according to various qualities. It must be noted, however, that none of these lists purports to rank the law schools by their overall quality. Nor should any combination of the categories we've chosen here be construed as representing the raw ingredients for such a ranking. We have made no attempt to gauge the "prestige" of these schools, and we wonder whether we could accurately do so even if we tried. What we have done, however, is present a number of lists using information from two very large databases—one of factual information gathered from various sources (e.g., the American Bar Association) and another of subjective information gathered in our survey of more than eleven thousand current law students at the 170 law schools profiled in this book. On the basis of the information from these two sources, we have put together a number of "top ten" lists and, where meaningful and appropriate, corresponding "bottom ten" lists.

ADMISSIONS INDEX

At least in terms of numerical admissions standards, these are the twenty toughest law schools in the country to get into. To calculate this, we combined the average undergraduate GPA and the average LSAT score of entering students into a single index. Our top-twenty list is heavily populated by the traditional powerhouses of American legal education. It should come as no surprise to hear that Yale and Harvard students possess the highest numerical credentials of all U.S. law students. In fact, this list very closely resembles most traditional "top 20" lists.

Applicants to any of these schools had better have their numbers somewhere near the stratosphere, for though grades and LSAT scores are not the only factors that law schools consider when assessing applicants, the importance of numerical credentials in the admissions process should not be underestimated. Simply stated, a great GPA and LSAT score may not be enough to get you into a school like Yale, but a mediocre GPA and an unimpressive LSAT score will almost surely keep you out.

Top Twenty

1. Yale University
2. Harvard University
3. University of Chicago
4. Stanford University
5. New York University
6. University of California, Berkeley
7. Columbia University
8. Duke University
9. University of Michigan
10. University of Pennsylvania
11. University of Virginia
12. Cornell University
13. Georgetown University
14. Vanderbilt University
15. University of Minnesota
16. Washington and Lee University
17. University of California, Los Angeles
18. Northwestern University
19. University of Washington
20. Boston College

DEMAND INDEX

If you are hoping to gain admission to one of these twenty law schools, prepare to fight tooth and nail. In an effort to convey the popularity of certain law schools with applicants, we have calculated the "Demand Index" of the twenty most in-demand law schools in the country. This value is an indicator of more than simply the number of applicants to each school. It also takes into account the rate at which admitted applicants accept offers of admission to a given law school. Fellow geeks, follow along: To arrive at our demand index, we have taken the number enrolled divided by the number accepted and divided the resulting number by the percent accepted of those who applied.

$$\frac{\dfrac{\#\ \text{enrolled}}{\#\ \text{accepted}}}{\dfrac{\#\ \text{accepted}}{\#\ \text{applied}}} = \text{demand index}$$

Top Twenty

1. Yale University
2. Harvard University
3. Campbell University
4. Stanford University
5. Brigham Young University
6. North Carolina Central University
7. Arizona State University
8. New College of California
9. Northern Kentucky University
10. University of Minnesota
11. University of Georgia
12. University of Oklahoma
13. University of Texas
14. University of South Carolina
15. University of Chicago
16. Georgia State University
17. University of Alabama
18. University of California, Berkeley
19. University of New Mexico
20. University of Washington

QUALITY OF LIFE

Some may subscribe to the popular myth that law school is, by definition, a kind of hell. It appears, however, that even hell has its relatively nice neighborhoods. In our survey of more than twenty thousand current law students, clear differences emerged regarding what we have chosen to call the "Quality of Life" enjoyed by students at the 170 American law schools we surveyed.

To arrive at our quality-of-life index, we factored in students' responses to questions concerning three aspects of their law-school experience: the degree of competitiveness among students, the "sense of community" among students, and the quality of relations between students and faculty. As you can easily see, the quality of the education available to students at a given law school has nothing to do with their quality of life.

A few years ago, when Harvard also ranked last in this category for the second time, the Dean of the Harvard Law School was moved to say that our survey instrument must be "seriously flawed." This criticism is fair only in part. Yes, our survey is decidedly unscientific, and our calling this index a measure of the quality of overall life at a law school is, perhaps, presumptuous. But the fact remains that our unscientific survey method is equally unscientific for all of the law schools we profile. Harvard students had the same opportunity as all others to voice their degree of satisfaction with their law school. Furthermore, we have updated numbers on all of the schools for this year's edition and we resurveyed 70 schools as well. The result: Harvard came out last for the fourth year in a row.

Top Ten

1. Howard University
2. Baylor University
3. Brigham Young University
4. University of Wyoming
5. Regent University School of Law
6. Thomas Jefferson School of Law
7. Texas Southern University
8. Dickinson School of Law of the Pennsylvania State
9. Campbell University
10. University of Hawaii, Manoa

Bottom Ten

1. Harvard University
2. Santa Barbara College of Law
3. State University of New York at Buffalo
4. University of California, Berkeley
5. City University of New York
6. Columbia University
7. University of Pittsburgh
8. Yale University
9. George Washington University
10. Indiana University, Indianapolis

COMPETITIVENESS

Anyone who is at all familiar with the popular literature on life in law school—see *The Paper Chase* or *One L*—knows that cutthroat competitiveness characterizes relations among struggling first-year students. At least that's how legend would have it. Whether such a perception was ever accurate is difficult to say, but the perception remains. There is a popular myth among law students, for instance, concerning the hyper-competitive student—always at "some other school, like Harvard"—who will, in order to render his classmates unprepared for class or an exam, remove pages containing key cases from every volume of the *Federal Reporter*. Suffice it to say that students in every discipline, like humans in general, perform some necessary psychological function by trafficking in such myths, which often have little basis in fact.

That said, it is quite clear that competition is a fact of life in law school. To some students at some schools, grades take on an importance that they never did in college. Coveted spots on a school's law review staff are awarded solely on the basis of class rank, and jobs with the most prestigious private law firms and government agencies are tough to come by for those who have not distinguished themselves in this arena. Add to this the way in which grades are determined in most law school classes—on the basis of a single exam at semester's end—and you have a volatile mixture. Those who give in to stress easily should have no problem finding the motivation to do so while in law school, but those who seek to avoid such stress do have their options. We asked students in our survey to characterize the degree of competitiveness among students at their schools, and we got strikingly different results.

Top Ten/Most Competitive

1. Texas Southern University
2. University of Alabama
3. University of the Pacific
4. Thomas M. Cooley Law School
5. Southwestern University
6. Baylor University
7. University of Florida
8. University of Mississippi
9. University of Texas
10. Emory University

Bottom Ten/Least Competitive

1. University of Virginia
2. Washington and Lee University
3. William and Mary
4. University of California, Davis
5. Northeastern University
6. Yale University
7. Vanderbilt University
8. City University of New York
9. University of Montana
10. University of Notre Dame

THE BEST TEACHING FACULTIES

Nobody who has been to college should be surprised to hear that the quality of instruction varies widely from law school to law school and, indeed, from professor to professor within a given law school. Like most institutions of higher education, law schools are not immune to the publish-or-perish ethic, and most law-school faculty rankings are based narrowly on those faculties' scholarly output (read: number of law review articles published). It is, of course, impossible to quantify something as intangible as quality of teaching, but we took a stab simply by asking students how they would rate their faculty in this regard.

Top Ten

1. Boston University
2. University of Chicago
3. Washington and Lee University
4. Western New England College
5. University of Notre Dame
6. William and Mary
7. University of Texas
8. University of Virginia
9. New England School of Law
10. Vanderbilt University

Bottom Ten

1. University of Arkansas at Fayetteville
2. Detroit College of Law at Michigan State University
3. Northern Kentucky University
4. City University of New York
5. Texas Southern University
6. University of Akron
7. John Marshall Law School
8. University of Alabama
9. University of Idaho
10. Southern University

MOST FAVORABLE STUDENT/FACULTY RATIOS

When the Socratic Method reigned supreme as the dominant teaching method, relatively high student-faculty ratios were the norm in most law schools. By and large, first-year classes at most law schools still follow the old format, with one professor holding class before up to one hundred students. The introduction of alternate teaching methods (i.e., seminars and lectures) and, more important, the increasing emphasis of many schools on clinical education, have changed matters considerably. In a hands-on legal clinic, one instructor cannot adequately serve more than a handful of students, so it is not surprising to see that several of the law schools on our list—Yale and NYU, for instance—are schools that boast particularly large clinical programs.

Note: This list is derived from figures reported by the schools themselves. The rankings reflect the relative size of teaching faculty (full-time and part-time) only. They do not include administrators and staff.

Top Ten

1. Washington University
2. Southern California Institute of Law
3. University of Colorado
4. Humphreys College
5. University of Arkansas at Fayetteville
6. University of Richmond
7. Washington and Lee University
8. West Virginia University
9. Yale University
10. Quinnipiac College

Bottom Ten

1. Whittier College
2. University of Akron
3. Gonzaga University
4. University of California
5. University of San Francisco
6. Capital University Law School
7. University of Detroit
8. University of Michigan
9. University of Tulsa
10. American University

MINORITY REPRESENTATION AMONG STUDENTS

Just twenty-five years ago, the list of law schools with minority enrollments exceeding 30 percent would have been mighty short: Howard, North Carolina Central, Southern, and Texas Southern. Those historically black institutions were once the only significant sources of nonwhite lawyers in the nation, and they still occupy four of the top five slots on our list. Over the course of the last twenty-five years, however, the rest of the country has gone a long way toward closing the gap. Today, nearly all of the nation's elite law schools boast minority enrollments that surpass the national average of 18 percent. Though they do not rank among the top ten, such elite schools as Yale and Columbia also boast minority populations that comfortably exceed the national average.

Top Ten

1. Howard University
2. Texas Southern University
3. University of Hawaii, Manoa
4. Southern University
5. University of Utah
6. North Carolina Central University
7. University of Washington
8. Loyola Marymount University
9. University of New Mexico
10. University of Southern California

Bottom Ten

1. Empire College
2. Campbell University
3. University of North Dakota
4. University of South Dakota
5. West Virginia University
6. University of Montana
7. Widener University
8. University of Wyoming
9. Creighton University
10. Duquesne University

MINORITY REPRESENTATION AMONG FACULTY

The highly publicized case of New York University's Derrick Bell, one of the nation's most prominent law professors, brought to the general public's attention the controversial issue of ethnic diversity among law school faculty. Professor Bell, an African American, was formerly a member of the Harvard Law School faculty, where he was one of only five nonwhites among sixty-seven full-time professors. When HLS students formally protested the law school's failure to grant tenure to a black woman professor (she would have been the first), Professor Bell took a leave of absence in a show of support for the protesters. Two years later, the Harvard Corporation chose to call Professor Bell's bluff, ruling that Bell could not extend his leave of absence any longer. Noting that the law school had not taken significant steps in the interim to rectify the situation that prompted his departure, Bell chose to remain at NYU. Confrontation had not prompted Harvard to take action. Today, its faculty remains disproportionately white and male.

Top Ten

1. Texas Southern University
2. Howard University
3. North Carolina Central University
4. Southern University
5. University of Hawaii, Manoa
6. University of San Francisco
7. William Mitchell College of Law
8. City University of New York
9. Golden Gate University
10. St. Mary's University

Bottom Ten

1. Franklin Pierce Law Center
2. University of South Dakota
3. University of South Carolina
4. Brigham Young University
5. Creighton University
6. Drake University
7. Indiana University, Bloomington
8. University of Missouri, Kansas City
9. University of Montana
10. Northwestern University

PROPORTION OF WOMEN STUDENTS

Women did not begin entering law school in significant numbers until the 1970s, and equal representation remains only an ideal at most U.S. law schools despite the dramatic increase in women applicants in the last decade. Nationally, women make up a bit more than 42 percent of all law students, but a sizable number of schools stray far from the average in both directions. On the top of the scale, a handful of schools actually enroll more women than men, and one, the Northeastern University School of Law, has almost reversed the national average. Fully 60 percent of Northeastern's nearly 600 J.D. students are women, and the law schools at American University and Howard University are not far behind. On the opposite end of the scale, a number of law schools fall well behind the national average. To be fair, the student bodies at the schools near the bottom of this list do tend to reflect the makeup of those schools' applicant pools. Until women begin to apply to these schools in greater numbers, they will remain underrepresented on these campuses.

Top Ten

1. Northeastern University
2. Howard University
3. American University
4. University of Colorado
5. Loyola University, Chicago
6. City University of New York
7. Golden Gate University
8. North Carolina Central University
9. University of Hawaii, Manoa
10. University of San Francisco

Bottom Ten

1. Brigham Young University
2. University of Kentucky
3. Thomas M. Cooley Law School
4. Franklin Pierce Law Center
5. Mercer University
6. Mississippi College
7. Ohio Northern University
8. Samford University
9. Touro College
10. George Mason University

PROPORTION OF FEMALE FACULTY

Although women now make up more than 40 percent of the law student population in the United States, such relative balance has yet to be achieved among law professors. Nationally, only 25 percent of all full- and part-time law teaching faculty members are women. In large part, of course, the tenure system creates a time-lag between female law school enrollment and female faculty representation. Equal representation for women will surely come, it could be argued, but until members of the overwhelmingly male old guard retire, women wishing to enter legal academia must bide their time.

Top Ten

1. City University of New York
2. University of Detroit
3. Duke University
4. Nova Southeastern University
5. Vermont Law School
6. University of New Mexico
7. University of Akron
8. Brooklyn Law School
9. North Carolina Central University
10. University of Hawaii, Manoa

Bottom Ten

1. University of South Carolina
2. Louisiana State University
3. University of Nebraska
4. George Mason University
5. Brigham Young University
6. University of South Dakota
7. Yale University
8. Empire College
9. Campbell University
10. University of Chicago

1. City University of New York
2. Northeastern University
3. Northwestern University
4. University of California
5. University of Dayton
6. Duke University
7. State University of New York at Buffalo
8. Hamline University
9. North Carolina Central University
10. American University

PUBLIC INTEREST PLACEMENT

In 1991, the average starting salary for recent law grads in public-interest positions was only $25,000 per year—less than half of the average starting salary of first-year associates in private law firms. And while a big-firm lawyer five years out of school might make well over $100,000 per year, most public-interest lawyers do not enjoy the same kind of salary growth. Of course, this salary differential alone does not explain why only 2 percent of all law-school graduates begin their careers practicing law in the public interest. Indeed, more than 10 percent of current law students express a desire to do this kind of work despite its relatively low pay. Unfortunately, a sad economic reality faces nearly all would-be public-interest lawyers, and especially those who attend private law schools; because of skyrocketing tuition rates, the debt incurred by many graduates of private law schools forces them to seek more lucrative employment. Many of the nation's private law schools are beginning to establish loan-forgiveness programs intended to allow their graduates to pursue low-paying public-interest jobs. In the meantime, it is fortunate that inexpensive options exist.

CLERKSHIP PLACEMENT

Nationwide, roughly 12 percent of all law-school graduates begin their careers as judicial clerks, the worker ants of the judicial system. Most of those who serve clerkships do so as a prelude to a career in private practice, while some do so before entering a career in academia. Whatever the case, these one- or two-year positions typically go to graduates who excelled in law school. Law-school grades are an important factor in many employers' hiring decisions, but grades are especially important for those who seek to land a judicial clerkship. These research and writing jobs demand many of the same sorts of skills as law school coursework does. Furthermore, the most prestigious positions tend to go to those who attended one of the nation's elite schools, so the proportion of a school's graduates who land clerkships is often a function of that school's prestige. It is also true, however, that judges tend to hire graduates of their own alma maters. Because of this fact, one can also roughly gauge the strength of the regional connections of a law school by the rate at which it sends its graduates into these positions. In the case of Harvard and Columbia, their places on this list clearly reflect the prestige of the degrees they confer. First-year clerks from these schools are likely to serve not local alumni but judges at the highest levels of state and federal judiciaries.

Top Ten

1. Louisiana State University
2. University of Hawaii, Manoa
3. Rutgers University, Camden
4. University of South Dakota
5. Harvard University
6. Washington and Lee University
7. University of Idaho
8. Rutgers University, Newark
9. Villanova University
10. Columbia University

PRIVATE PRACTICE

The proportion of recent law-school graduates entering private practice has risen steadily in this last decade, reaching a peak of about 70 percent in 1991. Not coincidentally, law school tuition was up sharply in the same period. While the employment patterns of most individual schools conform closely to the national average, a few stand out on either extreme. The schools on this list send a disproportionately high percentage of their graduates to work in private practice. Interestingly, four of these schools are very inexpensive public institutions, a fact that calls into question the assumption that high debt burden alone can explain this trend.

Top Ten

1. Louisiana State University
2. Texas Tech University
3. University of Southern California
4. Northwestern University
5. University of Pennsylvania
6. Vanderbilt University
7. Duke University
8. Pepperdine University
9. Southern Methodist University
10. University of Virginia

CHAPTER 11
HOW TO USE THIS BOOK

Each of the ABA-accredited law schools listed in this book has its own two-page spread, with two sidebars containing general, mostly factual, information; text with a general overview of the school; and a paragraph on admissions. The information used in compiling the profiles in this book comes from several different sources, including student surveys, questionnaires filled out by the schools, and the American Bar Association's *Review of Legal Education in the United States*. In gathering information on each of the schools, we have surveyed more than twenty-five thousand law students over the past several years. We asked them dozens of questions on such matters as the quality of their relations with faculty and the quality of their schools' facilities. We also sent the entries to the administration for their comments. We have done our best to provide a balanced picture of each school. Do keep in mind, however, that while we do our best to choose only representative quotes, one student may express herself more strongly than another and the words are her opinion, not those of every student at the school. Use the information presented in this book as a guide to your own further exploration.

Material in the sidebars covers the following:

OVERVIEW

Type of School
Whether the school is public or private.

Environment
Whether the campus is located in a metropolis (big urban environment), city (smaller urban environment), suburb, or town.

Scholastic Calendar
How the school breaks up its academic year (i.e., semesters, trimesters).

Schedule
Whether the school offers full-time or part-time schedules.

STUDENTS

Enrollment of Parent Institution
Total number of students in the institution, including the law school.

Enrollment of Law School
Total number of students in the law school.

Percent Men, Percent Women, Percent Out-of-State, Percent Part-Time, Percent Minorities, Percent International Students, Number of Countries Represented, Average Age at Entry
Demographic breakdown of last year's entering class.

APPLICANTS ALSO LOOK AT

Other schools applicants consider.

SURVEY SAYS...HITS AND MISSES

Strengths and weaknesses of the school as reflected by our student surveys.

EMPLOYMENT PROFILE

General demographics from the administration regarding the number of firms recruiting on campus, the job placement rate, the percentage of students employed immediately after graduation, the percentage employed within six months, the average starting salary, and the percentage breakdown by fields.

ACADEMICS

Student/Faculty Ratio, Percent Female Faculty, Percent Minority Faculty, and Hours of Study Per Day
The faculty makeup of a school and how much work that faculty piles on.

FINANCIAL FACTS

The first set of numbers covers how much it will cost you to get the degree—tuition, books, and fees. The second set of numbers tells you how students pay the first set of numbers—percent first-year students receiving aid, percent of students receiving loans and assistantships, and number of students receiving scholarships, how much they're getting, and how much they'll have to pay off after graduation.

ADMISSIONS

How many applications a school receives and what those applicants look like. This section includes the percent of applicants accepted, the percent of acceptees attending, the average LSAT score, and the average undergraduate GPA. We also tell you the application fee for the 1996–97 school year, whether or not the school has an early application and/or early notification program, the regular application deadline, when regular notification occurs, and possible admission deferment.

THE GOURMAN REPORT RATING

This is a numerical score from 2 to 5 that assesses the strengths and weaknesses of each school. It is compiled using material from educators and administrators at the schools themselves. These individuals are permitted to evaluate only their own programs. In addition, the Gourman Ratings draw on many external resources that are a matter of record. Finally, the Gourman Report is fortunate to have among its contributors a number of individuals, associations, and agencies whose business it is to make correct projections of the success graduates from given schools will enjoy in the real world. Using all these factors, Gourman Ratings rank schools and assign them a number that sums up their strengths and shortcomings in a nutshell.

SCHOOL
PROFILES

UNIVERSITY OF AKRON
School of Law

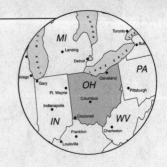

OVERVIEW

Type of school	public
Environment	city
Scholastic calendar	semester
Schedule	full-time or part-time

STUDENTS

Enrollment of parent institution	25,000
Enrollment of law school	640
% male/female	60/40
% out-of-state	25
% part-time	29
% minorities	8
% international (# of countries represented)	1 (3)
Average age at entry	27

APPLICANTS ALSO LOOK AT

Case Western Reserve University
Cleveland State University
Ohio State University
University of Dayton
Ohio Northern University

SURVEY SAYS...

HITS
Socratic method
Diverse faculty

MISSES
Quality of teaching
Library staff
Not enough courses

EMPLOYMENT PROFILE

Firms recruiting on campus	26
Job placement rate (%)	97
% grads employed within six months	97
Average starting salary	$37,047

Grads employed by field (%):

Academia	3
Business/industry	24
Government	16
Judicial clerkships	9
Military	1
Private practice	44
Public interest	3

The University of Akron School of Law's hometown, the former "Rubber Capital of the World," now prefers to be called the world's leader in "polymer research." Technological issues aside, one understands why. The University of Akron itself is a well-funded research and teaching institution with particular strength in materials science and engineering. Students at the Akron law school, however, tend to busy themselves not with plastics and polymers but with more familiar, if less malleable, subjects like torts and contracts that are the mainstay of the law school's solid, traditional curriculum.

Akron does, however, supplement its straightforward J.D. program with a number of clinical programs and skills courses, among which the trial advocacy program draws many participants. In addition to its own considerable resources, the law school puts at students' disposal the vast resources of the broader university, through which they can pursue various joint-degree programs (e.g., J.D./MBA, J.D./Master's in taxation or public administration). Like so many public law schools, Akron experienced an increase in applications during the late eighties that far outpaced the overall increase in law-school applications nationwide. In 1986, the law school admitted 63 percent of the candidates it evaluated. Since then, however, applications have almost tripled, and Akron now admits a much less generous percentage of those who apply. Though this clearly indicates that the numerical qualifications of the law school's students have risen, admissions standards at Akron remain moderate.

Students at Akron paint a picture of a law school that does little more than meet their basic needs. Their most consistent complaint concerned the unevenness of teaching abilities among the law school's faculty. Some, however, dissented from the majority opinion on this matter. "The school's greatest strength," said one 3L, "is the faculty's commitment to teaching and to maintaining contact with students." Few shared that specific opinion, but many Akron students did praise their faculty's academic abilities. As one put it, "Our professors are very knowledgeable and, most importantly, very approachable. I could have transferred to a so-called elite law school after my first year, but I believe that I

Lauri S. File, Director of Admissions and Financial Assistance
Akron, OH 44325-2901
Tel: 800-4-AKRON-U • Fax: 330-258-2343
Email: lawadmissions@uakron.edu
Internet: www.uakron.edu/law/index.html

University of Akron

couldn't receive a higher quality legal education anyplace else—Ivy Leagues included." Several Akron students praised the school's emphasis on legal writing. Akron students also were notably charitable toward their placement staff. As one 3L about to enter a difficult job market said: "The alumni and staff are very supportive of recent graduates, which is good, because nobody else out there is."

Many students' criticisms of Akron centered on its lack of a national name. Said one 3L, "Probably the school's greatest problem is the lack of an effective public relations program." Others complained loudly about the facilities, despite recent renovations. On the academic front, even those students who offered praise for Akron's existing skills courses expressed their desire to see even "more access to courses imparting practical knowledge." Others criticized the law school administration for not supporting more extracurricular activities and student organizations. Of course to be fair, the responsibility for what one student called a "blah" atmosphere on campus may rest as much on the students themselves: "We are subdued, down-to-earth and realistic. We simply expect to get a degree, get a job, and get on with our lives."

ADMISSIONS

Overall selectivity at the University of Akron School of Law is moderate, and numerical standards are relatively low, but a dramatic rise in total applications over the last several years has made the admissions process at this inexpensive public law school more competitive. The average GPA and LSAT scores of entering students are less than stellar, and candidates with above average numerical credentials are virtually guaranteed admission, thanks in part to an extremely generous overall acceptance rate.

ACADEMICS	
Student/faculty ratio	27:1
% female faculty	41
% minority faculty	10
Hours of study per day	3.36

Academic specialties:
Criminal, International, Taxation

FINANCIAL FACTS	
Tuition (in/out-state)	$7,041/$12,083
Cost of books	$600
Room & board (on/off-campus)	$2,025/$3,600
% first-year students receiving aid	NR
% all students receiving aid	92
% aid that is merit-based	7
% of all students receiving loans	80
% receiving scholarships	27
% of all students receiving assistantships	3
Average grant	$3,000
Average graduation debt	$29,500

ADMISSIONS	
# applications received	1,456
% applicants accepted	46
% acceptees attending	32
Average LSAT	153
LSAT range	143-173
Average undergrad GPA	3.09
GPA range	2.00-4.00
Application fee (in/out-state)	$35/$35
Early notification	November 1
Regular application	rolling
Regular notification?	rolling
Rolling notification?	Yes
Early decision program?	Yes
Admission may be deferred?	Yes
Maximum length of deferment	1 year
Evening division offered?	Yes
Part-time accepted?	Yes
Gourman Report Rating	**2.88**

UNIVERSITY OF ALABAMA
School of Law

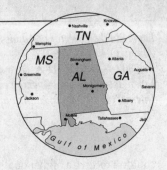

OVERVIEW

Type of school	public
Environment	city
Scholastic calendar	semester
Schedule	full-time only

STUDENTS

Enrollment of parent institution	13,167
Enrollment of law school	566
% male/female	60/40
% out-of-state	17
% part-time	NR
% minorities	11
% international (# of countries represented)	1 (1)
Average age at entry	23

APPLICANTS ALSO LOOK AT

Samford University
Florida State University
University of Mississippi
Baylor University
Dickinson College Of Law

SURVEY SAYS...

HITS
Broad range of courses
Research resources

MISSES
Quality of teaching
Faculty-student relations
Practical lawyering skills

EMPLOYMENT PROFILE

Firms recruiting on campus	105
Job placement rate (%)	91
% grads employed immediately	68
% grads employed within six months	85
Average starting salary	$36,044

Grads employed by field (%):

Academia	11
Business/industry	5
Government	8
Judicial clerkships	15
Military	1
Private practice	62
Public interest	2
Other	2

Located in the midsize college town of Tuscaloosa, the University of Alabama School of Law has served the state for almost 125 years, and while it has few pretensions to national status, Alabama's law school enjoys a very solid regional reputation. Alabama should not be tagged a local law school, however, if that description is meant to cast doubt on the breadth and quality of its offerings. This modern, well-staffed law school offers a J.D. program that is strong within traditional bounds and is administered by an able and relatively large faculty. As part of a major public university with some of the best research resources in the Southeast, it offers its students access to services uncommon at schools of its size.

Alabama's self-described goal is to live up to the concept of a "law center," an institution fully integrated with and involved in the surrounding community. Its efforts to meet that goal are aided by the fact that the overwhelming majority of its students are Alabama residents and that most of them remain within the state after completing their degrees. (It should be noted that the University of Alabama lags behind many of the nation's law schools in terms of the racial and gender diversity of its student body. More than anything, however, this fact reflects a broader problem facing many universities in the Gulf Coast states, most of which have not gone as far as Alabama has in opening themselves up to historically excluded minorities.) Admissions standards at Alabama are competitive, and those who are admitted possess solid mid- to high-range numerical credentials.

Students at Alabama say the law school satisfies them only up to a point. Though most of those we heard from expressed a fairly high degree of satisfaction with the quality of their training at the law school, many lamented Alabama's old-school emphasis on the Socratic Method and other trappings of the traditional curriculum. When asked to name the school's greatest strengths, however, few had difficulty responding: "Our faculty are all outstanding in their fields and bring a great deal of expertise to the classroom," wrote one. "They are, generally, very friendly with the students and very accessible." Though such sentiments

Betty McGinley, Admissions Coordinator
Box 870382
Tuscaloosa, AL 35487
Tel: 205-348-5440 • Fax: 205-348-3917
Email: admissions@law.ua.edu
Internet: www.law.ua.edu

University of Alabama

were expressed by Alabama students with less frequency and enthusiasm than students elsewhere, they were still quite noticeable. Moreover, one point on which nearly all agreed was on the quality of relations among students themselves: "One of the greatest attributes of the University of Alabama," said one, "is the sense of community that you feel here. Most people don't notice your race, sex, or economic status—they simply see a fellow law student and know what you're going through. It's comforting to know there are people here who understand you and that you can count on them for support and guidance."

Such compassion is especially important at a school like Alabama, where academic intensity often breeds unhealthy competitiveness. One 1L put it simply: "The quality of students and the level of competitiveness here far exceeded my expectations." Another 1L wrote that "the legal community itself is competitive and cutthroat, and these traits are ingrained in law school." Speaking for students at many of the nation's law schools, she continued: "Shouldn't the environment in law school focus more on learning than on rank?" Indeed, many here agreed that "the format is too traditional, overly rigid, and authoritarian." Criticism was also expressed concerning the perceived narrowness of the school's curriculum. "I'd like to see less of a focus on business courses and more on theoretical courses," went one fairly typical remark. On balance, however, even the most critical of the students we heard from were unable to say that the school's shortcomings completely outweighed its strengths, particularly considering its incredible affordability.

ADMISSIONS

The University of Alabama School of Law is one of the most selective in the entire Southeast. Indeed, Alabama ranks among the top 20 percent of all law schools nationally in terms of its numerical admissions standards. Since 1986, the average LSAT score of incoming students has leapt fifteen percentile points while the average GPA has inched up to a very respectable 3.4. Applications volume has risen steadily at this bargain law school to the point where slightly fewer than one in three applicants gains admission. Candidates whose numbers fall below Alabama's average face an uphill climb.

ACADEMICS

Student/faculty ratio	17:1
% female faculty	21
% minority faculty	7
Hours of study per day	3.00

FINANCIAL FACTS

Tuition (in/out-state)	$3,578/$7,712
Cost of books	$550
% first-year students receiving aid	65
% all students receiving aid	65
% aid that is merit-based	67
% of all students receiving loans	74
% receiving scholarships	66
% of all students receiving assistantships	7
Average grant	$2,588
Average graduation debt	$36,158

ADMISSIONS

# applications received	814
% applicants accepted	37
% acceptees attending	62
Average LSAT	156
Average undergrad GPA	3.40
Application fee (in/out-state)	$25/NR
Regular application	rolling
Regular notification	rolling
Rolling notification?	Yes
Early decision program?	No
Admission may be deferred?	No
Evening division offered?	No
Part-time accepted?	No
Gourman Report Rating	**3.23**

AMERICAN UNIVERSITY
Washington College of Law

No city is more densely packed with both lawyers and law students than Washington, D.C., which boasts one lawyer for about every 12 residents (the national average is one lawyer for every 350) and six law schools with an average enrollment of more than 1,000. Even with 1,167 students in its day and evening divisions, American University's Washington College of Law is only the third-largest law school in its home city. And although it places third in most other rankings behind Georgetown and George Washington law schools, this has more to do with the crowded law school neighborhood than with the quality of the school. American's reputation rests on the solidity of its traditional academic program and on the scope of its clinical programs. The latter were recently cited by a national magazine as among the top five programs in the U.S. Law students at American also have great opportunities for a wide array of externships in the D.C. area.

One aspect of the Washington College of Law that sets it apart from its D.C. rivals is its commitment to women. Celebrating its hundredth anniversary in 1996, the WCL was founded by two women who wished to ensure the inclusion of those who had historically been outside the mainstream of the legal profession. Today women make up nearly half the student body and the university offers a feminist law journal and associations. WCL students overall appear to be a tolerant and non-competitive group. "The best thing about WCL is the cooperative atmosphere among students," said a 1L. This congeniality may have worked its way down from the faculty who is, according to the school, dedicated to developing caring and responsible people as well as successful lawyers. In fact, many students we heard from cited what they termed a more "humane" approach to teaching as one of the university's main strengths. American "fosters a positive learning environment by encouraging teamwork and not competition," said one 2L. A 3L appreciated the school's "continuing commitment to public interest law, community activism, and humanizing legal experiences." American University also offers four joint-degree programs, a distinct advantage for students interested in cross-disciplinary studies.

Sandra Oakman, Director of Admissions
4801 Mass Avenue, NW
Washington, DC 20016
Tel: 202-274-4101 • Fax: 202-274-4107
Email: wc\admit@wcl.american.edu
Internet: www.wcl.american.edu

American University

Law students at American are generally pleased with their professors and curriculum. Students we spoke with called the "open door policy" most faculty members maintain very helpful. "Professors treat students fairly and are willing to do whatever they can to assist with schoolwork, employment, and even just surviving law school," said a 1L. The Washington College of Law's legal clinics were also frequently praised by students, although several mentioned that there were not enough spots available. (Approximately 25 to 30 percent of all third-year students participate in clinics.)

On the downside, several students we spoke with would like to see a more diverse faculty at the law school. One student called for "more women professors in non-clinical classes;" and another called for "more black professors." It is true that American's approximate 11 percent minority composition among the faculty is on the low side.

Since our last visit to the WCL, the construction of new, technologically advanced and state-of-the-art building has been completed. This multi-million-dollar project came none too soon, as students were becoming very frustrated with the poor facilities. In fact, nearly every student we surveyed in the past mentioned the new law school and how badly it was needed.

ADMISSIONS

American University College of Law's solid numerical standards place it among the sixty most selective law schools in the country. With more than 13 applications filed for every spot in its entering class of about 370, this is hardly surprising. Statistically, an applicant with an undergraduate GPA between 3.00 and 3.25 and an LSAT score between 155 and 159 stands a 14 percent chance of getting in.

ACADEMICS	
Student/faculty ratio	23:1
% female faculty	32
% minority faculty	11
Hours of study per day	3.68

Academic specialties:
Commercial, Govt Services, Human Rights, International

FINANCIAL FACTS	
Tuition	$20,528
Cost of books	$750
Fees	$340
Room & board (on/off-campus)	$8,739/$8,739
% first-year students receiving aid	84
% all students receiving aid	81
% aid that is merit-based	2
% of all students receiving loans	81
% receiving scholarships	NR
% of all students receiving assistantships	17
Average grant	$6,600
Average graduation debt	$66,000

ADMISSIONS	
# applications received	4,600
% applicants accepted	40
% acceptees attending	20
Average LSAT	157
LSAT range	141-170
Average undergrad GPA	3.29
GPA range	2.15-4.00
Application fee	$55
Regular application	March 1
Regular notification	rolling
Rolling notification?	Yes
Early decision program?	No
Admission may be deferred?	Yes
Maximum length of deferment	1 year
Evening division offered?	Yes
Part-time accepted?	Yes
Gourman Report Rating	**3.80**

ARIZONA STATE UNIVERSITY
College of Law

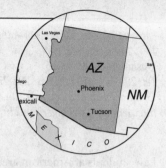

Few parts of the country saw the kind of growth in the last decade that Arizona did, and few parts of Arizona saw more growth than Phoenix, now the nation's ninth-largest city. More to the point, on the strength of an economy that is growing and diversifying nearly as quickly as its population, Phoenix—like Arizona generally—has become a major consumer of legal services, catapulting it into the top twenty job markets for recent law school graduates.

This surely goes a long way toward explaining the phenomenal success of the city's relatively young law school, Arizona State University School of Law. (Tempe, the actual site of the ASU campus, is a suburb of Phoenix.) Founded in 1966, ASU took no time to achieve local prominence, and national recognition as a top public law school wasn't far behind. Still, the law school remains primarily a regional institution, drawing the vast majority of its students from inside the state and sending a similar proportion of its graduates to work within Arizona. When one considers ASU's strong academic program, its incredibly low tuition and its location in a city where "winter" must be put in quotes, one understands why few Arizona residents feel a need to look elsewhere for their legal education and why few ASU grads feel compelled to look elsewhere for work. Thanks to an enormous increase in applications volume in the late eighties and early nineties, ASU admissions have become highly competitive. The law school's diverse student body possesses strong numerical credentials.

On the whole, students enrolled at ASU are highly satisfied with the fundamental quality of their program and with the extent to which it is preparing them for entry into the profession. The college has a multi-faceted clinical program—an in-house client clinic, a public defender clinic, and a prosecutor clinic. ASU also offers a variety of practical skills courses—practice court, alternative dispute resolution, mediation, arbitration, and negotiation. They are also starting a lawyering theory and practice course this year. According to the administration, the school's "Indian Legal Program. . .has been cited as a model at a national level. We have many Native American law students and provide a number of curricular offerings in that area."

Christine Smith
Armstrong Hall, Box 877906
Tempe, AZ 85287
Tel: 602-965-6181 • Fax: 602-965-5550
Internet: www.asu.edu/law

Arizona State University

When asked to name the strengths of their school, many students cited "the faculty, the clinics and the location near the state and federal courts." ASU's location drew strong words of praise not only for its proximity to legal institutions that provide its students with significant co-curricular opportunities, but also for its overall pleasantness. "The campus atmosphere is wonderful here," was one typical remark, "and the student body is really diverse, which makes for interesting discussions in and out of class." Others agreed: "ASU law students are intelligent and serious about their studies. For the most part they bear little resemblance to the [insult deleted] types who populate the undergrad campus." "The faculty is available for questions and to help, and all staff members are helpful and responsive to individual students' needs."

ADMISSIONS

The admissions process at Arizona State is highly competitive. In part because of its strong program and in part because of its low tuition, the law school is inundated with applications from candidates with strong numerical credentials. (The average LSAT score of ASU students is slightly above the 80th percentile.) Numbers count heavily in the selection process. Factoring in both its low acceptance rate and the rate at which admitted applicants accept offers from the law school, Arizona State is in the top 30 percent of all law schools nationally in terms of overall demand for spots in its relatively small first-year class.

ACADEMICS	
Student/faculty ratio	17:1
% female faculty	28
% minority faculty	16
Hours of study per day	3.99

FINANCIAL FACTS	
Tuition (in/out-state)	$3,940/$10,308
Cost of books	$700
% first-year students receiving aid	80
% all students receiving aid	82
% aid that is merit-based	NR
% of all students receiving loans	82
% receiving scholarships	28
% of all students receiving assistantships	NR
Average grant	$10,755
Average graduation debt	$23,000

ADMISSIONS	
# applications received	2,087
% applicants accepted	18
% acceptees attending	39
Average LSAT	157
Average undergrad GPA	3.36
Application fee (in/out-state)	$35/NR
Regular application	March 1
Regular notification	January-April
Rolling notification?	No
Early decision program?	NR
Admission may be deferred?	Yes
Gourman Report Rating	**3.29**

UNIVERSITY OF ARIZONA
College of Law

OVERVIEW

Type of school	public
Environment	metropolis
Scholastic calendar	semester
Schedule	full-time only

STUDENTS

Enrollment of parent institution	21,511
Enrollment of law school	472
% male/female	55/45
% out-of-state	27
% minorities	27
% international (# of countries represented)	1 (4)
Average age at entry	27

APPLICANTS ALSO LOOK AT

Arizona State University
University of California, Los Angeles
University of San Diego
University of Texas
University of Colorado

SURVEY SAYS...

HITS
Academic reputation
Sleeping
Quality of teaching

MISSES
Not enough courses

EMPLOYMENT PROFILE

Firms recruiting on campus	75
Job placement rate (%)	90
% grads employed immediately	55
% grads employed within six months	90
Average starting salary	$39,110

Grads employed by field (%):

Academia	2
Business/industry	6
Government	9
Judicial clerkships	19
Military	4
Private practice	46
Public interest	5
Other	6

Law students know a bargain when they see one, and they clearly see one in the University of Arizona College of Law, one of only two law schools in the state. Retirees have long flocked to the high Arizona desert for its clean air and year-round sunny climate, but it takes a bit more than the promise of a great suntan to provoke the dramatic increase in applications that Arizona, like so many public law schools, saw in the early '90s. It takes a strong academic program, a high success rate for graduates, and a small price tag, all of which Arizona has. The university itself is a premier research and teaching facility, a rising academic star through which the law school offers a wide array of joint-degree programs. Arizona's law curriculum, administered by a large, highly respected faculty, is strong in all traditional areas. Many of Arizona's offerings unmistakably reflect the law school's setting. In addition to the kind of government placements that are available to students at almost any law school, Arizona offers internship programs with the governments of the Navaho, Pascua Yaqui, and Tohono O'odham tribes. The University of Arizona turns out a small, well-prepared group of graduates who have little difficulty finding employment in a state that needs more lawyers than it produces. And, perhaps most important, even the nonresident tuition here is on the low end of the scale for law schools of this caliber. Arizona also stands out for the true ethnic and racial diversity of its student body.

Arizona's J.D. program is highly demanding, and students acknowledge the high degree of competitiveness that keeps everyone from being numbed by the year-round stunningly beautiful weather. As nearly all the students we heard from pointed out, however, the law school sees to it that incoming Arizona students make a smooth transition to the academic rigor. This is achieved by separating the entering class into small groups and keeping those students together in all of their first-year courses. Arizona students attest to the success of this program as it keeps them from being lost in the shuffle during the demanding first year. As one 3L reported, "The small sections during first year, first semester were extraordinarily helpful in integrating into law school." This integration is made even easier by a faculty that most students seem to regard as "dedicated and accessible."

Terry Sue Holpert, Assistant Dean for Admissions
P.O. Box 210176, College of Law
Tucson, AZ 85721-0176
Tel: 520-621-3477 • Fax: 520-621-9140
Email: admissions@law.arizona.edu
Internet: admissions@lawArizona,edu

University of Arizona

Naturally, Arizona students have their share of gripes about their chosen school. A large number, for instance, complained about inconsistency in the quality of classroom instruction, and few had kind words for the school's facilities. However, the school is beginning a major building program which will add several new seminar rooms and refurbish all existing classrooms and seminar rooms. More fundamental criticisms centered on the limited availability of practical skills courses and the limited array of courses available on a regular basis. "Don't advertise aggressively the environmental and international programs when they barely exist," wrote one particularly disappointed 2L. To present the other side, the school said that they have made progress in international law, recently adding an additional faculty member to the program. Even though the law school's student body is incredibly diverse relative to the rest of the nation (as is its faculty), quite a few students called for even greater representation of historically excluded minorities. Still, most Arizona students seem satisfied with their overall experience at the law school. They all agree that the price is right, and as one student put it, "Where else can you eat lunch outside in January?"

ADMISSIONS

The University of Arizona has become one of the most highly selective law schools in the country. The size of its first-year class (around 150) allows the admissions committee to admit only about one in five of the 1,800 candidates it considers annually. With their very solid undergraduate grade-point averages and a median LSAT score at the 89th percentile, Arizona students possess numerical credentials that rank them among the top 25 percent nationally. Compounding the already low acceptance rate is the fact that a very high percentage of those admitted (around 40 percent) actually choose to enroll at the law school. Arizona is, quite simply, in great demand.

ACADEMICS

Student/faculty ratio	16:1
% female faculty	34
% minority faculty	11
Hours of study per day	3.49

Academic specialties:
Constitutional, Corporation Securities, Criminal, International, Legal Philosophy, Taxation

FINANCIAL FACTS

Tuition (in/out-state)	$0/$6,368
Cost of books	$700
Fees (in/out-state)	$4,010/$4,010
Room & board (on/off-campus)	$8,100/$11,802
% first-year students receiving aid	80
% all students receiving aid	80
% aid that is merit-based	51
% of all students receiving loans	80
% receiving scholarships	60
% of all students receiving assistantships	10
Average grant	$2,000
Average graduation debt	$35,000

ADMISSIONS

# applications received	1,773
% applicants accepted	26
% acceptees attending	31
Average LSAT	161
LSAT range	143-173
Average undergrad GPA	3.45
GPA range	2.27-4.00
Application fee (in/out-state)	$45/$45
Regular application	March 1
Regular notification	Bet. Dec. & May
Rolling notification?	Yes
Early decision program?	No
Admission may be deferred?	Yes
Maximum length of deferment	2 years
Evening division offered?	No
Part-time accepted?	No
Gourman Report Rating	**3.32**

UNIVERSITY OF ARKANSAS AT LITTLE ROCK
School of Law

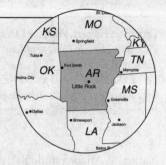

Thanks to a certain former governor and his wife, the capital of Arkansas today enjoys a cachet previously unimaginable: lawyers and Little Rock now go hand in hand in the minds of millions of Americans. Despite this fame, the University of Arkansas at Little Rock School of Law remains primarily a local institution, and most of its graduates choose to work within the state. Since 1965, the school has grown from a part-time division of its companion school in Fayetteville into an independent entity offering its own day and evening programs to over 400 students, most of whom are Arkansas residents. The law school recently experienced a comfortable expansion, thanks to its move into new, significantly larger quarters adjacent to MacArthur Park near downtown Little Rock.

The curriculum at Arkansas, Little Rock is relatively rigid, with a greater than average number of required courses. Its traditional classroom offerings are supplemented by several clinical programs in which enrollment is extremely limited. UALR is notable for its 3L requirement of a trial advocacy course; the addition of this trials-skills requirement is part of the law school's continuing effort to increase its emphasis on practice skills. The volume of applications to the law school is relatively low, making the overall acceptance rate quite high, although it has declined significantly in recent years. More than half of each entering class is admitted solely on the basis of a numerical index, so moderately high GPAs and LSAT scores virtually insure admission.

Many students wrote enthusiastically about their school's relatively new facilities; however, the kudos were not reserved for inanimate objects. Many of the respondents praised the school's faculty, and the pervading sense of community. One 3L wrote, "The professors are intelligent, scholarly, and very accessible. The students, facility, and staff coalesce to make a wonderful experience." A 1L stated, "The overall commitment to help you succeed is the school's strongest strength." Another first year wrote, "The environment is of course demanding—but surprisingly friendly and positive." Some first years singled out the "mentor program" as an invaluable aid in getting through the first semester.

Jean Probasco, Director of Admissions
1201 McAlmont
Little Rock, AR 72202-5142
Tel: 501-324-9439 • Fax: 501-324-9433
Internet: www.ualr.edu/~lawlib/index.htm

University of Arkansas at Little Rock

While most students praised their school, they still cited areas where improvement was needed. A few respondents called for greater diversity among both students and faculty. By far, though, the most consistent criticism called for expanding the selection of courses. One 3L suggested that a more varied course catalogue "would allow for...further specialization." Although students were satisfied with the school, some complained that it's "undermarketed." As a 1L put it, "Not enough people realize the quality and successes of the school and its graduates."

ADMISSIONS

UALR's numbers-driven admissions process allows the applicant to calculate her chances of admission much more accurately than she could for most other law schools. The average incoming Arkansas student has a respectable undergraduate GPA of 3.12 and moderately low LSAT score at about the 55th percentile. Since the law school's overall acceptance rate is relatively high, any applicant whose UGPA and LSAT exceed the Arkansas average probably stands a better than 50/50 chance of getting in—far better odds than at most law schools in the country.

ACADEMICS

Student/faculty ratio	14:1
% female faculty	38
% minority faculty	9
Hours of study per day	3.38

FINANCIAL FACTS

Tuition (in/out-state)	$4,004/$9,072
Cost of books	$800
Fees (in/out-state)	$173/$173
Room & board (on/off-campus)	NR/$9,000
% first-year students receiving aid	66
% all students receiving aid	61
% aid that is merit-based	5
% of all students receiving loans	62
% receiving scholarships	13
% of all students receiving assistantships	5
Average grant	$2,620
Average graduation debt	$25,000

ADMISSIONS

# applications received	467
% applicants accepted	52
% acceptees attending	54
Average LSAT	153
Average undergrad GPA	3.20
Application fee (in/out-state)	$40/$40
Regular application	rolling
Regular notification	rolling
Rolling notification?	Yes
Early decision program?	No
Admission may be deferred?	No
Evening division offered?	Yes
Part-time accepted?	Yes
Gourman Report Rating	**2.41**

UNIVERSITY OF ARKANSAS AT FAYETTEVILLE
School of Law

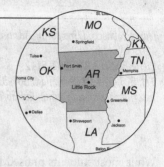

OVERVIEW

Type of school	public
Environment	town
Scholastic calendar	semester
Schedule	full-time only

STUDENTS

Enrollment of parent institution	14,692
Enrollment of law school	394
% male/female	60/40
% out-of-state	40
% minorities	8
% international (# of countries represented)	NR (3)
Average age at entry	26

APPLICANTS ALSO LOOK AT

University of Arkansas at Little Rock
Southern Methodist University
Vanderbilt University
University of Texas
Tulane University

SURVEY SAYS...

HITS
Socratic method
Legal writing

MISSES
Quality of teaching
Practical lawyering skills
Library staff

EMPLOYMENT PROFILE

Firms recruiting on campus	22
Job placement rate (%)	93
% grads employed immediately	38
% grads employed within six months	93
Average starting salary	$32,810

Grads employed by field (%):

Academia	2
Business/industry	21
Government	15
Judicial clerkships	9
Private practice	51
Public interest	2
Other	1

The University of Arkansas School of Law at Fayetteville, the older of Arkansas's two state law schools, holds the distinction of having been the first private-sector employer of President Clinton. (Both Bill and Hillary Rodham Clinton taught here briefly in the mid-1970s, although neither attended the school.) While this small public law school, which has served its home state for over seventy years, may not always feature a president-to-be on its faculty, it will no doubt continue to produce its share of well-prepared attorneys.

Arkansas at Fayetteville draws most of its students from within the state, and puts them through a traditional, rigorous course of study that is particularly demanding in the first year, when students are required to take five full courses and a legal research class. The requirements lessen considerably after the first year. The elective curriculum includes four client-based clinics, including the Federal Practice clinic, and a number of other professional skills courses. If approved, J.D. students may also take courses offered through the Law School's highly regarded graduate program in agricultural law. This program reflects the school's responsiveness to the imperatives of its home state, which has a substantial agricultural industry. Arkansas students also feel the effects of this civic commitment in the extremely low tuition at the school, which ranks among the least expensive in the nation.

Not surprisingly, many students surveyed felt that they were receiving a good value for their money. As a 1L described it: "This school has the most bang for the buck in the country." Its location seems agreeable to students as well. Even out-of-state students readily characterized Fayetville as "a great place to live." Most students seemed to be content with most of their professors, who were called "fantastic" and "accessible." Some professors, though, were criticized for being, in one student's words, "a little self-important and impolite." A 1L summed up another concern of some classmates, stating, "While many of our instructors are excellent, a few are inexperienced in the actual practice of law, and this is evident in their inability to inspire interest in their subjects." Other students called for a "greater diversity of classes offered." A number of students were also dissatisfied with the

James Miller, Associate Dean for Students
Leflar Law Center
Fayetteville, AR 72701
Tel: 501-575-3102 • Fax: 501-575-3320
Email: keaudle@comp.uark.edu
Internet: www.law.uark.edu

University of Arkansas at Fayetteville

grading system. One 3L complained, "We suffer from a bad case of grade deflation here."

While some criticisms of faculty and administration were voiced, the most common area of concern surrounded the school's facilities, which, as many students suggested, are in need of renovation. As one student tactfully stated, "they could use a facelift." Despite all these areas of concern, most students seemed satisfied with the quality of their legal education thus far. In the words of one third-year student, "Overall, I've had a great experience here and would recommend this school over many of the more expensive and supposedly 'better' law schools."

ADMISSIONS

Like many state schools, the University of Arkansas, Fayetteville School of Law is constrained to admit a certain proportion of its students solely on the basis of their numerical credentials. At Arkansas, a complicated formula is used to arrive at an index score for each applicant. On the basis of this formula, the law school admits more than half of its class without considering other factors. What this means to you is that if your own numbers exceed the relatively modest average you see printed here, you can be virtually assured of gaining admission. Take note, however: Numerical standards are on the rise here, and may not remain at this level for long.

ACADEMICS

Student/faculty ratio	9:1
% female faculty	28
% minority faculty	4
Hours of study per day	3.64

Academic specialties:
Agricultural

FINANCIAL FACTS

Tuition (in/out-state)	$3,496/$7,528
Cost of books	$1,000
Room & board (on/off-campus)	$3,790/NR
% first-year students receiving aid	27
% all students receiving aid	57
% aid that is merit-based	5
% of all students receiving loans	54
% receiving scholarships	24
% of all students receiving assistantships	NR
Average grant	$2,622
Average graduation debt	NR

ADMISSIONS

# applications received	733
% applicants accepted	48
% acceptees attending	44
Average LSAT	152
LSAT range	135-169
Average undergrad GPA	3.20
GPA range	2.29-4.00
Application fee (in/out-state)	$0/$0
Regular application	rolling
Regular notification	rolling
Rolling notification?	Yes
Early decision program?	No
Admission may be deferred?	No
Evening division offered?	No
Part-time accepted?	No
Gourman Report Rating	**2.85**

UNIVERSITY OF BALTIMORE
School of Law

OVERVIEW

Type of school	public
Environment	metropolis
Scholastic calendar	NR
Schedule	full-time or part-time

STUDENTS

Enrollment of parent institution	NR
Enrollment of law school	1,034
% male/female	53/47
% out-of-state	20
% part-time	41
% minorities	18
% international (# of countries represented)	NR (NR)
Average age at entry	28

APPLICANTS ALSO LOOK AT

University of Maryland
American University
George Washington University
Catholic University of America
Georgetown University

SURVEY SAYS...

HITS
Legal writing
Socratic method

MISSES
Not enough courses
Quality of teaching
Library staff

EMPLOYMENT PROFILE

Firms recruiting on campus	35
Job placement rate (%)	88
% grads employed immediately	67
% grads employed within six months	88
Average starting salary	$38,285

Grads employed by field (%):

Business/industry	19
Government	13
Judicial clerkships	21
Military	4
Private practice	40
Public interest	3

The city of Baltimore is home to two public law schools in the University of Maryland system. While the nearby University of Maryland School of Law is the older and better known, the University of Baltimore is actually a bigger school. With more than 1,000 J.D. students (approximately a whopping one-fourth of them in the part-time evening division) UB is one of the largest law schools in the nation.

The obvious benefits provided by a large school are all part of the University of Baltimore experience. Founded in 1925, UB has dedicated significant resources to its clinical programs. In fact, this is one of very few law schools in the country that has a clinical requirement. All students must satisfy an advocacy requirement by participating in one of the Law School's several clinics, taking an advanced advocacy course, or competing on one of the eleven interscholastic advocacy teams. UB has also developed a new curriculum, which offers most students a choice of twelve areas of concentration.

The combination of these activities seems to lead to a high degree of student satisfaction with the education they receive. As one 3L stated, "Students have the opportunity to gain practical experience that is invaluable." Another wrote, "The University of Baltimore has a practical approach to the law that provides students with the knowledge to be effective in their profession." The students were also generally enthused about the quality of teaching available. A 2L commented that the school's greatest strength was, "Professors who are extremely dynamic and sincerely interested in the success of their students." The school's location in Baltimore and its proximity to Washington, D.C. were also viewed as big advantages for students seeking practical experience or jobs. While some students called for UB to offer a broader range of courses, most respondents seemed quite content with the quality of their education.

Claire Valentine, Director of Admissions
1420 North Charles Street
Baltimore, MD 21201
Tel: 410-837-4459 • Fax: 410-837-4450
Email: lwadmiss@ubmail.ubalt.edu
Internet: www.ubalt.edu/www/law

University of Baltimore

ADMISSIONS

In terms of the numerical standards to which it holds applicants, the University of Baltimore School of Law ranks in the bottom third of all U.S. law schools, but its bargain-basement tuition draws an applicant pool that is large enough to make the overall admissions process quite competitive. Nearly eight applicants vie annually for each spot in Baltimore's entering class of about 300. Those whose credentials fall short face very long odds.

ACADEMICS

Student/faculty ratio	19:1
% female faculty	35
% minority faculty	10
Hours of study per day	3.37

Academic specialties:
Commercial, Criminal, Environmental, Govt Services, International, Labor, Legal History, Legal Philosophy, Property

FINANCIAL FACTS

Tuition (in/out-state)	$7,812/$13,940
Cost of books	$850
Fees (in/out-state)	$540/$540
Room & board (on/off-campus)	NR/$9,250
% first-year students receiving aid	NR
% all students receiving aid	68
% aid that is merit-based	NR
% of all students receiving loans	68
% receiving scholarships	7
% of all students receiving assistantships	NR
Average grant	$1,500
Average graduation debt	$38,300

ADMISSIONS

# applications received	1,862
% applicants accepted	53
% acceptees attending	31
Average LSAT	153
Average undergrad GPA	3.00
Application fee (in/out-state)	$35/$35
Regular application	rolling
Regular notification	rolling
Rolling notification?	Yes
Early decision program?	No
Admission may be deferred?	Yes
Maximum length of deferment	1 year
Evening division offered?	Yes
Part-time accepted?	Yes
Gourman Report Rating	**2.61**

BAYLOR UNIVERSITY
School of Law

As a rule, Texas's eight law schools, which together enroll nearly 7,000 students, are a bit larger than average. The exception that proves the rule sits smack-dab in the middle of the Lone Star State: the Baylor University School of Law, Texas's oldest law school. The only concession this small, inexpensive private law school makes to the bigger-is-better ethos is its outsize reputation for training great lawyers. Located in the central Texas town of Waco, the Baylor law school has been in nearly continuous operation since 1857 on the campus of this midsize university, affiliated with the Texas Baptist Convention. Baylor's unassailable regional reputation owes much to the success of its graduates, a disproportionate number of whom hold or have held positions of power in the state's legal and political institutions. But the law school has seen to it that even its less prominent graduates distinguish themselves by the quality of their training. Baylor's J.D. curriculum, which is geared as much to practical as to intellectual training, includes far more required courses than does the traditional law school. Among these is a rare third-year requirement for which Baylor is well known, the Practice Court course. The broad-based advocacy training that this course provides has helped Baylor grads to continue to succeed in an increasingly competitive job market. Baylor operates on a quarter system, admitting students in fall, spring, and summer. Admissions are highly selective and numerical standards high.

Students come to Baylor for the excellent litigation training the school is known for, and in true Texas hyperbolic style, boast that their practical law preparation is unbeatable: "The program here is without a doubt the best trial preparation in the country; other law schools don't even come close to preparing their students for the practice of law, they prepare their students for malpractice," said one proud 2L. Baylor students offered gratitude for the small class size. They greatly admired their "firm but fair" professors and said that the faculty open-door policy cuts the edge off the intense competition and makes the rigorous course load bearable. One happy student said, "The faculty comprise some of the best attorneys in Texas who teach out of a desire to teach!"

Becky L. Beck, Admission Director
P.O. Box 97288
Waco, TX 76798
Tel: 254-710-1911 • Fax: 254-710-2316
Email: Becky_Beck@baylor.edu
Internet: www.baylor.edu/~law

Baylor University

Through gritted teeth, students expressed understanding of and appreciation for the intense workload that prefigures the now standard interminable office hours most will endure in private practice. However, they wholeheartedly denounced the administration's grade deflation policy. One 1L explained it's not "just 'grade deflation' but 'grade depression!'…This system has resulted in high prestige for some students and for Baylor, but low self-esteem and job opportunities for others."

According to one student, "The small student body of approximately 400 permits a close-knit family atmosphere." However, students commented on the lack of diversity at Baylor. As one student told us, "Diversity at this law school is practically non-existent, and therefore, the levels of tolerance are low for people who aren't white males (Protestant of course!)" Many complained this southern conservative school needs to "focus on attracting a diverse student body with a broader array of experiences, political, and social ideas, and goals!"

Applicants to Baylor should remember this 2L's comments: "If you want to have fun in law school and slide through third year, don't come to Baylor. They will work you like no other. But be assured that you will have a top rate education."

ADMISSIONS

Unlike most law schools, Baylor welcomes new students three times during the course of the year, in September, January, and June. If you hope to be among the roughly 180 people annually who take seats in one of these entering classes, be prepared to fight. The numerical credentials of Baylor students are astoundingly high. Their stellar GPAs and average LSAT score above the 90th percentile rank them among the most highly qualified student bodies in the nation. Taking into account both the low overall acceptance rate and the percentage of admitted applicants who accept offers to attend the law school, Baylor ranks among the 50 most in-demand schools in the country.

ACADEMICS

Student/faculty ratio	19:1
% female faculty	33
% minority faculty	9
Hours of study per day	5.15

FINANCIAL FACTS

Tuition	$11,357
Cost of books	$945
Fees	$450
Room & board (on/off-campus)	$4,431/$6,639
% first-year students receiving aid	86
% all students receiving aid	86
% aid that is merit-based	12
% of all students receiving loans	75
% receiving scholarships	62
% of all students receiving assistantships	NR
Average grant	$3,217
Average graduation debt	$42,082

ADMISSIONS

# applications received	792
% applicants accepted	39
% acceptees attending	24
Average LSAT	159
LSAT range	152-173
Average undergrad GPA	3.50
GPA range	2.44-4.00
Application fee	$40
Regular application	March 1
Regular notification	rolling
Rolling notification?	Yes
Early decision program?	No
Admission may be deferred?	No
Evening division offered?	No
Part-time accepted?	No
Gourman Report Rating	**3.30**

BOSTON COLLEGE
Law School

OVERVIEW

Type of school	private
Environment	metropolis
Scholastic calendar	semester
Schedule	full-time only

STUDENTS

Enrollment of parent institution	13,618
Enrollment of law school	814
% male/female	55/45
% out-of-state	63
% part-time	NR
% minorities	17
% international (# of countries represented)	NR (NR)
Average age at entry	24

APPLICANTS ALSO LOOK AT

Boston University
Harvard University
Georgetown University
George Washington University
Suffolk University

SURVEY SAYS...

HITS
Sense of community
Sleeping
Academic reputation

MISSES
Not enough courses

EMPLOYMENT PROFILE

Job placement rate (%)	93
% grads employed within six months	93

Grads employed by field (%):

Academia	1
Business/industry	8
Government	10
Judicial clerkships	13
Private practice	66
Public interest	2
Other	3

Boston is not only America's number one college town, but also the nation's top law school town. Every year, close to 30,000 applications are filed by prospective 1Ls seeking to fill one of the 2,000 first-year slots in Boston's six law schools. More than 5,000 of those applications are addressed to the Boston College Law School, located on the city's outskirts in Newton. After its neighbor in Cambridge (the one that starts with an "H"), BC, which was founded in 1929, is probably the most esteemed law school in the entire region, with a reputation for excellence that extends beyond New England.

This reputation was built on the strength of the law school's faculty and the traditional curriculum they administer—a curriculum that is continually revised to keep up with the evolving profession. In addition to variety, there's no shortage of advanced courses and clinical programs, in which a large portion of BC law students participate. With the resources of both the college and the city's legal community (the nation's fifth largest) close at hand, students do not lack learning or employment opportunities. Slightly more than half of Boston College law grads remain in New England. Given the law program's strength and the sheer volume of applicants, it isn't surprising that admissions standards are quite high; incoming BC students have numerical credentials that rank among the nation's highest.

Remarkably, given the credentials of the school and its students, competition is reported to be moderate at best. Students were incredibly positive about their experiences at what one termed a "warm and fuzzy law school." A 2L commented, "The sense of community and the strive for excellence, without excessive competition among students, makes BC a really special place to be." Students described each other as compassionate and supportive, but did not reserve their praise for their peers. The school as a whole was termed, in the words of another 2L, "a 'humane' place. If you have a problem, the school works quickly and diligently to find creative solutions. Their goal is to keep you in law school and to enable you to perform well." This high opinion of BC is retained by students after they graduate. A current student reported, "While interviewing this fall, I found that alumni from

Elizabeth Rosselot, Director of Admissions
885 Centre Street
Newton, MA 02159
Tel: 617-552-4350 • Fax: 617-552-2615
Email: bclawadm@bc.edu
Internet: www.bc.edu/lawschool

BC are among the only ones who 'enjoyed' law school." Students also cited a "top notch" library, and "down to earth and approachable" professors as strong points of the school. Plans to further improve the facilities were also applauded.

While the overall experience was deemed very positive, BC law students also found room for improvement. Many commented on the difficulties of finding parking and easy transportation to and from the school. Reviews of career services were mixed at best. Voicing a criticism heard at many schools, a 2L wrote, "Programs for those students outside the top 10 percent are not very beneficial." Other students felt that career services was too region-oriented. "They have a lot of contacts with large firms in Boston, but that's about it. They don't have any connections, nor have they attempted to get any, with anything international," claimed a 3L. Another 2L observed that the office was "very limited in regards to opportunities outside of Massachusetts for a national school. If you wanted a job outside of Massachusetts, you're better off looking on your own."

Even those students who found fault with some aspects of Boston College Law School were able to keep a light shining on the positive. One 3L wrote, "I have received an excellent legal education and feel well-prepared to embark on my legal career." Most students were even more enthusiastic about their experiences at BC, and agreed with the student who wrote, "If you have to go to law school, go to BC."

ADMISSIONS

While it is true that many applicants to the nation's five or six super-elite schools consider Boston College a "safety," it is hardly a safe bet that even well-qualified applicants will gain admission. If you hope to gain a spot in BC's entering class of almost 300, you'll have to earn it. Applications volume at the law school is extraordinarily high, and the qualifications of those applying are impressive. Those who are admitted and go on to enroll at BC possess very strong numerical credentials, including an average LSAT score above the 90th percentile. These credentials are stronger, in fact, than those of students at 85 percent of the nation's fully accredited law schools.

ACADEMICS

Student/faculty ratio	17:1
% female faculty	27
% minority faculty	11
Hours of study per day	3.41

FINANCIAL FACTS

Tuition	$22,300
Cost of books	$740
% first-year students receiving aid	75
% all students receiving aid	75
% aid that is merit-based	NR
% of all students receiving loans	76
% receiving scholarships	32
% of all students receiving assistantships	NR
Average grant	NR
Average graduation debt	$60,500

ADMISSIONS

# applications received	4,644
% applicants accepted	26
% acceptees attending	22
Average LSAT	162
Average undergrad GPA	3.41
Application fee	$65
Early application	November 1
Early notification	December 16
Regular application	March 1
Regular notification	rolling
Rolling notification?	Yes
Early decision program?	Yes
Admission may be deferred?	Yes
Maximum length of deferment	1 year
Evening division offered?	No
Part-time accepted?	No
Gourman Report Rating	**4.32**

BOSTON UNIVERSITY
School of Law

Established in 1872, Boston University School of Law is a large and highly esteemed private law school that enrolls almost 1,100 students on the urban campus of its well-respected parent institution. BU's extremely well-qualified law students pursue a course of study that is an interesting mix of innovation and tradition. Unlike many schools of its size and strong reputation, Boston University has not resisted the trend toward practical-skills training at the J.D. level. The law school's clinical program is large and multifaceted, and few schools have made a greater commitment to emphasizing legal writing skills. Students give the First Year Research and Writing Seminar high marks for the quality of instruction. However, BU retains a strong grasp on the traditional through the medium of the Socratic method.

BUSL students were quick to dispel the long-standing notion that their school is an ultra-competitive place to study law. A 1L commented, "I was very pleasantly surprised to find that the level of competitiveness among the students is lower than I'd anticipated. The sense I'm getting is that my classmates want to do well, but they're not going to step on their classmates to achieve that." Many others echoed these sentiments. It's clear that the students are a hard-working and motivated group, striving to do well and secure jobs in the shadow of Harvard, one of the best known law schools/universities in the world. A 3L wrote, "When I first got here, it seemed that all my classmates had applied to BU as a backup school and hadn't gotten in to their schools of choice. Since then, I've witnessed a certain amount of pride come about in the student body. We did make the right choice in coming to BU law."

Students at BU certainly have a lot to be proud of. They overwhelmingly consider their faculty first rate. "Our faculty is incredibly accessible and really cares about the students. They want us to learn in class, but they are also very supportive of career efforts outside the classroom," observed a 3L. An impressed 1L wrote that "[The faculty] are constantly asking us to step back and ask what the societal purpose of the laws are. It's not just black letter law. The faculty seemed like very experienced lawyers, as well as academics." Motivated students can take

Erika Schwab, Associate Director
765 Commonwealth Avenue
Boston, MA 02215
Tel: 617-353-3100 • Fax: 617-353-2547
Email: bulawadm@bu.edu
Internet: www.bu.edu/LAW

advantage of concentrations in six different areas of the law and dual degrees in six disciplines, not to mention the overseas programs in three countries. "The study abroad program at Oxford was one of the best educational experiences of my life," wrote a satisfied 3L.

BUSL students were not uniformly satisfied with their experience, though. If you want to hear somebody strive to use adjectives that conjure up the frightful, ask a BU student about the law building. It was described as "the ugliest building in the nation," "the single biggest architectural nightmare in all of Boston," and a "late 1950s post-modern nightmare," among other things. "We try to blame it on a Harvard architect," joked a 3L. Aesthetics weren't the only problem. The heating, classroom acoustics, and elevator system of this tall building were all thoroughly criticized. The Career Placement Office was also singled out for criticism by students who felt that it catered to the top students in the class. A 2L commented that the office "could use a major overhaul. Since it is an avenue to the outside world, you would think that it should be the most polished and accessible office in the school. On the contrary, it has a very provincial approach to your job search." On the other hand, some students found the staff there to be helpful and supportive.

Overall, students were quite positive about the entire BU law experience. A 2L stated, "As much as people slam the school and its facilities, they would have to admit that it has been an amazing experience. If you take the initiative here, you will succeed, and there will be a job for you upon graduation. It's a question of self-initiative and motivation and making the best of your time here."

ADMISSIONS

Though competition among enrolled students at the Boston University School of Law reportedly runs much higher than at neighboring Boston College, the admissions process at BU is (ever so slightly) less selective. Still, the numerical credentials of students here rank them in the top quarter of all law students nationally, and with more than 4,500 applications filed annually, the BU admissions committee must choose carefully. Mercifully, however, almost five candidates are admitted for every spot in the law school's entering class of roughly 330.

ACADEMICS

Student/faculty ratio	17:1
% female faculty	29
% minority faculty	8
Hours of study per day	4.22

FINANCIAL FACTS

Tuition	$20,570
Cost of books	$950
Fees	$264
Room & board (on/off-campus)	$8,635/$8,635
% first-year students receiving aid	85
% all students receiving aid	85
% aid that is merit-based	2
% of all students receiving loans	85
% receiving scholarships	38
% of all students receiving assistantships	0
Average grant	$8,500
Average graduation debt	$61,960

ADMISSIONS

# applications received	4,585
% applicants accepted	34
% acceptees attending	22
Average LSAT	161
LSAT range	146-177
Average undergrad GPA	3.42
GPA range	2.35-3.99
Application fee	$50
Regular application	March 1
Regular notification	rolling
Rolling notification?	Yes
Early decision program?	No
Admission may be deferred?	Yes
Maximum length of deferment	1 year
Evening division offered?	No
Part-time accepted?	No
Gourman Report Rating	4.45

BRIGHAM YOUNG UNIVERSITY
J. Reuben Clark Law School

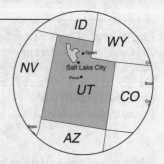

Brigham Young University, founded over 100 years ago, is the largest privately owned, religiously affiliated university in the United States. Since the J. Reuben Clark Law School was established in 1973, it has steadily gained a reputation for academic excellence. That reputation now extends well beyond the Mountain West, a region heavily populated by graduates of BYU's rigorous, traditional J.D. program.

Although BYU's many successes have not gone unnoticed, admissions standards at the law school have not changed much in recent years. This has as much to do with the fact that standards have always been high and the volume of yearly in-coming applications has not increased significantly, despite the law school's growing reputation. While BYU is attractive to prospective law students for several reasons, it is clear that the university is not for everyone. The Law School encourages attendance by members of all faiths, but the influence of the Church of Jesus Christ of Latter-Day Saints is inescapable. BYU, for instance, is the only law school with a dress code (no sleeveless shirts or skirts above the knee) and a total ban on alcohol and tobacco and caffeine. Of course, at least one effect of the school's Mormon affiliation is universally appealing: Its extremely low tuition. Because of heavy church subsidies, the tuition at BYU is, by a fairly wide margin, the lowest of any private law school in the nation.

Even if the tuition were considerably higher, it's safe to say that the students of BYU would be more than satisfied with their law school experiences. Most students did not restrict their praise to one area of the law school, choosing instead to rave about the entire experience. A 1L declared, "At J. Reuben Clark Law School, I have found precisely what I looked for in a law school: A stimulating environment, reputable faculty, fantastic facilities, and, most of all, a cooperative friendly student body." In fact, "friendly" was the adjective of choice of many respondents, whether they were describing the highly regarded faculty, or their fellow students. The fact that the students unwaveringly consider each other friendly is all the more remarkable given how hard BYU students seem to work. A 3L described the situation: "The competition for grades is cutthroat for two reason: a tight job market in the Mountain West [region], and a very strict grading curve. Despite the competition, students are very kind to each other and there is a strong sense of community."

Lola Wilcock, Director of Admissions
Brigham Young University Law School
Provo, UT 84602
Tel: 801-378-4277 • Fax: 801-378-5897
Email: wilcock1@lawgate.byu.edu

By far, though, students were most impressed by the law school's new library. It's no wonder, either, as it appears to be better equipped than some students' apartments at other schools. At BYU, each student is assigned his or her own carrel, which is equipped with locking storage area, electrical outlets, and Internet access. So great was the allure of this facility that some students even lobbied for twenty-four-hour access to the library (its current hours are 6:00 A.M. to 1:00 A.M.). As this 1L boasted, "Harvard has the name, but we have tangible resources that even the Ivies don't."

Indeed, most complaints had to do more with the tough job market in Utah than with the school itself. A 3L claimed that "We have very few on-campus interviewers due to oversupply of lawyers in the Salt Lake City area and we have a problem attracting firms from outside the Mountain West." Students seemed to feel that Career Services was working hard for them, but many expressed frustration that their school was not more highly regarded by prospective employers and national rankings. Another common complaint, even among those who otherwise spoke highly of BYU, was the lack of ethnic and geographic diversity among the students. "Everyone is married and went to BYU as an undergrad," reported a first-year student. Yet even though the majority of the student body is politically conservative, students reported that those with liberal viewpoints are treated with respect by their colleagues.

ADMISSIONS

The admissions process at Brigham Young University's J. Reuben Clark Law School is both kind and brutal. Because of its relatively small applicant pool, BYU's overall acceptance rate is moderate. Numerical admissions standards, however, are very high. In fact, with an average LSAT score at the 89th percentile and a very high average GPA, the student body at BYU ranks, by our calculations, among the 20 most qualified in the entire nation.

ACADEMICS

Student/faculty ratio	18:1
% female faculty	15
% minority faculty	3
Hours of study per day	4.67

Academic specialties:
Commercial, Constitutional, International, Property, Taxation

FINANCIAL FACTS

Tuition	$4,950
Cost of books	$1,080
Fees	$20
Room & board (on/off-campus)	$5,290/$6,500
% first-year students receiving aid	84
% all students receiving aid	85
% aid that is merit-based	33
% of all students receiving loans	86
% receiving scholarships	53
% of all students receiving assistantships	15
Average grant	$2,000
Average graduation debt	$22,000

ADMISSIONS

# applications received	710
% applicants accepted	30
% acceptees attending	72
Average LSAT	160
LSAT range	156-176
Average undergrad GPA	3.60
GPA range	3.00-4.00
Application fee	$30
Regular application	February 1
Regular notification	rolling
Rolling notification?	Yes
Early decision program?	No
Admission may be deferred?	Yes
Maximum length of deferment	1 year
Evening division offered?	No
Part-time accepted?	No
Gourman Report Rating	**3.77**

BROOKLYN LAW SCHOOL

Separated from bustling Manhattan by the narrow East River, Brooklyn Law School sits in one of the most historic and scenic neighborhoods in all of New York City, appropriately located just a few blocks from the federal and state courts. Since it opened its doors in 1901, the number of students has grown from 18 to almost 1,500, about a third of whom are members of the part-time division. The school's solid regional reputation allows many graduates to obtain positions at nearby law firms and government offices. Many Brooklyn grads owe thanks to the network of over 13,000 alumni, most of whom live and practice around New York City, for their help in keeping the school's job placement rate relatively high. Having a strong regional reputation does not limit the geographical representation of the student body, though; according to statistics from the admissions office, the number of students from across the United States and around the world has increased over the past several years.

What truly distinguishes the Brooklyn Law School curriculum from others is its diverse in-house and external clinical programs, which take full advantage of the school's proximity to several important offices: the U.S. District Court, the State Supreme and Family Courts, the City Civil and Criminal Courts, the offices of the U.S. Attorney, the King's County D.A., and the Legal Aid society. Students appreciate the opportunities that their school's location provides. As a 2L wrote, "The clinical programs provide a great experience to obtain practical lawyering skills."

Students were also generally happy with their professors. "In my years of higher education, I have never seen a school whose faculty cares as much about the difficulties of students with material ... the 'open door policy' of the faculty is wonderful and provides an amazing chance to interact with your professors on a 'real' level," commented a 1L. While many students were quick to praise the faculty, others were just as quick to criticize the school's administration. The registrar's office was often cited as being extremely slow. Opinion was divided about the Career Center, with the most common complaint being that it focused too much on the top students. There was also some disapproval voiced about the grading curve, which a 3L claimed had "de-

Joan Wexler, Dean of Admissions and Financial Aid
250 Joralemon Street
Brooklyn, NY 11201
Tel: 718-780-7906
Internet: www2.brooklaw.edu

Brooklyn Law School

stroyed morale among 2Ls and 3Ls, often resulting in a significant number of students cutting classes for long stretches at a time." Respondents were willing to admit that there was a degree of competitiveness at Brooklyn Law, but also pointed out that it did not lead to uncomfortable interaction between students.

Students expressed satisfaction with a new library and cafeteria, but acknowledged that the school, historically a commuter school, needed more than the new eating facility to increase its sense of community. Several suggested that the school "build a gym." A 1L wrote about the difficulty of "finding housing within the local area," although the nearby neighborhoods of Cobble Hill and Carroll Gardens are not only charming, but within reasonable walking distance. However, one 3L thought that the sense of community might improve in the near future, stating that, "I have noticed in my three years here that more people are moving close to the school." Others also expressed optimism for the future of Brooklyn Law, and general contentment with their experiences there.

ADMISSIONS

Although a few better-known schools in Manhattan are far more selective than Brooklyn, a prospective student's numerical standards have to be fairly solid to gain admittance. Before you count yourself a shoe-in, consider that in 1995 the average incoming Brooklyn Law School student had an undergraduate GPA of 3.31 and an LSAT score at about the 80th percentile. Applicants whose numerical credentials exceed these numbers are highly likely to gain admittance to Brooklyn.

ACADEMICS	
Student/faculty ratio	20:1
% female faculty	41
% minority faculty	9
Hours of study per day	3.53

FINANCIAL FACTS	
Tuition	$17,600
Cost of books	NR
% first-year students receiving aid	NR
% all students receiving aid	NR
% aid that is merit-based	NR
% of all students receiving loans	NR
% receiving scholarships	NR
% of all students receiving assistantships	NR
Average grant	NR
Average graduation debt	NR

ADMISSIONS	
# applications received	2,678
% applicants accepted	37
% acceptees attending	27
Average LSAT	157
Average undergrad GPA	3.32
Application fee	$50
Regular application	NR
Regular notification	rolling
Rolling notification?	Yes
Early decision program?	No
Admission may be deferred?	Yes
Maximum length of deferment	1 year
Evening division offered?	Yes
Part-time accepted?	Yes
Gourman Report Rating	**3.62**

CALIFORNIA WESTERN
School of Law

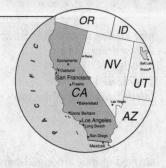

They may not realize it, but when Easterners imagine California, they are imagining San Diego. This fast-growing metropolis, the sixth largest in the United States, is blessed with the kind of climate that makes a mockery of winter and turns many casual visitors into lifetime residents. With 325 annual days of sunshine and 70 miles of brilliant beaches, San Diego County promises quality of life writ large, a fact that one of the city's two law schools, the California Western School of Law, sees fit to point out at the very beginning of its admissions materials.

Indeed, this midsize private law school understands quite well the power of its location, which surely helps explain why it draws such a great proportion of its students from outside California. From within the state and without, competition is tough for the more than 200 seats in Cal Western's first-year class. Those students who do succeed in gaining admission pursue a fairly straightforward J.D. program on the law school's downtown San Diego campus, a program that has been supplemented recently with special offerings in the growing fields of biotechnology law and telecommunications law. Like most law schools that lack weighty and long-standing reputations, however, Cal Western has seen to it that its students gain practical lawyering experience before graduation, experience that will prove invaluable when seeking employment. Between Cal Western's extensive clinical internship program and its classroom trial-advocacy program, a great majority of its students gain such experience.

As for their experience while at the law school, most Cal Western students express a fairly high degree of satisfaction with many fundamental aspects of their chosen school. By all accounts, for instance, the quality of the relations among students and between faculty and students is quite high. Asked to name their law school's greatest strengths, most Cal Western students cite its "good educational environment," "student camaraderie," and the "availability of faculty to students." "The faculty are very helpful," reported one 2L, "and have not forgotten what it is like to be a law student." As for their program itself, most of those we heard from were most enthusiastic about Cal Western's practical focus, in particular its trial advocacy program. "I've never learned

Ruth Briscoe, Assistant Director
225 Cedar Street
San Diego, CA 92101
Tel: 800-255-4252, ext. 1401 • Fax: 619-525-7092
Email: admissions@cwsl.edu
Internet: www.cwsl.edu

more or been more challenged to expand my skills than on the moot trial team," said one 2L. "The practical, 'black-letter' approach to most classes helps with bar preparation," wrote another.

Most students at Cal Western have little difficulty pointing out areas in which the law school could stand to improve. Few students, for instance, had anything charitable to say about the law school's physical plant. In most cases, their criticism focused not on the quality of Cal Western's facilities but, rather, on the lack of facilities. "I would love to have access to all the facilities that a law school affiliated with an undergraduate campus has," said one. Less charitably, one out-of-state student complained that "the law school does not make prospective students who cannot afford to visit the law school aware of the fact that there is no campus whatsoever." Indeed, many students complained that their immediate physical surroundings worked against any sense of community among students, though the recent addition of a new administrative building should do much to mitigate these complaints.

All in all, Cal Western students seem unenthusiastic about some aspects of their experience at the law school, though nearly all seem to agree that they feel well prepared to enter the profession. This general assessment from one satisfied 3L nicely summed up the sentiments of many: "Cal Western is near enough to the beach, but with a seriousness and practicality that should create effective attorneys."

ADMISSIONS

The allure of the San Diego area is strong enough to draw roughly 3,000 applications annually to the California Western School of Law. But while only about 250 first-year students enroll annually, this midsize private law school sends acceptance letters to a relatively large group in order to fill this class. The result is that Cal Western ranks somewhere on the lower end of the midrange of all law schools in terms of overall selectivity. An applicant with an undergraduate GPA over 3.0 and an LSAT score above 155, for instance, should be virtually certain of gaining admission.

ACADEMICS

Student/faculty ratio	20:1
% female faculty	45
% minority faculty	17
Hours of study per day	4.08

FINANCIAL FACTS

Tuition	$19,100
Cost of books	$650
Fees	$70
Room & board (on/off-campus)	NR/$6,850
% first-year students receiving aid	75
% all students receiving aid	85
% aid that is merit-based	10
% of all students receiving loans	85
% receiving scholarships	NR
% of all students receiving assistantships	48
Average grant	$10,000
Average graduation debt	$78,000

ADMISSIONS

# applications received	1,934
% applicants accepted	65
% acceptees attending	19
Average LSAT	151
LSAT range	136-168
Average undergrad GPA	3.10
GPA range	2.21-3.93
Application fee	$45
Regular application	April 1
Regular notification	Rolling
Rolling notification?	Yes
Early decision program?	No
Admission may be deferred?	Yes
Evening division offered?	No
Part-time accepted?	No
Gourman Report Rating	**2.87**

UNIVERSITY OF CALIFORNIA, BERKELEY

Boalt Hall School of Law

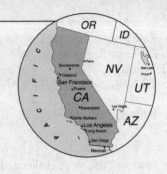

The University of California's flagship campus is located in a town that Pat Buchanan and his ilk still enjoy referring to as "The People's Republic of Berkeley." But as apt a moniker as that might be for a city that celebrates Indigenous Peoples' Day instead of Columbus Day and virtually refuses to enforce marijuana laws, the broad-based leftist activism of Cal students is mostly the stuff of nostalgia, a memory that is fond or bitter depending on one's political leanings. These days, politics takes a distant backseat to academics as the focus of Berkeley's faculty, administration, and student body. The university is consistently ranked as the strongest overall graduate institution in the country, thanks in part to the strength of its hugely respected law school, Boalt Hall. The alma mater of former Chief Justice Earl Warren and longtime comics-page star Joanie Caucus of Doonesbury, Boalt is generally regarded as one of the nation's top ten law schools and as probably the best bargain in American legal education.

The curriculum here is staunchly traditional in the first year; the Socratic Method is alive and well. In their second and third years, however, Boalt Hall students have a wide range of courses from which to choose. In recent years, programs of informal but organized concentration have been added at the J.D. level, and the law school's program in Jurisprudence and Social Policy is one of the country's finest interdisciplinary legal-studies programs. Upon completing their degrees, roughly 75 percent of Boalt students choose to remain in California, where they have their choice of top jobs. Berkeley's stellar reputation and very down-to-earth price combine to produce a torrent of applications every year. In recent years, the law school has admitted around 10 percent of all applicants. Said a 1L: "The whole first-year hazing experience is very minimal here. They let you have a life and the Bay Area is a great place to have one."

The unique Boalt attributes that draw the lucky, talented, and driven people who are admitted, in addition to those mentioned above, are the school's excellent reputation; its profusion of journals; proximity to Silicon Valley; the fantastic Intellectual Property, Immigration, International, and Environmental law programs; and perhaps most importantly, the enriching diversity

Edward G. Tom, Director of Admissions
5 Boalt Hall
Berkeley, CA 94720-7200
Tel: 510-642-2274 • Fax: 510-643-6222
Email: admissions@boalt.berkeley.edu
Internet: www.law.berkeley.edu

University of California, Berkeley

of Boalt's "brilliant" students. One 2L spoke for many when she counted her blessings: "Great student body. I hope it will get to stay so diverse given the recent U.C. Regents' decision [to no longer consider race, gender, or ethnicity in applications]."

"I really like that it's a public school because I think the institution and the people are more concerned with their communities," one student said. As for their scholastic community, Boalt students would make certain changes if they could. A great majority wish that the faculty would initiate diversification efforts as one first-year told us, the "faculty is too conservative, too white male dominated and too many 1L classes are taught by visiting professors." Some students wished course offerings were more numerous and broader as well.

However, the most frequent and negative comments bashing the facilities have been answered with completed renovation and expansion of the library and buildings.

In general, most students would agree with this man: "Boalt is terrific. It exceeded all my expectations."

ADMISSIONS

The student body at the Boalt Hall School of Law is one of the most qualified in the nation, so if you are considering sending an application to Berkeley, take this simple advice: Apply to a backup school as well. This is straight up one of the four or five hardest schools in the country to get into, even for those with extraordinarily high numerical credentials. Demand for spots in Boalt's entering class of about 270 is so great that even an applicant with a GPA around 3.6 and an LSAT score at the 98th percentile stands a better chance of being rejected than of getting in.

ACADEMICS

Student/faculty ratio	18:1
% female faculty	26
% minority faculty	11
Hours of study per day	3.02

Academic specialties:
Environmental, International, Law and Tech, Intellectual Property, Traditionally Disadvantaged Groups

FINANCIAL FACTS

Tuition (in/out-state)	$0/$8,394
Cost of books	$937
Fees (in/out-state)	$10,800/$10,800
Room & board (on/off-campus)	$7,947/$8,802
% first-year students receiving aid	88
% all students receiving aid	81
% aid that is merit-based	2
% of all students receiving loans	80
% receiving scholarships	58
% of all students receiving assistantships	4
Average grant	$6,000
Average graduation debt	$37,783

ADMISSIONS

# applications received	4,684
% applicants accepted	18
% acceptees attending	30
Average LSAT	165
Average undergrad GPA	3.70
Application fee (in/out-state)	$40/$40
Regular application	February 1
Regular notification	rolling
Rolling notification?	Yes
Early decision program?	No
Admission may be deferred?	Yes
Maximum length of deferment	1 year
Evening division offered?	No
Part-time accepted?	No
Gourman Report Rating	**4.88**

UNIVERSITY OF CALIFORNIA, DAVIS
School of Law

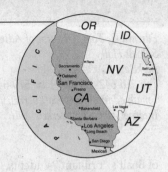

OVERVIEW

Type of school	public
Environment	suburban
Scholastic calendar	quarter
Schedule	full-time only

STUDENTS

Enrollment of parent institution	17,596
Enrollment of law school	489
% male/female	55/45
% out-of-state	2
% minorities	32
% international (# of countries represented)	NR (10)
Average age at entry	25

APPLICANTS ALSO LOOK AT

University of California
University of California, Berkeley
University of California, Los Angeles
Santa Clara University
Stanford University

SURVEY SAYS...

HITS
Sense of community
Faculty-student relations
Sleeping

MISSES
Not enough courses

EMPLOYMENT PROFILE

Firms recruiting on campus	110
Job placement rate (%)	94
% grads employed immediately	46
% grads employed within six months	94
Average starting salary	$47,500

Grads employed by field (%):

Academia	3
Business/industry	16
Government	15
Judicial clerkships	7
Military	1
Private practice	54
Public interest	4
Other	2

The youngest of California's four outstanding public law schools, the School of Law at the University of California, Davis has a solid regional reputation for excellence and a stubborn case of sibling rivalry. The Law School's excellent academic program and low tuition are no secret to residents of northern California, but to the consternation of many of its students, Davis does not command the national name recognition of its older companion schools in the UC system. Of course, trying to match the name recognition of two of the nation's best known law schools—Berkeley and UCLA— is no small feat.

There can be no doubt that Davis is widely regarded as one of the finest public law schools in the country. With twenty applicants per first-year slot, it is obvious that Davis is not the best-kept secret in the world of law schools. Not surprisingly, many of the applications come from California residents, for whom a Davis legal education is an extraordinary bargain. Davis charges virtually the same tuition as the other UC schools, but the cost of living in this Central Valley college town of 50,000 is very low. Given the extreme selectivity of the admissions process, those candidates who are admitted possess very strong numerical credentials.

While the competition for acceptance is stiff, it seems to end as soon as students are admitted to Davis. Students were almost universally positive about the atmosphere on campus. They were so positive, that a visitor, after reading students' comments, might expect to see them walking around singing "We Are Family," while passing around course outlines for others to share. A 1L commented, "One of the reasons I chose Davis was because I had been told and had read that the student environment was very friendly and noncompetitive. I have not been disappointed ...The atmosphere is one of cooperation not competition." A 2L raved, "After numerous warnings, I came to law school prepared to have no life. Funny, instead I've found a new life better than I could've hoped for. It's been a blast."

Don't think that Davis students don't work. They do, but they seem to do so in a less pressurized atmosphere. A 2L observed, "Academic standards are high, but competition between students is nonexistent." A 3L related this anecdote: "At other

Sharon L. Pinkney, Director of Admissions
School of Law-King Hall
Davis, CA 95616-5201
Tel: 916-752-6477
Email: admissions@lawadmin.ucdavis.edu
Internet: kinghall.ucdavis.edu

University of California, Davis

schools when you look up the reserved reading, you find the book missing or the page ripped out. At Davis, the page is flagged and there is a big arrow pointing to the section you are looking for." Not only do the students like each other, they also had praise for their professors as well. A 2L wrote, "We have some of the best minds in the state [in the faculty] … and they like to meet with students. They are clear and usually entertaining." Students also had praise for small class sizes and the clinical programs. Though the town of Davis is relatively small, a 2L noted that its "proximity to Sacramento, the seat of government power in California, affords a wide range of both government and private sector opportunities."

Some of the school's strengths lead to its weaknesses. Some students complained that the course selection was too limited—not a surprising complaint at a small school. Others noted that Career Services was understaffed and too small, "even for a small school." The town of Davis also received some criticism for being less than exciting. But, as a 1L astutely observed, "The town of Davis's proximate location to San Francisco, Lake Tahoe, and Napa Valley is its redeeming quality." Wherever they may wander off-campus, though, Davis students know that they have a supportive environment waiting for them back at school. Not a bad way to go through law school!

ADMISSIONS

Demand for spots in Davis's small first-year class is still extremely high. It may be less selective than Berkeley and UCLA, the crown jewels in the University of California system, but considering how high the standards of those other schools are, that isn't saying much. Admissions at Davis are extremely competitive. With its very strong academic reputation and its super-low tuition, Davis draws a flood of applications from highly qualified candidates. Of the roughly 2,900 candidates it considers annually, the law school admits only one in four.

ACADEMICS

Student/faculty ratio	15:1
% female faculty	29
% minority faculty	16
Hours of study per day	4.03

Academic specialties:
Criminal, Environmental, Human Rights, International

FINANCIAL FACTS

Tuition (in/out-state)	$8,726/$8,984
Cost of books	$864
Room & board (on/off-campus)	$8,819/$8,673
% first-year students receiving aid	87
% all students receiving aid	83
% aid that is merit-based	NR
% of all students receiving loans	80
% receiving scholarships	73
% of all students receiving assistantships	1
Average grant	$5,278
Average graduation debt	$30,000

ADMISSIONS

# applications received	2,621
% applicants accepted	31
% acceptees attending	18
Average LSAT	161
Average undergrad GPA	3.40
Application fee (in/out-state)	$40/$40
Regular application	rolling
Regular notification	rolling
Rolling notification?	Yes
Early decision program?	No
Admission may be deferred?	No
Evening division offered?	No
Part-time accepted?	No
Gourman Report Rating	**4.36**

UNIVERSITY OF CALIFORNIA, LOS ANGELES

School of Law

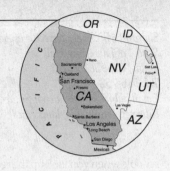

OVERVIEW

Type of school	public
Environment	metropolis
Scholastic calendar	NR
Schedule	full-time only

STUDENTS

Enrollment of parent institution	NR
Enrollment of law school	919
% male/female	50/50
% out-of-state	24
% part-time	NR
% minorities	13
% international (# of countries represented)	NR (30)
Average age at entry	24

APPLICANTS ALSO LOOK AT

University of California, Berkeley
University of California, Hastings College of Law
Stanford University
Georgetown University
University of California, Davis

SURVEY SAYS...

HITS
Practical experience
Practical lawyering skills
Grads expect big bucks

MISSES
Library staff
Not enough courses

EMPLOYMENT PROFILE

Firms recruiting on campus	250
Job placement rate (%)	92
% grads employed immediately	62
% grads employed within six months	92
Average starting salary	$61,333

Grads employed by field (%):

Academia	2
Business/industry	10
Government	6
Judicial clerkships	5
Military	1
Private practice	58
Public interest	3
Other	1

No list of the nation's top law schools will fail to include the School of Law at the University of California at Los Angeles. Inevitably, however, these lists rank UCLA somewhere behind its older companion school at Berkeley. If, in fact, there are any objectively verifiable reasons for this, you would be hard-pressed to find them. And if lists measured subjective factors such as pure popularity with other applicants and enrolled students, the balance might well tip the other way.

There are very good reasons for the fact that UCLA ranks behind only the massive law schools at Harvard, Georgetown, and George Washington in terms of applications volume. Among them are the sheer strength of the law school's J.D. program and the size and quality of the faculty that administers it. The traditional curriculum is supplemented by one of the largest and best-equipped clinical programs in the country, and the law school's overall student-faculty ratio is the most favorable of any of the UC schools. Combine these qualities with UCLA's incredibly low tuition and you get to the heart of the matter: value. No appreciably better bargain is to be found among the country's 175 fully accredited law schools.

In addition to all the enthusiastic comments we heard regarding the school's great location and climate, students at UCLA are quite content with their atmosphere of the school itself. Perhaps it can be attributed to the abundance of sun and fun to be had in Los Angeles, but this is, by all accounts, a laid-back and social group of students. In fact, survey respondents praised their fellow students and the supportive and noncompetitive atmosphere at UCLA most highly. "The people here are extremely open and helpful. Everyone smiles and pitches in to work together. There is no cutthroat competition," said a 1L. Another student, a 3L, offered: "I have been very impressed with the quality of students here. I think that most students at UCLA get into higher ranked schools but choose to come to UCLA because of the quality of student life here." And a 2L went so far as to make this bold statement in naming the student body as the school's greatest strength: "The quality, depth, and diversity of these highly qualified students make even the professors blush with

Michael Rappaport, Dean of Admissions
University of California, Los Angeles, School of Law
Los Angeles, CA 90024
Tel: 310-825-4041
Email: admit@law.ucla.edu
Internet: www.law.ucla.edu

University of California,
Los Angeles

envy." It is true that the student body at UCLA is well diversified; 40 percent of it is made up of traditionally underrepresented ethnic groups, a fact that many students we spoke with appreciated. While students applaud the diversity of UCLA's student body, they fault the lack of it among the faculty, composed of only a little under 10 percent minority groups.

Students are happy to report that a new grading system has replaced the strict curve the school used to adhere to, which many students described as "unfair." The new system, reported one student, has made UCLA "a kinder, gentler law school." Prospective students will also be happy to hear that their loudest complaints—about the poor, out-of-date facilities—have been heard, and the facilities are being renovated.

It is not surprising that when it comes time to find employment, the majority of UCLA students remain in L.A., the nation's fourth-largest and second-highest-paying legal job market. As a rule, they have no difficulty finding great jobs there and elsewhere.

ADMISSIONS

As large as its student body is, the University of California at Los Angeles still must turn away more than three-quarters of those who apply. Although not as selective as the law school at Berkeley, the average numerical credentials at this "first-tier" law school are very strong: a median LSAT of 162 and an undergraduate GPA of 3.50. An applicant with a GPA between 3.25 and 3.50 and an LSAT score between 155 and 159 stands only a 6 percent chance of getting in.

ACADEMICS	
Student/faculty ratio	18:1
% female faculty	32
% minority faculty	8
Hours of study per day	3.58

Academic specialties:
Civil Procedure, Commercial, Constitutional, Corporation Securities, Criminal, Environmental, Govt Services, Human Rights, International, Labor, Legal History, Legal Philosophy, Property, Taxation

FINANCIAL FACTS	
Tuition (in/out-state)	$10,861/$20,155
Cost of books	$1,222
Room & board (on/off-campus)	$6,366/$8,717
% first-year students receiving aid	88
% all students receiving aid	84
% aid that is merit-based	15
% of all students receiving loans	83
% receiving scholarships	49
% of all students receiving assistantships	15
Average grant	$4,759
Average graduation debt	$37,507

ADMISSIONS	
# applications received	4,417
% applicants accepted	22
% acceptees attending	30
Average LSAT	162
Average undergrad GPA	3.50
Application fee (in/out-state)	$40/NR
Regular application	rolling
Regular notification	January15-May
Rolling notification?	No
Early decision program?	No
Admission may be deferred?	No
Maximum length of deferment	none
Evening division offered?	No
Part-time accepted?	No
Gourman Report Rating	**4.76**

UNIVERSITY OF CALIFORNIA
Hastings College of Law

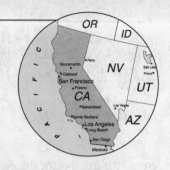

The University of California's Hastings College of the Law is the oldest law school in the University of California system and the one that supplies the most lawyers to its home state. Since its founding in 1878, Hastings has enjoyed a strong reputation within the state; especially within its immediate setting, the San Francisco Bay Area. Over 14,000 Hastings alumni serve the legal community as lawyers, judges, and elected officials—80 percent of whom live and work in California.

It is not surprising that a sizable proportion of Hastings grads remain in San Francisco—arguably the legal capital of the West Coast—where the law school's connections to the legal community are strongest. The law school is located adjacent to the Civic Center, on the edge of a community called "the Tenderloin," an area as negatively urban as San Francisco gets, which isn't bad compared to some other large cities. Although Hastings students can be quick to point out how undesirable their neighborhood can be, they are also quick to point out how happy they are to be located within one of the nation's most beautiful and diverse cities. Though some students bemoaned the lack of campus greenery at the Hastings location, most seemed to look on the bright side of studying in the city by the bay. As one student wrote, "Come on, we're in San Francisco."

We can't discuss Hastings without mentioning the issue of competitiveness. While the school has a reputation for being competitive, students greatly differ as to how competitive it really is, and how it affects their law school experiences. Our respondents rated the school as more than moderately competitive, but many still felt that the reality didn't live up to the school's reputation for ultracompetitiveness. Some shared the thoughts of the first-year student who wrote, "Prior to coming to Hastings I heard from everyone that Hastings was absolutely the worst place to be. I heard that [it] was ultracompetitive and cutthroat. Based on my first semester, I don't see any of those things." Some students offered solutions to combat the competitiveness, such as instituting a more lenient grading system that might take some pressure off of students.

Cornelius H. Darcy, Director of Admissions
200 McAllister Street
San Francisco, CA 94102
Tel: 415-565-4623
Email: admiss@uchastings.edu
Internet: www.uchastings.edu

University of California

Students also seemed to feel that the school lacked a strong sense of community. However, numerous students commended the amount of extracurricular activities that are offered, and most students seemed impressed by and happy with their fellow students. A 3L wrote, "There are many active student groups that represent every point of view, so it is easy to find a group of sympathetic and supportive spirits." The average age of entering students (twenty-five) may also affect student interaction. Another 3L stated, "I really enjoy the fact that many people here have life experience outside of college. I was amazed by the number of students, like myself, who have returned because they want to and not because they have to." Still other students expressed great satisfaction with the Thursday evening "Beer on the Beach" program.

Whatever the atmosphere is, students seemed genuinely impressed by the faculty. A 3L wrote, "Hastings is a great place to study. It's in the heart of a great legal market—the faculty and administration recognizes this and lets students get involved and learn important practical skills." Others were impressed by the accessibility of the professors. A 2L commented that "The intermingling of students and professors reminds students that professors are not as scary as they appear to be, and that students do have intelligent things to say."

Despite whatever criticisms students might have about competitiveness, location, or the facilities (some thought that it was time to renovate), most seemed remarkably upbeat and willing to concentrate on Hastings's considerable benefits. As a 1L stated, "The environment here is exhilarating, intimidating, and never dull. You are challenged as a complete individual at Hastings."

ADMISSIONS

The University of California's Hastings College of Law was not spared in the massive surge in applications volume during the last decade. Last year nearly 5,300 applicants vied to be among the entering class of 420 students. Those who were admitted possessed extremely impressive numerical credentials. With an average GPA of 3.38 and a median LSAT score of 162, the student body is more highly qualified than the student bodies at about 80 percent of the country's 178 ABA-accredited law schools.

ACADEMICS

Student/faculty ratio	26:1
% female faculty	31
% minority faculty	17
Hours of study per day	3.65

Academic specialties:
Civil Procedure, International, Taxation

FINANCIAL FACTS

Tuition (in/out-state)	$7,488/$8,392
Cost of books	$835
Room & board (on/off-campus)	$10,215/$10,215
% first-year students receiving aid	84
% all students receiving aid	85
% aid that is merit-based	2
% of all students receiving loans	85
% receiving scholarships	71
% of all students receiving assistantships	14
Average grant	$3,190
Average graduation debt	$41,318

ADMISSIONS

# applications received	4,352
% applicants accepted	40
% acceptees attending	27
Average LSAT	162
Average undergrad GPA	3.30
Application fee (in/out-state)	$40/$40
Regular application	rolling
Regular notification	rolling
Rolling notification?	Yes
Early decision program?	No
Admission may be deferred?	No
Evening division offered?	No
Part-time accepted?	No
Gourman Report Rating	**4.61**

CAMPBELL UNIVERSITY
Norman Adrian Wiggins School of Law

OVERVIEW

Type of school	private
Environment	rural
Scholastic calendar	semester
Schedule	full-time only

STUDENTS

Enrollment of parent institution	2,160
Enrollment of law school	318
% male/female	58/42
% out-of-state	25
% part-time	NR
% minorities	3
% international (# of countries represented)	1 (NR)
Average age at entry	25

APPLICANTS ALSO LOOK AT

University of North Carolina
Wake Forest University
University of Richmond
North Carolina Central University
University of South Carolina

SURVEY SAYS...

HITS
Socratic method
Practical lawyering skills
Students feel well-prepared

MISSES
Library staff
Not enough courses

The youngest of North Carolina's five law schools, Campbell University's Norman Adrian Wiggins School of Law is a Southern Baptist institution established in 1976 in semi-rural Buies Creek, thirty miles from the greater Raleigh area. With only a few hundred students, it is one of the smallest fully accredited private law schools in the country, and though its name is little recognized outside its immediate region, Campbell is certainly noteworthy—not for having a world-famous faculty or a world-class library, but, rather, for the very tangible evidence of its commitment to a simple goal: training good lawyers.

In a state well stocked with solidly established traditional law schools, Campbell probably had little choice but to distinguish itself from the norm somehow. It chose to do so by instituting what is surely legal education's most complete and rigorous required course of study in trial advocacy. Over the course of Campbell's four-semester litigation program, every student will receive extensive simulated training before trying two actual cases through to the appellate level. Of course, the maintenance of this innovative program has its downside. This kind of practical training cannot be accomplished in large classes, so the law school must dedicate enormous financial and faculty resources to its trial-advocacy programs. As a result, Campbell's traditional classroom curriculum is limited in breadth. The J.D. program is heavy in required courses, and students are allowed few electives.

Despite expected frustration over the lack of elective courses, most Campbell students expressed satisfaction with the school's chosen path and the practical knowledge the Trial Advocacy Program imparts. Upon graduation, Campbell students know they will possess an enviable confidence when they enter a courtroom. As one student said, they will be "off and running. The school is recognized for the strength of the trial lawyers it produces." Another student framed his praise even more strongly: "Campbell's greatest strength is that it is a leader, not a follower, in its approach to the teaching of law. Its conservative core curriculum, once thought to be backwards and outdated, is now being regarded as the way to produce practicing attorneys for the

Box 158
Buies Creek, NC 27506
Tel: 910-893-1750

real world, as evidenced by the school's 100 percent bar passage rate in 1993 and 94."

Many survey respondents noted and appreciated the important sense of inclusion the faculty provides its small student body, thanks to the "individual attention students receive" and the "dedication of faculty." However, some women enrolled at Campbell complained that condescension directed specifically at minority and female students sometimes hampers their efforts to succeed.

Although Campbell students voiced adamant pride for their legal education, they just as loudly demanded better recognition from the world at large. Campbell law students agreed with this 2L's sage words: "With age, the name will improve itself; this is an excellent school." Many students blamed that ever-static target, the placement office, for this lack of recognition, but a few simply told us, and thence the world, to wake up to the fact that "Campbell is highly regarded by students, practicing attorneys, and the general public as the best law school in N.C. The most common example of this today is the high number of Duke, Carolina, and Wake law school grads who say that if they were to do it all over again, they would go to Campbell."

ADMISSIONS

Very small and relatively unknown outside the immediate region, the law school at Campbell University selects its students from a relatively small pool of applicants. This fact has one obvious consequence: Numerical admissions standards are fairly low—lower, in fact, than numerical standards at about 60 percent of all U.S. law schools. Less obvious, however, is another advantage. Applications volume is low enough that Campbell can do something that is virtually unheard of among law schools: grant interviews to almost half of the candidates it considers. As a result, applicants to Campbell can be assured of getting the fullest consideration.

ACADEMICS

Student/faculty ratio	20:1
% female faculty	17
% minority faculty	7
Hours of study per day	4.01

FINANCIAL FACTS

Tuition	$12,400
Cost of books	NR
% first-year students receiving aid	NR
% all students receiving aid	NR
% aid that is merit-based	NR
% of all students receiving loans	NR
% receiving scholarships	NR
% of all students receiving assistantships	NR
Average grant	NR
Average graduation debt	NR

ADMISSIONS

# applications received	1,000
% applicants accepted	16
% acceptees attending	70
Average LSAT	157
Average undergrad GPA	3.10
Application fee	$40
Regular application	May 1
Regular notification	NR
Rolling notification?	Yes
Early decision program?	NR
Admission may be deferred?	No
Gourman Report Rating	**2.24**

CAPITAL UNIVERSITY LAW SCHOOL

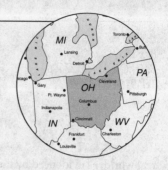

OVERVIEW

Type of school	private
Environment	metropolis
Scholastic calendar	semester
Schedule	full-time or part-time

STUDENTS

Enrollment of parent institution	4,071
Enrollment of law school	814
% male/female	56/44
% out-of-state	17
% part-time	42
% minorities	11
% international (# of countries represented)	1 (4)
Average age at entry	27

APPLICANTS ALSO LOOK AT

Ohio State University
University of Dayton
University of Akron
University of Cincinnati
University of Toledo

SURVEY SAYS...

HITS
Socratic method
Studying
Diverse faculty

MISSES
Quality of teaching
Library staff
Not enough courses

EMPLOYMENT PROFILE

Firms recruiting on campus	32
% grads employed within six months	70
Average starting salary	$40,585

Grads employed by field (%):

Academia	4
Business/industry	21
Government	17
Judicial clerkships	4
Military	1
Private practice	42
Public interest	2

Bigger and better things are undeniably in the future for Capital University Law School, and the students we polled were buzzing with excitement. At the beginning of the 1997 academic year, the Law School relocated to a "very large," newly renovated building in downtown Columbus, "two blocks from the Ohio Supreme Court." This new facility will provide more than 140,000 square feet of space for "state of the art" classrooms, library, and student services.

On the academic front, Capital's course of study is largely traditional, though some students told us that the curriculum would improve if Civil Procedure were taught during the first year. Course offerings are supplemented by the highly regarded clinical and externship programs, which make good use of the school's downtown location. Among the most interesting of these programs is the innovative "Night Prosecutors Program," which allows students to mediate, under attorney supervision, complaints brought by area residents against other residents. The university also supports the Center for Dispute Resolution, which produced a significant international "first" when it helped train personnel for and institute non-litigious methods of resolution at a national level in Jamaica. "Legal writing is strong," and Capital also offers joint degrees in taxation and business. Students applauded Capital's "pleasant learning environment" and "very solid" legal education. According to some, the faculty is "intelligent, insightful, and extremely helpful." Said one 1L: "Professors are not as intimidating as I expected. The profs here are very personable and often funny." Others disagreed, and warned that "the quality of teaching varies a great deal." Students reported that the administration "cares," and that even the "wonderful financial aid department" is "organized, knowledgeable, and helpful." Ultimately, Capital's greatest strength may be is its "ability to produce strong, intellectual, and well-prepared lawyers." For evidence of this claim, look no further than the Ohio bar passage rates, where you'll find Capital "consistently at or near the top."

The law school enrolls almost 800 students, over half of them in its part-time and evening divisions. "The school's night program

Linda Mihely, Assistant Dean of Admissions and Financial Aid
303 E. Broad Street
Columbus, OH 43215-3201
Tel: 614-236-6310 • Fax: 614-236-6972
Email: law-admissions@capital.edu
Internet: www.capital.edu/law/law.htm

Capital University Law School

makes an effort to accommodate folks who work forty hours a week," said a part timer. Capital is truly a "working persons' law school," with "great cohesion among students" and a "laid-back" atmosphere.

The vibrant city of Columbus, with its strong economy, is "a booming center of banking, insurance, and other service industries." Since it's also home to the mammoth Ohio State University, there's a very student-friendly vibe in this metropolitan city of over one million people. The headquarters of many progressive national and international corporations are located here, including CompuServe and Banc One. Capital Law students have access to "a full array of social, cultural, and academic activities. Columbus offers Broadway and community theater, symphony, ballet, opera, jazz, art galleries, and much more, all of which rivals the cultural activities in cities twice its size." With plenty of entertainment and practical lawyering training at their disposal, students here were generally very happy. "Aside from the typical complaints about the parking and the thermostat," asserted a 1L, "our weakest area is that we're consistently underrated by law school reviewers." Agreed another 1L: "Capital is a diamond in the rough. I feel I'm getting a better education than I would elsewhere."

ADMISSIONS

Capital Law School considers the entire application, putting less emphasis on the LSAT and GPA than other schools. Though this school is considerably more expensive than Ohio's state law schools, it is the least expensive of Ohio's private law schools. It also awards a great deal of scholarship and grant money. Capital chooses its first-year class of about 260 students from a large applicant pool, many of whom seek admission to the school's comprehensive evening and part-time divisions. Six out of ten candidates for admission to Capital are unsuccessful, despite the school's relatively low numerical standards.

ACADEMICS

Student/faculty ratio	25:1
% female faculty	19
% minority faculty	8
Hours of study per day	4.24

Academic specialties:

Corporation Securities, Govt Services, International, Labor, Legal History, Taxation

FINANCIAL FACTS

Tuition	$14,993
Cost of books	$887
% first-year students receiving aid	94
% all students receiving aid	93
% aid that is merit-based	38
% of all students receiving loans	93
% receiving scholarships	23
% of all students receiving assistantships	7
Average grant	$3,787
Average graduation debt	$44,887

ADMISSIONS

# applications received	955
% applicants accepted	68
% acceptees attending	42
Average LSAT	151
LSAT range	138-168
Average undergrad GPA	3.00
GPA range	2.01-3.98
Application fee	$35
Regular application	rolling
Regular notification	rolling
Rolling notification?	Yes
Early decision program?	No
Admission may be deferred?	Yes
Maximum length of deferment	1 year
Evening division offered?	Yes
Part-time accepted?	Yes
Gourman Report Rating	**2.81**

CASE WESTERN RESERVE UNIVERSITY
School of Law

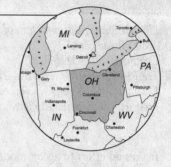

Although it has long commanded respect within its region as an important major research institution, Case Western Reserve University has not always enjoyed such recognition nationally. Until recently, the same held true for the Case Western law school, but with dramatic changes in recent years, its reputation has grown to extend beyond the state of Ohio. In 1986, Case drew the vast majority of its applicants from the immediate region, accepting almost 70 percent of them. Judging from the current competitiveness of its admissions process and the markedly increased geographic diversity of its student body, Case Western's law school has since gone national: it now denies admission to more than half of all applicants, and its students come in significant numbers from nearly every state in the union.

Why the apparent rush to Cleveland? Well, Paris on Lake Erie it's not, but neither is it a rusting urban wasteland. With two million people in the metropolitan area, Cleveland supports a sizable and successful legal community, to which Case Western annually adds a large group of capable law-school graduates. Ten years ago, if you asked a random sample of people living more than 500 miles from Cleveland what "Case Western Reserve" was, many would have guessed it was a savings and loan. Ask the same question today, and more than a few will be able to tell you it's a law school on the rise. The curriculum is strong in all the traditional areas, and the law school has, in recent years, added significantly to its clinical and skills offerings. Although these programs are limited in size (see below), they are admirable in scope.

The current students we heard from had nothing but praise for the law school's special programs, but many lamented their limited availability. "Case entices students with its 'hands-on' courses taught by well-known faculty members," complained one 3L, "but the sad truth is that only a few lucky students get into these courses." He was far from alone in voicing such frustration. "The administration needs to pay more attention to the needs of its students," went one typical remark, "specifically by increasing the availability of practical skills programs." Frustration runs high among Case Western students on this matter.

Barbara Andelman, Assistant Dean
11075 East Boulevard
Cleveland, OH 44106
Tel: 216-368-3600 • Fax: 216-368-6144
Email: lawadmissions@po.cwru.edu
Internet: lawwww.cwru.edu

Case Western Reserve
University

Students were almost invariably positive, however, about the quality of their academic preparation at the law school. Nearly every criticism of any aspect of their experience at Case was prefaced with a favorable remark about the "outstanding" faculty, with a significant number of students even naming names. Case Western students seem to feel sincere admiration and even affection for this "highly approachable, highly qualified" group of instructors. "They are all excellent at teaching," noted one surprised second-year.

Most students, however, had nothing kind to say about Case Western's career-placement office, which several called "inadequate." Some students went even further: "Career Services is the worst aspect of this school." Opinion was mixed when it came to the overall quality of life at the law school, but for every student who called the sense of community poor and the degree of competitiveness too high, there were two who praised the school's "great, supportive atmosphere." Like most things, it appears, an education at this respected private law school is what you make it.

ADMISSIONS

The admissions landscape at the Case Western Reserve University School of Law changed radically during the late 1980s. Not only did overall applications volume increase by 70 percent, but the numerical qualifications of those applying to the law school also increased significantly. With a solid average GPA and an average LSAT score at the 84th percentile, the credentials of current Case students are stronger than students at about two-thirds of fully accredited U.S. law schools. And if one believes in the law of supply and demand, the steadily increasing percentage of admitted candidates who accept offers to attend Case Western is a sure sign of this school's rising prestige.

ACADEMICS

Student/faculty ratio	16:1
% female faculty	23
% minority faculty	6
Hours of study per day	4.04

Academic specialties:

Commercial, Constitutional, Corporation Securities, Criminal, International, Taxation, Health

FINANCIAL FACTS

Tuition	$19,500
Cost of books	$730
Fees	$40
Room & board (on/off-campus)	$8,250/$8,250
% first-year students receiving aid	NR
% all students receiving aid	75
% aid that is merit-based	100
% of all students receiving loans	75
% receiving scholarships	27
% of all students receiving assistantships	NR
Average grant	$9,000
Average graduation debt	$45,000

ADMISSIONS

# applications received	1,458
% applicants accepted	52
% acceptees attending	25
Average LSAT	157
Average undergrad GPA	3.36
Application fee	$40
Regular application	rolling
Regular notification	NR
Rolling notification?	Yes
Early decision program?	No
Admission may be deferred?	Yes
Maximum length of deferment	1 year
Evening division offered?	No
Part-time accepted?	Yes
Gourman Report Rating	**3.74**

CATHOLIC UNIVERSITY OF AMERICA
Columbus School of Law

OVERVIEW

Type of school	private
Environment	metropolis
Scholastic calendar	semester
Schedule	full-time or part-time

STUDENTS

Enrollment of parent institution	5,974
Enrollment of law school	980
% male/female	54/46
% out-of-state	96
% part-time	30
% minorities	16
% international (# of countries represented)	1 (8)
Average age at entry	24

APPLICANTS ALSO LOOK AT

George Washington University
American University
Georgetown University
University of Maryland
Boston College

SURVEY SAYS...

HITS
Practical experience
Sense of community
Students feel well-prepared

MISSES
Not enough courses

EMPLOYMENT PROFILE

Firms recruiting on campus	164
Job placement rate (%)	89
% grads employed within six months	89
Average starting salary	$46,207

Grads employed by field (%):

Academia	2
Business/industry	23
Government	19
Judicial clerkships	13
Private practice	40
Public interest	3

The Catholic University of America Columbus School of Law, which celebrated its 100th anniversary in 1997, is the product of the 1954 merger of Catholic University's School of Law with the Law School of Columbus University in Washington, D.C., an institution created three decades earlier by the Knights of Columbus. This large, well-equipped private law school is located within ten minutes of downtown Washington, D.C., and with the Supreme Court, the Capitol, and roughly 6,000 other law students within the city limits, the District of Columbia may well be a law student's heaven on earth. As its name would imply, Catholic University is surely more concerned than other schools with that other heaven, but students of all faiths are encouraged to apply and attend—and do so.

Both tradition and innovation are evident in Catholic's curriculum, and the law school allows a student to balance them as the he or she sees fit. Students at Catholic are lucky to be able to take advantage of the "brand new and state of the art facilities" (the new law building was completed in 1994) and the city's vast resources. As one 1L stated, "The greatest strength of this law school is its location coupled with its connections in the community." Such connections give students "access to prominent public officials and policy makers," added a 3L. Not surprisingly, externship and clinical opportunities are numerous. Few students pass their three years at Catholic without serving some kind of externship at a government agency, federal court, or one of the thousands of private advocacy groups located in the capital. Catholic also provides students with an opportunity to study diverse areas of law. J.D. candidates at Catholic can now pursue official certificate programs of specialization in comparative and international law, communications law, and the law and public policy. Several respondents praised the Communications Law Institute, especially its placement program, which, one student wrote, "put me in competition with students from higher ranked schools for communications law jobs."

While Catholic students can take advantage of all of these opportunities, they also feel a great sense of community and little sense of competition. "I inherited 700 great friends when I came to

George Braxton, Director of Admissions
Cardinal Station
Washington, DC 20064
Tel: 202-319-5151 • Fax: 202-319-4459
Email: braxton@law.cua.edu
Internet: www.law.cua.edu

Catholic University of America

Catholic," raved one 2L. Another wrote of "the feeling of community that is pervasive throughout all aspects of the school—from the students who are involved in numerous community service projects to the friendly library staff and accessible professors." Students from various backgrounds all voiced approval of the upbeat atmosphere at the school, though some warned incoming students to be prepared for conservatism. A 1L noted, "I really appreciate the Catholic heritage of the school, but I feel like the church sometimes interferes with the information we are given about different educational and career opportunities."

While almost all respondents were overwhelmingly positive about their choice of law school, some suggested areas that needed improvement. There were some complaints about the strict grade median, and suggestions that financial aid be improved, especially with respect to loan repayment assistance programs. Overall, though, students at Catholic were extremely pleased with all that their school and city had to offer.

ADMISSIONS

Although often overshadowed by neighboring law schools like Georgetown and George Washington, The Catholic University Columbus School of Law has maintained a relative selectivity in composing its entering classes. After rising for the past few years due to increased admissions, Catholic's numerical admissions averages have leveled off. Although certainly solid, Catholic's standards remain moderate when compared to the better-known schools in Washington. Today, with roughly 2,700 applicants from which to choose, Catholic admits only about 42 percent of all candidates, putting together a well-qualified entering class of approximately 310 students. The average numerical credentials of students at Catholic University (average undergraduate GPA of 3.20 and LSAT score of 156) are stronger than the credentials of students at more than half of all fully accredited law schools in the country.

ACADEMICS

Student/faculty ratio	21:1
% female faculty	32
% minority faculty	13
Hours of study per day	4.17

FINANCIAL FACTS

Tuition	$20,874
Cost of books	$760
Fees	$459
Room & board (on/off-campus)	$6,019/$6,019
% first-year students receiving aid	81
% all students receiving aid	84
% aid that is merit-based	25
% of all students receiving loans	25
% receiving scholarships	33
% of all students receiving assistantships	82
Average grant	$3,113
Average graduation debt	$66,807

ADMISSIONS

# applications received	2,273
% applicants accepted	49
% acceptees attending	27
Average LSAT	155
LSAT range	148-157
Average undergrad GPA	3.14
GPA range	2.80-3.40
Application fee	$55
Early application	November 1
Early notification	December 15
Regular application	March 1
Regular notification	rolling
Rolling notification?	Yes
Early decision program?	Yes
Admission may be deferred?	Yes
Maximum length of deferment	1 year
Evening division offered?	Yes
Part-time accepted?	Yes
Gourman Report Rating	**3.89**

UNIVERSITY OF CHICAGO
Law School

No law school holds its students to more exacting standards or sets forth a course of study that is more rigorous or interdisciplinary than The Law School (always capitalized) at the University of Chicago. Since its founding in 1902, Chicago has taught law within the context of the social sciences, and the faculty has always included highly accomplished scholars from fields once considered outside the law, most notably economics. Perhaps most importantly, Chicago grads get good jobs. The Law School's reputation is outstanding, and its graduates enjoy full and lucrative employment. A law degree from the University of Chicago gives the prospective practicing attorney virtual carte blanche in the legal profession.

Students at Chicago speak with one voice about many aspects of their program. They unanimously laud the excellent and accessible faculty. A 3L noted, "The professors are brilliant and, by and large, very generous with their time." A 2L wrote, "You cannot do better than U. of C.'s faculty. They are as brilliant as they are philosophically diverse. If you're looking for real moral leaders who blend scholarship with a belief in social justice, we've got some of the greats." The Bigelow legal writing program was also singled out for praise, though it is graded and quite rigorous. Students also had compliments for the use of the Socratic method, which is probably put into use more at Chicago than at other law schools.

One might expect a competitive atmosphere at a school whose students are held to such high standards (both during and after the admissions process), but according to most students, this isn't the case. A 2L commented, "Cooperation is the rule. Outlines, notes, and ideas are shared freely. And this, despite a horrendous and bizarre grading structure that provides a dis-incentive to be helpful to one's classmates." Another student characterized her classmates as "very motivated, intelligent, and diverse, yet committed to keeping The Law School a cooperative experience." A 2L concluded, "It's not really competitive because everyone's going to get a great job."

The Law School has a conservative reputation because it was the birthplace of the Law and Economics approach, which applies economic analysis to legal problems and tends to promote legal approaches that rely on the market rather than on government intervention. A sizable number of Chicago's current faculty members are Law and Economics adherents. Despite this orientation, many students took pains to stress that Chicago was not as conservative as it is reputed to be. A 3L summed up the thoughts of many of her classmates when she wrote, "UChicago is known for being conservative and there are certainly many conservative students and faculty who are outspoken. But there are equally as many middle of the road and liberal students and faculty. Regardless, all viewpoints are equally respected and encouraged." Though this last sentiment was echoed by respondents of various backgrounds and political outlooks, some students feel that The Law School needs a more diverse faculty, with more minority representation.

Some students expressed disapproval with the quarter system of grading, which, in one 3L's words, "makes life less pleasant than it could be." Most acknowledged that Chicago was a great place despite the weather. One respondent, however, suggested moving the campus to the East or West Coast. But no matter where the school is located, it will never suffer from lack of qualified applicants, all yearning to be admitted to a school that features incredible professors, incredible students, and an atmosphere that seems to foster serious legal discourse and learning—not to mention great job prospects.

ADMISSIONS

With Chicago, one can dispense quickly with the question that preoccupies most law-school applicants: "What are my chances of getting in?" Slim. Like its counterparts in the traditional "top five," the University of Chicago admits only a few hundred of its thousands of applicants. Indeed, it chooses more carefully than most: Chicago is the only elite law school that offers interviews to a substantial number of candidates as a matter of course. Although this would seem to offer hope to those whose numerical credentials do not make a strong case for admission, don't be fooled. Not only are numerical admissions standards extraordinarily high, applications volume is incredible heavy. The Law School is one of the most difficult schools to gain admission to in the country.

ACADEMICS	
Student/faculty ratio	19:1
% female faculty	17
% minority faculty	13
Hours of study per day	3.68

FINANCIAL FACTS	
Tuition	$20,499
Cost of books	NR
% first-year students receiving aid	NR
% all students receiving aid	NR
% aid that is merit-based	NR
% of all students receiving loans	NR
% receiving scholarships	NR
% of all students receiving assistantships	NR
Average grant	NR
Average graduation debt	NR

ADMISSIONS	
# applications received	3,367
% applicants accepted	17
% acceptees attending	30
Average LSAT	170
Average undergrad GPA	3.65
Application fee	$45
Regular application	NR
Regular notification	NR
Rolling notification?	Yes
Early decision program?	NR
Admission may be deferred?	NR
Gourman Report Rating	**4.89**

CHICAGO-KENT COLLEGE OF LAW
Illinois Institute of Technology

OVERVIEW

Type of school	private
Environment	metropolis
Scholastic calendar	semester
Schedule	full-time or part-time

STUDENTS

Enrollment of parent institution	6,287
Enrollment of law school	1,187
% male/female	54/46
% out-of-state	40
% part-time	29
% minorities	16
% international (# of countries represented)	1 (NR)
Average age at entry	26

APPLICANTS ALSO LOOK AT

Loyola University, Chicago
DePaul University
John Marshall Law School
Northwestern University
University of Chicago

SURVEY SAYS...

HITS
Legal writing
Classroom facilities
Research resources

MISSES
Not enough courses

EMPLOYMENT PROFILE

Firms recruiting on campus	129
Job placement rate (%)	92
% grads employed within six months	92
Average starting salary	$45,851

Grads employed by field (%):

Academia	1
Business/industry	30
Judicial clerkships	4
Private practice	51
Public interest	2
Other	5

"If you build it, they will come." Over the last decade or so, the Chicago-Kent College of Law at the Illinois Institute of Technology has followed this advice with a great deal of success. For most of its first 100 years of existence, the school was largely a regional phenomenon, admired within the sizable legal community of Chicago and the Midwest, but largely unknown elsewhere. Lately, though, the school has become much more noticeable on the national legal radar, thanks to an ambitious campaign that built up several areas of the school. This campaign includes: building a first-rate faculty whose scholarship has bolstered the school's reputation within the academic community; foreseeing the importance of changes in communications technology to the legal profession by establishing a Center for the Law and Computers; building a new physical plant with a massive library and state of the art facilities; exploiting the strengths of the parent institution by adding special programs in environmental and energy law and intellectual property law; and increasing students' marketability by improving the trial advocacy program and instituting a rigorous three-year course of study in legal research and writing.

These ambitious improvements paid off. Between 1991 and 1992, shortly after being dubbed an "up and coming" law school by one well-known national magazine, the volume of applications at Chicago-Kent increased by an impressive 25 percent. Those students who did come to the school have been impressed by the areas the institution built up. Current students almost uniformly praise the quality of the school's "computer technology and emphasis on the future." As a first-year student boasted, "We attend the most technically advanced law school in the country." Another student proclaimed the law building "a perfectly designed learning environment." Of course, good facilities without a good faculty would be worthless; but students were generous in complimenting their professors as well. A 1L stated, "The professors are excellent; they are laid back, easily approachable, and eager to make students learn." A third-year student commented, "[The professors] care about us, not just publishing."

Students also seemed to think that the school did a good job of preparing them for legal jobs. The comprehensive legal writing

Michael S. Burns, Assistant Dean for Admissions
565 West Adams Street
Chicago, IL 60661
Tel: 312-906-5020 • Fax: 312-906-5274
Email: admitq@kentlaw.edu
Internet: www.kentlaw.edu

Chicago-Kent
College of Law

program was often singled out for praise. As one self-deprecating 2L described it: "[The] legal writing program takes idiots like me and makes us into the top writers in the city." Naturally, some students thought the program was a little too comprehensive. One complained, "I'm a law student, not a novelist." In addition to praising various programs, students were also satisfied with the school's location. Attending law school in downtown Chicago affords students ample opportunities to seek legal experience by clerking at law firms, doing pro bono litigation, or pursuing other options that a big city provides.

While the law school seems to have done a commendable job in improving its facilities and faculty, students suggested several areas for improvement. Although Chicago-Kent apparently enjoys a solid reputation within Chicago, its national reputation has not risen enough to satisfy students. One second-year student commented, "I have discovered through interviews that Kent's reputation in this city is phenomenal. I don't know why the 'national' rankings have failed to recognize this." Another stated, "The [school's] name needs to cross state boundary lines— not enough people know of this school." Money was also an issue, as many students complained that the tuition was too high. However, this could be the price of attending a school that appears intent on improving itself.

ADMISSIONS

After being dubbed an "up-and-coming" school by a leading U.S. magazine in the early 1990s, applications volume at the law school increased by an astonishing 25 percent. Numerical admissions standards consequently rose and have since leveled off at a quite respectable average. Still, admission standards at IIT's Chicago-Kent College of Law are somewhat more lax than those at the more elite regional law schools. But, as the school's applications pool rises as it has during the past several years, so does the school's selectivity. Approximately 2,500 prospective students vie annually for a place in the school's entering class of 400. Numerical admissions standards at the school would rank Chicago-Kent among the 85 most selective schools in the country if it were not for the law school's extremely generous overall acceptance rate of 40 percent.

ACADEMICS	
Student/faculty ratio	17:1
% female faculty	38
% minority faculty	22
Hours of study per day	3.82

FINANCIAL FACTS	
Tuition	$18,850
Cost of books	$737
Fees	$80
Room & board (on/off-campus)	$9,000/$9,000
% first-year students receiving aid	79
% all students receiving aid	73
% aid that is merit-based	NR
% of all students receiving loans	73
% receiving scholarships	36
% of all students receiving assistantships	NR
Average grant	$4,948
Average graduation debt	$75,000

ADMISSIONS	
# applications received	2,175
% applicants accepted	67
% acceptees attending	28
Average LSAT	156
Average undergrad GPA	3.20
Application fee	$40
Regular application	April 1
Regular notification	rolling
Rolling notification?	Yes
Early decision program?	No
Admission may be deferred?	Yes
Maximum length of deferment	1 year
Evening division offered?	Yes
Part-time accepted?	Yes
Gourman Report Rating	**3.90**

UNIVERSITY OF CINCINNATI
College of Law

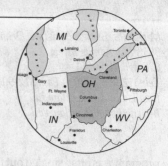

The College of Law at the University of Cincinnati, which bills itself as the fourth-oldest continuously operating law school in the United States, offers a solid, traditional legal education to a small, dedicated, and extremely able student body. UC draws the vast majority of its students from within Ohio, thanks to an extremely low in-state tuition. Its regional reputation is very good and it serves its graduates well in a metropolitan region of almost 2 million people that is home to such corporate biggies as Procter & Gamble. Another regional plus, Cincinnati boasts "more four- and five-star restaurants than anywhere in the country except San Francisco," so sticking around to enjoy the fruits of the Ohio River Valley after receiving a fine low-tuition legal education is an idea that many UC grads find very palatable.

One half of all Cincinnati graduates choose to remain in the greater Cincinnati area, but the school's catalogue is quick to point out that UC law grads are not shy about taking steps outside of this Ohio city's metropolitan boundaries. Indeed, a law degree from the University of Cincinnati can travel. Students with less-regional plans are well served by the programs of the school's major international research center, the Urban Morgan Institute for Human Rights. As for admissions, this has been a factor that has definitely undergone some change over the last ten years. In 1988, UC accepted nearly 50 percent of all the candidates it considered. Today, the law school draws its small first-year class from a greatly enlarged and more highly qualified pool of applicants, accepting a far higher percentage of top students.

Current students seem justifiably proud of their school's solid regional reputation. According to a 3L, "The strong academic reputation allows access to a large job market." Another adds that, "having the Sixth Circuit in the area is a definite bonus." Students also appreciated the benefits of the small size of their school. A 1L wrote, "The small class size encourages a great deal of interaction between the students and faculty. Everybody can get involved." A 2L praised the quality of the teaching, commenting that, "The diversity and educational background of the university's law professors is excellent. The individual characters of most professors make both the material and themselves quite

Al Watson,
Assistant Dean and Director of Admission and Financial Aid
P.O. Box 210040
Cincinnati, OH 45221
Tel: 513-556-6805
Email: admissions@law.uc.edu
Internet: www.law.uc.edu

University of Cincinnati

memorable." Students also seemed quite happy with the school's library, which has ample room for each student to study. Respondents were not so happy with the computer facilities, complaining about their availability and quality.

While some students yearned for a higher national ranking (not an odd wish for students at a strong, regionally recognized school) a more common request was for greater diversity among the population. A third-year student wrote, "The school needs to put more effort into creating a more positive academic environment for minorities. While minorities are accepted on a social level, they are noticeably absent from academic organizations, such as law review and moot court." Overall, though, students seemed quite content with the quality of student life and the legal education they were receiving, especially considering the low tuition. As a 3L stated, "I'm no longer an adoring 1L who thinks there are no problems, but UC Law remains an excellent facility with great resources that gives great opportunities."

ADMISSIONS

Considering it is one of the best public law schools in its region, it is hardly surprising that competition for spots in the University of Cincinnati School of Law's very small first-year class is heated. Applications volume is moderate in absolute terms, but limits on the size of the entering class allows Cincinnati to admit only about one in every four of the more than 1,200 candidates it considers annually. Those who are admitted possess very strong numerical credentials. In fact, with its very solid average GPA and its average LSAT at the 89th percentile, the student body at Cincinnati is among the 40 most qualified in the entire country.

ACADEMICS	
Student/faculty ratio	16:1
% female faculty	32
% minority faculty	8
Hours of study per day	4.03

FINANCIAL FACTS	
Tuition (in/out-state)	$6,897/$13,404
Cost of books	NR
% first-year students receiving aid	70
% all students receiving aid	90
% aid that is merit-based	10
% of all students receiving loans	70
% receiving scholarships	65
% of all students receiving assistantships	NR
Average grant	NR
Average graduation debt	NR

ADMISSIONS	
# applications received	1,202
% applicants accepted	28
% acceptees attending	35
Average LSAT	160
Average undergrad GPA	3.47
Application fee (in/out-state)	$35/NR
Regular application	April 1
Regular notification	rolling
Rolling notification?	Yes
Early decision program?	No
Admission may be deferred?	Yes
Maximum length of deferment	1 year
Evening division offered?	No
Part-time accepted?	No
Gourman Report Rating	3.27

CITY UNIVERSITY OF NEW YORK
School of Law at Queens College

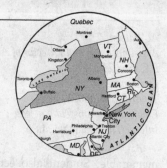

OVERVIEW

Type of school	public
Environment	metropolis
Scholastic calendar	semester
Schedule	full-time only

STUDENTS

Enrollment of parent institution	200,000
Enrollment of law school	448
% male/female	45/55
% out-of-state	23
% minorities	28
% international (# of countries represented)	NR (NR)
Average age at entry	30

APPLICANTS ALSO LOOK AT

New York Law School
St. John's University
Brooklyn Law School
New York University
Pace University

SURVEY SAYS...

HITS
Left-leaning politics
Diverse faculty
Practical experience

MISSES
Quality of teaching
Not enough courses

EMPLOYMENT PROFILE

Grads employed by field (%):

Academia	7
Business/industry	5
Government	16
Judicial clerkships	5
Private practice	25
Public interest	41

Superlatives are unavoidable when discussing the City University of New York School of Law at Queens College. Without question, this is the most genuinely innovative law school in the country. From the day it opened in 1983, this small legal institution has chartered its own course, questioning every premise of the traditional law school curriculum and setting a unique agenda that could actually make the world a better place. CUNY's motto, "Law in the Service of Human Needs," does not alone tell the story. All schools exalt the ethical principles of public service, but many do nothing more than pay it lip service. CUNY Law School, the conscience of American legal education, makes even those schools that do back their words with action look like little more than corporate-lawyer factories. Nationally, only a very small percentage of all recent law school graduates choose to practice law in the public interest. At CUNY, nearly half of graduates do so. At no point in their three years at the law school do CUNY students simply plow through appellate-court cases and regurgitate abstract principles. Classroom courses emphasize legal theory as it tangibly affects human relations. The school's nationally recognized clinical programs are designed to involve all students in those relations throughout their training. CUNY's mission to keep its students involved in the society they will one day serve is greatly aided by the degree to which its faculty and students resemble that society. Diversity is no empty phrase here, where over half of all full-time professors are women and nearly a third of all students are members of historically underrepresented minority groups.

To judge from the results of our survey, those CUNY students who most embrace the ideals espoused by the school itself are the happiest here. Conversely, those whose interests might be better served at more traditionally oriented schools are the least happy. A 1L summed up CUNY's appeal, stating, "The school's greatest strength is its ideological commitment to producing public interest lawyers with a respect for all individuals, regardless of race, class, religion, ethnicity, or sexuality. All those issues are frankly discussed." Another praised student/professor interaction, stating, "Professors insist on being addressed by their first name and consider the student a lawyer in training and not someone who

William Perez, Director of Admissions
65-21 Main Street
Flushing, NY 11367
Tel: 718-340-4200

should be beat into submission." Others did not appreciate the atmosphere at the school, complaining of rampant political correctness or calling the school "too liberal." Some students, especially third years, had more practical complaints about their legal education. One 3L stated, "I feel there is a need for more courses in preparation for the bar, particularly in N.Y. state law." Another wrote that there was, "Way too much theory and not enough black letter law." There were other negative comments regarding uneven quality of teaching, particularly in the "big six" topics.

Perhaps because of the low tuition, and the fact that the school is funded by New York City, there were also some complaints about the quality of the facilities, especially the lack of a cafeteria. Most students, though, seemed to be quite happy where they were, extolling the virtues of faculty accessibility, student cooperation rather than competition, and, "The practical lawyering skills and experiences that are part of the curriculum from the first semester of first year on."

ADMISSIONS

To report simply that the numerical credentials of the average CUNY law student are lower than those of the average student at all but six of the law schools in this book would be dangerously misleading. The admissions process at CUNY, Queens is as different from the norm as the school's curriculum is. Consider this: When one factors in both relative applicant volume and the rate at which admitted students choose to enroll, this innovative school ranks among the 20 most selective in the nation. Indeed, CUNY admits nearly the same proportion of its applicants as do the national powerhouses NYU and Columbia. Hopeful candidates for admission here had better have more than just numbers, though the admissions committee will be looking very carefully for other hopeful signs.

ACADEMICS

Student/faculty ratio	12:1
% female faculty	59
% minority faculty	35
Hours of study per day	4.33

FINANCIAL FACTS

Tuition (in/out-state)	$5,700/$8,930
Cost of books	NR
Room & board (on/off-campus)	NR/$3,802
% first-year students receiving aid	78
% all students receiving aid	79
% aid that is merit-based	0
% of all students receiving loans	79
% receiving scholarships	NR
% of all students receiving assistantships	0
Average grant	$1,850
Average graduation debt	$42,000

ADMISSIONS

# applications received	1,647
% applicants accepted	32
% acceptees attending	31
Average LSAT	147
Average undergrad GPA	3.00
GPA range	2.05-4.00
Application fee (in/out-state)	$40/$40
Regular application	March 15
Regular notification	NR
Rolling notification?	Yes
Early decision program?	No
Admission may be deferred?	Yes
Maximum length of deferment	1 year
Evening division offered?	No
Part-time accepted?	No
Gourman Report Rating	**2.19**

CLEVELAND STATE UNIVERSITY
Cleveland-Marshall College of Law

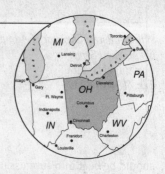

OVERVIEW

Type of school	public
Environment	city
Scholastic calendar	semester
Schedule	full-time or part-time

STUDENTS

Enrollment of parent institution	16,000
Enrollment of law school	888
% male/female	54/46
% out-of-state	19
% minorities	9
% international (# of countries represented)	NR (NR)
Average age at entry	27

APPLICANTS ALSO LOOK AT

Case Western Reserve University
University of Akron
Ohio State University
New England School of Law
Ohio Northern University

SURVEY SAYS...

HITS
Diverse faculty
Legal writing

MISSES
Quality of teaching
Library staff
Not enough courses

EMPLOYMENT PROFILE

Firms recruiting on campus	70
Job placement rate (%)	89
% grads employed immediately	78
% grads employed within six months	86
Average starting salary	$42,486

Grads employed by field (%):

Academia	4
Business/industry	29
Government	13
Judicial clerkships	3
Private practice	49
Public interest	2
Other	2

In a state that's heavily stocked with law schools and law students, the Cleveland-Marshall College of Law is the largest of all. Descended from two private schools (Cleveland and Marshall) founded in the early part of the century, this public law school became affiliated with the state university in 1969. Both the Cleveland State Law School and the university itself are vital resources for this major urban center, which is otherwise lacking in opportunities for inexpensive higher education. Cleveland-Marshall has established itself as the most convenient and affordable option in the area for would-be lawyers for whom financial and/or scheduling constraints preclude full-time study at a private institution. Its low tuition (remarkably lower at the residential rate than the tuition charged by its better-known neighbor, Case Western Reserve) and its evening J.D. program attracts a career-minded, older-than-average group of students, the vast majority of who come from within Ohio. Upon completing their degrees, the majority also remain in or around the city of Cleveland, one of the highest-paying legal job markets in the Midwest.

Cleveland-Marshall offers a straightforward, traditional J.D. curriculum that is supplemented by a modest number of clinical programs and an increasing number of practical-skills courses, particularly in the area of trial advocacy. In conjunction with the broader university, the law school offers a joint J.D./M.B.A. program and a joint J.D./M.P.A. degree in law and public policy. Applications volume for the law school is moderate considering the school's size, and a little more than a third of all candidates gain admission.

Those students at Cleveland-Marshall who responded to our survey (the percent of respondents was lower than at most other schools) seemed satisfied with the practical education they were receiving. A 2L commented that, "Our school places a great emphasis on legal writing and practical application...I feel that I am gaining practical experience through legal writing and clinics as well as being afforded a terrific opportunity to get involved with the community." Others complimented the school's local reputation. "The school is highly regarded among judges, attorneys, and the Cleveland community in general. This is what

Margaret McNally, Assistant Dean for Admissions
1801 Euclid Avenue
Cleveland, OH 44115
Tel: 216-687-2304 • Fax: 216-687-6881
Email: mmcnally@trans.csuohio.edu
Internet: www.law.csuohio.edu

Cleveland State University

enabled me to obtain a job upon graduation at a large firm," reported a satisfied 3L. Another wrote that the school, "teaches you what you need to know to be a good lawyer in the Cleveland area—and you don't overextend yourself financially."

The educational process was also praised by respondents, who liked the quality of the faculty and found their fellow students helpful. The "diversity of students, programs, and organizations," was appreciated by a 1L. "It's a friendly environment where students are not competitive, but rather cooperative. I think the camaraderie at Marshall is due to the diversity of our student body, many of whom work part time," added a 3L. At the time of our survey, students were looking forward to the opening of the new library, which was expected to be completed in the spring of 1997. This new feature was expected help quell traditional student discontent with the school's facilities. One student described the new library as a "beautiful addition to a law school on the move." A 3L lamented that there had been, "too much damn construction. Cleveland-Marshall will be in great shape in a couple of years…too bad I won't be around to enjoy it."

While students did not report feeling that the school was inordinately competitive, there were some complaints about the tough grading curve. Other students desired a wider variety of courses. Some students also regretted that while the school had a friendly atmosphere, its status as a commuter school prevented a greater feeling of community.

ADMISSIONS

Admissions at the Cleveland-Marshall College of Law are not terribly competitive in comparison with other law schools in the region. But the mission of this midsize public law school has always been more about inclusion than exclusion. Over 1,400 prospective law students file applications every year, the majority of them several years older than the average law student. Roughly one half of those who apply will gain admission, and those who go on to enroll will have only moderate numerical credentials: a respectable undergraduate grade point average and an LSAT score at about the 63rd percentile.

ACADEMICS
Student/faculty ratio	19:1
% female faculty	32
% minority faculty	9
Hours of study per day	3.40

FINANCIAL FACTS
Tuition (in/out-state)	$6,408/$13,302
Cost of books	$660
Fees (in/out-state)	$528/$528
Room & board (on/off-campus)	$4,944/$6,370
% first-year students receiving aid	75
% all students receiving aid	80
% aid that is merit-based	31
% of all students receiving loans	80
% receiving scholarships	40
% of all students receiving assistantships	NR
Average grant	$1,330
Average graduation debt	$41,500

ADMISSIONS
# applications received	1,401
% applicants accepted	56
% acceptees attending	33
Average LSAT	151
Average undergrad GPA	3.10
Application fee (in/out-state)	$35/$35
Regular application	rolling
Regular notification	May 1
Rolling notification?	No
Early decision program?	No
Admission may be deferred?	No
Evening division offered?	Yes
Part-time accepted?	Yes
Gourman Report Rating	**3.09**

UNIVERSITY OF COLORADO
School of Law

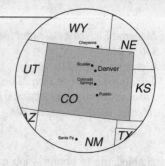

OVERVIEW

Type of school	public
Environment	city
Scholastic calendar	semester
Schedule	full-time only

STUDENTS

Enrollment of parent institution	24,622
Enrollment of law school	497
% male/female	44/56
% out-of-state	14
% minorities	19
% international (# of countries represented)	1 (3)
Average age at entry	26

APPLICANTS ALSO LOOK AT

University of Denver
University of California, Davis
Georgetown University
Hastings College of Law
George Washington University

SURVEY SAYS...

HITS
Sleeping
Quality of teaching
Library staff

MISSES
Practical lawyering skills
Not enough courses

EMPLOYMENT PROFILE

Firms recruiting on campus	55
Job placement rate (%)	89
% grads employed within six months	89
Average starting salary	$37,900

Grads employed by field (%):

Business/industry	10
Government	11
Judicial clerkships	15
Military	4
Private practice	54
Public interest	5

The University of Colorado School of Law at Boulder lives up to its solid reputation for "high quality education at a low tuition" by offering the strongest legal preparation for miles around. Colorado's broad curriculum is supplemented by an array of clinical programs. Especially notable is the Natural Resources Law Center, which "promotes education and scholarship in natural resources law and policy." Students also lauded the legal aid clinic and trial advocacy programs. The student-faculty ratio at CU is one of the lowest in the nation, with "very able and accessible" professors, who are known to "invite entire sections to their houses for barbecues." For the most part, students said that "first-rate professors" are plentiful, "especially in the fields of Constitutional and Criminal Law, and Natural Resources Law." Students noted, however, that CU would improve with "more female faculty" and more political diversity. "Most of our professors are laid back and approachable but still very competent and Socratic," explained a 2L, "sort of like a Socratic Lite." Legal Writing is a different story. A frustrated 3L offered this comment: "I would vaporize the entire program and find people who could teach and write." But, the "well-qualified" and "responsive" administration, earned high-marks from CU students.

Many CU students expressed concern about their futures. "This school is ranked as one of the highest academically and has stringent admissions requirements, yet only the top few can get a decent job after graduation," complained a 2L. The "supersaturated" job market in Denver is at the root of this problem. "A lot of students are dissatisfied with our Career Services Office," observed a 2L. "The staff is quite helpful, so I guess there just aren't a lot of good jobs out there. It seems to me that CU needs to work on its alumni relations and networking opportunities." Other students were more optimistic. Noted a 3L: "The school's name seems to carry a good reputation in the other areas where I am seeking employment, like Portland and the South." Facilities are a mixed bag. Respondents praised the "excellent" library as the "best in the region, public or private" and it received tons of ringing endorsements. What remains of the "uncomfortable, dark, and poorly maintained" facilities "could use a major overhaul." Students noted, though, that extensive renovations are

Carol Nelson-Douglas, Director of Admissions
Campus Box 403
Boulder, CO 80309-0401
Tel: 303-492-7203 • Fax: 303-492-2542
Internet: www.colorado.edu/law

University of Colorado

budgeted and should be coming soon. Computer facilities are "cutting edge," said a 3L, "for the Eisenhower era."

CU students couldn't be more pleased with their "proximity to great mountains" and "absolutely beautiful" surroundings. There are "a lot of skiers, bikers, and climbers" here. "Boulder itself is as much of a reason to attend as the educational opportunities," explained one. "The environs of Boulder are unsurpassed," and, for better or worse, "the most politically correct town this side of San Francisco."

Since the Law School is somewhat isolated from the larger university and the enrollment is fairly small, "you get to know your classmates well." They are a "mellow, friendly," and "tremendously supportive" bunch. "People are always willing to help their fellow students with notes, outlines, etc. It is a very healthy environment for this very stressful endeavor," explained a 2L. The atmosphere "is not very competitive at all, which is refreshing and pleasant given the extremely high quality of students at the school. This makes the entire law school experience much more enjoyable." Another 2L concurred: "It's very relaxed. Students are friendly and cooperative. There is strong participation by 2Ls and 3Ls in the 1L orientation and mentoring programs. Student groups are active in bringing a diversity of speakers to address a wide variety of legal issues and career options. Students also organize social events and community service projects." The many "fun school-sponsored social events" include "post-finals chair massages." Even Law Review is a less competitive, "egalitarian operation at CU. All positions are write-on, so the top 10 percent are not necessarily selected."

ADMISSIONS

With its solid academic reputation, affordable price, and dream location, it shouldn't be at all surprising that demand for the precious spots in the University of Colorado's small entering class of about 170 is extraordinarily high. Numerical admissions standards alone rank this excellent law school among the thirty most selective in the country. The average entering student at Colorado boasts an undergraduate GPA and an LSAT score above the 90th percentile.

ACADEMICS

Student/faculty ratio	7:1
% female faculty	26
% minority faculty	19
Hours of study per day	3.88

Academic specialties:
Environmental, Taxation

FINANCIAL FACTS

Tuition (in/out-state)	$3,984/$14,742
Cost of books	$625
Fees (in/out-state)	$518/$518
Room & board (on/off-campus)	$5,060/$6,273
% first-year students receiving aid	80
% all students receiving aid	82
% aid that is merit-based	5
% of all students receiving loans	80
% receiving scholarships	49
% of all students receiving assistantships	21
Average grant	$2,639
Average graduation debt	$41,632

ADMISSIONS

# applications received	2,299
% applicants accepted	30
% acceptees attending	25
Average LSAT	162
LSAT range	147-176
Average undergrad GPA	3.50
GPA range	2.31-4.00
Application fee (in/out-state)	$45/$45
Regular application	February 15
Regular notification	rolling
Rolling notification?	Yes
Early decision program?	No
Admission may be deferred?	No
Evening division offered?	No
Part-time accepted?	No
Gourman Report Rating	**3.49**

COLUMBIA UNIVERSITY
School of Law

OVERVIEW

Type of school	private
Environment	metropolis
Scholastic calendar	semester
Schedule	full-time only

STUDENTS

Enrollment of parent institution	20,000
Enrollment of law school	1,073
% male/female	56/44
% out-of-state	72
% part-time	NR
% minorities	34
% international (# of countries represented)	5 (32)
Average age at entry	24

APPLICANTS ALSO LOOK AT

Harvard University
New York University
Yale University
Georgetown University
Stanford University

SURVEY SAYS...

HITS
Grads expect big bucks
Broad range of courses
Intellectual challenge

MISSES
Practical lawyering skills
Not enough courses

EMPLOYMENT PROFILE

Firms recruiting on campus	650
Job placement rate (%)	99
% grads employed immediately	93
% grads employed within six months	99
Average starting salary	$70,425

Grads employed by field (%):	
Academia	1
Business/industry	4
Government	1
Judicial clerkships	22
Military	1
Private practice	67
Public interest	4

The reputation of the Columbia University School of Law as one of the undisputed leaders in legal education dates back to 1858, when the establishment of a law school on the campus of one of the country's oldest and finest universities lent much-needed credibility to the incipient movement toward academic preparation for the practice of law. Columbia rose to eminence in the field on the strength of its faculty, and particularly on the strength of the leadership of Theodore Dwight, one of the founding fathers of the American law school. Over the course of its first 138 years, this large, private law school on Manhattan's Upper West Side has employed some of the most respected legal scholars in the nation. The current faculty is as strong as they come. They may not be the most accessible bunch, but the quality and breadth of their scholarship is felt by every Columbia law student in the form of a curriculum that is exceedingly strong in all the traditional areas and particularly rich in fields, like Human Rights Law and Legal History, that receive little or no attention in most law schools. The vast resources of the law school, of the broader university, and, not least, of New York City itself have consistently drawn to Columbia a group of law students whose qualifications match those of students at any school.

While legend would have it that the law school is little more than a brutally competitive breeding ground for future corporate lawyers, and though the employment patterns of the law school's graduates do little to dispel that notion, Columbia is a far cry from the shark pool it is widely reputed to be. Students paint a picture of a law school that offers a tremendously rich academic experience but also has clear shortcomings. On the positive side, most students list Columbia's stellar faculty and the quality of the scholarship they demand from students. And, of course, they list Columbia's ability to land them top jobs. "This place is great (really great, awesome, the best) if you want to do corporate law," wrote one student who does. "The school's greatest strength is its reputation," wrote another. "Really, it gets you jobs." Just as important, most Columbia students we heard from had something like this to say: "There is a myth that CU is cutthroat, which I have found to be more or less false. People are helpful, concerned and supportive both academically and personally." That

James Milligan, Dean of Admissions
435 West 116th Street
New York, NY 10027
Tel: 212-854-2670 • Fax: 212-854-7946
Internet: www.columbia.edu/cu/law

Columbia University

from a 1L in the middle of a notoriously rigorous first-year program. It should be noted that dissenting voices were also heard. From another 1L: "Students are snobby and the stress here can be unbearable."

When it comes to the faults of their school, Columbia students are forthcoming. Their loudest complaints concerned the overall quality of life within the law school. "With notable exceptions," said one LL.M. candidate, "faculty members are not accessible and do not put much effort into relations with students." Others disagreed, and noted that relations have been warming recently, with many students referring to professors as "friendly." By far the most common lament of Columbia students was summarized by one 3L: "Facilities suck." She refers not to Columbia's research facilities, which students unanimously praise, but, rather, to the law building itself. Prospective applicants, however, need not be deterred by past tales of woe, as a dramatic, $20 million renovation and expansion project is currently underway, aimed at improving the student experience at Columbia. A new building, and the vastly overhauled original building, thanks to the renovation of the library, up-to-the-nanosecond classroom computer capabilities, and a "new front door" (37-foot high atrium), greets each lucky incoming class. The changes were driven by "the need for informal, social, study, and personal spaces," which hopefully will facilitate the faculty-student, student-student community, the lack of which current J.D. candidates decry.

Accordingly, even Columbia students' criticisms often conveyed a tone of optimism for the school's future, and many students offered unsolicited votes of confidence in their administration, and particularly in their new dean. "This is a dynamic place," was the judgment of one 3L. "Columbia is making a valiant effort to change with the times."

ADMISSIONS

The rumor mill would have it that the law school at Columbia is a bastion of cutthroat competitiveness. This reputation is very much overstated, and possibly wholly inaccurate. One area where ruthless competition certainly exists, however, is in the admissions process. Fewer than one in every six of the roughly 6,000 candidates Columbia considers annually will gain admission to the law school. Those who are admitted and actually go on to enroll possess numerical credentials that are higher than those of students at all but five of the nation's fully accredited law schools.

ACADEMICS

Student/faculty ratio	16:1
% female faculty	29
% minority faculty	11
Hours of study per day	3.32

Academic specialties:

Civil Procedure, Constitutional, Corporation Securities, Criminal, Environmental, Human Rights, International, Labor, Legal History, Legal Philosophy, Property, Taxation

FINANCIAL FACTS

Tuition	$25,128
Cost of books	$700
Fees	$1,215
Room & board (on/off-campus)	$10,710/$10,710
% first-year students receiving aid	71
% all students receiving aid	72
% aid that is merit-based	0
% of all students receiving loans	72
% receiving scholarships	22
% of all students receiving assistantships	8
Average grant	$9,142
Average graduation debt	$58,672

ADMISSIONS

# applications received	5,510
% applicants accepted	20
% acceptees attending	32
Average LSAT	168
Average undergrad GPA	3.60
Application fee	$65
Early application	December 1
Early notification	December 15
Regular application	February 15
Regular notification	rolling
Rolling notification?	Yes
Early decision program?	Yes
Admission may be deferred?	Yes
Maximum length of deferment	2 years
Evening division offered?	No
Part-time accepted?	No
Gourman Report Rating	**4.86**

UNIVERSITY OF CONNECTICUT
School of Law

OVERVIEW

Type of school	public
Environment	metropolis
Scholastic calendar	NR
Schedule	full-time or part-time

STUDENTS

Enrollment of parent institution	NR
Enrollment of law school	612
% male/female	54/46
% out-of-state	34
% part-time	30
% minorities	16
% international (# of countries represented)	NR (5)
Average age at entry	25

APPLICANTS ALSO LOOK AT

Boston College
Boston University
Yale University
Georgetown University
George Washington University

SURVEY SAYS...

HITS
Broad range of courses
Sleeping
Academic reputation

EMPLOYMENT PROFILE

Job placement rate (%)	92
% grads employed within six months	92
Average starting salary	$51,250

Grads employed by field (%):

Academia	2
Business/industry	25
Government	14
Judicial clerkships	6
Military	3
Private practice	47
Public interest	2

The University of Connecticut School of Law offers a "good balance of theory and practical skills" and, "on the whole, a very conducive academic atmosphere." UConn's traditional course offerings are broad considering the school's size, which students say is "just right. It's large enough so you don't know everyone, yet classes are fairly small, which results in a higher level of student participation." The "friendly, engaging, and extremely accessible" faculty here "comprises a wonderful mix of outstanding academic scholarship and approachability." Professors "really care about the students' understanding of the subjects. They are not too hung up on 'being published.'" Said a 2L: "I have never encountered a professor who was unwilling to go the extra mile academically or professionally." However, students do perceive too much "subjectivity in grading." They also griped about a lack of funding for Connecticut's broad and numerous legal clinics, which include a program dedicated to the state legislative process and an array of judicial externships.

UConn Law is situated in the nation's insurance capital, only a few minutes from the Capitol building in Hartford. This location affords students "many opportunities for practical experience outside the classroom." Students also touted their "charming little campus," which is listed on the National Register of Historic Sites. "When you enter the campus, you feel like you are in Camelot" because of the "beautiful Gothic buildings and verdant landscaping." The newly completed "state of the art" law library is "a shining temple of legal research" that "should make UConn a national player among U.S. law schools." The "fabulous" new library has "more study carrels than could ever be used at one time" and "enough space to house all residents of the state in the event of nuclear war." About the only complaint we heard is that it "could be open more." Alas, not all the facilities here are as pleasing. The computer facilities and classrooms "need updating." The cafeteria, the parking situation, and access for disabled students "need a lot of work" as well. Perhaps more than anything, though, UConn needs new or better maintained photocopiers.

Ellen Rutt, Assistant Dean
55 Elizabeth Street
Hartford, CT 06105
Tel: 860-570-5100 • Fax: 860-570-5153
Email: admit@law.uconn.edu
Internet: www.law.uconn.edu

The current market for legal employment is highly competitive, especially in the Northeast, a corner of the world certainly not lacking in fine law schools. But students here seem relaxed. "I am confident that UConn has given me enough ammunition to compete successfully," said a 2L. The Office of Career Services has "good local connections" and "does a lot to help students get jobs." As a 1L pointed out: "One of the main career benefits of UConn is its low cost. Students will graduate with much lower debts than had they gone to private institutions. This lower debt allows broader choices when making career decisions." The majority of students are Connecticut residents who are happy to take advantage of the low in-state tuition. The law school also gives tuition breaks to students from Massachusetts, New Hampshire, Rhode Island, and Vermont. (They pay more than in-state students, but less than out-of-state students.) Most students are eligible to establish Connecticut residency for tuition purposes after one full year in the state.

Students here have "a team spirit ethos," Explained one: "Everyone obviously wants to do well. Thus, there is some competitiveness. However, it's a healthy competition and the few that become 'cutthroat' stand out like sore thumbs. Their behavior is generally looked upon unfavorably." Though several students called for increased diversity, they told us that "UConn is the place to be for a low-stress environment. All the students get along and work with one another. There are no horror stories." Says a 2L: "Student groups are constantly organizing activities ranging from visiting lectures to beer bashes. Both inside and outside the classroom, this law school provides an enjoyable atmosphere in which to learn the law." "My experience at Connecticut has been excellent," concluded a 3L.

ADMISSIONS

Drawn as much by UConn's affordability as by its academic strengths and solid reputation, about 2,200 applicants vie annually to be among the roughly 200 day and evening students chosen to admission. This "second-tier" law school (whatever that means) ranks among the top 25 percent of all law schools in the nation, both in terms of its numerical admissions standards and in terms of applicant demand for spots in its first-year class. The 1996 day division entering class had a median GPA of 3.29 and a median LSAT of 159. Two out of every three students that apply to UConn are rejected.

ACADEMICS

Student/faculty ratio	12:1
% female faculty	27
% minority faculty	11
Hours of study per day	4.23

FINANCIAL FACTS

Tuition (in/out-state)	$10,320/$21,766
Cost of books	$900
Fees (in/out-state)	$172/$172
Room & board (on/off-campus)	NR/$7,634
% first-year students receiving aid	79
% all students receiving aid	71
% aid that is merit-based	2
% of all students receiving loans	65
% receiving scholarships	24
% of all students receiving assistantships	NR
Average grant	$5,148
Average graduation debt	$39,625

ADMISSIONS

# applications received	1,427
% applicants accepted	37
% acceptees attending	36
Average LSAT	159
LSAT range	156-161
Average undergrad GPA	3.29
GPA range	3.03-3.50
Application fee (in/out-state)	$30/$45
Regular application	March 15
Regular notification	rolling
Rolling notification?	Yes
Early decision program?	No
Admission may be deferred?	Yes
Maximum length of deferment	1 year
Evening division offered?	Yes
Part-time accepted?	Yes
Gourman Report Rating	**3.37**

CORNELL UNIVERSITY
Law School

OVERVIEW

Type of school	private
Environment	suburban
Scholastic calendar	semester
Schedule	full-time only

STUDENTS

Enrollment of parent institution	18,000
Enrollment of law school	550
% male/female	60/40
% out-of-state	75
% minorities	27
% international (# of countries represented)	10 (18)
Average age at entry	24

APPLICANTS ALSO LOOK AT

Harvard University
Georgetown University
New York University
Columbia University
Yale University

SURVEY SAYS...

HITS
Academic reputation
Grads expect big bucks
Studying

MISSES
Practical lawyering skills
Not enough courses

EMPLOYMENT PROFILE

Firms recruiting on campus	400
Job placement rate (%)	95
% grads employed immediately	90
% grads employed within six months	95
Average starting salary	$70,000

Grads employed by field (%):

Academia	1
Business/industry	7
Government	8
Judicial clerkships	15
Private practice	65
Public interest	2

With very good reason, Cornell Law School appears perennially on nearly everybody's list of top law schools in the United States. Its stellar national reputation, its affiliation with an Ivy League university, and its strength in all the traditional areas—most notably international law—Cornell attracts (and will continue to attract) thousands of highly qualified applicants every year. Only one out of four applicants is accepted, and around 180 first-year students enroll each year. The intimacy that such a small group of students engenders is notable among the nation's elite schools, and the physical beauty of the small town environs at Cornell's upstate New York campus draws many students who could likely have their pick of urban law schools. Though Cornell has been mysteriously described as a "corporate" law school, the career choices of its graduates are no more skewed toward corporate law than at any top law school. Even if they were, it would not be the result of any bias in the school's curriculum. The Cornell Law School offers a program that is broad-based and flexible, and it boasts one of the country's better loan-forgiveness programs for graduates who choose to practice law in the public interest.

The fact remains, though, that the vast majority of Cornell grads do choose a "corporate" career path upon graduating. Many students praised the career placement office for its ability to help them gain such jobs, especially since the school is not located in a major metropolitan area. While the placement office was lauded for its connections to New York City, opinion was split as to its efficacy in assisting students who were interested in jobs outside that area. There was little argument that the students themselves were extremely bright and highly motivated. As a 3L wrote, "The line that separates the top 50 percent from the bottom 50 percent is completely arbitrary."

Perhaps because there is so much quality in a relatively small school, students freely acknowledge that the atmosphere is competitive. However, most respondents saw that quality as natural in an environment in which students "are extremely bright and work extra hard to do well," and were unwilling to describe the atmosphere as "cutthroat." Some placed the blame on the school's

R. Geiger, Dean of Admissions
Myron Taylor Hall
Ithaca, NY 14853
Tel: 607-255-5141
Email: lawadmit@law.mail.cornell.edu
Internet: www.law.cornell.edu/admit/admit.htm

Cornell University

isolated location, which was described as a "cold and lonely place to be." Many students expressed frustration at being unable to escape the tight academic grip, saying that there was nothing to do except study. One student, though, offered a solution, urging others to "broaden their Cornell experience outside of law school" by taking advantage of a true university setting and exploring the offerings of some of the other schools at Cornell. The student extolled the virtues of taking classes on wine and desserts offered by the School of Hotel Management.

Even if one is unable to escape school at Cornell, the quality of the schooling makes it worthwhile. Students do not hesitate to praise their instructors. "I never doubt that what I am being taught is anything less than first-rate," noted a 3L. While students here rated the quality of their faculty more highly than did students at nearly every other law school in the country, they were not as enthusiastic about the grading. The tight grading curve was criticized for making Cornell students look worse than students from other top-tier schools. A 2L wryly cautioned, "Make sure your self-worth isn't tied to your grades."

Students planning to attend Cornell must be prepared for a competitive and intellectually demanding experience in a setting whose isolation sometimes outweighs its natural beauty. For students who can handle the Cornell experience, the benefits are more than worth it. As described by a 2L, "Internally, [Cornell Law] provides quality professors, and externally, the name of the school helps to open many doors and opportunities."

ADMISSIONS

It should come as no surprise to hear that this Ivy League law school—traditionally considered one of the twenty finest in the nation—is tremendously selective in filling its first-year class of about 200 students. In fact, the average numerical credentials of incoming Cornell students rank them, by our calculations, as one of the ten or so most qualified in the nation. Unfortunately for the highly qualified applicant, however, even very impressive numbers do not come close to guaranteeing admission to Cornell. When estimating your own chances, consider that in 1993, only half of those applicants with undergraduate GPAs over 3.5 and LSAT scores above the 84th percentile were admitted.

ACADEMICS

Student/faculty ratio	12:1
% female faculty	26
% minority faculty	10
Hours of study per day	4.69

Academic specialties:
International

FINANCIAL FACTS

Tuition	$23,100
Cost of books	$760
Room & board (on/off-campus)	$7,150/$7,150
% first-year students receiving aid	80
% all students receiving aid	82
% aid that is merit-based	NR
% of all students receiving loans	80
% receiving scholarships	40
% of all students receiving assistantships	NR
Average grant	$8,000
Average graduation debt	NR

ADMISSIONS

# applications received	3,000
% applicants accepted	25
% acceptees attending	22
Average LSAT	165
Average undergrad GPA	3.55
Application fee	$65
Regular application	February 1
Regular notification	rolling
Rolling notification?	Yes
Early decision program?	No
Admission may be deferred?	Yes
Maximum length of deferment	2 years
Evening division offered?	No
Part-time accepted?	No
Gourman Report Rating	**4.80**

CREIGHTON UNIVERSITY
School of Law

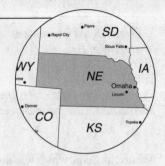

The larger of Nebraska's two law schools, the Creighton University School of Law is located in downtown Omaha, the state's largest business center and the largest metropolitan area in the immediate region. The 118-year-old Jesuit university is widely regarded as one of the finest private institutions in the Midwest. The law school, founded in 1904, enjoys a solid regional reputation as a training ground for extremely competent attorneys. The highest levels of the bench and bar of Nebraska and its neighboring states are heavily populated with Creighton graduates, whose successes are as responsible as anything else for the law school's standing.

With fewer than 500 students in its J.D. program, and a combined full- and part-time teaching faculty of forty-five, Creighton has the resources to offer a broad curriculum. In terms of traditional course offerings, it clearly does just that. The range of courses available to upper-level students is great, particularly within the category of commercial law. If the curriculum is lacking anywhere, it is in the area of clinical training. Creighton offers only one legal clinic, though it does sponsor numerous externships with the many government agencies and private law firms located in Omaha. The law school receives almost 1,000 applications annually, so competition to be among Creighton's entering class of about 150 students is fairly high, even though numerical admissions standards are moderate.

Students at Creighton were not the most opinionated group of respondents we encountered, but on the whole, the strongest shouts were heard about the great school faculty. While they considered the quality of teaching to be quite good, students reserved their highest praise for the accessibility of the "friendly" professors. A 1L described the open door policy as "not just a goal or admissions ploy; it's a reality at Creighton." The professors are "so easy to talk to, we invited them to join us in a round of golf," offered another first-year student. Of the courses, the legal writing program was singled out for its effectiveness.

In general, students found their law school to be a relatively friendly place, in part due to its small size, which allows students to easily get to know one another and develop a sense of commu-

School of Law Admissions Office
2500 California Plaza
Omaha, NE 68178
Tel: 402-280-2872 • Fax: 402-280-2244
Email: admit@culaw.creighton.edu
Internet: www.creighton.edu/CULAW

Creighton University

nity. Some students, however, criticized the school for the lack of diversity within the student body. One 3L critically but simply described the school: "Creighton is an Omaha school for Omahans. Outsiders need not apply." A first year observed, "Creighton needs to catch up with the 1990s . . . I think the law students here need to remember that the world is not primarily composed of white, male, upper-middle-class, single, childless people." It was observed that the law school offers ample opportunities to help out in the community, and that students take advantage of these charitable venues. This is not surprising in light of the comments of a 2L who wrote, "I want to change the world— but I'll start with Nebraska. That's not an uncommon perspective here."

It seems these student attempts at contributing to their surrounding environment is contagious: The administration has also taken steps to improve their immediate surroundings. Though students have complained in the past about the quality of the facilities, a 3L acknowledged that, "The school has undertaken an effort to improve the classrooms [and other] physical aspects of the law school." Though some students observed that more improvements still need to be made, most Creighton students seemed to feel that they chose wisely when they chose Creighton.

ADMISSIONS

Creighton resides in the lower end of the mid-range of all fully accredited U.S. law schools when it comes to the competitiveness of its admissions process. Still, its regional reputation is strong enough that, despite its much higher tuition, Creighton draws a larger applicant pool than, and is very nearly as selective as, Nebraska's fine public law school in Lincoln. In large part, this is due to the relatively higher percentage of non-Nebraskans who apply to and enroll at Creighton, whose reasonable tuition is competitive with the University of Nebraska's nonresident rate. Numerical standards are moderate: The average GPA of Creighton students is 3.21 and the average LSAT score is a 153— the 63rd percentile.

ACADEMICS	
Student/faculty ratio	19:1
% female faculty	31
% minority faculty	3
Hours of study per day	3.88

FINANCIAL FACTS	
Tuition	$14,936
Cost of books	$700
Fees	$464
Room & board (on/off-campus)	$10,700/$10,700
% first-year students receiving aid	91
% all students receiving aid	89
% aid that is merit-based	33
% of all students receiving loans	86

ADMISSIONS	
# applications received	711
% applicants accepted	63
% acceptees attending	36
Average LSAT	151
Average undergrad GPA	3.25
Application fee	$40
Regular application	May 1
Regular notification	Rolling
Rolling notification?	Yes
Early decision program?	No
Admission may be deferred?	Yes
Gourman Report Rating	3.10

UNIVERSITY OF DAYTON
School of Law

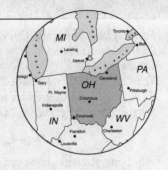

The University of Dayton School of Law is a small private law school on the campus of one of the largest Catholic universities in the Midwest. The city of Dayton is home to nearly one million people, the university to 10,000, the law school to fewer than 500, a sizable number of them Ohio natives. The course of study they follow includes a modest variety of traditional classroom offerings and several notable nontraditional offerings, including a required three-semester skills program ("Legal Profession") and an informal but organized program of specialization in law and technology. (The "Law and Tech" program focuses on computer-related law and on intellectual property law.) Although it is relatively small in absolute terms, the faculty that administers these programs is quite large for the law school's size. Dayton has undergone significant growth in the past decade, with the faculty size increasing by 50 percent. In the fall of 1997, Keller Hall, a new $23 million facility, was dedicated. The state-of-the-art facility integrates sophisticated technology in classrooms, the law library, and all student study areas, and nearly doubles the school's current space. For a private school, Dayton charges a reasonable tuition, and the cost of living in the surrounding area is low. Because of its relative affordability, Dayton draws a sizable group of applicants, and members of the student body possess solid mid-range numerical credentials.

Part of Dayton's self-described mission is to train lawyers who are "sensitive to the impact of Judeo-Christian ethics on the law." That the law school sees fit to state this as an operating principle is surely not insignificant, but it would be a mistake to take this as a sign of religious zealotry. The impact of the school's affiliation with the Marianist order is benevolent and, aside from one course on Judeo-Christian ethics and the law, mostly intangible.

Dayton students are certainly not without their criticisms, but most of those we heard from expressed a fairly high—though hardly enthusiastic—degree of satisfaction with many aspects of their experience. When asked to name the greatest strengths of their chosen school, most cited the quality of Dayton's skills programs, the career placement services, and the overall pleas-

Charles Roboski, Assistant Dean, Director of Admissions and
Financial Aid
300 College Park
Dayton, OH 45469-2760
Tel: 937-229-3555 • Fax: 937-229-2469
Email: lawinfo@udayton.edu
Internet: www.udayton.edu/~law

University of Dayton

antness of the law school's academic environment. "The Legal Professions program provides much practical experience for students," reported one, "and our professors are always accessible and willing to help when asked." Most others agreed: "Professors here encourage insightful discussion during class time and are respectful of divergent opinions," said one 3L, "and the kegs on Friday afternoons make for a relaxed, friendly atmosphere." And while many of the students we heard from voiced their frustration with Dayton's lack of a nationally recognized "name," many others went out of their way to express their appreciation for the solidity of its program and for their feelings of professional preparedness. "Dayton is an above-average law school," began one such remark. "I worked the last two summers, and I was at least as competent as the students from other schools, and probably more competent in terms of practical skills." The student was possibly also more likely to pass the bar; Dayton has had the second-highest first-time bar passage rate in the state for 1993–95.

In offering criticism of their law school, Dayton students are every bit as practical-minded as they are in praising it. In part, their negative comments focused directly on academic issues. "I have found the curriculum terribly narrow," wrote one 3L. Other negative comments concerned the lousy facilities, although some students pointed out that an upgrade was slated for 1997. Indeed, though the majority expressed satisfaction with the quality of the courses they have taken, many complained about the limited selection of courses from which they could choose. "This school needs more classrooms, more professors, and a much broader offering of courses for every semester," said one 2L.

ADMISSIONS

After the state's big three law schools (Case Western, Cincinnati, and Ohio State), the University of Dayton School of Law is the most selective of Ohio's nine schools. A moderately priced private school, Dayton competes quite well with the state's many public law schools for well-qualified prospective students. Dayton students, more than half of whom come from outside Ohio, possess solid numerical credentials that rank them smack-dab in the middle of all law students nationally. The law school's overall acceptance rate, however, is a bit lower than average, so even those applicants whose numbers approach Dayton's average are far from assured of gaining admission.

ACADEMICS	
Student/faculty ratio	19:1
% female faculty	31
% minority faculty	8
Hours of study per day	4.30

Academic specialties:
Commercial, Constitutional, Corporation Securities, Criminal, International, Property, Taxation, Intellectual Property, Computer

FINANCIAL FACTS	
Tuition	$16,900
Cost of books	$900
Fees	$130
Room & board (on/off-campus)	$5,500/$6,200
% first-year students receiving aid	80
% all students receiving aid	75
% aid that is merit-based	30
% of all students receiving loans	80
% receiving scholarships	25
% of all students receiving assistantships	NR
Average grant	NR
Average graduation debt	$57,000

ADMISSIONS	
# applications received	1,550
% applicants accepted	43
% acceptees attending	25
Average LSAT	153
LSAT range	139-172
Average undergrad GPA	3.33
GPA range	2.50-3.92
Application fee	$40
Regular application	May 1
Regular notification	rolling
Rolling notification?	Yes
Early decision program?	No
Admission may be deferred?	Yes
Maximum length of deferment	1 year
Evening division offered?	No
Part-time accepted?	No
Gourman Report Rating	**2.59**

UNIVERSITY OF DENVER
College of Law

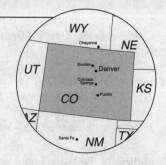

"Location, location, location" is one enormous strength to note at the University of Denver College of Law. According to our student respondents, "the Rocky Mountains are wonderful" and "the quality of life is second to none." Outdoor activities abound, and students said their city "logs more annual hours of sunshine than San Diego or Miami." The "free-beer-on-Thursdays policy of the campus pub" is a nice bonus as well.

This huge law school delivers a mammoth variety of courses, flexible class schedules, and vast resources. Denver's solid traditional J.D. curriculum offers programs of specialization in Business Planning, Natural Resources and the Environment, Lawyering Skills, and International Legal Studies. In cooperation with its parent institution and other area universities, Denver Law offers dual degree programs in anthropology, business administration, international studies, psychology, social work, and urban planning, as well as the nation's only joint J.D./Master's in Mineral Economics. "There is a pretty amazing selection of classes offered each semester," wrote one student. "So many, in fact, that I wish the program allowed for more electives than it does." For those willing to put forth the effort, DU engenders "a lot of challenging opportunities."

Denver has sought to differentiate itself from other law schools with a required 1L course called Lawyering Process. In this class, students work on client counseling, research, writing, and litigation skills in a simulated law firm setting. While the course received a smattering of praise, most students viewed it as a big waste of time. "Every week, two-thirds of the class skips. The class is a great concept, but it needs a major overhaul." Another student charged that this "pseudo-simulation attempts a lot and achieves very little."

DU students said they were satisfied with the majority of their "demanding" professors. "Most of the new and old (and I mean old) faculty genuinely care about students and teaching," quipped a 2L. The faculty "has a strong bent toward public interest" and "they may not publish, but they can really teach!" The "walking zombies" in the administration, on the other hand, received some harsh criticism. "The school's administration, and especially the registrar, runs this school like a Mom and Pop operation. It is disorganized, understaffed, slow, and the technology is out-

Claudia Tomlin, Director
7039 East 18th Avenue
Denver, CO 80220
Tel: 303-871-6135 • Fax: 303-871-6135
Internet: www.law.du.edu

University of Denver

dated." The "high cost of tuition" was another delicate issue among students.

As DU is "the only law school in Denver"—the capital of Colorado—students here have "many, many opportunities for internships, clerkships, and other practical experience in the field." Because students can intern at firms and for judges, many are able to establish "inroads to the Denver legal market." This is a very good thing, considering the area's growing popularity with recent law school grads. "The Denver market is getting tighter, as DU grads compete with nationally ranked universities for jobs. Why? Denver is a great place to live," explained a 1L. The facilities are "good," though a few students complained that DU needs "better classroom facilities" and improved technology. However, argued a 3L, "I have visited a lot of other law schools because I am on the traveling trial team, and I can't find another school with better library, computer, and research facilities."

According to one student: "With a child-care facility on campus and a very positive atmosphere, DU has made law school bearable for myself and a good experience for my child." However, lamented a 2L, "I wish we had a more diverse student population." Some students here claimed that everyone gets along reasonably well. Others noted that negative competition runs rampant. "People may act friendly, but I think folks are pretty competitive here. They like you, but they like you better when you are ranked lower," said a disillusioned 2L. A 1L begged to differ: "I had heard law school was ultra-competitive, but I don't find that here."

ADMISSIONS

The numerical standards to which it holds applicants fall slightly below the national average, but the University of Denver is in a position to be relatively selective thanks to the size of the applicant pool from which it draws its 350-member entering class of day and evening students. Overall, roughly half of the candidates for admission are rejected. Statistically, an applicant to the University of Denver who has an undergraduate GPA between 3.00 and 3.25 and an LSAT score between 155 and 159, inclusive, stands only a 27 percent chance of getting in.

ACADEMICS

Student/faculty ratio	20:1
% female faculty	30
% minority faculty	16
Hours of study per day	3.88

Academic specialties:
Environmental, Human Rights, International, Taxation, Criminal, Civil, Environmental Arbitration and Mediation

FINANCIAL FACTS

Tuition	$17,732
Cost of books	$700
Room & board (on/off-campus)	$6,036/$6,036
% first-year students receiving aid	75
% all students receiving aid	80
% aid that is merit-based	33
% of all students receiving loans	80
% receiving scholarships	23
% of all students receiving assistantships	13
Average grant	$6,860
Average graduation debt	$45,000

ADMISSIONS

# applications received	1,852
% applicants accepted	52
% acceptees attending	32
Average LSAT	156
LSAT range	154-174
Average undergrad GPA	3.15
GPA range	2.40-4.34
Application fee	$45
Regular application	May 1
Regular notification	rolling
Rolling notification?	Yes
Early decision program?	No
Admission may be deferred?	Yes
Maximum length of deferment	1 Year
Evening division offered?	Yes
Part-time accepted?	Yes
Gourman Report Rating	**3.81**

DePaul University
College of Law

After years of creditable, quiet service in its historical role of providing legal education to aspiring attorneys from Chicago's working class, and after producing thousands of fine lawyers and sending a substantial number of graduates into positions of political power, the DePaul University College of Law has seriously stepped up efforts to enhance its reputation beyond the bounds of downtown Chicago's Loop. Recent statistics point to the success of this endeavor, and under its current leadership this midsize Catholic law school seems poised to attract more attention.

Much of DePaul's success stems from its long-respected skills-training programs, which offer "a great practical legal education" and continue to be the centerpiece in a varied curriculum that includes one of the nation's most highly regarded programs in health law. "We have the greatest balance of theory and legal practice," says a 1L. "The externship program affords students a great opportunity to gain experience working in the legal community while earning credit for it." The "competent" and "humorous" professors here are "excited about their work." Though, as a harried 1L observed, "law school itself can kick your butt, the faculty are fantastic at helping everyone learn and keep their sanity." Another 1L explains, "DePaul wants to make lawyers out of those they've accepted. They are not trying to 'weed out' students." "The professors are very accessible and there is a great focus on hands-on experience. Also, women here seem to be treated with more respect and equality, judging from what I hear about other schools," says a 2L. "My one true gripe is aimed at a small portion of the faculty that believes they are much too smart to be teaching at such a 'second rate' school." Also, though most students express satisfaction with the DePaul's practical focus, some bemoan what they perceive as an "unintellectual" atmosphere. Other students contend that profs "encourage" and "facilitate lively discussion."

DePaul's three-year renovation program has just recently been completed ("except for the ninth floor"). The facilities here are accommodating and aesthetically pleasing. Students report a

Dennis Shea, Director of Admissions
25 East Jackson Boulevard
Chicago, IL 60604
Tel: 312-362-6831 • Fax: 312-362-5448
Email: lawinfo@wppost.depaul.edu
Internet: www.depaul.edu

DePaul University

high degree of satisfaction with the "fantastic" library, the classrooms and computer labs, and even the administrative offices.

Despite DePaul's desire to improve its national reputation, most students still consider its "outstanding reputation" and "excellent location" in "the heart of Chicago's legal community" as the school's most significant attributes. "It's right in The Loop, where all the law firms are," wrote one. "There are a lot of alumni in prominent legal positions in Chicago willing to help new grads." Students told us that "you really get a feeling that DePaul is an active part of Chicago's legal community" once enrolled here. These days, though not nearly as many DePaul law students come from the Chicago area, most still envision themselves as having lifelong careers in metropolitan Chicago. A meaningful sign of DePaul's rising reputation is the ever-increasing proportion of its graduates who go to work in the city's largest and richest firms.

The "down-to-earth and realistic" students here are "warm and friendly," if they do say so themselves. "There seems to be a bond between the students in my section that I didn't expect," says a 1L. "It is a very enjoyable atmosphere. The other students have all been extremely helpful." Diversity, however, is somewhat lacking. The "essentially homogeneous" nature of the student body is "the most frustrating thing about DePaul," says one. But students are "bright and intelligent," and the environment is "non-competitive." As a 2L concludes, "the school encourages a cooperative, ethical atmosphere, which allows students to participate in a legal community."

ADMISSIONS

Applications volume at DePaul is up sharply in recent years, and the law school's entering classes possess increasingly stronger numerical credentials. Though DePaul is only moderately selective when compared to its strong rivals in the Chicago area, admissions at this large law school are nonetheless competitive. A 3.0 GPA and an LSAT score above 155 give you a solid chance of getting into DePaul.

ACADEMICS

Student/faculty ratio	21:1
% female faculty	35
% minority faculty	14
Hours of study per day	4.11

FINANCIAL FACTS

Tuition	$18,700
Cost of books	$500
Fees	$110
Room & board (on/off-campus)	NR/$11,800
% first-year students receiving aid	80
% all students receiving aid	80
% aid that is merit-based	20
% of all students receiving loans	NR
% receiving scholarships	NR
% of all students receiving assistantships	NR
Average grant	$1,776
Average graduation debt	NR

ADMISSIONS

# applications received	2,449
% applicants accepted	57
% acceptees attending	24
Average LSAT	155
LSAT range	145-172
Average undergrad GPA	3.23
GPA range	2.10-4.00
Application fee	$40
Regular application	April 1
Regular notification	March 1
Rolling notification?	Yes
Early decision program?	No
Admission may be deferred?	Yes
Maximum length of deferment	1 year
Evening division offered?	Yes
Part-time accepted?	Yes
Gourman Report Rating	**3.46**

DETROIT COLLEGE OF LAW AT MICHIGAN STATE UNIVERSITY

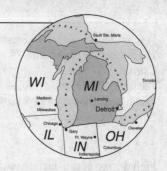

OVERVIEW

Type of school	private
Environment	metropolis
Scholastic calendar	NR
Schedule	full-time or part-time

STUDENTS

Enrollment of parent institution	NR
Enrollment of law school	664
% male/female	63/37
% out-of-state	3
% part-time	34
% minorities	13
% international (# of countries represented)	13 (2)
Average age at entry	28

APPLICANTS ALSO LOOK AT

Wayne State University
University of Detroit
University of Michigan
Thomas M. Cooley Law School
George Mason University

SURVEY SAYS...

HITS
Sleepless nights
Studying
Socratic method

MISSES
Faculty-student relations
Library staff

EMPLOYMENT PROFILE

Firms recruiting on campus	35
Job placement rate (%)	91
% grads employed immediately	54
% grads employed within six months	79
Average starting salary	$39,070

Grads employed by field (%):

Academia	1
Business/industry	22
Government	9
Judicial Clerkships	6
Military	1
Private practice	53
Public Interest	1
Other	3

Established in 1891, the Detroit College of Law at Michigan State University is the oldest law school in the "Motor City." Through all the changes the city has seen, this mid-size private law school has remained a reliable source of well-trained lawyers. The bench and bar of Michigan are well populated by DCL/MSU alumni, many of whom occupy some of the most powerful positions of judicial authority. In its second century, the school is seeking to adapt itself to the changing face of the region's economy and to the changing face of the legal profession in general. To this end, beginning in fall 1996, the school started offering classes in East Lansing, on the campus of Michigan State University, with which it developed joint programs. DCL/MSU's new law school building, with a new library and state-of-the-art technology throughout the facility, was completed in July, 1997.

The law school's efforts to remain competitive are evident in its curriculum. In response to the trend toward specialization in the profession, DCL/MSU has recently introduced two programs of formal concentration at the J.D. level. Students may elect to specialize in either Taxation or International and Comparative Law. The law school is particularly strong in the latter category, but while "International Law" may conjure up images of European capitals and a glamorous jet-set lifestyle, DCL/MSU's international focus is decidedly less exotic. The law school offers one of the nation's greatest variety of courses relating to the legal system of Canada, our country's biggest trading partner. DCL/MSU will soon be offering students the opportunity to participate in an electronic classroom for their Contracts I course, using laptop computers. It should be noted that virtually all specialization at DCL/MSU must occur in the third year of studies, since the relatively rigid curriculum leaves room for only two electives in the first and second years.

On the basis of the many comments we heard from students at the Detroit College of Law at MSU, the degree of a DCL/MSU student's satisfaction has to do mainly with how he or she feels about the demanding program. "They really pound the law into you," was one typical remark—delivered as a compliment—from one 2L. The most highly satisfied students generally sub-

Andrea Heatly, Director of Admissions
N110 North Business Complex
East Lansing, MI 48201
Tel: 517-432-0222 • Fax: 517-432-0098
Email: dcl@pilot.msu.edu
Internet: www.dcl.edu

scribed to this evenhanded assessment from another 2L: "The quality of education here is extremely high. Some students do not like it, but professors make strict use of the Socratic Method and enforce rigid attendance requirements. Education by coercion—a method that DCL is very good at employing—may be unpleasant, but it is definitely effective." In fact, of the students we heard from, many share this belief. "The professors are outstanding," reported a 1L. "They challenge students every day, but they present the material in an easily understandable manner." "The professors are practical and demanding," agreed another, "so competition is inevitable, but I've experienced no alienation among students." On the negative side, for every student who praised the rigor of Detroit's J.D. program, there were two who found it far too traditional and rigid. When asked to name the specific strengths of their chosen school, many students sound a common note: "This school is thought of as a factory school that pumps out good litigators," said one participant in the law school's popular trial advocacy program. "That image may not be great, but from day one after graduation you are ready to litigate."

ADMISSIONS

Though numerical admission standards are not particularly high at either of Detroit's two private law schools, overall selectivity is much greater at the Detroit College of Law than at the larger, neighboring University of Detroit School of Law. Indeed, total applicant volume at Detroit College of Law has nearly doubled since 1986, when the law school admitted fully 75 percent of all the candidates it considered. Today, DCL turns away almost three out of four applicants in assembling its small first-year class. Still, the relatively low average GPA and LSAT scores of entering students virtually guarantee that applicants with moderately strong numerical credentials will gain admission.

ACADEMICS

Student/faculty ratio	19:1
% female faculty	22
% minority faculty	8
Hours of study per day	4.25

Academic specialties:
International, Taxation

FINANCIAL FACTS

Tuition	$14,300
Cost of books	$800
Fees	$0
Room and board (on/off-campus)	$0/$0
% first-year students receiving aid	73
% all students receiving aid	80
% aid that is merit-based	7
% of all students receiving loans	80
% receiving scholarships	12
% of all students receiving assistantships	NR
Average grant	$10,033
Average graduation debt	$48,000

ADMISSIONS

# applications received	1,029
% applicants accepted	53
% acceptees attending	38
Average LSAT	151
Average undergrad GPA	2.95
Application fee	$50
Regular application	rolling
Regular notification	NR
Rolling notification	Yes
Early decision program?	No
Admission may be deferred?	Yes
Maximum length of deferment	1 year
Evening division offered?	Yes
Part-time accepted?	Yes
Gourman Report Rating	**3.33**

UNIVERSITY OF DETROIT MERCY
School of Law

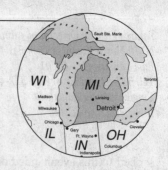

OVERVIEW

Type of school	private
Environment	metropolis
Scholastic calendar	NR
Schedule	full-time or part-time

STUDENTS

Enrollment of parent institution	NR
Enrollment of law school	762
% male/female	54/46
% out-of-state	9
% part-time	27
% minorities	16
% international (# of countries represented)	3 (1)
Average age at entry	28

APPLICANTS ALSO LOOK AT

Wayne State University
University of Michigan
Detroit College of Law at Michigan State University
Thomas M. Cooley Law School
University of Notre Dame

SURVEY SAYS...

HITS
Socratic method
Academic reputation

MISSES
Practical lawyering skills
Not enough courses

EMPLOYMENT PROFILE

Average starting salary	$40,000

Located across from the "Renaissance Center" in the heart of downtown Detroit, this Jesuit law school has served its city and the state of Michigan for more than eighty years. It has also served—and continues to serve—the neighboring city of Windsor, Ontario, which is only five minutes away by bridge or tunnel. In conjunction with the University of Windsor Law School, the University of Detroit Mercy School of Law offers its programs to Canadian law students and lawyers interested in practicing in the United States. The two law schools also allow cross-registration on an elective course-by-course basis.

Detroit Mercy offers a straightforward curriculum that stays well within traditional bounds. Explained a 2L, "You are taught to be a lawyer, not just how to pass the bar exam." Beyond the "intense first-year curriculum," the bulk of course offerings fall under the general heading of business law, and a high percentage of grads pursue private-practice careers in the immediate region. Students described their profs as "young and dynamic," "knowledgeable, accessible, helpful, fair," and "sarcastic." The overall consensus was the faculty is the best reason to come here. Many students felt "stonewalled" by the "inefficient" administration, but others praised the administration for being "fair" and "responsive." Observed a 2L, "Student issues are addressed by the student council and the administration pretty promptly." Detroit Mercy offers a handful of special programs, including notable ones in Intellectual Property Law and Health Law. The Law School also operates a clinical program of modest size and sponsors various externships and judicial clerkships for upper-level students. Students acknowledged that the clinical programs are the "best part" of the experience here and "an invaluable addition to anyone's legal education." The Moot Court Board also "has a great reputation. It placed third in last year's national competition."

Though they seemed reasonably satisfied with many of Detroit Mercy's academic aspects, students here painted a general picture of the law school that is, at best, negative and disappointing. The complaints were numerous: "Improving our so-called 'placement' office" is a must," as is updating the "drafty and cold" law

Bernard Dobranski, Admissions Counselor
651 East Jefferson Avenue
Detroit, MI 48226
Tel: 313-596-0200
Email: udmlawao@udmercy.edu

University of Detroit Mercy

school building. "Acoustics can be a problem in the classrooms," and computer resources, to the extent that they exist at all, are insufficient. "The facility needs immediate attention," urged a 2L. And to judge from the sheer number of respondents who mention it, "No toilet paper in the bathrooms" is a constant dilemma that needs to be resolved.

There are "major divisions between day and evening students," but most everyone here avoids competition and "works together fairly well." Wrote one student, "I've never felt the presence of any really cutthroat types." Said another: "This is a very friendly school. People will go out of their way to help you succeed." However, the atmosphere at Detriot doesn't exactly resemble a big, happy family. Detroit Mercy students appear to bond together more out of frustration than satisfaction.

According to a disgruntled 2L, "'I hate this place' is a common response to 'How's it going?'" Though many students expressed a fairly high degree of fundamental satisfaction with their education, discontent appeared to afflict a large proportion of the Detroit student body. Concluded one student: "If they did something about the facilities and were more responsive to student needs in general, this would be a much more pleasant place to be."

ADMISSIONS

The University of Detroit Mercy School of Law ranks among the twenty-five least selective in the nation, thanks in large part to the relatively small applicant pool from which it selects and stiff competition with nearby law schools for many of the same students. Forty-seven percent of all applicants are admitted, and the average numerical credentials of recent incoming classes have been modest: A mean GPA of 3.15 and an LSAT score at the fiftieth percentile. As long as the volume of law school applicants across the country continues its downward drift, the admissions process here will remain comparatively kind.

ACADEMICS

Student/faculty ratio	25:1
% female faculty	51
% minority faculty	8
Hours of study per day	3.58

FINANCIAL FACTS

Tuition	$14,400
Cost of books	$500
% first-year students receiving aid	NR
% all students receiving aid	99
% aid that is merit-based	5
% of all students receiving loans	68
% receiving scholarships	61
% of all students receiving assistantships	NR
Average grant	$2,300
Average graduation debt	$50,000

ADMISSIONS

# applications received	1,021
% applicants accepted	47
% acceptees attending	43
Average LSAT	150
Average undergrad GPA	3.15
Application fee	$50
Regular application	April 15
Regular notification	rolling
Rolling notification?	Yes
Early decision program?	No
Admission may be deferred?	Yes
Maximum length of deferment	1 year
Evening division offered?	Yes
Part-time accepted?	Yes
Gourman Report Rating	**3.45**

DICKINSON SCHOOL OF LAW OF THE PENNSYLVANIA STATE UNIVERSITY

OVERVIEW

Type of school	public
Environment	town
Scholastic calendar	NR
Schedule	full-time only

STUDENTS

Enrollment of parent institution	NR
Enrollment of law school	530
% male/female	56/44
% out-of-state	29
% minorities	10
% international (# of countries represented)	2 (8)
Average age at entry	24

APPLICANTS ALSO LOOK AT

University of Pittsburgh
Villanova University
Temple University
Widener University
Duquesne University

SURVEY SAYS...

HITS
Sleeping
Sense of community
Faculty-student relations

MISSES
Not enough courses

EMPLOYMENT PROFILE

Firms recruiting on campus	50
Job placement rate (%)	94
% grads employed immediately	50
% grads employed within six months	94
Average starting salary	$35,913

Grads employed by field (%):

Business/industry	2
Government	15
Judicial clerkships	22
Military	3
Private practice	54
Public interest	2
Other	2

Founded in 1834, Dickinson School of Law, the smallest of seven law schools in its home state, bills itself as "one of the best buys in legal education." This is a rather audacious claim for a small private school in central Pennsylvania, but one that is not entirely without merit. To be sure, as a private institution, Dickinson charges fees that are significantly higher than those of almost any public school, but its "best buy" claim has more to do with what you get than it does with what you pay. Dickinson's reasonable tuition buys the law student access to a fine, long-established law school that offers a broad academic and practical curriculum in a peaceful small-town setting. By any measure, this program has been quite successful in preparing its graduates for law practice. The large proportion of Dickinson grads who begin their careers in prestigious judicial clerkships is a sure sign of the esteem or, at the very least, the connections the law school enjoys. The school itself attributes much of this success to the fact that a large portion of Dickinson's students gain direct practical experience during their second and third years by holding legal positions in nearby Harrisburg, the state capital.

Some schools that offer a "best buy"' try to deliver by cutting corners on service. This is definitely not the case with Dickinson. The small group of students admitted each year receive their fair share of attention. "The school is interested in student concerns and offers numerous speakers and seminars to address these concerns. The school also has an open-door policy for students to approach their professors as well as the staff and administration," wrote a 3L. Students held high opinions of the teaching abilities of their professors. A 2L stated that "the overall teaching style of the faculty allows for a more 'real world' view of the practice of law, rather than engulfing us in too much of a theoretical atmosphere." Students are also easily able to satisfy their desire for practical application of the law in the school's clinical programs. "I intern with one of the local district attorney's offices and I have had the opportunity to prosecute three jury trials during the first semester of my third year," a student related. Such practical experience, combined with the school's strong in-state reputation, was described as helpful in trying to secure a job.

Barbara W. Guillaume, Director of Admissions Services
150 South College Street
Carlisle, PA 17013
Tel: 800-840-1122 • Fax: 717-243-4366
Email: admssion@dsl.edu
Internet: www.dsl.edu

Dickinson School of Law of the Pennsylvania State University

The friendly atmosphere at this small school can be attributed to the strong sense of campus community. Several "older" students made sure to note that they felt accepted at the school. One 3L stated, "I don't spend a lot of time outside of class at the school; however, I still feel a part of things." While most agreed that classmates were collegial, opinions varied as to the social life at Dickinson. "Social life here is nonexistent. It's either drink or nothing," a 1L wrote, echoing the sentiments of many respondents. Some compared the atmosphere to high school or even junior high, "where the rumors abound, the cliques are everywhere, and alcohol consumption is encouraged," according to a 3L. The size of the school definitely contributes to this atmosphere. As a 2L observed, "there is little opportunity for privacy in this small school environment." The school's surroundings offer little relief, because, as a 1L politely stated, "the town of Carlisle is somewhat lacking in entertainment value."

Students could entertain themselves by debating whether their school should retain its independent status. While some felt that this status affords the school the luxury of deciding its own direction, others believed that combining with Penn State would help the school gain national recognition and valuable resources. Most students were quite content with the school's current facilities. Not all students would agree with the enthused 3L who wrote that "the combination of social and academic aspects of Dickinson School of Law make it the greatest school in America in which to study the law," but most probably would agree that the school at least comes close to its claim of being one of the best buys in legal education.

ADMISSIONS

Overall, the admission's process at the Dickinson School of Law is only slightly more competitive than average. Of course, these days, average is still quite competitive, so hopeful applicants to Dickinson had better get their act together. The numerical credentials of the incoming students at Dickinson are quite solid; their average GPA of 3.30 and average LSAT score at the 66th percentile rank them among the top 40 percent of all law students nationally.

ACADEMICS

Student/faculty ratio	17:1
% female faculty	22
% minority faculty	6
Hours of study per day	4.02

Academic specialties:
Civil Procedure, Commercial, Constitutional, Corporation Securities, Criminal, Environmental, Human Rights, International, Labor, Property, Taxation

FINANCIAL FACTS

Tuition (in/out-state)	$14,500/$14,500
Cost of books	$700
Fees (in/out-state)	$100/$100
Room & board (on/off-campus)	$2,700/$7,230
% first-year students receiving aid	81
% all students receiving aid	85
% aid that is merit-based	10
% of all students receiving loans	84
% receiving scholarships	41
% of all students receiving assistantships	NR
Average grant	$3,435
Average graduation debt	$42,069

ADMISSIONS

# applications received	1,287
% applicants accepted	52
% acceptees attending	26
Average LSAT	153
Average undergrad GPA	3.30
Application fee (in/out-state)	$50/$50
Regular application	March 1
Regular notification	rolling
Rolling notification?	Yes
Early decision program?	No
Admission may be deferred?	Yes
Evening division offered?	No
Part-time accepted?	No
Gourman Report Rating	**3.26**

DRAKE UNIVERSITY
Law School

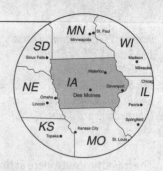

OVERVIEW

Type of school	private
Environment	city
Scholastic calendar	semester
Schedule	full-time or part-time

STUDENTS

Enrollment of parent institution	3,219
Enrollment of law school	454
% male/female	59/41
% out-of-state	52
% part-time	1
% minorities	10
% international (# of countries represented)	1 (7)
Average age at entry	26

APPLICANTS ALSO LOOK AT

University of Iowa
Creighton University
University of Wisconsin
University of Minnesota
Hamline University

SURVEY SAYS...

HITS
Practical experience
Practical lawyering skills

MISSES
Not enough courses

EMPLOYMENT PROFILE

Firms recruiting on campus	35
Job placement rate (%)	92
% grads employed immediately	43
% grads employed within six months	92
Average starting salary	$34,672

Grads employed by field (%):

Academia	2
Business/industry	18
Government	15
Judicial clerkships	7
Military	1
Private practice	55
Public interest	3

Accredited in 1923, the Drake University School of Law is one of the oldest continuously operating law schools west of the Mississippi. This midsize, private, "blue-collar law school" offers a "nuts and bolts" legal education and "a tremendous amount in the way of experiences and resources." A 2L beamed: "Drake is a solid school which turns out lawyers ready to practice."

The notably traditional curriculum at Drake is grounded in the practical application of the law and is very narrow in its scope. Students complained that "not enough courses" are available each semester. The "very accessible" and "down-to-earth" professors here "are an eclectic mix of liberal-minded idealists and pragmatic cynics." Students claimed that "all of the profs were active attorneys before becoming instructors." The administration runs the school efficiently and benevolently. "I came from a public university in California where they treat you like a social security number," reflected a 2L. Many students, however, wish that the top brass would take steps to enhance (or, perhaps, initiate) Drake's reputation outside of the Midwest.

"Fabulous" clinical experiences that prepare students "to hit the ground running" are what really make Drake shine. "Drake offers numerous opportunities to apply what we learn. The clinical, internship, and clerkship offerings are great." For many years, Drake has recognized the importance of "really emphasizing practical experience." Its clinical offerings are impressively broad for a law school of its size, thanks in large part to its location in Des Moines, Iowa's center of business and government. The legal community in this city of nearly 400,000 is large and diverse. Between it and the institutions of the state government, there are numerous opportunities for clerkships and externships. About 80 percent of students participate in one or more clinical programs. On campus, Drake operates a well-funded general legal aid clinic and two specialized programs: the Senior Citizens Legal Services Program and the Criminal Defense Program. A strong, though not-altogether popular Legal Writing Program received mostly negative reviews.

Susan Unkrich Guilford, Director of Admissions and Financial Aid
2507 University Avenue
Des Moines, IA 50311
Tel: 515-271-2782 • Fax: 515-271-4118
Email: lawadmit@drake.edu
Internet: www.drake.edu

Drake University

Armed with all these practical skills, Drake students said they "will be ready to walk out of here and step into a courtroom." It's a good thing, too, because the law school "strongly encourages judicial clerkships." Be that as it may, several students here seem to be fretting about employment prospects. "I know it will be difficult to find a job outside the Midwest," said a 2L, "because no one has heard of Drake." Another student lamented: "Most students leave Iowa to practice, but employers are reluctant to come here to interview." As far as facilities go, there's an "exceptional library" that's "huge and well-equipped, with lots of quiet hideaways and study rooms." Drake has "the best facilities of any school" in the Midwest, "public or private," according to its students.

The students here are "pretty homogenous." Many complained that the lack of student diversity—ethnic, geographic, etc.—could stand some serious improvement. On a positive note, "there are no obstacles for women at Drake." The environment is "friendly" and "very supportive" as well, and "almost like an extended family." It's a conservative family, but with "no hotbed of political activity." A fairly harsh grading system "promotes mistrust and deceit." Nevertheless, students claimed they are "competitive, but not extremely" so. "It's more like 'you help me, I'll help you, and we'll both do well.'" A 1L told us: "Perhaps one of the best examples of the excellent student environment is shown by a three-string display of Christmas lights which surrounded a student's carrel in the library at Christmas-time."

ADMISSIONS

In terms of admissions selectivity, the Drake University Law School ranks on the low end of the midrange of all fully accredited U.S. law schools. In part because of the presence of a hugely respected public law school in the state, Drake receives only a moderate number of applications. Drake admits about half of the roughly 900 candidates it considers annually. Applicants whose GPAs exceed Drake's average and whose LSAT scores are higher than about the 70th percentile are virtually guaranteed admission. "The median LSAT score for students who enrolled in 1995 was 155; the median GPA for the entering class in 1995 was 3.23."

ACADEMICS

Student/faculty ratio	23:1
% female faculty	29
% minority faculty	3
Hours of study per day	4.25

FINANCIAL FACTS

Tuition	$16,330
Cost of books	$900
Room & board (on/off-campus)	NR/$5,900
% first-year students receiving aid	95
% all students receiving aid	91
% aid that is merit-based	7
% of all students receiving loans	93
% receiving scholarships	65
% of all students receiving assistantships	8
Average grant	$3,386
Average graduation debt	$55,318

ADMISSIONS

# applications received	917
% applicants accepted	52
% acceptees attending	31
Average LSAT	153
Average undergrad GPA	3.10
Application fee	$35
Regular application	rolling
Regular notification	rolling
Rolling notification?	Yes
Early decision program?	No
Admission may be deferred?	Yes
Maximum length of deferment	1 year
Evening division offered?	No
Part-time accepted?	Yes
Gourman Report Rating	**3.07**

Duke University
School of Law

The Duke University School of Law in Durham, North Carolina, is one of the finest and most selective law schools in the country. In just about every respect—academic standards, campus life, location, facilities—Duke stands head and shoulders above most other law schools in the United States.

The law school's solid curriculum is peppered with innovative courses in emerging specialty areas of law. The range of course offerings is broad, and students have access to the full academic resources of the entire university through numerous joint degree programs. However, one student pointed out that "Duke definitely could use more clinical programs." Existing programs and series of note include a very impressive Visiting Lecture Series; the Center on Law, Ethics, and National Security; and Duke's Pro Bono and Public Interest programs, which offer students the chance to test their legal mettle in the real world. A "general liberal bent" characterizes the "interesting and unique" faculty, which many students described as "highly accessible." "What better way to learn civil procedure or property than from the nation's most respected scholars?" pondered one 1L. Other students noted that professors vary noticeably in quality, with "teaching styles ranging from genius to megalomaniac." The faculty is "predominantly male" and "seems to take the men more seriously," according to one student. "As a male, I was blind to this, but after some female classmates pointed it out, I've observed several instances in which it appeared true." This claim notwithstanding, "women excel here, and typically dominate the editorial board of the Law Review." The administration "is a huge bundle of red tape" that "is sometimes more concerned with self-congratulatory meetings instead of doing its job."

There's "lots of really great stuff going on" at Duke, including "scads of extracurricular clubs, speakers, panel discussions, etc." While students at most other schools complained about a scarcity of electronic media, students here applauded Duke's "outstanding use of technology and the Internet." This school is definitely wired, and use of cutting-edge technology in the classroom enhances learning opportunities and provides a classroom dynamic that few schools can equal. Also, the facilities here—

Cynthia L. Rold, Assistant Dean for Admissions and Financial Aid
P.O. Box 90393
Durham, NC 27708-0393
Tel: 919-613-7200 • Fax: 919-613-7231
Email: admissions@law.duke.edu
Internet: www.law.duke.edu

Duke University

highlighted by twenty-four-hour access to the law library—are "very conducive to getting things done." On the down side, the law school's architecture has "the Death Star look" and seems to be undergoing perpetual renovations. When students begin searching for employment, ... "Career Services works like a charm. So many employers come to campus, it's almost too much." A helpful alumni network provides "connections all over the country," and "employers respect a Duke Law education and genuinely want to hire students from the school."

Duke mostly attracts "well-rounded, friendly, and abundantly talented people"; there are "very few pretentious bores for a top law school." The "really dynamic" students here come from all over to enjoy the "best vibe in the country." A 1L reflected: "I don't know how the culture evolved here, but it's a puzzlingly happy place. Although we all feel tense as exams approach, the result (surprisingly) is an increased level of collaboration and cooperation." A seasoned 2L offered this explanation: "The better the rank, the less the stress." Another 1L agreed, reasoning, "We all know we have great futures ahead of us, so why bother competing with one another." Unfortunately, "Duke is not in the most hip, happening town." In fact, "Durham is not a pleasant place. Do not be fooled by Duke's Gothic Wonderland campus." Though it's not ideal in some ways, the surrounding area is "quiet and affordable," and "65 degrees in December ain't bad." Many students said that "the environment at Duke is its best asset. Duke affords a challenging atmosphere. We hear horror stories about professors' methods and students' attitudes elsewhere, but don't have to experience them ourselves."

ADMISSIONS

More than 2,500 applicants vie annually for one of the coveted 200 or so slots in Duke's first-year law class. If you have set your sights on this top ten law school, you'd better have some very impressive numbers. A GPA approaching a 3.6 and an LSAT score of 166 or better puts you in the thick of the competition here. A GPA of 3.2 and an LSAT above 160 gives you a dim ray of hope. While Duke's acceptance rate is a bit higher than the rate of its closest competitors, nearly 2,000 applicants are turned away each year.

ACADEMICS

Student/faculty ratio	17:1
% female faculty	50
% minority faculty	12
Hours of study per day	3.62

FINANCIAL FACTS

Tuition	$23,350
Cost of books	$1,200
Fees	$535
Room & board (on/off-campus)	NR/$6,990
% first-year students receiving aid	NR
% all students receiving aid	75
% aid that is merit-based	75
% of all students receiving loans	75
% receiving scholarships	54
% of all students receiving assistantships	NR
Average grant	$15,000
Average graduation debt	$21,043

ADMISSIONS

# applications received	2,744
% applicants accepted	29
% acceptees attending	22
Average LSAT	168
Average undergrad GPA	3.62
Application fee	$65
Early application	November 1
Early notification	December 15
Regular application	April 1
Regular notification	rolling
Rolling notification?	Yes
Early decision program?	Yes
Admission may be deferred?	Yes
Maximum length of deferment	1 year
Evening division offered?	No
Part-time accepted?	No
Gourman Report Rating	**4.85**

DUQUESNE UNIVERSITY
School of Law

Nearly one-third of all the practicing lawyers in western Pennsylvania graduated from Duquesne (pronounced doo-KANE) University School of Law. If you want to attend a law school that has a strong sense of community, a provincial atmosphere, and active alumni, then Duquesne may be for you. A 1L who likes the small, intimate nature of the law school explained: "If you want to go where everyone knows your name, this is the place." Duquesne University, a private, Catholic institution, established the School of Law in 1911. It has remained relatively small, with approximately 650 students, and relatively inexpensive, with its tuition ranking as one of the lowest for private U.S. law schools.

Duquesne School of Law is situated in downtown Pittsburgh, only blocks away from the city's courthouses. The school attracts students and working professionals who are from the area and want to remain there. With nearly half of its students enrolled in the evening division, the law school has a strong hold on the fairly sizable market for legal education for older working professionals in western Pennsylvania. The average age of Duquesne day students is 24, while that of night students is 32. The close proximity to the Pittsburgh legal community, many of whose members are Duquesne alumni, allows students to network and make important contacts during their three years at the school. Several students noted that nearby alumni are a great resource when it's time to get an internship or job. Of course, the student who does not want to remain in the Keystone State may be in a bit of a bind. "[The school needs] to keep in mind that not everyone who attends Duquesne wants to practice in Pittsburgh or even Pennsylvania," said one 3L. Perhaps this is the reason many students said that the law school's career services office needs improvement. However, according to the administration, the school has a hard time persuading students to leave the area, though it schedules out-of-town interview trips.

The students at Duquesne are a tightly knit group who reflect the university's traditional and conservative leanings. "There is a strong sense of community among students due, in large part, to the small size of the school," said one 3L. Another 1L agreed: "It's comfortable here, and you aren't just a number. People are very

Dean of Admissions
900 Locust Street
Pittsburgh, PA 15282
Tel: 412-396-6296
Email: ricci@duq.z.cc.duq.edu

friendly and helpful." However, with just under 10 percent of its student body composed of minorities, Duquesne School of Law ranks as one of the least ethnically diverse schools in the Mid-Atlantic.

Since the new administration came into being at Duquesne in 1993, six skills courses have been added to the curriculum, and the school has dramatically expanded its externship program, with opportunities throughout western Pennsylvania and as far afield as Hawaii, Zimbabwe, and Ireland. Although the vast majority of students are content with their education at Duquesne, we did hear from several students who feel that course offerings need to be improved, particularly the writing program. One 1L said, "The writing program does is no way teach me how to write like a lawyer," and, "We are given assignments and told to do them with no directions how to do them." The administration has heard and agreed with student assessments and responded by creating four and a half new faculty positions for teaching legal writing and research in 1996. Responsiveness such as this might be one reason Duquesne students seem particularly pleased with the faculty and administration. "The faculty are very helpful," said one 3L, and "[the] faculty and [the] dean are concerned about students' welfare." However, a small but vocal group of students spoke of a few less than stellar professors who seem to get by the administration. "We have a very few exceptionally poor professors," said one student, and added, "The administration seems deaf to the caterwauls of the students about these awful profs." But overall, students are content with their education and surroundings at Duquesne University School of Law.

ADMISSIONS

Admissions at Duquesne are fairly competitive with an acceptance rate of about one-fourth. Only slightly less selective in its admissions process than the nearby public law school at the University of Pittsburgh, the Duquesne University School of Law maintains relatively high numerical standards. The strong grade point average of the typical admitted student combined with a respectable LSAT score places Duquesne's student body in the top 40 percent nationally in terms of numerical qualifications. These standards are particularly high in comparison with many other law schools that maintain large part-time divisions.

ACADEMICS	
Student/faculty ratio	23:1
% female faculty	21
% minority faculty	20
Hours of study per day	3.62

FINANCIAL FACTS	
Tuition	$12,215
Cost of books	NR
% first-year students receiving aid	40
% all students receiving aid	35
% aid that is merit-based	50
% of all students receiving loans	75
% receiving scholarships	NR
% of all students receiving assistantships	NR
Average grant	NR
Average graduation debt	NR

ADMISSIONS	
# applications received	NR
% applicants accepted	26
% acceptees attending	NR
Average LSAT	156
Average undergrad GPA	3.25
Application fee	$50
Regular application	April 1, May 1
Regular notification	rolling
Rolling notification?	Yes
Early decision program?	No
Admission may be deferred?	Yes
Maximum length of deferment	1 year
Evening division offered?	Yes
Part-time accepted?	Yes
Gourman Report Rating	**3.19**

EMORY UNIVERSITY
School of Law

OVERVIEW

Type of school	private
Environment	metropolis
Scholastic calendar	semester
Schedule	full-time only

STUDENTS

Enrollment of parent institution	10,000
Enrollment of law school	706
% male/female	59/41
% out-of-state	79
% part-time	NR
% minorities	18
% international (# of countries represented)	NR (14)
Average age at entry	22

APPLICANTS ALSO LOOK AT

Duke University
Georgetown University
Vanderbilt University
Boston University
George Washington University

SURVEY SAYS...

HITS
Practical experience
Quality of teaching
Intellectual challenge

MISSES
Not enough courses

EMPLOYMENT PROFILE

Firms recruiting on campus	115
Job placement rate (%)	93
Average starting salary	$48,378

Grads employed by field (%):

Academia	1
Business/industry	20
Government	7
Judicial clerkships	8
Private practice	63
Public interest	5
Other	1

To hear the admissions brochures of nearly every American law school tell it, there is not a city in this country that is neither "vibrant" nor "livable." Personal experience tells us that these terms are at times used so freely as to lose any sense of their original meanings. Some places, however, seem to embody the accepted definitions of these words. Atlanta, Georgia, is one. The city exudes confidence in its own future, as does the midsize private law school that calls Atlanta home. A fast-rising star in the firmament of U.S. law schools, the Emory University School of Law is no longer a very well-kept secret.

Emory has long enjoyed an unchallenged reputation as one of the finest law schools in the Southeast, but in recent years it has garnered praise from all quarters for its strong traditional curriculum and its model skills programs. Besides its broad and numerous academic course offerings and its various clinical programs, Emory runs an intensive two-week "trial training" workshop that is required of all students at the end of their second year. The success of this program has helped to boost Emory's reputation as a training ground for well-prepared young attorneys. Emory now attracts the vast majority of its very qualified students from outside the Southeast. A good many of these transplants choose to stay in Atlanta, a large and lucrative legal job market, after completing their degrees. Applications volume is very heavy, having nearly doubled over the last decade. Accordingly, the admissions process is extremely competitive, and numerical standards are high.

Just as high, it seems, are the standards to which Emory students hold their school. Although their fundamental satisfaction with their program and confidence in their futures is high, they criticize certain aspects of their experience at the law school. On the positive side, few students we heard from had anything but praise for Emory's outstanding faculty, opinions of which ran the gamut from "excellent" to "superb." Students also lauded the accessibility and diversity of the faculty. Most also offered unsolicited endorsements of the law school's innovative trial techniques program. "The litigation courses are very strong," went

Lynell Cadray, Assistant Dean for Admissions
Emory University School of Law
Atlanta, GA 30322
Tel: 404-727-6801
Internet: www.law.emory.edu

one typical remark, "and the clinical programs in general offer fabulous experience in a broad range of legal fields."

But Emory students seem more eager to point out their law school's shortcomings than to belabor its obvious strengths. Most of their criticisms relate to the fairly high degree of competitiveness among students. This was a typical comment: "The quality of the student body is exceptionally high, and the faculty is solid, but the administration needs to work to alleviate the competitiveness and recognize the high quality of all its students and not just the upper tier." Most blame a strict and unforgiving grading curve for this competitiveness, and if the remarks we heard are any indication of the general mind-set of Emory students, grades are indeed the focus of much concern, particularly in regard to their effect on employment prospects. For example: "Great job opportunities if you are in the top 20 to 25 percent of class. More difficult if your grades are not up to par"; "Career services seems to cater only to the top 20 percent"; "Emory is not ranked among the top ten law schools, but job prospects for students who succeed academically are equivalent." It is understandable that some students would perceive some relative difficulty in landing good jobs when their most successful classmates get some of the best jobs in the nation, but top 10 percent of the class or no, Emory grads are among the most employable in the region.

ADMISSIONS

Thanks in part to its anointment by a major U.S. magazine as one of the country's "up-and-coming" law schools, the Emory University School of Law has become extremely popular with highly qualified applicants around the nation. In terms of the numerical standards to which it holds applicants, Emory is one of the forty most selective law schools in the nation. Statistically, an applicant with an undergraduate GPA between 3.00 and 3.25 and an LSAT score between about 155 and 159 stands only a 8 percent chance of getting in.

ACADEMICS

Student/faculty ratio	16:1
% female faculty	18
% minority faculty	4
Hours of study per day	4.00

Academic specialties:

Commercial, Criminal, Environmental, Human Rights, International, Taxation

FINANCIAL FACTS

Tuition	$22,500
Cost of books	$1,000
Fees	$190
Room & board (on/off-campus)	$9,120/$9,120
% first-year students receiving aid	81
% all students receiving aid	79
% aid that is merit-based	1
% of all students receiving loans	74
% receiving scholarships	24
% of all students receiving assistantships	18
Average grant	$11,512
Average graduation debt	$48,918

ADMISSIONS

# applications received	2,805
% applicants accepted	37
% acceptees attending	19
Average LSAT	160
Average undergrad GPA	3.40
Application fee	$50
Regular application	rolling
Regular notification	rolling
Rolling notification?	Yes
Early decision program?	No
Admission may be deferred?	Yes
Maximum length of deferment	1 year
Evening division offered?	No
Part-time accepted?	No
Gourman Report Rating	**3.83**

FLORIDA STATE UNIVERSITY
College of Law

Few states have experienced a higher rate of population growth in the last decade than Florida. In struggling to keep up with the demand for legal services placed on it by an ever-increasing populace, the Sunshine State's legal community and its six law schools have thrived, especially Florida State University's College of Law. In its relatively short history, Florida State has matured from a tiny start-up operation into a midsize public law school that is widely regarded as one of the finest in the Southeast. The law school's curriculum is solid in all the traditional areas and is supplemented by a wide variety of clinical externship programs available through the legal and governmental institutions of Tallahassee, the state capital. Much of the strength of Florida State's academic program stems from its faculty, which is large and well-qualified.

The same can certainly be said of the applicant pool, which is already immense and growing. Thanks in part to its incredibly low tuition, Florida State now processes almost three times as many applications annually as it did just eight years ago. The numerical credentials of entering students are solid and comparable with those of students at Florida's other top schools. The gender balance and ethnic diversity in the student body at Florida State, however, certainly put other schools to shame. FSU is well ahead of almost every other school in the region.

Students at Florida State painted a picture of a fairly pleasant learning environment, and though they had their gripes, their overall level of satisfaction with their chosen school was high. "I really like FSU," endorsed a 2L student. "The professors overall are highly motivated to teach us how to be good lawyers. Perhaps it is because the school is trying to build a reputation, rather than rest on one." In addition to the high marks given to the quality and accessibility of the faculty, nearly every student we heard from also praised FSU's extensive cocurricular offerings. By exploiting the resources of the capital city, the students have plenty of legislative and clerkship opportunities "to see first hand how laws are created and interpreted."

Marie Capshew, Director of Admissions and Records
425 West Jefferson Street
Tallahassee, FL 32306-1601
Tel: 850-644-3787 • Fax: 850-644-7284
Email: admissions@law.fsu.edu
Internet: www.law.fsu.edu

Florida State University

Needless to say, students here saw room for improvement. Not only did they feel the need for improved computer facilities, many also expressed dissatisfaction with the Legal Writing program and the lack of practical courses. A 3L advised that the school would benefit from "less 'cutting edge' theoretical instruction and more practical instruction." And it wouldn't be a public school if there weren't numerous complaints about bureaucracy. "I wish," confided one student, "the law school was more personal, more concerned, and actually took notice of the students." One of her classmates warned us: "The administration is currently in a state of instability." Perhaps FSU is still recovering from some growing pains accumulated in its short history.

Overall, Florida State attracts a diverse student body. "There are students here of all ages, sizes, and persuasions," boasted a forty-one-year-old 1L. The atmosphere at the school is relaxed and sociable according to many students. Despite the report of one who claimed that students become "more and more competitive" as coursework progresses, the responses indicated a reduced amount of competitiveness since we last surveyed. One student assured us that, "the enforcement of the student honor code has prevented any abusive incidents of competition or harassment." Another summarily conceded that, "Florida State is a wonderful place."

ADMISSIONS

Like so many other respected public law schools, Florida State experienced a dramatic increase in application volume during the late 1980s. Between 1987 and 1993, the number of applicants to the law school more than doubled, and though FSU expanded its total enrollment during the same period, overall selectivity has climbed. Only one in four of the roughly 2,000 candidates considered annually will gain admission, and almost half of those admitted will actually choose to attend. Numerical standards are impressive: The average GPA of entering students is a solid 3.30, and the average LSAT score is 157, a score at the 80th percentile.

ACADEMICS

Student/faculty ratio	17:1
% female faculty	34
% minority faculty	11
Hours of study per day	3.58

Academic specialties:
Environmental, International

FINANCIAL FACTS

Tuition (in/out-state)	$3,952/$12,411
Cost of books	$800
Room & board (on/off-campus)	NR/$9,000
% first-year students receiving aid	97
% all students receiving aid	98
% aid that is merit-based	10
% of all students receiving loans	74
% receiving scholarships	21
% of all students receiving assistantships	NR
Average grant	NR
Average graduation debt	$55,500

ADMISSIONS

# applications received	2,107
% applicants accepted	31
% acceptees attending	31
Average LSAT	156
Average undergrad GPA	3.30
Application fee (in/out-state)	$20/$20
Regular application	rolling
Regular notification	rolling
Rolling notification?	Yes
Early decision program?	No
Admission may be deferred?	No
Evening division offered?	No
Part-time accepted?	No
Gourman Report Rating	**3.41**

UNIVERSITY OF FLORIDA
College of Law

One of the Southeast's finest law schools, the University of Florida College of Law is the oldest in the state and, arguably, the best. Located on the Gainesville campus of one of the biggest universities in the country, this large, inexpensive public law school has served its home state since the beginning of the century. Importing an enormous number of law-school graduates, Florida may be as favorable a job market as exists these days, and its most respected source of home-grown lawyers is UF.

Florida's curriculum is traditional and modestly broad, and it includes a limited assortment of clinical programs and skills courses. The law school distinguishes itself less through any curricular innovations than through its overall academic solidity. The faculty is large and strong, the law library huge and well-staffed, the students serious and well-qualified. Add to that already impressive list of ingredients the super-low tuition, and you can see why applications volume at Florida has gone through the roof. The overwhelming majority of those who take advantage of the strong program at this bargain law school are native Floridians. A similar proportion of Florida grads remains in the state after completing their degrees. The law school enrolls around 400 new students each year, half in September and half in January. Numerical admissions standards are very high.

Equally high, it seems, are the standards to which Florida law students hold their chosen school. No student we heard from was totally negative in assessing his experience at the law school, but nearly all see real room for improvement. On the positive side, UF students voiced nearly unanimous praise for certain fundamentals, chief among them the law school's strong regional reputation, fine facilities (especially the library), and very low tuition. But Florida students also had kind words for their instructors and, not least, for themselves. Asked to name their law school's greatest strengths, most cited the "quality of students and faculty." As one 2L explained: "The one phrase that sums this place up is that no one phrase could sum this place up—very diverse individuals with diverse goals and attitudes, laid-back on the outside but on the whole very driven and ambitious."

Michael Patrick, Assistant Dean for Admissions
Box 117620
Gainesville, FL 32611
Tel: 352-392-2087 • Fax: 352-392-8727
Email: patrick@law.ufl.edu
Internet: www.nersp.nerdc.ufl.edu~lawinfo

University of Florida

The assessment of this 3L, however, does seem to sum up the opinion of the majority of students we heard from: "Our tuition is very low, and because admissions are so competitive, the students here are possibly better than the school." Specifically, some UF students are dissatisfied with the limitations of their curriculum, which they consider far too narrow. "Due to a lack of funds," reported one 3L, "students suffer from over-crowded classes and poor choice of courses." "They really should provide for specialization in fields other than tax," said another. (Florida is generally considered one of the nation's leaders in tax law.) "I understand that resources are limited, but what is really bad is that the faculty and the deans and career placement encourage students only to go into corporate, commercial, or tax law. They need to provide more opportunities for public interest, judicial clerkships, and clinical programs."

These constructive criticisms, however, should not be taken as a sign of serious discontent among Florida students. Critical though they may be, few had difficulty reciting the law school's many strengths, and many went out of their way to say that they couldn't think of another school in the region that they would rather have attended.

ADMISSIONS

The University of Florida College of Law is one of the most selective in the Southeast and, indeed, in the nation. In the mysteriously derived national rankings of law schools that you have probably seen, this excellent law school generally resides somewhere in the "second tier." But try telling that to the country's most highly qualified law-school applicants in search of a great bargain. The average GPA and LSAT scores of incoming Florida students rank them among the top twenty-five in this book. This should come as no surprise given the remarkable value of this school's highly regarded J.D. program. Hopeful applicants to the U of F College of Law face a steep uphill climb.

ACADEMICS

Student/faculty ratio	15:1
% female faculty	22
% minority faculty	9
Hours of study per day	3.60

Academic specialties:
Civil Procedure, Commercial, Constitutional, Corporation Securities, Criminal, Environmental, Govt Services, Human Rights, International, Labor, Legal History, Legal Philosophy, Property, Taxation, Other

FINANCIAL FACTS

Tuition (in/out-state)	$4,320/$13,860
Cost of books	NR
Room & board (on/off-campus)	$2,960/$3,900
% first-year students receiving aid	85
% all students receiving aid	82
% aid that is merit-based	90
% of all students receiving loans	82
% receiving scholarships	5
% of all students receiving assistantships	NR
Average grant	NR
Average graduation debt	$30,000

ADMISSIONS

# applications received	1,549
% applicants accepted	512
% acceptees attending	43
Average LSAT	158
LSAT range	136-178
Average undergrad GPA	3.49
GPA range	2.37-4.00
Application fee (in/out-state)	$20/$20
Regular application	February 1
Regular notification	rolling
Rolling notification?	Yes
Early decision program?	No
Admission may be deferred?	No
Evening division offered?	No
Part-time accepted?	No
Gourman Report Rating	**3.78**

FORDHAM UNIVERSITY
School of Law

OVERVIEW

Type of school	private
Environment	metropolis
Scholastic calendar	semester
Schedule	full-time or part-time

STUDENTS

Enrollment of parent institution	4,293
Enrollment of law school	1,404
% male/female	57/43
% out-of-state	31
% part-time	25
% minorities	26
% international (# of countries represented)	NR (5)
Average age at entry	25

APPLICANTS ALSO LOOK AT

Emory University
Boston College
Brooklyn Law School
Boston University
George Washington University

SURVEY SAYS...

HITS
Grads expect big bucks
Broad range of courses
Practical experience

MISSES
Library staff
Not enough courses

EMPLOYMENT PROFILE

Firms recruiting on campus	250
Job placement rate (%)	95
% grads employed immediately	84
% grads employed within six months	92
Average starting salary	$61,000

Grads employed by field (%):

Academia	1
Business/industry	9
Government	12
Judicial clerkships	4
Private practice	65
Public interest	1

If New York is the cultural capital of the United States, then Lincoln Center is the cultural capital of New York, by which logic the approximately 1,500 students of the adjacent Fordham University School of Law should be about the most sophisticated group of law students in the country. As it stands, the demanding J.D. program at this highly regarded nearly hundred-year-old law school requires that most students get their culture by osmosis, giving up champagne and evenings at the Met and sticking to coffee and long nights in the library. Although it may not approach NYU and Columbia in the slippery terms of prestige, Fordham is probably New York City's most highly regarded law school after these two, and in many quantifiable respects—the size and qualifications of its faculty, the breadth of its curriculum, the success of its graduates—it doesn't give away much to its powerhouse neighbors. An excellent law school by any objective measure, Fordham can surely lay claim to offering the most respected part-time J.D. program in the entire Northeast. Indeed, Fordham is a godsend to several hundred highly qualified working professionals who would otherwise be forced to step down a rung on the ladder of prestige in order to earn a law degree. Whether in the day or evening division, Fordham students follow a rigorous course of study that is strong in all the traditional areas and is supplemented by a wide variety of clinical programs, including the recently instituted disability law, tax, and domestic violence clinics, most of which combine simulations with live client contact under faculty supervision. These programs, along with a mandatory moot court exercise and a significant writing requirement, are part of Fordham's growing emphasis on practical-skills training, professional ethics, and public service.

Students at Fordham paint a very consistent picture of their chosen school, both in terms of its strengths and weaknesses. One matter on which nearly all seem to agree is the quality of their preparation for the actual practice of law. "FLS has prepared me very well," wrote one. "I was a summer associate at a large Wall Street law firm, and I felt very well trained to compete with and even surpass students from the top Ivy League schools." Students raved about the quality of the faculty, who reportedly maintain

John Chalmers, Assistant Director of Admissions
140 West 62nd Street
New York, NY 10023
Tel: 212-636-6810

Fordham University

an "open door" policy. Fordham's alumni network also was lauded for the role it plays in helping graduates land jobs in New York City. "One of the absolute best things about Fordham," wrote one 2L, "is its fanatically loyal alumni. They are very helpful and enthusiastic." While most of the comments we heard could hardly be called fanatically enthusiastic, they did, for the most part, convey a strong sense of well-being. "We have a dynamic young faculty and a Dean who lives, breathes, eats and sleeps Fordham," reported another 2L. "God is our Dean, how can we lose?"

All of which is not to say that Fordham students see no room for improvement in their school. Past complaints included, "This school has a truly horrible physical plant" and "The library is hideous and the cafeteria abominable." The administration has heard these complaints and several renovations designed to improve study space in the library and triple the space devoted to clinical programs were completed. More generalized complaints were often heard from Fordham's night students. "As an evening student," wrote one, "I am a member of a discrete and insular minority, and have a substantially worse selection of classes." This fairly representative remark did, however, go on to conclude that "on the other hand, my fellow students are grown-ups, so it evens out." In spirit, most of the criticisms we heard matched this last one. Fordham students may wish for more, but also appreciate what they've got.

ADMISSIONS

After Columbia and NYU, whose students' numerical credentials are among the highest in the nation, the Fordham University School of Law is the most selective in the New York metropolitan area. In fact, the admissions process at Fordham is one of the forty most competitive in the entire country. The average incoming student here has a solid undergraduate GPA of 3.30 and an LSAT score above the 90th percentile. Applicants to Fordham whose numbers fall below these face an uphill climb. Consider this: In 1993 only 9 percent of all applicants with GPAs between 3.25 and 3.49 and LSAT scores between 155 and 159 were offered admission.

ACADEMICS

Student/faculty ratio	22:1
% female faculty	22
% minority faculty	8
Hours of study per day	3.42

Academic specialties:

Civil Procedure, Commercial, Constitutional, Corporation Securities, Criminal, Environmental, Govt Services, Human Rights, International, Labor, Legal History, Legal Philosophy, Property, Taxation

FINANCIAL FACTS

Tuition	$21,520
Cost of books	$669
Fees	$174
Room & board (on/off-campus)	$9,198/NR
% first-year students receiving aid	46
% all students receiving aid	49
% aid that is merit-based	4
% of all students receiving loans	45
% receiving scholarships	48
% of all students receiving assistantships	8
Average grant	$4,054
Average graduation debt	$71,900

ADMISSIONS

# applications received	3,916
% applicants accepted	32
% acceptees attending	27
Average LSAT	163
Average undergrad GPA	3.30
Application fee	$60
Regular application	rolling
Regular notification	rolling
Rolling notification?	Yes
Early decision program?	No
Admission may be deferred?	No
Evening division offered?	Yes
Part-time accepted?	No
Gourman Report Rating	4.44

FRANKLIN PIERCE LAW CENTER

OVERVIEW

Type of school	private
Environment	suburban
Scholastic calendar	semester
Schedule	full-time only

STUDENTS

Enrollment of parent institution	470
Enrollment of law school	412
% male/female	65/35
% out-of-state	73
% part-time	NR
% minorities	13
% international (# of countries represented)	1 (16)
Average age at entry	28

APPLICANTS ALSO LOOK AT

Boston University
George Washington University
Boston College
John Marshall
University of Maine

SURVEY SAYS...

HITS
Practical experience
Practical lawyering skills
Sense of community

MISSES
Quality of teaching
Not enough courses

EMPLOYMENT PROFILE

Firms recruiting on campus	25
Job placement rate (%)	87
% grads employed immediately	37
% grads employed within six months	87
Average starting salary	$46,457

Grads employed by field (%):

Academia	2
Business/industry	19
Government	9
Judicial clerkships	2
Military	1
Private practice	63
Public interest	3

Wherever you attend law school, it goes without saying that you will be tortured as a 1L. While Franklin Pierce Law Center is no exception, this "'little law school that cares' tortures you empathetically." One of the smallest private law schools in the country, Franklin Pierce bills itself as an institution very much opposed to rigidity, impersonality, unhealthy competitiveness, and many of the negatives associated with a traditional legal education. The staff works very hard to satisfy each student's individual needs. Insofar as anyone could ever call a law school "touchy-feely," it's a good description of FPLC. "The library is small" but "most of the school's facilities are brand-new and excellent." The campus itself is located in New Hampshire's capital of Concord, "a very small town" that provides "many legal opportunities in the state legislature, district court, county court, and New Hampshire Supreme Court." As a result, students "are swamped with externship possibilities." The clinical experiences available here provide a wealth of additional hands-on training. "This is a good thing," explained a 3L, because while "academics are important, it's lawyering skills that get you a job." FPLC's curriculum is flexible, with few requirements existing beyond the first year, and all students are encouraged to devise independent study projects that combine academic research with practical experience. Students at Franklin Pierce choose from one of several organized but informal programs of concentration, most of which revolve in some way around Intellectual Property (IP) law, a growing field in which FPLC has gained worldwide recognition as a leader. No J.D. program in the country can boast a larger full-time IP faculty, let alone supplement it with domestic and foreign adjuncts, nor claim a more extensive or intensive IP curriculum. There's also a full-time IP librarian who maintains a widely acclaimed Intellectual Property Mall on the Internet.

The FPLC faculty, most of whom continue to practice in one fashion or another, is large enough to ensure a degree of personal attention, to which most bigger law schools can only pay lip service. The "masters of the universe" who teach IP received especially high marks from respondents. "The program allows you to leave the school with in-depth knowledge of the topic," said one student, "which definitely puts you ahead of graduates

Lisa Deane, Assistant Dean for Admissions
2 White Street
Concord, NH 03301
Tel: 603-228-9217 • Fax: 603-228-1074
Email: admissions@fplc.edu
Internet: www.fplc.edu

Franklin Pierce Law Center

from other schools." Overall, the "very accessible and witty" professors "are great teachers and entertaining speakers." The Legal Writing program "could use great improvement" and some students felt that Torts at FPLC leave much to be desired. "I think that first-year classes, Torts especially, should teach us black-letter law," remarked one student, "not the professor's idea of what the class is." A 2L warned: "Be prepared to study extra for Torts on the bar." Most students here get along well and "help each other in ways that scream community." However, some students commented that this cozy environment could "get annoying after awhile." But all in all, the small size and out-of-the-way location of FPLC are conducive to cooperation, sharing of expertise, and employment leads.

On the downside, many students criticized FPLC for dedicating much of their resources to the Intellectual Property program. Furthermore, many of the same students who praised FPLC's untraditional approach and the noncompetitive atmosphere expressed concern that it goes a bit too far. The law school "should remember that we do have to take the bar exam after three years." One 2L chided: "This school can't decide whether to foster cooperation among the students, or competition. We do some teamwork on exams, yet now the school wants to institute a tougher grading policy and 'laude,' 'magna,' etc., on diplomas. Are we to keep our unique character or become a clone of the rest of the legal education system?" However, even students with serious criticisms, (including this one) told us they were generally satisfied with their experience.

ADMISSIONS

The average incoming student at Franklin Pierce possesses numerical credentials lower than those of students at many of the law schools in this book. FPLC is no cakewalk to get into, though: Nearly two out of every three applicants are denied admission. Mature, self-motivated law students thrive here. The average Franklin Pierce student is a good deal older than the national average and has often accumulated significant career experience prior to enrollment.

ACADEMICS

Student/faculty ratio	20:1
% female faculty	24
% minority faculty	1
Hours of study per day	3.97

Academic specialties:
Civil Procedure, Commercial, Criminal, International, Family, Intellectual Property, Health , Community

FINANCIAL FACTS

Tuition	$15,832
Cost of books	$550
Fees	$25
% first-year students receiving aid	87
% all students receiving aid	85
% aid that is merit-based	57
% of all students receiving loans	96
% receiving scholarships	79
% of all students receiving assistantships	5
Average grant	$1,702
Average graduation debt	$61,443

ADMISSIONS

# applications received	1,137
% applicants accepted	47
% acceptees attending	28
Average LSAT	153
LSAT range	135-170
Average undergrad GPA	2.97
GPA range	1.87-3.92
Application fee	$45
Early application	December 1
Early notification	January 15
Regular application	May 1
Regular notification	rolling
Rolling notification?	Yes
Early decision program?	Yes
Admission may be deferred?	Yes
Maximum length of deferment	1 year
Evening division offered?	No
Part-time accepted?	Yes
Gourman Report Rating	**2.65**

GEORGE MASON UNIVERSITY
School of Law

Until very recently, the old guard of legal education in the United States clung defiantly to a promise that has now been called into question: that law school should not engage in the business of specialized training. This was all well and good when the legal profession was still dominated by general practitioners, but those days are gone. Curricula within American law schools increasingly reflect the trend toward specialization within the legal profession, but most schools are only beginning to test the waters into which the George Mason University School of Law has already dived headfirst.

While most law schools have only dabbled with informal programs of specialization that merely suggest a particular combination of courses, George Mason has established five organized programs or "tracks": Corporate and Securities Law, International Business Transactions, Litigation Law, and Patent Law. All were designed to provide George Mason graduates with levels of expertise that might otherwise take years of work experience to achieve. Students in these tracks follow a course of study that is almost entirely prescribed and so bears little resemblance to the traditional legal education offered in most U.S. law schools.

One does not drift through the George Mason School of Law. In addition to its specialization tracks, GMU operates a rigorous, highly regarded standard J.D. program. Even this program is unusual in one important respect: its inclusion of a two-semester first-year requirement in Quantitative Methods, a course that gives GMU a truly unique flavor. The law school contends that all future lawyers must possess a grounding in the basic principles of economics, accounting, and statistics. GMU is a bastion of the conservative Law and Economics school of legal thought, so rigorous economic analyses are the stock-in-trade of many of the school's excellent faculty members.

Most students come from in-state for the bargain tuition rate, so they are well-aware of and, for the most part, drawn by the Law and Economics focus and staunchly conservative atmosphere. Most are extremely happy with just about everything they came looking for and found at GMU. One student proclaimed his pride of place in the strong tones we heard over and over: "I believe this

Wendy E. Payton, Acting Director of Admissions
3401 North Fairfax Drive
Arlington, VA 22201
Tel: 703-993-8010 • Fax: 703-999-8088
Email: wpayton@gmu.edu
Internet: web.gmu.edu/departments/law

George Mason University

is the strongest pillar in Virginia's triumvirate of great public law schools (UVA and William and Mary). Its innovative, strong writing program, metropolitan location, [and] low price probably make it one of the best law school bargains in the country." He answered those who complain about "comparatively more work and a lower grading scale than at other law schools" with this comment: "It's not supposed to be easy." Another listed very specifically why GMU appeals to him: "The faculty is mostly young and brilliant. The atmosphere is most accurately characterized as 'libertarian' than as 'conservative.' Minorities get no breaks here, and PC behavior gets no lip service. This school is absolutely colorblind. The quality of the education is the best in the D.C. area, and employers are beginning to notice. GMU places an inordinate number of graduates in judicial clerkships." And one 2L explained further: "The mandatory two-year Legal Research and Writing Program is a winner with employers-they are very impressed with GMUL's emphasis on good writing skills."

A few changes would impress some students, however, like more clinical programs and perhaps a few more women faculty members. It should be noted that although many students agreed that diversity is lacking, this is one of the few schools where many students actually listed this as a positive characteristic. One change that should improve academic and nonacademic life is the new law school building planned to open in June 1998.

ADMISSIONS

Judging by UGPA and LSAT score, GMU students rank in the top 20 percent nationally, with an average undergraduate GPA of 3.08 and an average LSAT score of 159, or the 84th percentile. Obviously the law school selects very highly qualified candidates, but there is more to selectivity than just that. If you consider both relative applications volume and the rate at which admitted students actually choose to attend the law school, George Mason ranks behind only Yale, Stanford, and Haaarvard in terms of popularity with prospective law students.

ACADEMICS

Student/faculty ratio	21:1
% female faculty	11
% minority faculty	11
Hours of study per day	4.29

Academic specialties:
Civil Procedure, Corporation Securities, International, Legal Philosophy, Intellectual Property

FINANCIAL FACTS

Tuition (in/out-state)	$7,280/$17,948
Cost of books	$710
Room & board (on/off-campus)	NR/$14,378
% first-year students receiving aid	NR
% all students receiving aid	NR
% aid that is merit-based	9
% of all students receiving loans	43
% receiving scholarships	7
% of all students receiving assistantships	7
Average grant	$9,457
Average graduation debt	NR

ADMISSIONS

# applications received	2,022
% applicants accepted	38
% acceptees attending	28
Average LSAT	159
Average undergrad GPA	3.08
Application fee (in/out-state)	$35/$35
Regular application	March 1
Regular notification	March 15 - June 30
Rolling notification?	No
Early decision program?	No
Admission may be deferred?	Yes
Maximum length of deferment	1 year
Evening division offered?	Yes
Part-time accepted?	Yes
Gourman Report Rating	**2.31**

GEORGE WASHINGTON UNIVERSITY
Law School

OVERVIEW

Type of school	private
Environment	metropolis
Scholastic calendar	semester
Schedule	full-time or part-time

STUDENTS

Enrollment of parent institution	18,986
Enrollment of law school	1,496
% male/female	54/46
% out-of-state	94
% part-time	14
% minorities	30
% international (# of countries represented)	1 (5)
Average age at entry	24

APPLICANTS ALSO LOOK AT

Georgetown University
American University
Boston University
Boston College
New York University

SURVEY SAYS...

HITS
Academic reputation
Broad range of courses
Grads expect big bucks

MISSES
Practical lawyering skills
Library staff

EMPLOYMENT PROFILE

Firms recruiting on campus	250
% grads employed immediately	87
% grads employed within six months	94
Average starting salary	$65,000

Grads employed by field (%):

Academia	1
Business/industry	8
Government	18
Judicial clerkships	9
Private practice	61
Public interest	3
Other	11

The George Washington University Law School is one of the oldest, largest, and most respected legal training grounds in the country. Its prime location in the heart of the nation's capital gives GW "a big-time, big-city" feel. The Supreme Court and the Library of Congress are readily accessible, as are all federal trial and appellate courts, a wealth of federal legislative resources, federal agencies galore, and offices of every national and international ilk.

GW offers a "huge variety of classes," which fill up quickly. The rich curriculum here is particularly strong in International Law and Intellectual Property and Patent Law. Strong clinics and internship programs offer ample opportunities for hands-on lawyering experience in the very corridors of federal power. Students credited the "witty, dynamic," and "practically sound" faculty as being "undoubtedly the greatest strength" of GW. Professors are "available, dedicated, and capable." However, "the faculty is not as diverse as the student body warrants." A few students also charged that excessive subjectivity on the part of their profs had adversely affected their grades. The "bureaucratic" administration, though it "has made an obvious commitment to its faculty [is] typical of D.C.," observed a 1L. "Everyone means well but it seems hard to change anything." Students claimed that GW is "in denial over technology issues, specifically the availability of computers." On the plus side, "they treat minorities very well and that translates into a better environment for everyone."

While GW has all the advantages of a large school, it also has its shortcomings, which are magnified by the "third-world-like conditions" of the current physical plant. "Two words," urged a 1L, "modern facility. We need one." GW is literally "too big for its britches" and "the school's facilities are atrocious when you take into account the ridiculously high cost of tuition." Students "feel boxed in like sardines." Restrooms "are a health hazard. Bacteria and no ventilation make for a cess pool." A 3L argued: "With Catholic and American moving into new facilities this year and Georgetown touting its beautiful edifice, it is time for GW, Fred, Wilma, Barney, and Betty to pack up, grab the kids, and move out

Robert V. Staneck, Assistant Dean
2003 G Street, NW
Washington, DC 20052
Tel: 202-994-7230 • Fax: 202-994-3597
Email: jd@admit.nlc.gwu.edu
Internet: www.law.gwu.edu

George Washington
University

of Bedrock." Career Development fares only slightly better. "The trap of GW is that you need to be in the top quarter of the class for this huge investment to pay off. The placement program is really geared toward the top students," explained a 2L. Luckily, employment opportunities "abound" inside the Beltway. "I got a great job despite lousy grades," chirped one student. "The name works."

Don't look for a warm and fuzzy glow around GW. The "high pressure environment can be unnecessarily intense," especially around finals time. "One moment you can be talking about vacations. The next you are talking about who had the best vacation," observed a 3L. Other students strongly disagreed with this assessment, instead applauding the ubiquitous "cooperation" at GW. Though "the size of the school and its city location create less of a sense of community than schools with well-defined campuses," there are plenty of clubs and activities available, both academic and social. Also, explained a 2L: "It is widely known that GW law students have the most fun in D.C. The students here party more than any other law school in the area. When we plan a joint function with other law schools, our students make up the overwhelming majority." Beamed another student: "It's more fun than college."

ADMISSIONS

At $55 a pop, the 6,471 applications that were filed by prospective George Washington students in 1995 filled the law school's coffers to the tune of $355,900. Of course, a sizable chunk of that kitty must be used to pay an admissions staff large enough to sort through the second-highest pile of applications in the country. When all is said and done, more than 4,000 people will be denied admission to GW, a great deal more than will even apply to most schools. Those who are admitted and go on to enroll possess tremendous numerical credentials. With an extremely high average GPA and an average LSAT score at the 90th percentile, the GW student body is in the top 20 nationally in terms of numerical qualifications.

ACADEMICS

Student/faculty ratio	18:1
% female faculty	29
% minority faculty	9
Hours of study per day	3.49

FINANCIAL FACTS

Tuition	$20,870
Cost of books	$740
Fees	$915
Room & board (on/off-campus)	$7,400/$7,400
% first-year students receiving aid	78
% all students receiving aid	63
% aid that is merit-based	10
% of all students receiving loans	63
% receiving scholarships	60
% of all students receiving assistantships	4
Average grant	$8,000
Average graduation debt	$67,500

ADMISSIONS

# applications received	6,454
% applicants accepted	29
% acceptees attending	24
Average LSAT	161
Average undergrad GPA	3.42
Application fee	$55
Regular application	March 1
Regular notification	rolling
Rolling notification?	Yes
Early decision program?	No
Admission may be deferred?	Yes
Maximum length of deferment	1 year
Evening division offered?	Yes
Part-time accepted?	Yes
Gourman Report Rating	**4.30**

GEORGETOWN UNIVERSITY
Law Center

Set almost literally in the shadows of the U.S. Capitol and the Supreme Court, in the most lawyer-rich city on earth, the Georgetown University Law Center is the law school of Washington insiders past, present, and future. One cannot study law any closer to the halls of power than at this nearly one-hundred-year-old Jesuit institution, whose own halls are crowded with the largest student body of any American law school. Widely regarded as one of the 10 or 15 finest law schools in the country, and undoubtedly the most highly esteemed law school to offer a part-time J.D. program, Georgetown enrolls more than 2,000 highly qualified students in its day and evening divisions.

Within the confines of the classroom, these students follow a course of study that is rich in academic possibilities. Georgetown's top-notch faculty administer a tremendously broad traditional curriculum that is particularly strong in areas like international law and public interest law. Georgetown's unique Public Interest Law Scholars Program provides a very small number of students with a rich array of academic and extra-academic support programs meant to facilitate their goal of practicing law in the public interest. With the recent addition of an optional "Plan B" first-year curriculum, a segment of Georgetown's class has the option of following a less traditional course of study emphasizing "the sources of law in history, philosophy, political theory and economics." The law school also operates what has been called the nation's finest and most comprehensive clinical program, the greatly varied offerings of which reflect and exploit Georgetown's proximity to the institutions of the federal government. If one is willing and able to brave the crowds, the opportunities here are almost limitless. This fact is clearly not lost on prospective law students, more of whom apply to Georgetown than to just about any other law school in the country. In terms of sheer popularity with applicants, Georgetown far exceeds even Harvard, with more than 9,000 files processed annually.

Current Georgetown students have remarkably consistent feelings toward their chosen school. "Ambivalent" is the word that comes to mind. Although we heard almost uniformly positive reviews for things like Georgetown's excellent clinical program

Susan Brooks, Associate Director
600 New Jersey Avenue, NW
Washington, DC 20057
Tel: 202-662-9010 • Fax: 202-662-9459
Email: admis@law.georgetown.edu
Internet: www.ll.georgetown.edu/lc/

Georgetown University

and cultural diversity, most of those we heard from were quicker to criticize than to praise. No single remark, perhaps, summed up the sentiments expressed by many as well as this one from a one 1L: "Each class, I've calculated, costs approximately the same as a Broadway show, and the audience is not much smaller. I'd get much more out of Georgetown if most of my classes didn't have so many damn people in them." Indeed, the students we heard from seem to appreciate the advantages such a large school offers—"vast and up-to-date research resources, widely varied course offerings"—but many were quick to point to the drawbacks—"lots of diversity and opportunities, but classes should be smaller so that people wouldn't be so intimidated to talk." In the eyes of some, such disadvantages are inconsequential when balanced against Georgetown's "excellent" facilities and other opportunities. "Everything's really big," wrote one such 2L, "and nothing is made very easy for you, but between the school itself and the city of D.C., there's enough here for any self-starter to do anything she pleases." And although a few students remarked on the competitiveness of the student body, most praised Georgetown's success in establishing a "sense of community" in a large school.

ADMISSIONS

Little more need be said about admissions at the Georgetown University Law Center than this: Nearly 10,000 prospective law students apply annually. From that fact, the rest follows obviously: The overwhelming majority of all candidates are denied admission, and those who are admitted possess incredibly strong numerical credentials. Sure, this gigantic law school must admit 2,000 applicants in order to fill its first-year class of more than 600, but those lucky 2,000 will have some serious numbers. In fact, by our calculation, the average undergraduate GPA and LSAT score of Georgetown students rank them as the twelfth most qualified in the nation.

ACADEMICS	
Student/faculty ratio	17:1
% female faculty	34
% minority faculty	11
Hours of study per day	3.57

FINANCIAL FACTS	
Tuition	$23,375
Cost of books	NR
Room & board (on/off-campus)	$14,575/$14,575
% first-year students receiving aid	NR
% all students receiving aid	NR
% aid that is merit-based	0
% of all students receiving loans	NR
% receiving scholarships	NR
% of all students receiving assistantships	0
Average grant	NR
Average graduation debt	$62,917

ADMISSIONS	
# applications received	7,500
% applicants accepted	28
% acceptees attending	31
Average LSAT	166
Average undergrad GPA	3.50
Application fee	$60
Early application	November 1
Early notification	December 10
Regular application	Feb. 1, March 1
Regular notification	January-June
Rolling notification?	Yes
Early decision program?	Yes
Admission may be deferred?	Yes
Maximum length of deferment	1 year
Evening division offered?	Yes
Part-time accepted?	Yes
Gourman Report Rating	**4.69**

GEORGIA STATE UNIVERSITY
College of Law

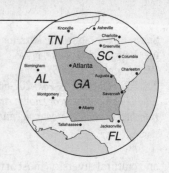

OVERVIEW

Type of school	public
Environment	metropolis
Scholastic calendar	quarter
Schedule	full-time or part-time

STUDENTS

Enrollment of parent institution	7,664
Enrollment of law school	668
% male/female	52/48
% out-of-state	14
% part-time	38
% minorities	22
% international (# of countries represented)	NR (8)
Average age at entry	28

APPLICANTS ALSO LOOK AT

University of Georgia
Emory University
Mercer University
University of South Carolina
Florida State University

SURVEY SAYS...

HITS
Diverse faculty
Legal writing
Practical lawyering skills

MISSES
Library staff
Not enough courses

EMPLOYMENT PROFILE

Firms recruiting on campus	60
Job placement rate (%)	92
% grads employed within six months	93
Average starting salary	$42,806

Grads employed by field (%):

Academia	1
Business/industry	15
Government	11
Judicial clerkships	4
Military	1
Private practice	57
Public interest	4

The curriculum at Georgia State University College of Law does not venture very far into the abstract. This urban law school focuses on training future attorneys with practical lawyering skills and a pragmatic understanding of the working world and the law as it relates to the state of Georgia. Though students called the faculty "great," they also said that professors are somewhat unapproachable. "Some of the faculty are accessible but others lock themselves in their fortresses and do not return phone calls." Red tape is easily avoided here, as "the administration is fairly decent and responsive to student concerns." Without a doubt, though, the opportunities available beyond the classroom are GSU's biggest asset. The school's laudable tax clinic, externships, and trial-advocacy and moot court programs afford its law students innumerable opportunities to use and cultivate their professional skills in the burgeoning Atlanta legal community. "The campus's access to the local courts in Atlanta and myriad programs with the real world are great," said a 2L. Students at Georgia State can also take advantage of its flexible programs for evening and part-time study.

Nearly 80 percent of GSU's students are Georgia natives. Once they obtain their degrees, an equally high percentage of graduates find employment in the city of Atlanta, the star of the New South and one of the country's fastest-growing and highest-paying legal job markets. Students told us that the school's geographic location is high on their lists of what originally attracted them to GSU. Students certainly benefit from the school's connection to Atlanta firms and government offices. They also enjoy its low tuition, which is an "excellent value" for anyone, and an incredible bargain for state residents.

Students here are a "very diverse group of people." In fact, Georgia State's student body is far and away the most diverse—in terms of both ethnicity and age—of any in the state Its faculty is relatively balanced in terms of both gender and ethnicity as well. "The best thing about GSU is the diversity of the students," said a 3L. "I don't know if it's because the students are older or because many students are starting second careers, but there seems to be an atmosphere of sophistication in this school." As a

Cheryl Jackson, Director of Admissions
P.O. Box 4049
Atlanta, GA 30302-4037
Tel: 404-651-2048
Email: lawcry@langate.gsu.edu
Internet: www.gsu.edu/~lawadmn/gsulaw.html

Georgia State University

result, "most people don't get too worked up about things," including "community spirit outside of class," which many students called "weak." Explained a 2L: "With many professional night students who already have accomplished careers as stockbrokers and accountants, the collegial atmosphere of most other places is not as evident at GSU. Many students are older, married, etc." One 1L observed: "People seem to make friends here, but not to the extent that they socialize outside of school. However, groups form fairly readily for the purpose of studying and outlining." Some students felt that the university could improve by developing a more campus-like atmosphere and "a sense of community."

The school's urban location and lack of a traditional campus does little to promote fellowship and community spirit. "The school is just not a place to be at night," either, said one student. Downtown Atlanta is "vibrant, close to firms, and dangerous," so much so that "security is a big concern, especially on weekends and late nights." Also, the parking situation is a problem that has yet to be alleviated.

ADMISSIONS

According to law school rankings, this young institution takes its place as a "third-tier" law school. However, a simple calculation of supply and demand yields Georgia State University College of Law a stellar rating. Each year, the school denies admission to over 80 percent of those who apply. In fact, the school is among the twenty most in-demand law schools in the entire nation. One big reason why: In three years of law school at Georgia State, a Georgia resident will pay less in tuition than he or she would pay in one semester at many elite law schools like Duke and Georgetown (which have higher acceptance rates, by the way). While its numerical admissions standards still don't approach those of the traditional elite, consider the statistics for the 1995 class: There were 2,800 applications for 190 seats in the entering class, the average LSAT score was an impressive 157, and the median undergraduate GPA was 3.2.

ACADEMICS

Student/faculty ratio	16:1
% female faculty	37
% minority faculty	16
Hours of study per day	3.86

Academic specialties:
Civil Procedure, Commercial, Corporation Securities, Environmental, Human Rights, International, Taxation

FINANCIAL FACTS

Tuition (in/out-state)	$3,058/$10,550
Cost of books	$4,902
Fees (in/out-state)	$282/$282
Room & board (on/off-campus)	$7,760/$7,806
% first-year students receiving aid	86
% all students receiving aid	57
% aid that is merit-based	2
% of all students receiving loans	54
% receiving scholarships	6
% of all students receiving assistantships	10
Average grant	$2,858
Average graduation debt	$19,537

ADMISSIONS

# applications received	2,358
% applicants accepted	23
% acceptees attending	39
Average LSAT	157
Average undergrad GPA	3.20
Application fee (in/out-state)	$30/$30
Regular application	rolling
Regular notification	rolling
Rolling notification?	Yes
Early decision program?	No
Admission may be deferred?	No
Evening division offered?	Yes
Part-time accepted?	Yes
Gourman Report Rating	**2.20**

UNIVERSITY OF GEORGIA
School of Law

Even before the last decade's dramatic rise in law-school tuition, the prospective law student who was not independently wealthy had a lot of financial planning to do. Apart from the prominent public law schools in Michigan, Virginia, and California, the giants of American legal education have traditionally been expensive private institutions. The bargain hunter should be heartened, however, by the recent rise to prominence of a few inexpensive public law schools in other parts of the nation. With its rock-bottom tuition rates and top-notch faculty and facilities, the School of Law at the University of Georgia is one such school. Even for nonresidents, three years at the excellent law school in Athens ranks among the great bargains in legal education. The Georgia J.D. program is traditional in the best sense. Requirements are few and offerings extensive, giving the student ample academic and cocurricular options from which to choose an individual course of study. Among its special programs, the school of law is particularly proud of its perennially successful moot court teams and the programs offered through its Dean Rusk Center for International and Comparative Law, named for the former U.S. Secretary of State. Also at the law student's disposal are the extensive recourses of UGA itself, a major research and teaching facility with 30,000 students. Admissions are highly selective, and admitted applicants have extremely strong numerical credentials. It should come as no surprise that Georgia grads have little difficulty finding very good jobs.

Dreams of future glory, however, cannot quite eradicate the stress of the present for some students, especially those on financial aid. Since UGA draws many bright students away from other schools with the lure of a low price and financial aid, the unrealistic loan amounts authorized by the aid office (run by the university itself, not the law school, many students point out) create enormous problems. Other problems include the dearth of practical skills and legal writing offerings, and the "horrendous grading curve." A particularly well-noted unfriendly aspect of the school has to do with certain traditions to which UGA unfortunately clings, such as the refusal to diversify its faculty and student body or incorporate the feminist courses many students cry for. Regarding the students UGA chooses, one

Athens, GA 30602
Tel: 706-542-7060 • Fax: 706-542-5556
Internet: www.lawsch.uga.edu

person notes, "If Newt Gingrich were a student at GA, he'd surely be labeled a moderate, so overwhelmingly conservative is the student body here. At the same time, those of us who still believe in the rights of civil plaintiffs and criminal defendants are able to do so without interference. The right-wingers pity us, I think, but they pretty much let us be."

Like the comment above suggests, most students (especially those not dependent on aid) are happy at UGA. They delight in the excellent activities the school provides: "UGA has a diverse selection of student organizations, ranging from academic (The Law Practice and Technology Association) and service (Phi Alpha Delta) to social (Student Bar Association) organizations." Students also relish the outstanding International Law program and the local reputation: "if anyone wants to practice law in GA, they'd be foolish to not go here." According to one satisfied 2L: "We have the nicest faculty, administration, and support staff…Since all law schools are competitive, demanding, and most fall miserably short of their goal to prepare you to practice, wouldn't you rather be in a place where people smile, students have fun, and every day is not some hellacious experience? Oh yeah, the University of Georgia has a damn good law school."

ADMISSIONS

By all measurable standards, the University of Georgia School of Law is one of the most selective in the nation. Not only are the law school's numerical admissions standards higher than those of 85 percent of America's law schools, but applicant volume is so great that UGA admits a smaller proportion of its applicants than do many of the nation's so-called top-20 schools. Georgia's academic strength and bargain-basement tuition help explain the popularity of this excellent, inexpensive law school.

ACADEMICS

Student/faculty ratio	17:1
% female faculty	25
% minority faculty	5
Hours of study per day	3.69

FINANCIAL FACTS

Tuition (in/out-state)	$2,736/$9,438
Cost of books	$925
% first-year students receiving aid	70
% all students receiving aid	70
% aid that is merit-based	10
% of all students receiving loans	70
% receiving scholarships	20
% of all students receiving assistantships	NR
Average grant	$2,000
Average graduation debt	NR

ADMISSIONS

# applications received	2,315
% applicants accepted	22
% acceptees attending	42
Average LSAT	162
Average undergrad GPA	3.48
Application fee (in/out-state)	$30/NR
Regular application	March 1
Regular notification	rolling
Rolling notification?	Yes
Early decision program?	No
Admission may be deferred?	Yes
Maximum length of deferment	case by case
Gourman Report Rating	**3.87**

GOLDEN GATE UNIVERSITY
School of Law

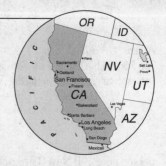

OVERVIEW

Type of school	private
Environment	metropolis
Scholastic calendar	trimester
Schedule	full-time or part-time

STUDENTS

Enrollment of parent institution	454
Enrollment of law school	713
% male/female	47/53
% out-of-state	27
% part-time	34
% minorities	21
% international (# of countries represented)	NR (NR)
Average age at entry	26

APPLICANTS ALSO LOOK AT

University of San Francisco
Santa Clara University
McGeorge School of Law
University of California, Hasting College of Law
California Western

SURVEY SAYS...

HITS
Practical lawyering skills
Diverse faculty
Practical experience

MISSES
Library staff

EMPLOYMENT PROFILE

Job placement rate (%)	76
% grads employed within six months	76
Average starting salary	$48,897

Grads employed by field (%):

Academia	1
Business/industry	25
Government	8
Judicial clerkships	4
Military	1
Private practice	57
Public interest	6
Other	14

Students who want to be spend their three years of law school in one of the country's most beautiful and diverse cities have an opportunity to do so at Golden Gate University School of Law. Golden Gate has cashed in on the growing appeal of its location: the heart of downtown San Francisco. In fact, the San Francisco Bay Area has become so popular with law-school applicants that the Golden Gate University School of Law could probably hold its classes in a bus station and still draw students in droves. In a region dominated by the world-class law schools of Berkeley, Stanford, and the increasingly prestigious Hastings, several lesser-known law schools with moderate admissions standards, including Golden Gate, have long filled a niche by offering part-time and evening programs. Golden Gate makes a point of accommodating the schedule of the working law student, whether he or she is right out of college or has spent twenty years in the workplace. Its mid-year admissions option and flexible scheduling for even full-time students reflect Golden Gate's unusual commitment to making legal education accessible to working professionals.

Overall, Golden Gate students had only positive comments to make regarding their professors and the quality of their legal education. One thing is certainly true of the school's curriculum: It prepares students for the courtroom. Golden Gate, said students, is not a school for would-be professors; its practical approach focuses on "real-world lawyering skills." The litigation program at Golden Gate is quite comprehensive. After completing the basic courses such as Trial Advocacy, Civil Litigation, and Lawyering Skills, students can choose from a wide array of advanced practical skills courses. Students praise these opportunities at Golden Gate as this 3L does: "The clinical and practical programs are excellent. I've been able to get a wide variety of legal experience and hone my research, writing, and advocacy skills." In addition, the faculty, who were often described as "unbelievable" and "always available," were ranked among the top twenty law-school faculties in the nation in the April/May 1996 issue of The National Jurist. The same survey called Golden Gate the 11th best law school for women.

Cherie A. Scricca, Assistant Dean
536 Missions Street
San Francisco, CA 94105
Tel: 415-442-6630
Email: lawadmit@ggu.edu
Internet: www.ggu.edu

Golden Gate University

Where students gave glowing reports of their instructors, they had few kind words to say overall about the school's administration. An uncharitable grading system was the main focus of a deep frustration that many GGU students feel. Griping about grading procedures is a favorite leisure-time activity of most law students, but in most cases students complain about mechanics: one semester, one exam, one grade. Students at Golden Gate, however, have far more serious and fundamental complaints about their school's grading system. Specifically, their complaint was that the law school has actively decided to deflate grades, thereby, students said, flunking about 20 to 25 percent of the first-year class. The administration said the actual figure is closer to 15 percent, and that it has modified the curve." While concluding that many Golden Gate law students are generally relatively happy with their school, it is important to keep such statements in mind.

ADMISSIONS

Selectivity at Golden Gate has been on the rise in recent years as the volume of applications filed at the law school has inched up steadily. Now more than 2,500 students vie annually for spots in the law school's entering class of about 230. Because so many applicants of the Bay Area schools use Golden Gate as their "safety school," the law school must admit a relatively large portion of the candidates it considers in order to be sure of filling its class. Nearly one half of all applicants to the law school gain admission, and slightly fewer than a quarter of those admitted chose to enroll. Those who do tend to possess decent numerical credentials: a 3.0 undergraduate GPA and an LSAT score of 154.

ACADEMICS

Student/faculty ratio	17:1
% female faculty	34
% minority faculty	32
Hours of study per day	4.23

Academic specialties:
Commercial, Constitutional, Criminal, Environmental, International, Labor, Taxation

FINANCIAL FACTS

Tuition	$18,850
Cost of books	$3,605
Fees	$239
Room & board (on/off-campus)	NR/$7,425
% first-year students receiving aid	90
% all students receiving aid	95
% aid that is merit-based	8
% of all students receiving loans	91
% receiving scholarships	46
% of all students receiving assistantships	3
Average grant	$4,500
Average graduation debt	$67,000

ADMISSIONS

# applications received	2,157
% applicants accepted	56
% acceptees attending	16
Average LSAT	154
Average undergrad GPA	3.00
Application fee	$40
Regular application	April 15
Regular notification	rolling
Rolling notification?	Yes
Early decision program?	No
Admission may be deferred?	Yes
Maximum length of deferment	1 year
Evening division offered?	Yes
Part-time accepted?	Yes
Gourman Report Rating	**3.42**

GONZAGA UNIVERSITY
School of Law

OVERVIEW

Type of school	private
Environment	city
Scholastic calendar	semester
Schedule	full-time only

STUDENTS

Enrollment of parent institution	2,707
Enrollment of law school	535
% male/female	64/36
% out-of-state	65
% part-time	3
% minorities	14
% international (# of countries represented)	NR (2)
Average age at entry	27

APPLICANTS ALSO LOOK AT

University of Washington
Willamette University
Lewis and Clark College
University of Montana
University of Oregon

SURVEY SAYS...

HITS
Legal writing
Faculty-student relations
Sleeping

MISSES
Quality of teaching
Not enough courses
Library staff

EMPLOYMENT PROFILE

% grads employed immediately	50
% grads employed within six months	82
Average starting salary	$35,180

Since opening its doors in 1912, Gonzaga University School of Law has built a solid regional reputation as a training ground for highly competent attorneys. A new Integrated Curriculum strongly emphasizes Jesuit ethics and continual substantive training. The students we polled acknowledged that Gonzaga offers "lots of personal attention in a small classroom setting." Said a 2L: "I particularly enjoy the small classes because it gives you a chance to get to know your fellow students." The "enthusiastic" and "very knowledgeable" professors "sincerely care about the students" and they're "a lot of fun" Some faculty members rank "at the top of their field." Others "have been here so long they could teach classes in their sleep. Sadly, many do." according to one 3L. Most, however, are "very accessible and helpful for problems." Clinics and skills-building programs are solid, and Gonzaga is the "only law school to make National Moot Court Finals seven years straight."

Unfortunately, students were not nearly as upbeat about Gonzaga's physical plant. "The facilities are res ipsa loquitor," according to a 1L, who said this is Latin for "sucky." The library is "a farce" and, like the out-of-service restrooms, antiquated classrooms, and crowded study areas, in desperate need of attention. The administration noted that help is on the way, in the form of a $15 million law school building project tentatively scheduled to be completed in 1999. Until then, though, "$17,000 a year tuition gets you a law school housed in a former grade school building," quipped a 3L. "I keep waiting to hear the bell so we can go to recess."

Gonzaga has an "incredibly hard-working career services director" who sees to it that jobs are "available for students." However, "going to a small, private, regional law school has extreme disadvantages," explained one student. "Most people I know think I'm attending an off-shore alternative law school near the coast of Mexico." A 2L added: "I realize that after school loan payments of $1,000 per month for ten years, law school wasn't the most fiscally sound decision I've ever made. But the intellectual growth is incredible." For the record, Gonzaga has the "highest bar passage rate in the state of Washington."

Sharon Day, Admissions Administrator
P.O. Box 3528
Spokane, WA 99258
Tel: 509-328-4220
Internet: www.law.gonzaga.edu

Gonzaga University

Diversity at Gonzaga appears to be a problem. The school has a low percentage of minority students and one of the lowest percentages of minority faculty members nationwide. "Recently, there were a couple of racial harassment incidents here. The school responded by requiring attendance at a Diversity Workshop during Orientation. It seems very cosmetic and preachy," asserted a 1L. "I think Gonzaga should really concentrate on changing its demographics. If a law student is racist, I doubt one class will have much of an effect. Day-to-day contact with different people may or may not change minds, but at least it will demonstrate that we have to share the world with people who aren't just like us." Beyond these "isolated" diversity problems, Gonzaga students reported a "laid-back" and "congenial" environment. The law school is located in Spokane, near the city's law firms, courts, and government offices. "Spokane is a wonderful place to attend law school," observed a sarcastic 3L. "There is absolutely nothing here to divert students from the drudgery of studying law." Other students noted that there are "many incredible golf courses with very, very low prices" nearby and, during the winter, "skiing is only thirty to forty-five minutes away." Socially, "relations among students are a little too much like undergraduate school, probably due to the fact that many are from out-of-town." Students are "friendly," though, and "there is a genuine sense of cooperation and helping here." Concluded a 2L, "The whole system is geared toward making us the best lawyers we can be. It's a very supportive atmosphere, from the administration to the faculty to the students."

ADMISSIONS

The Gonzaga University School of Law continues to be one of the least selective in the country. That's good news for applicants whose numbers might otherwise prevent them from pursuing a legal education. The average incoming student at Gonzaga possesses numerical credentials lower than those of students at all but one of the law schools in the West, and lower than the credentials of students at 75 percent of all the law schools in the country.

ACADEMICS	
Student/faculty ratio	27:1
% female faculty	27
% minority faculty	9
Hours of study per day	4.00

Academic specialties:

Taxation

FINANCIAL FACTS	
Tuition	$17,050
Cost of books	$900
% first-year students receiving aid	NR
% all students receiving aid	81
% aid that is merit-based	NR
% of all students receiving loans	90
% receiving scholarships	43
% of all students receiving assistantships	3
Average grant	$23,000
Average graduation debt	$65,000

ADMISSIONS	
# applications received	1,198
% applicants accepted	67
% acceptees attending	20
Average LSAT	155
Average undergrad GPA	3.00
Application fee	$40
Regular application	rolling
Regular notification	NR
Rolling notification?	No
Early decision program?	No
Admission may be deferred?	No
Evening division offered?	No
Part-time accepted?	Yes
Gourman Report Rating	**3.47**

HAMLINE UNIVERSITY
School of Law

Though there are plenty of recent college graduates at this law school, the student population at "small, warm, and friendly" Hamline University School of Law is remarkably diverse in terms of age. Over 1,000 degree-seeking students, ranging in age from twenty-two to sixty-nine, take courses primarily in the evening, on weekends, and during the summer. The average student here has professional and family commitments that require the sort of flexible scheduling that Hamline provides. Formal options of morning-only or afternoon-only reduced enrollment are what allow many of the older, "nontraditional" students to pursue a legal education in a university setting. Hamline students said that their curriculum "could be more nuts-and-bolts-oriented" and could probably schedule more "traditional academic courses," but they had few other complaints. "Hamline is a young, dynamic, progressive educational community," asserted one student. "The staff is remarkable" and the "very approachable" professors are "willing to answer questions." Said a 1L: "The professors are committed to helping students understand and realistically apply the subject matter in the courses." Several students also fawned over the admissions office. "Most people I know who chose Hamline over another school say it was because of the admissions process," claimed a 2L. Comments regarding other administrative areas were mixed. Many students credited the top brass with doing a fine job. Others believe that the "arbitrary and heavy-handed" administration perpetuates an "old boy network."

Clinical resources are limited, but Career Services offers "wonderful internship experiences" and "many opportunities to receive practical experience in the legal field." Hamline alumni are also "committed to helping students." According to a 1L, "Twenty percent of last year's class got clerkships. I haven't decided if I'm willing to take the necessary pay cut to receive a clerkship, but it's nice to know the opportunity is there." As a result of its grads making so many dents in the local legal community, Hamline (which only opened its doors in 1976) "has developed a very strong academic reputation in a very short period of time. The graduates are well-respected by the local and regional elite." Students here are said to be so career-oriented that an older 1L remarked, "I wish the student body had more people with a

Elizabeth A. Schmitt, Director of Admissions
1536 Hewitt Avenue
St. Paul, MN 55104-1284
Tel: 612-523-2461 • Fax: 612-523-2435
Email: lawadm@seq.hamline.edu
Internet: www.hamline.edu

Hamline University

broader range of interests beyond just the expected job in a law firm practicing x, y, z"

In the fall of 1997, Hamline Law will open the doors to a "long overdue" new facility. Current students shared their wish list for this building with us. "We need windows in the classrooms," they said, and to get rid of "the vintage 1976, patriotic carpet." In addition, the "library needs improvements" and, as long as they are making requests, students said "it would be nice to have a library staff that knows more than I do about the library." On the bright side, "the Twin Cities provide great resources for law students."

"Political correctness" is a divisive topic here. "Hamline is quite liberal," acknowledged one student, "which is okay because I am too. I just don't like being pressured into a certain way of thinking. There is a sense of pressure from faculty and students that you are bad if you express conservative views, no matter how well reasoned." Once they got past their political differences, students proudly described themselves as "good, smart, confident" types "who don't need to ride on the coattails of an institution's reputation." There are "lots of opportunities for students to get involved" and "2Ls and 3Ls are very supportive." The atmosphere here is either competitive or it's not, depending on who you talk to. "My biggest competitor is myself," beamed a 2L. "Students are cooperative with one another. I love this law school and look forward to being an active alum." Other students spoke to us of "occasional behind-the-scenes tactics to sabotage research and job-hunting." However, one 3L told us: "We all seem to have a good time together, when we're not studying." Overall, students are pleased with their law school. "The school prides itself on making the law school experience enjoyable while not compromising on academics," said a 2L. "There are some areas that need improvement here, but we are a young school and only getting better."

ADMISSIONS

The numerical credentials of the average admitted student are respectable. The average undergraduate GPA is a relatively solid 3.1, and the average LSAT score is at or about the 67th percentile. But Hamline admits students of diverse ages and backgrounds and, hence, across a broad range of grade point averages and test scores. Hamline is more adamant than other law schools in insisting that its admissions process is driven by more than just numbers. This may offer a glimmer of hope to students who had once been thought of as underachievers.

ACADEMICS

Student/faculty ratio	23:1
% female faculty	35
% minority faculty	6
Hours of study per day	4.18

Academic specialties:
Commercial, Corporation Securities, Criminal, Govt Services, International, Labor, Law and Religion

FINANCIAL FACTS

Tuition	$15,500
Cost of books	$400
Fees	$150
Room & board (on/off-campus)	$5,000/$5,000
% first-year students receiving aid	90
% all students receiving aid	90
% aid that is merit-based	8
% of all students receiving loans	90
% receiving scholarships	23
% of all students receiving assistantships	NR
Average grant	$6,179
Average graduation debt	$55,000

ADMISSIONS

# applications received	1,162
% applicants accepted	55
% acceptees attending	29
Average LSAT	154
Average undergrad GPA	3.10
Application fee	$50
Regular application	rolling
Regular notification	rolling
Rolling notification?	Yes
Early decision program?	No
Admission may be deferred?	Yes
Maximum length of deferment	1 year
Evening division offered?	No
Part-time accepted?	Yes
Gourman Report Rating	**2.80**

HARVARD UNIVERSITY
Law School

OVERVIEW

Type of school	private
Environment	metropolis
Scholastic calendar	semester
Schedule	full-time only

STUDENTS

Enrollment of parent institution	18,310
Enrollment of law school	1,646
% male/female	59/41
% out-of-state	94
% minorities	28
% international (# of countries represented)	5 (20)
Average age at entry	24

APPLICANTS ALSO LOOK AT

Yale University
New York University
Columbia University
University of Chicago
Stanford University

SURVEY SAYS...

HITS
Broad range of courses
Grads expect big bucks
Library staff

MISSES
Faculty-student relations
Practical lawyering skills

EMPLOYMENT PROFILE

Firms recruiting on campus	600
Job placement rate (%)	96
% grads employed immediately	96
% grads employed within six months	98
Average starting salary	$72,000

Grads employed by field (%):

Academia	2
Business/industry	4
Government	1
Judicial clerkships	27
Private practice	60
Public interest	2

Few observers of U.S. law schools would disagree that Harvard University Law School provides one of the best legal educations in the country. Harvard, in fact, has long served as the quintessential American law school as portrayed in the movie The Paper Chase: tough, cutthroat, and imperious. Today this image of Harvard law is only partially true. The school certainly boasts some of the best and brightest students and legal scholars in the country. But, for the most part, the days of cruel professors and browbeaten students are gone; you will now find a law school that is much more humane but no less demanding. The school has maintained its theoretical, rather than pragmatic, approach to the law. Harvard's mission to "impart the enduring principles of law, legal philosophy, and the historical development of legal institutions," is successfully met through the instruction of a first-rate faculty, which includes several famous legal personalities.

The power that a law degree from HLS grants is still unparalleled among U.S. schools. One 2L, when asked to name Harvard's strengths, put it this way: "PRESTIGE, PRESTIGE, PRESTIGE." It is true that Harvard grads, even those who coast through with average grades, are virtually assured of jobs upon graduation. This fact has not escaped students, who note that unlike their peers at other law schools, they do not have to worry too much about gaining employment. "HLS is a basically a job factory; regardless of expansion or contraction of the legal industry, there will always be jobs for HLS grads," said one confident 2L.

Students were quick to point out that a Harvard education puts them in touch with great people: the best professors and a dynamic, intellectual student body. "The strengths of Harvard Law School are its excellent faculty, who are on the cutting edge of research and practice in their fields, as well as its student body. I feel that I'm constantly learning from my fellow students...." said one 2L. The majority of students agreed that the level of competition among students at Harvard is not above the norm. However, many did criticize the law school's lack of community and the large class sizes. "Because of the large class sizes, I've had virtually no contact with my professors," said a 2L.

Contrary to what one might expect at a institution composed of such high-achievers, students claim that fun can be had at Harvard

Joyce Curll, Assistant Dean for Admissions & Financial Aid
1563 Massachusetts Avenue
Cambridge, MA 02138
Tel: 617-495-3109
Internet: www.law.harvard.edu

Law School. In fact, several students we spoke with referred to their "active social lives," including Thursday night Bar Reviews at local pubs and other forms of relaxation. "I have found the student body much more diverse and more social than I expected. I'm actually able to go out drinking and dancing at many of Boston's great night spots at least once a week," said a 1L. However, some students noted that the school itself has little community space for its law students and that the recreational facilities, particularly the gym, are too limited.

Topping the list of student complaints was the Harvard Law School administration, often described as "inflexible" and "uncaring." One 3L, who referred to her time at HLS as "an incredibly alienating experience," said: "The administration is not the least bit interested in student concerns. Students arrive here first year full of interest and enthusiasm which usually gets sucked out of them by second year."

We heard sharply differing opinions regarding the school's support of public interest law from students and the administration. Many students cited the administration's—and more pointedly, the dean's—lack of support for public-interest law. "The administration is openly hostile to public-interest oriented students," said one 3L. Another suggested that the dean "tries periodically to cut the public interest career office and the clinical programs." We must say that the school's actions, including the creation of a public-interest professorship, the purchase and renovation of the Legal Services Center teaching clinic, and the establishment of the Human Rights Journal, appear to strongly support public interest law.

Overall, Harvard is Harvard, a school which provides one of the most distinguished law degrees in the country.

ADMISSIONS

Last year nearly 6,800 prospective students competed to be among the 559 men and women admitted to the Harvard Law School's entering class, making this premier law school the second most selective in the country. However, most of those unlucky applicants could likely have their pick of most other law schools. With an overall acceptance rate of about 12 percent, it is inevitable that Harvard will reject thousands of very well qualified candidates. Those whose numbers fall even slightly short of stunning face long odds. But it never hurts to try.

ACADEMICS

Student/faculty ratio	17:1
% female faculty	27
% minority faculty	22
Hours of study per day	3.49

Academic specialties:

Civil Procedure, Commercial, Constitutional, Corporation Securities, Criminal, Environmental, Govt Services, Human Rights, International, Labor, Legal History, Legal Philosophy, Property, Taxation

FINANCIAL FACTS

Tuition	$21,700
Cost of books	$860
Fees	$654
Room & board (on/off-campus)	$8,550/$8,550
% first-year students receiving aid	75
% all students receiving aid	75
% aid that is merit-based	0
% of all students receiving loans	75
% receiving scholarships	28
% of all students receiving assistantships	NR
Average grant	$9,075
Average graduation debt	$62,814

ADMISSIONS

# applications received	6,493
% applicants accepted	12
% acceptees attending	66
LSAT range	166-173
GPA range	3.70-3.93
Application fee	$50
Regular application	February 1
Regular notification	rolling
Rolling notification?	Yes
Early decision program?	No
Admission may be deferred?	Yes
Maximum length of deferment	2 years
Evening division offered?	No
Part-time accepted?	No
Gourman Report Rating	**4.92**

UNIVERSITY OF HAWAII, MANOA
William S. Richardson School of Law

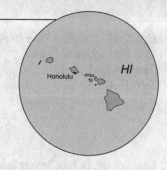

Honolulu   HI

A "paradise setting" provides the backdrop for the 250 or so students who study at the tiny William S. Richardson School of Law, a public school affiliated with the University of Hawaii. Richardson is "the only law school" in this sun-drenched state, where "the beaches are clean, the surf's up," and "Aloha spirit" is alive and kicking. Due largely to the law school's Pacific Rim location, an "Asian/Pacific focus" prevails. Special offerings bolster this reputation, including the comprehensive Pacific-Asian Legal Studies (PALS) program. Environmental awareness is another major issue here, and a formal certificate of specialization in environmental and natural resources law is available. Taken in its entirety, though, course selection is somewhat limited, mostly because of the school's small size. Clinical programs are sparse as well. "Richardson could benefit from more clinics so that all interested students could participate in them," wrote one student.

"Classes are small and personal" at Richardson, and "you are given a lot of individual attention by an exceptionally bright and dedicated staff." Students attested that virtually all faculty members are very approachable and readily available for assistance. "At Hawaii, you can talk to anyone (deans, profs), anywhere (office, class, parties), and anytime (call 'em at home)." The faculty is also remarkably diverse. It includes many native Hawaiians; leaders in Chinese and Japanese law; and a notable percentage of women. Since admitting its first class of 56 students in 1973, Richardson has graduated more than 1,200 attorneys, most of whom continue to serve in the state of Hawaii. Countless bigwigs in Hawaii's legal profession, including the state's current governor, are Richardson alums. According to a 3L, "Connections in Hawaii are absolutely vital" to students "who are not in the top 5 to 10 percent of the class." Luckily, "opportunities to meet and socialize with political leaders such as members of Congress, district attorneys, and federal judges" are plentiful.

The grading system here is somewhat unique. "What I really like is the fact that our first semester is not graded," said a 1L, "so we can just relax and get to know other students." The free ride ends there, though. During the second semester, an uncompromising

Joanne K. Punu, Assistant Dean
2515 Dole Street
Honolulu, HI 96822
Tel: 808-956-3000 • Fax: 808-956-3813
Email: lawadm@hawaii.edu
Internet: www.hawaii.edu/catalog/school-law.html

University of Hawaii, Manoa

grading system kicks in, bringing with it a palpable increase in tension. As a 2L explained, "the strict 'C' curve is absolutely demoralizing and no matter how much the administration explains this fact to potential employers, a 'C' looks much worse than a 'B'. This mandate needs to go." Other students praised the grading system for fostering a "competitive environment among very bright, qualified people."

Complaints about Richardson's facilities were abundant. The library "needs to have expanded hours" and is "probably the coldest spot" in the state. "Hey, we're in Hawaii!" observed a 1L, "why do I need to use a quilt in the library?" Classrooms were said to be "dirty and musty," and an increase in research hardware, computer terminals, and the number of copy machines would also be much appreciated. Another area of student discontent that surrounded the 1996-97 school year focused on the school's price tag, which saw a "steep (100 percent) tuition increase."

On the positive side, Richardson is home to a diverse and friendly population. The "tight-knit group" of "extremely heterogeneous" students here is "good-natured, opinionated, confident," and represents "a successful meeting across the political spectrum." There is a "great ethnic mix between local people, mainland people, as well as people from foreign countries"; over 70 percent of the students are members of what are referred to elsewhere as minority groups.

ADMISSIONS

Applications volume at Hawaii is low in comparison to other law schools, but the size of its entering classes (around eighty) necessitates a highly selective admissions process. Since the University of Hawaii primarily seeks to provide the state with talented and highly trained attorneys and judges, strong preferences are given to state residents. Given the constraints of its mission, it is somewhat surprising that Hawaii is able to enroll a student body with numerical credentials better than those of students at 70 percent of American law schools.

ACADEMICS

Student/faculty ratio	13:1
% female faculty	40
% minority faculty	37
Hours of study per day	4.07

Academic specialties:
Environmental, International, Pacific-Asian

FINANCIAL FACTS

Tuition (in/out-state)	$4,800/$12,800
Cost of books	$800
Fees (in/out-state)	$59/$119
Room & board (on/off-campus)	$6,900/$9,600
% first-year students receiving aid	NR
% all students receiving aid	54
% aid that is merit-based	26
% of all students receiving loans	44
% receiving scholarships	46
% of all students receiving assistantships	2
Average grant	$4,800
Average graduation debt	NR

ADMISSIONS

# applications received	668
% applicants accepted	26
% acceptees attending	38
Average LSAT	157
LSAT range	150-176
Average undergrad GPA	3.40
GPA range	2.80-4.00
Application fee (in/out-state)	$30/$30
Regular application	March 1
Regular notification	April 1-15
Rolling notification?	No
Early decision program?	No
Admission may be deferred?	No
Evening division offered?	No
Part-time accepted?	No
Gourman Report Rating	**2.60**

HOFSTRA UNIVERSITY
School of Law

For more than 20 years, heavily populated suburban Long Island has made do with only two law schools, one of them the midsize Hofstra University School of Law. Established in 1971 on the Hempstead campus of its 12,000-student parent university, Hofstra is a regionally respected law school that draws the vast majority of its students from and sends the vast majority of its graduates to the metropolitan New York area. Its traditional curriculum is solid and its faculty strong, and Hofstra graduates have historically had little difficulty securing good jobs. To better prepare its students for a tightening job market, however, Hofstra places great emphasis on practical-skills training, both in the classroom and in the community.

The law school administers a broad variety of special-subject workshops and externship programs, and it has long operated its own Neighborhood Law Office. Hofstra recently augmented its skills curriculum with a special three-credit Trial Techniques program held in January before the beginning of the spring semester. These and other programs in the law school's impressive array of simulated and live-action clinical courses involve a significant proportion of the Hofstra student body. The law school admits more than one in three applicants, but with a pool of more than 2,500 from which to choose, it holds candidates to high standards. The numerical credentials of admitted applicants are moderately strong.

For the most part, those who actually go on to enroll at the law school express overall satisfaction with their surroundings. Almost unanimously, in fact, Hofstra students praise their "often brilliant" faculty. As a 1L put it: "Our professors are intelligent, well prepared, open, and concerned about their students' academic and personal welfare." Most others agreed. "They have a nurturing attitude rather than trying to push out those who can't make it." Many also had words of praise for the practical focus of their curriculum, and particularly for its trial advocacy program. When asked to name their law school's greatest strength, quite a few cited its "growing reputation for producing great trial lawyers."

Amy Engle, Dean for Admissions
121 Hofstra University
Hempstead, NY 11550
Tel: 516-463-5916
Email: lawale@Hofstra.edu
Internet: www.hofstra.edu

Hofstra students do, of course, have their gripes, but other than the small but vocal minority of students we heard from who called for more ethnic diversity in the law school's faculty, few had specific complaints. (Note: Only a tiny percentage of Hofstra's full-time teaching faculty are members of minority groups, far fewer than at most schools in the metropolitan area, and the entire nation.) By far the most prevalent concern of Hofstra students seems to be their future employment prospects. In many cases, this concern took the form of complaints about the limited number of slots on the school's single law journal. In most cases, however, it took the form of nonspecific criticism—even from 1Ls—of the law school's career placement office. Many also expressed their desire that the law school "improve its national reputation." Of course, things are not quite that simple. Given the lack of geographical diversity in the student body, Hofstra can't really aspire to the kind of standing that some of its neighboring schools enjoy. But when one considers the fact that practically all Hofstra graduates go to work in the New York area, one sees that concerns about the law school's perceived lack of "national" status are misplaced. New York is home to the single-largest legal job market in the world, and though the upper echelon of the city's legal community may still be the almost exclusive province of lawyers from "top-ten" schools, plenty of jobs await the graduates of strong regional schools like Hofstra.

ADMISSIONS

As highly selective as the 11 law schools in the metropolitan New York region are, it would be misleading to claim that admissions at Hofstra are much less competitive than at most of these schools. In the grand scheme of things, Hofstra is quite selective. With a solid average GPA and an average LSAT score at the 70th percentile, the numerical credentials of students in Hofstra's entering class of about 270 are stronger, in fact, than those of students at about 40 percent of the country's fully accredited law schools. These high numerical standards, however, are mitigated somewhat by a relatively generous overall acceptance rate.

ACADEMICS

Student/faculty ratio	15:1
% female faculty	21
% minority faculty	5
Hours of study per day	3.59

Academic specialties:

Civil Procedure, Commercial, Constitutional, Corporation Securities, Criminal, Environmental, International, Labor, Legal Philosophy, Property, Taxation

FINANCIAL FACTS

Tuition	$19,840
Cost of books	$900
Fees	$398
Room & board (on/off-campus)	$8,350/$8,350
% first-year students receiving aid	65
% all students receiving aid	62
% aid that is merit-based	36
% of all students receiving loans	33
% receiving scholarships	50
% of all students receiving assistantships	10
Average grant	$3,462
Average graduation debt	NR

ADMISSIONS

# applications received	1,912
% applicants accepted	42
% acceptees attending	31
Average LSAT	157
Average undergrad GPA	3.20
Application fee	$60
Regular application	rolling
Regular notification	rolling
Rolling notification?	Yes
Early decision program?	No
Admission may be deferred?	No
Evening division offered?	No
Part-time accepted?	No
Gourman Report Rating	4.15

UNIVERSITY OF HOUSTON
Law Center

OVERVIEW

Type of school	public
Environment	metropolis
Scholastic calendar	semester
Schedule	full-time or part-time

STUDENTS

Enrollment of parent institution	31,000
Enrollment of law school	998
% male/female	61/39
% out-of-state	17
% minorities	20
% international (# of countries represented)	8 (NR)
Average age at entry	25

APPLICANTS ALSO LOOK AT

University of Texas
South Texas College of Law
Southern Methodist University
Texas Tech University
Baylor University

SURVEY SAYS...

HITS
Grads expect big bucks

MISSES
Faculty-student relations
Library staff
Quality of teaching

EMPLOYMENT PROFILE

Firms recruiting on campus	150
Job placement rate (%)	88
% grads employed immediately	60
% grads employed within six months	88
Average starting salary	$48,600

Grads employed by field (%):

Academia	1
Business/industry	16
Government	8
Judicial clerkships	6
Private practice	67
Public interest	1
Other	2

One of three mega-law schools in the nation's seventh-largest legal job market, the University of Houston Law Center is home to more than 1,000 full- and part-time students. The law school's excellent faculty and high-caliber student body are both causes and effects of its long-established reputation as one of the finest law schools in the South. Its low public-school tuition is to thank for its standing as one of the better bargains anywhere.

The law school at Houston has succeeded in augmenting its overall strength by establishing several highly regarded special programs. In 1978, for example, it established its Health Law and Policy Institute in conjunction with the University of Texas Health Science Center. Since then, the law school has been recognized as a national leader in the growing field of health law, an area of specialization that is particularly appropriate in a city whose largest employer is the world's biggest medical complex. Besides including a wide array of health-law courses in its standard J.D. curriculum, Houston offers a master of laws (LL.M.) and two concurrent-degree programs in the field: a master's in public health and a Ph.D. in medical humanities, both through UT. The law school has also established special programs in international law and environmental liability law, as well as an Intellectual Property Law Institute. All of these subjects are areas of curricular strength at Houston.

Outside the classroom, Houston students can participate in several clinical programs, including the Family and Poverty Law Clinic and other clinical curricula dedicated to some of the fields of law discussed above. This broad-based strength has earned the law school increasing notice, not least from highly qualified applicants, who have driven Houston's numerical admissions standards significantly higher in recent years. As it stands, it is a law school in great demand.

Although they were vocally critical about particular aspects of their experience at the law school, those applicants who actually went on to become students at Houston were fundamentally satisfied with their chosen school. They found their curriculum solid and their faculty competent, and they exuded a confidence about their professional futures, which a large percentage of

Sondra Richardson, Assistant Dean for Admissions
4800 Calhoun
Houston, TX 77204-6371
Tel: 713-743-1070 • Fax: 713-743-2194
Email: info@lawlib.uh.edu
Internet: www.law.uh.edu

University of Houston

graduates spend in private practice. This confidence, in most cases, seems to have a basis in reality, since so many Houston students have gained practical experience in the field before earning their degrees. Asked to name their school's greatest strengths, many cited "its proximity to major law practices and its relationship with them." "I've been able to interact and network with many area lawyers," said one student only in her second year. "Our location in this major metropolitan area allows employment opportunities galore," reported another. "This law school is secretly striving to become a top-twenty school. It has the best reputation in town and growing." And, quite naturally, Houston students credited the low tuition they pay for a good part of their overall contentment. As one student asserted, Houston gives "the best bang for the buck." Future students will benefit from the recent extensive overhaul of and additions to the computer facilities and the much needed refurbishment to the library and grounds.

Houston students' criticisms ranged from the purely aesthetic to the truly substantive. Since the vast majority commented on the "drab, lifeless appearance" of the physical plant, we can only assume that now that this problem has been addressed, they have nothing major to complain about. However, quite a few students who praised the quality of the Houston program expressed their frustration with the relatively limited selection of courses, which one student said "is not diverse enough during any given semester." These and other relatively minor criticisms aside, however, most Houston students are basically content.

ADMISSIONS

The University of Houston's respected J.D. program and its attractive tuition attract applications from the 2,650 prospective law students annually. The size and quality of this applicant pool allow the law school to choose its students quite carefully. Successful candidates for admission to Houston possess solid numerical credentials. Those who are admitted and actually go on to enroll have solid average UGPAs and LSAT scores.

ACADEMICS

Student/faculty ratio	21:1
% female faculty	17
% minority faculty	11
Hours of study per day	3.89

Academic specialties:
Environmental, International

FINANCIAL FACTS

Tuition (in/out-state)	$4,500/$9,000
Cost of books	$560
Fees (in/out-state)	$1,369/$1,369
% first-year students receiving aid	86
% all students receiving aid	89
% aid that is merit-based	15
% of all students receiving loans	89
% receiving scholarships	45
% of all students receiving assistantships	NR
Average grant	$2,750
Average graduation debt	$37,500

ADMISSIONS

# applications received	2,600
% applicants accepted	32
% acceptees attending	36
Average LSAT	159
Average undergrad GPA	3.30
Application fee (in/out-state)	$50/$50
Early application	November 1
Early notification	January 15
Regular application	rolling
Regular notification	May 1
Rolling notification?	No
Early decision program?	Yes
Admission may be deferred?	Yes
Maximum length of deferment	1 year
Evening division offered?	Yes
Part-time accepted?	Yes
Gourman Report Rating	**3.68**

HOWARD UNIVERSITY
School of Law

OVERVIEW

Type of school	private
Environment	metropolis
Scholastic calendar	semester
Schedule	full-time only

STUDENTS

Enrollment of parent institution	6,274
Enrollment of law school	444
% male/female	43/57
% out-of-state	NR
% part-time	NR
% minorities	85
% international (# of countries represented)	NR (NR)
Average age at entry	25

APPLICANTS ALSO LOOK AT

Georgetown University
University of Maryland
George Washington University
American University
New York University

SURVEY SAYS...

HITS
Sense of community
Legal writing
Academic reputation

MISSES
Library staff
Not enough courses

EMPLOYMENT PROFILE

Firms recruiting on campus	200
% grads employed immediately	50
% grads employed within six months	88
Average starting salary	$48,260

Grads employed by field (%):

Academia	1
Business/industry	20
Government	26
Judicial clerkships	16
Military	2
Private practice	27
Public interest	5
Other	7

In the wake of the Civil War, the Reconstruction-era Congress established Howard University in the District of Columbia. The university's mission was to provide the educational means by which newly freed slaves could redeem their constitutional rights and claim the practical, social, and economic standing necessary to make those rights meaningful. Though accomplishing this mission has been and continues to be a struggle, the Howard University School of Law has maintained a "strong commitment to civil rights" and a commitment to hiring and admitting members of the African American community and other minority groups. The overwhelming majority of both students and full-time faculty represent minorities.

Using its curriculum as its vehicle, Howard makes an "earnest effort to develop the total person." The course of study here is straightforward and traditional, though somewhat limited. "A wider range of classes from which to choose" would be gladly received. The performance of the "very accessible and very encouraging" faculty "varies widely," but most are "intellectually stimulating and quite demanding." They are "enthusiastic, organized, and have practical experience" as well. One student complained of "ridiculous levels of favoritism," but most seem to agree with this 2L who asserts: "The faculty members really want us to succeed. They challenge us to the utmost and test our ability to analyze and articulate our ideas in a clear fashion." The administration, notorious for its "five-hour lunch breaks," drew considerably fewer raves, primarily because it "appears to have the art of giving students the run-around down to an art form." A 2L cautioned: "From financial aid to health services, everything administrative is a nightmare."

Students do rave about their "strong legal writing program, clinical programs, and an extremely active, politically powerful alumni network. Career Services also "provides an array of employment opportunities." Most of the students here planned to seek employment in either public service or government where they will make a modestly large salary, or in the corporate world where, to judge from their expectations, they will be set for life. The rate at which HU grads choose to begin their careers in private practice is well below the national average, and the proportion of Howard graduates who enter government positions is one of the highest.

Ted Miller, Assistant Dean
2900 Van Ness Street
Washington, DC 20008
Tel: 202-806-8008
Email: admission@law.howard.edu

Howard University

Chief among students' criticisms are complaints about the lack-luster facilities here. "The computer lab is inadequate," said a 2L. "There is usually a line." The library "could use some remodeling," but "because we're surrounded by law schools, it's not a huge problem," noted a 2L. "The research facilities were borderline when I first arrived, but there have been vast improvements since then," observed another 2L. Still, most students agreed that "the Howard experience would be greatly improved if broken facilities were repaired in a timely fashion."

Despite their gripes, it is apparent that Howard students hold their law school very dear. It's "the psychic energy you feel when you walk down the corridors knowing that you are where some of the pioneers of civil rights litigators once started." It's an atmosphere where "if you want to use Howard as a springboard to greatness, you will be encouraged, not mocked." It's knowing that Howard "attempts to make Supreme Court Justices, not just lawyers." It's the belief that "law is not an occupation, but a chance to devote your life to the protection of groups that have been historically oppressed." No doubt about it, "the 'Howard Legacy' is a big thing here." Subsequently, "the legacy of civil rights advocacy and public service permeates every area and students are encouraged to live, think, and breathe 'concern for each other and society'" constantly. "We are on a mission," concluded a 1L. "Ninety percent of the students here could probably be at law schools with objectively higher rankings. We come here because it's Howard."

ADMISSIONS

Howard's strong tradition, its relatively low tuition (for a private school), and its generous financial aid programs combine to draw a large pool of applicants every year. As a result, the admissions process here is selective. Although the numerical credentials of the average member of the Howard University School of Law fall below the national average, admissions at Howard is no joke. Applications volume at this long-established law school is so great that Howard accepts a smaller proportion of its applicants than do some of the country's elite law schools.

ACADEMICS

Student/faculty ratio	16:1
% female faculty	34
% minority faculty	80
Hours of study per day	4.58

FINANCIAL FACTS

Tuition	$11,920
Cost of books	$1,000
Fees	$505
Room & board (on/off-campus)	$8,537/$8,537
% first-year students receiving aid	90
% all students receiving aid	95
% aid that is merit-based	28
% of all students receiving loans	95
% receiving scholarships	45
Average grant	$9,555
Average graduation debt	$44,800

ADMISSIONS

# applications received	1,350
% applicants accepted	29
% acceptees attending	32
Average LSAT	152
Average undergrad GPA	3.00
Application fee	$60
Regular application	rolling
Regular notification	NR
Rolling notification?	Yes
Early decision program?	No
Admission may be deferred?	Yes
Maximum length of deferment	1 year
Evening division offered?	No
Part-time accepted?	No
Gourman Report Rating	**2.86**

UNIVERSITY OF IDAHO COLLEGE OF LAW

OVERVIEW

Type of school	public
Environment	town
Scholastic calendar	semester
Schedule	full-time only

STUDENTS

Enrollment of parent institution	7,398
Enrollment of law school	266
% male/female	57/43
% out-of-state	25
% part-time	NR
% minorities	10
% international (# of countries represented)	NR(NR)
age at entry	27

APPLICANTS ALSO LOOK AT

Gonzaga University
Brigham Young University
University of Oregon
University of Utah
Willamette University

SURVEY SAYS...

HITS
Studying
Socratic method
Library staff

MISSES
Not enough courses
Quality of teaching
Practical lawyering skills

EMPLOYMENT PROFILE

Firms recruiting on campus	32
Job placement rate (%)	89
% grads employed immediately	55
% grads employed within six months	81
Average starting salary	$32,871

Grads employed by field (%):

Business/industry	12
Government	22
Judicial clerkships	25
Private practice	36
Public interest	1
Other	11

The University of Idaho College of Law is a "good school" with "good opportunities" in a "good location." This small and inexpensive law school has been the sole in-state provider of employees in the legal sector since its inauguration in 1909. Idaho provides "excellent preparation to work in the Northwest" and "turns out well-prepared lawyers." "In this respect," said a 1L, "it serves the state rather well." Students here follow a traditional and strictly prescribed course of study, with relatively few electives even in the second and third years. The "lack of diversity in the curriculum" was a source of frustration for some Idaho students. "I wish the school could offer more courses besides those needed to pass the bar," wrote one. On the other hand, classrooms here are far from overcrowded. "The small class size is the greatest strength. It allows for more personal contact with classmates and with professors," explained a 2L. "With the small classes, you can't hide from the Socratic method," though. "One cannot avoid participating in class, which is, of course, both good and bad."

Students disagreed substantially over the quality of the Idaho faculty. Students who liked their professors called the faculty "incredibly knowledgeable and helpful" and said that "the law school's size and the individual attention we receive are definitely its strong points." According to one student: "I do perceive a genuine concern on the part of the profs that we learn the law. Most are very willing to pace themselves with the students." Also, "The deans teach as well as administer, so if you have a concern or gripe, a dean is quite accessible." Another camp viewed professors here quite differently. "Some professors are dead wrong many times about what the black letter of the law should be," said one student. A 3L pointed out: "The majority of the faculty are not even members of the Idaho bar. It seems odd that they are not required to pass the very test they are supposed to be preparing us to take." And while some lauded Idaho for its "desire to help students prepare for the 'real world,'" others clamored for "more practical experience." "Too much theory, not enough law," was the opinion of some respondents.

Paige Wilkins, Admissions Coordinator
Sixth and Rayburn
Moscow, ID 83844-2321
Tel: 208-885-6423 • Fax: 208-885-7609
Internet: www.uidaho.edu/law/lawcoll.html

University of Idaho

The law school's home of Moscow is a "sleepy college town" of 18,000 located in Idaho's panhandle, surrounded by "rolling hills" and, no kidding, amber waves of grain. "No crime. No pollution. No traffic. Beautiful." Although the snowy winters "could be warmer," students gave the area high marks for livability. Clean air and water aren't something you have to drive out of town to find; they're abundant, and numerous outdoor activities are easily accessible. Spokane is only eighty miles to the northwest and Washington State University is only eight miles away. The law school draws the overwhelming majority of its students from within Idaho or from nearby Washington. However, a few students remarked that the law school "should be in Boise," where there is more legal action and more opportunities to mingle with potential employers.

Students here form a "tight-knit community" and are "generally tolerant of opposing views and helpful toward each other." The "close, comfy atmosphere" is friendly enough that "all students know one another by name." Underneath the surface, though, there is "a silent, highly competitive atmosphere lurking." Students told us that the degree of competitiveness is spawned by Idaho's strict grading system. "Low averages do not help students get jobs when other surrounding western schools grade high." Socially, "people tend to group themselves by religion, age, or gender, so there's not a lot of interaction (other than in class)."

ADMISSIONS

Since most of the school's students hail from the Northwest (or, specifically, a relatively small population base in eastern Washington and Idaho itself) the volume of applications is relatively moderate. Numerical admissions standards are moderate as well, but the small size of the law school's entering class necessitates a careful screening process. Only about one-third of the roughly 700 candidates Idaho considers annually will gain admission. One-third of those who are accepted will actually choose to enroll.

ACADEMICS

Student/faculty ratio	12:1
% female faculty	33
% minority faculty	4
Hours of study per day	4.76

FINANCIAL FACTS

Tuition (in/out-state)	$3,260/$8,640
Cost of books	$1,020
% first-year students receiving aid	90
% all students receiving aid	90
% aid that is merit-based	39
% of all students receiving loans	90
% receiving scholarships	40
% of all students receiving assistantships	NR
Average grant	$1,300
Average graduation debt	NR

ADMISSIONS

# applications received	482
% applicants accepted	50
% acceptees attending	34
Average LSAT	153
Average undergrad GPA	3.20
Application fee (in/out-state)	$30/$30
Regular application	February 1
Regular notification	April 1
Rolling notification?	Yes
Early decision program?	No
Admission may be deferred?	No
Evening division offered?	No
Part-time accepted?	No
Gourman Report Rating	**2.78**

UNIVERSITY OF ILLINOIS
College of Law

OVERVIEW

Type of school	public
Environment	metropolis
Scholastic calendar	semester
Schedule	full-time only

STUDENTS

Enrollment of parent institution	13,491
Enrollment of law school	616
% male/female	61/39
% out-of-state	20
% part-time	NR
% minorities	27
% international (# of countries represented)	NR (NR)
Average age at entry	24

APPLICANTS ALSO LOOK AT

Northwestern University
University of Michigan
Loyola University, Chicago
DePaul University
University of Wisconsin

SURVEY SAYS...

HITS
Sleeping
Quality of teaching
Faculty-student relations

MISSES
Practical lawyering skills

EMPLOYMENT PROFILE

Firms recruiting on campus	116
% grads employed immediately	75
% grads employed within six months	95
Average starting salary	$50,680

Grads employed by field (%):

Academia	4
Business/industry	13
Government	4
Judicial clerkships	8
Military	1
Private practice	68
Public interest	1
Other	6

The University of Illinois College of Law has long enjoyed a strong reputation as one of the country's finest law schools. A satisfied 3L told us: "There's a feeling among the students that we're very lucky to be here, given the cost and the excellent legal education."

Though a few students complained that Illinois is "too business-oriented," most saw a "balance between the intellectual pursuit of legal theory and practical skills." The law school offers a traditional J.D. program, with few prescribed courses after the first year. "Course selection is a little weak," but "if students pick classes carefully, they can almost always take professors who are entertaining and truly know how to teach (after first year, of course)." The nationally recognized program in trial advocacy—taken by over half the student body—received universal praise, while the revamped Legal Writing program, which divides students into mock law firms that prepare mock cases, drew mixed reviews. A "good legal clinic just started," but many students here continue to call for a greater emphasis on clinical training, especially since externships and opportunities for practical experience tend to be sparse. Many 1Ls and 2Ls argued that U of I's location is less than ideal "compared to students at Chicago schools because we can't work at firms in the city during the school year." Summer internship programs, though available, have "too many hoops to jump through." For the most part, the "highly acclaimed" faculty is "so accessible it's ridiculous." Most professors have both outstanding teaching skills and a serious interest in scholarly output. Students agreed that "the administration is very open to suggestions and complaints and acts promptly on them." "Nonresidents should know that it is not very easy to obtain state residency," though. Cautioned a 2L: "It took me three semesters."

The "beautiful, immaculate, and highly maintained" facilities here were remodeled in 1994, and sit directly across from an art museum and cafe. The library received rave reviews, but the "computer network is unreliable and the systems are slow" according to many students, and "There aren't enough computers." "Also," grumbled a 3L, "the university nickels and dimes us with parking fees and tickets." U of I students described Career Services as "extremely supportive," especially for job searches in

Pamela B. Coleman, Director of Admissions
504 East Pennsylvania Avenue
Champaign, IL 61820
Tel: 217-244-6415
Email: dfalls@law.uiuc.edu
Internet: www.law.uiuc.edu

University of Illinois

the Chicago metropolitan area. However, if you are interested in working in another city, "the law school does not help a lot." Salary expectations are high here, particularly among students in the top third of their classes.

Illinois students "are smart, but there is a little bit of bitterness," explained a 1L. "Most were within striking distance of the Top Ten, so there's always 'I could've gone to Harvard, but ...'" The environment here is "very competitive," but "not destructive or disruptive." Maintained a 2L: "I've yet to see examples of people trying to get ahead at the expense of others." The 2Ls and 3Ls "always hand down outlines and study aids to 1Ls. Old exams are on file in the library." Illinois students are also quite sociable, "which is probably why there is so much camaraderie." Every week, there are "a lot of social activities and private parties," to which "Even faculty members have been known to show up." Politically, "a libertarian point of view is the prevailing philosophy" at Illinois. "As a flaming liberal, I have found my views to be out of sync with the general law school population, but I have not had too much difficulty finding like-minded friends," said a 2L.

"U of I is a very practical school, set up to teach the nuts and bolts, and to get you a job," concluded a 2L. "It succeeds at both. Unlike other schools, everything here is geared toward making law school as painless as possible for the students." A satisfied 1L threw down the gauntlet: "I challenge anyone to find a better atmosphere at a Top Twenty law school."

ADMISSIONS

Though the overall acceptance rate is relatively generous, competition for admission to this superb public law school is heated because the University of Illinois is flooded with applications from highly qualified bargain hunters. Candidates lucky enough to gain admission possess very strong numerical credentials. In an average year, more than 10 applicants vie for each spot in the law school's entering class of about 200. Data for the 1996 entering class indicated a median LSAT score of 161 and a median GPA of 3.41. Illinois natives are viewed favorably, and obtaining ethnic diversity is definitely a goal of the admissions committee.

ACADEMICS	
Student/faculty ratio	22:1
% female faculty	25
% minority faculty	6
Hours of study per day	3.52

FINANCIAL FACTS	
Tuition (in/out-state)	$6,012/$15,605
Cost of books	$800
Fees (in/out-state)	$1,002/$1,002
Room & board (on/off-campus)	$6,394/NR
% first-year students receiving aid	NR
% all students receiving aid	44
% aid that is merit-based	NR
% of all students receiving loans	NR
% receiving scholarships	17
% of all students receiving assistantships	NR
Average grant	$5,242
Average graduation debt	NR

ADMISSIONS	
# applications received	1,792
% applicants accepted	33
% acceptees attending	30
Average LSAT	161
LSAT range	143-176
Average undergrad GPA	3.41
GPA range	2.10-4.00
Application fee (in/out-state)	$30/$30
Regular application	March 15
Regular notification	NR
Rolling notification?	Yes
Early decision program?	No
Admission may be deferred?	Yes
Maximum length of deferment	1 year
Evening division offered?	No
Part-time accepted?	No
Gourman Report Rating	**4.20**

INDIANA UNIVERSITY, BLOOMINGTON
School of Law

The Indiana University School of Law at Bloomington is one of the oldest and most respected public law schools in the nation. Attached to one of the nation's largest teaching and research universities, Indiana has the vast academic resources to provide its students with a rich, interdisciplinary legal education. The IU approach is never just about law; it's always about law in action and how it relates to something else, like society or technology or literature. As a result, the education here is definitely one of the more "theory-driven" available in the Midwest.

IU maintains a strong awareness of the ways in which the growing abundance of information technology continuously changes and globalizes the practice of law. The up-to-date curriculum is broad in scope. "Classes are too large," said one student, and actual course selection leaves much to be desired. Indiana mixes its mostly "effective, engaging," but "homogenous" resident faculty with visiting professors from around the world, creating an international flavor. Many "accomplished" and "fabulous" faculty members are cutting-edge theorists in their fields, with "long histories of teaching the law." Nevertheless, students noticed an unmistakable inconsistency in teaching quality. Also, according to one student, "there's a shortage of teaching practical things—like how the legal system really works." In an effort to better provide the practical training that students are clamoring for, IU has increased its clinical offerings. Students called the administration "somewhat bureaucratic," and questioned why "offices are closed for the one hour at noon when most students have the time to do things." Out-of-state applicants should heed this 1L's warning: "You will never ever receive resident tuition if you moved here as a nonresident."

Indiana students couldn't say enough about their "wonderful and bright" facilities. Also, "the research facilities are the best in the country, bar none." On the minus side, "parking sucks." Career Services "needs to be more aggressive" and "could be more helpful to those not interested in working in firms." IU maintains a strong network alumni relations. In a recent moot court, which Chief Justice William Rehnquist helped preside over, alums teamed with current students in a trial of Shakespeare's *Richard III.*

Frank Motley, Assistant Dean for Admissions
211 South Indiana Avenue
Bloomington, IN 47405
Tel: 812-855-4765 • Fax: 812-855-0555
Email: lawadmis@law.indiana.edu
Internet: www.law.indiana.edu

**Indiana University,
Bloomington**

The quintessential college town of Bloomington offers "a wide variety of activities and experiences" and "is as diverse as a town its size could ever be." Student life is greatly enhanced by the 1,860 acres of beautifully wooded campus. The University offers plenty of cultural activities as well as Big Ten sporting events. "Socializing beyond the confines of the Law School" is common. "On any given night of the week, it is possible to find a group of law students to play basketball or go bar-hopping with."

Some students complained that minority enrollment is low and the IU Law School is overflowing with "nameless, faceless frat boys" and "obnoxious white kids from Indianapolis suburbs." Others contended that "there is quite a mix of people—people who've been working for a few years in everything from social work to construction work." Students are "competitive, but not unreasonably so," and there are "no back-stabbers." Again and again, students gushed about the "unexpectedly wonderful" atmosphere. "I remember reading these kinds of books during my law school search and thinking, 'Who really cares whether the students are nice?' But that's false. You need other students who are going through what you're going through. Your family doesn't always understand, but your fellow students, especially during the first year, mean everything. They push you to do better than you would have. Everyone here is so sympathetic to what's going on in your life. It's terrific."

ADMISSIONS

It's tough to get into the University of Indiana at Bloomington. Over 1,500 candidates vie annually for spots in the entering class of about 200. Successful candidates possess strong numerical credentials. Recently, the average LSAT score of enrolled students has been at least 158 and the average GPA has ranged from 3.3 to 3.5. In 1996, only 23 percent of applicants with LSAT scores below the 75th percentile and 17 percent of applicants with GPAs under 3.0 were accepted. By design, Indiana natives tend to get luckier than out-of-state applicants.

ACADEMICS

Student/faculty ratio	17:1
% female faculty	33
% minority faculty	3
Hours of study per day	3.98

Academic specialties:

Civil Procedure, Commercial, Constitutional, Corporation Securities, Criminal, Environmental, Government Services, Human Rights, International, Labor, Legal History, Legal Philosophy, Property, Taxation, Communications

FINANCIAL FACTS

Tuition (in/out-state)	$5,019/$13,811
Cost of books	$982
Fees (in/out-state)	$331/$331
Room & board (on/off-campus)	$5,439/NR
% first-year students receiving aid	73
% all students receiving aid	80
% aid that is merit-based	11
% of all students receiving loans	78
% receiving scholarships	31
% of all students receiving assistantships	3
Average grant	$1,500
Average graduation debt	$35,000

ADMISSIONS

# applications received	1,524
% applicants accepted	44
% acceptees attending	33
Average LSAT	159
LSAT range	139-169
Average undergrad GPA	3.40
GPA range	2.15-4.00
Application fee (in/out-state)	$35/$35
Regular application	rolling
Regular notification	rolling
Rolling notification?	Yes
Early decision program?	No
Admission may be deferred?	Yes
Maximum length of deferment	2 years
Evening division offered?	No
Part-time accepted?	Yes
Gourman Report Rating	**4.33**

INDIANA UNIVERSITY, INDIANAPOLIS
School of Law

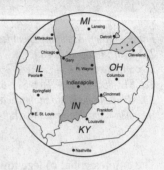

Weighing in with an enrollment of about 850 students, the Indiana University School of Law at Indianapolis is the largest law school in the Hoosier state. IU-Indy "provides a solid education and the Indianapolis location allows you to begin networking and searching for jobs right away." The bar-pass rate is "extraordinary." In-state tuition is quite low, and the higher rate for nonresidents (who face an uphill climb in achieving resident status) is reasonable as well. The "mostly accessible" and "very knowledgeable" faculty includes "several outstanding professors," but also "some really lousy" ones. Though "some are stand-offish," most profs "tell wonderful stories and are challenging without being malicious," asserted a 1L. In their spare time, professors "write questions for the Bar, as well as participate in writing state laws." Students said that the administration "is generally helpful but there's too much red tape," and it needs some work as "a cheerleader" for the school, "especially outside of Indiana."

The "clinical opportunities" and "practical-skills emphasis" draw raves from our student respondents. "I've heard from many attorneys in Indiana, especially in the Indianapolis area, that IU-Indy grads are better prepared than IU-Bloomington grads," boasted a 1L. At students' disposal are the significant resources of both the broader university and the city itself. The "downtown location provides opportunities for employment, internships, and contacts." The institutions of the state government are mere blocks away, affording IU-Indianapolis students ample opportunities for both research and employment in Indianapolis, "the county seat, state capitol, and base for the federal district." Students also applauded the "extensive clerkship possibilities" and "abundant" career opportunities that "students can explore while still in school. With part-time work and the many internships and externships, the opportunities can be endless."

Loyal IU-Indy grads hold many prominent positions in the local legal community. As a result, according to students, the law school has a "monopoly" on jobs in Indianapolis, the nation's twelfth-largest city and twentieth-largest legal-job market. Ca-

Angela M. Espada, Assistant Dean of Admissions
735 West New York Street
Indianapolis, IN 46202
Tel: 317-274-2459 • Fax: 317-274-3955
Email: kmiller@wpo.iupui.edu
Internet: www.iulaw.indy.indiana.edu

reer expectations are especially bright for students with GPAs on the sunny side of 3.0. For less fortunate students, the placement office seems to be an unhelpful "glorified help wanted page."

The IU-Indianapolis School of Law is currently housed in an "architecturally unique" (translation: old) building on the campus of Indiana University–Purdue University at Indianapolis. "The facilities are dated," but "a new building is in the works." For now, while the "research facilities are sufficient," the classrooms and the library are less than dazzling. IU-Indy "needs two or three times the current number of computers" and "parking is awful."

This school attracts an older student body—the average age of 1Ls is just under thirty. Students noted a "strong distinction between evening and day students. Evening students still have a hard time making our voice heard by the administration," griped a part-timer. Perhaps because of the age variations and the urban location, the environment here is "very impersonal." According to a 2L: "Since it's a commuter campus, there's not a real sense of community. Many of the students have families and other commitments." Nevertheless, to the extent that they are able, "people cooperate and help each other out." The majority of IU-Indy students are more or less united by their "conservative" political beliefs, though "the full political spectrum is represented." A 3L told us: "The school seems to attract students with state and national political aspirations. The level of involvement in local politics and the emphasis by the student body on the political process is unprecedented in my experience." Perhaps that student was referring to Dan Quayle, one of the law school's most prominent alumni.

ADMISSIONS

The IU-Indianapolis School of Law receives only a moderate number of applications, so its overall acceptance rate is fairly high. Accepted students, however, tend to possess strong numerical credentials. The most recent class of full-time and evening division students had a median GPA of 3.2. The average LSAT score for all applicants was 157. Statistically, applicants with an undergraduate GPA between 3.00 and 3.25 and an LSAT score between 150 and 154, inclusive, stands only a 13 percent chance of getting in.

ACADEMICS

Student/faculty ratio	18:1
% female faculty	32
% minority faculty	6
Hours of study per day	3.01

Academic specialties:
Constitutional, Criminal, Government Services, International, Labor, Taxation

FINANCIAL FACTS

Tuition (in/out-state)	$5,430/$12,960
Cost of books	$800
% first-year students receiving aid	NR
% all students receiving aid	60
% aid that is merit-based	20
% of all students receiving loans	55
% receiving scholarships	10
% of all students receiving assistantships	3
Average grant	$1,500
Average graduation debt	$39,000

ADMISSIONS

# applications received	1,042
% applicants accepted	47
% acceptees attending	53
Average LSAT	157
LSAT range	141-168
Average undergrad GPA	3.20
GPA range	2.00-4.10
Application fee (in/out-state)	$35/$35
Regular application	March 1
Regular notification	rolling
Rolling notification?	Yes
Early decision program?	No
Admission may be deferred?	Yes
Maximum length of deferment	1 year
Evening division offered?	Yes
Part-time accepted?	Yes
Gourman Report Rating	3.14

UNIVERSITY OF IOWA
College of Law

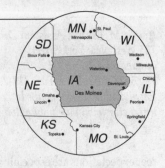

OVERVIEW

Type of school	public
Environment	suburban
Scholastic calendar	semester
Schedule	full-time only

STUDENTS

Enrollment of parent institution	25,778
Enrollment of law school	682
% male/female	58/42
% out-of-state	32
% part-time	NR
% minorities	21
% international (# of countries represented)	5 (12)
Average age at entry	26

APPLICANTS ALSO LOOK AT

University of Minnesota
University of Wisconsin
Drake University
Northwestern University
University of Illinois

SURVEY SAYS...

HITS
Research resources
Academic reputation
Classroom facilities

MISSES
Practical lawyering skills

EMPLOYMENT PROFILE

Firms recruiting on campus	200
Job placement rate (%)	95
% grads employed immediately	75
% grads employed within six months	95
Average starting salary	$44,000

Grads employed by field (%):

Academia	2
Business/industry	11
Government	8
Judicial clerkships	13
Military	2
Private practice	59
Public interest	4
Other	1

Located in picturesque Iowa City, the University of Iowa College of Law is a generously funded state school that has long enjoyed a regional reputation for the highest academic excellence. "If you can find a place to park" and "if you can stand the absolutely brutal arctic conditions," then this is the best bang for your buck. Said a 1L: "I'm getting just as good an education here as I would at the Ivies. My friend at Harvard Law and I both know the same stuff. He had Alan Dershowitz for Criminal Law, but I am $20,000 less in debt."

Iowa offers a broad curriculum, which is especially strong in international law, antitrust, jurisprudence, and minority issues, including federal Indian law. The J.D. program is "much more theoretical than practical," and places a heavy emphasis on legal writing. The clinic is large and well staffed, and its writing requirements are extensive. Some students called the practical skills curriculum "shameful," though, and suggested that "a greater emphasis could be placed on lawyering (like, how do you handle a real estate closing?)" Others disagreed, and singled out client counseling, trial advocacy, and moot court programs for praise. A favorable student-faculty ratio contributes to an intimate academic atmosphere. Professors run the gamut from "adequate" to "knock-your-socks-off." They "utilize discussion well" and "are very open to argumentation and analysis." However, a 2L complained that too much class time is wasted "figuring out what the law should be," and not what it is." Profs maintain a "true open-door policy" outside of class ("no appointments, no muss, no fuss"). The administration "bends over backwards" to take care of students. For the most part, "the facilities (especially the Writing Resource Center) are excellent." The "outstanding" library is "one of the largest in the country" but "not open enough." And, though "Iowa is a school where you can take courses in everything from Critical Race Theory to International Banking, you can't print out a course assignment because of a remarkably low regard for technology."

An "excellent sense of community" is definitely ubiquitous here. "We study together, work together, and party together," said a 3L. "Students get along very well. There is a high level of partici-

N. William Hines, Director of Admissions
Melrose at Byington Streets
Iowa City, IA 52242
Tel: 319-335-9071 • Fax: 319-335-9019
Email: ldw-admissions@uiowa.edu

University of Iowa

pation in student activities, especially Law Night, which is held at a different Iowa City bar each week." A 2L disagreed: "The student body is less active than I would like, probably less from lack of interest than a Midwestern work ethic, which tells them to get all of their work done first." While the law school is "not cutthroat competitive," explained a 3L, "there is still an atmosphere riddled with strong attitudes." The political atmosphere here is hard to figure. According to some students, there are many "women and minorities holding leadership positions" and they argued that Iowa is the "best school in the country for lesbian law students." Others complained of a "good old boys' network" and too many "portraits of constipated-looking white males in the halls." Still others said that PC-overload is a real problem: "In order to promote diversity, diverse opinions are squelched." Whatever the case, the student population is diverse in terms of race and ethnicity.

Students here seem interested in obtaining "mainstream corporate" jobs in the urban centers of the Midwest. Most are successful. "I was concerned about the marketability of my degree," admitted a 2L, "but after interviewing for jobs this fall, I am confident of my ability to get a good, well-paying job in the field I desire." Jobs outside the Midwest are hard to come by, and students here would like to see Iowa address this weakness. But complaints were few and far between. Said a 3L, "If you consider quality and accessibility of faculty, school facilities, the excellence of the writing program, tuition, the great college town of Iowa City, and great classmates, there is no better law school in the nation."

ADMISSIONS

The University of Iowa College of Law is one of the nation's finest and least expensive law schools, and one of its most selective. The numerical credentials of the enormously well-qualified students rank it among the fifty in the entire nation. State residents will have a much easier time gaining admission. Just less than 70 percent of each incoming class is from Iowa, while 30 percent attended the University of Iowa as undergraduates.

ACADEMICS

Student/faculty ratio	13:1
% female faculty	26
% minority faculty	14
Hours of study per day	4.01

Academic specialties:

Constitutional, Corporation Securities, Criminal, Human Rights, International, Legal History, Legal Philosophy, Property

FINANCIAL FACTS

Tuition (in/out-state)	$5,166/$14,020
Cost of books	$1,252
% first-year students receiving aid	100
% all students receiving aid	100
% aid that is merit-based	3
% of all students receiving loans	74
% receiving scholarships	35
% of all students receiving assistantships	9
Average grant	$8,156
Average graduation debt	$32,652

ADMISSIONS

# applications received	1,261
% applicants accepted	43
% acceptees attending	40
Average LSAT	158
LSAT range	140-179
Average undergrad GPA	3.41
GPA range	2.00-4.00
Application fee (in/out-state)	$20/$20
Regular application	March 1
Regular notification	rolling
Rolling notification?	Yes
Early decision program?	No
Admission may be deferred?	Yes
Maximum length of deferment	1 year
Evening division offered?	No
Part-time accepted?	No
Gourman Report Rating	**4.49**

JOHN MARSHALL LAW SCHOOL

OVERVIEW

Type of school	private
Environment	metropolis
Scholastic calendar	semester
Schedule	full-time or part-time

STUDENTS

Enrollment of parent institution	NR
Enrollment of law school	1,110
% male/female	61/39
% out-of-state	38
% part-time	29
% minorities	15
% international (# of countries represented)	2 (22)
Average age at entry	26

APPLICANTS ALSO LOOK AT

Loyola University, Chicago
DePaul University
Illinois Institute of Technology
University of Illinois
Northern Illinois University

SURVEY SAYS...

HITS
Legal writing
Grads expect big bucks

MISSES
Quality of teaching
Library staff
Not enough courses

EMPLOYMENT PROFILE

Firms recruiting on campus	21
Job placement rate (%)	86
% grads employed immediately	74
% grads employed within six months	86
Average starting salary	$45,041

Grads employed by field (%):

Academia	1
Business/industry	21
Government	20
Judicial clerkships	5
Private practice	52
Public interest	1
Other	3

The John Marshall Law School, named for the venerable chief justice of the United States Supreme Court (1801–35), is "a big-city school." With a student population of well over 1,200, John Marshall weighs in as one of the largest law schools in both the city of Chicago and the nation. Students called JMLS a "good 'nuts and bolts' law school" with a "high bar passage rate." A distinguished Trial Advocacy program and an emphasis on legal writing are its greatest strengths. A solid judicial externship program, extensive moot court competitions, and a Fair Housing Clinic are also notable.

John Marshall is one of a small number of law schools that allows for specialization at the J.D. level, and the awesome variety of courses offered is commensurate with the school's size. Students who choose to specialize may combine their own concentrations from a wealth of options, including international law (with programs in China and the Czech Republic), real estate, and informatics (information and communications technologies) law. Nevertheless, most students follow a traditional course of study and find the curriculum "challenging." Many students gave the entire faculty low marks for being "arrogant intellectuals who could not make it in the real world." Some felt that the "cold, distant" professors are "either great or terrible, no in-between." Other students called the profs "excellent" and praised the hypertraditional, Socratic teaching method often utilized here. Explained one student: "Profs work you hard and make you stand to recite answers in class, but they are largely good-natured and extremely competent." Many students harbored complaints about the rigorous grading curve at JMLS. "We need to increase the grading scale so we do not look like idiots when compared with students from schools with grade inflation," urged one student. To some extent, this change has already occurred. A 3L pointed out that: "Most people need to know that John Marshall is no longer a school that flunks 25 percent of its first-year class."

Of the facilities, students say classrooms are "poor" and "too cold." In the library, there are "not enough computer stations." Career Services also received a bad rap. "Anyone who relies solely on Career Services is unemployed," insisted a 3L. "Many

William B. Powers, Assoc. Dean for Admissions & Student Affairs
315 South Plymouth Court
Chicago, IL 60604
Tel: 800-537-4280 • Fax: 312-427-5136
Email: 6powers@jmls.edu
Internet: www.jmls.edu

John Marshall Law School

firms in the Chicago area traditionally hire from their old school, and the job market is extremely tight." Luckily, John Marshall's program is well respected and "well connected" in the sizable legal community of Chicago, where thousands of the law school's graduates form an alumni network that represents an invaluable resource to current students preparing to enter the job market.

Life outside the classroom received mixed reviews. While some students found that JMLS offered "a great sense of family," many others agreed that "John Marshall is a school populated by students who pass like ships in the night." A 2L claimed that: "Morale is low. Students here are very apathetic and for the most part vow not to support the school as alumni." The atmosphere at JMLS was said to be "very tense, especially during final examinations." Students remarked that the evening division tends to be "more cooperative" and "forms fewer cliques," while the day division is "more competitive."

Students also remonstrated JMLS for its failure to "enhance its reputation outside the Chicago area." However, most agreed that "the program really concentrates on how to teach you to be a good lawyer in Chicago" and expressed fundamental satisfaction with the training they received. JMLS "cranks out very practical lawyers with great writing, speaking, and trial skills." John Marshall "teaches its students how to practice law" and "provides an excellent practical education." One 3L was confident that, "From day one, a graduate can hold his or her own in any legal practice." Another 3L agreed: "In my work experiences, I believe I've had an advantage over students (coworkers) from schools that emphasize theory."

ADMISSIONS

On paper, John Marshall is the least selective of the six law schools in Chicago. Students with GPAs above 3.0 and LSAT scores above 150 can rest fairly assured of a positive admissions decision. For applicants who fall below the standards at JMLS, admission is doubtful. The JMLS application asks several pointed questions, though, and offers a ray of hope to those who can express their true desire to enter the legal profession through their writing. John Marshall is a good place for more nontraditional students, since the law school enrolls students of very diverse backgrounds and ages.

ACADEMICS

Student/faculty ratio	17:1
% female faculty	27
% minority faculty	8
Hours of study per day	3.85

Academic specialties:

International, Taxation, Community Economic and Housing Development, Law and Tech, Intellectual Property, Real Estate, Trial Advocacy

FINANCIAL FACTS

Tuition	$16,950
Cost of books	$700
Fees	$80
Room & board (on/off-campus)	NR/$12,224
% first-year students receiving aid	70
% all students receiving aid	70
% aid that is merit-based	3
% of all students receiving loans	67
% receiving scholarships	13
% of all students receiving assistantships	NR
Average grant	$17,380
Average graduation debt	$50,864

ADMISSIONS

# applications received	1,637
% applicants accepted	62
% acceptees attending	23
Average LSAT	150
Average undergrad GPA	2.99
Application fee	$50
Regular application	April 1
Regular notification	rolling
Rolling notification?	Yes
Early decision program?	No
Admission may be deferred?	Yes
Maximum length of deferment	1 year
Evening division offered?	Yes
Part-time accepted?	Yes
Gourman Report Rating	**2.14**

UNIVERSITY OF KANSAS
School of Law

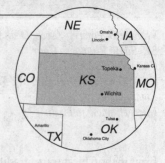

Among the advantages of residence in the Plains states is cheap and easy access to some of the nation's finest institutions of higher education. Kansas is no exception when it comes to the size and quality of its flagship public university. With 28,000 students and nearly 2,000 faculty members, the highly respected University of Kansas is one of the nation's largest comprehensive universities, and its midsize School of Law is one of the best in the region. The law school, which entered its second century in 1993, has long enjoyed a solid reputation in the professional and academic legal communities, a reputation that today derives in large part from the excellence of its 25-member faculty.

Current students had no problem defining those attributes that make KU such a good regional law school: the incredible price and their capable teachers. "Faculty! Faculty! Faculty!—the faculty is open and friendly and they make an effort to be available for students," cheered one 1L. Although many complained about the inconsistency of their teachers' abilities, most were extremely impressed by the quality of those teachers they liked.

The course of study that this faculty administers is notable not so much for any innovations as for its sheer strength within traditional bounds. The breadth of course offerings at Kansas is necessarily limited by the size of its faculty, and its clinical program, while broad in scope, is limited in size. Still, a wide range of joint-degree programs with various well-respected departments in the broader university's graduate division provides numerous opportunities for Kansas students to diversify their academic experiences.

Several students praised the tax and commercial law programs and the school's commitment to bestowing not only theoretical tools, but a strong ethical tradition. One 2L expressed gratitude that his pessimistic expectations of law school went unmet at Kansas: "The faculty expect you to behave like a professional.... The faculty are not interested in intimidating or humiliating students.... Ethical behavior is something you are expected to consider the moment you enter this program."

The happiest students we heard from were those particularly comfortable in a conservative Midwestern atmosphere. One cur-

Diane Lindeman, Director of Admissions
15th and Burdick Drive
Lawrence, KS 66045
Tel: 785-864-4378 • Fax: 785-864-5054
Email: admit@law.wpo.ukans.edu
Internet: www.lark.cc.ukans.edu/~kalaw/index.html

rent 1L gave his sound and simple reasons for feeling so content: "We are a healthy community, offering a Midwestern relaxed and yet urban environment with a good entertainment district, good shopping, and close proximity to Kansas City—America's best-kept secret."

Dissatisfaction was high among students approaching moving out of law school into the unfriendly legal market. As at many other schools, we heard a great deal of past criticism focused on the career services department. The jury is still out on the changes made by the new career services director.

Besides these standard gripes in the age of a downsized legal economy, there were also substantial (and some not so substantial) criticisms that the school may have more power to change, like increasing the number of practical-skills courses and providing a smoking lounge. One uncommonly perturbed 3L told us. "Much of what I've learned in law school isn't practical. Nothing that I've learned in law school was helpful or even applicable to the clerking that I've done over the summer." We heard repeated cries to diversify hiring and enrollment. A 1L offered a simple three-pronged solution to make the school a more perfect place: Bring in "more computers, more clinical programs, more chicks."

ADMISSIONS

Like every excellent public law school, the University of Kansas School of Law is swamped with applications from highly qualified prospective law students. Okay, 819 applications isn't quite a swamp, but it's all relative. With a first-year class of only about 170, Kansas must deny admission to the majority of applicants. Indeed, its numerical admissions standards rank Kansas among the fifty most selective law schools in the nation.

ACADEMICS

Student/faculty ratio	20:1
% female faculty	25
% minority faculty	12
Hours of study per day	3.73

FINANCIAL FACTS

Tuition (in/out-state)	$4,689/$11,620
Cost of books	$600
Fees (in/out-state)	$209/$209
% first-year students receiving aid	75
% all students receiving aid	75
% aid that is merit-based	NR
% of all students receiving loans	75
% receiving scholarships	34
% of all students receiving assistantships	7
Average grant	$8,500
Average graduation debt	$25,000

ADMISSIONS

# applications received	819
% applicants accepted	46
% acceptees attending	49
Average LSAT	157
LSAT range	143-171
Average undergrad GPA	3.40
GPA range	2.53-4.00
Application fee (in/out-state)	$40/NR
Regular application	March 15
Regular notification	rolling
Rolling notification?	Yes
Early decision program?	No
Admission may be deferred?	No
Evening division offered?	No
Part-time accepted?	No
Gourman Report Rating	**3.71**

UNIVERSITY OF KENTUCKY
College of Law

OVERVIEW

Type of school	public
Environment	city
Scholastic calendar	semester
Schedule	full-time only

STUDENTS

Enrollment of parent institution	22,731
Enrollment of law school	421
% male/female	66/34
% out-of-state	14
% minorities	8
Average age at entry	23

APPLICANTS ALSO LOOK AT

University of Louisville
Northern Kentucky University
Vanderbilt University
Wake Forest University
University of Virginia

SURVEY SAYS...

HITS
Socratic method
Library staff

MISSES
Practical lawyering skills
Not enough courses
Quality of teaching

EMPLOYMENT PROFILE

Firms recruiting on campus	75
Job placement rate (%)	94
% grads employed immediately	59
% grads employed within six months	94
Average starting salary	$36,000

Grads employed by field (%):

Academia	1
Business/industry	5
Government	3
Judicial clerkships	15
Private practice	69
Public interest	6
Other	1

The University of Kentucky College of Law is located in Lexington, a charming, safe city of 250,000 in Kentucky's beautiful Bluegrass region. The law school facility is "not in a great area of town," but it is "isolated from the main campus, and self-contained," which "allows the law school to function as its own social and educational community." While students contended that "UK is nationally underrated," few denied that this midsize public law school enjoys an unshakable reputation for excellence within Kentucky and the broader Ohio Valley area, where the vast majority of its graduates choose to practice. Alumni hold such positions as chief justice of the State Supreme Court, attorney general, and secretary of state of Kentucky. "UK College of Law is considered a major stepping stone for those who want to pursue a career in Kentucky politics."

Students here follow a traditional course of study, fully prescribed in the first year and almost completely elective in the second and third. Many of the respondents complained that UK needs to "expand curriculum" and add more opportunities for "real world experience" and "a larger offering of practical skills courses." UK is "very strong in business-related courses" and has "a good curriculum if you want to practice corporate law." There was little interest "in social issues or non-business areas of the law," though, "which results in a very narrow educational experience." Students said that "the dedication and accessibility of the faculty is UK's greatest strength." The Socratic method can become a bit stale at times but, overall, the "unpretentious" and "extremely personable" profs are "entertaining, knowledgeable, and explain things very well." However, some UK students said a few profs "interject entirely too many of their personal beliefs." The administration is "student-friendly," research resources are strong, and the library and library staff received high marks. Students griped that the 1970s-style facilities "probably looked cool twenty-five years ago" but are "uncomfortable and dirty" now. Also, a disgruntled 3L suggested, "Just get rid of Career Services, so we'll know up front not to rely on them." Other students offered positive comments about UK's placement program: "They do everything possible to help students find jobs [and] negotiate salaries."

Drusilla V. Bakert, Associate Dean
209 Law Building
Lexington, KY 40506
Tel: 606-257-1678 • Fax: 606-323-1061
Email: dbakert@pop.uky.edu
Internet: www.uky.edu/law/welcome.html

University of Kentucky

According to some responses, many students here are "high-strung" and "self-important twenty-two-year-olds" who "study constantly." One student claimed that "there is no sense of community among the students, because we are all trying to figure out how to beat each other for the extremely limited number of clerkships." A 2L disagreed, contending that "students are cool as hell" and there is only "friendly competition." Said one student, "We have parties together, play on sports teams, and even have 'prom' (Barrister's Ball)." A 3L told us: "I go to school with a lot of great people who look out for one another, hang out together, and party together. There are also some of the most evil, back-stabbing bastards I have ever met." UK has many students organizations, including a well-received Student Bar Association and a popular Women's Law Caucus.

Diversity could probably stand to improve at this "exceedingly white school." A 1L noted, "There are few African American students in my class. My entering class has more women than the 2L or 3L classes, but women are still far from equal in terms of numbers." Racial tension occasionally simmers, but as one student argued, "We are a southern school with the expected racial issues. However, at this school there does exist an awareness of the problem and a good faith effort on all sides to address the problems honestly, not merely from the need for political correctness."

ADMISSIONS

The University of Kentucky student body can compete numerically with some of the best law schools in the Midwest and nationally. In the last decade, application volume has grown by more than 250 percent, and the overall acceptance rate has plummeted from 61 percent to about 30 percent. The 1996 class had a median LSAT score of 159 and a median GPA of 3.40. In recent years, the profile for the entering class has been 34–48 percent women, 6–8 percent minority, and 14–22 percent out-of-state. The average age has ranged from twenty-two to twenty-five.

ACADEMICS	
Student/faculty ratio	19:1
% female faculty	34
% minority faculty	6
Hours of study per day	3.62

Academic specialties:
Civil Procedure, Commercial, Constitutional, Corporation Securities, Criminal, Environmental, Human Rights, International, Labor, Property, Taxation

FINANCIAL FACTS	
Tuition (in/out-state)	$4,620/$12,460
Cost of books	$500
Fees (in/out-state)	$336/$336
Room & board (on/off-campus)	$6,554/$6,554
% first-year students receiving aid	NR
% all students receiving aid	NR
% aid that is merit-based	90
% of all students receiving loans	71
% receiving scholarships	31
% of all students receiving assistantships	NR
Average grant	$2,800
Average graduation debt	$36,000

ADMISSIONS	
# applications received	891
% applicants accepted	38
% acceptees attending	39
Average LSAT	159
Average undergrad GPA	3.40
Application fee (in/out-state)	$25/$25
Regular application	rolling
Regular notification	rolling
Rolling notification?	Yes
Early decision program?	No
Admission may be deferred?	Yes
Maximum length of deferment	1 year
Evening division offered?	No
Part-time accepted?	No
Gourman Report Rating	**3.25**

LEWIS AND CLARK COLLEGE
Northwestern School of Law

OVERVIEW

Type of school	private
Environment	metropolis
Scholastic calendar	semester
Schedule	full-time or part-time

STUDENTS

Enrollment of parent institution	1,837
Enrollment of law school	631
% male/female	54/46
% out-of-state	74
% part-time	29
% minorities	11
% international (# of countries represented)	3 (8)
Average age at entry	26

APPLICANTS ALSO LOOK AT

University of Oregon
Willamette University
University of Washington
University of Colorado
University of California, Berkeley

SURVEY SAYS...

HITS
Left-leaning politics
Sleeping

MISSES
Practical lawyering skills
Library staff
Not enough courses

Though "it's difficult and stressful" like any other law school, Lewis and Clark's "challenging and effective" law program offers an "unintimidating" and "very user-friendly" educational experience. Nearly all of our survey respondents mentioned the "nationally renowned" and "truly top-notch" environmental law program as Lewis and Clark's greatest strength. The law school offers an LL.M. program for graduate law students and a formal certificate of specialization for J.D. candidates in this popular and growing field. Given the school's location in the Pacific Northwest, "opportunities to intern and extern are large." L&C has also cultivated a strong business and tax law curriculum. Other specialties, like criminal law, need improvement. L&C also "needs far more commercial classes" and an updated Legal Writing program. "Rudimentary technology" and classrooms that "resemble bunkers" drew extensive criticism. "The strength of the facility is its location," said one 2L. "Otherwise, it looks like a combination wood-grain bomb shelter and Ewok village." Also, "there simply aren't enough sections of popular classes, so scheduling can be a nightmare." On a positive note, L&C is home to "excellent research facilities," including Oregon's largest law library.

The "accessible" faculty at Lewis and Clark received massive praise for being "highly qualified, interesting," and "very knowledgeable." Students claimed that their "even-handed" professors are "funny" and "very conscientious about presenting arguments from all sides." First-year profs "ensure that you know the basics." Many employ the Socratic method, "but never to torture or embarrass" anyone. Students and faculty members often dine together, continuing to discuss questions long after classes end. "Mutual support" among faculty, students, and the "efficient administration" reigns supreme.

The "motivated" and "geographically diverse" student population here "tends to break down into crunchy, Birkenstock-clad, left-wing environmentalists or suit-wearing, corporate types," explained a 3L, but there are "very few minority students." L&C is "small enough that just about everyone knows everyone else, which can be either good or bad. If you are a super-liberal who

Grace Walters, Admissions Director
10015 Southwest Terwilliger Boulevard
Portland, OR 97219
Tel: 503-768-6613 • Fax: 503-768-6671
Email: lawadmss.@lclark.edu

Lewis and Clark College

voted for Ralph Nader, you will have plenty of friends. If you have a more pragmatic outlook, you may eat a few meals by yourself," explained a 2L. Others—liberal and conservative alike—disagree, saying that discussions in and out of class are open and tolerant. There is "some competition" here, but L&C still maintains a "close-knit feel." Students described themselves as "cooperative, friendly, and encouraging," and asserted that "student relations are perhaps the most significant attribute of this school."

Located six miles from downtown Portland, the L&C campus is "nestled adjacent to a sprawling 600-acre state park, within striking distance of the Pacific Ocean and Mount Hood, and near more microbreweries per capita than any other U.S. city. What more could a law student want?" asked a 2L. A glimpse of the sun, perhaps? The "rainy city" of Portland may provide "a great place to spend three years," but the weather "is as bad as everyone claims." Parking is also a drag, especially for 1Ls, who "have to hike from the undergraduate campus." When students aren't studying or running to their cars, "nature trails, camping, and fishing" are popular. The "quality of life here is extremely high." Occasionally, "classes will be held outside." Claimed a 2L: "This is the only place where you can be happy and be in law school at the same time."

ADMISSIONS

Lewis and Clark admits few students outside a relatively narrow range of high grade-point averages and test scores. The law school enrolls about 220 law students each fall, approximately 65 percent of whom are from outside Oregon. Competition to be among the chosen has grown increasingly fierce as national awareness of and respect for Lewis and Clark continues to increase. A decade ago, 77 percent of all applicants were admitted. Those days are long gone, as application volume has soared well over 200 percent. Consequently, numerical admission standards have skyrocketed, with the average LSAT score of entering students jumping an eye-popping 23 percentage points. Lewis and Clark's most recent entering class ranked among the sixty most highly qualified in the nation.

ACADEMICS

Student/faculty ratio	18:1
% female faculty	29
% minority faculty	5
Hours of study per day	4.10

FINANCIAL FACTS

Tuition	$14,740
Cost of books	NR
% first-year students receiving aid	NR
% all students receiving aid	NR
% aid that is merit-based	NR
% of all students receiving loans	NR
% receiving scholarships	NR
% of all students receiving assistantships	NR
Average grant	NR
Average graduation debt	NR

ADMISSIONS

# applications received	1,822
% applicants accepted	46
% acceptees attending	20
Average LSAT	161
LSAT range	139-179
Average undergrad GPA	3.25
GPA range	2.24-4.02
Application fee	$50
Regular application	March 15
Regular notification	rolling
Rolling notification?	Yes
Early decision program?	No
Admission may be deferred?	Yes
Maximum length of deferment	1 year
Evening division offered?	Yes
Part-time accepted?	Yes
Gourman Report Rating	**3.16**

LOUISIANA STATE UNIVERSITY
Paul M. Hébert Law Center

The Louisiana State University Law Center is a midsize public law school in close proximity to the offices of the state government in Baton Rouge. Founded in 1906, the law school has been providing a solid, inexpensive legal education to Louisiana residents as long as any school in the state. Like all the state's law schools, LSU must cover both Louisiana's civil law and the common law of the other 49 states. Unlike some Louisiana schools, however, LSU does not deal with the divergent systems separately. Instead, the law school has configured most courses so that the subject matter they address is considered within both contexts. This approach has its advantages. Because the Roman Law doctrine of the Napoleonic Code of France and Las Siete Partidas of Spain form the cornerstone of Louisiana law and that of many other countries, such as Canada, Japan, Thailand, the Philippines, Turkey, and much of Europe and Latin America, LSU is somewhat justified in regarding its entire curriculum as a course of study in comparative law. Some added bonuses available thanks to this focus on international law are a summer study program at the University of Aix-Marseille III Law School at Aix-en-Provence, France, and the master of Civil Law (M.C.L.) option.

LSU offers a unique and useful program even for the future lawyer who does not plan to practice in Louisiana. Be that as it may, most LSU students do choose to remain in the state after completing their degrees. Applications volume at LSU has risen significantly in recent years, but the overall selectivity of the admissions process remains moderate.

According to the admissions brochure, the faculty is a strong suit of LSU Law Center. Says the brochure: "The Journal of Legal Education recently reported that the LSU law faculty ranked second out of 68 schools of similar size in the quality of published works. When compared to the 169 law schools approved by the American Bar Association, the Law Center was listed as tenth in the nation. The quality of faculty writings, according to the Journal of Jurimetrics, has been displayed by consistent citation of LSU faculty work in reported cases throughout the country, in

Beth Loup, *Director of Admissions*
Room 210, LSU Law Center
Baton Rouge, LA 70803
Tel: 504-388-8646 • Fax: 504-388-8202

other journals and books, and by the ranking of the Louisiana Law Review as one of the top 15 law reviews in the United States."

LSU requires 97 hours of credit for graduation, "one of the highest and most demanding curriculums in the nation," according to its own publication, and class attendance and daily preparation are mandatory for every one of those credit hours. All second-year students not on Law Review are required to participate in a year-long moot court case. "Grade inflation is unknown at LSU." The solid work ethic the school instills will hopefully make the long hours most students look forward to in private practice seem luxurious.

Overall, LSU Law Center offers a singular, strong education that prepares students for law practice in Louisiana and beyond.

ADMISSIONS

Happily for the prospective student, the Louisiana State University Law Center ranks in the bottom half of all law schools in terms of the numerical admission standards to which it holds applicants. But despite the law school's very generous overall acceptance rate of 46 percent, those applicants whose numbers aren't quite in line with the averages you see at right are not likely to be offered admission to LSU.

ACADEMICS

Student/faculty ratio	16:1
% female faculty	9
% minority faculty	6
Hours of study per day	3.97

FINANCIAL FACTS

Tuition (in/out-state)	$3,922/$8,542
Cost of books	$400
Room & board (on/off-campus)	$5,200/$9,000
% first-year students receiving aid	NR
% all students receiving aid	41
% aid that is merit-based	NR
% of all students receiving loans	NR
% receiving scholarships	NR
% of all students receiving assistantships	NR
Average grant	NR
Average graduation debt	NR

ADMISSIONS

# applications received	947
% applicants accepted	28
% acceptees attending	
Average LSAT	153
Average undergrad GPA	3.32
Application fee (in/out-state)	$25/$25
Regular application	February 1
Regular notification	Early spring
Rolling notification?	Yes
Early decision program?	No
Admission may be deferred?	No
Evening division offered?	No
Part-time accepted?	No
Gourman Report Rating	**3.38**

UNIVERSITY OF LOUISVILLE
Louis D. Brandeis School of Law

OVERVIEW

Type of school	public
Environment	metropolis
Scholastic calendar	semester
Schedule	full-time or part-time

STUDENTS

Enrollment of parent institution	21,218
Enrollment of law school	504
% male/female	51/49
% out-of-state	18
% part-time	17
% minorities	12
% international (# of countries represented)	1 (4)
Average age at entry	25

APPLICANTS ALSO LOOK AT

University of Kentucky
Northern Kentucky University
University of Cincinnati
University of Dayton
Vanderbilt University

SURVEY SAYS...

HITS
Research resources
Library staff
Sleeping

MISSES
Practical lawyering skills
Not enough courses

EMPLOYMENT PROFILE

Firms recruiting on campus	26
% grads employed immediately	38
% grads employed within six months	95
Average starting salary	$32,000

Grads employed by field (%):

Academia	2
Business/industry	7
Government	11
Judicial clerkships	6
Private practice	60
Public interest	3
Other	11

Founded in 1846, the University of Louisville School of Law is Kentucky's oldest law school and the nation's fifth oldest in continuous operation. Tradition is definitely a watchword at this school and in this city, which has a decidedly more southern atmosphere than its geographic location might lead one to believe. The school is particularly proud of the legacy it inherited from former Supreme Court Justice Louis D. Brandeis, who gave the university his personal library and also left a legacy of public service. The University of Louisville was one of the first law schools in the nation—and the only one in Kentucky—to institute a thirty-hour pro bono requirement for all students. In fact, the school's Samuel L. Greenbaum Public Service Program has served as a model for many other ABA-accredited law schools that are interested in increasing their service to their communities.

Many students cited the mandatory pro bono work and the school's commitment to public service as Louisville's greatest strengths. They were equally quick to praise the traditional classroom instruction at their school. "The professors are the greatest strength at UL," opined one 2L. "Access to the best legal minds provides the edge to success in law school." Another 2L offered a slightly different view: "Some professors are extremely accessible. Others are standoffish. The new faculty tend to be in the first category; the tenured faculty tend to be in the second."

There was a high degree of satisfaction in terms of the school's atmosphere. Many found it to be better than expected. A first-year student wrote, "Before enrolling, I had heard that this school was fairly competitive. Thus far, I have not experienced any competitiveness. The vast majority of my classmates are very friendly and helpful." A classmate concurred, stating, "We all share our resources and try to help each other." Another first year described Louisville as "a joint venture between students, faculty, and administration all working together toward a common goal."

If that goal is employment, the joint venture seems to be working. Many students thought that the greatest strength of the school was its local reputation. As one student said, "The school is the

Jerie Torbeck, Assistant Dean for Admissions
2301 South Third Street
Louisville, KY 40292
Tel: 502-852-6358 • Fax: 502-852-0862
Email: jltorb01@ulkyvm.louisville.edu
Internet: www.louisville.edu/brandeislaw/

University of Louisville

only [law] school in the city of Louisville, so it has a monopoly on the legal resources of the community." The school's strong regional reputation is not enough for some students, who suggested that the school work on developing a more national reputation. Amazingly, not a discouraging word was voiced about the career placement program. One second year student glowingly reported, "The director of the program works tirelessly for the benefit of students and alumni."

While most students shared a positive view of their law school, they still mentioned areas where improvement is needed. Surprisingly, one of those areas was public service. A 2L wrote that when the school begins to provide "debt relief for students who go into public service, funding internships for summer placements, and increasing internship opportunities, the school will become a desperately needed center for public interest law." Like most critics of the school, he found a bright side: "The foundation is there, though. Now we just need some motivated student leaders and a bit more vision in the administration." Other students complained that the physical plant of the law school could stand improvement, especially in terms of correcting heat and air conditioning problems, and providing a cafeteria.

Most of the students we polled called for an increase in the number of minorities at the law school. However, students were happy that the "student body does have an excellent diversity of age [because] older students bring great real world perspective to classroom discussions." Whatever their criticisms of the school, though, students generally appeared satisfied. As a 1L wrote, "There is never a reason to be bored at Louisville. There's always something interesting to do."

ADMISSIONS

A solid regional reputation and a bargain basement tuition make the University of Louisville School of Law's admissions process fairly competitive. While the numerical credentials of the average Louisville student are equal to or slightly higher than the national average, the overall acceptance rate at the law school, particularly for out-of-state applicants, is relatively low at 39 percent. Happily for the prospective Louisville student, the law school does admit applicants across a range of grade point averages and test scores.

ACADEMICS

Student/faculty ratio	18:1
% female faculty	29
% minority faculty	11
Hours of study per day	3.47

Academic specialties:
Commercial, Corporation Securities, Environmental, International, Taxation, Intellectual Property, Health

FINANCIAL FACTS

Tuition (in/out-state)	$4,620/$12,460
Cost of books	$752
Fees (in/out-state)	$230/$230
Room & board (on/off-campus)	$4,986/$5,988
% first-year students receiving aid	30
% all students receiving aid	79
% aid that is merit-based	7
% of all students receiving loans	69
% receiving scholarships	12
% of all students receiving assistantships	7
Average grant	$5,216
Average graduation debt	$39,135

ADMISSIONS

# applications received	922
% applicants accepted	39
% acceptees attending	45
Average LSAT	155
LSAT range	132-171
Average undergrad GPA	3.30
GPA range	1.63-3.97
Application fee (in/out-state)	$30/$30
Regular application	rolling
Regular notification	rolling
Rolling notification?	Yes
Early decision program?	No
Admission may be deferred?	Yes
Maximum length of deferment	1 year
Evening division offered?	Yes
Part-time accepted?	Yes
Gourman Report Rating	**3.28**

LOYOLA MARYMOUNT UNIVERSITY
Loyola Law School

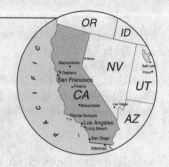

Loyola's recently completed expansion, designed by architect Frank O. Gehry, has radically transformed the previously nondescript downtown campus of California's largest law school into one of Los Angeles's many architecturally significant spaces. The new campus reflects Loyola's "energy and self confidence," according to the Dean, who calls the architecture "both provocative and congenial."

Loyola's admissions brochure describes a law school whose strong day and evening J.D. programs have earned it a well-deserved reputation in the L.A. legal community as a training ground for highly skilled practical attorneys. Loyola has always emphasized practical training: Its traditional academic curriculum is supplemented by a number of well-run clinical programs and a highly-regarded trial advocacy program. The Externship Program, available to second- and third-year students, places them in judicial clerkships, public interest organizations, and government organizations. There is also an entertainment law practicum, which provides hands-on experience and has a required classroom component. While students appreciated the practical training, they had some critical comments for the legal research and writing courses, which they said should be integrated and improved. Effective for the 1997–98 academic year, these courses have been combined into one skills course.

All students matriculating after fall 1994 must complete a mandatory public service requirement in order to graduate. Each student must contribute 40 hours of uncompensated supervised legal service to the disadvantaged in the community. The school hopes the experience will improve students' practical skills and impress upon them the need for lawyers to give back to society.

Overall, students were satisfied with the education they were getting at Loyola. Many respondents highlighted their professors' practical knowledge. Said one, "Teachers know a lot about being a lawyer, as opposed to having only theoretical knowledge." Professors are not "ivory tower academics," commented another. Professors are also very accessible and approachable. Loyola students believe they graduate ready to "hit the ground

Carmen Ramirez, Assistant Director of Admissions
919 South Albany Street
Los Angeles, CA 90015
Tel: 213-736-1180 • Fax: 213-736-6523
Email: lawadmis@lmulaw.lmu.edu
Internet: www.law.lmu.edu

**Loyola Marymount
University**

running." Many students praised the "sense of community" and "willingness to help one another," although they said the competition was "intense." They called their classmates "wonderfully diverse."

On the negative side, some students criticize the administration as "unresponsive" and "obsessively image-conscious." According to one 3L, "The administration is openly mistrusted and maligned by students, and has earned at least part of its poor reputation." Specifically, a few say communication between students and the administration could be improved, and that student input should be heeded. Like law students nearly everywhere, Loyola students criticize the placement office, specifically the policy of charging firms to interview on campus and the focus on top-ranked students. Recently, students panned Loyola's facilities, especially the computer facilities and the library; however, since then, the school has improved its technological facilities, and now offers 45 general-use terminals, 30 Lexis or Westlaw terminals, and laptops.

All in all, Loyola is home to a relatively happy and confident student body ("We're #3 in LA and rising"), which nonetheless sees real room for improvement. This evenhanded assessment of the school's strengths and weaknesses offered by a Loyola 3L sums things up: "Loyola is a school blessed with many intelligent and inspiring professors, and cursed with administrators more interested in architecture and alumni donations than in career services or alumni access to the school's resources."

ADMISSIONS

Applications volume is very heavy, and Loyola admits less than 40 percent of the more than 3,000 who apply annually. Numerical admissions standards are high, having risen significantly in recent years as more qualified applicants have added Loyola to their lists.

ACADEMICS	
Student/faculty ratio	22:1
% female faculty	34
% minority faculty	21
Hours of study per day	3.19

FINANCIAL FACTS	
Tuition	$20,474
Cost of books	$620
Fees	$260
Room & board (on/off-campus)	NR/$8,955
% first-year students receiving aid	81
% all students receiving aid	82
% aid that is merit-based	8
% of all students receiving loans	75
% receiving scholarships	12
% of all students receiving assistantships	NR
Average grant	$12,800
Average graduation debt	$45,000

ADMISSIONS	
# applications received	3,021
% applicants accepted	39
% acceptees attending	37
Average LSAT	158
LSAT range	148-177
Average undergrad GPA	3.25
GPA range	2.40-4.00
Application fee	$50
Regular application	rolling
Regular notification	rolling
Rolling notification?	Yes
Early decision program?	No
Admission may be deferred?	No
Evening division offered?	Yes
Part-time accepted?	Yes
Gourman Report Rating	**4.22**

LOYOLA UNIVERSITY, CHICAGO
School of Law

Founded in 1870 by Jesuit priests, Loyola is Chicago's oldest university. Just as its hometown has long since put away any inferiority complex stemming from its designation as America's Second City, the School of Law of Loyola University, Chicago has no reason to doubt itself even if it is thought of as the city's "third" law school. A law school could certainly do worse than to occupy the third slot behind heavy hitters Northwestern and U. Chicago. And a law school could certainly do worse on its own terms than this fine midsize institution: Loyola, Chicago not only enjoys an extremely solid regional reputation, but it also appears to have one of the happier student bodies in the region. The program that Loyola's roughly 500 day and 250 evening students follow is quite comprehensive.

The breadth of its traditional classroom curriculum is enhanced by the programs of its Institute for Health Law, and its practical-skills offerings are extensive. Loyola, a nationally recognized leader in the growing field of health law, runs one of the nation's few graduate law programs in this field, and its J.D. students have access to a broad array of courses in this subject. Other special programs include: International Law, in which students can travel to London or Rome to study law for a brief period; and the CIVITAS Child Law Center, which prepares students "for professional careers in the service of children." The school runs two clinics: the Loyola University Community Law Center, which provides legal assistance to those who cannot afford private legal representation; and a Federal Tax Clinic. Loyola also takes great pride in its skills programs, particularly in its trial advocacy courses, which, along with the extensive variety of other clinical offerings, draw many students.

The strength of these programs appears to figure highly in students' overall satisfaction with their experience at Loyola. Asked to name their school's greatest strengths, many cited "the focus of the curriculum on the practical aspects of being a lawyer in addition to the theoretical underpinnings of the law." Indeed, few of the students we heard from expressed any doubts about the quality of their professional preparation. "Loyola is primarily a school for the Midwestern general practitioner or litigator,"

Karen Scribano, Office of Admission and Financial Aid
1 East Pearson
Chicago, IL 60611
Tel: 312-915-7170 • Fax: 312-915-7906
Email: law-admissions@luc.edu
Internet: www.luc.edu/schools/law

Loyola University, Chicago

explained one 2L, "and a great one at that." As often as not, Loyola students explained their satisfaction with the school in terms of its atmosphere. "If you're looking for a place with a comfortable atmosphere in which everyone becomes friends as opposed to competitive enemies," wrote another 2L, "then Loyola is the place to be." Nearly all agreed on this matter. "The atmosphere is very friendly," said one 3L, "which makes coping with the pressures of law school much easier." Students gave as much credit for this state of affairs to their faculty and administration as to themselves. "The most prestigious professors here also enjoy teaching," wrote a 3L, "and they contribute to a strong sense of community by being available and interacting with students." "Loyola has a strong commitment to providing students full value for their tuition," she continued, "and to being responsive to their input. The student here is an integral part of an ambitious academic community."

Loyola recently added a new law library, with seating for 378 students, and 142 study carrels with the capability of connecting a laptop to the school's computer network. The Student Computer Center at the library offers a number of computer terminals and access to Lexis and Westlaw systems of legal research.

We heard some complaints about the inconsistency of teaching abilities among their faculty. "There are some excellent professors here," allowed one 3L, "but there are others who are very poor. Unfortunately, some of the poorer ones teach the required first-year bar courses." Several evening students also complained about the relative lack of flexibility in part-time scheduling and the perceived lack of attention given the evening division in general. Overall, however, even those students who were most critical on this and other matters expressed a clear sense of well-being and of satisfaction with their decision to attend Loyola.

ADMISSIONS

Any law school that receives more than 10 applications for every spot in its first-year class is going to disappoint more than a few well-qualified applicants. Such is the case with the Loyola University, Chicago School of Law. Although the law school admits 40 percent of all applicants—a relatively generous acceptance rate for a school of this caliber—it holds those applicants to high numerical standards.

ACADEMICS

Student/faculty ratio	19:1
% female faculty	26
% minority faculty	11
Hours of study per day	3.34

FINANCIAL FACTS

Tuition	$19,390
Cost of books	$900
Room & board (on/off-campus)	NR/$13,250
% first-year students receiving aid	NR
% all students receiving aid	NR
% aid that is merit-based	54
% of all students receiving loans	77
% receiving scholarships	33
% of all students receiving assistantships	1
Average grant	$5,500
Average graduation debt	$47,500

ADMISSIONS

# applications received	2,329
% applicants accepted	40
% acceptees attending	26
Average LSAT	158
Average undergrad GPA	3.27
Application fee	$45
Early application	January 15
Early notification	February 15
Regular application	April 1
Regular notification	rolling
Rolling notification?	Yes
Early decision program?	Yes
Admission may be deferred?	Yes
Maximum length of deferment	1 year
Evening division offered?	Yes
Part-time accepted?	Yes
Gourman Report Rating	**3.48**

LOYOLA UNIVERSITY, NEW ORLEANS
School of Law

OVERVIEW

Type of school	private
Environment	metropolis
Scholastic calendar	semester
Schedule	full-time or part-time

STUDENTS

Enrollment of parent institution	2,772
Enrollment of law school	687
% male/female	53/47
% out-of-state	53
% minorities	20
% international (# of countries represented)	NR (3)
Average age at entry	26

APPLICANTS ALSO LOOK AT

Tulane University
Southern University
Florida State University
University of Florida
Nova Southeastern University

SURVEY SAYS...

HITS
Studying
Legal writing
Students feel well prepared

MISSES
Quality of teaching
Not enough courses
Library staff

EMPLOYMENT PROFILE

Firms recruiting on campus	85
Job placement rate (%)	84
% grads employed immediately	71
% grads employed within six months	85
Average starting salary	$40,000

Grads employed by field (%):

Academia	1
Business/industry	5
Government	11
Judicial clerkships	18
Private practice	63
Public interest	3
Other	1

The Loyola University School of Law in New Orleans is located just a few miles from the heart of the city's French Quarter. Indeed, Loyola is very much a Louisiana school and its curriculum reflects the state's unique history and blend of legal traditions. The law of every state but Louisiana is rooted in the English common law, a system in which the law is derived both from statutes and judicial decisions or precedent. Louisiana's French and Spanish past has influenced its civil law system, in which law is explicitly codified. The two legal systems, common law and civil law, are very different, and to practice in Louisiana a lawyer must know both.

At Loyola, both common law and civil law programs are available in the day division, but only the civil law curriculum is taught at night. Students may elect either course of study, or choose to set up a curriculum containing elements of both. However, those who must take both civil law and common law classes sometimes say that they would like fewer required classes and more electives. One disgruntled 2L commented, "Loyola is one of the few schools that have required courses all three years. The faculty claims these required courses help to better prepare us for the bar. Loyola, however, has a lower bar-passage rate than other Louisiana schools, who do not require courses after first year. Go figure." Loyola also offers joint degree programs in communications, religious studies, business administration, urban and regional planning, and public administration. Not surprisingly, in light of the curriculum, nearly half of Loyola's students come from and practice in Louisiana.

Another thing that sets Loyola apart from most other law schools is its emphasis on the Jesuit tradition. According to the school's philosophy, "While the Christian tradition is not wedded to any one philosophical, scientific, aesthetic, or political ideology, it is not compatible with every point of view. The Christian view of reality is concerned ultimately with choice and action, and is premised on the concept of moral responsibility. . . . [I]t is also deeply concerned with the promotion of service to others rather than self-aggrandizement." The Jesuit tradition also stresses intellectual rigor and individual excellence. A 2L wrote that "the Jesuit tradition focuses on the entire person and this is reflected in our diverse student body. While most law schools tend to look

Michele Allison-Davis, Dean of Admissions
Box 904, 7214 Saint Charles Avenue
New Orleans, LA 70118
Tel: 504-861-5575 • Fax: 504-861-5772
Email: 1admit@beta.loyno.edu
Internet: www.loyno.edu

solely at GPA and LSAT scores, Loyola looks deeper, including life experiences, and this is reflected in more interesting classroom discussion."

Students at Loyola can take advantage of numerous opportunities to gain practical experience. One 2L praised the law clinic, which "affords 3Ls a chance to actually try cases and develop necessary skills prior to graduation." Others praised the clinical experiences, which include the Gillis Poverty Law Center and the Public Law Center, but wished that there were more such opportunities available. Clinic participation is limited to third years, and space is limited.

However, other opportunities are available. A second year related his experiences: "I have gotten great internships, externships, and clerkships. Virtually all of the judges on the state supreme court, federal district court, and various city courts are Loyola grads." Many respondents listed the school's reputation within the Louisiana legal community as one of its strongest points. Although some complained of a tough grading curve, others pointed out that a student's class rank rather than GPA was often more important to potential employers familiar with Loyola. "The school's greatest strength is in the alumni base," said a 2L. "The resources available throughout the community far outweigh those made available to students enrolled at the three other law schools in the state."

Besides complaining about the "C" curve, which "makes everyone's GPA ridiculously low," some students also voiced concerns over the competitive atmosphere at Loyola. A 1L wrote, "Overall, I am very unimpressed with the way students treat each other. There is a great deal of backstabbing going on and I do not like it." The student did note, "There are many people who are not involved in what I am referring to." A few respondents also expressed disapproval of the research/computer facilities. "I've seen elementary schools with better facilities," observed one first-year student.

ADMISSIONS

Loyola University Law School, New Orleans, can provide an opportunity for students who may not have stellar academic pasts, but aim for outstanding futures. The school's overall acceptance rate of 57 percent does not hold its students to particularly high numerical standards.

ACADEMICS

Student/faculty ratio	22:1
% female faculty	20
% minority faculty	12
Hours of study per day	4.23

FINANCIAL FACTS

Tuition	$17,515
Cost of books	$600
Fees	$476
Room & board (on/off-campus)	$5,660/$8,500
% first-year students receiving aid	84
% all students receiving aid	87
% aid that is merit-based	NR
% of all students receiving loans	83
% receiving scholarships	25
% of all students receiving assistantships	5
Average grant	$6,572
Average graduation debt	$63,840

ADMISSIONS

# applications received	1,433
% applicants accepted	57
% acceptees attending	29
Average LSAT	152
LSAT range	143-164
Average undergrad GPA	3.00
GPA range	2.19-4.00
Application fee	$20
Regular application	rolling
Regular notification	rolling
Rolling notification?	Yes
Early decision program?	No
Admission may be deferred?	Yes
Maximum length of deferment	2 years
Evening division offered?	Yes
Part-time accepted?	Yes
Gourman Report Rating	2.49

UNIVERSITY OF MAINE
Maine School of Law

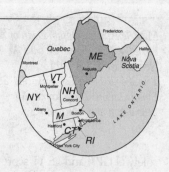

How small is the University of Maine School of Law? With a total student population of 277, it is one of the smallest nationally accredited law schools in the U.S. Many courses have enrollments of fewer than thirty, and it isn't uncommon for upper-level courses to have under ten students. The intimate size and "close relationships with professors" are the school's greatest strengths. Maine also has the rare distinction of being the state's only law school, a fact that sits well with students looking for local externships and employment in the state.

Maine's solid core curriculum offers "a strong emphasis on the traditional meat and potatoes courses." The law school's special strengths lie in environmental and marine law, international law, and business. Though a few distinctive programs are offered within these specialties—including the Ocean and Coastal Law Program, the Marine Law Institute, and exchange programs with two Canadian law schools—a 1L griped that "Maine doesn't take enough advantage of the strengths that it has." Additional complaints stem from the rather limited number of clinical programs and lack of electives. Students were divided on the quality of the legal writing program. Some said it "needs a lot of improvement," while others contended that "the first-year legal writing and research program is excellent." The "witty, accessible, and unpretentious" professors here are "dedicated to doing their jobs the right way" and "very involved in student life." Many profs are "the experts in the state of Maine." Mused a 1L: "I sometimes feel the professors are retired comedians, but when you've stopped laughing, you realize how much you've learned." Other students say the "mostly white male faculty" varies widely "politically, intellectually, and in ability to inspire." The disaffected urge their administration to hire "more profs who are still practicing law and who can bring their experiences to the classroom."

According to students, "very old and inadequate facilities," including a "leaky library" that "needs to be expanded and modernized" and a "cramped and uncomfortable 1L lecture room," are Maine's most glaring negatives. Maine "needs more computers" and a more comfortable lounge and cafeteria area. Also, in terms of support for incoming 1Ls, students warned:

[title line in header]

Barbara Gauditz, Assistant Dean
246 Deering Avenue
Portland, ME 04102
Tel: 207-780-4341 • Fax: 207-780-4239
Internet: www.usm.maine.edu

"You're on your own for housing, logistics, and information." On a more positive note, "Career Services is surprisingly well staffed, well organized, and effective," especially for students looking for jobs in the New England area.

Outside the confines of the building itself, students say Maine offers a fabulous environment in which to "spend three years or the rest of your life." The surrounding area of Portland—Maine's largest city—has all the charm you might expect, with spectacular scenery, friendly people, and clean air to boot. The school is also "within walking distance of the ocean, and within half hour of some of the best skiing and hiking in the East." One student said, "Portland is the greatest city in the world for law students" because there are "not too many distractions but enough to keep school from getting to you." And, believe it or not, "the nightlife and the social opportunities are endless." Students describe themselves as "intelligent, educated, and ambitious" as well as "concerned with Maine's political issues" and the environment. The school's uncommonly small size allows for a "a real sense of togetherness" found at few other institutions. "This school has 'real people,'" observed a 2L, "which makes for a pleasant environment in which to study and prepare for a career in the law." While the atmosphere is not exactly "chummy," it's definitely "noncompetitive" and "extremely cooperative." "It reminds me a lot of a small, top-rate liberal arts school," comments a 1L. Maine "seems to have a penchant for attracting students who are willing to work together to try and get through" the law school experience. "Everyone is friendly here. I don't think you find that at many law schools," said a 2L. "In general, law school sucks," advised another 1L, "but if you are going to go anywhere, go to Maine."

ADMISSIONS

If your dream is to attend law school in the state of Maine, this public institution is your only shot. Although numerical standards here are relatively moderate (roughly a B+ GPA combined with an LSAT score at about the 70th percentile), the school is relatively selective. With an entering class of approximately one hundred, the admissions committee affords careful consideration to whom it will invite into each entering class. The average age of entering students is twenty-nine years old.

ACADEMICS

Student/faculty ratio	17:1
% female faculty	35
% minority faculty	0
Hours of study per day	4.32

FINANCIAL FACTS

Tuition (in/out-state)	$8,280/$16,440
Cost of books	$1,050
Fees (in/out-state)	$300/$300
Room & board (on/off-campus)	$6,780/$6,780
% first-year students receiving aid	80
% all students receiving aid	80
% aid that is merit-based	20
% of all students receiving loans	81
% receiving scholarships	41
% of all students receiving assistantships	NR
Average grant	$2,961
Average graduation debt	$38,000

ADMISSIONS

# applications received	672
% applicants accepted	50
% acceptees attending	32
Average LSAT	155
LSAT range	134-173
Average undergrad GPA	3.27
GPA range	2.31-3.96
Application fee (in/out-state)	$25/$25
Regular application	February 15
Regular notification	rolling
Rolling notification?	Yes
Early decision program?	No
Admission may be deferred?	Yes
Maximum length of deferment	1 year
Evening division offered?	No
Part-time accepted?	No
Gourman Report Rating	**2.56**

MARQUETTE UNIVERSITY
Law School

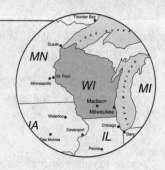

OVERVIEW

Type of school	private
Environment	metropolis
Scholastic calendar	semester
Schedule	full-time only

STUDENTS

Enrollment of parent institution	6,890
Enrollment of law school	475
% male/female	59/41
% out-of-state	62
% minorities	14
% international (# of countries represented)	NR (5)
Average age at entry	25

APPLICANTS ALSO LOOK AT

University of Wisconsin
University of Minnesota
DePaul University
Loyola University, Chicago
Hamline University

SURVEY SAYS...

HITS
Practical lawyering skills
Practical experience
Library staff

MISSES
Not enough courses

EMPLOYMENT PROFILE

Job placement rate (%)	88
% grads employed immediately	50
% grads employed within six months	88
Average starting salary	$36,126

The Marquette University Law School is a "lawyer's law school" that "provides an extremely practical education." The traditional J.D. curriculum emphasizes the "basic lawyering skills" and ethics typical of a Jesuit education. It is supplemented by a growing number of skills courses and stimulating, hands-on clinical internship programs. Students applaud the D.A. and Public Defender clinics as well as Marquette's affiliation with the National Sports Law Institute. The "caring administration" is highly regarded, including the dean, who "takes an active interest in the students." Praise for the "helpful and accessible" faculty here is abundant. Although some students responded that the professors are "intellectual giants" who "have all practiced the type of law they are teaching," their "attitude of superiority" can be annoying. The administration "seems to be trying to attract a younger, newer breed of faculty with some success," a strategy that has resulted in a noticeable gap between "old-line faculty" who "are very traditional and Socratic" and the younger faculty who "are quite liberal."

"Fortunately, the Marquette faculty is much brighter than the lighting in the library," quipped a 2L. While some students crowed that they have access to "the best law library in Wisconsin," others couldn't get past the noise level. Said one, "I've had quieter moments waiting for the bus." The library and its staff received mixed reviews. According to one student, "The library space was designed by intoxicated architects." However, others felt that once the "gradual overhaul" of the computer system is complete, "it will add tremendously to the entire school's success."

The ethnic diversity here is not much to write about. "I think the student body would be greatly improved if there were more minority students, particularly African Americans," argued a 2L. "The interjection of more diverse opinion would greatly improve discourse in this school." One positive outcome of the homogeneity here is a great degree of community. "Marquette's strength is its people," asserted a 2L. "The Law School offers a supportive, friendly," and "very comfortable" environment. Study groups are "quite popular," and "older students are helpful in giving

Steven M. Barkan, Assistant Dean for Admissions
1103 West Wisconsin Avenue
Milwaukee, WI 53233
Tel: 414-288-6767 • Fax: 414-288-5914
Internet: www.mu.edu/dept/law

Marquette University

advice to younger students about classes, professors, and job prospects." A 1L agreed: "Marquette is striving to become a 'kinder, gentler' law school. The curriculum is challenging, but supported by student interaction, faculty encouragement, and strong community involvement."

Social opportunities are plentiful. Milwaukee is the economic center of Wisconsin and "a fantastic city." A 1L contended: "If you've never checked out the summer and winter festivals in downtown Milwaukee, you've missed some of the greatest social events ever put together." A "great way to meet your classmates and students from other classes" is the unique "Thursday Night Bar Review," a migrating event during which students inspect a different Milwaukee bar each week.

Marquette's "career-minded" law students told us that "it's very difficult to find jobs outside the Midwest coming from Marquette," but "if you want to build contacts in Milwaukee, this is the place to be." A "huge alumni base," made up of senior partners, judges, and local bigwigs, offers many opportunities to work in firms, corporations, government offices, and public interest organizations. Students asserted that their school's most appealing characteristics stem from its close ties to Milwaukee's courts and law community, providing graduates with a strong, practical legal education and likely venues to market their degrees. "Marquette is a great school. We know we aren't a Minnesota or Northwestern, but…at Marquette you receive a practical education that prepares you to be an attorney right away."

ADMISSIONS

Marquette admits more than one-third of the candidates it considers and ranks in about the middle of all U.S. law schools in terms of numerical admissions standards. The 1996 entering class of 150 students broke down like this: 44 percent women, 7 percent ethnic minorities, and 66 percent Wisconsin residents. The average LSAT score was 156 (73.4 percentile) and the average GPA was 3.07. Roughly 33 percent had worked for two or more years before applying. The average age of 1996 incoming students was twenty-five.

ACADEMICS
Student/faculty ratio	22:1
% female faculty	30
% minority faculty	8
Hours of study per day	3.70

FINANCIAL FACTS
Tuition	$17,310
Cost of books	$800
% first-year students receiving aid	85
% all students receiving aid	90
% aid that is merit-based	11
% of all students receiving loans	85
% receiving scholarships	30
% of all students receiving assistantships	NR
Average grant	NR
Average graduation debt	$48,000

ADMISSIONS
# applications received	1,086
% applicants accepted	39
% acceptees attending	32
Average LSAT	156
Average undergrad GPA	3.07
Application fee	$35
Regular application	April 1
Regular notification	rolling
Rolling notification?	Yes
Early decision program?	No
Admission may be deferred?	No
Evening division offered?	Yes
Part-time accepted?	No
Gourman Report Rating	4.18

UNIVERSITY OF MARYLAND
School of Law

OVERVIEW

Type of school	public
Environment	metropolis
Scholastic calendar	semester
Schedule	full-time or part-time

STUDENTS

Enrollment of parent institution	6,311
Enrollment of law school	856
% male/female	50/50
% out-of-state	21
% part-time	30
% minorities	29
% international (# of countries represented)	1 (NR)
Average age at entry	26

APPLICANTS ALSO LOOK AT

University of Baltimore
George Washington University
American University
Georgetown University
Catholic University of America

SURVEY SAYS...

HITS
Practical experience
Broad range of courses
Practical lawyering skills

MISSES
Quality of teaching
Not enough courses

EMPLOYMENT PROFILE

Firms recruiting on campus	50
Job placement rate (%)	85
% grads employed immediately	50
% grads employed within six months	85
Average starting salary	$43,479

Grads employed by field (%):

Academia	1
Business/industry	18
Government	10
Judicial clerkships	21
Military	2
Private practice	42
Public interest	6

According to the students at the University of Maryland, their law school is "arguably the best public law school in the country." It's definitely one of the oldest and, with very low tuition, numerous clinics, and extensive resources (which rival those of many larger, more expensive law schools), UM is easily one of the best buys on the East Coast. The law school's traditional curriculum, administered by a large, respected faculty, is strong and broad. The first-year program here is "rigorous" and innovative, "and grades are on a very strict curve." In addition to a legal methods requirement for all 1Ls, Maryland students must take either "Legal Theory and Practice" (effectively a clinical offering) or a clinical offering in the second or third year. "Maryland puts a high priority on giving students practical skills," and the many clinical programs available here "make the degree very marketable." Part of the school's mission is to "provide a wellspring of pro bono legal services by training students to represent citizens who are dispossessed or disenfranchised." Students represent real clients, arguing their cases in court under faculty supervision. Another notable program is the Law and Entrepreneurship Program, which enables students to work with cutting-edge start-up companies.

Despite a low student/teacher ratio of 14:1, there were some complaints about the faculty. UM has made great strides in hiring student-friendly instructors, but some students continue to express displeasure with the teaching methods. One cause of some students' unhappiness is the "flaming liberal bent." A 2L contended that UM "needs greater emphasis on lawyering, not on furthering the political agendas" of professors. Other students found the progressive disposition of the faculty to be quite refreshing.

A "pleasant southern mood without egos or fierce competition" and a general sense of camaraderie seem pervasive here. Reported a 1L, "People seem to be able to be serious without becoming obsessed or becoming a huge ball of stress." The student body at Maryland is "very diverse" in "both student population and thought," which "makes classroom discussions interesting." Students at the top of each class "tend to form

James Forsyth, Associate Dean
500 West Baltimore Street
Baltimore, MD 21201
Tel: 410-706-3492 • Fax: 410-706-4045
Email: admissions@law.ab.umd.edu
Internet: www.ab.umd.edu

University of Maryland

cliques," and "there is a stronger sense of community among students who live near the school (within one to three blocks) than among those who commute."

Both day and night students complained about the facilities. "We need land! And buildings!" clamored one. Currently, the "cramped and dirty" main building "looks like a high school and is very unimpressive." In response to complaints, we heard from the Dean that "a major addition and renovation is planned for the near future." We should also add that the administration has been promising improvements for a while now, but hasn't yet delivered the goods—or even broken ground. "Just waiting on state funding" was the official story. The school is located in less than stunning downtown Baltimore, where "all around are pawn shops and heroin addicts." If you like baseball, the UM School of Law is within walking distance of Baltimore Oriole Park at Camden Yards. One 2L noted: "I was able to skip Torts and go to Opening Day." According to the school, UM's location combines the advantages of Baltimore, Washington, D.C., and Maryland's capital, Annapolis, by providing access to national, state, and local courts, legislatures, and administrative agencies. "If you want to practice in Baltimore, a Maryland Law degree carries as much weight as one from Harvard or Yale," wrote one student. "Most Baltimore firms are obsessed with summer law clerks making a lifetime commitment to Baltimore, probably because no one in their right mind would want to live in Baltimore forever." Since UM students already live in the city, "the firms usually recruit heavily out of UM."

ADMISSIONS

Everybody knows that UM is a great bargain among East Coast law schools. Demand for spots in the entering class of about 260 is extremely high. Approximately 2,500 candidates applied for admission to Maryland's 1996 entering class. The median LSAT score among entering candidates was 156; the median GPA was 3.30. Obtaining a very diverse entering classes is also very important to the UM admissions staff. The 1995 entering class was 21 percent African American, 9 percent Asian American, and 2 percent Latino American. More than 20 percent of all accepted students already had graduate degrees.

ACADEMICS

Student/faculty ratio	14:1
% female faculty	39
% minority faculty	24
Hours of study per day	4.11

Academic specialties:
Environmental, Health Care

FINANCIAL FACTS

Tuition (in/out-state)	$8,914/$16,298
Cost of books	$1,200
Fees (in/out-state)	$305/$305
Room & board (on/off-campus)	$7,254/$8,820
% first-year students receiving aid	80
% all students receiving aid	79
% aid that is merit-based	NR
% of all students receiving loans	77
% receiving scholarships	40
% of all students receiving assistantships	NR
Average grant	$3,328
Average graduation debt	$46,510

ADMISSIONS

# applications received	2,534
% applicants accepted	38
% acceptees attending	27
Average LSAT	156
LSAT range	137-170
Average undergrad GPA	3.30
GPA range	2.23-3.99
Application fee (in/out-state)	$42/$42
Regular application	rolling
Regular notification	rolling
Rolling notification?	Yes
Early decision program?	No
Admission may be deferred?	Yes
Maximum length of deferment	1 year
Evening division offered?	Yes
Part-time accepted?	Yes
Gourman Report Rating	**3.63**

UNIVERSITY OF MEMPHIS
Cecil C. Humphreys School of Law

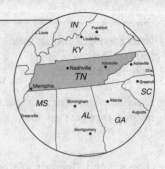

OVERVIEW

Type of school	public
Environment	urban
Scholastic calendar	semester
Schedule	full-time or part-time

STUDENTS

Enrollment of parent institution	20,000
Enrollment of law school	473
% male/female	59/41
% out-of-state	20
% part-time	5
% minorities	11
% international (# of countries represented)	NR (NR)
Average age at entry	27

APPLICANTS ALSO LOOK AT

University of Tennessee
Vanderbilt University
University of Mississippi
University of Georgia
Emory University

SURVEY SAYS...

HITS
Socratic method
Library staff

MISSES
Not enough courses

EMPLOYMENT PROFILE

Firms recruiting on campus	75
Job placement rate (%)	90
% grads employed immediately	32
% grads employed within six months	96
Average starting salary	$35,230

Grads employed by field (%):

Academia	2
Business/industry	14
Government	6
Judicial clerkships	3
Military	3
Private practice	58
Other	10

Since its inception in 1962, the Cecil C. Humphreys School of Law at The University of Memphis has developed a reputation for excellent classroom instruction, and graduated a diverse and outstanding group of lawyers who have made extensive contributions to the legal profession, especially in Tennessee and the mid-South. The J.D. program is generously sprinkled with Contracts, Torts, Income Tax, Procedure, and other solidly traditional, prescribed courses—so much so that first- and second-year students here are allowed only one elective. Those wishing to chart individual courses of study must wait until the third year, which has only one required course. In keeping with the national trend, the University of Memphis offers many practical-skills courses. Among these, the trial advocacy courses and moot court competitions drew the highest rates of participation and the most praise from students. Most students cited the "structured, practical," and "rigorous" curriculum and the "emphasis on Tennessee law and preparation for the bar" as the school's greatest strengths. They absolutely raved about the fact that the bar passage rate at Memphis "is the best in the state," beating out the University of Tennessee and Vanderbilt. "Most of our grads will make very fine, hard-working attorneys," argued one student. "Most have worked hard both inside the classroom and in the real world to get to where they are."

Most of the students here heaped praise upon the "committed" and "very knowledgeable" faculty, whose "willingness to offer personal assistance anytime" does not go unnoticed. An "excellent 1L mentoring program, which matches a first-year student with a practicing attorney," helps students develop their practical skills. The facilities, on the other hand, "need drastic improvement." Students described the library as "laughable" and urged that the "computers should be updated." The air conditioning and heating system in the "poor" physical plant of the school "is in disarray." A jaded 3L charged that the lower floors have flooded twice this year. "We've had to change carpet three times and rescue the library books," said one student. The administration also received low marks, with students "on their own to get jobs" with "almost no help from Career Services." Luckily, at

Dr. Sue Ann McClellan, Director of Law Admissions & Recruitment
Campus Box 526513
Memphis, TN 38152-6513
Tel: 901-678-2073 • Fax: 901-678-5210
Email: uofmlaw@profnet.law.memphis.edu
Internet: www.people.memphis.edu/~law

University of Memphis

these "great" prices, occasional battles with red tape are more acceptable.

Memphis, Tennessee, is a "fairly conservative," reasonably peaceful, and prosperous city of about 1 million located on the banks of the Mississippi River. While it's not exactly a mecca of legal opportunity, it's a relaxed and fairly inexpensive metropolis. According to the law school, the city is "home to numerous transportation and distribution firms, a substantial health care services industry, and many judicial and administrative branches of state and federal government. These community resources provide clerking and field placement opportunities to students and an exciting environment in which to pursue your interest in law." While Memphis manages to remain "devoid of aggressive and antagonistic competition," one student told us that the environment here "is one of the most racially polarized I have ever been in." Another said: "Jobs, families, the great variations in age, and the commuter nature of the school amount to none of the 'family' feeling of a college of the same size."

Judging from their responses to our survey, many students are frustrated with the University of Memphis's lack of status and see the school as worthy of finer distinction. "We have great things to offer, and it's time the world knew about it!" was a typical response. "The dean comes from an impeccable background and is very forward-thinking. There are new programs being offered that are on the cutting edge. The professors are experienced. The march is on to expand this school's reputation."

ADMISSIONS

Around 40 percent of all applicants to the University of Memphis School of Law are admitted, and numerical standards for admission are quite moderate. The school's bargain-basement tuition, however, draws a relatively large pool of applicants, ensuring a competitive admissions process. About 1,000 applicants competed for approximately 160 seats in the 1996 entering class. Applicants from disadvantaged backgrounds and minority and nontraditional student groups will find the admissions process a bit more forgiving, as will residents of Tennessee.

ACADEMICS

Student/faculty ratio	21:1
% female faculty	31
% minority faculty	5
Hours of study per day	3.71

Academic specialties:
Civil Procedure, Commercial, Constitutional, Corporation Securities, Criminal, Environmental, International, Labor, Property, Taxation

FINANCIAL FACTS

Tuition (in/out-state)	$3,784/$9,612
Cost of books	$1,400
Fees (in/out-state)	$68/$68
Room & board (on/off-campus)	$4,370/$4,370
% first-year students receiving aid	76
% all students receiving aid	80
% aid that is merit-based	15
% of all students receiving loans	76
% receiving scholarships	15
% of all students receiving assistantships	6
Average grant	$4,790
Average graduation debt	$42,000

ADMISSIONS

# applications received	1,000
% applicants accepted	42
% acceptees attending	35
Average LSAT	154
LSAT range	139-172
Average undergrad GPA	3.27
GPA range	2.02-4.00
Application fee (in/out-state)	$15/$15
Regular application	February 15
Regular notification	March 15
Rolling notification?	No
Early decision program?	No
Admission may be deferred?	Yes
Maximum length of deferment	1 year
Evening division offered?	No
Part-time accepted?	Yes
Gourman Report Rating	**2.68**

MERCER UNIVERSITY
Walter F. George School of Law

With "strong alumni backing" and a "rich tradition of providing students with a comprehensive legal education and preparation for positions of leadership," the Walter F. George School of Law at Mercer University may very well be the "best damn law school that no one has ever heard about." Mercer offers a strong emphasis on ethics, a comfortable and intimate learning environment, and, despite its somewhat limited number of course offerings, "one of the lowest student-faculty ratios in American legal education." According to students, the "approachable and readily available" faculty is mostly "excellent." Said a 2L: "This school's greatest asset is about 85 percent of the faculty. It's worst problem is the other 15 percent." The majority of the professors are "personable human beings who help us learn, instead of spending their time intimidating us." Mercer's "open-door policy" is taken very seriously by students, professors, and administrators alike, and individual attention is always available. Though classes are small, "don't expect too much debate in the classroom." Warned one student, "It's a yes-man's paradise." Mercer has revamped its curriculum to include "skills" workshops at the start of every year and has introduced a sixth-semester "pre-practice" program designed to combat the feeling of drift that envelops most 3Ls come springtime. However, a third-year student complained: "Many 3Ls still have never been in a courtroom." Each summer, Mercer sponsors a National Criminal Defense College that is "nationally known among criminal defense lawyers."

"When you walk in the front door" of the law facility, "Mercer looks very impressive with marble floors and woodwork." However, "the interior screams Brady Bunch." Though "the facilities are in much need of repair," optimistic students told us that "the school is planning to remodel." Pessimists retorted: "The administration says they are working on it, but who knows if it will ever get done." Renovations notwithstanding, nearly all students agreed that Mercer offers a "warm, conducive atmosphere for legal learning." Said a 2L: "We have an excellent library and computer facilities that give us access to any and all research resources we need."

Kathleen O'Neal, Director of Admissions
Admissions Office, 1021 Georgia Avenue
Macon, GA 31201
Tel: 912-752-2605 • Fax: 912-752-2989
Internet: www.mercer.edu/~law/index.html

Annually, Mercer boasts one of the highest Georgia bar passage rates (sometimes the highest). Employment prospects are fabulous for the high percentage of Mercer grads who want to practice in the state. "Few firms interview on campus," though, and Mercer's "great reputation for producing excellent Georgia lawyers" does not reach very far beyond the state line. The school's lack of recognition outside the area was frustrating for some. Said one student: "They need to do a better job of spreading Mercer's reputation outside of Georgia and Florida." Several students also complained that Mercer is "very expensive."

The law school is "well-situated overlooking downtown Macon," a "sleepy town" known for its beautiful ante-bellum architecture, and "located in the heart of southern hospitality." While it's certainly no Mecca, "it is close to Atlanta" and "there are few distractions, which can be irritating when you need a break. But at the same time, it helps you focus on the task at hand." Students said the intimate atmosphere allows them to "create lasting friendships" and, despite the fact that "Macon is a drag," most seemed quite content with their social lives. "School-funded cocktail parties, enigmatic Sixties renegades teaching classes, and a social life equaled only by Melrose Place all at a Baptist school! Who'da thought?" A 2L concluded: "It's been a great experience. It's a great school. If you want a small school with a personal touch, Mercer is the place for you."

ADMISSIONS

The Walter F. George School of Law is situated in the lower-middle range of all nationally ranked law schools. The average Mercer student has a moderate undergraduate GPA of 3.10 and a solid LSAT score at about the 75th percentile. Since Mercer admits a very small class, though, the admissions process is quite selective. The law school's overall acceptance rate is only about 30 percent.

ACADEMICS

Student/faculty ratio	15:1
% female faculty	30
% minority faculty	6
Hours of study per day	4.21

FINANCIAL FACTS

Tuition	$17,490
Cost of books	$600
% first-year students receiving aid	92
% all students receiving aid	88
% aid that is merit-based	9
% of all students receiving loans	85
% receiving scholarships	23
% of all students receiving assistantships	NR
Average grant	$8,804
Average graduation debt	$64,000

ADMISSIONS

# applications received	1,117
% applicants accepted	NR
% acceptees attending	NR
Average LSAT	156
Average undergrad GPA	3.10
Application fee	$45
Regular application	March 15
Regular notification	rolling
Rolling notification?	Yes
Early decision program?	No
Admission may be deferred?	Yes
Maximum length of deferment	1 year
Evening division offered?	No
Part-time accepted?	No
Gourman Report Rating	**2.93**

UNIVERSITY OF MIAMI
School of Law

OVERVIEW

Type of school	private
Environment	suburban
Scholastic calendar	semester
Schedule	full-time or part-time

STUDENTS

Enrollment of parent institution	7,297
Enrollment of law school	1,554
% male/female	57/43
% out-of-state	43
% part-time	19
% minorities	33
% international (# of countries represented)	1 (11)
Average age at entry	26

APPLICANTS ALSO LOOK AT

University of Florida
Florida State University
Nova Southeastern University
Tulane University
Emory University

SURVEY SAYS...

HITS
Broad range of courses
Library staff

EMPLOYMENT PROFILE

Job placement rate (%)	83
% grads employed immediately	40
% grads employed within six months	83
Average starting salary	$47,644

Grads employed by field (%):

Academia	2
Business/industry	8
Government	18
Judicial clerkships	5
Private practice	60
Other	1

The University of Miami School of Law is located just a few miles south of Miami in the smallish community of Coral Gables. "The warm climate, tropical landscape, and proximity to the beach create a magnificent ambiance." Many might be surprised to learn that the University of Miami is more than just sunshine and perennially powerful football teams; it is one of the largest and best-funded research universities in the nation. It is also home to a large and well-equipped law school with solid academic credentials and a broad traditional curriculum that is supplemented by an increasing commitment to skills training and special offerings. The vast resources of the broader university have begun to play a larger role within the law school as well, as interdisciplinary research in areas like economics and the behavioral sciences has gained popularity within the field of law. A 1L rhapsodized, "My professors have the artful skill of Shakespeare, the intellect and wisdom of Thurgood Marshall, and the caring concern of a grandmother. They are friends, colleagues, and the greatest teachers of the law." Not all students felt the same, however, as this 3L called the profs "pompous, inaccessible, and often downright humiliating." Another student said, "The professors orchestrate personal attacks upon the students."

According to students, a new dean arrived not so long ago and began implementing major changes to the quality of life and education at Miami. The majority of respondents cheered the progress the new dean has made toward significantly reshaping this law school. "Dean Thompson forced out all of the old, dry, Socratic professors and replaced them with younger, more interesting professors." A 3L attested, "The dean is a godsend. He is taking the entire school on his back and dragging it into the Top Twenty." Most students seemed to agree that "the administration is working very hard to meet the needs of the students." Others argue that "information falls out of the sky," and administrative changes are usually communicated poorly, if at all. Also, though "Miami does a decent job with job prospects, it could be much better," admitted a 2L.

Therese Lambert, Director of Student Recruiting
P.O. Box 248087
Coral Gables, FL 33124
Tel: 305-284-2523 • Fax: 305-284-3084
Email: admissions@law.miami.edu
Internet: www.law.miami.edu

University of Miami

Students at Miami bragged that their "ideal facilities" are "the best in the country." Miami's Law Library and research facilities are definitely something to behold. Accordingly, the legal community of southern Florida is also well aware. "It's annoying to wait behind the scores of attorneys using the copiers when I need to copy my cases for an assignment," griped a 1L. "But it gives me a good opportunity to network for a job."

Miami draws more than half of its nearly 2,500 applicants from outside Florida. The "great melting pot" that is the law school population here is composed of "a large diversity of students, not only from different states but also from different countries and cultures and ethnic groups." But diversity is not without its problems. One student told us: "It is a very tense environment for minority students." It's definitely a tense environment for law students harboring hopes of good grades. "Very highly competitive" or even "very hostile" might be a better description. As a result, "law school can be a drag, but it doesn't seem so bad when you walk out of class to sunshine and palm trees." A 2L had this to say: "My main concern is the negativism here. There are groups of students who can compete with anyone in the nation, and others that are not serious about the law. This latter group is very bitter and expresses itself in a very loud voice. Most students I know like their experience here and have learned a tremendous amount. Unfortunately, the few who are bitter make it seem like everyone here is unhappy. This is an excellent school on the rise. I am extremely proud and happy to be a part of its future."

ADMISSIONS

Although the size of the entering class at the University of Miami School of Law requires the admissions committee to admit a large number of applicants, competition to be among those admitted is growing. Still, this expensive private law school offers admission to over half of the candidates it considers—a very generous acceptance rate for a school of its caliber. Numerical admissions standards are moderate.

ACADEMICS

Student/faculty ratio	16:1
% female faculty	24
% minority faculty	11
Hours of study per day	4.00

FINANCIAL FACTS

Tuition	$20,600
Cost of books	$700
Fees	$388
Room & board (on/off-campus)	$5,204/$8,324
% first-year students receiving aid	85
% all students receiving aid	85
% aid that is merit-based	9
% of all students receiving loans	85
% receiving scholarships	17
% of all students receiving assistantships	5
Average grant	$11,262
Average graduation debt	$65,000

ADMISSIONS

# applications received	2,451
% applicants accepted	59
% acceptees attending	34
Average LSAT	154
Average undergrad GPA	3.20
Application fee	$45
Early application	rolling
Early notification	rolling
Regular application	July 31
Regular notification	rolling
Rolling notification?	Yes
Early decision program?	Yes
Admission may be deferred?	Yes
Maximum length of deferment	1 year
Evening division offered?	Yes
Part-time accepted?	Yes
Gourman Report Rating	**3.34**

UNIVERSITY OF MICHIGAN
School of Law

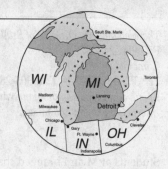

With its nonresident annual tuition rate exceeding $20,000 and its resident rate not far behind, the University of Michigan School of Law does not have the bargain attractions of your typical public law school, but never mind. By any yardstick—from the purely academic to the purely aesthetic—this large, old institution is widely acknowledged to be among a handful of law schools that can legitimately be called the best in the country.

In the classroom, Michigan's program is extremely flexible and terrifically strong. With virtually no requirements after the solidly traditional first year, and with a broad range of innovative courses from which to choose, Michigan students control their own academic fates. Outside the classroom setting, the law school's clinical programs are limited in neither capacity nor scope. Fully one-half of Michigan students participate in these programs, which include a clinic dedicated to AIDS and public health and another to women and the law. The Michigan faculty, which includes some of the country's top legal scholars, still favors the Socratic Method, and traditional case analysis forms the basis of many upper-division courses. Still, the law school is not without its structural innovations. One-quarter of each entering class is admitted to what the law school calls the "new section," in which the traditional disciplinary barriers within the first-year curriculum are eschewed in favor of a more integrated, less structured course of study. Michigan admits another quarter of its first-year class for study beginning in June. These summer admittees can use their head start to graduate early by attending summer sessions, to slow the pace of their legal education, or simply to prepare themselves for the Ann Arbor winter.

Not that winter could foster discontent among the highly qualified, satisfied students at Michigan. Though certainly not without their criticisms, the Michigan students we heard from expressed a very high degree of satisfaction not only with the quality of their program, but also with the overall quality of their experience at the law school. "The atmosphere created by the students, the community, the faculty, and even the facilities is excellent," wrote one 1L, "probably the best in the country." Though that last claim would be difficult to verify, prevailing opinion among Michigan

Dennis Shields, Assistant Dean
312 Hutchins Hall
Ann Arbor, MI 48109
Tel: 313-764-0537
Email: law.jd.admissions@umich.edu
Internet: www.law.umich.edu

students appears to be very consistent with the judgment of another 1L who said that "this is an easy place to love." Most give credit for this fact to their fellow students—"Students here are incredibly intelligent and, just as importantly, incredibly human"—and to their faculty—"Most members of the faculty are absolutely outstanding, both as scholars and as teachers."

When asked to name areas in which their school could stand to improve, many lamented the degree of competitiveness among students and the perceived inaccessibility of their "otherwise excellent" professors. For the most part, their substantive criticisms had little or nothing to do with the quality of any of the law school's existing programs. More often, their remarks concerned the future. "I want to work for a small public-interest firm, or for the Department of Justice," wrote one 2L, "but the debt required by this school forces students to go after the big firms and the big $$." Furthermore, many others complained that the school's placement office was of little help to those whose career plans fell outside the mainstream. "The placement office has limited ties to the legal community," reported one 3L. "Students are left mostly to their own initiative, particularly if they don't want to work in a large firm." Those Michigan students who do want such work, however, are as employable and as happy as any in the nation.

ADMISSIONS

Simply stated, the University of Michigan Law School is one of most selective law schools in the nation. How difficult is it to gain admission to this world-class school? Well, every year Michigan receives nearly 3,000 applications from prospective students with LSAT scores below 165—the 95th percentile. These luckless applicants stand a cumulative 26 percent chance of getting in. Bear this in mind when considering whether to write that application-fee check.

ACADEMICS

Student/faculty ratio	25:1
% female faculty	32
% minority faculty	9
Hours of study per day	4.40

Academic specialties:

Civil Procedure, Commercial, Constitutional, Corporation Securities, Criminal, Environmental, Government Services, Human Rights, International, Labor, Legal History, Legal Philosophy, Property, Taxation

FINANCIAL FACTS

Tuition (in/out-state)	$16,678/$22,678
Cost of books	$720
Room & board (on/off-campus)	$12,000/$12,000
% first-year students receiving aid	95
% all students receiving aid	95
% aid that is merit-based	24
% of all students receiving loans	80
% receiving scholarships	32
% of all students receiving assistantships	NR
Average grant	$7,540
Average graduation debt	$36,000

ADMISSIONS

# applications received	3,677
% applicants accepted	30
% acceptees attending	28
Average LSAT	167
Average undergrad GPA	3.50
Application fee (in/out-state)	$70/$70
Regular application	rolling
Regular notification	NR
Rolling notification?	No
Early decision program?	NR
Admission may be deferred?	Yes
Evening division offered?	No
Part-time accepted?	No
Gourman Report Rating	**4.91**

UNIVERSITY OF MINNESOTA
Law School

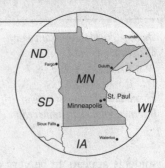

OVERVIEW

Type of school	public
Environment	metropolis
Scholastic calendar	semester
Schedule	full-time only

STUDENTS

Enrollment of parent institution	16,457
Enrollment of law school	810
% male/female	55/45
% out-of-state	47
% minorities	17
% international (# of countries represented)	NR (8)
Average age at entry	25

APPLICANTS ALSO LOOK AT

University of Michigan
University of Wisconsin
Harvard University
Northwestern University

SURVEY SAYS...

HITS
Library staff
Broad range of courses
Research resources

MISSES
Not enough courses

EMPLOYMENT PROFILE

Job placement rate (%)	96
% grads employed immediately	75
% grads employed within six months	96
Average starting salary	$52,000

Grads employed by field (%):

Academia	2
Business/industry	15
Government	6
Judicial clerkships	27
Private practice	47
Public interest	3

There are two ways in which one might interpret the fact that the University of Minnesota School of Law keeps its library, one of the largest in the nation, open twenty-four hours a day, seven days a week. On the one hand, it could be viewed as a sign of the law school's commitment to fostering scholarship by maintaining wonderfully accessible, top-notch facilities. On the other hand, it could be seen as a sign that the law school's students spend relatively little time anywhere else. Both interpretations, it seems, would be accurate. Minnesota is generally considered to be among the finest public law schools in the nation, and it has never chosen to rest on its laurels. Since 1913, for instance, Minnesota has recognized the importance of practical training as a supplement to the standard classroom curriculum in law schools. Its current clinical program, one of the largest in the country and in which 68 percent of students participate, has served as a model for other schools around the nation since its inception in 1968. Ninety percent of students participate in the clinics or practical skills courses. The school revamped its writing program in 1994 in response to student complaints; according to the administration, the new program has also been used as a model for other schools.

The law school's facilities, housed on the Minneapolis side of the university's Twin Cities campus, are first-rate, and its faculty is very highly regarded. The greatly varied co-curricular activities available to students are far too numerous to mention, and the opportunities for interdisciplinary study through the many highly rated graduate departments of the broader university are tremendous. In terms of the substance of the legal education it provides, this top law school is as progressive as any of its peers. But be forewarned: The University of Minnesota is very much of the old school when it comes to style. The Socratic Method may elsewhere have been consigned to the ash heap of history, but it continues to thrive in Minnesota. The workload here is heavy, and competition among students is high. Still, one cannot argue with the results. Minnesota graduates tend to get very good jobs, and get them with relative ease.

Edward Kawczynski, Director of Admissions
229 19th Avenue South
Minneapolis, MN 55455
Tel: 612-625-5005
Internet: www.umn.edu/law

University of Minnesota

And despite their criticism of aspects of their chosen school, Minnesota students seem to appreciate the advantages they have. "Our faculty and our facilities (especially the library) are excellent," said one 2L, "and the student body is strong and diverse." The law school's "reputation and location are excellent," wrote another, who, like many others, chose Minnesota for its perceived "prestige."

Their satisfaction with certain fundamentals notwithstanding, however, Minnesota students expressed frustration with some faculty members as well. "Some teachers are excellent," said one, "and all are open to talking with students one-on-one, but we need more teachers who focus on teaching and teaching well."

Minnesota has both a new placement director, and a new, expanded placement office. According to an associate dean, "the director is so popular the students invited her to an otherwise 'students only' graduation party." The school also has a new dean of students "who is immensely popular." Overall, Minnesota students are quite satisfied with their experience at the law school.

ADMISSIONS

As a result of the University of Minnesota Law School's huge reputation and its status as a relative bargain among Midwestern law schools, competition for spots in its entering class of about 270 is quite fierce. The overall acceptance rate is a very selective 25 percent, and the quality of the law school's average applicant pool of about 2,100 is very high. As a result, Minnesota's numerical admissions standards are among the highest in the country. In fact, the Minnesota student body is, by our calculations, one of the 20 most highly qualified in the nation.

ACADEMICS

Student/faculty ratio	16.7:1
% female faculty	37
% minority faculty	11
Hours of study per day	3.99

FINANCIAL FACTS

Tuition (in/out-state)	$7,981/$13,875
Cost of books	NR
Fees	$468
% first-year students receiving aid	85
% all students receiving aid	85
% aid that is merit-based	35
% of all students receiving loans	85
% receiving scholarships	21
% of all students receiving assistantships	12
Average grant	$5,000
Average graduation debt	NR

ADMISSIONS

# applications received	1,800
% applicants accepted	25
% acceptees attending	49
Average LSAT	163
Average undergrad GPA	3.57
Application fee (in/out-state)	$40/$40
Regular application	March 1
Regular notification	rolling
Rolling notification?	Yes
Early decision program?	No
Admission may be deferred?	No
Evening division offered?	No
Part-time accepted?	No
Gourman Report Rating	**4.63**

MISSISSIPPI COLLEGE
School of Law

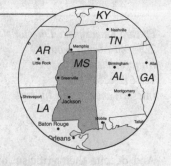

OVERVIEW

Type of school	private
Environment	city
Scholastic calendar	semester
Schedule	full-time only

STUDENTS

Enrollment of parent institution	3,241
Enrollment of law school	418
% male/female	65/35
% out-of-state	55
% minorities	11
% international (# of countries represented)	NR (2)
Average age at entry	26

APPLICANTS ALSO LOOK AT

University of Mississippi
Tulane University
Mercer University
Loyola University, New Orleans
Georgia State University

SURVEY SAYS...

HITS
Intellectual challenge
Diverse faculty
Students feel well prepared

MISSES
Library staff
Not enough courses

EMPLOYMENT PROFILE

Firms recruiting on campus	30
Job placement rate (%)	91.3
% grads employed within six months	91.3
Average starting salary	$36,100

Grads employed by field (%):

Business/industry	NR
Government	8.8
Judicial clerkships	17
Military	1
Private practice	70

Founded in 1975 and accredited in 1980, the Mississippi College School of Law is a "a strong, regional law school with a national focus." Operated by the Mississippi Baptist Convention, this tiny school "seeks to provide a superior legal education within the context of a Christian institution." The relatively limited curriculum here resembles the traditional liberal arts model. In addition to providing a grounding in common law and legal writing, courses at MC also explore emerging doctrine and "stress legal theory," so much so that some students call for "more practical" instruction, "i.e., how to draft a complaint, etc." Beyond the standard requirements, Mississippi College students must also complete a major research paper. The "concerned and easily accessible" faculty, though not very large, reflects "a wide variety of backgrounds and interests." Women currently constitute 21 percent of the MC faculty, which includes two African Americans. Students we polled spoke of professors who offer personal attention galore and are "as good as you will find at any Top Twenty school." The "open-door policy" at MC is taken quite seriously. Many professors even give out their home phone numbers. Explained a 1L: "Because the school is small, there are many opportunities to interact with professors. As a result, the quality of education is higher." Unfortunately, students did not give such ringing endorsements to the "very unresponsive" and "entirely too paternalistic" administration, which, "although improving, is simply bad."

The law school's location in downtown Jackson offers much, including mild weather virtually year-round and "convenience to the Mississippi Supreme Court and legislature." MC students are only a short walk away from many federal courts and the seat of Mississippi state government. Because of its location in a major southern legal center, MC is able to "draw on leading practitioners and judges as adjunct professors and as supervisors of externship programs." The Career Services Office "is genuinely concerned about helping students find employment that is suited to their talents and abilities." A 2L beamed, "This assistance is not only available to the top students, but also to the rest of the students."

Patricia H. Evans, Director of Admissions
151 East Griffith Street
Jackson, MS 39201
Tel: 601-353-3907
Email: pevans@mc.edu

Mississippi College

Mississippi College ain't much to look at. "The research facilities definitely need improving" and the "heinous" five-story law school facility is "a bit dated," to say the least. It's not in the best part of town, either, although the full-time presence of security guards does much to prevent crime. Improvements could be in the works, though. "There is a rumor going around that the school is going to move to another building in the downtown Jackson area," said a hopeful 1L. "If that comes through, I will have no complaints at all."

Lest we forget that Mississippi College is a Baptist-affiliated school, students reminded us that the political atmosphere here is largely "to the right of Atilla the Hun." There is "great southern hospitality and friendliness" here, and "a strong sense of community among the students." Said a 2L: "We enjoy many non-academic activities together. There are numerous planned social events." Nevertheless, many students told us that the academic environment here is "very cutthroat." On the plus side, female students are especially happy about the "great deal of support" they are afforded at MC. In fact, students say "this is a great school for females and minorities and older students." In general, students here praised MC as "a diverse, well-structured environment, which is very conducive to the study of law." Explained a 3L: "Mississippi College provides a quality legal education. The school is Christian-oriented and the students seem to care about each another."

ADMISSIONS

As the size of the law school's applicant pool has grown in recent years, admissions standards at the Mississippi College School of Law have risen appreciably. However, numerical admissions standards here are still among the most lenient in the country. Of the applicant pool for the 1996 entering class, 63 percent were accepted. The median GPA of accepted candidates was 3.00. The median LSAT score was 152. A healthy 61 percent of accepted students hailed from out-of-state. The average age of incoming students was twenty-six.

ACADEMICS

Student/faculty ratio	21:1
% female faculty	38
% minority faculty	10
Hours of study per day	3.90

FINANCIAL FACTS

Tuition	$13,170
Cost of books	$850
Fees	$262
% first-year students receiving aid	88
% all students receiving aid	87
% aid that is merit-based	24
% of all students receiving loans	87
% receiving scholarships	24
% of all students receiving assistantships	NR
Average grant	$9,000
Average graduation debt	$55,000

ADMISSIONS

# applications received	732
% applicants accepted	64
% acceptees attending	34
Average LSAT	152
Average undergrad GPA	3.00
Application fee	$25
Regular application	rolling
Regular notification	rolling
Rolling notification?	Yes
Early decision program?	No
Admission may be deferred?	No
Evening division offered?	No
Part-time accepted?	No
Gourman Report Rating	**2.22**

UNIVERSITY OF MISSISSIPPI
School of Law

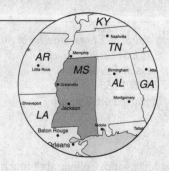

If you had only one day in which to experience the American South, you could do worse than to start in Oxford, Mississippi, the former home of William Faulkner and still the home of one of the finest law schools in the Southeast, the University of Mississippi School of Law. As evidenced by the namesake of the law school's main building—Lucius Quintus Cincinnatus Lamar—and the nickname by which even serious-minded scholars refer to the modern, comprehensive university of which it is a part—"Ole Miss"—this is a quintessentially southern institution. From its architecture to its curriculum, this law school—the fourth-oldest state-supported law school in the country—is steeped in tradition, one that dates back over 120 years to its founding in the aftermath of the Civil War.

There is one aspect of the Ole Miss tradition, however, that the law school is working very hard to overcome: a shameful history of racial exclusion. The population of Mississippi includes a larger proportion of African Americans than does any other state in the union, but until very recently the state's flagship public university was almost completely white, and defiantly so. To its credit, the law school has made minority recruitment a high priority, and if the trend in recent years continues, the law school at Mississippi will soon be much closer to reflecting the population of the state it has served for so long.

Indeed, the law school's regional reputation, built on the quality of its extremely traditional curriculum, couldn't be stronger. Ole Miss is the alma mater of a sizable majority of Mississippi's lawyers, and this alumni network represents a significant resource for the law school's graduates when they enter the job market. This fact is certainly not lost on students at Ole Miss, who have nothing but praise for their chosen school when it comes to its ability to prepare them for practice within the state. And although most of those we heard from complained that an unforgiving grading curve fosters competitiveness among students, most did agree that the overall atmosphere at the law school is made livable by the "terrific relationships between professors and students." "The faculty is both interested and interesting,"

Barbara Vinson, Coordinator of Admissions
Room 310
University, MS 38677
Tel: 601-232-6910 • Fax: 601-232-1289
Email: lawmiss@olemiss.edu
Internet: www.olemiss.edu/depts/law_school/law-hom.html

University of Mississippi

said one. "They seem strongly and genuinely interested in their students."

But the criticism of Mississippi students for certain aspects of their law school is every bit as heartfelt as their praise for others. Most of the negative reviews we heard concerned the general dissatisfaction with the lack of flexibility in the law school's highly prescribed curriculum. "We need more practice/clinical classes," said one 2L, "and more classes in general." Indeed, Mississippi students have relatively few courses from which to choose their electives and little access to clinical courses. As one student who criticized the rigidity of his program put it, "They need to quit relying on the 'ole' and bring in some 'new.'"

All in all, it seems that those Mississippi students who are most satisfied with their law school are those who are most satisfied with their geographical and cultural surroundings generally. To some, the "old South" atmosphere is a bit stifling. Said one such student, a non-Mississippian, "Unfortunately, the degree...is good for one ticket, valid only in the state of Mississippi and surrounding area." One even-handed 3L counseled, "If you are a Mississippi native this is the school for you. Oxford is a small, historical town that personifies the Old South and provides a positive and unique learning atmosphere." On the basis of the remarks we heard, this latter judgment is by far more indicative of the consensus among students at Ole Miss.

ADMISSIONS

In terms of the numerical standards to which it holds applicants, the University of Mississippi School of Law ranks as one of the sixty least selective law schools in the country. Still, all but the most highly qualified of hopeful applicants would be wrong to conclude that this long-established law school represents a sure bet. Applications volume at Ole Miss is quite heavy, and the overall acceptance rate is very low.

ACADEMICS

Student/faculty ratio	21:1
% female faculty	17
% minority faculty	17
Hours of study per day	4.04

FINANCIAL FACTS

Tuition (in/out-state)	$3,081/$7,003
Cost of books	NR
Fees (in/out-state)	$118/$314
Room & board (on/off-campus)	$9,085/$9,085
% first-year students receiving aid	NR
% all students receiving aid	29
% aid that is merit-based	NR
% of all students receiving loans	NR
% receiving scholarships	NR
% of all students receiving assistantships	NR
Average grant	NR
Average graduation debt	$30,000

ADMISSIONS

# applications received	1,098
% applicants accepted	44
% acceptees attending	46
Average LSAT	151
LSAT range	132-168
Average undergrad GPA	3.27
GPA range	2.00-4.00
Application fee (in/out-state)	$20/$20
Regular application	March 1
Regular notification	April 15
Rolling notification?	No
Early decision program?	NR
Admission may be deferred?	No
Evening division offered?	No
Part-time accepted?	No
Gourman Report Rating	3.24

UNIVERSITY OF MISSOURI, COLUMBIA
School of Law

OVERVIEW

Type of school	public
Environment	suburban
Scholastic calendar	semester
Schedule	full-time or part-time

STUDENTS

Enrollment of parent institution	15,086
Enrollment of law school	485
% male/female	61/39
% out-of-state	15
% part-time	NR
% minorities	10
% international (# of countries represented)	2 (5)
Average age at entry	24

APPLICANTS ALSO LOOK AT

University of Missouri, Kansas City
Washington University
St. Louis University
University of Illinois
University of Iowa

SURVEY SAYS...

HITS
Classroom facilities
Faculty-student relations
Quality of teaching

MISSES
Not enough courses

EMPLOYMENT PROFILE

Firms recruiting on campus	60
Job placement rate (%)	100
% grads employed immediately	60
% grads employed within six months	92
Average starting salary	$37,000

Grads employed by field (%):

Academia	1
Business/industry	5
Government	16
Judicial clerkships	21
Military	4
Private practice	53
Public interest	1
Other	2

Located "on a wonderful campus" in a great college town about halfway between St. Louis and Kansas City, the School of Law at the University of Missouri, Columbia has been producing well-trained lawyers since 1873. Mizzou enjoys a solid reputation as a regional powerhouse and as one of the nation's finest state-supported law schools. It ranks as one of the best bargains in legal education, and MU students give their school consistently high marks on most issues relating to the fundamental quality of their education.

The traditional course of study here is straightforward and, especially during the first and second years, largely prescribed. Much of the curriculum has a "practical emphasis." While students say they "can't complain about the quality of most of the courses," many told us that the range of courses offered is "often too limited." This shortcoming notwithstanding, Mizzou's curriculum is supplemented by a rich variety of clinical offerings. The law school takes particular pride in its highly regarded Trial Practice program and "strong" Center for the Study of Alternative Dispute Resolution, which promotes and fosters research in this burgeoning field. The integration of dispute-resolution problems into the entire curriculum—even first-year courses—is lauded by many students. Despite their not-very-metropolitan location, MU students felt confident about the "good 'real world' application" and clinical experience offered here. "The practical skills courses and clinics take learning to a higher level, combining theoretical and legal accuracy with solid, hands-on experience," boasted a 2L.

Students applauded the "excellent" and "extremely accessible" faculty and administration. "Some of our professors have been teaching for over forty years. Imagine the resulting expertise," said a 2L. Another student swore, "If someone asked me which five people I would want to have to dinner and I could have anyone, three would be my professors." On the minus side, a 1L lamented: "We need more women professors." Also, of class discussions, a 2L asserted, "The vast majority of students become mute the moment they enter the classroom." And though "the

Kenneth Dean, Associate Dean
231 Hulston Hall
Columbia, MO 65211
Tel: 888-882-6042
Email: gregory@law.missouri.edu
Internet: www.law.missouri.edu

University of Missouri, Columbia

administration is extraordinarily concerned with students," the financial aid department can be "rather discouraging."

The "very new and very nice" facilities here are "well designed" and among the best in the nation." The library—though it "needs to be open longer"—is "first-rate." The law building has become "painfully overcrowded," though, to the extent that there are "not enough lockers" for all the students. Technology is not exactly on the cutting edge, either. "They make us write on stone tablets," charged a 1L. Really? "Well, not really, but the matrix printers are way old." Finally, dozens of students pointed out that "parking blows." Warned a 2L: "Expect to hike several miles a day." When it comes time to begin practicing, Career Services "seems to be only open to those in the top of the class," complained a 2L. "If you're in the bottom 90 percent, you must find your own job." Disheartened students tell us that "the average salary coming out of MU is $28,000."

Socially, Mizzou Law is "like high school." One 3L told us that her peers are "cliquier than a bunch of junior high school students." Other students took a more positive stand, citing "numerous activities" and "proximity to bars." Some students claim the atmosphere here is "very competitive." Others disagreed, calling it "surprisingly cooperative." One student explained the environment this way: "While there is a healthy amount of competitiveness among the students, there is also a general feeling that 'we're all in this together.'" A huge percentage of the law school's students and alumni hail from Missouri and choose to remain in the Show-Me State upon graduation.

ADMISSIONS

Small, strong, and inexpensive, it is no surprise that the University of Missouri, Columbia is a tremendously popular destination for aspiring attorneys. Like all of the nation's better public law schools, Mizzou draws a relatively large volume of applications by virtue not only of its quality, but also of its value. Consequently, Missouri is in a position to be selective in choosing members of its entering class. Still, the numerical standards are only slightly above the national average. The average LSAT score of entering classes here is around 157. The average GPA is about 3.3.

ACADEMICS	
Student/faculty ratio	20:1
% female faculty	27
% minority faculty	5
Hours of study per day	3.60

Academic specialties:
Corporation Securities, Environmental, Labor, Property, Taxation

FINANCIAL FACTS	
Tuition (in/out-state)	$7,800/$8,033
Cost of books	$1,097
Fees (in/out-state)	$8,481/$16,514
Room & board (on/off-campus)	$4,735/$6,346
% first-year students receiving aid	70
% all students receiving aid	70
% aid that is merit-based	20
% of all students receiving loans	70
% receiving scholarships	20
% of all students receiving assistantships	2
Average grant	NR
Average graduation debt	$33,000

ADMISSIONS	
# applications received	750
% applicants accepted	65
% acceptees attending	40
Average LSAT	157
Average undergrad GPA	3.30
Application fee (in/out-state)	$40/$40
Regular application	rolling
Regular notification	rolling
Rolling notification?	Yes
Early decision program?	No
Admission may be deferred?	No
Evening division offered?	No
Part-time accepted?	No
Gourman Report Rating	**3.72**

UNIVERSITY OF MISSOURI, KANSAS CITY

School of Law

OVERVIEW

Type of school	public
Environment	metropolis
Scholastic calendar	semester
Schedule	full-time or part-time

STUDENTS

Enrollment of parent institution	9,931
Enrollment of law school	536
% male/female	52/48
% out-of-state	42
% part-time	3
% minorities	11
% international (# of countries represented)	1 (4)
Average age at entry	27

APPLICANTS ALSO LOOK AT

University of Kansas
University of Missouri, Columbia
Washburn University
St. Louis University
University of Tulsa

SURVEY SAYS...

HITS
Research resources
Classroom facilities

MISSES
Practical lawyering skills
Not enough courses

EMPLOYMENT PROFILE

Firms recruiting on campus	35
Job placement rate (%)	93
% grads employed immediately	42
% grads employed within six months	93
Average starting salary	$37,553

Grads employed by field (%):

Academia	2
Business/industry	15
Government	22
Judicial clerkships	8
Military	2
Private practice	52
Public interest	1
Other	3

The University of Missouri, Kansas City School of Law is located in a "pleasant" residential district of one of the Midwest's most livable metropolitan areas. The law school's low tuition and Kansas City's eminently reasonable cost of living combine to make a legal education here affordable. "Dollar for dollar," wrote one student, "I'm more than satisfied with my decision to go here."

The "highly challenging" UMKC curriculum is a traditional one supplemented by a handful of clinical programs. "Beyond the basics," though, "there's not a whole lot to choose from"—and students clamored for "a wider variety of electives." The "very knowledgeable" faculty has a "zeal for the subject matter" and "experience in the practice of law." Many students agreed that "the professors' enthusiasm, encouragement, and guidance more than compensate for the 'average academic rank' of the school." However, while some students raved that the "accessibility of the faculty and their willingness to relate to students creates a very cooperative learning atmosphere," others complained of "arrogant" professors who "dodge requests for appointments." One student told us: "The professors are, with notable exceptions, good teachers as well as scholars." Student views of the administration were even more mixed. Though many applauded the "advancements" of recent years, many others castigated the administration for being "unfriendly" and somewhat apathetic to student concerns. "A Supreme Court justice (Scalia) spoke just blocks away from our school, and the reaction from the administration was a collective yawn," said a 2L.

UMKC "is striving to prepare its students for the legal practice by offering courses in practical skills such as trial and appellate advocacy classes, and practical legal writing skills," explained a 3L. "The law school has an outstanding Career Services office that does a great job assisting with judicial clerkships, big firm jobs," and others positions. Once they complete their degrees, nearly all graduates remain in the Kansas City region, one of the Midwest's largest legal job markets. "The location gives us an edge in the Kansas City job market," asserted a 2L. "Law firms in Kansas City know that this is a good school and they are eager to hire from

Jean Klosterman, Director of Admissions
5100 Rockhill Road
Kansas City, MO 64110
Tel: 816-235-1644 • Fax: 816-235-5276
Email: klosterj@smtpgate.umkc.edu
Internet: www.law.umkc.edu

**University of Missouri,
Kansas City**

here." Though "UMKC has a lower median salary, grads are having great success in getting on with large firms that pay over $55,000. UMKC also has had great success in placing students with federal judges (four in 1997) and the Missouri Supreme Court (one in 1997)." Unfortunately, students don't have as much luck finding employment outside of the local legal community. "Our isolation makes us the forgotten stepchild of Missouri law schools," griped one student.

According to our surveys, the facilities at UMKC are acceptable. Though it's "not open late enough," the law library is designed in a novel fashion: 2Ls and 3Ls have individual assigned spaces in office "suites" that are shared by faculty members. Students told us that the research and computer facilities "are excellent and improving every year." The lounge and classrooms, however, "look like the 1970s threw up all over the place."

Most of the "very white" student population hails from within Missouri and from nearby counties in Kansas. The political bent of the majority of students is "conservative," which causes some strain with the "liberal, liberal, liberal" faculty. UMKC is largely a "commuter-based law school" with "no campus atmosphere." It's small enough, though, that "everyone knows everyone." Both negative competition and "a good deal of anxiety-producing stress" definitely rear their ugly heads here, at least on occasion. One student explained: "There are some that are competitive and some that are very laid back. There doesn't seem to be a middle ground."

ADMISSIONS

Although significantly less celebrated than its companion school in Columbia, the University of Missouri, Kansas City School of Law enjoys a solid regional reputation. As entering classes at UMKC tend to be relatively small, the admission is somewhat selective. However, since the law school uses a straight index to make most of its admissions decisions, applicants with solidly mid-range numerical credentials are virtually guaranteed admission. Numerically, UMKC ranks in the middle of all U.S. law schools in terms of admissions selectivity, and has a very generous overall acceptance rate of 64 percent.

ACADEMICS	
Student/faculty ratio	17:1
% female faculty	30
% minority faculty	3
Hours of study per day	3.88

Academic specialties:

Taxation

FINANCIAL FACTS	
Tuition (in/out-state)	$8,548/$16,581
Cost of books	$750
Fees (in/out-state)	$316/$316
% first-year students receiving aid	89
% all students receiving aid	86
% aid that is merit-based	52
% of all students receiving loans	84
% receiving scholarships	23
% of all students receiving assistantships	12
Average grant	$4,100
Average graduation debt	NR

ADMISSIONS	
# applications received	766
% applicants accepted	64
% acceptees attending	36
Average LSAT	153
LSAT range	141-166
Average undergrad GPA	3.10
GPA range	2.10-4.00
Application fee (in/out-state)	$25/$25
Regular application	rolling
Regular notification	rolling
Rolling notification?	Yes
Early decision program?	No
Admission may be deferred?	No
Evening division offered?	No
Part-time accepted?	Yes
Gourman Report Rating	**3.36**

UNIVERSITY OF MONTANA
School of Law

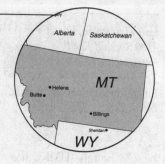

The "small, nurturing," and "inexpensive" University of Montana School of Law offers a low student-to-faculty ratio and a creative curriculum that combines legal theory with a "heavy emphasis on practical experience." In addition to strong Native American law and general practice curriculums, UM offers a broad range of courses in environmental and natural resources law, including a clinical program in conjunction with the U.S. Forest Service. The first year covers a lot of ground, and 1Ls learn team-oriented problem-solving techniques. The required "practical law firm program" enables 1Ls to "use substantive course material in practical situations." As part of the program, a group of six or seven 1Ls forms a hypothetical firm in conjunction with a 3L junior partner. "This program helps orient and familiarize students from day one," said a 1L, and "fosters a cooperative environment." Some students complained that UM "needs to have more classes that focus on legal theory," and that the practical program places "too much emphasis on 'busy work' classes like legal research." Also, participation in clinical programs is "mandatory" and, according to some, "a thorn in the side of every 3L." Other students disagreed, and gushed about the required clinical programs. There is a strong bond between UM students and the "very well qualified and helpful" faculty. "It is amazing that they all make an effort to know not only the names of all the students, but also concern themselves with knowing who the students are in terms of interests, social life, etc." The professors "love to teach" and "have an affection for the state." Many "make their own casebooks that incorporate Montana law into the curriculum, and it really prepares students for the bar (we have a very high pass rate in Montana)."

Facilities-wise, "the building is not huge or top-flight, but they are making improvements." The library "could be bigger" as well, and "the computer labs are a disgrace." UM is "the only law school in a very large state" and it enjoys a solid reputation throughout the Northwest and "Big Sky" states. "The school is geared to prepare you to practice in Montana," which is fine by most students. "UM graduates practicing in the region do not face the severe competition per capita" frequently present in large metropolitan areas. Other students took a more negative

Christine Sopko, Admissions Officer
Admissions Office
Missoula, MT 59812
Tel: 406-243-2698 • Fax: 406-243-2576
Email: lawadmis@selway.umt.edu
Internet: www.umt.edu/law/homepage.htm

University of Montana

view: "Montana just doesn't have the market to accommodate seventy-five new lawyers each year." The average student here expects to begin working at a salary of less than $40,000. That's a pittance on Wall Street, but it goes pretty far in Montana, where "the cost of living is lower." The few here who wish to practice out-of-state were are very confident of their abilities to find good jobs.

UM students said they were happy overall, thanks in large part to the "beautiful surroundings" and ample outdoor sporting opportunities. Located in Missoula, a city of 50,000-plus that sits on the western slope of the Rocky Mountains, UM offers a "low-stress environment." "Competition is negligible" and "upper-class students freely pass out their outlines." Roughly once a month during "Fridays at 5:00," the school "provides beverages and food and an opportunity for lots of students to socialize." On the downside, UM does not attract many minority students, "though there have been some efforts to recruit Native Americans."

If you want the opportunity to be a big fish in a small pond, Montana is worth checking out. "Those of us studying law at the University of Montana are not here because we could not get into a Top Twenty-Five law school," asserted a 2L. "We are here because we recognize the value of studying law at a small school focused on both legal theory and its practical application. The Montana Supreme Court regularly travels to Missoula to meet with our classes, and student interaction with local judges and attorneys occurs on a regular basis."

ADMISSIONS

Each entering class at the University of Montana is limited to seventy-five students. According to the admissions office, there are about eight applicants for every slot in the first-year class. Nevertheless, overall admissions standards are moderate. For the fall 1995 entering class, the average LSAT score was 157 and the average GPA was 3.21. Montana residents will find the admissions process much easier than out-of-staters, since the law school strictly limits nonresident enrollment to 33 percent.

ACADEMICS

Student/faculty ratio	13:1
% female faculty	26
% minority faculty	3
Hours of study per day	3.75

FINANCIAL FACTS

Tuition (in/out-state)	$5,755/$10,412
Cost of books	$850
Room & board (on/off-campus)	$2,600/NR
% first-year students receiving aid	74
% all students receiving aid	78
% aid that is merit-based	3
% of all students receiving loans	78
% receiving scholarships	39
% of all students receiving assistantships	16
Average grant	$1,482
Average graduation debt	$37,500

ADMISSIONS

# applications received	478
% applicants accepted	43
% acceptees attending	38
Average LSAT	156
LSAT range	139-171
Average undergrad GPA	3.25
GPA range	2.24-4.00
Application fee (in/out-state)	$60/$60
Regular application	rolling
Regular notification	rolling
Rolling notification?	Yes
Early decision program?	No
Admission may be deferred?	No
Evening division offered?	No
Part-time accepted?	No
Gourman Report Rating	**2.83**

UNIVERSITY OF NEBRASKA
College of Law

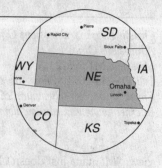

It is indeed true that $80,000 starting salaries do not await most graduates of the College of Law at the University of Nebraska, Lincoln. Neither Lincoln nor Omaha, Nebraska's other major job market, is New York or Los Angeles. But this suits Nebraskans just fine. The obsession with salaries and rankings that preoccupies so many law students on both coasts is a distant phenomenon in Lincoln. While a share of its graduates do venture out to the major markets, the University of Nebraska College of Law is, in the best sense, a regional institution. U of N holds the franchise when it comes to supplying the state's lawyers: More than half of Nebraska's practicing attorneys are Nebraska Law graduates. Few law schools of its size can match the educational resources the Nebraska law school offers its students. In a part of the country where higher education is dominated by state-supported schools, the University of Nebraska is one of the finest. Numerous joint-degree programs are available to the university's law students, including a highly regarded course of study leading to a J.D./Ph.D. in psychology. As residents of the state, the majority of Nebraska students pay a tuition that is as low as that of practically any law school in the country.

Equally moderate is the praise that we heard from Nebraska law students for their school. Most of those we surveyed expressed satisfaction with the basic quality of their program, but few did so enthusiastically. This remark from one 2L was typical of those we heard: "Some of my classes have been great, and a few of my professors have been excellent, but certainly not all.... Only when I consider how much students at some private schools pay for the same thing do I really appreciate UNL as much as I probably should." Indeed, such praise seems far less faint when one considers how many other law schools utterly fail to satisfy their students in fundamental areas in which Nebraska students seem to want for very little. As one 3L put it, "The facilities here are excellent, and there are enough talented and helpful members of the faculty and staff that you can, if you try, get just about anything you need here." Most seem to share this opinion, giving Nebraska very high marks for its research facilities and the Nebraska faculty better-than-average marks for its teaching abilities.

Glenda J. Pierce, Assistant Dean
P.O. Box 830902
Lincoln, NE 68583
Tel: 402-472-2161 • Fax: 402-472-5185
Email: lawadm@unlinfo.unl.edu
Internet: www.unl.edu/lawcoll

University of Nebraska

That said, it must be noted that students here see room for serious improvement in several areas. There is general agreement among Nebraska law students—as there appears to be among law students almost everywhere—that their curriculum, however strong, fails to prepare them for the daily demands of law practice. As one 3L lamented, "There are no courses that teach billing practices or how to find a courthouse. Law schools in general are geared to produce research associates (for big firms), not individual lawyers." This complaint was quite common, especially among the relatively large number of Nebraska students who expressed a desire to become solo practitioners. At the same time, the administration said it has offered clinical education programs every semester for over 20 years. "In the civil clinic, our third-year students represent indigent clients in a wide variety of matters, and in our criminal clinic, our students conduct most of the misdemeanor prosecutions for Lancaster County." Perhaps the discrepancy between student and administrative opinions can be explained by student comments on lack of class selection.

Nebraska students also expressed dissatisfaction in several areas where many smaller law schools appear to fall short: career services and class selection. "They need to offer more classes on a regular basis," wrote one 2L, "rather than once a year or even less." "The selection of classes is too limited," agreed a 3L, "and you're basically on your own when it comes to career services." The latter opinion appears to be widely held, and cannot easily be dismissed. As for course selection, which is often a function of faculty size, Nebraska students may not realize how lucky they are.

ADMISSIONS

In 1986, the University of Nebraska College of Law admitted nearly 70 percent of all applicants. Today, Nebraska is hardly among the most selective of law schools, but gone are the days when practically all one had to do to get into this fine public law school was have a pulse and file an application. The numerical credentials of the average Nebraska student are only slightly above the national average for current law students, and the law school's overall acceptance rate is still quite generous.

ACADEMICS

Student/faculty ratio	14:1
% female faculty	9
% minority faculty	5
Hours of study per day	3.81

Academic specialties:
Corporation Securities, Environmental, Labor, Taxation, Skills, Clinical Education

FINANCIAL FACTS

Tuition (in/out-state)	$3,510/$9,009
Cost of books	$765
Fees (in/out-state)	$988/$988
Room & board (on/off-campus)	$5,915/$8,000
% first-year students receiving aid	55
% all students receiving aid	55
% aid that is merit-based	52
% of all students receiving loans	86
% receiving scholarships	55
% of all students receiving assistantships	NR
Average grant	$2,598
Average graduation debt	$20,000

ADMISSIONS

# applications received	685
% applicants accepted	56
% acceptees attending	36
Average LSAT	154
LSAT range	151-158
Average undergrad GPA	3.45
GPA range	3.16-3.71
Application fee (in/out-state)	$25/$25
Regular application	March 1
Regular notification	rolling
Rolling notification?	Yes
Early decision program?	No
Admission may be deferred?	Yes
Maximum length of deferment	1 year
Evening division offered?	No
Part-time accepted?	No
Gourman Report Rating	**3.22**

NEW ENGLAND SCHOOL OF LAW

OVERVIEW

Type of school	private
Environment	city
Scholastic calendar	semester
Schedule	full-time or part-time

STUDENTS

Enrollment of parent institution	NR
Enrollment of law school	968
% male/female	53/47
% out-of-state	48
% part-time	42
% minorities	12
% international (# of countries represented)	3 (12)
Average age at entry	27

APPLICANTS ALSO LOOK AT

Suffolk University
Boston College
Northeastern University
Boston University
Western New England College

SURVEY SAYS...

HITS
Students feel well-prepared
Practical experience
Faculty-student relations

EMPLOYMENT PROFILE

Firms recruiting on campus	12
Job placement rate (%)	87
% grads employed immediately	40
% grads employed within six months	84
Average starting salary	$36,568

Grads employed by field (%):

Academia	7
Business/industry	21
Government	16
Judicial clerkships	9
Military	4
Private practice	49
Public interest	4
Other	2

"Sadly underrated." That, in a nutshell, is how students at the New England School of Law summed up the prevailing national view of their institution. Originally established in 1908 as the all-women's Portia Law School, NESL has been coeducational since 1938 and fully accredited by the ABA since 1973. NESL now enrolls over 1,100 full- and part-time students, more than half of whom are male. In the 1980s, the school relocated to its current location "in downtown Boston near the centers of government" and just one block from the Public Garden. Students at New England admitted that their law school is "a great bargain in legal education" and "the best kept secret in Boston," a city that itself is "a tremendous place to live and study."

Beyond a traditional first-year course of study, the "demanding" curriculum here is straightforward, with relatively few required courses. NESL offers concentrated programs in environmental law, international law, and tax law, as well as several specialized seminars. "There is great diversity in courses" here and an emphasis on "producing practical lawyers" with "real legal skills." The curriculum stresses "learning via problem-solving" and students boasted that "NESL graduates possess a strong, working knowledge of the law as well as an almost instinctual awareness of courtroom strategy." One 3L claimed that "public interest emphasis is extremely lacking. Unless you are interested in tax or business law, there is little support." Students reserved enormous praise for the "young, energetic, intelligent, accessible" and "utterly first-rate" NESL faculty. Professors "teach with passion and evoke debate" and "make a tremendous effort to ensure that students grasp and understand the legal concepts and theories." They also bring "a lot of practical experience" to the classroom. Unfortunately, the staff lacks diversity and "minority faculty are almost nonexistent."

A wide variety of clinical programs and clerkships give 2Ls and 3Ls numerous opportunities to gain "hands-on" experience. Most of these programs take the form of external placements that run concurrently with courses. For instance, an NESL student might work with the Department of Public Health while taking the law school's course in health and hospital law. NESL students

Pamela Jorgensen, Director of Admissions
154 Stuart Street
Boston, MA 02116
Tel: 617-422-7210 • Fax: 617-422-7200
Email: admit@admin.nesl.edu
Internet: www.nesl.edu

New England School of Law

also applauded the "excellent part-time program" and flexible scheduling options (full-time day, part-time evening, flex time). On a negative note, NESL "needs more journals."

Many students had complaints about the physical quality of their school. The "tiny box" that constitutes the facilities at NESL "desperately needs new elevators" and additional computer terminals. While research resources are "good," NESL "could use a bigger, better library." "The lack of an actual campus hurts the camaraderie," suggested a 1L. "We should have student lounges—places where students can come together instead of the hallways." The Student Bar Association provides plenty of programs and "turnout is good" for extracurricular activities and guest lectures by "top-notch" speakers like Janet Reno. In keeping with the school's "family" atmosphere, "everyone exchanges notes and outlines" and gets along well. "We push each other to work hard, and we support each other every step of the way," said a 2L. Many students here are Massachusetts natives and intend to practice in lawyer-saturated Boston. The thought of competing in this jam-packed legal market causes some anxiety. "Career Services does a lot, but they fight an uphill battle because employers flock to the more nationally known schools."

School pride runs exceptionally high at NESL, as does frustration with arbitrary law school rankings. "The school's reputation does not match how good it is," complained a 2L. "Other schools may have a 'name' and 'prestige,' but look at the facts, and don't be biased or prejudiced. Our bar passage rate is on a par with Harvard." Declared an optimistic 1L: "Students realize that NESL is not recognized among the best Boston law schools, but we are all very hard workers with big goals, and are willing to work to change this perception."

ADMISSIONS

Admissions standards at the NESL have crept up slightly over the decade, but the numerical credentials of the average NESL student are still lower than those of students at nearly all other ABA-approved law schools in the competitive Northeast.

ACADEMICS

Student/faculty ratio	20:1
% female faculty	34
% minority faculty	5
Hours of study per day	3.89

Academic specialties:
Environmental, International, Taxation

FINANCIAL FACTS

Tuition	$13,350
Cost of books	$500
Fees	$150
Room & board (on/off-campus)	NR/$11,250
% first-year students receiving aid	78
% all students receiving aid	78
% aid that is merit-based	10
% of all students receiving loans	76
% receiving scholarships	28
% of all students receiving assistantships	NR
Average grant	$2,400
Average graduation debt	$45,600

ADMISSIONS

# applications received	2,408
% applicants accepted	65
% acceptees attending	16
Average LSAT	149
LSAT range	137-166
Average undergrad GPA	2.92
GPA range	2.05-3.83
Application fee	$50
Regular application	June 1
Regular notification	rolling
Rolling notification?	Yes
Early decision program?	No
Admission may be deferred?	Yes
Maximum length of deferment	1 year
Evening division offered?	Yes
Part-time accepted?	Yes
Gourman Report Rating	**3.08**

UNIVERSITY OF NEW MEXICO
School of Law

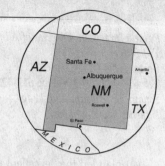

Many previously insulated law schools are only now awakening to the realities of the communities they exist to serve. The University of New Mexico School of Law has been awake and making progress now for years. Small, innovative, inexpensive, and well-funded, New Mexico seems to fulfill the ideal of the dynamic public law school, reflecting both academically and demographically the state that supports it.

The law school's curriculum is strong in the traditional areas, but it stands out most for its regional (and generally social) consciousness. The law school operates several respected research and training institutes, most notably the American Indian Law Center, the Transboundary Center, which is itself concerned with natural resource management on an international scale. New Mexico students can choose from numbers of courses in all these areas and can earn their J.D.'s with a formal certificate of specialization in Natural Resources Law. The law school's commitment to practical-skills training is exceptionally strong: New Mexico is one of a handful of schools nationwide that require significant clinical participation by all students. Most UNM students fulfill this requirement on campus, in the school's well-staffed Law Practice Clinic. The student body at New Mexico is definitely a student body of New Mexico. The vast majority are state residents and almost half members of minority groups, giving UNM a level of student diversity unmatched by any public law school, "save the University of Hawaii." UNM's tiny class size insures an enormously favorable student-faculty ratio and extremely selective admissions process. UNM admits less than 20 percent of all applicants, and gives strong preference to state residents. (Overall, however, numerical admissions standards are rather moderate.)

Decidedly immoderate is the enthusiasm current students express for their chosen school and the very particular attributes that draw them here. Students include among their many blessings the incredible location, the small size and corresponding "incredible closeness of the community and the amount of caring shown among faculty, staff, and students," the excellent Environmental Law and Indian Law programs, an inspiring faculty

Corina Gonzales, Administrative Assistant
1117 Stanford, NE
Albuquerque, NM 87131
Tel: 505-277-0958 • Fax: 505-2779958
Internet: www.unm.edu/unmlaw

which are "the greatest asset. They are accessible and always willing to help," and, most of all, each other. One first year explains, "Fellow students help me 'see' things in new ways. The diversity of experience and background is astounding." Many students love sharing their teacher's commitment to changing the makeup of law practitioners who will in turn transform and humanize the law and the country it serves. One first-year tells us: "There aren't 'too many' lawyers in society. Those people who have access to lawyers make up a small percentage, however. There are too many lawyers representing the interests of the upper classes/corporations of society. This must change." One 3L adds that UNM is "a great law school for people who want to learn how to use the law to help people solve their problems." And these students will certainly have the chance to do so, as their job-prospect confidence predicts, thanks to UNM's reputation and their excellent legal writing and practical lawyering training which makes them especially attractive to future employers.

Some UNM students do muster a few complaints, but these are generally tempered with (or canceled out by) general satisfaction. One 2L hesitantly asks for "more courses, but that would compromise its size, which is ideal." Many students agree that UNM needs "more money for library and computers" since these facilities are not sufficient to meet student needs. And a few would like more business law, critical race relations, and feminist jurisprudence courses. The general level of content must surely be pretty high when an otherwise happy student requests "more gothic architecture."

ADMISSIONS

If one looks only at the grade-point average and LSAT score of the average student at the University of New Mexico School of Law, one runs the risk of seriously underestimating the competitiveness of the law school's admissions process. Extremely high demand for spots in New Mexico's tiny entering class makes this fine, inexpensive law school one of the most selective in the nation. No applicants save those with stratospheric numerical credentials can be certain of gaining admission—New Mexico accepts and rejects applicants across a broad range of GPAs and test scores.

ACADEMICS

Student/faculty ratio	11:1
% female faculty	43
% minority faculty	24
Hours of study per day	3.66

FINANCIAL FACTS

Tuition (in/out-state)	$3,283/$11,015
Cost of books	$668
Fees (in/out-state)	$135/$135
Room & board (on/off-campus)	$7,220/$10,164
% first-year students receiving aid	NR
% all students receiving aid	NR
% aid that is merit-based	NR
% of all students receiving loans	NR
% receiving scholarships	NR
% of all students receiving assistantships	NR
Average grant	$3,284
Average graduation debt	NR

ADMISSIONS

# applications received	825
% applicants accepted	29
% acceptees attending	47
Average LSAT	156
LSAT range	141-176
Average undergrad GPA	3.24
GPA range	2.16-4.10
Application fee (in/out-state)	$40/$40
Regular application	February 15
Regular notification	NR
Rolling notification?	No
Early decision program?	No
Admission may be deferred?	Yes
Evening division offered?	No
Part-time accepted?	No
Gourman Report Rating	2.84

NEW YORK LAW SCHOOL

For the price of a single subway token, and without changing trains, you could get yourself within about two blocks of all of Manhattan's five law schools. Near the end of the line for the downtown No. 1 Train—probably the most law-school-rich subway line in the world—sits one of the city's and country's oldest law schools, the New York Law School. Established in 1891 by former students and administrators from Columbia's young law school, New York Law has put in a century of solid service to the nation's largest legal community. Additionally, this private law school has, through its operation of one of the country's largest evening divisions, put in a century of service to the working men and women of New York City.

Today, New York Law has a total enrollment of almost 1,400, approximately one-third of them part-time students, most of whom are already working professionals. The course of study they follow at the law school represents a good mix of tradition and innovation. Through a variety of classroom courses in "Lawyering Skills," through one of the law school's several clinical programs, or through one of a number of opportunities for external placement, students at New York Law have ample opportunity to gain practical skills before entering the profession. However, some students are unhappy with the current legal writing program. One 3L had some visionary advice, shared in the confident style of the New York Law School students we heard from: "All law schools should provide concentration programs so students will be prepared for a specialization. Also, the future of law is in mediation. This should be a required course."

Current NYLS students wish that people would pay attention to the fact that NYLS consistently turns out "successful business leaders and politicians." Their vocal ambition and self-esteem is admirable and absolutely necessary in a city chock-full of prestigious law schools. One student declared, "New York Law School is underrated and its students have the ability to compete with the surrounding likes of Columbia, NYU, Fordham, etc., intellectually, academically, and ethically. Let's get an update on those statistics, our ratings should be going up. NYLS is being treated unfairly, the curriculum and grading system are far more strin-

Pamela McKenna, Director of Admissions
57 Worth Street
New York, NY 10013
Tel: 212-431-2888 • Fax: 212-966-1522
Email: admissions@nyls.edu
Internet: www.nyls.edu

gent than those schools formerly mentioned." In response to such outcries, the school has revised its grading system to be comparable to its New York brethren. Another student articulated the general perception, "It's better than its reputation." If the tide of national opinion could be turned by force of sheer will alone, Columbia and NYU would soon be considered merely second-rate New York law schools.

Many students expressed dissatisfaction with several areas more within the realm of their administration's ability to change, such as instituting longer library hours. Relations between students, between students and faculty, and between students and the president were also cited as impediments to the strong sense of community that most students said the school currently lacks. One student commented that the school must "improve representation of students to reflect diversity of the surrounding geographic area."

Most NYLS students who responded to our survey expressed typical worry over that precarious step out the law school door and the likelihood that a welcome mat into some friendly office or another would present itself, but they proclaimed adamant pride and enthusiastic confidence in their school.

ADMISSIONS

Although its numerical admissions standards are lower than those of many law schools in the New York region, a massive applicant pool allows the New York Law School to be somewhat selective. Still, New York Law represents by far the safest bet for law-school-bound Manhattanites. Statistically, an applicant with an undergraduate GPA between 3.00 and 3.25 and an LSAT score between about 155 and 159 stands a 95 percent chance of gaining admission. And to make the school even more friendly to applicants, the admissions office tells us that "every applicant is assigned to a specific counselor in Admissions."

ACADEMICS	
Student/faculty ratio	22:1
% female faculty	30
% minority faculty	11
Hours of study per day	2.96

Academic specialties:

Constitutional, Corporation Securities, Government Services, Human Rights, International

FINANCIAL FACTS	
Tuition	$19,777
Cost of books	$800
Fees	$278
Room & board (on/off-campus)	NR/$9,945
% first-year students receiving aid	NR
% all students receiving aid	79
% aid that is merit-based	12
% of all students receiving loans	94
% receiving scholarships	42
% of all students receiving assistantships	NR
Average grant	NR
Average graduation debt	$34,700

ADMISSIONS	
# applications received	4,113
% applicants accepted	55
% acceptees attending	19
Average LSAT	154
LSAT range	147-171
Average undergrad GPA	3.01
GPA range	2.50-4.00
Application fee	$50
Regular application	rolling
Regular notification	rolling
Rolling notification?	Yes
Early decision program?	No
Admission may be deferred?	Yes
Maximum length of deferment	1 year
Evening division offered?	Yes
Part-time accepted?	Yes
Gourman Report Rating	**3.35**

NEW YORK UNIVERSITY
School of Law

OVERVIEW

Type of school	private
Environment	metropolis
Scholastic calendar	semester
Schedule	full-time only

STUDENTS

Enrollment of parent institution	13,464
Enrollment of law school	2,059
% male/female	60/40
% out-of-state	48
% part-time	16
% minorities	17
% international (# of countries represented)	NR (58)
Average age at entry	NR

APPLICANTS ALSO LOOK AT

Columbia University
Harvard University
Georgetown University
Yale University
University of Pennsylvania

SURVEY SAYS...

HITS
Grads expect big bucks
Left-leaning politics
Practical lawyering skills

MISSES
Library staff
Not enough courses

EMPLOYMENT PROFILE

Job placement rate (%)	100
% grads employed immediately	94
% grads employed within six months	97
Average starting salary	$69,000

If you were to set about ranking law schools, you would be forced to make some idiosyncratic, even arbitrary decisions as to what criteria to consider. Whatever formulas you chose to try out, however, three little letters would start to look mighty familiar at the top of your list: N-Y-U. Established more than 150 years ago just off Washington Square Park in the heart of Greenwich Village, the New York University School of Law is a leader among American law schools in nearly every category. Its students are enormously well qualified, its admirably gender-balanced faculty is world-class, and the ratio of the latter to the former is marvelously low. Its research resources are vast, and its facilities are state-of-the-art. Its traditional classroom curriculum is strong and terrifically broad, and its widely respected clinical programs are innovative and numerous. Upholding the NYU motto, "A private university in the public service," NYU is currently involved in programs offering unparalleled support for students who wish to pursue public interest law, expanding resources in scholarships and loan repayment. Though its tuition is one of the highest charged by any of the nation's 178 ABA-approved law schools, its graduates are, on average, some of the most highly compensated in the nation. Beyond these manifold strengths, however, there is something equally important. NYU students are, by our reckoning, among the happiest of all the students at the nation's elite schools.

We could certainly go further, but perhaps that is best left to current NYU students, a highly qualified, remarkably self-assured bunch whose lavish praise for their chosen school speaks for itself. As one student reported: "This school has its attitude as its greatest asset." Indeed. From a 1L asked to assess her law school: "How do I love thee? Let me count the ways....With every part of the law school on your side, it's hard not to feel like you'll be a success." Students praise the "laid-back attitude" of their fellow students, a "diverse" and "community-oriented" group. From one of the many students who lionized NYU's career placement staff: "NYU gets its students jobs.... Placement takes it personally if you are not employed." From various others who declined to enumerate their beloved's many strengths: "I love NYU"; "Best school in the country"; "NYU=Godhead." When

Nan McNamara, Assistant Dean of Admissions
Admissions, West Third Street, 2nd Floor
New York, NY 10012
Tel: 212-998-6060

New York University

asked to name their school's weaknesses, the majority of NYU students we heard from could muster little more than "There could perhaps be..." this or that. And several asserted that the only ways in which NYU could improve would be through the addition of "more copiers in the library," "hors d'oeuvres carts," and "back rubs for all."

In a more serious vein, some students at NYU do see real room for improvement. The law school's clinical programs for instance, whose quality students rightly praise, are criticized by many for their limited enrollment. "Clinics should be open to all who want them," argued one 2L. A number of students also voiced complaints like this one: "NYU has some of the top academics in the country teaching here, which gives us prestige but not necessarily good teaching." While most seem to consider this only a relative weakness, they nevertheless cry out for more "professors who put teaching before their own careers and publishing records."

In the end, it is hard to ignore the near unanimity of opinion and the preponderance of evidence supporting this conclusion from one NYU 2L: "If you are ridiculous enough to go to law school, this is the place to go. The quality of life is better than any other place, and the prestige and respect of going to this school goes a long way."

ADMISSIONS

Once classes begin, cutthroat competitiveness among NYU students is clearly considered unseemly, but they all had to scratch and claw their way in. NYU is universally regarded as a "top-ten" school, and the selectivity of its admissions process is very much in keeping with that status. Numerical admissions standards couldn't be much higher; the average credentials of entering NYU students place them, by our calculations, among the eight or nine most qualified student bodies in the nation. Numbers aren't everything when it comes to getting into a school like this, but they certainly play a major role.

ACADEMICS	
Student/faculty ratio	11:1
% female faculty	27
% minority faculty	9
Hours of study per day	3.41

Academic specialties:
Corporation Securities, International, Taxation

FINANCIAL FACTS	
Tuition	$22,144
Cost of books	NR
% first-year students receiving aid	72
% all students receiving aid	74
% aid that is merit-based	5
% of all students receiving loans	74
% receiving scholarships	24
% of all students receiving assistantships	20
Average grant	$11,100
Average graduation debt	$62,000

ADMISSIONS	
# applications received	6,525
% applicants accepted	20
% acceptees attending	30
Average LSAT	168
Average undergrad GPA	3.65
Application fee	$65
Early application	October 15
Early notification	December 1
Regular application	April 15
Regular notification	rolling
Rolling notification?	Yes
Early decision program?	Yes
Admission may be deferred?	Yes
Maximum length of deferment	2 years
Evening division offered?	No
Part-time accepted?	No
Gourman Report Rating	**4.79**

NORTH CAROLINA CENTRAL UNIVERSITY
School of Law

The cities of Raleigh, Durham, and Chapel Hill, North Carolina, form what has come to be known as the "Research Triangle," a burgeoning center for industrial and governmental research. The triangle also encompasses three law schools: the nationally prominent law schools at Duke and UNC and the North Carolina Central University School of Law. NC Central is the smallest of the three, and it is certainly the least well known. This public law school cannot compete, perhaps, with its larger, better-known neighbors in terms of prestige, but then it has never tried to. Instead, NC Central has dedicated itself to serving and reflecting the population of the state it serves, and it has succeeded admirably. Founded as the country's first public liberal-arts college for African Americans, NC Central joined the UNC system in 1972, and it now stands as a tremendously important complement to the system's flagship campus in Chapel Hill. The same is true of its law school, which enrolls over 90 percent North Carolina residents, 55 percent of them African Americans. (At Chapel Hill, these statistics are about 70 percent and 9 percent.) In terms of both its student body and its faculty, NC Central is very nearly the most racially diverse of the country's ABA-approved law schools.

The law school's J.D. curriculum is highly structured, with relatively few elective courses even in the third year, but co-curricular opportunities are ample and varied. NC Central also offers a limited clinical program and a joint-degree program with the School of Library and Information Sciences. Overall admissions are relatively selective because of the small size of entering classes, but numerical standards are fairly low.

The law school operates the only evening division available in any of North Carolina's five law schools. The evening students we heard from expressed a heartening combination of excitement, thrill and gratitude that this wonderful program exists and at such an affordable price, enabling working people "to pursue a life-long dream, the best legal representation to clients."

We did hear some negative comments, of course, especially from day students, many of whom expressed dissatisfaction with limitations stemming from those characteristics that draw people to NCCU. Many claimed the night students receive better treat-

Jacqueline Faucett, Admissions Coordinator
NCCU Law, 1512 South Alston Avenue
Durham, NC 27707
Tel: 919-560-6333

North Carolina Central University

ment. The low class size and tuition restrict NCCU's ability to provide all the physical comforts and extensive course offerings which many students said would make NCCU a more perfect place. Future NCCU students need not be unduly concerned, however, since, according to one student, "The school has undergone and will continue to undergo some much needed change under the leadership of Dean Luney. New life has been breathed into the school." What troubles students most, besides the perceived lack of effort on the part of Career Services, is the misperception on the part of other schools and employers in the area, who refuse to take proper account of NCCU. One student told us, with typically positive emphasis: "My only concern is traditional employers' limited way of thinking that only certain law schools produce exceptional attorneys....At the NCCU School of Law 'Excellence Without Excuse' is not just a motto, but a way of life."

ADMISSIONS

The admissions process at the North Carolina Central University School of Law is competitive despite the low numerical standards to which the law school holds its applicants. The numerical credentials of the average NC Central student are lower than those of students at most other law schools, but Central's small size necessitates a high degree of selectivity since the law school enrolls only about 100 new students annually.

ACADEMICS

Student/faculty ratio	15:1
% female faculty	41
% minority faculty	59
Hours of study per day	4.19

FINANCIAL FACTS

Tuition	$1,890
Cost of books	$1,250
Room & board (on/off-campus)	$4,200/$6,850
% first-year students receiving aid	NR
% all students receiving aid	NR
% aid that is merit-based	NR
% of all students receiving loans	NR
% receiving scholarships	NR
% of all students receiving assistantships	NR
Average grant	NR
Average graduation debt	NR

ADMISSIONS

# applications received	1,152
% applicants accepted	19
% acceptees attending	45
Average LSAT	149
Average undergrad GPA	3.00
Application fee	$30
Regular application	rolling
Regular notification	NR
Rolling notification?	Yes
Early decision program?	No
Admission may be deferred?	NR
Evening division offered?	Yes
Part-time accepted?	Yes
Gourman Report Rating	**2.26**

UNIVERSITY OF NORTH CAROLINA
School of Law

The University of North Carolina School of Law, located on the campus of the nation's oldest state university, enjoys a long-established reputation as one of the finest law schools in the country, public or private. For a combination of reasons, some more tangible than others, thousands of highly qualified applicants vie annually for one of the roughly 235 slots in North Carolina's first-year class. Some of this popularity is easily explained by the law school's obvious strengths. The broad traditional curriculum is administered by a large and esteemed faculty and is supplemented by numerous opportunities for interdisciplinary study in several of the university's widely respected graduate departments and by a modest variety of clinical programs. But two other factors do a better job of explaining the flood of applications that inundate UNC's admissions committee every year: value and location. The law school is a bargain if ever there was one. Resident tuition is almost negligible, while non-resident tuition is extremely low. As for location, Chapel Hill is the archetypal college town that, to a degree, both defines and is defined by the university. While a large percentage of Carolina students are state residents, the vast majority of applicants are not, which makes the admissions process, which is competitive for all, extraordinarily selective for non-residents.

Carolina students were quite happy with their school, and many pointed to the quality of teaching as a major factor in their contentment. One 3L exclaimed, "The professors at Carolina are the best! Their doors are always open and I have never left a class where the professor wasn't fielding more questions or engaging in a discussion with students." Some respondents mentioned their fellow students as a stand-out quality of the school. "The diversity of students and backgrounds is one of the school's greatest assets. I strongly believe there is something for everyone here," wrote a 3L, "Even with [all the] wide-ranging views, there is no hostility." Some students noted that the school seemed to have a slightly liberal/progressive bent, and one 3L even claimed, "There isn't much tolerance for conservative viewpoints."

J. Elizabeth Furr, Assistant Dean for Admissions
Campus Box 3380
Chapel Hill, NC 27599
Tel: 919-962-5109 • Fax: 919-962-1170
Email: law_admission@unc.edu
Internet: www.law.unc.edu

University of North Carolina

However, most students reported that everybody from students to faculty to administrators got along pretty well. Despite respect for the intellectual attributes of other students, and for a "healthy mix of cooperation and competition," some students we heard from agreed with the 2L who wrote, "There is not a strong sense of community among students as a whole, although we have several cohesive student groups." The sense of community that students did feel often seemed to come as much from being part of the overall university as it did from being a law student.

While some students complained that physically the law school was too small and cramped, all acknowledged that construction that should more than adequately solve such problems was underway. One 2L wryly commented, "If they really were going to finish the construction before we graduate, then the facilities would be awesome. I'm not holding my breath. Maybe they'll include a nice Alumni Lounge . . ." Students were generally enthusiastic about their prospects as alumni thanks to their faith in the career placement office. "We are fortunate to have a very energetic director of Career Development and Placement, who works 12-hour days helping us find jobs." Some did note that the school's excellent reputation and networking opportunities worked better for those students planning to remain in the state.

The Carolina students we heard from had few suggestions for improvement. Some suggested that the school improve faculty diversity. The school's low tuition may actually be problematic in that some students admitted that the school didn't have the available funds to implement some of their suggestions. Better alumni fund-raising was suggested as a potential remedy.

ADMISSIONS

Like all the nation's elite public law schools, the University of North Carolina School of Law is extremely selective. The law school has the luxury of denying admission to hundreds of candidates whose numbers would get them into almost any law school in the country. Nonresident applicants be forewarned: You will face stiffer competition and be held to even higher standards.

ACADEMICS

Student/faculty ratio	20:1
% female faculty	32
% minority faculty	10
Hours of study per day	3.50

Academic specialties:
Civil Procedure, Commercial, Constitutional, Corporation Securities, Criminal, Environmental, Government Services, Human Rights, International, Labor, Legal History, Legal Philosophy, Property, Taxation

FINANCIAL FACTS

Tuition (in/out-state)	$2,717/$13,989
Cost of books	$700
Room & board (on/off-campus)	$6,362/$6,362
% first-year students receiving aid	NR
% all students receiving aid	18
% aid that is merit-based	84
% of all students receiving loans	72
% receiving scholarships	NR
% of all students receiving assistantships	NR
Average grant	$2,500
Average graduation debt	$29,087

ADMISSIONS

# applications received	2,281
% applicants accepted	27
% acceptees attending	39
Average LSAT	160
LSAT range	142-178
Average undergrad GPA	3.41
GPA range	2.30-4.00
Application fee (in/out-state)	$60/$60
Early application	October 15
Early notification	January 1
Regular application	rolling
Regular notification	rolling
Rolling notification?	Yes
Early decision program?	Yes
Admission may be deferred?	Yes
Maximum length of deferment	1 year
Evening division offered?	No
Part-time accepted?	No
Gourman Report Rating	4.43

UNIVERSITY OF NORTH DAKOTA
School of Law

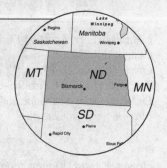

In the spirit of full disclosure, the bulletin of the University of North Dakota School of Law reports that the average temperature in Grand Forks, ND, for the month of January is 4 degrees Fahrenheit. Low temperatures during what is laconically termed the "cold period" tend to reach -25 degrees. Less-than-hardy prospective law students probably needn't read any further. Located in the fertile Red River Valley, in the northeastern part of sparsely populated North Dakota, this small, inexpensive public law school draws the majority of its students from within the state and from nearby Minnesota, a state with which North Dakota has a reciprocal residency agreement for purposes of tuition. Other states in the upper Midwest are also well represented. The curriculum at North Dakota is decidedly traditional, but clinical programs and skills courses are on the rise. Many of the course offerings reflect regional priorities: "Oil and Gas Law," and "Water Law." The Scandinavian roots of many of the state's residents are reflected not only in the law library (named for former dean Olaf Thormodsgard) but also in the school's exchange program with the University of Oslo in Norway. Those who wish to become part of the roughly eighty new students who bundle up each year and join the first-year class at North Dakota will want to know that fewer than half of all applicants are admitted. Numerical admissions standards, however, are moderate.

Maybe it's just that the chilly weather makes people huddle together for warmth, but the degree of closeness and camaraderie that current North Dakota law students claim to feel for both their colleagues and their professors is striking. Though not without their criticisms, the students we surveyed expressed a solid sense of satisfaction with their chosen school, particularly when it came to quality-of-life issues. A sampling of the comments we heard follows: "There is very close faculty-student contact here. Professors are your friends and are very concerned with students' learning." "Our size allows you to get to know fellow students very well—there is a family atmosphere despite the inevitable degree of competition among students." "The faculty treat you more like a peer than like a lowly student. That makes for a comfortable classroom environment that stimulates lively discussion."

But for all of the good will which seems to stem from the advantages of North Dakota's size, few of the students we heard from failed to mention some of the disadvantages. "There are not enough professors here to offer the kind of class selection I would ideally like to have," wrote one 3L. "This is basically a meat-and-potatoes law school where you learn the basics to become a competent attorney," added a 2L. "If you want more specialized training, look to a larger school." Indeed, most seem to agree that UND does at least an adequate job of "stick[ing] to the basic general-law courses," but that it "lacks the sort of curricular diversity (not to mention ethnic diversity) that you might find in a larger, more cosmopolitan setting."

Such criticisms are probably inevitable from students at a school as small as this one. What is not inevitable, however, is the fact that, much to its credit, the University of North Dakota School of Law appears to be populated by satisfied customers. The following remark from a UND 2L was typical of most we heard: "North Dakota's lack of financial resources has led to its poor national 'rank' among law schools. But while the library is not gigantic, it is adequate. Although the faculty do not earn comparatively high salaries, they are for the most part talented, knowledgeable, and enthusiastic. They know and care about the students here, which is probably not the case at most larger schools. If you're looking for an inexpensive legal education in a small school with a family atmosphere, UND is ideal.

ADMISSIONS

With a first-year class as tiny as that of the University of North Dakota School of Law, any law school would have to be quite selective. With an applicant pool that is, in relative terms, as large as those of some "top-twenty" schools, North Dakota must be somewhat selective. Still, the numerical credentials of the average student here are lower than those of students at two-thirds of all U.S. law schools.

ACADEMICS	
Student/faculty ratio	14:1
% female faculty	38
% minority faculty	5
Hours of study per day	3.35

FINANCIAL FACTS	
Tuition (in/out-state)	$3,848/$8,074
Cost of books	NR
% first-year students receiving aid	NR
% all students receiving aid	NR
% aid that is merit-based	NR
% of all students receiving loans	NR
% receiving scholarships	NR
% of all students receiving assistantships	NR
Average grant	NR
Average graduation debt	NR

ADMISSIONS	
# applications received	446
% applicants accepted	40
% acceptees attending	49
Average LSAT	151
Average undergrad GPA	3.31
Regular application	April 1
Regular notification	NR
Rolling notification?	No
Early decision program?	NR
Admission may be deferred?	NR
Gourman Report Rating	**2.34**

NORTHEASTERN UNIVERSITY
School of Law

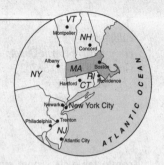

OVERVIEW

Type of school	private
Environment	metropolis
Scholastic calendar	quarter
Schedule	full-time only

STUDENTS

Enrollment of parent institution	11,022
Enrollment of law school	614
% male/female	40/60
% out-of-state	63
% minorities	24
% international (# of countries represented)	1 (5)
Average age at entry	24

APPLICANTS ALSO LOOK AT

Boston College
Boston University
Suffolk University
Harvard University
New England School of Law

SURVEY SAYS...

HITS
Practical experience
Students feel well-prepared
Left-leaning politics

MISSES
Not enough courses

EMPLOYMENT PROFILE

Firms recruiting on campus	35
Job placement rate (%)	91
% grads employed within six months	91
Average starting salary	$41,839

Grads employed by field (%):

Business/industry	8
Government	7
Judicial clerkships	22
Private practice	46
Public interest	16
Other	1

As the job market for young attorneys has tightened, employers have come to place a high premium on practical experience from recent law school graduates. While many law schools have been slow to take meaningful action, the Northeastern University School of Law has led the pack in bridging that gap and providing students with a legal education that should make it easy for them to step into the practice of law. By virtue of its unique co-op program, this midsize Boston law school promises prospective students that they will not enter the legal profession without the skills needed to succeed.

After a traditional first year of academic studies, Northeastern students alternate every three months between classroom instruction and full-time work in the legal field. They finish school in the same amount of time as any full-time law student, but by foregoing summer breaks, they graduate with a J.D. and a full year of legal work experience on their resumes. All students are encouraged to take one of their co-op placements with a public-service organization, and most choose to do so. The law school administers a number of stipend programs designed to make such low-paying work possible for students demonstrably in need.

Northeastern students picked their law school with its unique attributes in mind, so it is not surprising to hear how satisfied they are with their choice. Naturally, the co-op program was mentioned most often as the school's greatest strength. A 2L related, "It is commonly said that at minimum you'll find four areas of law you don't want to practice in, and at a maximum you'll find your future legal career." Opportunities within the program are quite varied, both substantively and geographically. A third-year student reported "Through the co-op program I have clerked with a state supreme court justice in the Midwest, interned with an environmental law center in the Southwest, received a fellowship for a summer in legal services in the Northeast, and intend to go to the Southeast for my final internship." Another 3L summed up the prevailing attitude: "The co-op program makes all petty complaints about Northeastern fade into the background!"

Students did relate complaints and cautionary words about NUSL. The orientation of the very diverse student body is decid-

Paul D. Baluer, *Assistant Dean and Director of Admissions*
400 Huntington Avenue
Boston, MA 02115
Tel: 617-373-2395 • Fax: 617-373-8865
Email: wdoherty@slaw.nev.edu
Internet: www.slaw.neu.edu

Northeastern University

edly liberal—not a big surprise considering its reputation for focusing on social justice as well as legal education. Students warned that "conservatives may feel out of place," and that NU could be a "frustrating place" for those with a conservative bent. A 1L wrote "Northeastern is the liberal law school. Come with an open mind and beware of PC 'thuggery'—it is rampant." Other students wrote that while the atmosphere at NU is definitely cooperative, there is competition as well. Students work hard, but the competition is expressed in an "appropriately channeled way." The students we heard from seemed quite content with their surroundings. "We only have a couple of buildings, but the human and tangible resources are immense," commented a 3L.

While some students embraced Northeastern's nontraditional grading system, in which professors give written evaluations rather than grades and class rank is nonexistent, others expressed reservations about the system, alleging that "certain adjectives have grade equivalents." Other students pushed for a greater variety of course offerings. The relative lack of variety was blamed on the co-op system—which nobody seemed willing to give up. NU is not an inexpensive law school, and some students wished that there was better financial aid available.

Overall, Northeastern students come to the school with a good idea of what to expect and end up being very satisfied with what they encounter. A 3L summed up the unique experience: "With a strong focus on social justice, a diverse student body, and the co-op program, I think Northeastern is the best legal education in the country. If the rest of the world could duplicate Northeastern's open, dynamic, and accepting environment, we'd all be much better off."

ADMISSIONS

As Northeastern's unique program has become more widely known, both the size and quality of the law school's applicant pool has increased. In terms of numerical admissions standards, NU is still considerably less selective than most of the nation's traditional "elite" schools, but a fairly high degree of overall admissions selectivity is necessitated by the sheer size of its applicant pool. Northeastern denies admission to roughly 2,000 well-qualified candidates annually.

ACADEMICS

Student/faculty ratio	21:1
% female faculty	38
% minority faculty	17
Hours of study per day	3.97

Academic specialties:

Civil Procedure, Commercial, Constitutional, Corporation Securities, Criminal, Environmental, Human Rights, International, Labor, Property, Taxation

FINANCIAL FACTS

Tuition	$20,150
Cost of books	$950
Room & board (on/off-campus)	$14,400/$14,400
% first-year students receiving aid	74
% all students receiving aid	82
% aid that is merit-based	22
% of all students receiving loans	82
% receiving scholarships	44
% of all students receiving assistantships	14
Average grant	$5,810
Average graduation debt	$54,546

ADMISSIONS

# applications received	2,438
% applicants accepted	36
% acceptees attending	24
Average LSAT	157
LSAT range	140-172
Average undergrad GPA	3.30
GPA range	1.98-4.00
Application fee	$55
Regular application	March 1
Regular notification	rolling
Rolling notification?	Yes
Early decision program?	No
Admission may be deferred?	Yes
Maximum length of deferment	1 year
Evening division offered?	No
Part-time accepted?	No
Gourman Report Rating	**2.92**

NORTHERN ILLINOIS UNIVERSITY
College of Law

OVERVIEW

Type of school	public
Environment	suburban
Scholastic calendar	semester
Schedule	full-time only

STUDENTS

Enrollment of parent institution	23,171
Enrollment of law school	294
% male/female	58/42
% out-of-state	10
% minorities	22
% international (# of countries represented)	2 (2)
Average age at entry	27

APPLICANTS ALSO LOOK AT

John Marshall Law School
Southern Illinois University
Loyola University, Chicago
Illinois Institute of Technology
University of Illinois

SURVEY SAYS...

HITS
Diverse faculty
Sense of community
Library staff

MISSES
Not enough courses
Quality of teaching

EMPLOYMENT PROFILE

Firms recruiting on campus	8
Job placement rate (%)	91
% grads employed immediately	36
% grads employed within six months	70
Average starting salary	$35,056

Grads employed by field (%):

Academia	7
Business/industry	15
Government	23
Judicial clerkships	2
Military	2
Private practice	41
Public interest	1
Other	1

Statistically, the Northern Illinois University College of Law stands out among Illinois law schools in several respects. Founded in 1974, this public institution is the youngest, smallest, and one of the least-expensive of the state's nine law schools. This last statistic probably helps explain the most surprising and impressive fact of all; among the state's law schools, most of which are far better known, Northern Illinois ranks only behind national powerhouses Chicago and Northwestern in terms of overall admissions selectivity. Of course, the small size of its entering class accounts in large part for the low acceptance rate at NIU, and this very young law school has a long way to go before it will compete with these schools for the same applicants. But considering the fact that NIU recently experienced a huge surge in applications volume, it seems clear that at least a certain segment of students is seeking out the school. Located in DeKalb, a town of about 35,000 in the semi-rural area ("surrounded by cornfields" in one student's words) just outside of Chicago's suburban sprawl, NIU is the only public law school in the northern part of the state. Consequently, a significant proportion of the Law School's students are residents of the surrounding area. NIU's J.D. program is largely traditional, with relatively few formal clinical offerings. But like all law schools whose reputations alone do not guarantee graduates their jobs-of-choice, Northern Illinois is beefing up its assortment of "skills" courses.

While students appreciated various aspects the law school, its main appeal was summed up by a 3L: "There are two reasons I am glad I came here—the financial value and the close-knit community, fellow students are not the enemy and the professors are human beings." Students attributed the "close-knit" (a term that most used) atmosphere, in part, to the school's size. One 3L wrote that the community was "the mixing of Animal House and The Paper Chase. As long as there is beer and Chicago nearby, DeKalb is a nice place to sit back and put your head in the books for three years." Some students were pleasantly surprised by the value they received. "While I came to Northern expecting a low cost legal education, I found top

Judith Malen, Director of Admissions & Financial Aid
Swen Parson Hall-276
De Kalb, IL 60115
Tel: 815-753-9485 • Fax: 815-753-4501
Email: lawadm@niu.edu
Internet: www.niu.edu/claw/lawhome.html

Northern Illinois
University

quality professors, resources, and a great potential to succeed," asserted one first-year student.

However, students, who did not let the low cost of tuition diminish their expectations, were quick to point out areas in which NIU could improve. Some of the complaints stemmed from the school's lack of a national reputation. A few students felt that this hurt on-campus recruiting. Others, though, were more optimistic about job prospects. "Career services seems very active in getting you a job," noted one 2L. "It helps that a NIU College of Law graduate is running it!" Another second-year added, "There is a large number of NIU alumni who sit on the bench or work for the state's attorney, or public defender's office in Illinois. For a relatively young school, our alumni list is very impressive." As at most small schools, students were quite vocal about their desires to expand the number and scope of courses. Some suggested trying to hire more diverse professors. The most vehement comments were reserved for the Legal Writing program (though not all students were dissatisfied). "The legal writing instructors couldn't teach their way our of a paper bag," exclaimed one 2L. A slightly more charitable 1L wrote, "It seems that the legal writing department is just a big casserole that they threw together at the last minute because they had to have something."

Some students also thought that the "lame" facilities could use some upgrading. Almost uniformly, though, NIU students who made suggestions for improvements also noted their overall satisfaction with the school.

ADMISSIONS

With spots for only about 100 new students in its first-year class, it is hardly surprising that the Northern Illinois University College of Law must deny admission to as many applicants as it does. Indeed, increasing demand has driven NIU's overall acceptance rate steadily lower in recent years, so prospective students can expect to face stiff competition. Still, the law school's numerical admissions standards remain in the low-to-moderate range.

ACADEMICS

Student/faculty ratio	14:1
% female faculty	24
% minority faculty	16
Hours of study per day	3.90

Academic specialties:
Civil Procedure, Commercial, Constitutional, Corporation Securities, Criminal, Environmental, Government Services, Human Rights, International, Labor, Legal History, Property, Taxation

FINANCIAL FACTS

Tuition (in/out-state)	$4,632/$9,264
Cost of books	NR
Fees (in/out-state)	$835/$835
Room & board (on/off-campus)	$3,722/$4,522
% first-year students receiving aid	69
% all students receiving aid	78
% aid that is merit-based	90
% of all students receiving loans	74
% receiving scholarships	24
% of all students receiving assistantships	16
Average grant	$3,314
Average graduation debt	$20,000

ADMISSIONS

# applications received	1,073
% applicants accepted	35
% acceptees attending	27
Average LSAT	156
Average undergrad GPA	3.00
Application fee (in/out-state)	$35/$35
Regular application	rolling
Regular notification	rolling
Rolling notification?	Yes
Early decision program?	No
Admission may be deferred?	Yes
Maximum length of deferment	1 year
Evening division offered?	No
Part-time accepted?	Yes
Gourman Report Rating	**2.39**

NORTHERN KENTUCKY UNIVERSITY
Salmon P. Chase College of Law

OVERVIEW

Type of school	public
Environment	metropolis
Scholastic calendar	semester
Schedule	full-time or part-time

STUDENTS

Enrollment of parent institution	7,084
Enrollment of law school	407
% male/female	60/40
% out-of-state	41
% part-time	44
% minorities	9
% international (# of countries represented)	NR (1)
Average age at entry	28

APPLICANTS ALSO LOOK AT

University of Kentucky
University of Louisville
University of Cincinnati
University of Dayton
Ohio State University

SURVEY SAYS...

HITS
Socratic method
Intellectual challenge

MISSES
Quality of teaching
Library staff

EMPLOYMENT PROFILE

Job placement rate (%)	90
% grads employed immediately	81
% grads employed within six months	90
Average starting salary	$43,000

Grads employed by field (%):

Other	2

The thousands of people whose mental maps of the United States are woefully incomplete will be confused to learn that the law school at Northern Kentucky University is located in a suburb of Cincinnati, Ohio. In fact, for most of its history, the Salmon P. Chase College of Law was actually in Ohio, moving across the river only in 1971 to merge with NKU in Highland Heights, Kentucky. Though they came together only twenty-five years ago, the Salmon P. Chase law school and NKU share a similar history. Northern Kentucky University evolved from a two-year community college spun off of the University of Kentucky to serve a segment of the state's population that previously lacked easy access to higher education. Chase began life as a night-school program of the Hamilton County (Ohio) YMCA in 1893. Before the turn of the century, the YMCA founded many such law schools to make legal education available to the vast majority of Americans who couldn't possibly afford to attend school by day. The WASP-dominated ABA resisted the YMCA's efforts, fearing an influx of "undesirable elements" into the bar.

Those days are gone, but schools like Salmon P. Chase, with its evening and part-time programs, low tuition, and relatively open admissions standards, continue to perform the vital service of preserving some semblance of egalitarianism in American legal education. Of course, those same ingredients can also pose certain disadvantages. Except at the biggest and most established public law schools, low tuition sometimes means inadequate funding. And flexible scheduling, while improving overall access, can also mean that resources get spread too thin. On the basis of comments made by current Chase students, it seems that their law school meets their needs, but is not entirely immune to such problems.

Most students we heard from, especially the night students, were grateful for the wonderful opportunity the school provides by being geared to both working and traditional students. As one student wrote, "Chase is unique. Half of the student body are evening students who work full time. The school is dedicated to its students and shows a real interest in each student's success."

Victoria Garry, Assistant Dean for Admissions
Nunn Drive
Highland Heights, KY 41076
Tel: 606-572-6476

Northern Kentucky University

The word "nice" in relation to professors and the Dean was used far more frequently than one might expect from people in law school. More than one student remarked on the "good relations between professors and students." "Professors are very accessible and willing to help," said a 2L. Many students praised their teachers' abilities, echoing the 3L who said, "Professors . . . have a strong and genuine concern for their students." Although class size is kept low so teacher-student interaction works, nearly all respondents asked for more professors, as talented as the ones they so admire, to facilitate more classes at more convenient times for all students. As a 1L explained, NKU needs "more professors so once we get into second and third years we don't have to take so many night classes."

Many students said that additional practical skills courses, legal writing courses, clinical options and possibilities for specialization would vastly improve the education NKU offers. A few disheartened students went so far as to say that NKU could stand to upgrade in every area. Students we surveyed felt that a new building, away from the undergrads, would make the atmosphere more professional and serve as a declaration of commitment to the law students on the part of the Dean and the administration. However, simply continuing its commitment to provide an "excellent opportunity for non-funded students," not to mention both funded and non-funded working students, constitutes the main challenge NKU students hope their school will continue to meet.

ADMISSIONS

In terms of numerical admissions standards, the law school at Northern Kentucky is in the bottom of the midrange of all U.S. law schools, but the small size of its entering class necessitates a fairly high degree of overall selectivity. With about seven applicants for every spot in that class, the law school must deny admission to more than three out of four applicants. Successful candidates tend to possess moderate numerical credentials.

ACADEMICS

Student/faculty ratio	21:1
% female faculty	27
% minority faculty	5
Hours of study per day	3.21

FINANCIAL FACTS

Tuition (in/out-state)	$4,700/$12,300
Cost of books	$500
% first-year students receiving aid	100
% all students receiving aid	100
% aid that is merit-based	NR
% of all students receiving loans	NR
% receiving scholarships	NR
% of all students receiving assistantships	NR
Average grant	$4,939
Average graduation debt	NR

ADMISSIONS

# applications received	1,028
% applicants accepted	23
% acceptees attending	46
Average LSAT	155
Average undergrad GPA	3.19
Application fee (in/out-state)	$25
Regular application	May 15
Regular notification	rolling
Rolling notification?	Yes
Early decision program?	No
Admission may be deferred?	Yes
Maximum length of deferment	1 year
Evening division offered?	Yes
Part-time accepted?	Yes
Gourman Report Rating	**2.30**

NORTHWESTERN UNIVERSITY
School of Law

OVERVIEW

Type of school	private
Environment	metropolis
Scholastic calendar	semester
Schedule	full-time only

STUDENTS

Enrollment of parent institution	7,570
Enrollment of law school	619
% male/female	56/44
% out-of-state	65
% minorities	21
% international (# of countries represented)	NR (10)
Average age at entry	25

APPLICANTS ALSO LOOK AT

Harvard University
University of Chicago
Georgetown University
University of Michigan
Universuty of Pennsylvania

SURVEY SAYS...

HITS
Grads expect big bucks
Classroom facilities
Research resources

MISSES
Practical lawyering skills
Not enough courses

EMPLOYMENT PROFILE

Firms recruiting on campus	225
Job placement rate (%)	95
% grads employed immediately	89
% grads employed within six months	93
Average starting salary	$70,000

Grads employed by field (%):

Business/industry	6
Government	10
Judicial clerkships	10
Private practice	75
Public interest	9
Other	1

With a reputation for academic excellence and roots that go back nearly as far as those of any law school in the nation, the Northwestern University School of Law is a charter member of the club of elite law schools. Though it may be overshadowed by its neighbor in Hyde Park, the University of Chicago Law School, Northwestern's wonderful reputation is not limited to the large legal community in Chicago. Housed in beautiful facilities on a downtown Chicago campus (its parent institution is in nearby suburban Evanston), the law school is widely regarded as one of the Top Twenty in the nation. The curriculum at Northwestern is comprehensive, with a large and multifaceted clinical program adding a practical complement to Northwestern's richly diverse traditional course offerings. The highly respected faculty provides the school with one of the most favorable student-faculty ratios in the nation.

Between the law school's own offerings and those of the larger university, the Northwestern J.D. student does not want for intellectual opportunities. The law school encourages concurrent enrollment in the university's outstanding graduate division. The joint degree most often pursued by Northwestern J.D. candidates is the masters of management (MM), offered through the Kellogg School of Management, one of the top five business schools in the country. Apart from being enormously well-qualified, the Northwestern student body stands out for its admirable ethnic diversity—particularly in comparison with Chicago's five other law schools.

Students expressed a high degree of satisfaction with the education they were receiving. "Northwestern has much emphasis on practical courses," wrote one 3L, "from this point of view, I'm quite satisfied." A first-year commented, "The faculty at Northwestern is demanding, yet interested in seeing the students succeed. They're very careful not to leave anyone behind." Another 1L wrote, "For such a prestigious school, the law school community is amazingly down-to-earth. I expected a great many pompous, stuffy academics, but found just the opposite." In fact, most students felt that the school was only moderately competitive. "The students are the greatest strength," opined a 1L, "This

Donald L. Rebstock, Administrative Secretary
357 East Chicago Avenue
Chicago, IL 60611
Tel: 312-503-8465 • Fax: 312-503-0178
Email: nwlawadm@harold.law.nwu.edu
Internet: www.lawl.nwu.edu

is one of the least competitive and cut-throat schools in the Top Ten. Once you cut through the cut-throat machoism, we are all here to learn." At NU, the students realize this extremely early and this results in a cooperative environment. Students were equally enthusiastic about the faculty. According to one 1L, "The faculty bends over backwards to make themselves available and takes teaching very seriously even though they are serious scholars too." The administration was also singled out by some for being attentive and receptive to student concerns.

Northwestern students could find little grounds for complaint at their school. Any criticism that was expressed was generally constructive. Some students felt that the school was oriented a little bit to much toward corporate practice. Others pointed out that NU could improve itself by increasing racial and geographic diversity at the school. "As a minority female, I would like to see more diversity among faculty. The administration is listening to student concerns about this and hopefully the situation will improve," wrote one 2L. Despite occasional comments suggesting that the Legal Writing program was too much work for too few credits, or that the computer facilities could be better (in general, NU students were very please with the school's facilities), students at NU are walking, talking advertisements for their school. In the words of one 3L, "For a fabulous education that opens up a world of opportunities in an environment that is friendly and conducive to learning, come to Northwestern."

ADMISSIONS

The Northwestern University School of Law is one of the most selective law schools in the nation. In terms of numerical admissions standards it may rank second in the city of Chicago, but in terms of sheer applicant demand, Northwestern outranks its neighbor in Hyde Park. (Twenty-one applicants vie annually for each spot in Northwestern's entering class of about 200, twice as many as do so at the University of Chicago.) In any case, Northwestern is in the top 20 nationally in both categories.

ACADEMICS

Student/faculty ratio	11:1
% female faculty	26
% minority faculty	3
Hours of study per day	3.84

Academic specialties:
Business Assc., Civil Litigation, Dispute Resolution

FINANCIAL FACTS

Tuition	$21,316
Cost of books	NR
Fees	$0
Room & board (on/off-campus)	$8,235/$8,235
% first-year students receiving aid	75
% all students receiving aid	75
% aid that is merit-based	5
% of all students receiving loans	75
% receiving scholarships	45
% of all students receiving assistantships	0
Average grant	$8,500
Average graduation debt	$50,000

ADMISSIONS

# applications received	4,098
% applicants accepted	20
% acceptees attending	23
Average LSAT	164
Average undergrad GPA	3.50
GPA range	3.26-3.73
Application fee	$80
Regular application	February 1
Regular notification	rolling
Rolling notification?	Yes
Early decision program?	No
Admission may be deferred?	Yes
Maximum length of deferment	none
Evening division offered?	No
Part-time accepted?	No
Gourman Report Rating	**4.74**

UNIVERSITY OF NOTRE DAME
Notre Dame Law School

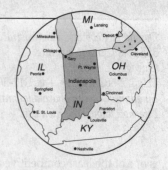

South Bend, Indiana is more than just the center of the college football universe. It is also the home of the nation's oldest and finest Catholic law school. On Saturdays in autumn, while men in gold helmets hit one another for the pleasure of millions of television viewers, more than 500 hardworking students at the University of Notre Dame Law School hit the books ... unless they have tickets to the game! Theirs is a highly regarded law school that offers a demanding, staunchly traditional legal education to a small, well-qualified group of students. The curriculum is highly prescribed, and class offerings tend to be very traditional, so those who seek innovation may be left wanting, though one of the schools numerous clinical programs may satisfy them. In any case, Notre Dame's sheer academic strength is undeniable, and variety can certainly be found by those who seek it.

Historically, Notre Dame's law students have always come from all parts of the country, and the Law School's large, loyal, and far-flung alumni network plays no small part in the success of its students in securing good jobs upon graduation. (Some students conducting job searches did comment, however, that they had yet to see that network in action.) Students at Notre Dame tend to possess very strong numerical credentials, but the school's unique "flavor" is really determined by the fact that over half of its students are Roman Catholics. Notre Dame is, by its own description, a humanistic institution that not only tolerates but also encourages the "manifestations of other faiths and commitment." However, the school is emphatic about maintaining its own commitment to the preservation of its religious character. Indeed, the university's affiliation with the Catholic church has an unmistakable effect on the atmosphere within all of its classrooms—attendance at the Law School's Sunday mass is reportedly very high, and some classes begin with a recitation of the Lord's Prayer. A 2L advised, "You'd better know the Hail Mary and Our Father by heart because you'll always begin class with a prayer (usually that you're not the one to be on the hot seat that day ...)"

As one might expect, such an atmosphere will not please everyone, but judging from our survey, students at Notre Dame Law School are among the most satisfied in the nation. Students

Anne Hamilton, Director of Admissions
Notre Dame Law School
Notre Dame, IN 46556
Tel: 219-631-6626 • Fax: 219-631-6371
Email: law.bulletin.1@nd.edu
Internet: www.nd.edu/~ndlaw

University of Notre Dame

certainly appreciated the high quality of academic instruction they received, but most reserved their highest praise for the atmosphere the Law School engenders. "The school offers a very thorough curriculum, maintaining moral and ethical strengths, while giving students a solid legal and technical background," wrote a 3L. A first-year student added that "[I] never expected the sense of family I feel in the Law School. Students treat each other with respect, often even while engaged in heated debates over various issues." Incoming students also praised the returning students for being incredibly cooperative and friendly "from Day One." The students' attitudes toward one another seem to have created an intellectually demanding, yet remarkably non-competitive atmosphere that only increases the quality of life. Other factors also contribute. "Football tickets are very reasonably priced," wrote one 1L, though he was not completely satisfied, adding, "I wish I didn't have to sit in the end zone, though."

Aside from that dubious hardship, students generally were unable to point out any negative aspects of their law school experience, except one. While some students agreed that the school was generally a friendly place, others bemoaned the lack of campus diversity. "The professors and deans embody both what is right and what is wrong with Notre Dame Law School," commented a 3L. "They are, on the one hand, energetic, dynamic and thought-provoking, but they are also closed-minded to 'non-conservative' thoughts." Some observed that the pervading conservatism was not limited to the faculty and administration.

ADMISSIONS

In every quantifiable respect, the Notre Dame Law School is one of the most selective in the nation. Not only does Notre Dame receive more than fifteen applications for every spot in its small entering class, but those it admits choose to attend the country's premier Catholic law school at a very high rate. All of this adds up to a very simple conclusion: Applicants whose numbers fall below the averages of a particular year's applicants are highly unlikely to be admitted while even those with credentials that exceed Notre Dame's average stand a less-than-even chance of admission. The administration asked us to point out that the "admissions office does consider each applicant's file individually, and special qualities may occasionally overcome lower numbers."

ACADEMICS

Student/faculty ratio	17:1
% female faculty	18
% minority faculty	9
Hours of study per day	4.33

Academic specialties:
Human Rights, International

FINANCIAL FACTS

Tuition	$20,390
Cost of books	$900
Fees	$27
Room & board (on/off-campus)	NR/$4,250
% first-year students receiving aid	77
% all students receiving aid	77
% aid that is merit-based	NR
% of all students receiving loans	77
% receiving scholarships	34
% of all students receiving assistantships	NR
Average grant	$6,750
Average graduation debt	$35,000

ADMISSIONS

# applications received	2,249
% applicants accepted	22
% acceptees attending	30
Average LSAT	162
Average undergrad GPA	3.40
Application fee	$45
Regular application	rolling
Regular notification	rolling
Rolling notification?	No
Early decision program?	No
Admission may be deferred?	Yes
Part-time accepted?	No
Gourman Report Rating	**4.68**

NOVA SOUTHEASTERN UNIVERSITY
Shepard Broad Law Center

OVERVIEW

Type of school	private
Environment	city
Scholastic calendar	NR
Schedule	full-time or part-time

STUDENTS

Enrollment of parent institution	NR
Enrollment of law school	906
% male/female	57/43
% out-of-state	19
% part-time	2
% minorities	26
% international (# of countries represented)	NR (NR)
Average age at entry	27

APPLICANTS ALSO LOOK AT

University of Miami
Florida State University
University of Florida
Stetson University
Georgia State University

SURVEY SAYS...

HITS
Classroom facilities
Diverse faculty

MISSES
Not enough courses
Library staff

EMPLOYMENT PROFILE

% grads employed within six months	73
Average starting salary	$32,161

Grads employed by field (%):

Other	6

Few people think of the Socratic method or constitutional law when the city of Fort Lauderdale, Florida is mentioned. More often, images of young, rowdy college students swarming to the city's beaches come to mind. But for 900 or so diligent law students enrolled at the Nova Southeastern University Shepard Law Center, Fort Lauderdale has less to do with criminal behavior and more to do with criminal procedure. In fact, applications to this private law school, which is a little over twenty years old, have been increasing recently. In need of more space, the school opened a new law building in 1992. In 1996, the Shepard Law Center began offering a part-time evening program limited to approximately sixty students.

The Law School's administrators hope that Nova's academic reputation can keep up with its growing size and popularity. With that goal in mind, the straightforward, traditional curriculum is supplemented by an impressively wide array of trial-skills courses and clinical programs designed to offer students the practical experience necessary to compete in a tightening legal job market. Among the more interesting special opportunities available to students at Nova are the King Disability Law Institute and the Center for the Study of Youth Policy. The school has also initiated a four-semester Lawyering Skills and Values curriculum that allows student to select either business or litigation tracks. Full semester clinics in various specialties are also available for third-year students. Students who responded to our survey were more than satisfied with the quality of the education they were paying for. "Nova has a very intensive law school," wrote a 2L. "Upon completion of the J.D. program you will definitely have the skills needed to be a successful lawyer." A 3L wrote, "I am very happy that I chose Nova. I attended a competitive Ivy League school undergrad, and I appreciate the level of academic challenge at NSU." The professors were generally praised for their contribution to the academic environment. "[Nova has] an unusually accessible faculty who encourage discussion after class," wrote one first-year student. A 2L praised "the availability of the faculty outside of class and the professors' excitement about what they are teaching."

Gail Levin Richmond, Assistant Dean
3305 College Avenue
Fort Lauderdale, FL 33314
Tel: 954-452-6117 • Fax: 954-452-6109
Email: admiss@law-lib.law.nova.edu
Internet: www.law.nova.edu/nova/nova.htm

*Nova Southeastern
University*

Some students, though, were unhappy with the lack of breadth in the curriculum. A 2L observed, "The curriculum cannot allow for formal specialization when programs such as the family law concentration are threatened to be cut before there is any attempt to observe its value." Others singled out the administration as a source of displeasure. "Nova has a lot to offer, and only one major defect," wrote a 1L. "The administration considers the students economic products, not future lawyers to be reasoned with. Expect no strong clubs or student life beyond your studies. There is minuscule money allocated for that ..." A 2L suggested: "The administration needs to find the correct balance between the students needs and the administration's desires." One critic noted that such "growing pains" were natural for a "young" school. Another common complaint centered around the cost of tuition. While students felt that they were receiving a good legal education, they wished that they were receiving more for their money. If Nova is able to address such student complaints, its reputation and standing are bound to improve

ADMISSIONS

Although the average numerical standards of those attending Nova Southeastern University's Shepard Broad Law Center are far from stellar, the sheer number of applications the school receives makes its admissions process quite competitive. Nova receives almost 1,500 applications from candidates with LSAT scores below about 150 and offers admission to only about 150 of them. A prospective student is only guaranteed admittance if his or her numerical credentials slightly exceed those listed. Because the law school is reducing the size of its first-year class, admissions is likely to become even more competitive.

ACADEMICS

Student/faculty ratio	23:1
% female faculty	45
% minority faculty	26
Hours of study per day	4.02

FINANCIAL FACTS

Tuition	$18,850
Cost of books	
% first-year students receiving aid	NR
% all students receiving aid	NR
% aid that is merit-based	NR
% of all students receiving loans	85
% receiving scholarships	27
% of all students receiving assistantships	20
Average grant	$3,531
Average graduation debt	NR

ADMISSIONS

# applications received	2,463
% applicants accepted	37
% acceptees attending	32
Average LSAT	150
Average undergrad GPA	2.93
Application fee	$45
Regular application	NR
Regular notification	March-April
Rolling notification?	No
Early decision program?	No
Admission may be deferred?	Yes
Maximum length of deferment	1 year
Evening division offered?	Yes
Part-time accepted?	Yes
Gourman Report Rating	**2.66**

OHIO NORTHERN UNIVERSITY
Claude W. Pettit College of Law

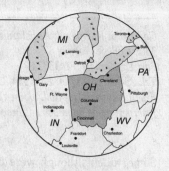

Ohio Northern University's Claude W. Pettit College of Law is a small private law school in the northwestern Ohio town of Ada. Actually, Ada is not officially a town but a village, which makes Ohio Northern the only U.S. law school to be located in a village besides NYU, but that's different. While tiny Ada (Pop. 5,000) offers all the distractions of Mayberry, its cost of living is exceedingly low, and its quiet atmosphere is cited by ONU students as being particularly conducive to the intensive study of law.

Ohio Northern offers the nation's only program leading to joint degrees in law and pharmacy. These programs are overseen by the school's Pharmacy-Law Institute, which was established in 1990 as a center for research and education in this growing field dealing with, among other things, the "regulatory problems of pharmaceutical, bio-technological, and genetically engineered substances." Of course, this subject is not one in which most ONU students become involved. The general curriculum at Ohio Northern is a traditional one supplemented by several clinical programs, including one focusing on the problems of the local poor and elderly. ONU students, an immoderately large percentage of whom are men, come, to a large extent, from Ohio and Pennsylvania and possess midrange numerical credentials. Each entering class is very small, however, so the overall admissions process is somewhat selective.

Those applicants who actually go on to enroll at Ohio Northern paint a picture of a law school environment that is pleasant. Although most had little difficulty naming areas in which their chosen school could stand to improve, most praised its comfortable, congenial atmosphere. "Because there is such a small number of students here," said one, "the whole program is more personalized." Most ONU students expressed similar sentiments, with many giving credit for their satisfaction to the law school's faculty, whose "concern for the quality of education that their students receive seems very genuine." Most of those we heard from also praised the law school for its efforts to keep class sizes small and the overall student-faculty ratio low in order to preserve the closeness and sense of community that students currently enjoy. On the strictly curricular front, mixed reviews were

George Justice, Director of Law Admissions
Ohio Northern University, Pettit College
Ada, OH 45810-1599
Tel: 419-772-2211 • Fax: 419-772-1875
Email: g-justice@onu.edu
Internet: www.law.onu.edu

Ohio Northern University

heard, though most students seem to agree on the quality of Ohio Northern's traditional classroom offerings and of its limited clinical programs. And though not all listed it as a strength, most ONU students remarked on the school's location, which "lets students do nothing else but study."

On the negative side, most of the Ohio Northern students we heard from focused their criticism on what they regard as a strong but disappointingly limited curriculum. "I'd really like to see greater diversity of classes and to see the curriculum expanded into new fields of law," went one typical remark from a slightly dissatisfied 2L. Indeed, Ohio Northern's J.D. program is much heavier in prescribed courses than that of most schools, and the breadth of its course offerings leaves something to be desired. Specifically, many students believe the law school could stand to beef up its practical-skills programs. "We could really use a class in the practical writing aspects of civil practice," suggested one 2L, who voiced a concern held by many regarding their professional preparedness. As one student put it: "I wish more attention were paid to the day-to-day demands of being a lawyer."

Finally, students griped about the school's facilities, especially the computing facilities and the building. With respect to the latter, students report that an addition should be complete within the next 2-3 years, which may solve the problem.

ADMISSIONS

If one considers only its numerical standards, the Ohio Northern University College of Law appears not to be very selective. With 9 applicants for every spot in its very small entering class, however, applicant demand at Ohio Northern is higher than it is at many better-known schools. Consequently, ONU has the luxury of choosing its students very carefully.

ACADEMICS

Student/faculty ratio	15:1
% female faculty	25
% minority faculty	3
Hours of study per day	4.79

Academic specialties:
Civil Procedure, Commercial, Constitutional, Criminal, Environmental, Human Rights, International, Labor, Legal History, Legal Philosophy, Property, Taxation

FINANCIAL FACTS

Tuition	$21,480
Cost of books	$800
Room & board (on/off-campus)	$5,230/$7,500
% first-year students receiving aid	91
% all students receiving aid	90
% aid that is merit-based	46
% of all students receiving loans	82
% receiving scholarships	38
% of all students receiving assistantships	15
Average grant	NR
Average graduation debt	$65,000

ADMISSIONS

# applications received	870
% applicants accepted	74
% acceptees attending	19
Average LSAT	149
Average undergrad GPA	2.98
Application fee	$40
Regular application	rolling
Regular notification	rolling
Rolling notification?	Yes
Early decision program?	No
Admission may be deferred?	Yes
Maximum length of deferment	1 year
Evening division offered?	No
Part-time accepted?	No
Gourman Report Rating	**2.63**

OHIO STATE UNIVERSITY
College of Law

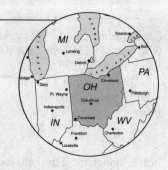

With very good reason, Ohio State University College of Law is widely regarded as the best law school in the state, and as one of the finest public law schools in the country. The university's 500,000 volume law library is the fourteenth largest in the United States. The other resources of the university, which is one of the biggest in the world, and of the state capital, are equally as vast, accessible, and first-rate. (Take note that while the university is huge, with almost 55,000 students, the Law School, with fewer than 700 students, is much smaller.) The school's broadly traditional curriculum is administered by an excellent faculty and Ohio State is also one of the country's best bargains in legal education, especially for residents of Ohio. Although the Law School's reputation carries weight around the country, the vast majority of its graduates choose to remain in one of the state's three sizable and well-paying legal centers.

When asked to cite their school's greatest strength, many students mentioned the newly renovated law building. A 1L called Ohio State "The only school in America where the faculty and staff have an 'edifice complex.' They love this building!" The library also drew many compliments. For the most part, students were happy with the quality of the teaching. "Professors make you want to learn," wrote one 2L. Another commented, "The faculty is outstanding and almost every professor I've had is very willing to talk after class or in their office."

While students praised the faculty, they were less enthusiastic about the administration. "The administration doesn't acknowledge or value student opinions or concerns," wrote a 3L. A second-year student elaborated: "The administration doesn't know we exist. They make decisions without our input, but that is typical of a school the size of OSU." Despite these feelings, it should be noted that the administration has attempted to institute some changes in response to student dissatisfaction with the traditional curriculum. First-year classes in criminal law, legislation, and legal writing and analysis were added in 1995. For those interested in practical experience, the school also operates five clinics.

Nancy B. Rapoport, Associate Dean
55 West 12th Avenue
Columbus, OH 43210
Tel: 614-292-2631 • Fax: 614-292-1383
Email: rapoport.3@osu.edu
Internet: www.acs.ohio-state.edu/units/law/index.htm

Ohio State University

Students had mixed reactions to the efforts of the placement office. A 3L observed, "The placement office is of little help to those who are not successful in the on-campus interview program." "Our placement office brings in all the big firms, but they don't do anything else," wrote one 2L. Another commented, "The placement office could stand some improvement in its sensitivity to student schedules; nevertheless, it provides good research facilities for the motivated job-seeker."

Although students felt that they were surrounded by "dynamic" and intelligent peers, some thought that the school was lacking in any sort of spirit or community feeling. One 2L suggested, "requiring pro bono projects as a cooperative effort by students would help build more of a sense of community." However, some law students do take advantage of the communal spirit that can be experienced at a large university; several mentioned the storied Ohio State football team as one of the school's strengths, though they noted that beating Michigan would be a nice change. Away from the gridiron, students can take advantage of the Law School's offering of joint degree programs with other colleges and departments within the university. Of course, Ohio state residents were quite happy with the price, as well as the quality, of their education. As a 3L stated, "Ohio State gives you a BMW-quality education for a Yugo price."

ADMISSIONS

The rush of law-school applicants to the nation's top public law schools in the late 1980s certainly didn't leave the excellent law school at Ohio State behind. Applications volume nearly doubled between '86 and '92, and, numerical admissions standards rose accordingly. As it now stands, the numerical credentials of the average entering OSU law student are stronger than those of students at 80 percent of the nation's fully accredited law schools. In comparison to other schools with such high standards, however, Ohio State is relatively generous in its overall acceptance rate.

ACADEMICS

Student/faculty ratio	20:1
% female faculty	30
% minority faculty	15
Hours of study per day	3.84

Academic specialties:
Environmental, International

FINANCIAL FACTS

Tuition (in/out-state)	$6,412/$14,932
Cost of books	$1,500
Room & board (on/off-campus)	$8,067/$8,067
% first-year students receiving aid	65
% all students receiving aid	65
% aid that is merit-based	2
% of all students receiving loans	65
% receiving scholarships	65
% of all students receiving assistantships	NR
Average grant	$1,500
Average graduation debt	$30,000

ADMISSIONS

# applications received	1,387
% applicants accepted	42
% acceptees attending	42
Average LSAT	159
LSAT range	140-173
Average undergrad GPA	3.40
GPA range	2.30-4.00
Application fee (in/out-state)	$30/$30
Regular application	rolling
Regular notification	rolling
Rolling notification?	Yes
Early decision program?	No
Admission may be deferred?	Yes
Maximum length of deferment	1 year
Evening division offered?	No
Part-time accepted?	No
Gourman Report Rating	**4.26**

OKLAHOMA CITY UNIVERSITY
School of Law

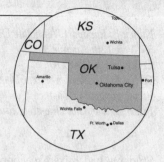

OVERVIEW

Type of school	private
Environment	metropolis
Scholastic calendar	semester
Schedule	full-time or part-time

STUDENTS

Enrollment of parent institution	4,660
Enrollment of law school	586
% male/female	62/38
% out-of-state	56
% part-time	32
% minorities	12
% international (# of countries represented)	1 (4)
Average age at entry	27

APPLICANTS ALSO LOOK AT

University of Oklahoma
University of Tulsa
South Texas College of Law
Texas Tech University
St. Mary's University

SURVEY SAYS...

HITS
Socratic method
Intellectual challenge

MISSES
Library staff
Not enough courses

EMPLOYMENT PROFILE

Firms recruiting on campus	10
Job placement rate (%)	78
% grads employed within six months	78
Average starting salary	$35,000

Grads employed by field (%):

Academia	2
Business/industry	20
Government	15
Judicial clerkships	1
Private practice	57
Other	1

The Oklahoma City University School of Law, established in 1907, was the first school in the state to train future lawyers. Since that time, Oklahoma has become home to two other law schools, and the Oklahoma City School of Law has grown to well over 600 students, a third of them in the evening division.

Students at OCU follow a traditional J.D. curriculum, with an ever-increasing number of opportunities to up their practical skills. All of the standard co-curricular activities, including law review and moot court, can be found here, and in the past few years, the school has added several practical and clinical courses, including a criminal practice seminar. The school's Center for Alternative Dispute Resolution trains students to be mediators, and provides them with opportunities to mediate disputes referred to the Center by state courts. OCU only operates one clinic, the Native American Legal Assistance Clinic, but it is quite notable. Through the clinic, law students provide free legal services to the area's large Native American population. In addition, the university's Native American Legal Resource Center, an institution within the School of Law, serves as a clearinghouse for scholars and attorneys practicing in the field.

OCU students certainly appreciate the opportunities afforded by their school. Many agreed with the 2L who cited "the emphasis on developing practical lawyering skills and particularly the emphasis placed on developing strong legal research and writing skills" as the school's greatest strength. Still, others suggested that the scope and depth of the course selection could be expanded and should include more clinical programs. In general, students were quite satisfied with in-class proceedings, praising the tough but good professors. A 1L wrote, "The professors are very willing to accommodate students when help is requested. They have high expectations from us . . . they expect nothing but your best efforts." Another first year commented on the accessibility of the professors: "Many first-year profs give opportunities to get to know them outside of the class, such as having lunch or dinner with them. This makes it extremely difficult to perform poorly because they know you." A 3L summed up his classroom experience: "Although the professors have high expectations and

Gary Mercer, Assistant Dean for Admissions
P.O. Box 61310
Oklahoma City, OK 73146-1310
Tel: 800-633-7242 • Fax: 405-521-5814
Email: ladmissions@frodo.okcu.edu
Internet: www.okcu.edu/~law/home.htm

Oklahoma City University

demands, the purpose seems to be to prepare us for the practice of law. We are expected to act like responsible attorneys from the first day."

In addition to praising teaching skills and experience of the faculty, students were also satisfied with the overall atmosphere at the Law School. One 1L commented, "The school's administration, professors, and career services are extremely concerned with the success of students . . . and their ability to balance the pressures of law school and the practicality of their personal lives." Another 1L wrote, "The attitude around here is: if you work hard and you want something bad enough, you can prevail. There isn't a strong sense of 'weeding out' that one experiences [elsewhere]." While acknowledging that there was some competition at OCU, most students did not seem to feel that it was overwhelming. According to one student, "As a first year, I have been impressed with the willingness of the upperclass students to help out and point us in the right direction."

Unlike students at many other schools, OCU students had almost unreserved praise for the career placement office. "Career placement is going beyond the call of duty to reach all students," wrote one 2L. Students also had kind words for the law school's "new, state of the art building," though a few complained that it was too hot. Some students also felt that the cost of their education was a little high. Others expressed a concern that the school's ranking was not as good as it should or could be. "[OCU] deserves far more credit for the quality of education," a 2L wrote. Whatever the school's ranking, it seems clear from student comments that they are happy with the practical education they receive, and are confident in the administration's responsiveness to their needs.

ADMISSIONS

Oklahoma City University School of Law's admissions standards are quite generous. Each year, 45 percent of applicants are granted admission. With an average LSAT score of 150 and undergraduate GPA of about 3.0, applicants with moderate credentials have a very good chance of being admitted. Those whose numbers exceed these averages are virtually assured of gaining admission.

ACADEMICS

Student/faculty ratio	17:1
% female faculty	26
% minority faculty	13
Hours of study per day	4.73

Academic specialties:
Civil Procedure, Commercial, Constitutional, Corporation Securities, Criminal, Environmental, International, Legal History, Property, Taxation, Litigation, Advocacy and Dispute Resolution, American Indian Law

FINANCIAL FACTS

Tuition	$13,330
Cost of books	$750
Fees	$162
Room & board (on/off-campus)	$6,509/$8,791
% first-year students receiving aid	83
% all students receiving aid	85
% aid that is merit-based	5
% of all students receiving loans	82
% receiving scholarships	25
% of all students receiving assistantships	2
Average grant	$4,099
Average graduation debt	$42,042

ADMISSIONS

# applications received	1,069
% applicants accepted	60
% acceptees attending	28
Average LSAT	150
Average undergrad GPA	3.00
Application fee	$35
Early application	April 1
Regular application	rolling
Regular notification	rolling
Rolling notification?	Yes
Early decision program?	No
Admission may be deferred?	Yes
Maximum length of deferment	1 year
Evening division offered?	Yes
Part-time accepted?	Yes
Gourman Report Rating	**2.76**

UNIVERSITY OF OKLAHOMA
College of Law

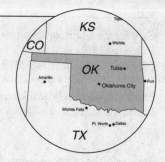

OVERVIEW

Type of school	public
Environment	metropolis
Scholastic calendar	semester
Schedule	full-time only

STUDENTS

Enrollment of parent institution	13,118
Enrollment of law school	661
% male/female	59/41
% out-of-state	15
% part-time	NR
% minorities	10
% international (# of countries represented)	NR (NR)
Average age at entry	24

APPLICANTS ALSO LOOK AT

Oklahoma City University
University of Tulsa
University of Texas
Southern Methodist University
Baylor University

SURVEY SAYS...

HITS
Socratic method
Library staff

MISSES
Practical lawyering skills
Quality of teaching
Not enough courses

The most respected of Oklahoma's three law schools is also the least expensive: the University of Oklahoma College of Law, established in 1909 on the Norman campus of the state's excellent public university. As the only publicly funded law school in the state, Oklahoma boasts vast resources in comparison with other schools in the region. The overall value of the legal education the school provides draws a large portion of the students. Tuition at Oklahoma makes it what one current student called "an unbeatable deal."

The law school's excellent reputation rests on the strength of its solid, traditional J.D. curriculum. After a fully prescribed first year, Oklahoma students can choose from a relatively broad array of course offerings, including a greater-than-average selection of courses in energy law and criminal law and corrections. Upper-level students can also participate in Oklahoma's fairly extensive clinical programs, which include an in-house legal aid clinic and numerous externship opportunities. Several students critiqued the school's legal writing program, though. One such student, a 1L, made this observation: "The writing program seems very weak compared to other schools." And another 1L said: "Research and writing is a joke. They don't teach you anything." Oklahoma students also expressed a desire to have a wider course selection at the law school. We heard the following suggestions: "The school needs more specialization-environmental law and health law" (2L); "[We need] more international law courses" (1L).

Many students spoke highly of the faculty who, they reported, go out of their way to help students achieve their goals inside and outside the classroom. One student, who dubbed Oklahoma a "simply outstanding law school," said: "The faculty here are incredible. They are very effective in teaching students the important material, yet they are also warm and personable." And another student, a 2L, said: "The entire faculty has an open door policy to help students in our pursuit of a J.D."

When asked to name the school's weaknesses, Oklahoma students frequently mentioned the school's facilities, but also noted

Sue E. Velie
300 Timberdell Road
Norman, OK 73019
Tel: 405-325-4699

that the law school is planning a move to a new building located on the main campus in the near future. The school's lack of racial and ethnic diversity were also noted by the students surveyed. "More female and minority faculty and students are needed," said one 3L. Oklahoma students join with the majority of other student bodies who feel their school's job placement office is not sufficient. Students who plan to look for employment after they receive their degree may face an additional challenge due to their location. "[This is] a good school, but Oklahoma has a very bad economy. [It] would be best to take advantage of the low tuition and then move to a better job environment," said a 3L. Considering the low tuition and fine instruction, prospective students should keep the following statement from an upbeat 2L in mind: "After working with law students from schools like NYU and UVA, [I realize] that those who apply themselves here are equipped to compete with students from the best law schools in the country."

ADMISSIONS

Although it is more selective than the state's other two law schools, the University of Oklahoma College of Law holds applicants to numerical standards that are slightly lower than the national average. The law school selects from a relatively small applicant pool, but still accepts only a third of all candidates who apply. Also, since the law school receives a moderate number of applicants for its size, and Oklahoma law limits enrollment of nonresidents to only 10 to 15 percent of the roughly 660 students in the school, admissions are far more selective for non-Oklahomans.

ACADEMICS	
Student/faculty ratio	23:1
% female faculty	22
% minority faculty	12
Hours of study per day	3.81

FINANCIAL FACTS	
Tuition (in/out-state)	$3,160/$9,198
Cost of books	NR
% first-year students receiving aid	NR
% all students receiving aid	NR
% aid that is merit-based	NR
% of all students receiving loans	NR
% receiving scholarships	NR
% of all students receiving assistantships	NR
Average grant	NR
Average graduation debt	NR

ADMISSIONS	
# applications received	1,153
% applicants accepted	31
% acceptees attending	59
Average LSAT	154
Average undergrad GPA	3.30
Application fee (in/out-state)	$25/NR
Regular application	March 15
Regular notification	rolling
Rolling notification?	Yes
Early decision program?	NR
Admission may be deferred?	NR
Gourman Report Rating	**3.40**

UNIVERSITY OF OREGON
School of Law

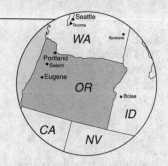

In one of the most beautiful parts of the country, on one of the loveliest college campuses in the West, you will find the highly respected—and popular—School of Law at the University of Oregon. Established in 1919, Oregon's only public law school is also its youngest, and probably its best. Oregon's curriculum is strong and broad, and while most law schools continue to resist offering areas of formal concentration at the J.D. level, U of O has embraced the trend toward specialization. Oregon now offers official "Statements of Completion" in a handful of subjects: environmental and natural resources law, ocean and coastal law, business law, criminal practice law, and estate planning. The law school's wide-ranging clinical programs afford a limited number of students the opportunity to supplement their academic training with hands-on experience in these and several other areas of law. The law school has a long established reputation for excellence in and around the Pacific Northwest, and if demand from highly qualified prospective law students is any indication, its reputation is well deserved. Since 1986, applications volume at Oregon has increased 160 percent and the average LSAT score of entering students has climbed by 15 percentile points. More than half of the law school's students now come from outside the state. People have begun to take notice, it seems, of Oregon's highly respected faculty, its strong, broad curriculum and its low tuition, all of which surely make it one of the better bargains anywhere— at least for state residents. (Residency requirements in Oregon are quite strict, and a large number of the law school's student body pay tuition at the nonresident rate.)

Students at Oregon, residents and nonresidents alike, are largely in agreement when it comes to the strengths of their chosen school. Although criticism of several fundamental aspects of their program was widespread, the vast majority of the U of O students we heard from expressed a high level of satisfaction with the overall quality of their experience, and most notably with their relations with faculty and fellow students. "U of O is not your average law mill," asserted one 3L, "student groups are active and the student body as a whole is involved, committed and supportive." As one 3L commented, "You can find a conservative male student sitting comfortably next to a woman with a nose

Katherine Jernberg, Admissions Director
1221 University of Oregon
Eugene, OR 97403
Tel: 541-346-3846 • Fax: 541-346-1564
Email: admissions@law.uoregon.edu
Internet: www.law.uoregon.edu

University of Oregon

ring in almost every class." Most echoed this sentiment, some even more enthusiastically. "My respect for the faculty here is exceeded only by the respect I have for my fellow students," wrote a 1L. "The academic program," she continued, "encourages us to maintain our idealism in the face of the oppressive cynicism which is often perpetuated by 'the system.'" This last remark likely referred to Oregon's strong record of encouraging public-interest work and in particular, environmental public-interest work. "The Enviro program, the Enviro clinic and the Enviro faculty are all excellent," reported one 3L. On the basis of the unanimously positive reviews we heard, it appears that such students have not been disappointed.

On the other hand, a large proportion of the students we heard from expressed a feeling that the law school has paid too little attention to other areas in its quest to build a highly respected environmental program. "The public-interest emphasis is great," wrote one, "but there is insufficient non-environmental public-interest instruction, and there is an insufficient number of spaces in all of the clinics." Another consistent area of criticism concerned the lack of diversity in Oregon's faculty. "The faculty is great," allowed a 2L, "but most profs are left-wing white males—we need more political, ethnic and gender diversity." The facilities were universally denounced, with two students describing the building as "butt-ugly." And just in case you've never been to Oregon, consider carefully this evenhanded assessment from one damp but happy law student: "Great school, but bring an umbrella."

ADMISSIONS

Like any excellent public law school, the University of Oregon School of Law has the luxury of choosing its students from a very large applicant pool. Even those applicants whose numbers slightly exceed Oregon's averages are in for a fight. A not-so-generous overall acceptance rate of 32 percent ensures that many highly qualified candidates will be turned away.

ACADEMICS

Student/faculty ratio	15:1
% female faculty	38
% minority faculty	13
Hours of study per day	3.84

FINANCIAL FACTS

Tuition (in/out-state)	$9,053/$13,537
Cost of books	$3,000
% first-year students receiving aid	NR
% all students receiving aid	97
% aid that is merit-based	NR
% of all students receiving loans	97
% receiving scholarships	77
% of all students receiving assistantships	3
Average grant	NR
Average graduation debt	NR

ADMISSIONS

# applications received	1,424
% applicants accepted	32
% acceptees attending	33
Average LSAT	158
Average undergrad GPA	3.39
Application fee (in/out-state)	$50/NR
Early application	December 15
Early notification	January 15
Regular application	April 1
Regular notification	rolling
Rolling notification?	Yes
Early decision program?	Yes
Admission may be deferred?	No
Evening division offered?	No
Part-time accepted?	No
Gourman Report Rating	**3.67**

PACE UNIVERSITY
School of Law

OVERVIEW

Type of school	private
Environment	city/suburban
Scholastic calendar	semester
Schedule	full-time or part-time

STUDENTS

Enrollment of parent institution	12,752
Enrollment of law school	799
% male/female	49/51
% out-of-state	30
% part-time	38
% minorities	15
% international (# of countries represented)	NR (8)
Average age at entry	28

APPLICANTS ALSO LOOK AT

Fordham University
New York University
New York Law School
St. John's University
Brooklyn Law School

SURVEY SAYS...

HITS
Socratic method

MISSES
Library staff
Not enough courses

EMPLOYMENT PROFILE

Firms recruiting on campus	21
Job placement rate (%)	89
% grads employed within six months	89
Average starting salary	$47,472

Grads employed by field (%):

Academia	1
Business/industry	23
Government	12
Judicial clerkships	4
Military	1
Private practice	58
Public interest	1

Founded in 1978, the Pace University School of Law is one of the youngest law schools in the Northeast, but it has come far in its short history. Like most latecomers to legal education, Pace has not had the luxury of resting on tradition. But as tradition has been called into question lately, this midsize private law school has tried, with much success, to turn its youth to its advantage. Pace has begun to set about building a national reputation not by imitating the established giants but by helping to usher in change. The most tangible sign of this is, perhaps, the law school's acceptance of the trend toward specialization at the J.D. level. Pace now offers certificates of specialization in three areas: health law and policy, international law, and environmental law. It is in this last area that the law school has drawn the most attention. By cannily choosing to dedicate substantial resources to such an up-and-coming field of study and practice, Pace fairly guaranteed the notice it has now received: Its curriculum in environmental law has been recognized as one of the most comprehensive in the nation. It also operates a clinical program dedicated to the subject and offers one of the country's few master of laws (LL.M.) and doctor of laws (S.J.D.) degrees in the field. While Pace has a way to go before it can hope to compete head-to-head with some of the region's powerhouse schools for the most highly qualified law-school applicants, standards are already high and rising. Admissions are quite selective (more so for the day division than for the evening division), and the average numerical credentials of entering students are now quite strong, having risen significantly in the last several years.

Students at Pace are remarkably consistent in their assessments of their chosen school—both in terms of its advantages and its drawbacks. Although nearly all express a fairly high degree of satisfaction with the uniqueness and overall quality of the law school's program, few could not point to areas in need of improvement. Not surprisingly, Pace students had strong words of praise for the school's specialization programs, especially the environmental program. "Pace is definitely an up-and-coming law school on the cutting edge of several expanding areas of law," went one fairly typical remark from a 3L. Another soon-to-be graduate agreed, noting that "I feel like the clinics here have

Angela D'Agostino, Assistant Dean & Director of Admissions
78 North Broadway
White Plains, NY 10603
Tel: 914-422-4210 • Fax: 914-422-4015
Email: admissions@genesis.law.pace.edu
Internet: www.law.pace.edu

Pace University

prepared me very well in a practical way to pursue my area of interest—environmental law." Some students also had kind words for their faculty, particularly one student who noted that "as an older student, it is a pleasure to be treated as an adult rather than an adolescent." Nearly all agreed that "the faculty is very involved with the student body and is very willing to interact with the students individually."

Specific and tangible criticisms were heard. For instance, although few had anything but praise for the quality of the law school's various clinical programs, a very large number of those we heard from lamented their limited enrollment. "The clinical programs here are quite good," wrote one 2L, "but they really need to find a way to accommodate more students." On balance, however, most here seem pleased with their surroundings and with their prospects. "More and more employers are becoming aware of Pace," claimed one student, "and I have found that Pace grads are looked upon with growing and well-deserved esteem."

ADMISSIONS

In its relatively short history, the Pace University School of Law has made significant progress toward achieving the goal of any rising law school: to attract students of the highest caliber possible. Since 1986, for instance, the average LSAT score of entering students has risen nearly twenty percentile points as applicant volume has grown by more than 50 percent. While Pace has a long way to go before it competes with the region's powerhouses for the most highly qualified students, its current admissions standards are anything but lenient. Purely in terms of numerical admissions criteria, Pace is in the top third of all U.S. law schools and rising steadily.

ACADEMICS

Student/faculty ratio	15:1
% female faculty	32
% minority faculty	8
Hours of study per day	4.18

Academic specialties:
Environmental, International, Health

FINANCIAL FACTS

Tuition	$19,394
Cost of books	$500
Fees	$50
Room & board (on/off-campus)	$9,108/$12,800
% first-year students receiving aid	78
% all students receiving aid	81
% aid that is merit-based	61
% of all students receiving loans	75
% receiving scholarships	30
% of all students receiving assistantships	NR
Average grant	$4,995
Average graduation debt	$58,000

ADMISSIONS

# applications received	2,117
% applicants accepted	42
% acceptees attending	27
Average LSAT	152
LSAT range	143-170
Average undergrad GPA	3.10
GPA range	2.00-4.00
Application fee	$55
Regular application	February 15
Regular notification	rolling
Rolling notification?	Yes
Early decision program?	No
Admission may be deferred?	Yes
Maximum length of deferment	1 year
Evening division offered?	Yes
Part-time accepted?	Yes
Gourman Report Rating	**2.36**

UNIVERSITY OF THE PACIFIC
McGeorge School of Law

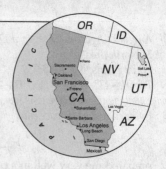

OVERVIEW

Type of school	private
Environment	city
Scholastic calendar	semester
Schedule	full-time or part-time

STUDENTS

Enrollment of parent institution	0
Enrollment of law school	1,226
% male/female	53/47
% out-of-state	NR
% part-time	29
% minorities	23
% international (# of countries represented)	1 (NR)
Average age at entry	24

APPLICANTS ALSO LOOK AT

U. of California, Davis
Santa Clara University
Pepperdine University
University of San Francisco
University of California, Berkeley

SURVEY SAYS...

HITS
Socratic method
Intellectual challenge

EMPLOYMENT PROFILE

% grads employed within six months	72
Average starting salary	$41,251

Grads employed by field (%):

Academia	1
Business/industry	11
Government	21
Judicial clerkships	8
Private practice	58
Public interest	1

Sacramento, the capital of California (the nation's most populous state), supports a large population of lawyers but only one law school: the McGeorge School of Law. Its name may be unfamiliar to those on the East Coast, but this very large private law school is one of the major sources of new blood for the sizable legal communities of northern California. Affiliated since 1966 with the University of the Pacific, California's oldest private university, 70-year-old McGeorge continues to emphasize the strengths on which its long established regional reputation for excellence was built.

McGeorge students we talked to offered almost unanimous praise for the quality of their program and for the extent to which it is preparing them for the demands of professional practice. As one 3L put it, "Practical training is emphasized at McGeorge instead of heady, yet impractical legal theory." Often cited by students was the university's prime location, minutes from downtown courts and the state's legislative offices. Sacramento is no cultural mecca, but the law school community is, by all reports, quite pleasant, and McGeorge students can satisfy their wanderlust through enrollment in international summer programs in Salzburg, London, and Budapest. For those interested in International Business Law, a growing legal specialization in this region of the country, McGeorge offers a concentration that can include special study abroad programs and moot court competitions.

McGeorge began to supplement its traditional curriculum with training in the practical skills of lawyering earlier than most law schools. It was, in fact, the first law school in the country to build a sophisticated mock-trial courtroom fully equipped with audio-visual teaching aids. This facility continues to be the focus of McGeorge's highly regarded trial-advocacy program, which is one of the many clinical programs offered through the law school. In addition to maintaining a relatively large in-house legal clinic, McGeorge sponsors externships through dozens of state and local government agencies, from Social Services to Seismic Safety.

McGeorge students praised the rigorous curriculum that has given the school the second-highest bar-passage rate in the state. "The discipline that one must develop here in order to survive

Jane Kelso, Dean of Students
3200 Fifth Avenue
Sacramento, CA 95817
Tel: 916-739-7015 • Fax: 916-739-7134
Email: admissionsmcgeorge@uop.edu
Internet: www.mcgeorge.edu

will later in our careers be a great strength, but right now it can be a pain," said a 2L. Most students, however, placed a great deal of blame on the university for instituting what is said to be an unfair and burdensome grading curve. "The grading system is on a 'C' curve, and that makes life difficult and scary, especially the first year," said a 2L. Another student, a 1L, told us, "The overwhelming sense of competition and difficult grading policy make the McGeorge environment somewhat counter productive." A 3L voiced concern that the school's "demoralizing" grading system makes it even more difficult for students to find jobs after graduation.

Without question, however, the majority of students seem quite pleased with the quality of their education at McGeorge and the practical skills training it affords. And as one 3L put it, "It is a tough time here, but that makes us work harder...thus preparing us very well for legal practice in any area."

ADMISSIONS

Although it is true that the McGeorge School of Law is in the lower tier of California's ABA-approved law schools in terms of numerical admissions standards, the long-established law school enjoys a regional reputation that is strong enough to draw a huge pool of applicants. The law school considers more than 2,000 applications annually, but the size of its entering class (around 450 total day and evening students) keeps overall admissions selectivity moderate.

ACADEMICS	
Student/faculty ratio	23:1
% female faculty	28
% minority faculty	7
Hours of study per day	4.34

FINANCIAL FACTS	
Tuition	$16,826
Cost of books	$610
% first-year students receiving aid	NR
% all students receiving aid	88
% aid that is merit-based	11
% of all students receiving loans	92
% receiving scholarships	28
% of all students receiving assistantships	NR
Average grant	NR
Average graduation debt	$64,510

ADMISSIONS	
# applications received	2,068
% applicants accepted	62
% acceptees attending	32
Average LSAT	150
Average undergrad GPA	3.01
Application fee	$40
Regular application	May 1
Regular notification	rolling
Rolling notification?	Yes
Early decision program?	No
Admission may be deferred?	No
Evening division offered?	Yes
Part-time accepted?	Yes
Gourman Report Rating	**4.28**

UNIVERSITY OF PENNSYLVANIA
Law School

The University of Pennsylvania Law School is one of the acknowledged giants of legal education. Situated on the Philadelphia campus of its Ivy League parent institution, it has been in continuous operation for over 140 years. Its reputation was built on the strength of its highly esteemed faculty and the strong traditional curriculum it administers. In the past decade, a changing of the guard within the Law School's faculty created the conditions for significant changes in the Penn curriculum—changes that have done nothing but bolster the law school's already golden reputation and ensure the continuing success of its graduates in entering the highest reaches of the legal profession.

Among the curricular innovations at Penn are two elective courses in the first year. This seemingly modest allowance is almost unheard of in the elite law schools, and it contributes to an overall first-year experience at Penn that is, by all reports, dynamic, exciting, and, perhaps most important, humane. Philadelphia itself is known as the City of Brotherly Love, and that attitude seems to have rubbed off on the school, which sports, by most reports, a collegial atmosphere. Any obsessive competitiveness at Penn seems limited to the search for employment at the nation's top firms, a search that begins almost on arrival. Given that the vast majority of Penn grads do go to work for these large, high-paying firms, the Law School's recent addition of a seventy-hour public service graduation requirement seems particularly appropriate and admirable. Some students greatly appreciate the requirement. A 1L commented, "The public service requirement means lots of groups drop by to recruit and many 1Ls are taking part. I began representing my first client just a few weeks after starting law school."

On the whole, Penn law students seemed quite satisfied with their choice of school. They were well aware of the advantages their degrees will give them when entering the profession, and they were thankful for a learning environment that spares them the blood-thirsty competitiveness. "For the most part, students save their competitiveness for on-campus recruiting at the start of second year," wrote a 2L. Another 2L stated, "The school is very

Janice Austin, Assistant Dean to Admissions
3400 Chestnut Street
Philadelphia, PA 19104-6204
Tel: 215-898-7400 • Fax: 215-573-2025
Email: adms@oyez.law.upenn.edu
Internet: www.law.upenn.edu

University of Pennsylvania

much a community...there is much camaraderie." While opinions differed regarding student stress levels, a 1L seemed to be speaking for his peers when he wrote, "The academic environment is a nice mix between cooperation and competitiveness. The pressure only comes from within and not from other students."

Students definitely appreciated the high quality of the faculty, but many reserved their highest praise for the recently rebuilt library, and for Lewis Hall, the original law school building which was recently reopened and reportedly features incredible architecture. "The library is the jewel of the entire Penn campus—that's why we have to keep the undergrads out," wrote a second-year student.

While many students acknowledged that one of the advantages of Penn was its ability to help students secure high-paying employment at law firms, a few students complained that Career Planning and Placement (CPP) was less effective at helping students who were not interested in employment at large firms in major metropolitan areas. Others found fault with the legal writing program, complaining that they were being taught by fellow students rather than by professionals. Students were overwhelmingly positive about Penn's offerings, though. "The greatest thing about this school is its constant striving to improve. Penn Law offers an outstanding and constantly improving academic community. It creates a positive attitude for students when you know your school is rapidly changing and improving," concluded a 1L.

ADMISSIONS

If you hope to earn a spot in the University of Pennsylvania Law School's entering class of around 230, plan to face stiff competition. Relative to many other top schools, the overall acceptance rate at Penn is fairly generous. Of course, it probably doesn't seem so to the more than two out of three well qualified candidates who are denied admission. Those who do manage to squeeze through and go on to enroll possess numerical credentials higher than those of students at all but seven American law schools. Their stellar average undergraduate GPA is very near the highest reported, and their average LSAT score stands impressively at the 94th percentile.

ACADEMICS

Student/faculty ratio	18:1
% female faculty	30
% minority faculty	6
Hours of study per day	3.77

Academic specialties:
Civil Procedure, Commercial, Constitutional, Corporation Securities, Criminal, Environmental, Government Services, Human Rights, International, Labor, Legal History, Legal Philosophy, Property, Taxation, Family

FINANCIAL FACTS

Tuition	$21,800
Cost of books	$740
Fees	$1,514
Room & board (on/off-campus)	$8,167/$8,167
% first-year students receiving aid	71
% all students receiving aid	80
% aid that is merit-based	2
% of all students receiving loans	80
% receiving scholarships	36
% of all students receiving assistantships	26
Average grant	$7,100
Average graduation debt	$54,000

ADMISSIONS

# applications received	3,956
% applicants accepted	29
% acceptees attending	24
Average LSAT	166
LSAT range	144-180
Average undergrad GPA	3.60
GPA range	2.60-4.00
Application fee	$65
Early application	November 1
Early notification	December 15
Regular application	March 1
Regular notification	February 1
Rolling notification?	Yes
Early decision program?	Yes
Admission may be deferred?	Yes
Maximum length of deferment	2 years
Evening division offered?	No
Part-time accepted?	No
Gourman Report Rating	**4.82**

PEPPERDINE UNIVERSITY
School of Law

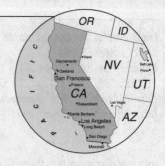

OVERVIEW

Type of school	private
Environment	city
Scholastic calendar	semester
Schedule	full-time only

STUDENTS

Enrollment of parent institution	2,661
Enrollment of law school	679
% male/female	52/48
% out-of-state	26
% part-time	NR
% minorities	24
% international (# of countries represented)	1 (3)
Average age at entry	23

APPLICANTS ALSO LOOK AT

University of California, Los Angeles
Loyola Marymount University
University of Southern California
University of San Diego
Southwestern University

SURVEY SAYS...

HITS
Faculty-student relations
Classroom facilities
Students feel well-prepared

EMPLOYMENT PROFILE

Firms recruiting on campus	120
Job placement rate (%)	89
% grads employed immediately	34
% grads employed within six months	85
Average starting salary	$54,000

Grads employed by field (%):

Business/industry	19
Government	7
Judicial clerkships	4
Private practice	70

The Pepperdine University School of Law is "only about thirty years old." In recent years, it "has made valiant efforts to increase its nationwide recognition," bringing in distinguished speakers," "young, exciting professors," as well as "upgrad[ing] its research facilities."

Pepperdine's traditional J.D. program offers an "excellent—but stringent—academic" curriculum. Special programs include International Law, Entertainment Law, and a comprehensive Institute for Dispute Resolution. "There is a strong emphasis on legal research and writing and preparation for the bar exam." A 3L claimed: "Despite the 'low' ranking we get, almost all the judges and law firms that have Pepperdine alums as employees rave about the quality of our work, especially written briefs." Other students complained that the Legal Research and Writing program is "ridiculously intense" and could stand to be redesigned. The "very accessible" and "committed" faculty "genuinely care about the welfare of the students." According to a 2L, "their theory seems to be: 'Law school is hard. Let us help you'" Professors are "a little—okay, really—conservative," but students told us they are "real people, not holier-than-thou egomaniacs." An "outstanding open-door policy" is near and dear to the hearts of both students and faculty.

"Career Services works extremely hard," but students complained that they're "not very useful if you are interested in working somewhere besides California." If you are interested in working California, Pepperdine grads do quite nicely for themselves in nearby Los Angeles, the nation's fourth-largest job market. Pepperdine students are second only to Stanford in passing the California Bar, and the law school has firmly established itself as a respected source of successful attorneys.

Students said that "there is no better library or computer lab anywhere" in Los Angeles. From its perch atop Pepperdine's Malibu campus, the law school commands a view of the Pacific Ocean and Catalina Island that is stunning. If you don't believe us, check out the school's promotional materials, which contain more full-color photographs of buildings and landscapes per page than perhaps any law school in the nation. A 3L suggests,

Ms. Shannon Phillips, Director of Admissions
24255 Pacific Coast Highway
Malibu, CA 90263
Tel: 310-456-4631 • Fax: 310-456-4266
Email: soladmis@pepperdine.edu
Internet: law-www.pepperdine.edu

Pepperdine University

"after first year, when you actually get a chance to look around and about you, try the beach right outside." One complaint we heard: the facility is "simply too cold."

The university was founded in 1937 by George Pepperdine, the devoutly Christian owner of a chain of auto-parts stores. Though officially nonsectarian, the whole institution "maintains a relationship" with the Church of Christ. This relationship is reflected in the law school's conservative bent. If you are a lover of Christianity, you'll probably "appreciate the emphasis on ethics as rooted in Christian principles and the absence of any conformist political correctness." If the Bible isn't your bag, you might find that "the hold the Church of Christ possesses over the students, faculty, and administration is counterproductive and detrimental to the pursuit of knowledge and intellectual growth." However, most students said "it's easy to fit in here. Being in southern California, individuality is accepted and even expected. It's great to be somewhere where students can be what they want to be without feeling pressures to conform." Just bear in mind that we're not talking pink hair and multiple body piercings.

Students reported that "there is enough competition to keep things interesting, but there is very little back-stabbing." "If you are looking for a law school with a very conservative environment, a noncompetitive atmosphere, accessible teachers, excellent educational opportunities, and immaculate and picturesque scenery," advised a 1L, "Pepperdine is your best choice."

ADMISSIONS

The view from the hilltop campus of the Pepperdine University School of Law is indeed spectacular, but you face a steep climb in getting there. More than twelve applicants vie annually for each spot in Pepperdine's entering class, so the Law School has the luxury of choosing its students very carefully. For the most recent entering class, the median LSAT score was 157; the median GPA was 3.0; and the average age was 23. The great majority of admitted students hail from California.

ACADEMICS

Student/faculty ratio	20:1
% female faculty	27
% minority faculty	9
Hours of study per day	3.42

Academic specialties:

Civil Procedure, Commercial, Constitutional, Corporation Securities, Criminal, Environmental, Human Rights, International, Labor, Property, Taxation, Family, Public interest

FINANCIAL FACTS

Tuition	$21,850
Cost of books	$700
Fees	$50
Room & board (on/off-campus)	$5,750/$9,200
% first-year students receiving aid	80
% all students receiving aid	82
% aid that is merit-based	67
% of all students receiving loans	82
% receiving scholarships	65
% of all students receiving assistantships	10
Average grant	NR
Average graduation debt	$67,000

ADMISSIONS

# applications received	2,517
% applicants accepted	40
% acceptees attending	20
Average LSAT	158
LSAT range	146-167
Average undergrad GPA	3.30
GPA range	2.20-3.97
Application fee	$50
Regular application	rolling
Regular notification	rolling
Rolling notification?	Yes
Early decision program?	No
Admission may be deferred?	No
Evening division offered?	No
Part-time accepted?	No
Gourman Report Rating	**3.85**

UNIVERSITY OF PITTSBURGH
School of Law

The University of Pittsburgh School of Law is a "highly intellectual and challenging" midsize public institution that has served this western Pennsylvania city for over 100 years. Pitt's numerous strengths include reasonable tuition (when compared to other schools of its caliber) and a "good mix of pragmatism and theory." Students told us that "legal opportunities abound," in "the Burgh," especially in the corporate headquarters that make their homes here. Not surprisingly, "being in an industrial, commercial center, the school's strength is business law."

The "sensible and challenging curriculum" here is traditional, with few requirements but many options. The law school's course offerings are vast, and include an increasing number of courses in the growing field of health law. "It's pretty much assumed that everybody wants to be a corporate lawyer," though, "if you didn't want to be one when you got here, you'll be one when you get out because those are the only courses offered." Pitt's "very talented, very driven professors" have been rated among the finest in the country in terms of scholarly output, and "student-faculty friendship is cherished" here. "They take a strong interest in seeing both the school, and the school's students, succeed." Even the "helpful and open" administration occasionally does something that warrants praise. Other times, "getting into the administration's offices is like getting into Fort Knox."

The city of Pittsburgh is one of the nation's top twenty legal job markets in terms of both volume and compensation, and Pitt is the city's primary supplier of lawyers. If you think these circumstances are cause for celebration, you're wrong. Pitt students begrudge their school for a lack of "practical skills development" and offer virtually nothing but grief to their Career Planning Office for "failing to market" graduates "aggressively to employers." Said a 3L, "As Pitt represents a middle-of-the-pack law school, Career Planning cannot afford to make sloppy mistakes." But students asserted that Career Planning has "no clue about jobs outside Pittsburgh" and "cannot seem to get its act together to serve those not on Law Review or Journal." Consequently, "the top 10 to 15 percent generally acquire high-paying jobs with larger law firms. The rest of the class is usually sent packing."

Fredi G. Miller, Dean
3900 Forbes Avenue
Pittsburgh, PA 15260
Tel: 412-648-1415 • Fax: 412-648-2647
Email: admissons@law.pitt.edu
Internet: www.law.pitt.edu

University of Pittsburgh

However, an optimistic 1L noted that it "seems like Career Planning is making a strong effort to improve."

The facilities received some pretty serious flack as well. According to a sarcastic 1L: "The physical plant is a rather sterile concrete bunker trimmed in lovely brown." A 2L agreed: "I love the East German Functionalist approach." Don't forget about the "ski-slope classrooms." Also, "the computer center is a disgrace. There are 16 computers for 750 students. The lab is hot, loud, and in disrepair," complained a fed-up 3L. "And the lab staff, in spite of their full-time positions, cannot manage to keep all 16 computers running at any one time."

Students described themselves as "bright and motivated" and "eager to make friends." And would you believe "Pitt Law students party like rock stars?" Well, "it's true," according to a 2L. Many respondents told us that the social life here "is like high school. Everybody knows everybody's business. Any time you put 750 people together in a closed environment, you can expect that," observed a 1L. The school's location on Forbes Street gives way to the nickname "Forbes High." There is some slight racial tension at Pitt. Many white students complained that minority students receive special and unfair treatment from the school. Minority students griped that they are not afforded equal treatment by other students. For all their bellyaching, though, Pitt students are ultimately pretty happy. In their gentler moments, they agreed that "students actually help one another" here and Pitt is "a wonderful place to grow, both in knowledge and friendship."

ADMISSIONS

If you'd like to attend law school at the University of Pittsburgh, you had better make sure that your numerical credentials are up to par. Although overall admission selectivity is relatively moderate, due to the high volume of applications the school receives, the qualifications of entering students are solid: an impressive average LSAT score of 155 and an undergraduate GPA of about 3.20. These standards are, in fact, higher than those of 60 percent of all American law schools.

ACADEMICS

Student/faculty ratio	21:1
% female faculty	40
% minority faculty	10
Hours of study per day	3.96

Academic specialties:
Environmental, International

FINANCIAL FACTS

Tuition (in/out-state)	$10,962/$16,970
Cost of books	$500
Fees (in/out-state)	$392/$392
Room & board (on/off-campus)	NR/$9,400
% first-year students receiving aid	25
% all students receiving aid	30
% aid that is merit-based	10
% of all students receiving loans	85
% receiving scholarships	31
% of all students receiving assistantships	NR
Average grant	$3,200
Average graduation debt	$45,000

ADMISSIONS

# applications received	1,367
% applicants accepted	62
% acceptees attending	30
Average LSAT	155
LSAT range	139-176
Average undergrad GPA	3.20
GPA range	2.04-3.99
Application fee (in/out-state)	$40/$40
Regular application	rolling
Regular notification	rolling
Rolling notification?	Yes
Early decision program?	No
Admission may be deferred?	Yes
Maximum length of deferment	1 year
Evening division offered?	No
Part-time accepted?	No
Gourman Report Rating	**3.75**

QUINNIPIAC COLLEGE
School of Law

OVERVIEW

Type of school	private
Environment	suburban
Scholastic calendar	semester
Schedule	full-time or part-time

STUDENTS

Enrollment of parent institution	3,772
Enrollment of law school	766
% male/female	68/32
% out-of-state	40
% part-time	31
% minorities	11
% international (# of countries represented)	NR (NR)
Average age at entry	26

APPLICANTS ALSO LOOK AT

University of Connecticut
Pace University
Western New England College
Saint John's University
New England School of Law

SURVEY SAYS...

HITS
Diverse faculty
Legal writing
Socratic method

MISSES
Library staff
Not enough courses

EMPLOYMENT PROFILE

Job placement rate (%)	90
% grads employed within six months	88
Average starting salary	$35,000

Grads employed by field (%):

Academia	2
Business/industry	18
Government	16
Judicial clerkships	9
Private practice	50
Public interest	1

Finding a decent apartment is hard enough when you have only yourself to please. Imagine trying to find a comfortable new dwelling on short notice for 29 professors, 700 law students and a 225,000-volume library. It boggles the mind, but that was the task that faced the former University of Bridgeport School of Law in early 1992 when its financially strapped parent institution began to unravel. While the ABA threatened to rescind the school's accreditation, the law schools administration cast about for new digs. It found them in March, 1992, and re-formed itself as the Quinnipiac College School of Law. Still, the law school's fight for survival is not over, and until the dust fully settles, to enroll at Quinnipiac is to take a calculated risk. So far, however, Quinnipiac's administrators have succeeded in making this huge transition as smooth as can be expected.

The new building, located in Hamden, Connecticut, sometimes referred to as the "Taj Mahal," affords a lovely view of the Sleeping Giant Mountains from its perch directly across from Sleeping Giant Park. In addition to the move, some other exciting changes happened in 1995. New hires who formerly taught at such estimable seats of learning as Vanderbilt, the University of Chicago, and Oxford University joined Quinnipiac's faculty. The school is making a name for itself by sponsoring events such as a conference on Forensics attended by most of the defense experts from the O.J. Simpson trial.

Even with all the change, the school happily continues its traditions of sound programs in Health Care Law and Tax Law, and its commitment to public service. According to the Quinnipiac School of Law bulletin, "The School of Law's curriculum reflects the belief that complete legal training includes a full understanding of ethical issues and values and an appreciation of a lawyer's professional and social responsibilities." To this end, the school operates three clinics, the Tax Clinic, the Civil Clinic, and the new Appellate Clinic, which provide vital legal services to the population of greater New Haven.

Many students expressed appreciation for the help their professors provide to improve their personal, more immediate futures. One 2L informed us, "Our professors are always available and

John Noonan, Dean of Law School Admissions
275 Mount Carmel Avenue
Hamden, CT 06518
Tel: 203-287-3400 • Fax: 203-287-3339
Email: adm@quinnipiac.edu
Internet: http:/www.quinnipiac.edu/law.html

Quinnipiac College

willing to provide help and answer questions outside the class-room." Many praised the Tax Clinic and the "stress on practical law," including Quinnipiac's extensive lawyering skills program. One said, "I would recommend Quinnipiac to anyone as a viable, nurturing school."

Thanks to all the recent changes, students we heard from are justifiably optimistic about the future of the school. We heard extensive gratitude for "the quality of the faculty and the effort of the administrators to improve the facilities and reputation of the school." The administration's efforts will surely go a long way to diminish students' greatest worry, the reputation, and increase name recognition. Another student spoke for many when she placed her praise in more guarded terms: "The school has great potential, and the faculty and administration seem willing to realize it." As a 1L told us, "The only direction this law school is going is up, especially with the devoted administration and motivated student body. Some predict the school will be among the top law schools in the nation within twenty years."

ADMISSIONS

The Bridgeport School of Law's much-publicized woes in 1992 did not fail to have an effect on the law school's admissions process. In the 1991 application year, Bridgeport received more than 3,300 applications for admission to its entering class of about 200. In 1993, it received fewer than 2,500. Furthermore, Bridgeport admitted almost 200 more students in order to fill its class. In other words, between '91 and '93 the acceptance rate here jumped from a low of 25 percent to the current, lenient rate of around 40 percent. Numerical standards, however, declined only slightly, and it is likely that Quinnipiac's overall admissions selectivity will once again increase as the law school settles in to its new home

ACADEMICS	
Student/faculty ratio	11:1
% female faculty	36
% minority faculty	5
Hours of study per day	4.14

Academic specialties:
Civil Procedure, Corporation Securities, Criminal, Taxation

FINANCIAL FACTS	
Tuition	$18,888
Cost of books	$800
Fees	$435
Room & board (on/off-campus)	NR/$11,535
% first-year students receiving aid	85
% all students receiving aid	85
% aid that is merit-based	30
% of all students receiving loans	80
% receiving scholarships	30
% of all students receiving assistantships	8
Average grant	$5,300
Average graduation debt	$70,500

ADMISSIONS	
# applications received	2,073
% applicants accepted	51
% acceptees attending	22
Average LSAT	150
Average undergrad GPA	2.80
Application fee	$40
Regular application	rolling
Regular notification	rolling
Rolling notification?	Yes
Early decision program?	No
Admission may be deferred?	Yes
Maximum length of deferment	1 year
Evening division offered?	Yes
Part-time accepted?	Yes
Gourman Report Rating	**2.22**

UNIVERSITY OF RICHMOND
The T.C. Williams School of Law

OVERVIEW

Type of school	private
Environment	suburban
Scholastic calendar	semester
Schedule	full time

STUDENTS

Enrollment of parent institution	2,872
Enrollment of law school	481
% male/female	50/50
% out-of-state	38
% part-time	1
% minorities	25
% international (# of countries represented)	8 (27)
Average age at entry	25

APPLICANTS ALSO LOOK AT

William and Mary
University of Virginia
George Mason University
Washington and Lee University
American University

SURVEY SAYS...

HITS
Studying
Practical lawyering skills
Classroom facilities

MISSES
Not enough courses

EMPLOYMENT PROFILE

Job placement rate (%)	86
% grads employed within six months	86
Average starting salary	$39,000

The T.C. Williams School of Law at the University of Richmond is a midsize private law school with a "small-class atmosphere" and a "practical emphasis." Given the law school's focus, it's not surprising that a good number of students see skills-training as Richmond's area of greatest strength. Explained a 2L, "The people who run this program try very hard to prepare their students well." The Richmond curriculum is solid and traditional, and notable for its programs, including environmental law as a requirement for 1Ls. "The professors are the best in their fields," contended a 2L, "from criminal law professors that participated in Iran–Contra to constitutional law professors that worked on resolving the Virginia Military Institute case." Students claimed that "profs are easily approachable and extremely attentive to your questions." The administration was said to be "very accessible" as well.

Richmond is the capital of Virginia, a state that has one of the biggest law-school graduate surpluses in the Union. Every year, the state's six law schools turn out more fledgling attorneys than its legal profession can absorb. But several of Virginia's law schools are among the nation's most elite, and a huge proportion of these schools' graduates leave the state for the greener, better-paying pastures of New York City and Washington, D.C. Thanks to "the Law School's membership in the Richmond Good Ole Boys' Network," and its solid and long-established regional reputation, Richmond fills the resulting void by sending the vast majority of its grads to work within the state. With a "strong Law Skills Program, clinics, and judicial placements," Richmond is committed to seeing that its graduates hit the ground running. Richmond's required two-year course in "Lawyering Skills" follows an uncommon but increasingly popular format: Students are divided into small simulated law offices in which they perform all the tasks associated with servicing real legal clients. This approach is intended to expose students early on to the sort of work they would otherwise have to learn on the job after graduation. "In three years working in a law firm before starting school, I saw attorneys who had recently graduated from top institutions who were not able to react and act in the 'real world' of the legal profession," explained one student. "I feel like U of R is doing its

University of Richmond, VA 23173
Tel: 804-289-8189 • Fax: 804-287-6516
Internet: www.urich.edu/^law

part to correct this all-too-prevalent problem." Students who want to practice law beyond the boundaries of Virginia—especially north of the Mason-Dixon line—do not fare exceptionally well. "I'm worried," admitted a 3L, "because I'm planning to move out of the state, and no one has heard of us."

Technology is big here, and entering students are "required to have laptops." Richmond was the first law school in the country to require this of its students. The facilities are "modern and user-friendly," and allow students to see and experience the cutting edge of the legal profession. "Computer training during orientation is inadequate," though, and, ironically, there is a "lack of computer knowledge among the staff in the library." Richmond's "acceptable" library and classrooms are nothing to write home about, but you could do much, much worse. The U of R's "classy moot courtroom" is a plus. Overall, complaints about the facilities were virtually nil.

The "intense but very well-guided" future attorneys at Richmond described themselves as "intelligent and talented." One student explained: "Generally, we are a very happy but very busy bunch." Competition for high grades is "not cutthroat" or negative. "This school is definitely not as competitive as I thought it would be. Most students are willing to do whatever they can to help you out," asserted a 2L. It's very much a "family-like atmosphere."

ADMISSIONS

Admissions are selective here, and admitted students possess strong numerical credentials. In purely numerical terms, the Law School at the University of Richmond is in the front half of the pack of American law schools, reflecting the extent to which admissions selectivity has increased nationwide. Seven or eight years ago, "moderate" admissions standards were truly moderate. Today, the term is relative. Consider, after all, the undeniable strength of the credentials of Richmond students. Their average undergraduate GPA and LSAT scores are solid.

ACADEMICS	
Student/faculty ratio	9:1
% female faculty	37
% minority faculty	13
Hours of study per day	4.54

FINANCIAL FACTS	
Tuition	$17,170
Cost of books	$900
% first-year students receiving aid	NR
% all students receiving aid	NR
% aid that is merit-based	25
% of all students receiving loans	86
% receiving scholarships	75
% of all students receiving assistantships	NR
Average grant	$3,164
Average graduation debt	NR

ADMISSIONS	
# applications received	1,631
% applicants accepted	34
% acceptees attending	31
Average LSAT	159
Average undergrad GPA	3.02
Application fee	$35
Regular application	January 15
Regular notification	May 1
Rolling notification?	Yes
Early decision program?	No
Admission may be deferred?	Yes
Gourman Report Rating	**2.69**

RUTGERS UNIVERSITY, CAMDEN
School of Law at Camden

OVERVIEW

Type of school	public
Environment	city
Scholastic calendar	semester
Schedule	full-time or part-time

STUDENTS

Enrollment of parent institution	47,800
Enrollment of law school	774
% male/female	56/44
% out-of-state	23
% part-time	21
% minorities	17
% international (# of countries represented)	2 (9)
Average age at entry	26

APPLICANTS ALSO LOOK AT

Temple University
Seton Hall University
Villanova University
Rutgers University, Newark
American University

SURVEY SAYS...

HITS
Academic reputation
Legal writing
Diverse faculty

MISSES
Not enough courses

EMPLOYMENT PROFILE

Firms recruiting on campus	75
Job placement rate (%)	96
% grads employed immediately	59
% grads employed within six months	95
Average starting salary	$38,764

Grads employed by field (%):

Academia	2
Business/industry	13
Government	8
Judicial clerkships	31
Military	2
Private practice	40
Public interest	3
Other	1

In 1950, the State University of New Jersey absorbed its second School of Law, one that was and is, in many positive respects, identical to the older state law school in Newark. The Rutgers University School of Law in Camden is a moderately large, inexpensive law school with an esteemed faculty, a favorable student-faculty ratio, academically strong day and evening programs, and a solid regional reputation. Both the Newark and the Camden schools attract highly qualified students, primarily in-state residents that are slightly older and significantly more diverse than average. The biggest difference between the two schools stems from their respective locations. The Newark location tends to be New York-oriented, while Camden is as much a part of Pennsylvania as it is of New Jersey. Many graduates of Rutgers, Camden find employment in the greater Philadelphia metropolitan area, the nation's fifth largest legal job market.

Academic options at Rutgers are many. The Law School's course offerings are quite extensive, and the programs of the university afford the law student ample opportunity for interdisciplinary study. Joint J.D./Master's degree programs are available through the departments of urban planning, business administration, and political science. The Law School also offers formal J.D. honors programs of specialization in taxation, and in international and comparative law. Both programs have limited enrollment due to the Law School's somewhat selective admissions requirements. Enrollment in general at the law school is also somewhat selective.

Many current students appreciate the low tuition at Rutgers, Camden, and think they're getting quite a bargain due to its low tuition. A first-year student stated, "For the quality education you receive here, you can't beat the price." A 3L claimed, "its low tuition attracts a wide variety of talented students who might otherwise have gone to the 'Ivies,' producing a smart student body with amazingly varied backgrounds." The faculty was praised for being supportive, approachable and, generally effective. One third-year student characterized the professors as, "well-informed, current in their subject, dedicated, and generally better than average in their ability to teach." A few students who

Maureen O'Boyle, Associate Director of Admissions
406 Penn Street, 3rd floor
Camden, NJ 08102
Tel: 609-225-6102 • Fax: 609-225-6537
Email: admissions@camlaw.rutgers.edu
Internet: www.comlaw.rutgers.edu

**Rutgers University,
Camden**

described themselves as "older" wrote glowingly about the positive reception they received at the school from both faculty and students. Several students, though, commented that the quality of the faculty was uneven.

The school's location was viewed as a mixed blessing. On the downside, the school is not exactly in a bucolic setting. One student described Camden "as dirty, threatening, and ugly." Others, while acknowledging that the campus was not ideally situated, characterized the campus as safe. On the upside, though, the school is in a perfect location for students seeking work; they can explore the legal markets in Philadelphia, New Jersey, New York City, and even Washington, D.C. with relative ease. (Another geographic advantage is that students seeking a break from work can easily hit the beaches on the Jersey shore.) Indeed, an overwhelming number of our respondents said that they chose the school because of its geographic location. Although the location is well-suited to job searches, some students found fault with the Career Services department. Whatever the school's weaknesses, most students agreed that they were getting a good law school experience for a great price.

ADMISSIONS

Numerical admissions standards at Rutgers, Camden, crept up steadily during the late 1980s, as they did at most of the nation's public law schools. Though Rutgers saw a less dramatic increase than some, standards were quite high to begin with. As it now stands, the law school is quite selective, denying admission to 70 percent of all applicants and admitting a midsize class of students with strong credentials: solid undergraduate GPAs and good LSAT scores at or about the 75th percentile. Rutgers's status as a true bargain is not unknown to successful candidates for admission. Admitted applicants accept offers to attend the law school at a high rate.

ACADEMICS
Student/faculty ratio	17:1
% female faculty	30
% minority faculty	6
Hours of study per day	3.40

Academic specialties:
Corporation Securities, International, Taxation

FINANCIAL FACTS
Tuition (in/out-state)	$8,550/$12,544
Cost of books	$1,000
Fees (in/out-state)	$992/$992
Room & board (on/off-campus)	$3,890
% first-year students receiving aid	82
% all students receiving aid	82
% aid that is merit-based	1
% of all students receiving loans	80
% receiving scholarships	25
% of all students receiving assistantships	NR
Average grant	$1,000
Average graduation debt	$45,000

ADMISSIONS
# applications received	1,656
% applicants accepted	44
% acceptees attending	31
Average LSAT	156
LSAT range	139-172
Average undergrad GPA	3.20
GPA range	2.20-4.00
Application fee (in/out-state)	$40/$40
Regular application	March 1
Regular notification	12/1-4/1
Rolling notification?	Yes
Early decision program?	No
Admission may be deferred?	Yes
Evening division offered?	Yes
Part-time accepted?	Yes
Gourman Report Rating	**3.69**

RUTGERS UNIVERSITY, NEWARK
School of Law

The history of Newark, a hardworking northern New Jersey city has been, in large part, a history of immigrants and industry. Over time, the origin of the immigrants and the identity of the industries changed, but the city has known one constant: a fine public law school that was once the country's second largest. The Rutgers University School of Law, Newark, boasts an excellent faculty and a highly qualified group of law students who are, in terms of both ethnicity and gender, among the most diverse in the nation. The law school's large evening division and its active alternative admissions program for applicants from under-represented minority groups are evidence of its dedication to making a quality legal education accessible to all New Jersey residents, who make up the great majority of the student body. The resources at the disposal of Rutgers law students are considerable, from the numerous clinical programs run by the law school to the extensive academic offerings of the university itself, through which interdisciplinary work is encouraged. The applicant pool from which Rutgers draws its first-year students is large and growing, so selectivity is high. Admitted applicants possess strong numerical credentials.

They also possess keen critical faculties, judging from the results of our survey. The students we heard from did not hesitate to criticize their chosen school on any number of matters, from its "decaying" facilities to its "mediocre" career services office. Yet nearly all of their criticism was constructive and offered in a manner that did not hide their overall satisfaction with the most basic aspect of their law-school experience: their academic and practical preparation for the practice of law. "The facilities at Rutgers-Newark leave much to be desired," began one fairly typical assessment from a 3L. "The library shows signs of neglect and the building is awful," it continued, "but the program itself is very strong and the tuition is so low that I cannot regret my decision to come here." It appears that most here would agree with that last judgment. Despite seeing real room for improvement elsewhere, most Rutgers students heaped praise on their school for its commitment to maintaining a strong, broad and nontraditional curriculum while keeping tuition low, at least in comparison with other schools in the region. As one 2L put it,

Olga Hunczak, Director of Admissions
SI Newhouse Center for Law and Justice
Newark, NJ 07102
Tel: 973-353-5557 • Fax: 973-353-1445
Email: rgeddis@andromeda.rutgers.edu
Internet: www.rutgers.edu/rusln

Rutgers University, Newark

"The clinical and public interest programs here are top-notch, particularly considering the low cost of an education." Indeed, many of the respondents to our survey used a similar cost-benefit analysis in assessing their overall feelings for their school. "There's a lot of things I would fix here if I could," wrote one such student, "but I don't think I'd have been willing to pay three times as much just to have a pretty campus."

Still, one cannot ignore the fact that many Rutgers students' complaints go deeper than the ugliness of their campus. Most see the condition of their physical plant as a serious drawback. "The students here are friendly, bright, and fairly relaxed, but there is almost no school social life," said one 2L. The reason? "Our building sucks and Newark's worse." Some went even further. "Sometimes it seems that it's not just the building that's falling apart," said one 2L. "The great reputation this school once enjoyed is threatened by the failure to replace some of our better retiring professors with high-caliber younger ones." In fact, though most students here seem to agree that their faculty is nothing if not uneven, the majority generally expressed more optimism: "Although the atmosphere and facilities at Rutgers-Newark are marginal, a new building is coming shortly, which should be a great improvement," went one fairly evenhanded assessment by one 3L, "[and] our new dean of placement and new dean of the school have injected some much-needed energy into a largely uninterested faculty." If that trend continues, it seems that future students at Rutgers-Newark will agree even more strongly that "This is a flawed but excellent school, and you can't beat it for the price."

ADMISSIONS

With a strong academic reputation and a bargain-basement price tag, it should come as no surprise to hear that the Rutgers School of Law, Newark, draws its students from a huge applicant pool. In fact, with more than 10 applicants for every spot in its first-year class, Rutgers, Newark, is in a position to select its students extremely carefully.

ACADEMICS

Student/faculty ratio	17:1
% female faculty	24
% minority faculty	15
Hours of study per day	3.76

Academic specialties:
Civil Procedure, Commercial, Constitutional, Corporation Securities, Criminal, Environmental, Human Rights, International, Labor, Legal History, Legal Philosophy, Property, Taxation, Other

FINANCIAL FACTS

Tuition (in/out-state)	$8,550/$12,544
Cost of books	$1,000
Fees (in/out-state)	$984/$984
Room & board (on/off-campus)	$8,192/$10,292
% first-year students receiving aid	NR
% all students receiving aid	66
% aid that is merit-based	5
% of all students receiving loans	65
% receiving scholarships	17
% of all students receiving assistantships	4
Average grant	$1,100
Average graduation debt	$34,000

ADMISSIONS

# applications received	2,678
% applicants accepted	25
% acceptees attending	33
Average LSAT	159
Average undergrad GPA	3.31
Application fee (in/out-state)	$40/$40
Regular application	March 15
Regular notification	rolling
Rolling notification?	Yes
Early decision program?	No
Admission may be deferred?	Yes
Maximum length of deferment	1 year
Evening division offered?	Yes
Part-time accepted?	Yes
Gourman Report Rating	**3.73**

SAMFORD UNIVERSITY
Cumberland School of Law

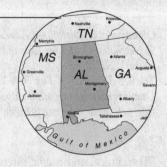

The Cumberland School of Law at Samford University is the larger of Alabama's two law schools. It began life in 1847, but in Lebanon, Tennessee. The law school did not become affiliated with Samford, a private Baptist university in suburban Birmingham until 1961. Since then, Cumberland has firmly established itself as a "great school for a traditional legal education." Occasionally, it's the kind of place where "people stand in the halls and debate esoteric principles" but the focus on "practical and therefore useful" aspects of the law is a bigger hit with current students. The "outstanding, competent, approachable" and "highly skilled" faculty runs the gamut "from nutty to serious." Students said "all the professors have great credentials and are very interested in seeing students succeed." Said a 1L, "I could not believe it when my professors stopped me in the hall to ask how I was doing in and out of class."

The traditional, requirement-heavy curriculum here "allows students to graduate with broad-based knowledge in most major areas of law—particularly business-oriented law." A "solid legal writing and research program" wins a great deal of praise, too. Through the broader university itself, law students can pursue dual degrees in education, business administration, public health, divinity, accountancy, and environmental management. That's the good news. Unfortunately, class sizes here are large, the variety of courses offered is very limited, and the curriculum itself is somewhat rigid. To compound these problems, "scheduling is a big problem." Argued a 3L, "Classes listed in the directory are not actually offered, and those electives that are offered always conflict."

Although it offers no more courses in the field than many law schools, Cumberland dedicates tremendous human and financial resources to instilling strong advocacy skills in its students. The law school's emphasis on courtroom skills is evident in its sponsorship of eight different on-campus mock trial competitions. The victors in these hotly contested competitions have had great success at the national level, drawing much attention to the school's strong suit. As a result, Cumberland has built a widely recognized reputation for its "excellent moot court" and generally strong practical-skills program, a fact which is not lost on the

Mitzi S. Davis, Assistant Dean for Admissions
800 Lakeshore Drive
Birmingham, AL 35229
Tel: 800-888-7213
Email: law.admissions@samford.edu
Internet: www.samford.edu

Samford University

enthusiastic, trial-happy students here. The "clinical programs are second to none in the Southeast," they said. "Based on my summer employment experience in North Carolina with students from other 'big name' law schools," asserted a 2L, "I felt as prepared if not more prepared (especially in legal research and writing) than these other students." Cumberland has also developed a "strong connection to the Birmingham legal community, providing many opportunities for learning and working." Nevertheless, students say "alumni networking" could use some fine-tuning.

"The campus is beautiful." The law school boasts an "unbelievable" $8.4 million new law library with modern research facilities," finished in March 1995. Students said that it's "functional, well-stocked, well-staffed, and technologically up-to-date." Cumberland's classrooms are "good for lectures," but the court rooms that have been converted to classrooms leave much to be desired in this capacity.

Cumberland is a "bastion of conservatism" and can be "difficult for liberals" at times. Students reported "some intellectual snobbery" and said that minorities are "not truly integrated," which provides for a smattering of tension. "Although the students do tend to form cliques here, there is still a strong sense of community. "I think this results from everyone being in 'the same boat' during first year," ventured a 2L. "Most students are supportive of others. Study groups are quick to form. Also, there are many parties to help everyone get to know one another and relax." For the most part, students seem satisfied. "Cumberland is an excellent law school. There is a great spirit of community throughout all three classes. Thus far, Cumberland has been an extremely positive experience," summarized a 2L. "I would not exchange my experience and friends here for anything in the world."

ADMISSIONS

Cumberland students, most of whom come from and stay in the Southeast, possess midrange numerical credentials. In most quantifiable respects, the Cumberland School of Law at Samford University resides in the middle of the pack of all U.S. law schools in terms of admissions selectivity. Still, a large applicant pool allows the law school to select its students rather carefully, denying admission to more than half of all candidates it considers.

ACADEMICS

Student/faculty ratio	20:1
% female faculty	18
% minority faculty	13
Hours of study per day	4.14

FINANCIAL FACTS

Tuition	$17,700
Cost of books	$1,003
Room & board (on/off-campus)	NR/$7,446
% first-year students receiving aid	97
% all students receiving aid	99
% aid that is merit-based	10
% of all students receiving loans	79
% receiving scholarships	28
% of all students receiving assistantships	15
Average grant	$6,224
Average graduation debt	NR

ADMISSIONS

# applications received	1,030
% applicants accepted	57
% acceptees attending	36
Average LSAT	152
Average undergrad GPA	3.10
Application fee	$40
Regular application	rolling
Regular notification	rolling
Rolling notification?	Yes
Early decision program?	No
Admission may be deferred?	No
Evening division offered?	No
Part-time accepted?	No
Gourman Report Rating	**2.77**

UNIVERSITY OF SAN DIEGO
School of Law

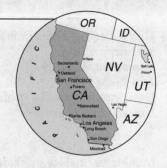

It is not difficult to understand why prospective law students would be attracted to the idea of studying in San Diego. Beautiful weather alone can, on occasion, go a long way toward relieving the stresses of law school. Indeed, the year-round sun and balmy temperatures of its home city must help explain the enormous popularity of the University of San Diego School of Law. During the early 1990s, the volume of applications filed at this large Catholic law school increased by more than 150 percent, and San Diego's overall acceptance rate was slashed in half. However, three years of sunshine is far from the only reason future lawyers come here.

Faculty vies with location as one of the greatest strengths of the school. Students praised their professors' willingness to help them understand material. We also heard many kind comments about the administration, a rare occurrence in the world of law schools. A 1L said that "professors as well as administrators sincerely care about our welfare and well-being." More than a few students called the administrative staff helpful, efficient, and friendly. One 2L said the "Dean of Students is always willing to help individual students." Another 2L proclaimed, "The records office staff is the best."

San Diego's J.D. program is rigorous, and its students serious-minded. The course of study they follow at the law school is straightforward: a fully prescribed first year and then a few required courses in the next two. A 1L praised the atmosphere of "group effort and broad learning." The school has relatively extensive course offerings within traditional bounds. The San Diego curriculum is supplemented by a considerable array of skills programs. The size of the clinical programs is limited, but the school offers a wide variety of them. USD takes particular pride in its advocacy programs; participation in San Diego's numerous moot-court competitions is reportedly quite high.

While the school's tuition is on a par with other private law schools, it is far steeper than that of California's higher-ranking state law schools. One student, who appreciated the school's "excellent library" and described the faculty as "helpful and

Carl Eging, Director of Admissions and Financial Aid
5998 Alcala Park
San Diego, CA 92110
Tel: 619-260-4528 • Fax: 619-260-2218
Email: jdinfo@acusd.edu
Internet: www.acusd.edu/~usdlaw

University of San Diego

insightful," still called the school's tuition "almost oppressive." Another voiced concerns that students were not getting their money's worth.

Students did express a need for more computer training and a greater use of computers in their legal research than they are currently receiving at San Diego. "For the money we pay and the technology available today, this and other law schools are using teaching methods that must come directly from the Dark Ages," said a 1L.

Unfortunately most students we heard from were far quicker to criticize than to praise, and those who did make positive comments lacked enthusiasm in their delivery. This possibly speaks of an alienation that many students seemed to feel, despite the friendly administration. "There could be more ways for students to voice their opinions without feeling threatened," said a 1L. "Student input needs to be seriously considered as opposed to offhandedly disregarded," said a 2L.

The positives we heard from students tended to focus on the school's environment—the great weather and the school's relaxed social climate. One student who noted that San Diego "affords students with an abundance of extracurricular activities," formed his list as such: "sailing, golfing, jogging…and tennis…" Another student, a 1L made this observation: "[This is a] very caring environment—no shark tank here."

ADMISSIONS

It is testimony to the popularity of all of California's law schools that the University of San Diego School of Law ranks only eighth of the state's sixteen in admissions selectivity. In terms of numerical standards to which it holds its applicants, San Diego is one of the seventy most selective law schools in the country.

ACADEMICS

Student/faculty ratio	20:1
% female faculty	26
% minority faculty	12
Hours of study per day	3.35

Academic specialties:
Civil Procedure, Commercial, Constitutional, Criminal, Environmental, Human Rights, International, Labor, Taxation

FINANCIAL FACTS

Tuition	$18,940
Cost of books	$750
Fees	$50
Room & board (on/off-campus)	$11,788/$11,788
% first-year students receiving aid	76
% all students receiving aid	76
% aid that is merit-based	NR
% of all students receiving loans	76
% receiving scholarships	21
% of all students receiving assistantships	15
Average grant	NR
Average graduation debt	$56,000

ADMISSIONS

# applications received	2,932
% applicants accepted	35
% acceptees attending	26
Average LSAT	160
Average undergrad GPA	3.20
Application fee	$40
Regular application	rolling
Regular notification	rolling
Rolling notification?	Yes
Early decision program?	No
Admission may be deferred?	Yes
Maximum length of deferment	1 year
Evening division offered?	Yes
Part-time accepted?	Yes
Gourman Report Rating	**3.86**

UNIVERSITY OF SAN FRANCISCO
School of Law

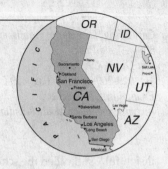

OVERVIEW

Type of school	private
Environment	city
Scholastic calendar	semester
Schedule	full-time or part-time

STUDENTS

Enrollment of parent institution	7,000
Enrollment of law school	691
% male/female	48/52
% out-of-state	8
% part-time	20
% minorities	21
% international (# of countries represented)	NR (NR)
Average age at entry	25

APPLICANTS ALSO LOOK AT

Santa Clara University
University of California, Hastings
University of California, Davis
University of California, Berkeley
University of California, Los Angeles

SURVEY SAYS...

HITS
Legal writing
Practical lawyering skills
Grads expect big bucks

MISSES
Not enough courses

EMPLOYMENT PROFILE

Firms recruiting on campus	35
Job placement rate (%)	83
% grads employed within six months	81
Average starting salary	$50,242

Grads employed by field (%):

Academia	1
Business/industry	18
Government	12
Judicial clerkships	6
Military	1
Private practice	58
Public interest	2
Other	2

For more than eighty years, the University of San Francisco School of Law has been a major supplier of fledgling attorneys to one of the nation's largest legal communities. USF is a relatively large Jesuit institution, and its law school has a strong regional reputation. As one of the only two schools in San Francisco that offers a part-time J.D. program, USF has a relatively secure place as a prominent regional law school.

USF's active efforts to stay on top of the trend toward more practical-skills training seem to reflect its desire to protect its regional status. Like many schools that lack hefty national reputations, USF has responded more quickly than the elite law schools to recent changes in the legal profession. As the job market for law school graduates has tightened, employers have come to place a higher premium on the practical skills of law practice, and USF is quick to tout its commitment to preparing its students accordingly. In the classroom this means an increased reliance on the case method. The level of discussion and intellectual instruction can even approach that found in one of the first-tier institutions."

Many student comments focused on the political climate at USF. This school seems to draw students with different, although equally vocal, political ideas and assumptions of what the social climate should be. Although the majority of students surveyed placed the school on the liberal side of the political spectrum, there are those at USF who find it too conservative and homogenous. One 3L said that USF espouses "a commitment to intellectual diversity and social justice that is simply not reflected in the course offerings, faculty, or administration. If you want to change the world—or even your law school—this is not the place to come." There were also students who felt the school was too liberal. When asked how USF could improve, a 3L made this suggestion: "Get some Republicans on the staff. [There are] too many liberals."

Students with both conservative and liberal leanings were in agreement on USF's facilities, which one student described as "tired." In particular, many students reported that the school's library and computer lab are in need of attention. Despite these

Saralynn Ferrara, Director of Admissions
2130 Fulton Street
San Francisco, CA 94117
Tel: 415-422-6586 • Fax: 415-422-6433

University of San Francisco

concerns, it appears that students at USF School of Law are content enough with their location and practical training to look positively on their educational experience.

As for the school's pragmatic approach to legal education, some students lamented the absence of theoretical instruction on campus. A 1L said, "I would prefer a less practical and more theoretical/critical-thinking approach." Another 1L said: "One is deluded if one believes that the level of discussion and intellectual instruction can even approach that found in one of the first-tier institutions."

ADMISSIONS

As the appeal of attending law school in the Bay Area has increased over the past several years, so has USF's applicant pool. The numerical standards of its students have increased accordingly, and USF now accepts only about one out of three candidates, the vast majority of whom are already Bay Area residents. In terms of numerical standards, USF ranks almost exactly in the middle of U.S. law schools. The class that entered in the 1996–97 term had a median LSAT score of 157 and an average undergraduate GPA of 3.1. For those whose averages exceed these figures, USF is very nearly a sure bet, but those whose numbers fall short face stiff competition.

ACADEMICS	
Student/faculty ratio	26:1
% female faculty	29
% minority faculty	37
Hours of study per day	3.88

Academic specialties:
Labor, Taxation, Business and Commercial, Constitutional and Public interest, Criminal Law and Procedure, Property and Environmental, Government Regulations, International and Comparative, Advocacy and Dispute Resolution, Jurisprudence and Professional Responsibility

FINANCIAL FACTS	
Tuition	$18,900
Cost of books	$750
Room & board (on/off-campus)	$10,389/$10,650
% first-year students receiving aid	100
% all students receiving aid	100
% aid that is merit-based	53
% of all students receiving loans	96
% receiving scholarships	75
% of all students receiving assistantships	15
Average grant	NR
Average graduation debt	NR

ADMISSIONS	
# applications received	3,000
% applicants accepted	42
% acceptees attending	19
Average LSAT	157
Average undergrad GPA	3.10
Application fee	$40
Regular application	April 1
Regular notification	rolling
Rolling notification?	Yes
Early decision program?	No
Admission may be deferred?	No
Evening division offered?	Yes
Part-time accepted?	Yes
Gourman Report Rating	**3.84**

SANTA CLARA UNIVERSITY
School of Law

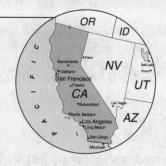

After nearby Stanford and the two area law schools in the University of California system, the Santa Clara University School of Law is probably the most highly regarded law school in the Greater Bay Area. Established more than eighty years ago in what is now the heart of the Silicon Valley—about an hour's drive south of San Francisco—this private law school has long enjoyed a solid reputation in and around Northern California. This region is the source of most of its well-qualified students and the destination of nearly all of its well-trained graduates. Santa Clara's J.D. curriculum is broad within traditional bounds and is supplemented by a relatively extensive clinical program, including an in-house clinic and a wide variety of externships with local courts and public agencies.

The law school also offers formal certificates of specialization in computer and high technology law, public interest law, and international law. Course offerings are richest, however, in the broader category of business and commercial law, and despite the curricular emphasis on public service, the overwhelming majority of Santa Clara grads begin their careers in private practice. A significant number of students pursue a joint J.D./M.B.A. through the university's regionally well-respected business school. Prospective students should note that the massive upsurge in law-school applications in the last decade has affected Santa Clara more than most private law schools. Since 1986, applications volume has more than doubled, and admissions standards have risen significantly. Members of Santa Clara's remarkably diverse entering classes now possess very solid numerical credentials.

They also appear to be satisfied with their chosen school. Although nearly all the students we heard from had their gripes, their overall sense of well-being was notable. "Santa Clara is a good school with very few low spots," said one 3L succinctly. "The academic atmosphere is generally very supportive," wrote another, "and though competition among students is strong, it is not so much so that learning is hindered." Indeed, Santa Clara students agreed almost unanimously that relations among students and between students and faculty are quite good. "The

Julia Yaffee, Assistant Dean
500 El Camino Real
Santa Clara, CA 95053
Tel: 408-554-4800 • Fax: 408-554-7897
Email: lawadmission@mailer.scu.edu
Internet: www.scu.edu/SCU/Departments/Law

Santa Clara University

availability of profs and their willingness to meet with students and work one-on-one with them is one of this school's greatest strengths," reported one 1L. "The attitude encouraged by the administration," he added, "is one of community and not of competition."

When asked to name areas in which their school could stand to improve, many students noted that while the academic elite (top 10 percent) are professionally provided for, the remainder of the students "feel the future looks bleak for the rest of us." Most criticisms were never harsh and were often followed by reiterated praise. Many students, for instance, called on the school to improve its job placement services outside the immediate region, but as one such student allowed, "there is great community support when trying to find a job in the San Jose area." "Most lawyers down here," she explained, "are Santa Clara graduates." "I wish Santa Clara had more of a national reputation," wrote another, "but I'm glad it's a place where you can still feel human. I think that's something important to consider." Though many other students expressed similar sentiments concerning their school's lack of national stature, they seemed to have a sense of humor and perspective on this matter. One student noted that "We almost don't care that the school's reputation isn't quite what it deserves to be—it's truly a fantastic school."

ADMISSIONS

Rising applications volume in the last several years has driven numerical admission standards at the Santa Clara University School of Law ever higher. As it now stands, Santa Clara ranks fifty-eighth among all U.S. law schools in terms of its students' numerical credentials. Happily for the hopeful applicant, however, Santa Clara's overall acceptance rate isn't very low.

ACADEMICS	
Student/faculty ratio	22:1
% female faculty	40
% minority faculty	11
Hours of study per day	4.27

Academic specialties:
International

FINANCIAL FACTS	
Tuition	$19,990
Cost of books	$878
Fees	$0
Room & board (on/off-campus)	$9,268/$9,268
% first-year students receiving aid	77
% all students receiving aid	79
% aid that is merit-based	5
% of all students receiving loans	73
% receiving scholarships	31
% of all students receiving assistantships	8
Average grant	$7,428
Average graduation debt	$60,379

ADMISSIONS	
# applications received	3,032
% applicants accepted	40
% acceptees attending	23
Average LSAT	157
Average undergrad GPA	3.20
GPA range	3.00-3.52
Application fee	$40
Early application	November 1
Regular application	rolling
Regular notification	rolling
Rolling notification?	Yes
Early decision program?	Yes
Admission may be deferred?	Yes
Maximum length of deferment	1 year
Evening division offered?	Yes
Part-time accepted?	Yes
Gourman Report Rating	**3.79**

SEATTLE UNIVERSITY
School of Law

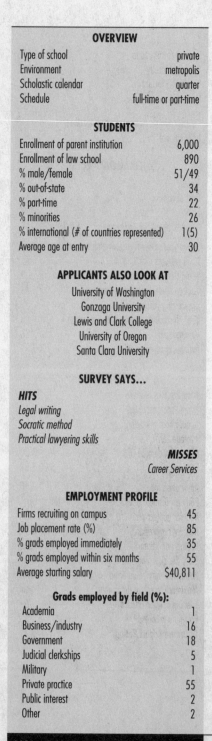

OVERVIEW

Type of school	private
Environment	metropolis
Scholastic calendar	quarter
Schedule	full-time or part-time

STUDENTS

Enrollment of parent institution	6,000
Enrollment of law school	890
% male/female	51/49
% out-of-state	34
% part-time	22
% minorities	26
% international (# of countries represented)	1(5)
Average age at entry	30

APPLICANTS ALSO LOOK AT

University of Washington
Gonzaga University
Lewis and Clark College
University of Oregon
Santa Clara University

SURVEY SAYS...

HITS
Legal writing
Socratic method
Practical lawyering skills

MISSES
Career Services

EMPLOYMENT PROFILE

Firms recruiting on campus	45
Job placement rate (%)	85
% grads employed immediately	35
% grads employed within six months	55
Average starting salary	$40,811

Grads employed by field (%):

Academia	1
Business/industry	16
Government	18
Judicial clerkships	5
Military	1
Private practice	55
Public interest	2
Other	2

The Seattle University School of Law (formerly known as the University of Puget Sound until 1994) in reality is located forty miles from Seattle in Tacoma. But not for very much longer! In 1999, the law school is packing its bags and hitting the road. Its destination is a brand-spanking new facility on a new campus in—rather sensibly—Seattle. Once the dust has settled, SU will still have the largest law school in the Northwest.

Seattle offers a program of study that includes more that 100 courses during fall, spring, and summer terms. Both day and evening courses are available to all students. SU has employs the largest number of full-time faculty of any private law school in the region. Students were divided on their effectiveness. One faction spoke of the "approachable" professors who "are always willing to help" and "really want us to learn." Students in this group told us that "most of the professors are great. A few are even outstanding." Another group of students saw the faculty as "a lot of Socrates wannabes" who "could stand to lighten up." For the most part, students agreed that "the administration is a problem at best. They are of the 'stonewall them' mentality." Financial aid, however, "bends over backwards to help students." The "solid legal writing program" here has been called "among the finest in nation" by the ABA. The "comprehensive" clinical programs and the Public Interest Law Foundation all received significant praise from students as well. "The school's concern for creating strong litigators and strong writing skills is apparent throughout all SU programs, competitions, and clinics," noted one student. "The entire student population can participate in three appellate mock trial competitions and two or more trial competitions."

Students boasted that SU's "bar-pass rate is consistently higher than other schools in the region" and that its "reputation for putting out skilled litigators is the best in the region." Career Services "is a joke," and "needs improving." The Pacific Northwest, especially the city of Seattle, is a hip, happening destination for young professionals these days, thus creating a tight legal labor market, at least temporarily.

Competition is keen at SU. Students complained about the "very tough mandatory grade curve for 1L classes" and the level of

Jennifer Freimund, Director of Admissions and Financial Aid
950 Broadway Plaza
Tacoma, WA 98402
Tel: 253-591-2252 • Fax: 253-591-6313
Email: lawadmis@seattleu.edu
Internet: www.law.seattleu.edu

Seattle University

competition here, which is "extremely high." One student pointed out that such competitiveness "is good because it raises the level of academic excellence, but bad because it limits the friendships you are able to develop." Nearly half of Seattle's students come from outside the state, and SU claims the largest ethnic minority population of any private law school in the Pacific Northwest. "Students represent a broad range of viewpoints" and are "diversified and probably older than at most schools." Many students are working professionals who are taking advantage of the flexibility of courses at SU. "Faculty and students tend to be open and 'gay-friendly' as well."

Socially, students tend to be "friendly, yet competitive." Many evening students noted a "strong esprit de corps" in their classes. That enthusiasm doesn't show up as much during the day, when "The people here are for the most part arrogant, uptight, and generally anally inclined," said a 2L, who noted that he has made many "lifelong friendships" here. Lately, SU has stepped up its efforts to "foster social life," but "a lot of students are commuters, so it's hard to have a sense of community," maintained a 2L.

On the whole, SU students were pretty satisfied. However, they'd still like to see more of the good things they already have: more clinical programs, more practical skills offerings, more diversity in hiring and enrolling, more public interest support, even better teachers, more amenities for nontraditional students (i.e., daycare facilities), and much more sensitivity towards students from diverse backgrounds.

ADMISSIONS

Seattle University School of Law considers almost 2,000 applications annually, which puts it in a position to select its students somewhat carefully. In recent years, the law school has seen a sizable increase in applications volume and a commensurate increase in the qualifications of its student body. Seattle continues to admit more than a third of all applicants, but numerical standards have become fairly high. The average LSAT is a 159 (80th nationally) and the average undergraduate GPA is a 3.3.

ACADEMICS

Student/faculty ratio	21:1
% female faculty	33
% minority faculty	14
Hours of study per day	4.12

Academic specialties:
Commercial, Constitutional, Corporation Securities, Criminal, Environmental, Labor, Taxation

FINANCIAL FACTS

Tuition	$17,040
Cost of books	$625
Fees	$46
Room & board (on/off-campus)	NR/$7,821
% first-year students receiving aid	85
% all students receiving aid	92
% aid that is merit-based	36
% of all students receiving loans	84
% receiving scholarships	36
Average grant	$4,511
Average graduation debt	$50,000

ADMISSIONS

# applications received	1,368
% applicants accepted	56
% acceptees attending	37
Average LSAT	158
LSAT range	153-159
Average undergrad GPA	3.30
Application fee	$50
Regular application	April 1
Regular notification	rolling
Rolling notification?	Yes
Early decision program?	No
Admission may be deferred?	No
Evening division offered?	Yes
Part-time accepted?	Yes
Gourman Report Rating	**2.94**

SETON HALL UNIVERSITY
School of Law

OVERVIEW

Type of school	private
Environment	metropolis
Scholastic calendar	semester
Schedule	full-time or part-time

STUDENTS

Enrollment of parent institution	4,160
Enrollment of law school	1,325
% male/female	55/45
% out-of-state	25
% part-time	27
% minorities	18
% international (# of countries represented)	1 (NR)
Average age at entry	26

APPLICANTS ALSO LOOK AT

New York Law School
New York University
Rutgers University, Newark
Fordham University
Brooklyn Law School

SURVEY SAYS...

HITS
Classroom facilities
Research resources
Broad range of courses

Seton Hall University is the only private legal education offered in New Jersey, and one of the largest Catholic universities in the United States. The "challenging, yet very rewarding" School of Law offers both day and evening divisions to its over 1,300 students. Seton Hall aims to provide its students with "the skills necessary to become an able practitioner." Thus the broad, traditional curriculum emphasizes "the practical side" of law. According to our surveys, professors here run the gamut from "the good" to "the bad" to "the ugly." The mostly "caring and compassionate faculty" received high marks overall, though. "Most of the professors are excellent and very receptive to out-of-class interaction," said a 2L. "They all know your name and will never hesitate to assist you." As a result, "it's impossible not to succeed here. You have to make an effort to do poorly." Seton Hall students are also in a distinct minority nationally in their ability to discuss their administration without resorting to angry epithets. The top brass "goes out of its way to accommodate students" and is "dedicated to student satisfaction." Of course, "red tape and favoritism" still rear their ugly heads, but sometimes the results are pleasing. "I asked the dean to keep the library open later," related a 2L. "Without hesitating, he said, 'no problem' and extended the hours." This is the same dean of students who "teaches a 1L class." The cordial relations among staff, faculty, and students at the law school seem to contribute significantly to a high overall level of satisfaction. "Once the school figures out how to register students over the phone, it will be perfect," predicted a 2L. "I mean that."

Cocurricular activities abound. The law school is "conveniently located close to state and federal courthouses." Seton Hall's regional reputation is quite solid, particularly within the sizable legal communities of Newark and, more generally, New Jersey. The extent to which the law school's alumni dominate the New Jersey bench and bar is evident in the employment patterns of its recent graduates. An unusually large number of Seton Hall grads begin their careers in judicial clerkships, nearly all of which are in the Tri-State area. Seton Hall points to its Christian heritage in explaining its commitment to community service. The university operates a large and exceptionally well-funded clinical program

Ronald J. Riccio, Acting Director of Admissions
One Newark Center
Newark, NJ 07102
Tel: 201-642-8757

Seton Hall University

that serves the dual purpose of providing much-needed legal services to Newark's citizens while also affording the law school's students the opportunity to gain practical lawyering experience.

Seton Hall students are nothing if not comfortable in their physical surroundings. Housed since 1991 in a modern office complex in downtown Newark, the law school is physically separate from its parent institution. The "terrific facilities" here are "beautiful" and "the library is state of the art." One student even claimed that "the building is the best in the Northeast." The Law School's virtually brand-new physical plant drew rave reviews, and it seems to have given the entire school a sense of modernity and confidence in its future. "The facility is first-rate in every regard," wrote one student. "Our research resources are top-notch, and the administration seems very responsive to students' needs. Unfortunately, "Newark is terrible" and "parking is an absolute nightmare."

The lack of geographical diversity in the student body is a major source of grief at Seton Hall. Students say the Law school "needs to make a commitment to attracting students from outside New Jersey." Competition for grades is "stiff" here, but not usually "cutthroat." Extracurricular associations and activities are popular. "There is an organization for everyone. There are also a number of functions for the entire school to attend that allows everyone to become friends." Concluded a cheery 2L: "I think a lot of people will probably practice in New Jersey, and it will be nice to already have many friendships in my field."

ADMISSIONS

Probably because of the law school's comparatively high tuition, applications volume at Seton Hall is lower than at the state's two public law schools. As a result, overall admissions selectivity is moderate. Admitted applicants, the vast majority of whom come from within New Jersey, tend to possess solidly midrange numerical credentials.

ACADEMICS	
Student/faculty ratio	21:1
% female faculty	39
% minority faculty	12
Hours of study per day	4.13

FINANCIAL FACTS	
Tuition	$17,214
Cost of books	$600
% first-year students receiving aid	62
% all students receiving aid	67
% aid that is merit-based	1
% of all students receiving loans	85
% receiving scholarships	86
% of all students receiving assistantships	11
Average grant	NR
Average graduation debt	$51,000

ADMISSIONS	
# applications received	3,176
% applicants accepted	43
% acceptees attending	32
Average LSAT	153
Average undergrad GPA	3.10
Application fee	$50
Regular application	April 1
Regular notification	NR
Rolling notification?	No
Early decision program?	No
Admission may be deferred?	Yes
Maximum length of deferment	1 year
Evening division offered?	Yes
Part-time accepted?	Yes
Gourman Report Rating	**3.43**

UNIVERSITY OF SOUTH CAROLINA
School of Law

Whatever else it has to import, when it comes to lawyers South Carolina may be the most self-sufficient state in the nation. The state's single law school churns out graduates at a rate that is almost perfectly in sync with the demand of the state's legal profession for new blood. This arrangement is so neat that in the well over 100 years since the University of South Carolina School of Law was established, its home state has had no need for another law school. The natural result of the law school's exclusive franchise on legal education is a bench and bar populated by men and women who needn't even return to campus to hold alumni reunions.

Located in the inland capital city of Columbia, South Carolina offers its nearly 800 students a strong, traditional legal education and ready access to the resources of the state government. The curriculum is broad within traditional boundaries and is supplemented by an increasing number of clinical programs designed to provide students with practical experience in a variety of fields. Carolina's most obvious shortcoming is the relative lack of diversity in the student body, which is disproportionately white. Minority representation is, however, on the rise, and the law school has increased its efforts to serve the community that supports it by instituting a voluntary but highly-organized pro bono program. Applications volume more than doubled between 1986 and 1991, and numerical admissions standards rose right along with it. Admitted students, a huge percentage of whom are South Carolina residents, possess very solid numerical credentials.

They also possess a fairly high degree of satisfaction with many aspects of their experience at South Carolina, though they speak clearly and almost unanimously when it comes to their school's shortcomings. On the positive side, most of those we heard from praised their faculty and the pleasant atmosphere that they help to foster. "Relationships between students and professors are excellent," went one typical remark. "This is a small, supportive school," went another, "with a beautiful campus and gorgeous weather." But South Carolina students reserve their strongest praise for something more pragmatic: "The networking [the law

John S. Benfield, Assistant Dean for Admissions
Columbia, SC 29208
Tel: 803-777-6605 • Fax: 803-777-7751
Email: usclaw@law.law.sc.edu

school] makes possible with practicing South Carolina attorneys." Indeed, students here express great appreciation for the professional contacts they will automatically have as SC alumni. As one 3L put it: "There are splendid opportunities here for meeting and developing relationships with members of the state bar, judiciary, and legislature."

Still, few South Carolina students had any difficulty naming areas in which their chosen school could stand to improve. The most commonly voiced complaint concerned the relative lack of diversity in course offerings. A vocal minority of South Carolina students also offered comments like this one from a 3L: "Students here are a little to the right of Jesse Helms." Although for some this fact appears to represent a real negative, others feel quite differently. "From what I hear," reported one 1L, "this is one of the most conservative law schools in America. I like that."

Opinion among South Carolina students is not so mixed, however, when it comes to the overall quality of their program, its value, and its success in preparing them to enter the profession. Most of those we heard from expressed great confidence in their professional futures, and most would probably agree with this endorsement from one soon-to-be graduate: "This is a great law school, and the only one to go to if you want to practice in South Carolina."

ADMISSIONS

The numerical standards to which the University of South Carolina School of Law holds applicants are just about equal to the average for all U.S. law schools, but like all good public law schools, South Carolina chooses its students carefully from a relatively large applicant pool. Those whose numbers fall even a bit short of South Carolina's averages have only an outside shot at gaining admission.

ACADEMICS

Student/faculty ratio	21:1
% female faculty	6
% minority faculty	2
Hours of study per day	3.80

Academic specialties:
Corporation Securities, International, Property, Taxation

FINANCIAL FACTS

Tuition (in/out-state)	$6,864/$13,606
Cost of books	$500
% first-year students receiving aid	NR
% all students receiving aid	NR
% aid that is merit-based	NR
% of all students receiving loans	NR
% receiving scholarships	NR
% of all students receiving assistantships	NR
Average grant	NR
Average graduation debt	$35,000

ADMISSIONS

# applications received	1,250
% applicants accepted	28
% acceptees attending	50
Average LSAT	156
Average undergrad GPA	3.23
Application fee (in/out-state)	$25/$25
Early application	December
Early notification	early February
Regular application	February 15
Regular notification	rolling
Rolling notification?	Yes
Early decision program?	Yes
Admission may be deferred?	Yes
Maximum length of deferment	1 year
Evening division offered?	No
Part-time accepted?	No
Gourman Report Rating	2.91

UNIVERSITY OF SOUTH DAKOTA
School of Law

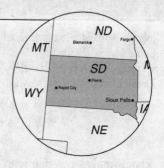

Do you suffer from a fear of wide-open spaces? Do you treasure the anonymity of a crowd? Do you hate large accumulations of snowfall? If so, then perhaps you should consider crossing the University of South Dakota School of Law off your list. But if the idea of sparsely populated, fruited plains and under-polluted, spacious skies and streams make your heart go pitter-patter, check out what USD students call "the best kept secret in the Midwest." Located on the Vermillion campus of its parent institution, this nearly 100-year-old public law school is one of the nation's smallest fully accredited bastions of legal education. With just a little over 200 students in its entire J.D. program, and only fifteen full-time faculty members, South Dakota offers the educational intimacy of "a small school in a small town." At the same time, if you feel the urge to be left alone, there's plenty of unrestricted spaces nearby for remote isolation.

South Dakota offers "a high quality legal education at an affordable cost, in a small, friendly school with many opportunities for specialized instruction and personal assistance. The curriculum here includes all the traditional subject areas, and law students have ample opportunity for interdisciplinary study through various graduate departments. "As long as you're interested in the nuts and bolts of a legal education, you'll be fine here," explained one student. "The library is great and the professors are usually very good, but your academic horizons are limited." The "small enrollment" translates into "small classes," which mean a slew of "personal attention" from the "extremely accessible" professors. "Our small size obviously permits a lot of student-faculty interaction," said another student, "and the quality of most of our professors makes that a really great opportunity." The USD administration is "easy to communicate with" as well. "There is no possibility of getting lost in the shuffle here, since everybody knows you and most faculty and staff seem to be genuinely concerned with seeing you do well."

Although both the law and legal education have evolved since the South Dakota School of Law was founded in 1901, the Law School maintains that its "commitment to provide students with an outstanding legal education at a comparatively low cost has also remained constant. The breadth of the co-curricular offerings at

Jean Henriques, Registrar
414 East Clark Street
Vermillion, SD 57069-2390
Tel: 605-677-5443 • Fax: 605-677-5417
Email: henri@jurist.law.usd.edu
Internet: www.usd.edu/law/legal.html

University of South Dakota

this full-service law school belies its diminutive size. A veritable wealth of joint-degree programs are available, from the ordinary JD/MBA to unique programs like a JD/MA in Agricultural Economics. Needless to say, a law school on this scale has its disadvantages, but they may be easily overlooked when that school charges a "reasonable tuition" like South Dakota does. And if you like the tuition, you'll love the local cost of living. This law school does little to add to the mountain of law-school debt in America. On the downside, Wall Street and K Street firms aren't going to be beating down many doors to recruit here. Students said the academic resources at USD "could use improvement, but they are getting better." Also, "technology needs to be more up-to-date."

Some students at South Dakota gripe that the typical student here is "apathetic and socially challenged." These same students and others complain that the population here is "not very diverse" and that "there is a lack of respect for opposing viewpoints and cultures." On the positive side, "everyone knows everyone," according to a 2L. "Because of its size, when you graduate from USD Law, you won't be just another alumnus."

ADMISSIONS

With only about eighty students, the first-year class at the University of South Dakota School of Law would barely fill the average city bus. South Dakota's size puts the law school in a position to choose its students very carefully, but the numerical standards to which South Dakota holds applicants are low. Statistically, an applicant with an undergraduate GPA between 3.00 and 3.25 and an LSAT score between about 150 and 154 stands about a 40 percent chance of getting in.

ACADEMICS	
Student/faculty ratio	15:1
% female faculty	15
% minority faculty	1
Hours of study per day	4.21

Academic specialties:
Environmental, Taxation

FINANCIAL FACTS	
Tuition (in/out-state)	$2,970/$8,610
Cost of books	$800
Fees (in/out-state)	$2,060/$2,060
Room & board (on/off-campus)	$1,700/$1,700
% first-year students receiving aid	NR
% all students receiving aid	NR
% aid that is merit-based	91
% of all students receiving loans	NR
% receiving scholarships	42
% of all students receiving assistantships	8
Average grant	$2,139
Average graduation debt	NR

ADMISSIONS	
# applications received	371
% applicants accepted	57
% acceptees attending	32
Average LSAT	154
LSAT range	145-167
Average undergrad GPA	3.20
GPA range	2.31-3.95
Application fee (in/out-state)	$15/$15
Regular application	rolling
Regular notification	NR
Rolling notification?	Yes
Early decision program?	No
Admission may be deferred?	No
Evening division offered?	No
Part-time accepted?	No
Gourman Report Rating	**2.43**

SOUTH TEXAS COLLEGE OF LAW

OVERVIEW

Type of school	private
Environment	city
Scholastic calendar	semester
Schedule	full-time or part-time

STUDENTS

Enrollment of parent institution	NR
Enrollment of law school	1,217
% male/female	59/41
% out-of-state	12
% part-time	32
% minorities	18
% international (# of countries represented)	1 (2)
Average age at entry	29

APPLICANTS ALSO LOOK AT

University of Houston
University of Texas
St. Mary's University
Southern Methodist University
Texas Tech University

SURVEY SAYS...

HITS
Practical experience
Socratic method
Broad range of courses

MISSES
Library staff
Not enough courses

EMPLOYMENT PROFILE

Firms recruiting on campus	48
Job placement rate (%)	79
% grads employed immediately	76
% grads employed within six months	77
Average starting salary	$42,857

Grads employed by field (%):

Academia	2
Business/industry	15
Government	6
Judicial clerkships	8
Private practice	57
Other	11

Everything's big in Texas and the "private, free-standing" South Texas College of Law is no exception. With over 1,200 students, South Texas has one of the largest law student populations in the country and claims to offer "an individualized education that can be tailored to fit each student's educational needs." The straightforward and "very demanding" traditional curriculum here is broad, with very few required courses beyond the first year. South Texas "emphasizes practical skills" and "prides itself in particular on its trial-advocacy program," which "prepares students for the 'real' practice of law" and "has helped build the law school's reputation as a respected source of strong litigators." As one student explained, "South Texas is no academic Ivory Tower. We have two appellate courts housed here permanently and we have what is arguably the strongest advocacy program in the country." In the "extremely challenging and fulfilling" classes "you hit the ground running," explained one student. "South Texas has the best instructors I've ever had," chirped a 1L. "They are genuinely interested in helping students further their legal careers." The professors are "readily available to students." Another student declared: "The personal attention we are given and the friendly, noncompetitive atmosphere among students are the school's greatest strengths." Students complained that South Texas "needs more sections for highly demanded classes" but, on the academic front, there were few gripes. "We could improve by being rated higher on these survey deals," suggested a 2L. "This school deserves more respect than the rigid ratings systems give it. So what if our library isn't huge; the quality of our skills teaching is very high." The "administration is excellent" and students told us that the "incredible" staff is "friendly and very well organized." There is even "personal service, no automatic phones."

Located in the middle of downtown Houston, America's fourth-largest city and seventh-largest legal job market, South Texas is the model of a working-person's law school. Like many other schools, South Texas offers both full- and part-time enrollment, but this law school is nearly unique in the scheduling flexibility it allows all of its students. Rather than being separated into distinct evening and day divisions, as they are at most law

Alicia K. Cramer, Director of Admissions
1303 San Jacinto
Houston, TX 77002-7000
Tel: 713-646-1810 • Fax: 713-646-2929
Email: acramer@stcl.edu
Internet: www.stcl.edu

South Texas College of Law

schools, students at South Texas choose their own schedules. Because the sheer size of the school's faculty and student body allows it to offer and fill classes at all hours of the day, students' options are numerous. The part-time program affords "many scholarship opportunities." The vast majority of students here seem (relatively) unconcerned about their professional futures, probably because most of them had several years of experience in the "real world" before entering law school.

Students griped about the "limited access to WestLaw/Lexis" and "no Internet access." They boasted about the "nice classroom facilities" and "extensive research facilities" The library is not awful, but it's not great, either. It's just small. "Lawyers need resources," pointed out a 1L. "We would benefit from a larger number of volumes."

You'll find a "very diverse student body" at South Texas. With a median age of about thirty, and a minority enrollment of about 20 percent, South Texas Law students are significantly older and more diverse than the national average. "What a great bunch of people," remarked a 1L. "These will be my friends for life." The atmosphere here is "very relaxed and friendly" with definitely competitive undertones. But in a good way. "Sheer, unadulterated hell with a splash of alcohol on Fridays" is how a 1L explained the environment. South Texas is largely a commuter school. In terms of camaraderie, the Law School has "a strong sense of community," but could probably use "a more cohesive group of students."

ADMISSIONS

Based on numerical standards for admission, the South Texas College of Law is less selective than three-quarters of the law schools profiled in this book. Applications volume has risen significantly in recent years, however, keeping the admissions process here somewhat competitive. Applications volume at South Texas is heavy, but a generous number of all candidates is admitted, and numerical admissions standards are moderate. About 2,000 applications are received annually for 450 seats. The median LSAT is 152; the median GPA is 2.96.

ACADEMICS	
Student/faculty ratio	22:1
% female faculty	19
% minority faculty	7
Hours of study per day	3.93

FINANCIAL FACTS	
Tuition	$13,800

ADMISSIONS	
# applications received	2,042
% applicants accepted	57
% acceptees attending	43
Average LSAT	152
LSAT range	139-168
Average undergrad GPA	2.96
GPA range	2.08-4.00
Application fee	$40
Regular application	March 1
Regular notification	June 1
Rolling notification?	No
Early decision program?	No
Admission may be deferred?	No
Evening division offered?	Yes
Part-time accepted?	Yes
Gourman Report Rating	**2.79**

UNIVERSITY OF SOUTHERN CALIFORNIA
Law School

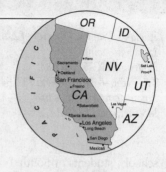

OVERVIEW

Type of school	private
Environment	metropolis
Scholastic calendar	semester
Schedule	full-time only

STUDENTS

Enrollment of parent institution	NR
Enrollment of law school	626
% male/female	55/45
% out-of-state	45
% minorities	37
% international (# of countries represented)	NR (2)
Average age at entry	24

APPLICANTS ALSO LOOK AT

University of California, Los Angeles
Stanford University
University of California, Berkeley
University of California, Hastings
New York University

SURVEY SAYS...

HITS
Library staff
Grads expect big bucks
Classroom facilities

MISSES
Not enough courses

EMPLOYMENT PROFILE

% grads employed immediately	85
% grads employed within six months	97
Average starting salary	$70,000

Grads employed by field (%):

Academia	1
Business/industry	1
Government	4
Judicial clerkships	12
Private practice	78
Public interest	4
Other	1

University of Southern California. In conversation they cast aspersions on USC's undergrad admissions standards by referring to it as the University of Second Choice. At football games, they jangle their car keys mockingly in reference to USC's high tuition and perceived status as a "rich-kid" school. Quite apart from Undergraduates at crosstown rival UCLA enjoy teasing their counterparts at the fact that law students tend not to involve themselves in such undergraduate rivalries, students at the University of Southern California Law School receive no such ribbing from anyone, least of all their neighbors in Westwood. While tuition at USC is indeed near the top of the scale, so is the average salary its graduates command. And one thing is certain: USC Law is practically nobody's second choice. Between 1985 and 1992, the number of applicants seeking entry into USC's small first-year class nearly doubled. In any quantifiable way, USC is a standout, and the numerical credentials of its small student body place it among the most highly qualified anywhere.

Those who make it through USC's increasingly competitive admissions process and enroll at the law school express a high degree of satisfaction with their decision to do so. After "the weather," most cite the law school's equally pleasant academic environment as one of its greatest strengths. "USC has a great atmosphere and a very diverse population," remarked one 2L, "and once you're in they do everything they can to keep you in. The atmosphere is very noncompetitive." Indeed, partly because of a strict grading curve that clumps two-thirds of the class within five points of one another on a 25-point scale, USC students enjoy relations that are, by all reports, "friendly, with little or no unhealthy competition." "USC Law School feels at times like a pleasant oasis in the living hell that is law school." Students give credit for much of their satisfaction to the quality and size of their faculty. "Most are excellent teachers," reported one 1L, "and all are, for the most part, readily available to students." Another student noted that "not only does the Dean teach first-year torts every year, but he is very proud of doing so without the assistance of teaching assistants or graders."

William Hoye, Director of Admissions
USC Law School, University Park
Los Angeles, CA 90089-0071
Tel: 213-740-7331 • Fax: 213-740-5502
Email: admissions@law.usc.edu
Internet: www.usc.edu/dept/law-lib/index.html

University of Southern California

When asked to name areas in which their chosen school could stand to improve, many called for greater "diversity of viewpoints" among faculty ("They should hire some [one?] conservative professors…All seem to share a mushy leftism.") and, more tangibly, for a lower price-tag. Right-wingers should not be daunted, however, as the "smaller Gingrich Gang is (annoyingly) vocal." As for the academic program itself, opinion ranged fairly widely among the USC students we heard from. While all praised the quality of their courses, quite a few called for greater variety. "They should really offer more classes each semester," went one fairly typical criticism. Specifically, several students expressed their frustration with what they perceive as an overemphasis on business-related courses in the USC curriculum. In fact, USC's course offerings are no more skewed toward the corporate than are the offerings at most comparable schools, but for one reason or another, USC grads enter private practice at a rate well above the national average and well above that of most elite schools.

ADMISSIONS

In keeping with its strong reputation, the University of Southern California Law School is one of the most selective law schools in the country. Not only are the numerical credentials of the average USC student very strong, but with more than 17 applicants for every spot, this excellent law school can pick and choose carefully. Fifty percent of admitted applicants have LSAT scores above 165—the 94th percentile.

ACADEMICS

Student/faculty ratio	14:1
% female faculty	21
% minority faculty	14
Hours of study per day	3.03

Academic specialties:
Civil Procedure, Commercial, Constitutional, Corporation Securities, Criminal, Environmental, Gov't Services, Human Rights, International, Labor, Legal History, Legal Philosophy, Property, Taxation

FINANCIAL FACTS

Tuition	$23,464
Cost of books	$600
Fees	$398
Room & board (on/off-campus)	$6,714/$7,650
% first-year students receiving aid	84
% all students receiving aid	85
% aid that is merit-based	NR
% of all students receiving loans	79
% receiving scholarships	48
% of all students receiving assistantships	3
Average grant	$10,000
Average graduation debt	$65,000

ADMISSIONS

# applications received	3,674
% applicants accepted	23
% acceptees attending	24
Average LSAT	165
Average undergrad GPA	3.40
Application fee	$60
Regular application	February 1
Regular notification	March-April
Rolling notification?	No
Early decision program?	No
Admission may be deferred?	Yes
Maximum length of deferment	1 year
Evening division offered?	No
Part-time accepted?	No
Gourman Report Rating	**4.39**

SOUTHERN ILLINOIS UNIVERSITY
School of Law

Nearly the youngest, smallest, and cheapest of the nine law schools in its home state, the Southern Illinois University School of Law has much to offer. This small, public law school has established a solid regional reputation that continues to grow. Remarkably, SIU has achieved its standing while keeping its tuition affordable and without growing beyond the intimate scale that distinguishes it from other area law schools.

With a tremendous student-to-faculty ratio of 11:1, and with a total enrollment of just under 350 students and a full-time teaching staff of 32, SIU is able to offer what it calls "an exceptionally dynamic and personalized style of education." Translation: anonymity is impossible here and there's "nowhere to hide in classes if you are not prepared." With such a small faculty, course offerings are necessarily "limited." The range of courses offered at SIU is relatively broad, though, and the required curriculum includes a sizable dose of skills-oriented courses. Nevertheless, quipped one student, "The classes here would be much more beneficial if the scheduling allowed us to take them." Students also griped that the Legal Writing program is "poorly instructed and lacking uniformity." There is very little ethnic diversity among the "extremely competent and intelligent" professors, with whom students say they are able to develop relationships outside of class. "I play poker weekly with one prof," admitted a 3L. "They provide so much individual attention that you almost feel like you are getting a massage," said a mellow 2L. While students are quite satisfied with their overall experience here, many lamented the fact that "all SIU lacks is reputation."

This "lack of a reputation" does nothing to help on the employment front. Compounding matters is the fact that the gods of geography have not looked favorably upon SIU when it comes to the legal market. With a resident population of about 27,000, SIU's home of Carbondale provides few outlets for employing graduates. Although St. Louis and Chicago are within reach, students reported that the university does not do enough to encourage on-campus recruiting. "If you want a job in southern Illinois, this is a good school. If you want to work anywhere else," counseled a 2L, "go anywhere else." Students also told us that

Thomas C. Britton, Associate Dean
Carbondale, IL 62901-6804
Tel: 618-453-8767
Email: lawadmit@siu.edu
Internet: www.siu.edu/~lawsch

"the Career Resource Center needs major improvements." A mere three clinical programs are open to third-year students here, but "SIU's emphasis on practical skills such as advocacy, alternative dispute resolution, clinical experience, and writing make students more prepared for practice than other programs with a more focused legal approach." The Law School's parent university has great resources, affording the students ample opportunity for interdisciplinary study. In addition to joint J.D./master's degree programs in business administration, public administration, and accountancy, SIU offers one of the country's few concurrent J.D./M.D. programs. Law students say they also have "twenty-four-hour access to the school and the library with our own keys." And, noted a 2L, "All of our research librarians also have J.D.s, so they are most helpful."

The "small-school environment" at SIU "discourages fierce competition" and promotes "strong spirit of cooperation." Explained a 1L: "The school atmosphere is truly relaxed." Another agreed: "There is a party almost every weekend where students are able to mix and talk. The classroom discussions allow you to voice your opinions—be they far right or extreme left. In fact, vocal expression is encouraged and expected." Carbondale is a "very small town." It's a "great place to have children" but the "rural area" is home to a faction of "Rednecks" who are "too conservative" and narrow-minded. A "mandatory class attendance" policy was not very popular with our respondents:

ADMISSIONS

Although the number of places in SIU's entering classes has increased slightly over the past few years, there is still room for only about 140 first-year students. SIU is one of the twelve smallest accredited law schools in the country. Consequently, the SIU admissions process is somewhat selective. The grades and test scores of the average southern Illinois law student are a little below the national average, but applicants to this very inexpensive law school face stiff competition from fellow bargain-hunters. The average age of first-year students here is twenty-six.

ACADEMICS

Student/faculty ratio	11:1
% female faculty	28
% minority faculty	17
Hours of study per day	4.03

Academic specialties:
Environmental, International

FINANCIAL FACTS

Tuition (in/out-state)	$4,312/$12,936
Cost of books	$810
Fees (in/out-state)	$988/$988
Room & board (on/off-campus)	$5,335/$5,335
% first-year students receiving aid	99
% all students receiving aid	99
% aid that is merit-based	99
% of all students receiving loans	99
% receiving scholarships	99
% of all students receiving assistantships	30
Average grant	$2,200
Average graduation debt	$24,000

ADMISSIONS

# applications received	740
% applicants accepted	49
% acceptees attending	34
Average LSAT	153
Average undergrad GPA	3.00
Application fee (in/out-state)	$25/$25
Regular application	rolling
Regular notification	rolling
Rolling notification?	Yes
Early decision program?	No
Admission may be deferred?	Yes
Maximum length of deferment	1 year
Evening division offered?	No
Part-time accepted?	No
Gourman Report Rating	3.15

SOUTHERN METHODIST UNIVERSITY
School of Law

The Southern Methodist University School of Law offers a "strenuous, yet fulfilling" academic environment and "an excellent balance of theory and practical application." The focus here is squarely on business law, and students pretty much agree that SMU's business and tax courses are superb. However, "The law school should refocus its curriculum to include an emphasis on other areas and not focus so intensely on business/tax courses," and make registering for classes easier, too. SMU recently began a public service program in which all students must complete thirty hours of law-related public service to graduate.

Many SMU students raved about the "good mix of litigation professors and theory professors" and the generally broad "diversity of instructors." The "quality of teaching is excellent" and profs "encourage office visits." One 1L told us: "I am constantly challenged to think critically." Other students said that SMU "needs to recruit more 'luminaries' for the faculty and weed out the merely passable professors." Library staff personnel are rarely saluted as often as they are at SMU, where administrators in general are given a collective thumbs up. "SMU is a new world compared to a giant public school," noted a 1L. "I still haven't become accustomed to administrators being polite and genuinely caring about my well-being."

There is a big payoff for students who successfully complete the J.D. program here. Literally. Southern Methodist is "very well-supported by the Dallas area, in both financial contributions and job opportunities." The School of Law has an "absolutely incredible reputation in the local legal community" and, since SMU is the only accredited law school in the city, students here are uniquely positioned to take advantage of one of the most thriving, high-paying legal markets in the nation. "Career Services is very good," asserted a 3L, "for all students, including those who are not planning to stay in Texas." Nevertheless, nearly 90 percent of SMU graduates remain in the Lone Star State after graduating. Many stay right in downtown Dallas because, as one student said, "a law degree from SMU in Dallas is worth its weight in gold."

Lynn S. Switzer, Director of Admissions
P.O. Box 750110
Dallas, TX 75275
Tel: 214-768-2550 • Fax: 214-768-2549
Email: 1 montes
Internet: www.smu.edu/~law

The facilities here received seriously mixed reviews. "The library is expansive" and Dallas offers "abundant legal resources." Many students called the research facilities "impressive" or, at the least, "adequately equipped." Others contended that the physical plant is "archaic and run down." They say the "rooms are drafty" and poorly designed. "Everything from bathrooms to electrical outlets needs repairs. Where does our $20,000 go?" asked a baffled 2L. "Fix this place up!" Students told us that SMU is "currently updating classrooms to provide more electronic media interfacing." No one can argue that "the Law School quad is beautiful and well-maintained." SMU's "pretty" and "tree-lined" residential campus "in the heart of one of the nation's most vibrant urban centers" received truckloads of approval.

The atmosphere here tends to be conservative and career-minded. Students from all fifty states and more than sixty-five foreign countries go to Dallas every year to study at SMU. They are "impeccable dressers" and "much less competitive than I anticipated," said a 1L. "A very strong sense of community" is pervasive, as is great diversity, particularly ethnic diversity. According to one student: "SMU is a shining example of a school that aims to increase minority participation in our legal system." Tuition is a tender topic here, and students warned that there are "absolutely no financial aid opportunities for out-of-state students." The relatively high price tag notwithstanding, SMU offers great opportunities to students interested in business law, or those who want to be near a thriving business community. As one student put it: "If you want to suffer through law school, SMU offers a beautiful campus set in the middle of a fabulous town, to help ease the suffering."

ADMISSIONS

The relatively modest applicant pool to the Southern Methodist University School of Law helps maintain the school's relatively generous overall acceptance rate. Over 40 percent of all candidates are granted admission, but the numerical standards are solid. The most recent entering class had a mean LSAT of 157.

ACADEMICS

Student/faculty ratio	15:1
% female faculty	29
% minority faculty	18
Hours of study per day	4.55

FINANCIAL FACTS

Tuition	$18,900
Cost of books	$1,000
Fees	$1,894
Room & board (on/off-campus)	$6,108/$4,500
% first-year students receiving aid	NR
% all students receiving aid	NR
% aid that is merit-based	NR
% of all students receiving loans	NR
% receiving scholarships	20
% of all students receiving assistantships	NR
Average grant	NR
Average graduation debt	$60,000

ADMISSIONS

# applications received	1,698
% applicants accepted	39
% acceptees attending	NR
Average LSAT	157
Average undergrad GPA	3.18
Application fee	$50
Early application	December 1
Early notification	January 31
Regular application	February 1
Regular notification	End of April
Rolling notification?	Yes
Early decision program?	Yes
Admission may be deferred?	Yes
Maximum length of deferment	1 year
Evening division offered?	No
Part-time accepted?	No
Gourman Report Rating	**4.25**

SOUTHERN UNIVERSITY
Law Center

OVERVIEW

Type of school	public
Environment	city
Scholastic calendar	semester
Schedule	full-time only

STUDENTS

Enrollment of parent institution	7,783
Enrollment of law school	339
% male/female	56/44
% out-of-state	15
% part-time	NR
% minorities	58
% international (# of countries represented)	NR (NR)
Average age at entry	27

APPLICANTS ALSO LOOK AT

Loyola University, Chicago
Howard University
Tulane University
Texas Southern University
Georgia State University

SURVEY SAYS...

HITS
Quality of teaching
Library staff

MISSES
Sleepless nights
Not enough courses

There was a time when law schools were semi-officially designated as either national or regional schools, depending on the make-up of their student bodies and the focus of their curricula. A regional school was one which drew its students predominantly from the immediately surrounding region and educated them in the law of that same region. The Southern University Law Center, which officially opened in 1947, is one law school that would probably embrace such a designation unapologetically. In terms of both its curriculum and the individuals who administer and follow it, Southern is truly a Louisiana school. Unlike other law schools in the state, for instance, Southern places primary curricular emphasis on Louisiana's civil law, hardly ignoring the common law for the rest of the nation, but definitely not attempting to give it equal time. This focus on the peculiar legal tradition of its home state is part of Southern's recognition of where the vast majority of its students come from and where the vast majority of its graduates go.

Southern runs three law clinics (Administrative, Criminal, and Juvenile), housed in spacious new quarters in the recently renovated Law Center Building, which provide practical experience to those students certified by the Louisiana Supreme Court for such activity and which prepares students to meet the specific needs of their fellow Louisiana citizens. Thanks to Southern's central location in Baton Rouge, the capital of Louisiana, a large industrial center and the nation's fifth largest port, and its proximity to the Crescent City of New Orleans, just 85 miles away, students have access to all the professional and cultural amenities of the two most important cities in their state.

Southern's dedication to its region is most clearly evident in the faces of its faculty and students. In comparison with Louisiana's other law schools, Southern, the smallest and least expensive of the four, has a makeup that reflects the population of the state it serves. Southern enrolls more than three times as many African Americans as some of its larger neighbors. The faculty is nearly half female and more than half African American.

Gloria Simon
A.A. Lenoir Hall
Baton Rouge, LA 70813
Tel: 504-771-5340

Southern University

A strong honor code lends an air of integrity and tradition to the school, which probably contributes an honorable air to a profession so often derided of late. Student associations include Law Review, Moot Court Board, Student Bar Association, Student ABA, two law fraternities, Black Students' Law Association, Women in Law, Sports and Entertainment Legal Association, Environmental Law Society, and the Advocates of Christ.

Southern students greatly appreciate the law school's commitment to teaching law "from a African American perspective," their professors' caring attitudes and strong teaching skills, the clinical and oral advocacy training, and the excellent new facilities. One 3L, who has watched many changes take place, said Southern "should win the most-improved school award." Another happy woman described her beloved law school this way: "Southern has a really nice facility, new classrooms, tons of computers, a good mix of ethnicities and genders, highly-qualified teachers, and a small college feel. It's located on the scenic Mississippi, atop the bluff, and is wooded with old, beautiful trees. The people are friendly, motivated, and smiley. Everyone here is determined to better themselves and those around them. Highly recommended."

When students complain, they have no fundamental qualms with Southern. Rather they request that the school extend itself even more towards prospective African American students, especially those in need of funds, and hire more teachers from diverse backgrounds, expand the curriculum, and strengthen the bar exam preparation. Most revel in the "diversity, scholarship, and the opportunity for an open, free exchange of ideas" to be had at Southern.

ADMISSIONS

If one considers only numerical standards, the Southern University Law Center appears to be one of the least selective law schools in the country. Simply stated, this is a law school that cares relatively little about numbers. Southern actually admits a larger proportion of applicants with LSAT scores between 145 and 149 than above 160. All hopeful applicants had better present the Southern admissions committee with a comprehensive and impressive picture in their applications.

ACADEMICS

Student/faculty ratio	12:1
% female faculty	35
% minority faculty	59
Hours of study per day	4.19

FINANCIAL FACTS

Tuition (in/out-state)	$3,088/$6,288

ADMISSIONS

# applications received	250
% applicants accepted	80
% acceptees attending	63
Average LSAT	145
Average undergrad GPA	3.62
Regular application	March 1
Regular notification	January-May
Rolling notification?	No
Early decision program?	NR
Admission may be deferred?	NR
Gourman Report Rating	**2.18**

SOUTHWESTERN UNIVERSITY
School of Law

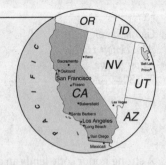

OVERVIEW

Type of school	private
Environment	metropolis
Scholastic calendar	semester
Schedule	full-time or part-time

STUDENTS

Enrollment of parent institution	1,160
Enrollment of law school	1,160
% male/female	51/49
% out-of-state	NR
% part-time	31
% minorities	33
Average age at entry	28

APPLICANTS ALSO LOOK AT

Loyola Marymount University
University of California, Los Angeles
University of Southern California
Whittier College
Pepperdine University

SURVEY SAYS...

HITS
Library
Grads expect big bucks
Diverse faculty

MISSES
Not enough courses
Administration

EMPLOYMENT PROFILE

Job placement rate (%)	86
% grads employed within six months	86
Average starting salary	$50,800

Grads employed by field (%):

Academia	1
Business/industry	28
Government	8
Judicial clerkships	3
Private practice	59
Public interest	1

Founded in 1911 in downtown Los Angeles, Southwestern University School of Law is one of the oldest law schools on the West Coast, with one of the newest state-of-the-art libraries as of the fall of 1996. In the years since its founding, law schools have proliferated in California, and Southwestern's reputation has long since been eclipsed by the state's many powerhouse schools. But to assess this law school in terms of such narrow and problematic qualities as "prestige" and "reputation" misses the point entirely. Southwestern is a law school that has always existed to serve its community and innovate, not merely to cultivate an image. A photo included in its promotional materials of a law school class from the 1920s is particularly telling: At a time when the legal profession was almost exclusively the domain of white men, Southwestern was graduating women and African and Asian Americans in more than token numbers. Since then, most law schools have caught up in those departments, but Southwestern has moved on to new territory. Through its unique SCALE (Southwestern's Conceptual Approach to Legal Education) program, established in 1974 with the aid of a substantial federal grant, Southwestern offers an alternative course of study leading to the J.D., which differs radically in both substance and form from the traditional law school curriculum. SCALE not only accelerates the process to two calendar years, but it also eschews traditional curricular divisions like torts and contracts, instead of trying to teach the law "as an integrated whole." In practical terms, this means that SCALE students, after an initial semester that is not entirely revolutionary, spend most of their remaining time in law school working as part of a simulated law firm within the school or as actual legal externs in the L.A. legal community. In addition to this relatively radical alternative, the Law School offers a traditional four-year evening program. The only law school to offer four different J.D. programs of study, Southwestern aims to make law school more accessible to a wide range of students. Not surprisingly, Southwestern students are significantly older than average, particularly those enrolled in SCALE or in the part-time division.

Anne Wilson, Director of Admissions
675 South Westmoreland Avenue
Los Angeles, CA 90005
Tel: 213-738-6717 • Fax: 213-383-1688
Email: admissions@swlaw.edu
Internet: www.swlaw.edu

Southwestern University

The new library is highly regarded by all the students we surveyed and many shared the sentiment expressed by one first-year who claimed, "It should make a great difference in the school's reputation as a major law school." Another 1L offered praise for the faculty, noting that they have a "sincere desire...to produce skilled, honest, and quick thinking lawyers." However, a number of students who had spent more time at Southwestern complained that in the second and third years the professors are not nearly as engaging. Nonetheless, students in the SCALE program expressed a tremendous degree of satisfaction, and students in general were pleased with the diversity at the school as well as the developing sense of camaraderie inspired by the new library. And many pointed out that even though Southwestern is traditionally viewed as a highly competitive institution, their fellow students are not only friendly, but also quick to offer help when asked.

The most ubiquitous complaint of the students was eloquently expressed by a 3L who wrote: "Never before have I seen such a group of well-meaning, good-hearted people operate under such apparently misguided leadership. The staff and faculty are great but the administration is done in such a cloak and dagger manner without student input that it seems quite disorderly and irrational at times." Harsh words, indeed, but echoed by many. Fortunately, besides some complaints about the financial aid office and the parking rates on school lots, it stands as the only pervasive criticism of Southwestern. With a budding sense of community forming in the stacks of the new library, the students at Southwestern should be able to find the voices they need to bend their administration's ear and ensure that their school's reputation and commitment to innovation doesn't get lost in a paper shuffle.

ADMISSIONS

Although nearly 3,000 prospective students apply annually, the numerical standards to which Southwestern University School of Law holds applicants rank in the bottom third of all U.S. law schools in terms of admissions selectivity. This is because of the size of Southwestern's first-year class and the relatively low rate at which admitted applicants choose to attend the Law School.

ACADEMICS

Student/faculty ratio	22:1
% female faculty	29
% minority faculty	16
Hours of study per day	3.63

FINANCIAL FACTS

Tuition	$19,020
Cost of books	$620
Fees	$100
Room & board (on/off-campus)	NR/$8,000
% first-year students receiving aid	89
% all students receiving aid	87
% aid that is merit-based	30
% of all students receiving loans	85
% receiving scholarships	25
% of all students receiving assistantships	8
Average grant	$4,772
Average graduation debt	$68,000

ADMISSIONS

# applications received	2,688
% applicants accepted	52
% acceptees attending	29
LSAT range	150-154
GPA range	2.72-3.27
Application fee	$50
Regular application	June 30
Regular notification	NR
Rolling notification?	Yes
Early decision program?	No
Admission may be deferred?	NR
Maximum length of deferment	1 year
Evening division offered?	Yes
Part-time accepted?	Yes
Gourman Report Rating	**3.39**

SCHOOL PROFILES • 401

St. John's University
School of Law

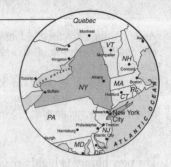

A list of graduates of the St. John's University School of Law from the not-too-distant past reads like a New York Democratic party hall of fame: Governors Hugh Carey and Mario Cuomo, Congressman Charles Rangel, and the late U.S. Commerce Secretary Ronald Brown. St. John's alumni aren't limited to New York, however; they can also head to warmer climates, like alums California Governor George Deukmajian and former Virgin Islands Governor Alexander Farrelly. This large, practical-minded Catholic law school located in Jamaica, Queens is home to nearly 1,200 students, most of them New York natives, and competition to be among them can be heated. As it has for more than seventy years, St. John's continues to play a significant role in New York's massive legal community, where its alumni are partners in many of the city's top corporate law firms. Both internal and external clinical programs and courses in lawyering skills have become a bigger part of the curriculum, which is evolving in order to give the school's graduates every advantage in the tightening job market by preparing them for the courtroom.

Students at St. John's expressed a moderate sense of satisfaction with their school, particularly in terms of the practical curriculum, which has resulted in a high bar-passage rate among graduates. Many students pointed out, though, that the course offerings are poorly planned. A 3L believed St. John's could provide "better scheduling of classes so that enrolling in one course doesn't prevent a student from taking three others." With its "strong concentration on New York law," a classmate offered words of reassurance: "St. John's gives me the skills and the opportunity to succeed in a tough New York market." This feeling is supported by the strong alumni network in the New York City area—frequently mentioned as one of the school's main strengths. But breaking into the job market starts in the school, according to another respondent. "Professors are extremely helpful in aiding students in finding employment," and the administration "has placed more emphasis on improving the quality of career services."

Mary A. Conlon, Assistant Dean
8000 Utopia Parkway
Jamaica, NY 11439
Tel: 718-990-6611 • Fax: 718-591-1918
Email: admisns@sjulaw.stjohns.edu
Internet: www.stjohns.edu/law

St. John's University

Overall, students offered positive comments on the faculty and the atmosphere at the school. "The professors are excellent," one student claimed, "with good reputations and vast knowledge and expertise." Many also highlighted the accessibility of the faculty. A first-year explained that the professors "have an open-door policy, even those professors who do not teach my specific classes." The sense of community at St. John's extends into the student body as well. One student we surveyed explained that the school "seems to create a very close-knit group of people. The competition is there but so is the helpfulness." As for extracurricular activities, the students described "an extremely involved Student Bar Association and a plethora of clubs and organizations." "If you are willing to participate and become involved," wrote a 3L student, "St. John's is the place for you."

The majority of St. John's students we surveyed focused their dissatisfaction on the school's administration. "The administration is lacking in its communication with its students, especially the dean," wrote one 2L—a comment that strikes at the heart of students' aggravation. Nearly all the students complained about the lack of communication that exists between the administrators and the students. However, a number of respondents mentioned that the Student Bar Association "tries to represent the students' needs as best as possible to the administration." And, to be fair, we must say that deans can be seen without an appointment in order to, among other things, advise on elective selection, and they frequently attend meetings to answer student concerns and write articles for the school paper on student issues.

ADMISSIONS

The strength of its regional reputation makes St. John's a perennially popular choice for law school applicants with numerical standards slightly lower than those necessary to gain admission to the area's top schools. Each year, St. John's turns away almost 2,000 applicants in selecting a class of about 300. Numerical admission standards are moderately high, as is the Law School's tuition. Only about 10 percent of all applications are filed by candidates with LSAT scores above 159. Consequently, competition is stiff among all others.

ACADEMICS

Student/faculty ratio	18:1
% female faculty	28
% minority faculty	15
Hours of study per day	3.63

FINANCIAL FACTS

Tuition	$21,000
Cost of books	$1,000
Room & board (on/off-campus)	NR/$2,700
% first-year students receiving aid	NR
% all students receiving aid	80
% aid that is merit-based	17
% of all students receiving loans	80
% receiving scholarships	33
% of all students receiving assistantships	8
Average grant	$3,509
Average graduation debt	$55,000

ADMISSIONS

# applications received	2,472
% applicants accepted	49
% acceptees attending	30
Average LSAT	156
Average undergrad GPA	3.30
GPA range	1.78-4.00
Application fee	$50
Regular application	rolling
Regular notification	rolling
Rolling notification?	Yes
Early decision program?	No
Admission may be deferred?	Yes
Maximum length of deferment	1 year
Evening division offered?	Yes
Part-time accepted?	Yes
Gourman Report Rating	**3.70**

St. Louis University

School of Law

Among U.S. law schools, the St. Louis School of Law scores in the middle of many quantifiable criteria. Its size is neither big nor small; its cost and its admissions standards are neither the highest nor the lowest. And this medium-sized city sits smack dab in the middle of the country. Yet this midsize, Midwestern law school actively sees to it that its midrange statistics do not add up to mediocrity.

One of the strongest features of SLU law school is its specialty programs. The School of Law is located on the grounds of St. Louis University, a Catholic Jesuit institution, and makes the most of its affiliation with the main campus. The university has strongly influenced the law school's widely recognized leadership in the growing field of health-care law. A longtime leader in this area, the School of Law's health law program was recently ranked by a major U.S. magazine as one of the top five in the U.S. St. Louis University School of Law also boasts one of the few employment law programs in the country. "Employment law is one of the fastest growing areas of law today," said one 2L, and, "SLU has one of the only employment law certificates in the country. [It's] a great program." The law school also offers areas of specialization in international and comparative law and professional skills. Many students we spoke with saw these opportunities to specialize, particularly in the health law program, as one of the law school's greatest strengths.

Students were quick to mention the "non-competitive," "unified," yet "diverse" atmosphere. "Students are willing to help each other out. [There is] no backstabbing," said one 2L. Another student, a 3L, agreed: "The student body is not that competitive; everybody works together so that every student can get the best possible legal education." At least one student, a 2L, feels that the lack of competition at the school stifles the exchange of ideas. "The non-confrontational posture possibly robs students of insight into the real legal world," he said. The law school community also seems to be open and encouraging to racial and ethnic diversity. SLU law school's percentage of minority students is slightly under 20 percent.

Valerie Lampe McFarlane, Assistant Dean
3700 Lindell Boulevard
St. Louis, MO 63108
Tel: 314-977-2800 • Fax: 314-977-3966
Email: admissions@lawlib.slu.edu
Internet: www.lawlib.slu.edu/home.htm

St. Louis University

Our surveys indicated a high level of satisfaction with the overall quality of teaching and range of courses offered at the School of Law. "The faculty is very interested, and the Dean is progressive in thinking," offered a 1L. "[The] professors are willing to answer questions outside of class about anything, including career options and classes you should take," said one 2L. The school offers over 25 professional skills courses each year, including simulated courses such as Moot Court, live clinic courses, and externships. While some students had only good things to say about the administration and faculty, a few law students are not so content. Frequently mentioned as an area of needed improvement was the law school's legal writing and research program. A 1L said, "The legal research and writing department is terrible. [It is] poorly organized and [has] poor instructors." Another student noted that there is "no consistency between the professors in that department. Some are excellent; some teach poorly." Apparently the law school's legal writing/research program was restructured recently, and although a few students noted these changes as positive, many responses were not so upbeat. A couple of students also mentioned a need for more emphasis on the Socratic method in the classroom.

The law school's physical plant also received much criticism. Complaints mentioned "very outdated" and "crowded" facilities. However, these complaints should be a thing of the past when the new facility, scheduled to be completed in August 1997, increases the size of the current facility by 40 percent. These and other criticisms aside, the general sense of well-being among students at St. Louis University School of Law seems strong.

ADMISSIONS

St. Louis University School of Law's numerical standards fall slightly below the average for all U.S. law schools. With a generous acceptance rate of over 40 percent, applicants have good reason to be hopeful. It should also be noted that the administration reports that, "Scholarship money is generous for students with outstanding credentials."

ACADEMICS

Student/faculty ratio	20:1
% female faculty	20
% minority faculty	6
Hours of study per day	3.93

FINANCIAL FACTS

Tuition	$18,150
Cost of books	$750
Fees	$40
Room & board (on/off-campus)	$8,520/$9,280
% first-year students receiving aid	89
% all students receiving aid	89
% aid that is merit-based	12
% of all students receiving loans	82
% receiving scholarships	48
% of all students receiving assistantships	NR
Average grant	$4,409
Average graduation debt	NR

ADMISSIONS

# applications received	1,140
% applicants accepted	54
% acceptees attending	41
Average LSAT	154
Average undergrad GPA	3.30
Application fee	$40
Regular application	rolling
Regular notification	rolling
Rolling notification?	Yes
Early decision program?	No
Admission may be deferred?	Yes
Maximum length of deferment	1 year
Evening division offered?	Yes
Part-time accepted?	Yes
Gourman Report Rating	**3.65**

ST. MARY'S UNIVERSITY
School of Law

San Antonio, Texas, America's tenth-largest city, is home to only one accredited law school, the 750-student St. Mary's University School of Law. This midsize Catholic law school was founded in 1934 and has been operated since 1948 by members of the Marianist order. Overall costs of a legal education at St. Mary's are kept down by the increasingly low cost of living in the San Antonio area and by the law school's tuition, which is reasonable by private-school standards.

Long known for its solid, traditional curriculum, St. Mary's law school describes itself as "a lawyers' law school." Many current law students we spoke with, however, feel that this mission is in jeopardy. The majority of students surveyed told us that they are content with the quality of teaching and the curriculum at St. Mary's, but there are some who worry that a more "theoretical approach" is replacing the historically pragmatic slant at the school. "[There are] too many courses on human rights and race and not enough practical skills [courses]" said one 3L.

Some of the concern over the curriculum seems to focus on what a few students perceive as a "new agenda" from the law school's current Dean. When asked how the school could improve, one such student, a 2L, said: "[We have an] extremely liberal Dean, and she only hires professors with her beliefs regardless of their teaching ability." Another student referred to his professors, who "turn Business Association classes into racial issues." Some of these students also cited the university's apparent drop in the percent of graduates who pass the state bar as proof of the change in focus at the school. "[The Dean's] perceived agenda of diversity at any cost is hurting the school's reputation. Look at the bar-passage rates," said one 2L. Whether these statements are isolated and more indicative of the political leanings of their authors, or whether they indicate a real shift in St. Mary's approach to providing a legal education, is not clear.

Where some students complained of a de-emphasis on traditional, practical lawyering skills at St. Mary's, others ask for a still broader curriculum and more opportunities to help make a change in the community. The majority of students are in agreement on the commitment of their professors, citing the popular

Yvonne Cherena-Pacheco, Associate Dean
One Camino Santa Marina
San Antonio, TX 78228-8601
Tel: 210-436-3523 • Fax: 210-431-4202
Internet: www.stmarylaw.edu

St. Mary's University

"open door policy" and the sense of community at the law school. Many students described St. Mary's as a "friendly," and "diverse" school. "The atmosphere of the school is friendly, and I don't feel the intense competition among students that you hear about regarding other law schools," said one 2L.

The law school offers an interesting array of clinical programs, including clinics in immigration and human rights, community development, civil justice, and criminal justice. According to the administration, nearly one quarter of the senior class is enrolled in live-client clinics. Participants in the Immigration and Human Rights Clinic gain hands-on lawyering experience in areas of particular concern to the Texas-Mexico border region. St. Mary's also operates a summer-study institute in Innsbruck, Austria, called the Institute on World Legal Problems, and conducts a summer study tour to Guatemala as part of its Institute on International Human Rights. In cooperation with other departments at St. Mary's University, the law school has also established seven joint-degree programs. The newest combines a Master of Arts in Justice Administration with a J.D.

When asked how the law school could improve, many students mentioned the library facilities and staff. "The law library needs to expand the resources available and improve the training of its staff," offered one 2L. Other students called for "longer library hours," an "expanded library," and "more Macintosh computers." The law school's career office was also the focus of several complaints. "The career services office is terrible and unable to place students in jobs," said a 2L. However, a school that offers a practical legal education at a relatively decent price can't be turned away from too quickly.

ADMISSIONS

The doors at St. Mary's School of Law are wide open. Although application volume is relatively heavy, St. Mary's admits 35 percent of all applicants in order to fill its entering class of about 250. As a result, numerical standards are moderate and candidates are admitted across a broad range of grade-point averages and test scores.

ACADEMICS

Student/faculty ratio	19:1
% female faculty	26
% minority faculty	27
Hours of study per day	4.18

FINANCIAL FACTS

Tuition	$16,213
Cost of books	$1,100
Fees	$300
Room & board (on/off-campus)	$2,104/$3,330
% first-year students receiving aid	85
% all students receiving aid	85
% aid that is merit-based	3
% of all students receiving loans	85
% receiving scholarships	NR
% of all students receiving assistantships	0
Average grant	$800
Average graduation debt	$70,000

ADMISSIONS

# applications received	1,270
% applicants accepted	56
% acceptees attending	36
Average LSAT	152
Average undergrad GPA	3.00
Application fee	$45
Early notification	November-May
Regular application	March 1
Regular notification	May/June
Rolling notification?	No
Early decision program?	Yes
Admission may be deferred?	No
Evening division offered?	No
Part-time accepted?	No
Gourman Report Rating	**2.52**

STANFORD UNIVERSITY
School of Law

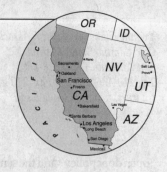

To call the Stanford University Law School the most highly esteemed law school west of the Mississippi is to risk understating the strength of its reputation. Along with the law schools at Harvard and Yale, Stanford forms a sort of holy trinity of American legal education. A generation ago, while California was still in the process of becoming the nation's most populous state, Stanford University was widely known as "the Harvard of the West." The days are long gone when Stanford, one of the world's preeminent universities, had to define itself on anything other than its own terms. The same can surely be said for its small, highly esteemed law school.

The curriculum at Stanford is traditional only in the freedom it affords the student to chart his or her own course of study. After completing their first semester in sunny Palo Alto, Stanford law students have virtually total control over the style and substance of their education. In their second and third years, Stanford students can cobble together their own programs or pursue studies in one of several informal but organized fields of concentration (e.g., "Business Law," "Comparative and International Law," and "Law and High Technology"). Stanford also actively encourages interdisciplinary and independent study. All students can earn up to eleven semester credits in relevant non-law fields, and it is not uncommon for third-year students to spend an entire semester engaged in a faculty-supervised independent research project. Only a tiny percentage of applicants to Stanford will gain admission, and those who do possess tremendously strong numerical credentials. In recent years, the law school has admitted and hired more and more women and minorities. Both Stanford's faculty and its student body are among the most ethnically diverse in the nation and among the most gender-balanced of the elite schools.

On the basis of what we heard from current students, it is also one of the more pleasant of the nation's top schools. Stanford's faculty and students are of absolutely the highest caliber, so intellectual challenge is a constant, but the atmosphere at the law school is, by most accounts, serious and scholarly without being unduly competitive. Competition does exist, but the general attitude of

Crown Quadrangle
Stanford, CA 94305
Tel: 415-723-49
Email: law-admissions@forsythe.stanford.edu

Stanford students is that they have overcome their toughest obstacle in gaining admission to the law school. "The tough part about Stanford Law School is getting admitted," said one 3L. "Once you're in, it's a piece of cake." Perhaps, but as one 2L put it, "You can be lazy and simply get through if you wish to, but the students and the faculty are all incredibly sharp, and they definitely keep you on your toes." Most seem to agree on this last count. "My class is astonishingly diverse and exciting," reported a 1L. "Stanford offers an outstanding climate for learning," added another. Not surprisingly, the students we heard from expressed even more enthusiasm for the outdoor climate at Stanford; asked to name their law school's greatest strengths, these students cited the "weather" even more often than "reputation."

All of which is not to say that Stanford students do not see room for improvement in their school. More often than not, their criticisms concerned the apparent lack of emphasis on practical skills in the law school's curriculum. Although Stanford operates what is surely one of the finest clinical programs in the nation, many students we heard from said they would like to see the law school encourage participation more actively. Others were more adamant: "Practical skills—particularly legal research and writing—are ignored here," asserted one 3L. Quite a few others criticized Stanford's perceived focus on private practice. Stanford does indeed send a smaller proportion of its graduates into public-interest work than do some other top schools (e.g., Yale), but it is just about right in line with the national average in this respect.

ADMISSIONS

Good Luck. The Stanford University Law School, one of the four most selective in the nation, denies admission to more extremely well qualified applicants than even Yale. Most others stand a better chance of winning the lottery. As a group, 95 percent of the applicants with LSAT scores below 167—the 95th percentile—are rejected. The Stanford admissions office would probably encourage such applicants to apply anyway. After all, at $65 a head, these luckless souls bring in more than a quarter of a million dollars annually.

ACADEMICS

Student/faculty ratio	14:1
% female faculty	29
% minority faculty	13
Hours of study per day	2.83

FINANCIAL FACTS

Tuition	$23,250
Cost of books	$1,074
	$160
Room & board (on/off-campus)	$10,845/$13,836
% first-year students receiving aid	NR
% all students receiving aid	NR
% aid that is merit-based	0
% of all students receiving loans	NR
% receiving scholarships	NR
% of all students receiving assistantships	NR
Average grant	$8,000
Average graduation debt	NR

ADMISSIONS

# applications received	4,034
% applicants accepted	12
% acceptees attending	35
Average LSAT	168
Average undergrad GPA	3.70
Application fee	$65
Regular application	rolling
Regular notification	NR
Rolling notification?	Yes
Early decision program?	No
Admission may be deferred?	Yes
Evening division offered?	No
Part-time accepted?	No
Gourman Report Rating	**4.87**

STATE UNIVERSITY OF NEW YORK AT BUFFALO

School of Law

The State University of New York at Buffalo is a mega-research university and home to the finest public law school in the Northeast. Buffalo offers a "broad range of courses" and class sizes that are "tolerable in some cases, and small in others." The law school has long prided itself on being "excellent in academic theory." Unfortunately, it has traditionally been "rather light on practical application" as well. A recently developed "new curriculum" suggests that the emphasis may be changing. "The school is going in the right direction by shifting the curriculum toward the practicalities of the law and encouraging specializations in certain areas," asserts a 2L. Interdisciplinary work by all students is encouraged, and the law school maintains its Baldy Center for Law and Social Policy to serve "as a focal point for interdisciplinary research and teaching." The Research and Writing program at UB "is one of the most useful and challenging courses provided." Many students say the "insightful" and "casually dressed" faculty is "down-to-earth" and "very eager to help." Others disagree, calling the professors here "book nerds with no experience" who "live their lives to promote" their own political agenda. "The faculty attitude toward students needs to improve. They could stand to take a much more caring attitude." The administration receives generally high marks for being "very open to new ideas" and "installing interesting programs." Nevertheless, "you have to deal with so much red tape to get anything done" that bringing about change can be frustrating.

Though UB has a "strong connection with the Buffalo legal community," a 1L tells us that many students "don't feel entirely comfortable finding a job through such a small Career Center." For what it's worth, the law school's emphasis on public policy and the social ramifications of the law give Buffalo grads a leg up in careers in public-interest positions. Starting salaries in this field are much higher than the national average.

The "dingy, dirty" and "isolated" facilities here are "aesthetically depressing." The main building "looks like somebody threw it together at the last minute," gripes a 1L. The "amazing, comfortable library" is highly applauded, though, as are the "immense resources" available "at a low cost relative to private schools." Tuition is, of course, very low for state residents, but even at the

Kim DeWaal, Assistant Director of Admissions and financial Aid
306A O'Brian
Buffalo, NY 14260
Tel: 716-645-2907 • Fax: 716-645-5940
Email: dewaal@msmail.buffalo.edu
Internet: www.buffalo.edu/law

State University of New York at Buffalo

nonresident rate, fees here are appreciably lower than those charged by New York's least expensive private law school. The remarkable value of the training they receive at the University at Buffalo is certainly not lost on students here, several of whom called the law school "easily the best for the money." Furthermore, Buffalo's J.D. program is greatly enhanced by the vast resources of the university itself. With more than 200 graduate and professional programs, UB is the largest and most comprehensive of the four SUNY schools. There are "tremendous resources for inter-disciplinary work" here. The upstate New York city of Buffalo is home to nearly one million people. The surrounding region, home to Niagara Falls and the Finger Lakes, is wonderfully scenic. For many, Buffalo itself conjures up images of ice storms and cold medicine, but the admissions materials assert that "Buffalo winters gain more fame than they deserve."

"Liberal ideology reigns supreme" at UB, and "students are diverse ethnically and in age, prior history," and most other areas. "Although there's not an overwhelming sense of community, there's a general atmosphere of friendliness" at UB. "Despite battles with staggering amounts of snow, students at Buffalo show up cheeky, cheery, and ready to learn." Once they are here, "the students get along very well with each other. There is no cutthroat competitiveness present here. This environment allows students to feel more comfortable in asking questions, in asking for help, and group studying. Although there are some advantages to a highly competitive environment, generally I think you learn more when the environment is a little less competitive," summarizes a 1L. "All in all, it is a very pleasing experience."

ADMISSIONS

With its solid academic reputation and its bargain-basement tuition, the University at Buffalo School of Law consistently attracts highly qualified applicants. In terms of its numerical standards, this is in fact one of the 70 most selective law schools in the nation. The University at Buffalo's overall acceptance rate, however, is quite generous for a law school of such high caliber. The administration reminds us that "numbers aren't the sole criterion. The admissions process is different from that at similar schools because of the unusual percentage of applications that receive active review from the Admissions Committee. In any given year, fewer than 20 percent will be admitted without committee review of the application."

ACADEMICS

Student/faculty ratio	14:1
% female faculty	31
% minority faculty	6
Hours of study per day	4.06

Academic specialties:

Commercial, Constitutional, Corporation Securities, Criminal, Environmental, Gov't Services, Human Rights, International, Labor, Legal History, Legal Philosophy, Property, Taxation, Family Health, Litigation, Administration and Regulation, Community Economic and Housing Development

FINANCIAL FACTS

Tuition (in/out-state)	$7,350/$12,000
Cost of books	$1,236
Fees (in/out-state)	$675/$675
Room & board (on/off-campus)	$6,529
% first-year students receiving aid	90
% all students receiving aid	88
% aid that is merit-based	0
% of all students receiving loans	85
% receiving scholarships	89
% of all students receiving assistantships	6
Average grant	$2,480
Average graduation debt	$35,056

ADMISSIONS

# applications received	1,023
% applicants accepted	51
% acceptees attending	39
Average LSAT	155
LSAT range	137-174
Average undergrad GPA	3.20
GPA range	1.85-4.12
Application fee (in/out-state)	$50/$50
Regular application	rolling
Regular notification	rolling
Rolling notification?	Yes
Early decision program?	No
Admission may be deferred?	Yes
Maximum length of deferment	1 year
Evening division offered?	No
Part-time accepted?	No
Gourman Report Rating	**4.19**

STETSON UNIVERSITY
College of Law

Founded in 1900, the Stetson University College of Law was the first law school in the state of Florida. Today, the "balanced" and "very demanding curriculum" at this midsize school provides "many opportunities to get practical knowledge" and "a great preparatory school for strong skills in lawyering and actual courtroom experience." Stetson is also one of only twelve schools nationwide to have a pro bono graduation requirement. The largely "outstanding faculty" here are "very accessible" and "helpful with practical advice on how to prepare and plan the job search" Another student added: "Most of our classes are small, and professors take the time to get to know individual students." While "each professor has been very memorable," reflected a 2L, "our teachers vary wildly from wonderful, caring professors to 'I-don't-give-a damn, I've-got-tenure' types." The administration can be "stuffy," but offers "lots of personal attention" and received a great deal of approval.

Here's a fun game: corner a Stetson student and ask about the trial advocacy program here. Then set your stopwatch, and see how long it takes for your unsuspecting mark to say, "Stetson is ranked #1 in Trial and Appellate Advocacy." Any time over ten seconds would be phenomenal. Stetson takes great pride in its role as the national leader in the development of trial practice. Under faculty scrutiny and "closed-circuit video systems," students at this "very litigation-oriented school" perform the functions of a trial lawyer, then observe and evaluate their own performances. There are also ample opportunities outside the classroom to participate in simulated and live-action clinical programs. Practice-based clinics include Labor, Criminal Prosecution, Poverty and Elderlaw, Public Defense, and Civil Government. "The judicial internship program and other programs are excellent and provide great opportunities for practical experience" as well. The Law School is particularly proud of the results these programs produce; Stetson students turn in consistently strong performances in interscholastic moot court competitions. "All competition teams rank high," according to a 2L.

Alexis Boles, Director of Admissions
1401-61st Street South
St. Petersburg, FL 33707
Ţel: 803-562-7801 • Fax: 813-343-0136
Email: lawadmit@hermes.law.stetson.edu
Internet: www.legal.law.stetson.edu

Stetson University

Despite the Law School's location in St. Petersburg, one of the twenty-five largest metropolitan areas in the United States, students complained that Stetson "needs to market itself in areas besides Tampa Bay." Stetson enjoys a strong reputation in and around the state, but the rep doesn't extend much beyond the Deep South. The school's "beautiful" facilities, housed in a group of low-slung, pale stucco buildings arranged in the fashion of a medieval Spanish village, include a well-appointed student courtroom in which actual sessions of the Florida Court of Appeals are occasionally held. Students told us Stetson "needs more classrooms" as well as "places for quiet study," which are few and far between. Apparently, the facility is also overrun with cats. Plans for a new library are in the works and it should be "completed by fall of 1998." Students said "the library staff is outstanding. They can always find anything and always have time for questions, no matter how silly."

Students from all parts of the country come to Stetson seeking the "great Florida weather." "Nothing can make hard work very pleasant," explained a 2L, "but the Stetson community makes it tolerable and worthwhile." A "rough grading curve" creates some "competitive separatism" among students in the same classes. Many sports-and-leisure-type activities are available here, everything "from intramural football to seasonal parties—there is always something to participate in." Some students complained about a few "snobby, rich" peers, and other immature ones who "seem like the people who never outgrew frat row."

ADMISSIONS

Although numerical standards remain moderate, the heavy volume of applications and the high rate at which those offered admission actually choose to attend Stetson make it one of the most in-demand law schools in the country. Stetson receives more than ten applications for every spot in its entering class of 225 and one quarter of those it admits choose to attend. While numerical admissions standards at Stetson do not come close to those at the country's elite schools, few but the most highly qualified can consider this school a sure bet. The median LSAT for entering students is about a 156 and the median GPA is about 3.21.

ACADEMICS

Student/faculty ratio	19:1
% female faculty	28
% minority faculty	7
Hours of study per day	3.87

Academic specialties:

International

FINANCIAL FACTS

Tuition	$18,975
Cost of books	$1,000
Fees	$170
Room & board (on/off-campus)	$4,140/$8,360
% first-year students receiving aid	83
% all students receiving aid	91
% aid that is merit-based	2
% of all students receiving loans	88
% receiving scholarships	68
% of all students receiving assistantships	10
Average grant	$4,400
Average graduation debt	$65,400

ADMISSIONS

# applications received	1,702
% applicants accepted	43
% acceptees attending	30
Average LSAT	154
LSAT range	140-167
Average undergrad GPA	3.20
GPA range	2.10-4.00
Application fee	$45
Regular application	rolling
Regular notification	NR
Rolling notification?	Yes
Early decision program?	No
Admission may be deferred?	Yes
Maximum length of deferment	1 semes
Evening division offered?	No
Part-time accepted?	No
Gourman Report Rating	**2.72**

SUFFOLK UNIVERSITY
School of Law

With a massive total enrollment of 1600 full- and part-time students, the Suffolk University Law School is the law school that put the mass in Massachusetts. Its evening division alone dwarfs many schools' entire student bodies. While a "large" law school certainly isn't for everyone, it does have abundant advantages. Chief among these perks is the awe-inspiring breadth of Suffolk's course offerings and the number and extent of its co-curricular programs available to students. Attending a big school has disadvantages as well. For instance, classes—especially required ones—can be entirely too large. And "sometimes you may feel like a number" here, despite the administration's moderately successful efforts to provide "personal attention" to individual Suffolk students. Much of the time, administrators are simply "too busy to help." Also, though the curriculum is richly diverse, Suffolk students complained that the heavily prescribed curriculum here prevents them from taking significant advantage of the Law School's extensive course offerings until their final year. "The number of required courses needs to be lowered," according to many. Students at Suffolk praised the "top-notch" faculty, but pointed out that not all the professors here are created equal. As a 2L observed, there are "some great professors and some horrible professors and nothing in-between" Also, the current facilities at Suffolk Law are "falling apart" and are "inadequate." However, a new "state of the art" building will be ready in 1999.

Because the law curriculum "is heavily centered on programmatic skills, legal writing, and clinical programs," students boasted that "lawyers who graduate from Suffolk are highly valued for their ability to apply knowledge immediately." For over sixty years, the Law School's traditional curriculum has been supplemented by clinical programs, which are now numerous and varied. They include a Volunteer Defenders Program in which students serve as public defendants, a Prosecutor Program in which students prosecute real cases under the guidance of the district attorney's office, and a Battered Women's Advocacy Program, which seeks to help victims of domestic violence. Students contended that Suffolk maintains "probably the best trial advocacy program in the region."

Gail N. Ellis, Director of Admissions
41 Temple Street
Boston, MA 02114
Tel: 617-573-8144
Email: g.ellis@suffolk.admin.edu
Internet: www.suffolk.edu/law

Suffolk University

The Law School "is deeply integrated within the greater Boston community" and "the alumni connections and the school's regional reputation in the legal field are excellent." Asserted a 2L: "If you look at the Boston Bar, Suffolk grads are continually achieving, prospering, and contributing to the legal community." The placement office didn't receive a lot of praise, but Suffolk has over 12,000 living alumni spread throughout the country and "one percent of all American lawyers are graduates of Suffolk Law." Thus, students have a tremendous networking base when it comes time to seek employment.

Students who choose Suffolk should be prepared for life at a "big-city school." A 3L warned: "Don't expect a campus quad and pep rallies at homecoming." In fact, don't expect a homecoming at all. The impersonal environment here is not eased by the fact that "the campus atmosphere is all-business." Another 3L speculated: "My classmates would benefit greatly if they would lighten up a bit." Nevertheless, "the city of Boston is a fantastic place to attend school," especially law school, as Beantown has a tremendous legal history and is, in many ways, at "the heart of American jurisprudence." Students boasted of a relatively noncompetitive atmosphere at Suffolk, which is surprising, considering the school's large size. Evening students also said their division is especially teeming with cooperation.

ADMISSIONS

Despite its size, the Suffolk University Law School has no difficulty filling all the seats in each entering class of more than 500 students. Suffolk is moderately selective, admitting less than half of the 2,600 candidates it considers annually. Those who actually go on to enroll at Suffolk possess numerical credentials stronger than those of students at 60 percent of all U.S. law schools. Still, Suffolk does admit students across a relatively broad range of grade-point averages and LSAT scores. In 1995, the average LSAT was 155. The average GPA was a 3.30.

ACADEMICS

Student/faculty ratio	20:1
% female faculty	27
% minority faculty	7
Hours of study per day	3.87

Academic specialties:
Civil Procedure, Commercial, Constitutional, Corporation Securities, Criminal, Environmental, Government Services, Human Rights, International, Labor, Legal History, Legal Philosophy, Property, Taxation

FINANCIAL FACTS

Tuition	$18,956
Cost of books	$800
Room & board (on/off-campus)	NR/$10,000
% first-year students receiving aid	100
% all students receiving aid	100
% aid that is merit-based	5
% of all students receiving loans	100
% receiving scholarships	30
% of all students receiving assistantships	NR
Average grant	$4,000
Average graduation debt	$60,000

ADMISSIONS

# applications received	2,000
% applicants accepted	65
% acceptees attending	42
Average LSAT	155
Average undergrad GPA	3.20
Application fee	$50
Regular application	rolling
Regular notification	rolling
Rolling notification?	Yes
Early decision program?	No
Admission may be deferred?	Yes
Maximum length of deferment	1 year
Evening division offered?	Yes
Part-time accepted?	Yes
Gourman Report Rating	**3.12**

SYRACUSE UNIVERSITY
College of Law

OVERVIEW

Type of school	private
Environment	city
Scholastic calendar	semester
Schedule	full-time or part-time

STUDENTS

Enrollment of parent institution	14,600
Enrollment of law school	738
% male/female	57/43
% out-of-state	55
% part-time	2
% minorities	22
% international (# of countries represented)	2 (6)
Average age at entry	25

APPLICANTS ALSO LOOK AT

Boston College
American University
George Washington University
Albany Law School of Union University
State University of New York at Buffalo

SURVEY SAYS...

HITS
Studying
Broad range of courses
Practical experience

MISSES
Library staff
Not enough courses

EMPLOYMENT PROFILE

Job placement rate (%)	89
% grads employed immediately	50
% grads employed within six months	81
Average starting salary	$43,240

Grads employed by field (%):

Academia	2
Business/industry	15
Government	10
Judicial clerkships	7
Military	2
Private practice	56
Public interest	2
Other	6

The Syracuse University College of Law, which celebrated its Centennial anniversary in 1995, provides a unique combination of tradition and innovation in its educational program. The "demanding but generally comprehensive curriculum" focuses on integrating legal theory with practice. Because the enormity of the University, the law school is able to offer formal dual-degree programs through more than a dozen separate graduate departments. "Programs such as the joint J.D./M.B.A. with the Maxwell School afford J.D.'s an opportunity many other schools do not," explains one student. The range of electives here is broad, from tax and corporate law to family law to computer law to jurisprudence courses to international policy. The notable Law, Technology, and Management Center prepares students for careers involving the development of new technologies. A 3L gushes: "The Law, Technology, and Management program is a truly unique and innovative program that allows law students to work with real clients on technology and Intellectual Property issues." Another student says, "I came here for this program and have been extremely satisfied." Students praise "the legal writing experience" they obtain in Syracuse's Law Firm course, which "combines legal theory, persuasive argument, research skills, and a focus on clear writing." While they complain about "insufficient training in day-to-day lawyering skills," students seem satisfied. "So far, my academic experience has been full of quality education, excitement, stress, and sense of accomplishment," relates a 1L, "all in one big bundle."

The "considerate and understanding" faculty is "obviously knowledgeable and able to teach." The professors and deans at Syracuse "know you by name" and "are very approachable. Their doors are always open and they are willing to talk." The Dean teaches a Civil Procedure course wherein "you learn that for every situation there is a rule, and for every rule there is a song," which the "singing Dean" will obliging belt out. However, cautions one student, "Syracuse has both the best and worst professors I have ever had. Every course seems to have a very strong professor and a very weak one teaching it. The problem is knowing who is who before you register for the class." And "teaching assistants should remain assistants," reasons a 1L, "for they are not teachers."

Mary Ellen Oyer, Director of Admissions
E.I. White Hall
Syracuse, NY 13244
Tel: 315-443-1962
Email: admissions@law.syr.edu
Internet: www.law.syr.edu

Syracuse offers a "variety of programs which include externships, clinics, study abroad, and Law Review" Programs like the Global Law and Practice Center, Business Law Center, and Family Law and Social Policy Center offer a wealth of hands-on experience. Syracuse Law takes particular pride in its trial-advocacy program, which has been cited by the New York State Bar Association as the best trial skills law program in the state for eight of the past fifteen years. Though students say that "job placement opportunities are high," they gripe that Career Services "could be more professional and more aggressive."

Many students say 'the building could stand to be renovated," and the administration has heard the message. "New facilities are on the way," including plans to expand the library. Construction and renovation are expected to be completed in 1998. "This is a good school that will be excellent when the new building is completed," predicts a 1L. In terms of technology, students have few complaints. On occasion "the library computers are unreliable."

Students say their peers are "competitive but supportive" and "extremely friendly." Declares a shocked 2L: "Ethics among the students at the law school are surprisingly high." In the eyes of many, political correctness remains a touchy issue here. "Political correctness has inundated the school and strikes terror into the hearts of those who might offend somebody, anybody, with what was said." A 1L disagrees: "The liberalness at this school is not nearly as prevalent as The Princeton Review reports. PC is on its way out here. If you are a conservative, you'll feel at ease at Syracuse." Outside the confines of the law school, "the city of Syracuse itself is boring." It's also snowy and cold. "Snow and lack of sunshine provide great incentives to study," though, and the weather provides what may be the perfect setting for law students in need of limited distractions. It's "definitely a learning atmosphere," as a 2L points out.

ADMISSIONS

Among the twenty-five schools in the highly competitive Mid-Atlantic region, Syracuse University College of Law is one of the least selective. According to the administration, "because we feel rigid use of cut-off LSAT scores and GPAs below which no candidate will be considered may deny qualified applicants a fair opportunity to gain admission to law school, Syracuse Law reviews all applications received for admission."

ACADEMICS

Student/faculty ratio	17:1
% female faculty	36
% minority faculty	6
Hours of study per day	4.32

Academic specialties:
Commercial, Criminal, Environmental, Human Rights, International, Family, Technology

FINANCIAL FACTS

Tuition	$20,640
Cost of books	$1,520
Fees	$496
Room & board (on/off-campus)	$8,764/$8,764
% first-year students receiving aid	43
% all students receiving aid	49
% aid that is merit-based	NR
% of all students receiving loans	86
% receiving scholarships	49
% of all students receiving assistantships	11
Average grant	$3,200
Average graduation debt	$60,000

ADMISSIONS

# applications received	1,893
% applicants accepted	60
% acceptees attending	22
Average LSAT	150
LSAT range	140-167
Average undergrad GPA	3.20
GPA range	2.20-3.90
Application fee	$50
Regular application	rolling
Regular notification	rolling
Rolling notification?	Yes
Early decision program?	No
Admission may be deferred?	Yes
Maximum length of deferment	1 year
Evening division offered?	No
Part-time accepted?	Yes
Gourman Report Rating	**3.76**

TEMPLE UNIVERSITY
School of Law

OVERVIEW

Type of school	private
Environment	metropolis
Scholastic calendar	semester
Schedule	full-time or part-time

STUDENTS

Enrollment of parent institution	32,000
Enrollment of law school	1,146
% male/female	53/47
% out-of-state	19
% part-time	32
% minorities	25
% international (# of countries represented)	NR (21)
Average age at entry	27

APPLICANTS ALSO LOOK AT

University of Pennsylvania
Villanova University
Rutgers University, Camden
American University
Dickinson School of Law

SURVEY SAYS...

HITS
Sleeping
Practical experience
Practical lawyering skills

MISSES
Not enough courses

EMPLOYMENT PROFILE

Firms recruiting on campus	70
Job placement rate (%)	93
% grads employed immediately	60
% grads employed within six months	93
Average starting salary	$45,192

Grads employed by field (%):

Academia	1
Business/industry	18
Government	11
Judicial clerkships	12
Military	1
Private practice	53
Public interest	5
Other	14

The north side of Philadelphia is home to the country's fifth-largest legal job market and one of the country's largest public law schools, the Temple University School of Law. Temple boasts a "great price" and enjoys "strong support from local alumni." The nearly 1,200 students in both day and evening divisions follow a regimen that is remarkably balanced between academic and practical preparation. Though the law school does not allow for formal specialization at the J.D. level, it has designated "areas of concentration" in areas such as litigation, business law, and public interest law. These concentrations combine, to varying degrees, traditional classroom work with practical instruction through Temple's highly regarded clinical programs. "The greatest strength of the law school is its emphasis on practical lawyering," says one student. "Little time is spent on inane, arcane issues that will never appear in practice. Temple turns out real world lawyers, not theoreticians."

"Although only three months into my law school career, I truly believe that I have begun to think, speak, and learn in a whole new way," testifies a 1L. "My experience with the faculty thus far has left me extremely impressed." Student after student tells us that "Temple has some incredibly bright, motivated instructors who really care about teaching." They also say the faculty is "very approachable." However, "sometimes, when they explain legal principles, they make them more difficult to understand instead of breaking them down." Also, many profs are not technologically savvy. "Some professors brag that they have computers in their offices and don't know how to turn them on." Students say that the administration is "very friendly," and they give a huge thumbs up to the Financial Aid for being "patient, knowledgeable, and exceptional."

The "fantastic" clinical opportunities available here include programs focusing on everything from Bankruptcy to Mothers with AIDS. "Temple does an excellent job in giving practical skills training," says a 1L. "The clinical education aspect is unmatched in breadth and scope, and this is one of the best places for trial advocacy!" About the only problem with Temple's clinical programs is that there are not enough to go around. "We should have more clinical access. I was only able to get one course in three years," laments a 3L. Unfortunately, the school's reputation

James Leipold, Director of Admissions
1719 North Broad Street
Philadelphia, PA 19122
Tel: 215-204-5949
Email: law@astro.ocis.temple.edu
Internet: www.temple.edu/departments/lawschool

Temple University

outside of Philadelphia "leaves a lot to be desired." Temple students keep their chins up, though. "It's a lot like *Rocky III* at Temple," explains a 2L. "The other name schools (like Rocky) in the region are riding on their laurels. We here at Temple are like Mr. T., using what we have, getting stronger every day. See ya in the job market, guys!"

The facilities at Temple are a "combination of the filmmaker Fritz Lang's *Metropolis* and a mausoleum from a Vincent Price movie." Translation: "The building is God-awfully ugly." To make matters worse, the location is "awful, dirty, and dangerous. It takes extreme bravery to live here." Other students disagree on this point: "The campus is very safe. Just don't go wandering around at night." The administration does its best to spin Temple's unfavorable location, calling it "a vibrant urban neighborhood conducive to the study of real law for the real world." Students say "the library is an architectural blunder" and the "research facilities are extremely poor." Temple is "way behind the times when it comes to Internet access" as well. In response to student concerns about the environment, the building has been improved in a number of ways recently, including additional lighting, new moot court and trial practice rooms, new computer labs, and revamped classrooms. A $10 million capital campaign should spawn additional progress.

"Basically, there is no student community" at Temple. Says a 2L, "People rarely socialize outside of lunch hour, so the law school experience is very boring." If diversity of students is what you crave, though, you'll love Temple. "From Second Amendment Pennsylvania conservatives to lefty liberals from New Yawk," they're all here. "The students are very diverse and have interesting backgrounds." Temple is also "a great place for gay and lesbian students." The student population may, in fact, be "diverse to the point of being a virtual mishmosh," as students say they "often cannot find a common ground other than our classes."

ADMISSIONS

Accepted applicants for fall 1996 had a median GPA of 3.29 and a median LSAT of 156. The average age of entering students was 27. Although the numerical standards to which it holds applicants are slightly lower than the national average, the Temple University School of Law chooses its students from a relatively large applicant pool and is selective in doing so.

ACADEMICS

Student/faculty ratio	20:1
% female faculty	32
% minority faculty	12
Hours of study per day	3.66

Academic specialties:

Civil Procedure, Commercial, Constitutional, Corporation Securities, Criminal, International, Property, Taxation

FINANCIAL FACTS

Tuition	$8,182
Cost of books	$1,200
Fees	$250
Room & board (on/off-campus)	$6,400/$6,400
% first-year students receiving aid	NR
% all students receiving aid	75
% aid that is merit-based	28
% of all students receiving loans	73
% receiving scholarships	57
% of all students receiving assistantships	7
Average grant	NR
Average graduation debt	NR

ADMISSIONS

# applications received	2,778
% applicants accepted	37
% acceptees attending	33
Average LSAT	155
Average undergrad GPA	3.20
Application fee	$50
Regular application	rolling
Regular notification	rolling
Rolling notification?	Yes
Early decision program?	No
Admission may be deferred?	Yes
Maximum length of deferment	1 year
Evening division offered?	Yes
Part-time accepted?	Yes
Gourman Report Rating	3.88

UNIVERSITY OF TENNESSEE
College of Law

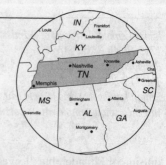

Located near the foothills of the Smoky Mountains in Knoxville, the University of Tennessee College of Law has provided a "solid legal education at a bargain price" to the bulk of the state's future attorneys for more than 100 years. A 1L calculates, "my three excellent years at UT will cost less than one semester at Vanderbilt" (Tennessee's powerhouse cross-state rival). The curriculum at Tennessee accentuates the practical and is strictly traditional during the first year, but includes several innovations thereafter. Upper-level students must complete three nontraditional requirements, in "Expository Writing," "Planning and Drafting" and "Interviewing, Counseling, and Dispute Resolution." These requirements, however, can be fulfilled through several different curricular offerings. Some students complain that the course selection at UT is too limited in any given semester. "The catalogue here may list hundreds of courses," exaggerates one student, "but you have very few electives to choose from in reality." The "outstanding" and "fantastic" professors here "balance wit with wisdom" and are "experts in their respective fields" A 1L beams: "They are the friendliest and most easily accessible group of people I have ever met."

In Tennessee's popular clinics, "students have support and freedom in actually putting together in practice what they learn as 1Ls and 2Ls." As one student observes, "The practical education offered here is a great plus; jobs are hard to come by now and we can use every advantage." Other students are very optimistic concerning their legal careers. These students say "the employment opportunities for UT graduates, especially in Tennessee, are outstanding. Those who do well here easily compete with the top students at other, more expensive private schools," particularly for in-state positions. Out-of-state positions are another story. "UT may get you in at law firms in Tennessee, but if you don't want to practice here, you might be in trouble." Career Services counters that the problem lies in getting UT graduates to leave the state, not in the lack of offers from out-of-state firms.

Karen R. Britton, Director of Admissions
1505 West Cumberland Avenue
Knoxville, TN 37996
Tel: 423-974-4131 • Fax: 423-974-1572
Email: lawadmit@libra.law.utk.edu
Internet: www.law.utk.edu

University of Tennessee

It seems like every law school is building new facilities these days, and Tennessee is no exception. A brand-spanking-new, "state-of-the-art" building, completed in 1997, was "designed with the student in mind." Students tell us that "the centralized facility should bring a sense of community that has been lacking" over the construction period. "Since the law school construction has spread the law students across campus, I have had a chance to interact with 'real' people who don't argue over everything," notes an enlightened 3L. "I love non-law students." Says one law student, "We've gotten a bad reputation because of our inadequate facilities, but UT offers a strong, practical education that prepares students for broad areas of legal work. Now that the new building is finished, this will once again be a top-notch state school. I'd recommend it to anyone."

Students at UT are a tad competitive. Though they "enjoy each other's company, day in and day out," the atmosphere here can get "intense" when finals roll around. But mostly, students say they are just happy with their school and excited about its prospects for the future. "The University of Tennessee must be the most underrated law school in the whole country," declares a 1L. "Tennessee is a real find and there is an attitude here that UT is on the rise," proclaims a 3L. "With the completion of the new, state-of-the-art law center coupled and with the incredible faculty already in place, UT is poised to move to the forefront of American law schools."

ADMISSIONS

In 1996, the median GPA of entering students was 3.37. The median LSAT was 156. Like all highly regarded public law schools, the University of Tennessee College of Law attracts a relatively large pool of applicants from which it chooses its students very carefully. The numerical standards to which Tennessee holds applicants are only slightly higher than the national average, but the size of the law school's entering class limits the overall acceptance rate to a stark 28 percent. Admitted applicants possess very solid numerical credentials.

ACADEMICS

Student/faculty ratio	15:1
% female faculty	30
% minority faculty	7
Hours of study per day	3.75

FINANCIAL FACTS

Tuition (in/out-state)	$3,514/$9,340
Cost of books	$1,032
Fees (in/out-state)	$380/$380
Room & board (on/off-campus)	$5,258/$5,258
% first-year students receiving aid	82
% all students receiving aid	81
% aid that is merit-based	53
% of all students receiving loans	74
% receiving scholarships	20
% of all students receiving assistantships	NR
Average grant	$4,000
Average graduation debt	NR

ADMISSIONS

# applications received	1,062
% applicants accepted	36
% acceptees attending	43
Average LSAT	156
LSAT range	138-170
Average undergrad GPA	3.37
GPA range	2.05-4.02
Application fee (in/out-state)	$15/$15
Regular application	February 1
Regular notification	Rolling
Rolling notification?	No
Early decision program?	No
Admission may be deferred?	Yes
Maximum length of deferment	1 year
Evening division offered?	No
Part-time accepted?	No
Gourman Report Rating	**3.11**

TEXAS SOUTHERN UNIVERSITY
Thurgood Marshall School of Law

OVERVIEW

Type of school	public
Environment	metropolis
Scholastic calendar	semester
Schedule	full-time only

STUDENTS

Enrollment of parent institution	5,595
Enrollment of law school	541
% male/female	57/43
% out-of-state	NR
% part-time	NR
% minorities	77
% international (# of countries represented)	NR (NR)
Average age at entry	NR

APPLICANTS ALSO LOOK AT

University of Houston
South Texas College of Law
Texas Tech University
University of Texas
Saint Mary's University

SURVEY SAYS...

HITS
Quality of teaching
Library staff
Studying

MISSES
Sleepless nights
Cut-throat competition
Not enough courses

EMPLOYMENT PROFILE

Grads employed by field (%):

Other	12

Originally established as the "Texas State University for Negroes" in 1947, the institution that was created under the provision of the state's separate-but-equal doctrine was renamed Texas Southern in 1951. Its school of law took the name of the late Justice Thurgood Marshall twenty-five years later. In its fifty years of service, the school continues the tradition of providing a sound legal education to all students. With over three-fourths of its student body and 85 percent of its faculty comprised of minorities, this midsize public law school is doing as much as any law school in the nation to diversify the legal profession.

Whatever their background, students at the Thurgood Marshall School of Law pursue a staunchly traditional, highly prescribed course of study. The law school's classroom curriculum is composed almost entirely of required courses in the first two years, and nearly all third-year electives fall under the broader heading of business. The school does operate a fairly broad clinical program that focuses on advancing the concept of equal justice under the law.

While far from being easy to get into or stay in, the law school does provide opportunities for many individuals to study law who would otherwise not be able to do so. Although the admissions committee relies on undergraduate GPA and LSAT scores, according to the school's promotional material it also "seeks to determine the applicant's level of motivation by reviewing personal experience indicating determination, patience, and perseverance." What is not included in the school's bulletin is the exceedingly high rate of attrition of 1L's at Thurgood Marshall School of Law, about 30 percent, say students. Students we spoke with repeatedly referred to the "grading curve" that "curves out" a sizable chunk of the first-year class. "My law school did a very poor job of communicating to its potential applicants the extremely high attrition rate among the first-year class," said a 1L, who added, "Had many of the students in the first-year class known of this high attrition rate, they most likely would not have attended law school here." Whether this substantial downsizing of the 1L class is formal policy or the result of tough standards is not clear, but its effects on students, particularly 1L's, as ex-

McKen Carrington
3100 Cleburne Avenue
Houston, TX 77004
Tel: 713-527-7114

Texas Southern University

plained by a 2L, is: "Because the attrition rate is so high, most 1L's spend too much time worrying if they will make it back," and, "Competition among 1L's is extremely fierce, which adds to the stress."

Many other students described the "cut-throat" atmosphere at Thurgood Marshall as one of the school's major drawbacks, and blame the administration and their instructors for it. "The faculty and the administration here at TSU promote a level of competition among students that could be likened to 'legal boot camp,'" said a 1L. The administration, particularly its financial-aid arm, was widely criticized, dubbed as "offensive" and "unprofessional" by students.

Although some students referred to an "uncaring" and "unsupportive" faculty, many others had only positive comments to make. "Professors encourage and maintain professional and working relationships with students to develop lawyering skills. They devote personal time to numerous tutorials and extend their office hours to accommodate student schedules," said a 1L.

One thing is certain of Thurgood Marshall School of Law: It is a place of great diversity and opportunity. "While most other schools rely on LSAT and GPA scores as their main concern, TSU looks at the overall package, which I think is great," said a 1L, who added, "My scores weren't the best but I know and always knew that I could succeed."

ADMISSIONS

As you would expect from a school named after the late Justice Thurgood Marshall, this law school's mission is to make legal education accessible to those who would elsewhere be excluded. The implications of that policy to the prospective student are fairly obvious: The admissions process at Thurgood Marshall is not driven by numbers.

ACADEMICS	
Student/faculty ratio	17:1
% female faculty	20
% minority faculty	83
Hours of study per day	5.09

FINANCIAL FACTS	
Tuition (in/out-state)	$3,900/$8,200
Cost of books	$275
% first-year students receiving aid	NR
% all students receiving aid	NR
% aid that is merit-based	NR
% of all students receiving loans	NR
% receiving scholarships	NR
% of all students receiving assistantships	NR
Average grant	NR
Average graduation debt	NR

ADMISSIONS	
# applications received	1,460
% applicants accepted	37
% acceptees attending	49
Average LSAT	38
Average undergrad GPA	3.00
Application fee (in/out-state)	$40
Regular application	NR
Regular notification	NR
Rolling notification?	No
Early decision program?	NR
Admission may be deferred?	NR
Gourman Report Rating	**2.33**

TEXAS TECH UNIVERSITY
School of Law

OVERVIEW

Type of school	public
Environment	city
Scholastic calendar	semester
Schedule	full-time only

STUDENTS

Enrollment of parent institution	24,717
Enrollment of law school	640
% male/female	63/37
% out-of-state	16
% part-time	NR
% minorities	14
% international (# of countries represented)	4 (4)
Average age at entry	26

APPLICANTS ALSO LOOK AT

University of Texas
University of Houston
Baylor University
Southern Methodist University
St. Mary's University

SURVEY SAYS...

HITS
Research resources
Classroom facilities
Faculty-student relations

MISSES
Not enough courses

EMPLOYMENT PROFILE

Firms recruiting on campus	61
Job placement rate (%)	94
% grads employed immediately	40
% grads employed within six months	94
Average starting salary	$51,300

Grads employed by field (%):

Government	14
Judicial clerkships	6
Military	1
Private practice	79
Other	1

The Texas Tech University School of Law is the youngest and westernmost law school of Texas's eight. It was established in 1967 on the Lubbock campus of its nearly 30,000-student parent institution. In its relatively short history, however, this midsize law school has built a very solid regional reputation. Law firms in and around west Texas are well stocked with Tech alumni. This fact is hardly surprising given the highly prescribed, traditional nature of Tech's J.D. program; even a student's second year at the Law School is dominated by required courses, most of which fall under the broad heading of business law. In short, Texas Tech has built a name for itself not on innovation, but on the undeniable quality of its traditional program.

Although the Law School does not operate an in-house legal clinic, it does sponsor a limited number of external placements, and its traditional classroom curriculum is supplemented by a variety of simulated clinical courses on topics such as trial advocacy. Participation in these skills programs and in Tech's extensive intraschool moot court competition is quite high.

Tech selects its well-qualified student body from a relatively large applicant pool, many of whom are drawn as much by Tech's price as by its academic reputation. Three years of Tech's tuition for residents costs less than a single year at most private law schools. Tech students acknowledged that they are getting more than just a good value for their money. According to one 2L, "Texas Tech is an excellent ground for the development of practical skills necessary to become a successful practicing attorney. The in-class teaching is able to achieve this goal without sacrificing a strong emphasis on theoretical underpinning of the law." Another 2L emphasized the practical emphasis of a Tech education: "I have spoken with attorneys, judges, etc., from across the state. One comment I consistently hear is that Tech graduates know how to practice law."

It is clear that the school is spending the students' money wisely, as students were nearly unanimous in their appreciation of the facilities and the faculty. "The facilities are second to none. Each law student gets a carrel and computer," wrote a second-year

Donna Williams, Admissions Assistant
1802 Hartford
Lubbock, TX 79409
Tel: 806-742-3985 • Fax: 806-742-1629
Email: xydaw@ttu.ttacs.edu
Internet: www.law.ttu.edu

Texas Tech University

student. A 1L expressed the views of many of his fellow students when he wrote, "What stands out at Texas Tech is faculty accessibility. You can always find them and they strongly encourage you to do so. I can honestly say that they care about their students." Another first-year praised the fairness of the professors: "Although the faculty is conservative as a whole, they conceal this aspect enough to allow meaningful discussion in class."

Despite generally positive feelings, Tech students saw room for improvement at their school. Some suggested broadening the range of courses, especially by adding courses in specialized fields. Others bemoaned the lack of clinical programs outside of the internship program. One student warned of the landscape, saying, "It's waaaay flat. Plenty to look at if you like skies and sunsets, but not so much if you like, say, hills." By far, though, the most common, and serious, complaint at Tech was the lack of national recognition. Convinced that they are receiving excellent legal educations (at a great price) that prepare them quite well for actual practice, Tech students are not content to be a well-kept secret. They want prospective students and employers to know about their quality. Who can blame them?

ADMISSIONS

Although the numerical standards to which the Texas Tech University School of Law holds applicants are only slightly higher than the national average, this law school's regional reputation is strong enough and its price tag low enough to draw a large pool of applicants. Those whose numbers fall more than a little short of Tech's averages face long odds.

ACADEMICS

Student/faculty ratio	23:1
% female faculty	29
% minority faculty	10
Hours of study per day	3.73

FINANCIAL FACTS

Tuition (in/out-state)	$4,500/$8,250
Cost of books	$770
Fees (in/out-state)	$1,870/$1,870
Room & board (on/off-campus)	$4,790/$4,790
% first-year students receiving aid	72
% all students receiving aid	72
% aid that is merit-based	76
% of all students receiving loans	67
% receiving scholarships	NR
% of all students receiving assistantships	0
Average grant	NR
Average graduation debt	$40,000

ADMISSIONS

# applications received	1,376
% applicants accepted	42
% acceptees attending	39
Average LSAT	155
LSAT range	139-175
Average undergrad GPA	3.37
GPA range	2.53-4.00
Application fee (in/out-state)	$50/$50
Early application	January 1
Early notification	Yes
Regular application	February 1
Regular notification	rolling
Rolling notification?	Yes
Early decision program?	Yes
Admission may be deferred?	Yes
Maximum length of deferment	1 year
Evening division offered?	No
Part-time accepted?	No
Gourman Report Rating	**3.17**

UNIVERSITY OF TEXAS
School of Law

OVERVIEW

Type of school	NR
Environment	city
Scholastic calendar	semester
Schedule	NR

STUDENTS

Enrollment of parent institution	48,008
Enrollment of law school	NR
% male/female	56/44
% out-of-state	17
% minorities	NR
% international (# of countries represented)	2 (15)
Average age at entry	NR

APPLICANTS ALSO LOOK AT

University of Houston
Southern Methodist University
Harvard University
Georgetown University
Baylor University

SURVEY SAYS...

HITS
Research resources
Broad range of courses
Quality of teaching

MISSES
Practical lawyering skills

EMPLOYMENT PROFILE

Job placement rate (%)	93
% grads employed within six months	93

Grads employed by field (%):	
Academia	1
Business/industry	6
Government	7
Judicial clerkships	9
Military	1
Private practice	53
Public interest	1
Other	10

When it comes to law schools, size alone may not guarantee variety and strength, but whether quantity or quality is your thing, the University of Texas at Austin School of Law is sure to satisfy. With around 1,500 full-time students in its J.D. program, this public law school is one of the largest in the nation, and the biggest in a state well stocked with giants. With a respected faculty, top-notch facilities, a broad and comprehensive curriculum, and one of the most highly qualified student bodies anywhere, it is also widely acknowledged as one of the fifteen or twenty finest law schools in the nation. With a ridiculously low tuition, it is also probably the best bargain in American legal education. Not for nothing do approximately 4,000 applicants vie annually to be among Texas's entering class of about 520.

Those who are fortunate enough to gain admission follow a course of study that is strong in all the traditional academic areas and increasingly rich in skills programs. UT's various clinical offerings run the gamut from "Children's Rights" to "Capital Punishment," and the law school takes great pride in its highly regarded trial-advocacy program. Texas is also notable for its emphasis on legal writing—an impressive number of the law school's students are member's of UT's ten law journals. More than any of these numerous strengths, however, the law school touts the teaching abilities of its faculty. A rarity among law schools—"elite" or not—Texas takes quite seriously the importance of quality instruction when making faculty hires and changes, and the results of this commitment are quite clear.

When asked to assess the strengths of their chosen school, Texas students enthusiastically endorsed many aspects of their program, most notably the teaching abilities of their faculty, about which the students were incredibly enthusiastic. "Our faculty is absolutely second to none," said one Texas 1L. "They are high-level scholars who can also teach," he continued, "and for a school of this size, it is surprising how much attention you get as an individual. The faculty makes a sincere attempt to help each student understand and succeed." Moreover, few students failed to mention their program's rigor. "You'll work quite hard here,"

727 East 26th Street
Austin, TX 78705-3299
Tel: 512-471-8268 • Fax: 512-471-6988

reported one 2L, "and you'll find it rather competitive, but the competition never gets too unhealthy, and it always feels like your fellow students support you." Predictably, UT students also trumpeted the virtues of their incredibly low overhead. "It's so inexpensive here," said one 2L, "that I'm almost embarrassed to talk about it with my friends at other law schools."

All of which is not to say that Texas students see no room for their school to improve. "As a traditional law school," began one fairly typical remark, "UT is a classic, but with its size and resources, it would be nice to see it be more innovative." Indeed, many of the students we heard from lamented the law school's relative lack of courses in specialized areas like environmental law and its focus on business and commercial law. They also wished the school emphasized practical skills more, especially legal writing, which is usually taught by third-year students. And, although such complaints are common among all law students, a large number of Texas students griped about the career placement office. Asked to list the areas in which Texas could stand to improve, one 2L wrote, "Career services, career services, career services, and, finally, career services." On balance, however, Texas students seem to be satisfied with their legal education—and the price is right.

ADMISSIONS

Although the entering class of the University of Texas School of Law is nearly as large as that of any U.S. law school, competition for those spots among applicants is fierce. Applications volume is heavy, and numerical standards are very high—in fact, the seventeenth-highest in the nation. All but the most highly qualified applicants must consider Texas a "reach" school.

ACADEMICS

% female faculty	27:1
Hours of study per day	3.34

FINANCIAL FACTS

Tuition	
Cost of books	$850
Fees	$2,162
Room & board (on/off-campus)	NR/$6,414
% first-year students receiving aid	75
% all students receiving aid	NR
% aid that is merit-based	25
% of all students receiving loans	NR
% receiving scholarships	78
% of all students receiving assistantships	6
Average grant	$2,144
Average graduation debt	$23,756

ADMISSIONS

# applications received	
% applicants accepted	
% acceptees attending	44
Average LSAT	162
LSAT range	147-176
GPA range	2.25-4.17
Regular application	February 1
Regular notification	NR
Rolling notification?	NR
Early decision program?	NR
Admission may be deferred?	NR
Gourman Report Rating	**4.77**

THOMAS JEFFERSON SCHOOL OF LAW

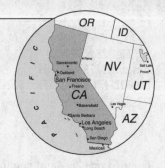

Founded in 1969 in the Old Town district of San Diego, Thomas Jefferson received provisional approval from the American Bar Association on August 6, 1996 and became the newest addition to the list of ABA accredited law schools. At this relatively young law school, the majority of growth in the has taken place over the last five years. In that time, the school has hired new faculty comprising well over half of the total number of educators at Thomas Jefferson. In 1994, a new dean was brought in to spearhead the campaign for ABA accreditation and ensure that the school will continue to grow to meet the needs of its students.

The average class size at Thomas Jefferson is under thirty students, allowing the professors to provide individual attention to each student in a relaxed atmosphere. By offering both day and evening programs and an accelerated two-and-a-half-year degree, the school caters to a diverse body of prospective applicants. Although Thomas Jefferson recognizes the traditional basis of legal education, the curriculum focuses primarily on practical lawyering skills, producing lawyers who are ready to enter the job market with strong real-world experience. The law school's low tuition costs and small student body combined with the clinical exposure it offers make Thomas Jefferson worthy of any prospective student's attention.

But it's not just the practical education that makes Thomas Jefferson an extremely popular school. Nearly everyone we heard from praised the quality of the faculty at TJ. Most echoed comments by a 1L who claimed the school's greatest strength was the "openness of the professors, and the devotion they give to help students learn the law and live the law, not just memorize or understand it." Students lauded the accessibility of their educators and boasted that the faculty "seems particularly concerned with our concerns and needs." Many were also pleased with the overall accessibility of the school. "Other schools are like Disney World...you are always waiting in line for something that only takes a minute to complete," according to one student. "Here, you are done with financial aid or registration with almost no wait."

2121 *San Diego Avenue*
San Diego, CA 92101
Tel: 619-297-9700
Internet: www.jeffersonlaw.edu

The time students save waiting in line may easily translate into more free time to enjoy one another's company, considering the high marks students given to the general atmosphere at the school. "There is a strong sense of community here at TJSOL," said one 2L. "Students support one another and the overbearing competitiveness complained about at other schools seems to be missing here." A classmate emphasized that, in addition to a strong camaraderie, Thomas Jefferson benefits from a student population composed of a diversity of backgrounds. "We have many knowledgeable students from different walks of life, which provides very interesting discussions."

Despite all the praise, students voiced a number of gripes about their chosen school. One 2L admitted: "The administration has done an excellent job in getting the school accredited, yet student issues understandably suffered during this time." Besides a few mentions of lack of funding for the Student Bar Association and missing nationwide recognition for the school, the most complaints surrounded the facilities. As a 1L summed up: "The school needs more building space for its continuing growth." Not to worry, the school has already purchased another building and is planning to finish renovations in the summer of 1997. This expansion will free up needed space for more classrooms and will allow the library to expand.

ADMISSIONS

Although less selective than almost all other law schools in California, the Thomas Jefferson School of Law may not remain that way for long. By the time this book goes to press, TJ will have received over 800 applications for the fall of 1997—greater than a 400 percent increase in the total number of applicants it received just one year before. Since the school is committed to a class size of about 200 students, there will be a considerable number of disappointed prospective students for this year and in years to come. And with the increase in applicants from around the country, the academic standards have climbed from a median LSAT of 148 last year to an average 152 this year. Still, Thomas Jefferson provides a good opportunity for students who might not have the numbers to apply elsewhere.

ACADEMICS

Hours of study per day	4.64

FINANCIAL FACTS

Tuition	
Cost of books	
% first-year students receiving aid	NR
% all students receiving aid	NR
% aid that is merit-based	NR
% of all students receiving loans	NR
% receiving scholarships	NR
% of all students receiving assistantships	NR
Average grant	NR
Average graduation debt	NR

ADMISSIONS

# applications received	
% applicants accepted	
% acceptees attending	
Regular application	NR
Regular notification	NR
Rolling notification?	NR
Early decision program?	NR
Admission may be deferred?	NR

Thomas M. Cooley Law School

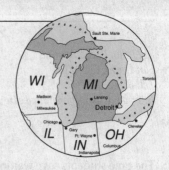

Michigan's largest and youngest law school, the Thomas M. Cooley Law School stands out for much more than its size and its relative youth. Established in 1973 and accredited by the ABA in 1978, Cooley pursues a mission that is similar enough to that of other law schools, but much of the form in which it does so is unique, or at least distinctive. Consider first that this law school has turned on its head the standard scheduling scheme: Nearly all of its students study year-round, part-time, and application must be made to study full time. For this reason, Cooley bills itself as the largest U.S. law school "for working people." (It is also notable for its Anglophile eccentricity: Cooley calls its autumn, spring and summer terms, respectively, Michaelmas, Hilary, and Trinity.)

As much as the law school dedicates itself to making legal education accessible to the working professional, it also actively rewards the dedication of the hardworking law student more than any other school. On the basis of their admissions index and their law school grades, Cooley students can qualify automatically for up to 100 percent tuition reimbursement in their second and third years. This aggressive attempt to attract highly qualified students to Cooley is, however, not the sum total of the law school's efforts to construct a true meritocracy. While the dominant admissions philosophy in legal education is that selectivity should be high and attrition near zero, Cooley has chosen to go the other way. Admissions to the law school are virtually open—new classes enter three time a year, and even applicants with a 2.0 and an LSAT score at the thirteenth percentile are "virtually guaranteed" admission. But be forewarned: matriculation at Cooley is no guarantee of graduation. Seventeen percent of entering students will be lost to academic failure. Depending on one's perspective—or actually, on one's grades—this innovation is either bold or brutal. In the same way, one can view the fact that around three-quarters of the courses in the law school's curriculum are required as a creative way to instill a sense of clear direction or as a heavy-handed way to limit creativity. What this all boils down to is this: The Thomas M. Cooley Law School is admirably unique, but it may not be for everyone.

Stephanie Gregg, Director of Admissions
217 South Capitol Avenue, P.O. Box 13038
Lansing, MI 48901
Tel: 517-371-5140
Email: cooleyadm@aol.com

Thomas M. Cooley Law School

So before enrolling, prospective students should be very sure they want the particularly rigorous, practical legal education Cooley provides and that their confidence can withstand the constant threat of Academic Probation and possible dismissal. If you are looking for a stepping stone to another school, look elsewhere; said one student, "Cooley—it's easy to get in but damn hard to graduate. We have the dreaded 'C' curve. If you come to Cooley, you might as well sign a three-year housing agreement because transferring out of here is next to impossible!!" Some students feel that the administration actively works against them: "I feel that the school keeps grades low to avoid paying academic scholarships to people. These GPAs will hurt us in the end when we are trying to seek employment. This does not benefit us or the school." Given such circumstances, competition between students is rather high and student morale is understandably lower than average.

Those who love a challenge thrive here. One 3L expressed appreciation for Cooley's "rigorous academic standards," saying, "Required courses give students firm background in business law and in practical lawyering skills." Some reveled in the school's punitive approach to learning: "They bust your ass so much that when you get out of here, you can challenge anyone." Most were grateful for the chance to enter that exclusive bastion, the legal profession; "Here, you don't have to be part of the cognitive elite with high grades and high scores on the LSAT to get in. They guarantee you a spot." Many emphasized Cooley's success: "I'll work harder here and get lower grades than other law students, but I feel I'll pass the bar more easily than those other students."

ADMISSIONS

Simply stated, the Thomas M. Cooley Law School has probably the most open admissions policies of any U.S. law school. The competition at Cooley is not to get in, but rather to earn a merit scholarship under the law school's unique financial-aid system. A certain UGPA and LSAT score, set by the school, qualifies Cooley students who earn honors in their first year for a tuition rebate on a sliding scale from 10 to 100 percent. If one is concerned simply with getting in, criteria are fairly low.

ACADEMICS

Student/faculty ratio	21:1
% female faculty	31
% minority faculty	7
Hours of study per day	4.93

FINANCIAL FACTS

Tuition	$16,905
Cost of books	$775
Fees	$60
Room & board (on/off-campus)	NR/$11,040
% first-year students receiving aid	NR
% all students receiving aid	97
% aid that is merit-based	NR
% of all students receiving loans	97
% receiving scholarships	35
% of all students receiving assistantships	NR
Average grant	$4,687
Average graduation debt	$58,343

ADMISSIONS

# applications received	1,934
% applicants accepted	79
% acceptees attending	71
Average LSAT	147
Average undergrad GPA	2.80
Application fee	$50
Regular application	rolling
Regular notification	rolling
Rolling notification?	Yes
Early decision program?	No
Admission may be deferred?	Yes
Evening division offered?	Yes
Part-time accepted?	Yes
Gourman Report Rating	**2.89**

University of Toledo
College of Law

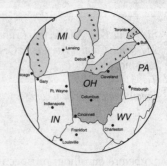

OVERVIEW

Type of school	public
Environment	metropolis
Scholastic calendar	semester
Schedule	full-time or part-time

STUDENTS

Enrollment of parent institution	22,000
Enrollment of law school	634
% male/female	57/43
% out-of-state	35
% part-time	31
% minorities	9
% international (# of countries represented)	NR (NR)
Average age at entry	27

APPLICANTS ALSO LOOK AT

Ohio State University
University of Akron
University of Cincinnati
University of Dayton
Cleveland State University

SURVEY SAYS...

HITS
Faculty-student relations
Broad range of courses
Quality of teaching

MISSES
Not enough courses

EMPLOYMENT PROFILE

Firms recruiting on campus	30
Job placement rate (%)	100
% grads employed within six months	80
Average starting salary	$35,000

Grads employed by field (%):

Academia	1
Business/industry	21
Government	18
Judicial clerkships	5
Private practice	51
Public interest	3
Other	3

The University of Toledo College of Law is an inexpensive law school with a long tradition and a solid regional reputation. Toledo is located in a peaceful residential neighborhood on the 25,000-student campus of its parent institution. With over 600 total students in its day and evening divisions, the law school is large enough to offer a comprehensive program yet small enough to maintain a comfortable learning environment. Students say Toledo's curriculum offers a "broad range of classes" within traditional bounds. After their first year, most students follow a recommended course of study—the "standard program"—in the basic bar exam topics. The "friendly, dedicated, approachable, and social" professors here are "very personable, accessible, and concerned about the welfare of the students." They are "very dedicated to teaching" as well. "I have a friend at a Southern law school who asked me what book we were using in Contracts because she didn't have a clue as to what was going on in that class," relates a 3L. "I told her it was my favorite class. As it turns out, my class and her class were using the same book. Unfortunately for her, she doesn't have the same teacher." Another student agrees: "The faculty are absolutely the greatest asset of UT. They could teach anywhere and we are lucky to have them here." Some students call the top brass "excellent"; others say the administration "treats us like babies" and have found it "hard to get straight answers." The heaviest criticism, however, is reserved for the "pathetic" Legal Research and Writing program. "They throw a book at you and expect you to produce legal writing," gripes a 2L.

Toledo operates a clinical program of modest size and sponsors a wide variety of co-curricular programs. Many students say these programs help students acquire "practical lawyer knowledge." At least one student disagrees with this assessment, seeing instead a "distinct lack of encouragement when it comes to developing practical skills." Whatever the case, students say "Career Services could do more in terms of locating jobs and scheduling people to come and talk about different areas of concentration." A palpable "concern about the job market" is apparent among some students here, especially those who don't want to work in the local area. "Career Services does little to make

Douglas Chapman, Associate Dean for Academic Affairs
2801 West Bancroft
Toledo, OH 43606
Tel: 419-537-4131 • Fax: 419-530-4526
Email: law0046@uoftol.utoledo.edu
Internet: www.utoledo.edu/law

University of Toledo

the school known to employers outside of the Ohio/Michigan area," complains a 2L. On the bright side, Toledo students have a perennially "high pass-rate" on the Ohio Bar exam. "If you like Ohio, Toledo is a great choice."

The "library is excellent" here, but students find the "drab" and "badly designed" facilities lacking. "The appearance of the building is a bit dismal" and classrooms are "too low-tech" and "outdated." Also, students say Toledo "needs more study space and study rooms available" and that "parking is too remote from the law building."

The atmosphere is "supportive and friendly," which is "very conducive to learning." Students say "competition is virtually nonexistent" here. "No Ex-Lax in your coffee tricks," remarks a regular 3L. Instead, "it's like a family. There are people you would go to the mat for." Is it possible to have too much of a good thing? "I wish sometimes that the student body was more competitive," argued a 1L, "just to spark interest." Another student concurred: "I almost wish it were a bit more rigorous, especially considering the difficult job market we face." Students also complained that Toledo "needs to recruit out-of-state students more aggressively." Observed a 2L, "It seems a bit too satisfied with its reputation as a good regional law school." Despite these criticisms, most Toledo students agreed that their law school is "a fairly pleasant place" to spend three years. "On my 30th birthday, homesick and wary of celebrating a milestone away from family and friends, I attended Property class," explained a non-traditional 2L. "My professor ended class early for a surprise party for me, which he and my classmates had been planning for two weeks. Needless to say, my mood was greatly improved and my 30th birthday proved memorable."

ADMISSIONS

With more than five applications filed for each spot in its first-year class, the University of Toledo College of Law is in a position to be somewhat selective, but a very generous overall acceptance rate makes this inexpensive law school a virtual sure thing for bargain-hunting applicants with moderately high numerical credentials. Those whose numbers fall below these values face less favorable but not insurmountable odds.

ACADEMICS

Student/faculty ratio	19:1
% female faculty	24
% minority faculty	4
Hours of study per day	3.46

Academic specialties:

Civil Procedure, Commercial, Constitutional, Corporation Securities, Criminal, Environmental, Gov't Services, Human Rights, International, Labor, Legal History, Legal Philosophy, Property, Taxation, Intellectual Property

FINANCIAL FACTS

Tuition (in/out-state)	$2,772/$5,722
Cost of books	$1,025
Fees (in/out-state)	$499/$499
Room & board (on/off-campus)	NR/$4,559
% first-year students receiving aid	25
% all students receiving aid	54
% aid that is merit-based	43
% of all students receiving loans	43
% receiving scholarships	11
% of all students receiving assistantships	NR
Average grant	$5,310
Average graduation debt	$39,480

ADMISSIONS

# applications received	928
% applicants accepted	63
% acceptees attending	34
Average LSAT	153
LSAT range	143-171
Average undergrad GPA	3.03
GPA range	2.11-3.97
Application fee (in/out-state)	$30/$30
Regular application	rolling
Regular notification	rolling
Rolling notification?	Yes
Early decision program?	No
Admission may be deferred?	Yes
Maximum length of deferment	1 year
Evening division offered?	Yes
Part-time accepted?	Yes
Gourman Report Rating	**2.47**

TOURO COLLEGE
Jacob D. Fuchsberg Law Center

OVERVIEW

Type of school	private
Environment	metropolis
Scholastic calendar	semester
Schedule	full-time or part-time

STUDENTS

Enrollment of parent institution	7,329
Enrollment of law school	893
% male/female	65/35
% out-of-state	15
% part-time	36
% minorities	21
% international (# of countries represented)	NR (NR)
Average age at entry	26

APPLICANTS ALSO LOOK AT

Hofstra University
Saint John's University
New York Law School
Brooklyn Law School
Pace University

SURVEY SAYS...

HITS
Diverse faculty
Practical experience

MISSES
Sleepless nights
Library staff
Not enough courses

The early 1980s saw a fairly sharp decline in law school applications, and it was widely believed that some of the country's less established law schools would be forced to close in response to this decreased demand. Yet in 1980, Touro College established its Jacob D. Fuchsberg Law Center in a region already saturated with law schools. Because of massive population growth in Long Island's Suffolk County, Touro survived during a tough time for legal education. As the only law school in this heavily-populated, suburban area to offer a part-time J.D. program, Touro filled a large void. Today Touro law school enrolls a total of about 800 students, approximately a third of them in its part-time and evening divisions. Touro's largely local and suburban student body is drawn from a sizable pool of applicants.

Touro University was established under Jewish auspices in 1970. The Law Center provides for the study of the Jewish legal experience through its Institute of Jewish Law. Other specialized programs offered at Touro law school include the Institute of Local and Suburban Law, the International Summer Law Internship Program, and a joint master's degree program in taxation through Long Island University. Students at the Law Center can take advantage of a wide range of legal clinics and externship programs. The Domestic Violence Externship Project and the Elderlaw Clinic are two examples of programs the school has instituted to meet the needs of surrounding communities.

Touro's admirably gender-balanced faculty administers a straight-forward and traditional course of study with a wide variety of elective courses. Law students at Touro appear to be reasonably happy with this curriculum and their surroundings. Students we spoke with repeatedly cited the faculty and the close relationship it shares with students as a major strength of the school. One 2L said, "Law school professors at Touro inspire students and push each student individually to achieve their maximum potential," and "The professors take an interest in knowing the students' names and pushing until they click with each individual." Touro students also praised the efforts of their faculty and administration to make their education manageable. In fact, Touro is one of the first law schools in the country to offer discussion sessions led

Director of Admissions
Jacob D. Fuchsberg Law Center
844 Sixth Avenue
New York, NY 11743
Tel: 516-421-2244

by third-year students. The Law Center's commitment to all students is also evident through its Legal Education Access Program (LEAP), a three-week summer program that introduces minority students to law school in a supportive and challenging way.

What concerns Touro students we spoke with most is the school's lackluster reputation. "I am disturbed by the reputation Touro has in comparison to other law schools...employers who are unfamiliar with the school, due to its age, are hesitant to employ graduates," said one 3L. Another student, a 2L, was somewhat more vocal: "I resent the classification of Touro as being one of the least selective law schools!..." "Our [bar] passage rate is 86 percent—not bad for a school with no 'quantifiable standards'." Some students believe the Law Center, particularly its placement office, need to take a more active role in selling the school. "Somehow the school should convey the standard of excellence it expects from its students to prospective employers," offered one 2L. A 3L suggested, "The career placement office could work harder to assist students in breaking the barriers to employment in New York City."

However, students themselves may be the best promoters of the school. Touro law students remain proud and spirited. Several spoke of their belief that Touro will soon gain the recognition it deserves. As one 2L put it: "Students from Touro will be the movers and shakers of the legal community...[the school's] reputation will increase trifold in the near future."

ADMISSIONS

The Touro College–Jacob D. Fuchsberg Law Center's numerical standards make it one of the least selective law schools in the nation. Because this is still a young law school, numerical standards may rise as the law school's applicant pool continues to grow; but for now, Touro remains a virtual sure thing for all prospective law students with even modest credentials.

ACADEMICS

Student/faculty ratio	19:1
% female faculty	39
% minority faculty	8
Hours of study per day	4.15

FINANCIAL FACTS

Tuition	$15,940
Cost of books	$500
% first-year students receiving aid	NR
% all students receiving aid	NR
% aid that is merit-based	NR
% of all students receiving loans	NR
% receiving scholarships	NR
% of all students receiving assistantships	NR
Average grant	NR
Average graduation debt	NR

ADMISSIONS

# applications received	2,028
% applicants accepted	43
% acceptees attending	34
Average LSAT	151
Average undergrad GPA	3.00
Application fee	$45
Regular application	May 1
Regular notification	rolling
Rolling notification?	No
Early decision program?	NR
Admission may be deferred?	NR
Gourman Report Rating	**2.21**

TULANE UNIVERSITY
School of Law

OVERVIEW

Type of school	private
Environment	city
Scholastic calendar	semester
Schedule	full-time only

STUDENTS

Enrollment of parent institution	11,158
Enrollment of law school	1,013
% male/female	52/48
% out-of-state	85
% part-time	1
% minorities	24
% international (# of countries represented)	2(17)
Average age at entry	24

APPLICANTS ALSO LOOK AT

Emory University
American University
Boston University
Vanderbilt University
George Washington University

SURVEY SAYS...

HITS
Broad range of courses
Classroom facilities
Research resources

EMPLOYMENT PROFILE

Job placement rate (%)	81
% grads employed immediately	60
% grads employed within six months	83
Average starting salary	$53,000

Grads employed by field (%):

Academia	1
Business/industry	10
Government	14
Judicial clerkships	15
Private practice	55
Public interest	5

Students at Tulane University Law School are living the good life, and not just for the reason you think. Yes, this private university, the twelfth oldest law school in the nation, is located in New Orleans, one of the most historic cities in the country, and is a short drive from the world-renowned French Quarter. Yes, students do get two days off for Mardi Gras. But the school has much more to offer than location. Tulane Law School is also bringing its graduates into the twenty-first century by becoming one of the most progressive and diverse law schools in the nation. The school recently opened a new state-of-the-art library in its brand-new law building and has added hundreds of computer terminals. Student satisfaction is running high, and it seems like it won't be long before public perception catches up with the reputation that the law school feels it deserves.

In several notable respects, Tulane is a leader among the nation's law schools. The school is known for its commitment to the public interest and ethical principled law practice in general (the law school operates several community law clinics and was the first law school to institute a pro bono graduation requirement), and its active recruitment and support of minorities in legal education. The school is also acknowledged as a leader in specialized fields such as admiralty and maritime law, in which Tulane offers the nation's only LL.M. degree and a formal certificate of specialization, European legal practice, environmental law, and sports law, in which Tulane offers formal certificates of specialization.

Tulane combines a solid core curriculum with a very broad range of upper-level courses and electives. Not surprisingly, students were lavish with praise for the specialty programs. The sports law program was termed "unparalleled" and "outstanding and unique." The international opportunities offered by the school also received kudos. "I picked up six units traveling the Middle East this summer," wrote one 2L, "How was your summer?" The praise was not reserved for specialty courses. A 1L described his Torts class as "the hardest course you'll ever love." Students were also enthusiastic about their professors. "The professors here are great," wrote one 2L, "When I'm finished asking them questions at their office, they'll often close the book, lean forward and ask, 'How are you doing outside of law school?'"

Nancy Montecalvo, Senior Admissions Specialist
6329 Freret Street
New Orleans, LA 70118
Tel: 504-865-5930 • Fax: 504-865-6710
Email: admissions@law.tulane.edu
Internet: www.law.tulane.edu

Indeed, students at Tulane seem to enjoy a good balance between school and life. "People have ample opportunity to go out and enjoy the New Orleans life," noted a 1L, "It's just a matter of time management." A strong sense of camaraderie was mentioned by many respondents. Students also pointed out that Tulane was a great school for minority students. "If you are a minority student, this is the place to be," a 2L flatly stated. A 1L wrote, "Tulane is far and away the best law school for gays and lesbians. Tulane goes way out of its way to make all students feel welcome." Another first year observed "all minority groups are treated with equal respect as the majority population." While Mardi Gras and Jazz Fest were mentioned as school strengths, students noted that they worked as hard as they played.

With all of these positive statements in mind, students must also consider the price of a legal education at Tulane, over $22,000, excluding living expenses. In light of the cost, it is easy to understand why the chief criticisms of the school relate to its ranking (students want it to be higher) and its ties to big cities on either coast (students want better ones to facilitate job hunts). A 2L suggested, "The career services office could improve by increasing our school's national reputation in popular areas like California, Washington, D.C., and New York."

While students may not be completely satisfied until the outside world's perception of Tulane school matches theirs, most seemed incredibly happy with their choice of school. As a 1L put it, "My experience at Tulane Law has been exhilarating and terrifying at the same time. I love it. This school truly brings out the best in students."

ADMISSIONS

Tulane's applicant pool has been on the rise in recent years, and today about 3,000 applicants vie for the 300 seats in the incoming class. Having its applicant pool more than double in the past several years, Tulane Law School is now much more selective than average in terms of both its acceptance rate and the numerical standards to which it holds its applicants. But do consider that 20 percent of the places in each class are reserved for "special admission students" whose predictors of success may be less objective than those of other applicants.

ACADEMICS

Student/faculty ratio	20:1
% female faculty	24
% minority faculty	12
Hours of study per day	3.74

FINANCIAL FACTS

Tuition	$21,364
Cost of books	$620
Room & board (on/off-campus)	$6,920
% first-year students receiving aid	75
% all students receiving aid	85
% aid that is merit-based	80
% of all students receiving loans	77
% receiving scholarships	36
% of all students receiving assistantships	0
Average grant	$10,000
Average graduation debt	$70,000

ADMISSIONS

# applications received	NR
% applicants accepted	NR
% acceptees attending	NR
Average undergrad GPA	3.24
Application fee	$45
Regular application	August 10
Regular notification	rolling
Rolling notification?	Yes
Early decision program?	No
Admission may be deferred?	Yes
Maximum length of deferment	1 year
Evening division offered?	No
Part-time accepted?	No
Gourman Report Rating	**4.35**

UNIVERSITY OF TULSA
College of Law

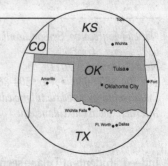

OVERVIEW

Type of school	private
Environment	metropolis
Scholastic calendar	semester
Schedule	full-time or part-time

STUDENTS

Enrollment of parent institution	2,699
Enrollment of law school	608
% male/female	61/39
% out-of-state	64
% part-time	30
% minorities	9
% international (# of countries represented)	1(NR)
Average age at entry	27

APPLICANTS ALSO LOOK AT

University of Denver
Tulane
Creighton
Drake
Washington University-MO

SURVEY SAYS...

HITS
Faculty-student relations
Diverse faculty
Studying

MISSES
Not enough courses

EMPLOYMENT PROFILE

Firms recruiting on campus	37
Job placement rate (%)	84
% grads employed immediately	48
% grads employed within six months	83
Average starting salary	$36,000

Grads employed by field (%):

Business/industry	22
Government	10
Judicial clerkships	3
Military	1
Private practice	55
Public interest	3
Other	6

The University of Tulsa College of Law traces its roots back to 1923, when a group of attorneys founded the Tulsa Law School. In those early days the school was housed in the city's courthouse and classes were taught in the evening after the faculty, all practicing attorneys, had finished a long day of work. An equally dedicated and knowledgeable faculty administers classes today at this midsize, private law school, located about three miles from downtown Tulsa, a city of 700,000. Tulsa's geography and climate—temperate and lush—may not fit many outsiders' images of Oklahoma as hot, flat, and dry. In many important aspects, however, the TU Law School is distinctly Oklahoma, and the majority of students come from Oklahoma and its neighboring states.

The course offerings at the University of Tulsa College of Law reflect the continuing regional importance of two subjects: Oil and Native Americans. The campus is home to the National Energy/Environmental Law and Policy Institute (NELPI) and to one of the nation's largest collections of materials relating to Native American law and history. The significant resources of NELPI, a national center for energy policy research, are at the disposal of TU law students who choose to pursue a concentration in energy law and policy. Students at Tulsa may also earn a Certificate in American Indian law, an appropriate option in a city that is second only to the Navajo reservation in Native American population. Many respondents mentioned the above programs when asked to list their school's greatest strengths. The curriculum at TU is not limited to regional concerns, though; students may also pursue certificates in dispute resolution, comparative and international law, public policy and regulation, and health law. The certificate programs were also praised by students.

A number of students cited the school's atmosphere as one of the positive aspects of TU. One first-year noted, "TU goes to great lengths to promote a positive and helpful environment, from 1L/3L mentor programs, to organizing small 1L groups to study together." The professors, who are of the "highest quality," play an important part in the mix. Numerous students simply listed

Velda Staves, Director of Admissions
3120 East Fourth Place
Tulsa, OK 74104-3189
Tel: 918-631-2709 • Fax: 918-631-2194
Email: Law_VLS@Centum.UTulsa.edu
Internet: www.UTulsa.edu

University of Tulsa

"faculty accessibility" as one of the school's strengths. Although one first-year wrote, "The teachers are a little bit too liberal; however, they do seem to provide a good environment for learning." That tolerance is reflected in the student body as well, according to a third-year. "TU has a very conservative student majority, but an extremely vocal and powerful liberal minority. There is a great deal of respect among the students for different viewpoints, and debate is healthy, challenging, and productive."

Students here voiced a common complaint heard at many law schools: TU is underrated. This was generally blamed on a tough grading curve. A 3L described the situation: "The curriculum is very difficult, and those of us who achieve higher grades must work much harder than those at other schools." Another 3L offered a slightly different take, writing, "We [the students] are a fired-up group. Generally this is everyone's second choice (not last) in where to go to law school—most of us are out to prove our first choice should have accepted us." Whatever the motivation, students here seem generally happy. They praised the school not only for its classroom opportunities, but for its extracurricular opportunities as well, ranging from high school tutoring to judicial internships.

Many TU students recommended improving classroom facilities. "We have Brady Bunch decor, but Masterpiece Theater faculty and students," wrote one television-minded 3L. Others criticized the administration for lack of planning and foresight. A 3L observed, "It would be nice for class offerings to be posted a year ahead so students can get the electives they want in time for graduation." Others groaned about the cost of TU, but these complaints were far outweighed by the remarks of TU students who praised the school for providing a solid education with diverse opportunities in a benign atmosphere.

ADMISSIONS

Between 1991 and 1993, the University of Tulsa College of Law reported a nearly 80 percent surge in applications volume. This dramatic jump would seem to indicate that admissions selectivity will very soon be on the rise here. As it stands now, however, Tulsa holds its applicants to lower numerical standards than do 85 percent of the law schools profiled in this book.

ACADEMICS	
Student/faculty ratio	25:1
% female faculty	33
% minority faculty	11
Hours of study per day	4.08

FINANCIAL FACTS	
Tuition	$15,200
Cost of books	$1,500
Fees	$65
Room & board (on/off-campus)	$5,000/$5,500
% first-year students receiving aid	87
% all students receiving aid	87
% aid that is merit-based	36
% of all students receiving loans	76
% receiving scholarships	39
% of all students receiving assistantships	6
Average grant	$3,964
Average graduation debt	$57,414

ADMISSIONS	
# applications received	951
% applicants accepted	63
% acceptees attending	35
Average LSAT	152
LSAT range	140-174
Average undergrad GPA	3.04
GPA range	2.00-4.00
Application fee	$30
Regular application	rolling
Regular notification	rolling
Rolling notification?	Yes
Early decision program?	No
Admission may be deferred?	Yes
Maximum length of deferment	1 year
Evening division offered?	Yes
Part-time accepted?	Yes
Gourman Report Rating	**3.20**

ALBANY LAW SCHOOL OF UNION UNIVERSITY

OVERVIEW

Type of school	private
Environment	city
Scholastic calendar	semester
Schedule	full-time or part-time

STUDENTS

Enrollment of parent institution	NR
Enrollment of law school	756
% male/female	49/51
% out-of-state	8
% part-time	5
% minorities	19
% international (# of countries represented)	1(6)
Average age at entry	26

APPLICANTS ALSO LOOK AT

Syracuse University
State University of New York at Buffalo
New York Law School
Brooklyn Law School
Western New England College

SURVEY SAYS...

HITS
Quality of teaching
Practical experience
Library staff

MISSES
Sleepless nights
Not enough courses

EMPLOYMENT PROFILE

Firms recruiting on campus	75
Job placement rate (%)	85
% grads employed immediately	67
% grads employed within six months	85
Average starting salary	$48,860

Grads employed by field (%):

Academia	1
Business/industry	22
Government	19
Judicial clerkships	4
Military	1
Private practice	50
Public interest	2

Albany Law School, an autonomous part of Union University, has served the upstate New York region continuously since 1851. The law school is the fourth oldest in the country, and its graduates have been prominent figures in state and national politics. Today it is a midsize school with moderate admissions standards and a solid regional reputation. The overwhelming majority of its students remains in New York after graduation. The bulk of the Albany Law School's facilities are housed in an imposing Tudor Gothic main building, but the tree-filled campus also includes a recently constructed modern library notable for its open, airy design.

Located, appropriately enough, in beautiful Albany, the capital of New York State and the setting for the novels of William Kennedy, the law school draws heavily on the city's resources. The proximity of both the state legislature and the Court of Appeals, the state's highest court, makes possible significant exposure to and participation in the workings of government by Albany law students. The school's Government Law Center encourages such participation through its sponsorship of symposia and other activities focusing on a broad range of issues relating to all branches and levels of government. These and numerous other co-curricular opportunities available to students at Albany are supplemented by an impressive range of clinical programs, including one of the country's few law-student clinics dedicated to AIDS law.

Albany students are a relatively happy group, satisfied with the fundamental academic quality of their chosen school. Above all, students here praise the general lack of unhealthy competitiveness. "The work is intense," said one, "but the atmosphere is comfortable and non-competitive." Most of those who expressed such sentiments also agreed on where to give due credit: "Our young faculty is excellent," reported one student, "and because of the small size of our classes, they offer us a great degree of personal attention." Others praised the general quality of life: "I am extremely pleased with my decision to come here. Albany Law School can actually be fun and painless."

Dawn M. Chamberlaine, Assistant Dean of Admissions and
Financial Aid
80 New Scotland Avenue
Albany, NY 12208
Tel: 518-445-2326 • Fax: 518-445-2369
Email: pfeid@mail.als.edu
Internet: www.als.edu

Albany Law School of Union University

The complaint most commonly voiced by Albany students had nothing to do with their experience at the law school per se, but, rather, with their prospects for employment after graduation. It must be noted, however, that these frustrations were expressed without a hint of anger toward those in charge of job placement. "The career planning center is very helpful," went one typical comment, "but their resources and contacts seem to be extremely limited." The concern that Albany students "really need better downstate job recruitment and placement" was very widely held.

Of course some students expressed little desire to break out of their immediate surroundings. As one put it, "Albany is a great city, and don't let anyone tell you otherwise." On balance, Albany students seem to be a relatively satisfied group, particularly when it comes to such fundamentals as the quality of their law school's curriculum.

ADMISSIONS

In terms of its numerical admissions standards, the Albany Law School ranks almost exactly in the middle of all U.S. law schools. This and the fact that Albany selects its students from a large applicant pool would seem to indicate a relatively high degree of admissions selectivity, but the law school's very generous overall acceptance rate indicates otherwise.

ACADEMICS

Student/faculty ratio	23:1
% female faculty	38
% minority faculty	11
Hours of study per day	4.06

Academic specialties:
Civil Procedure, Commercial, Constitutional, Corporation Securities, Criminal, Environmental, Gov't Services, International, Labor, Property, Taxation, Health , Criminal Law and Procedure, Business Transaction, Civil Litigation and Practice, Constitutional, Civil, Human Rights, Government Administration and Regulation, Labor and Employment , Family and Elder

FINANCIAL FACTS

Tuition	$18,795
Cost of books	$595
Fees	$110
Room & board (on/off-campus)	$4,550/$5,930
% first-year students receiving aid	90
% all students receiving aid	85
% aid that is merit-based	2
% of all students receiving loans	85
% receiving scholarships	47
% of all students receiving assistantships	5
Average grant	$5,900
Average graduation debt	$60,000

ADMISSIONS

# applications received	1,333
% applicants accepted	65
% acceptees attending	28
Average LSAT	153
LSAT range	138-173
Average undergrad GPA	3.10
GPA range	2.10-3.97
Application fee	$50
Regular application	March 15
Regular notification	rolling
Rolling notification?	Yes
Early decision program?	No
Admission may be deferred?	Yes
Maximum length of deferment	1 year
Evening division offered?	No
Part-time accepted?	Yes
Gourman Report Rating	**4.23**

UNIVERSITY OF UTAH
College of Law

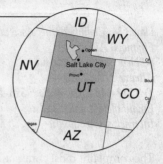

Located on the 25,000-student Salt Lake City campus of one of the most respected teaching and research universities in the nation, the tiny College of Law at the University of Utah ("The U" in local vernacular) is no less esteemed than its parent institution. Utah's only public law school enjoys a long-established reputation for excellence in the Mountain West, but the strength of its faculty and the qualifications of its students have also earned it recognition as one of the finest state-supported law schools in the United States. While dozens of schools offer programs of comparable or higher academic quality, few do so on such an intimate scale and at such a moderate price. With fewer than 400 exceptionally well-qualified students in its J.D. and graduate law programs and a relatively large complement of full-time teaching faculty, Utah boasts a tremendously favorable student-faculty ratio. With an exceptionally low in-state resident tuition, and a relatively low out-of-state tuition, The U can easily claim bargain status.

The curriculum at Utah was revamped several years ago, in an effort to add more structure to "the drift" that often characterizes the last two years of law school. Taking its imagery from architecture, Utah has organized its course offerings in three categories corresponding to the three years of the J.D. program. The law school envisions the three years of study as integrated parts that build upon one another: The first year is standard case-method "foundation" courses; second-year courses are termed "cornerstone" courses; and research seminars ("capstone" courses) round out the third year. While this reorganization may not have caused substantive change, at the very least it has given students a sense of direction.

Two words seem to be the source of Utah law students' satisfaction with their school: small size. Many respondents cited this as a key factor in creating an atmosphere that is collegial and conducive to getting to know professors. A 3L wrote, "The professors here are very intelligent and very accessible." Students found the administration and facilities to be of the same high quality as the professors. "The administration is very open," one 2L commented, "The deans are approachable and actually quite pleasant to talk with." The first year Legal Writing program was

Michelle McKenna, Coordinator
Salt Lake City, UT 84112
Tel: 801-581-7479
Email: admission@law.utah.edu

mentioned by some as demanding but worthwhile. While most students considered the school to be only moderately competitive, some students believed there was too much competition at times. According to one student, "The University of Utah strives to be the 'Harvard of the West,' not always the most appropriate goal. It encourages unhealthy competition and feelings of apathy and frustration."

Students do not have to go far to find relief from academic frustration. As a 2L wrote, "The spectacular scenery of Utah is right out the back door." Many students were extremely happy with the range of recreational opportunities available in the surrounding Wasatch Mountains, where skiing, mountain biking, and hiking seemed to be the most popular pursuits.

Students did have some concerns that an evening sojourn in the mountains could not cure. Some called for modernizing the "1960s retro-decor" of the Law School building. On a more serious note, many students mentioned the relative scarcity of jobs in the Salt Lake City legal market, and, consequently, the need for a stronger national reputation. The school's lack of diversity was the most common area of concern for a lot of students. There is a strong Mormon presence at the school, and the minority percentage is roughly akin to the ethnic makeup of Utah. "This is a great place if you want to ski," wrote one student, "but the school lacks diversity and divergent views are not tolerated." A 2L offered a slightly different view, "Yes, the conservative-LDS (Latter Day Saints) influence prevails throughout most of Utah. However, I think the College of Law (and the university as a whole) offers a balance to both conservative and liberally minded students." While students often characterized the school as "friendly," many acknowledged that there was a need for more minority representation on campus.

ADMISSIONS

As it does for all of the country's top public law schools, a combination of excellence and affordability puts the University of Utah College of Law in a position to be tremendously selective in its admissions process. Indeed, the rising numerical standards to which Utah holds applicants now rank it among the 25 most selective law schools in the nation.

ACADEMICS

Student/faculty ratio	12:1
% minority faculty	7
Hours of study per day	3.75

Academic specialties:
Commercial, Criminal, Environmental, International

FINANCIAL FACTS

Tuition (in/out-state)	$4,521/$10,120
Cost of books	$1,300
Fees (in/out-state)	$452/$452
Room & board (on/off-campus)	$6,633/$6,633
% first-year students receiving aid	75
% all students receiving aid	78
% aid that is merit-based	51
% of all students receiving loans	78
% receiving scholarships	40
% of all students receiving assistantships	2
Average grant	$4,700
Average graduation debt	$35,000

ADMISSIONS

# applications received	816
% applicants accepted	36
% acceptees attending	35
Average LSAT	161
LSAT range	147-172
Average undergrad GPA	3.56
GPA range	2.73-4.00
Application fee (in/out-state)	$40/$40
Regular application	February 1
Regular notification	rolling
Rolling notification?	Yes
Early decision program?	No
Admission may be deferred?	Yes
Maximum length of deferment	1 year
Evening division offered?	No
Part-time accepted?	No
Gourman Report Rating	**4.16**

VALPARAISO UNIVERSITY
School of Law

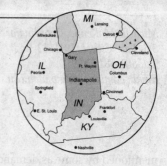

The Valparaiso (val-pa-RAY-zo) University School of Law is the smallest of Indiana's four law schools and the only Lutheran-affiliated law school in the country. Like most small schools, Valparaiso has a traditional and somewhat limited curriculum. Though many students consider the range of course offerings to be "inadequate," most agree that the curriculum is remarkably balanced. The standard first-year curriculum is "superbly taught by many of the school's best professors." The few upper-year requirements go beyond Constitutional Law and the universal professional responsibility courses to include a jurisprudence (or legal philosophy) course. Valpo's "very experienced, intelligent, and approachable" faculty "is a wonderfully diverse range of personalities," gushes a 2L. "The single greatest strength of Valparaiso is the enthusiasm of its professors. Not only do these men and women know the law, they are enthralled by it." Complaints about the professors are sparse. A few students suggest that "Valparaiso needs to do a little less hand-holding so that students will stand up more confidently on their own." The "great" administration is highly praised, especially for its ability to bring U.S. Supreme Court Justices on campus. "Our dean is the man," raps a 2L, "no one attracts more Supreme Court Justices than he can." A 2L beams: "Scalia even taught my Con Law class for a day."

Students disagree about the quality of Valpo's legal writing program. Some call it "very strong" while others speculate that students "would benefit" if it were "more coherent." Valparaiso operates a small in-house legal clinic that helps to balance academic preparation with practical skills training. Since 1989, Valparaiso has required all students to perform at least twenty hours of pro bono work prior to graduation. All the same, students here consistently gripe that there are "not enough clinical opportunities."

Career services is "excellent about making us aware of job opportunities and helping us with resumes," says a 1L. "They will do anything to help." Except, apparently, bring big city firms to campus. "We are only 45 minutes outside of Chicago and not one Chicago firm interviewed 3Ls on campus," complains one student. "The desire of many Valpo students to return to small town

Heike Sphahn, Director of Admissions and Student Relations
Wesemann Hall
Valparaiso, IN 46383
Tel: 219-465-7829 • Fax: 219-465-7872
Email: valpolaw@wesemann.law.valpo.edu
Internet: www.valpo.edu/law

Valparaiso University

firms has hurt our reputation in Chicago unfairly," laments a 3L. "Many students would make excellent associates in large private firms." Career services has a good track record at placing "top half" students in school-year externships. Facilities-wise, students offer few complaints, but not much praise. "The undergraduate campus is far enough away from the law school to make it seem like there is no connection between the law school and the rest of the university." The library "could use more materials," as "constantly squabbling over the same research materials for an assignment is extremely aggravating." Also, the computer network is "not very coordinated."

The "charming" city of Valparaiso (population roughly 25,000) is located in the extreme northern part of Indiana, minutes from Lake Michigan. While it's "not exactly a college town," Chicago "is only one hour away" and students say "there's a great small town atmosphere." There are "some background echoes of racial tension" here, but minority students tell us they "do not feel ostracized" in this "pleasant" environment. If problems arise, "students are vigorously encouraged to express their comments." Valparaiso draws a sizable proportion of its students from and sends a substantial number of its graduates to the major population centers of Illinois. Most students are "courteous" and "conservative, politically and religiously." Many hail "from small, private schools in the Midwest. Everyone is fairly friendly and makes a point of knowing everyone." Competition is not a problem at Valpo. "It is more likely that you will find students working together and helping one another rather than the stereotypical, competitive law school behavior." Says a satisfied 3L, "Valparaiso is the most inviting law school atmosphere I have ever experienced. From the first contact through the mail to orientation day when the staff knew my name, to my third year, I have always felt welcomed and appreciated."

ADMISSIONS

In strictly numerical terms, Valparaiso University ranks slightly lower than average among all U.S. law schools. The average LSAT of the most recent entering class was 150. Hopeful applicants' prospects of gaining admission here are made even better, however, by Valparaiso's generous overall acceptance rate. Applications volume at the law school is not particularly high, and about half of all applicants are admitted annually.

ACADEMICS

Student/faculty ratio	21:1
% female faculty	28
% minority faculty	9
Hours of study per day	4.08

FINANCIAL FACTS

Tuition	$15,660
Cost of books	$750
Fees	$450
Room & board (on/off-campus)	NR/$6,600
% first-year students receiving aid	90
% all students receiving aid	88
% aid that is merit-based	NR
% of all students receiving loans	88
% receiving scholarships	49
% of all students receiving assistantships	11
Average grant	NR
Average graduation debt	$60,716

ADMISSIONS

# applications received	797
% applicants accepted	64
% acceptees attending	30
Average LSAT	151
Average undergrad GPA	3.15
Application fee	$30
Regular application	April 15
Regular notification	rolling
Rolling notification?	Yes
Early decision program?	No
Admission may be deferred?	Yes
Maximum length of deferment	1 year
Evening division offered?	No
Part-time accepted?	Yes
Gourman Report Rating	**3.60**

VANDERBILT UNIVERSITY
School of Law

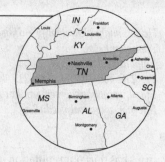

Ask the average American to name a major attraction in Nashville, the city synonymous with country music, and he will probably come up with the Grand Ole Opry. Ask the average American lawyer the same question, and she will almost certainly answer with the name of Tennessee's largest and most highly esteemed law school: The Vanderbilt University School of Law. This relatively small, private law school has long enjoyed coast to coast recognition as one of the finest law schools in the nation. Its high admissions standards, the notable geographic diversity of its student body, and the tremendous success of its graduates at landing good jobs make this fact perfectly clear.

Vanderbilt's reputation in the legal community derives in large part from its highly respected faculty, whose teaching abilities are touted by the law school as often as their scholarly achievements. Apart from its apparent quality, Vanderbilt's faculty is large enough to give the school a favorable student-teacher ratio.

The curriculum they administer is broadly traditional: Requirements are few, co-curricular activities are many, and Vandy's diverse course offerings are richest in the broader areas of business and commercial law. The school has recently made a change in its first-year curriculum. Formerly, 1Ls took courses that spanned the entire year, but now, with the exception of a Legal Research and Writing program that seeks to incorporate more practical skills, first-year courses are broken into semesters. Nonetheless, if curricular innovation is what you're looking for, you might look elsewhere. The curriculum here is relatively lacking in clinical programs and practical-skills courses. For sheer academic strength within a traditional mold, however, Vanderbilt cannot be overlooked.

Nearly all the students we heard from actually love going to law school and most attribute their pleasure to the quality of the professors who guide them. The professors "don't scare you into learning the law," boasted one student, "they lure you into loving the law." "Brilliant, stimulating, and always available for students," was how another described the faculty. Almost every student agreed with that statement wholeheartedly. A 2L noted, "Despite being in an out of the way location, I feel that Vanderbilt

Anne Brandt, Assistant Dean
School of Law, Vanderbilt University
Nashville, TN 37240
Tel: 615-322-6452 • Fax: 615-322-6631
Email: admissions@law.vanderbilt.edu
Internet: admission@law.vanderbilt.edu

Vanderbilt University

provides opportunities to work anywhere in the country; from small town to New York, Chicago, Atlanta, and Los Angeles, Vandy's alumnae are making their mark." Nashville may be "out of the way" for many, but the state capital gives students a chance "to participate in internships with judges, the DA's office, and the public defender's office," according to a 3L.

On the nonscholastic front, "The sense of community at this school separates it as an anomaly when compared to other top law schools." A number of the students we surveyed described Vanderbilt's greatest strength as its ability to foster "a cooperative rather than competitive nature between the students while maintaining high academic standards." And, although their education is grueling, students take advantage of the school-sponsored activities and Nashville's own resources to add a little variety and fun to the daily rigor.

However, there were numerous complaints about a lack of diversity at the school, both in the student body and among the faculty. Students also felt that Vanderbilt would benefit from a wider range of courses. A 3L explained, "The school needs to improve on [its] diversity of course offerings—it's currently too corporate orientated." Many agreed, but as a classmate explained, "The school's orientation is to private, big-firm hiring, which makes sense given the large debt you leave here with." Other gripes centered on the appearance of the law school; the current building was described by one as "a large box with airholes." The school is currently drawing up blueprints for a new facility, which they hope to erect within three years.

ADMISSIONS

Though an overall acceptance rate of 24 percent is hardly generous, the Vanderbilt University School of Law admits more applicants relative to its size than most of the nation's elite schools. More than three candidates are admitted for every spot in the law school's entering class of about 180. The good news for hopeful applicants stops there. In terms of the numerical standards to which it holds applicants, Vandy ranks thirteenth among the nation's law schools.

ACADEMICS

Student/faculty ratio	18:1
% female faculty	20
% minority faculty	7
Hours of study per day	3.88

FINANCIAL FACTS

Tuition	$21,750
Cost of books	$1,000
Fees	$200
Room & board (on/off-campus)	$11,300/$11,300
% first-year students receiving aid	85
% all students receiving aid	80
% aid that is merit-based	1
% of all students receiving loans	85
% receiving scholarships	42
% of all students receiving assistantships	NR
Average grant	$8,600
Average graduation debt	NR

ADMISSIONS

# applications received	2,452
% applicants accepted	29
% acceptees attending	25
Average LSAT	163
Average undergrad GPA	3.60
Application fee	$50
Regular application	April 1
Regular notification	April 1
Rolling notification?	No
Early decision program?	No
Admission may be deferred?	Yes
Maximum length of deferment	2 years
Evening division offered?	No
Part-time accepted?	No
Gourman Report Rating	**4.73**

VERMONT LAW SCHOOL
Vermont Law School

OVERVIEW

Type of school	private
Environment	town
Scholastic calendar	semester
Schedule	full-time only

STUDENTS

Enrollment of parent institution	NR
Enrollment of law school	480
% male/female	56/44
% out-of-state	91
% minorities	7
% international (# of countries represented)	2 (4)
Average age at entry	26

APPLICANTS ALSO LOOK AT

Lewis and Clark College
Pace University
Boston University
University of Maine
Northeastern University

SURVEY SAYS...

HITS
Sleeping
Sense of community
Practical experience

MISSES
Not enough courses

EMPLOYMENT PROFILE

Firms recruiting on campus	20
Job placement rate (%)	80
% grads employed immediately	30
% grads employed within six months	80
Average starting salary	$35,000

Grads employed by field (%):

Academia	1
Business/industry	16
Government	11
Judicial clerkships	13
Military	2
Private practice	50
Public interest	5
Other	2

Tucked away in a picturesque village in Vermont's Green Mountains sits the smallest and youngest private law school in New England and the only law school in the state of Vermont. In a region that reveres tradition, the upstart Vermont Law School has managed, in just over twenty years, to carve out a solid regional reputation and establish itself as one of the national leaders in environmental law education. VLS's Environmental Law Program is consistently ranked as one of the best in the country by a survey of law schools' environmental law faculties.

Vermont Law School's traditional core curriculum is supplemented with experiential programs such as its environmental law program. The school's Environmental Law Center (ELC), where students can pursue a joint Master of Studies in Environmental Law and J.D. degree or attend the school's summer session, open to both students and professionals, provides an interdisciplinary program of studies in environmental law and policy. Housed in its own building on the Law School campus, the center offers a broad array of courses on topics such as Global Impact of Energy Use, and Water Resources.

The Law School also offers several other notable innovative programs. In the General Practice Program, a limited number of students spend their second and third years working in a simulated law firm in addition to the library study. Students may also participate in the Semester in Practice Clinic, in which the classroom is abandoned for a semester of intensive field work. Students interested in government can take advantage of an internship in the Vermont General Assembly through the school's Legislation Clinic, or a fifteen-week stint in Washington, D.C. through the Environmental Semester in Washington Program.

It comes as no surprise that students at Vermont consistently cited the Environmental Law program and the availability of other progressive programs as the school's greatest strengths. Students were quick to point to the overall atmosphere at the school as an invaluable asset, characterizing the campus as "laid-back." "Our school's strengths lie in its strong sense of community, its dedication to advancing the interests of every individual, and its concern in providing a strong basis in necessary legal

Geoffrey R. Smith, Assistant Dean
Chelsea Street
South Royalton, VT 05068-0096
Tel: 888-APPLY-VLS • Fax: 802-763-7071
Email: admiss@vermontlaw.edu
Internet: www.vermontlaw.edu

Vermont Law School

skills, while allowing for personal discretion in educational direction," wrote a 3L. Students at Vermont Law School definitely seem to feel that there is more to law school than just learning law. A 1L stated, "VLS is a progressive law school geared to facilitate and enable social change. It is unlike traditional law schools in that they are part of the problem, and VLS is part of the solution."

The school's setting in the small town of South Royalton certainly contributes to a feeling of well-being. Some students observed that many of their colleagues owned dogs, and others reported that they felt comfortable enough to leave their bikes unlocked. A 1L commented, "Well, it's not like one can go to Taco Bell at 3:00 a.m., and maybe that's a good thing, but the setting is a bit stifling." While some observed that the school could do with more racial diversity, a 2L observed, "The interesting irony at VLS concerning student body composition is the fact that there are practically no minority students, yet this Wonder Bread white group spends most of its time searching [for] equality and justice."

There were very few complaints voiced by students we heard from. Some thought that the tuition was a little steep, while others noted that the school could improve its computer resources. Overall, though, many students would probably agree with the 3L who stated, "I had certain expectations of this place—that I would get a good education, live in a beautiful Vermont town, meet 'grounded' people with real interests in changing the world—all this has come true."

ADMISSIONS

In a short time, this young law school has become quite sought after, and by all indications Vermont Law School will continue to draw a large number of applicants who want to spend three years in Vermont's picturesque Green Mountains. About ten applicants now vie for each place in Vermont's entering class of 160 students, so overall selectivity is relatively high. Numerical admission standards, however, have remained moderate.

ACADEMICS

Student/faculty ratio	16:1
% female faculty	45
% minority faculty	3
Hours of study per day	4.15

Academic specialties:

Civil Procedure, Commercial, Constitutional, Corporation Securities, Criminal, Environmental, Human Rights, International, Labor, Legal History, Legal Philosophy, Property, Taxation, Other

FINANCIAL FACTS

Tuition	$18,490
Cost of books	$800
Fees	$75
Room & board (on/off-campus)	NR/$8,000
% first-year students receiving aid	85
% all students receiving aid	81
% aid that is merit-based	2
% of all students receiving loans	81
% receiving scholarships	36
% of all students receiving assistantships	0
Average grant	$5,500
Average graduation debt	$67,769

ADMISSIONS

# applications received	1,018
% applicants accepted	72
% acceptees attending	22
Average LSAT	156
LSAT range	145-176
Average undergrad GPA	3.10
GPA range	2.70-3.70
Application fee	$50
Regular application	February 15
Regular notification	April 1
Rolling notification?	Yes
Early decision program?	No
Admission may be deferred?	Yes
Maximum length of deferment	1 year
Evening division offered?	No
Part-time accepted?	No
Gourman Report Rating	**2.50**

VILLANOVA UNIVERSITY
School of Law

The youngest and—by a slim margin—the smallest of the three fine law schools in the greater Philadelphia area, the Villanova University School of Law is a highly respected midsize, Catholic institution. Located in the decidedly non-urban suburb from which it takes its name, Villanova is only about a half-hour's train ride from downtown Philadelphia. It is there, in the nation's fifth-largest legal-job market, that the law school's reputation is strongest. This reputation was built, in part, on the strength of the law school's highly successful graduates. These former students form a large and powerful alumni network that benefits current Villanova students greatly when it comes time to seek employment. The strength of this network is evident in the employment patterns of Villanova grads, a fairly large number of whom begin their legal careers in prestigious judicial clerkships.

The Villanova J.D. program is broadly traditional and quite strong, particularly in areas like taxation and commercial law. The law school is quite proud of its trial-advocacy program, and has started a new clinic, the Information Law and Policy Clinic, in an effort to broaden practical skills courses. Applications volume at the law school is only moderately heavy, but admissions standards are quite high. Entering Villanova students, the majority of whom come from Pennsylvania, possess strong numerical credentials.

Neither enthusiastically positive nor exceedingly negative about their experience at Villanova, students express a moderate but solid degree of satisfaction with most aspects of their chosen school. About their fellow students and faculty, for instance, Villanova students are nearly unanimously positive. "The students are all very closely knit," reported one, "and the faculty and administration are always there for you." "The people make Villanova a top-notch school." Most students we heard from seemed pleased with the law school's "very relaxed atmosphere" and with its very large, very able faculty. "The student body is very friendly and faculty members are always around for questions," said one 2L who also listed "ample parking" among her law school's greatest strengths. And, most seem pleased with

David Pallozzi, Director of Admissions
299 North Spring Mill Road
Villanova, PA 19085
Tel: 610-519-7010 • Fax: 610-519-6472
Internet: www.law.vill.edu

Villanova University

their general surroundings. "The school itself is excellent," said one 2L, "and Philadelphia is becoming an increasingly happening city."

But few Villanova students had any difficulty naming areas in which the law school could stand to improve. For the most part, their criticisms stemmed from what seems to be the overriding concern of most students here: their professional futures. Some of their most common complaints, for instance, concerned the perceived lack of support from the career-services office for those students not at the top of their class. Many students commented unfavorably about the physical plant, though not all as harshly as this dissatisfied student, "The facilities are like a junior high." It should be noted however, that since our survey, Villanova completed major renovations on the library, adding networked computers and study centers, which should brighten such dim perceptions of the school's facilities. Students at all levels lamented Villanova's grading policy, which many consider unfairly deflated.

More tangibly, a significant proportion of Villanova students voiced dissatisfaction with the relative lack of practical-skills courses in the law school's curriculum. "I would really like to see more clinical programs and a greater emphasis on legal writing and research," wrote one student. "We need greater opportunities to hone and develop these invaluable lawyering skills." Aside from some of these understandable but probably overstated concerns about their employment prospects in a tightening legal job market, most students at Villanova expressed fundamental satisfaction with their academic preparation for the practice of law.

ADMISSIONS

In terms of its numerical admissions standards, the Villanova University School of Law ranks forty-sixth overall among U.S. law schools. The prospects of the hopeful applicant to Villanova are made only a little bit brighter by the law school's relatively generous overall acceptance rate.

ACADEMICS

Student/faculty ratio	15:1
% female faculty	27
% minority faculty	4
Hours of study per day	3.84

FINANCIAL FACTS

Tuition	$18,750
Cost of books	$800
Fees	$30
Room & board (on/off-campus)	NR/$9,900
% first-year students receiving aid	77
% all students receiving aid	76
% aid that is merit-based	0
% of all students receiving loans	76
% receiving scholarships	4
% of all students receiving assistantships	NR
Average grant	$7,384
Average graduation debt	$62,472

ADMISSIONS

# applications received	1,270
% applicants accepted	54
% acceptees attending	34
Average LSAT	159
LSAT range	151-173
Average undergrad GPA	3.40
GPA range	2.39-3.90
Application fee	$75
Regular application	January 31
Regular notification	rolling
Rolling notification?	Yes
Early decision program?	No
Admission may be deferred?	No
Evening division offered?	No
Part-time accepted?	No
Gourman Report Rating	**3.64**

UNIVERSITY OF VIRGINIA
School of Law

OVERVIEW

Type of school	public
Environment	city
Scholastic calendar	semester
Schedule	full-time only

STUDENTS

Enrollment of parent institution	18,398
Enrollment of law school	1,148
% male/female	61/39
% out-of-state	45
% minorities	15
% international (# of countries represented)	NR (15)
Average age at entry	25

APPLICANTS ALSO LOOK AT

Harvard University
Georgetown University
Yale University
Duke University
Stanford University

SURVEY SAYS...

HITS
Quality of teaching
Sense of community
Broad range of courses

MISSES
Practical lawyering skills

EMPLOYMENT PROFILE

Firms recruiting on campus	469
Job placement rate (%)	99
% grads employed immediately	89
% grads employed within six months	99
Average starting salary	$76,000

Grads employed by field (%):

Business/industry	4
Government	3
Judicial clerkships	20
Private practice	70
Public interest	3
Other	1

From its architectural heart, the famous Thomas Jefferson-designed quadrangle, to its ethical backbone—a student-monitored honor code that is taken very seriously—the University of Virginia is steeped in tradition. So, to a great extent, is its highly respected School of Law. On the strength of its staunchly traditional curriculum, the UVA Law School enjoys a reputation as one of the finest in the nation. On the strength of the students' enthusiasm for the quality of its academic environment, it also enjoys a reputation as one of the best places to study law.

Academically, the J.D. program at Virginia is as strong as they come. After the first semester of their first year, students have almost complete control over their course of study, and with around 100 courses to choose from, they do not lack for options. Like many "first-tier" law schools, Virginia has remained focused on more theoretical aspects of the law. Amid rising criticism over the lack of practical experience, however, the school has begun offering limited clinical settings. The quality of the school's historically non-pragmatic instruction, though, cannot be questioned. UVA's faculty is both highly esteemed and well liked, and the classroom atmosphere they foster is, by all accounts, friendly and productive. A 1L wrote, "What has impressed me most is how the faculty has successfully incorporated their research into the classroom teaching experience." With a curve that puts 80 percent of students in the "B" range, and only 10 percent at either extreme, Virginia students have little reason to compete in any unhealthy way.

In fact, students generally had high praise for the attitudes of their fellow students and the "laid back" atmosphere they created. "Somehow the students remain intense and serious about their work without the level of competition you expect at a top law school," commented a 1L. Despite the relaxed academic atmosphere, rampant and frequent competition is an integral part of the UVA experience for many. Luckily, this competition takes place on the softball field. The overall institution is known for its emphasis on intramural activities and the Law School definitely contributes to the "softball and beer" image. While 1Ls all over the country are hitting the books, 1Ls at UVA are hitting for

Albert R Tumbull, Associate Dean of Admissions and Placement
580 Massie Road
Charlottesville, VA 22903-1789
Tel: 804-924-7351
Email: lawadmit@virginia.edu
Internet: www.law.virginia.edu

University of Virginia

average. One student wrote, "The only real area where I could see Virginia improving is implementing a few softball clinics to end the talent disparity." Students at UVA virtually flaunt their relaxed atmosphere. As one 1L said, "Bring your mitt." But they also take pains to ensure that their school is not just perceived as a place to party. "Anyone who thinks that Virginia is anything short of outstanding academically because we play a lot of softball is making a foolish assumption," stated a 1L, "Sometimes I marvel at how I ever got in with such a group of well-rounded, compassionate people."

What some see as the school's main strength (besides its impressive academics), some see as its main weakness. Some respondents did not like an atmosphere that one 1L likened to a "fraternity party for professionals." Others thought that the "strong sense of community" catered mainly to white males. A 2L wrote, "I have never seen such a homogenous group of people in my entire life. It's like a big J. Crew catalog come to life." On the other hand, a female second-year student warned, "Women shouldn't let the 'beer and softball' image put them off. On the surface it may smack of machismo, but it's a great way for small sections to bond their first year."

Students at UVA had some academic concerns as well. Many agreed with the 3L who suggested, "Less theory, more practice. Broader course areas and more diversity of teaching styles." A few suggested that career placement could use a little improvement. Even those who had suggestions for improvement, though, were usually satisfied overall. With new facilities ("We have doubled our space and are now totally buffed out," according to a 2L), a relaxed atmosphere, excellent academics, and a great reputation, the high level of satisfaction isn't surprising at all.

ADMISSIONS

UVA has recently been ranked by a national magazine as among the top ten most selective law schools in the country. In terms of both numerical standards and application volume, the hopeful applicant to Virginia faces the stiffest possible competition. About the only sure ticket into this world-class law school is to be a Virginia resident with more than stellar numerical credentials.

ACADEMICS	
Student/faculty ratio	17:1
% female faculty	20
% minority faculty	5
Hours of study per day	3.34

FINANCIAL FACTS	
Tuition (in/out-state)	$12,030/$19,178
Cost of books	$700
Room & board (on/off-campus)	NR/$9,720
% first-year students receiving aid	NR
% all students receiving aid	71
% aid that is merit-based	NR
% of all students receiving loans	67
% receiving scholarships	30
% of all students receiving assistantships	NR
Average grant	$6,500
Average graduation debt	NR

ADMISSIONS	
# applications received	3,782
% applicants accepted	26
% acceptees attending	37
Average LSAT	165
LSAT range	150-178
Average undergrad GPA	3.60
Application fee (in/out-state)	$40/$40
Regular application	rolling
Regular notification	April 15
Rolling notification?	Yes
Early decision program?	No
Admission may be deferred?	Yes
Evening division offered?	No
Part-time accepted?	No
Gourman Report Rating	**4.72**

WAKE FOREST UNIVERSITY
School of Law

In 1993, its ninety-ninth year, Wake Forest University School of Law opened the Worrell Professional Center for Law and Management. In fulfillment of its commitment to fully integrate the disciplines of law and management and to maintain state of the art facilities, this highly esteemed private law school in Winston-Salem, North Carolina now shares this new building with Babcock, its graduate business school. Not surprisingly, this effort also translated to a curricular focus on business and commercial law within the Law School. The Wake Forest curriculum is particularly rich in such offerings, and the majority of the school's graduates pursue careers in private practice. Wake Forest may not be quite as well known as the law schools at Duke and North Carolina–Chapel Hill, but in a state fairly bursting at the seams with fine law schools and able law students, being perceived as a close third is not a problem. This widely respected law school draws from a highly qualified, geographically diverse applicant pool, and its admissions standards and acceptance rates make it nearly as competitive as Chapel Hill. Although getting into Wake Forest is a competitive process, the school itself is not known for being ultracompetitive. First-year students characterized the school as "not cutthroat at all," and as having a "close-knit student body." A 3L wrote, "The student body is friendly with the exception of several complete freaks." Indeed, when it came to classroom issues, students were quite satisfied. With fewer than 500 students, the Law School has one of the most favorable student-faculty ratios in the nation. A 2L commented, "Faculty accessibility here is dumbfounding. Dedication to teaching here is sensational, and every firm I've interviewed with has pointed this out." A 3L praised the "active and involved faculty who achieve a good balance between teaching legal theory and practical legal skills." Not everybody is completely satisfied, though. A 1L, unhappy with the school's academic emphasis, wrote, "If one is looking to be a cold-hearted corporate lawyer, this is the place to be. Most of the curriculum is geared toward corporate practice." In general, students were content with course selection, enthusiastic about the faculty, and very happy with their surroundings. A 2L characterized the "brand new school facilities" as "unbelievable [due to the] access to computers, private carrels, and modern classrooms."

Melaine E. Nott, Director of Admissions and Financial Aid
P.O. Box 7206
Winston-Salem, NC 27109
Tel: 910-758-5437 • Fax: 910-758-4632
Email: admissions@law.wfu.edu
Internet: www.law.wfu.edu

Wake Forest University

Students at Wake Forest also clearly take the time to enjoy life outside of the classroom. Many of them praised the social aspects of the school. "A great SBA keeps things interesting," wrote a 3L. At least some of that interest revolves around alcohol, and the consumption thereof. A 1L simply wrote, "If you like beer, come here." A 2L commented that the school's greatest strength was "promoting alcohol abuse," while a 3L mourned "the passing of the happy hour kegs on the veranda." Not all were pleased with this aspect of social life. "It is a shame that single on-campus extracurricular activity centers around the consumption of alcohol, when chemical dependency is such an extraordinary problem in the legal profession," wrote an unamused 2L.

While opinion may be divided as to whether there is too much emphasis on drinking as a social outlet, students were able to achieve a near-consensus on another aspect of the Law School—the placement office. Comments were resoundingly negative, with the office described succinctly by one student as "awful." Another just wrote that it "sucks." More helpful observations were that the office "caters to the top 10 percent of the class," a common criticism of many such offices. Another student criticized its "career placement outside of North Carolina," while a 3L suggested that the placement office "should spend more time recruiting small firms to come."

ADMISSIONS

As popular as the Wake Forest University School of Law is with its current students, it is even more popular with prospective students. Over 1,600 applicants vie annually to be among the roughly 160 students in Wake Forest's first-year class, so competition is fierce and selectivity high. In fact, Wake Forest ranks among the 50 most selective law schools in the nation in terms of the numerical standards to which it holds applicants.

ACADEMICS

Student/faculty ratio	15:1
% female faculty	32
% minority faculty	4
Hours of study per day	4.25

Academic specialties:
Commercial, Labor, Taxation, International Business

FINANCIAL FACTS

Tuition	$19,500
Cost of books	$700
% first-year students receiving aid	20
% all students receiving aid	20
% aid that is merit-based	20
% of all students receiving loans	80
% receiving scholarships	20
% of all students receiving assistantships	15
Average grant	$8,600
Average graduation debt	$43,000

ADMISSIONS

# applications received	1,492
% applicants accepted	39
% acceptees attending	29
Average LSAT	160
Average undergrad GPA	3.31
Application fee	$60
Regular application	March 15
Regular notification	rolling
Rolling notification?	Yes
Early decision program?	Yes
Admission may be deferred?	No
Evening division offered?	No
Part-time accepted?	No
Gourman Report Rating	3.13

WASHBURN UNIVERSITY
School of Law

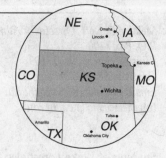

There are plenty of lawyer jokes in which lawyers receive "professional courtesy" from sharks, pitbulls, and the like. Apparently, Mother Nature does not recognize the concept, as the Washburn University School of Law found out when its Topeka, Kansas quarters were destroyed by a tornado in 1966. Luckily, students and faculty found out that there's no place like a new home. The Law School's new building, completed in 1968 and expanded in 1991, comfortably houses Washburn's more than 400 J.D. students, 50 percent of whom also work next door in the school's legal clinic. This high degree of participation reflects Washburn's long-standing and ongoing commitment to legal education outside the traditional classroom setting.

Washburn students come primarily from Kansas and nearby Missouri, and a healthy number of them choose careers in government. This is not surprising considering that the institutions and resources of the state capital play such a significant role in the education of students at Washburn. For example, they have free and easy access to the 200,000-volume library of the Kansas State Supreme Court (on which Washburn grads hold the majority). Washburn is a municipal university that is partially funded by the state. Nonresidents pay a bit more tuition than in-state residents, but still enjoy relatively low rates.

While low tuition and great facilities are certainly a draw, many students favor Washburn for its atmosphere. One 2L cited the school's "sense of community, strong camaraderie, and spirit of cooperation," adding, "Washburn is geared toward the needs of its students." The faculty was given credit for contributing to the friendly, relatively noncompetitive environment. "Intimidation does not exist at Washburn," wrote a 1L. "Faculty are friendly, open, and accessible. Even the dean is always there with an open door." Many respondents enthusiastically mentioned favorite professors by name. One 1L commented, "The professors are just like one of the crowd. They guide, but don't dominate the conversations. They only care about our learning experience." Students were also impressed with small class sizes.

Janet K. Kerr, Director of Admissions
1700 College
Topeka, KS 66621-1060
Tel: 785-231-1185 • Fax: 785-232-8087
Email: admissions@washburnlaw.edu
Internet: washburnlaw.edu

Washburn University

Although students clearly get along with each other and their professors, an odd duality exists at the school. Some characterized it as very liberal, while others felt it was a very conservative place. A 3L described the political climate: "There are two factions at Washburn: very liberal and somewhat-to-very conservative. The middle seems to be shrinking since my first year." The students were generally described as somewhat conservative, while the faculty was described as liberal. A 1L cautioned, "If you're expecting a strongly conservative Midwestern law school, you may be in for a surprise." Some students suggested that more conservative professors be added, while others suggested more diversity in the student body. Almost all, however, acknowledged that there was a high degree of acceptance at the school. "Individual differences are not only tolerated, but are encouraged," wrote a 2L. A 1L stated, "Overall, I think Washburn student life is moving in the right direction and I am happy to be a part of that evolution and growth."

Students did have suggestions for improvements, though there was no real area of consensus. One student complained that access for physically disabled students was limited, and such students were unable to sit in the front of classrooms as needed. Another suggested that the school could "grade boost like most schools do in the Midwest that are tier three or four. Instead everyone gets C's." Some students were less than enthusiastic about Topeka, and one suggested that the school "move to a different city." However, other students pointed out the advantages of being a law student in the state capital. One 3L noted, "The geographic location allows for a broad range of experiences outside the classroom, ranging from legislative internships to internships at the U.S. Attorney's office."

ADMISSIONS

According to the administration of the Washburn University School of Law, in terms of numerical admissions standards, they should be "somewhere in the middle third of the ABA-approved law schools," of which there are 178. Says the administration, "there are at least 58 schools that have both a lower UGPA and LSAT median than ours, at least 59 with a lower LSAT median, and at least 97 schools with a lower median UGPA."

ACADEMICS

Student/faculty ratio	16:1
% female faculty	33
% minority faculty	26
Hours of study per day	3.87

Academic specialties:
Criminal, Environmental, Gov't Services, Taxation

FINANCIAL FACTS

Tuition (in/out-state)	$6,810/$10,110
Cost of books	$700
Fees (in/out-state)	$40/$40
Room & board (on/off-campus)	$3,110/$5,500
% first-year students receiving aid	85
% all students receiving aid	85
% aid that is merit-based	95
% of all students receiving loans	80
% receiving scholarships	40
% of all students receiving assistantships	8
Average grant	$2,800
Average graduation debt	$35,000

ADMISSIONS

# applications received	719
% applicants accepted	60
% acceptees attending	42
Average LSAT	152
Average undergrad GPA	3.20
Application fee (in/out-state)	$30/$30
Regular application	March 15, September 15
Regular notification	June 1, Dec. 1
Rolling notification?	Yes
Early decision program?	No
Admission may be deferred?	No
Evening division offered?	No
Part-time accepted?	Yes
Gourman Report Rating	**3.31**

WASHINGTON AND LEE UNIVERSITY
School of Law

Besides being the only U.S. law school (that we know of) with Robert E. Lee's dead horse buried beneath its campus, the Washington and Lee University School of Law is remarkable for its extraordinary full-time faculty-to-student ratio of 1:10. The student body at this highly respected law school is very small as well, and W&L has a full-time faculty that is as large as those of many schools twice its size. If academic intimacy is your yardstick for judging law schools, W&L is hard to beat.

Though students applauded the "excellent mixture of the theoretical and practical in the classroom," W&L is far and away strongest in business law. "Washington and Lee is like a good restaurant that serves only one thing," explained one student. "If you like it, you're okay. If not, you're screwed." Students believed "a more diverse curriculum" would enhance the academic experience. The Legal Writing program, "which is incorporated into a substantive class and taught by full professors, is also very valuable." Remarked a 1L, "It is rewarding to go to a school where an actual law professor looks over writing assignments, thoroughly critiques them, and then gives you the opportunity to revise them." The "expert-but-not-aloof" faculty are "dedicated to teaching" and "really challenge you to think about the law and what it means to be a lawyer." Profs are also very accessible. According to one student, "You can even call them at home." The administration, on the other hand, "is distant, but perhaps that's better because when you talk to them you realize their incompetence."

The law school has a phenomenal placement rate, but that doesn't stop W&L students from feeling awfully goosey when their thoughts turn to life after law school. "Although W&L has been ranked highly in national surveys," lamented a 3L, "all the law students have had the distressing realization that many employers outside the Southeast have never heard of the school." The general perception that the placement office is "too low-tech and inadequate for a school of this caliber" does little to mollify fears. Warned one student: "The placement office can get you a job in Richmond, Charleston, Virginia, or Birmingham. Otherwise, you better get a clerkship."

Susan Palmer, Assistant Dean
Lewis Hall
Lexington, VA 24450
Tel: 540-463-8504 • Fax: 540-463-8586
Email: lawadm@wlu.edu
Internet: www.wlu.edu

Washington and Lee University

Students say the law school is "a blot on an otherwise attractive landscape." Computer resources are decent, but a 3L griped, "We need somebody whose only job is to keep the computer resources working." On a very positive note, "whether it is three o'clock in the afternoon or three o'clock in the morning, the library is open for students to use."

Social life at this "warm, fuzzy law school" rivals nirvana—especially if you like free beer. "Each student drinks several hundred dollars of free beer per semester at SBA functions," explained a 1L. "This is the only law school I know of that sets up kegs of beer outside the front door every Friday at five o'clock." Some complained that it "can become boring to see the same faces in the same places" all the time, but the small numbers seem to foster healthy competition. Student after student told us that "people share notes, outlines, and study tips constantly" and a "spirit of cooperation" is extremely pervasive.

W&L students called themselves "a little snobby and pretentious" and very conservative. "I'm a Republican," said a 3L, "but the folks here are too conservative for me. This place needs less emphasis on being a tool for big business and more heart." Said one student, "This is not a school where you can be really different in any way. And there's definitely a double standard for males and females insofar as what people can do with whom. The gossip chain is remarkable," explained a 2L. "Also, we're definitely a southern school. I feel it every day, especially as a African American female." Students told us that their law school offers "peace, love, and the only law school rugby team in the nation." Concluded a 2L, "Students actually enjoy law school here."

ADMISSIONS

The Washington and Lee University School of Law is one of the most selective in the nation. In fact, the numerical standards to which this excellent and inexpensive law school holds applicants rank it just outside of the notorious Top Twenty. A decidedly ungenerous overall acceptance rate only compounds matters for the prospective W & L student, who had better have very strong numerical credentials to have a shot at gaining admission. The median GPA of entering students in the 1996 first-year class was 3.51. This class's median LSAT score was 165.

ACADEMICS

Student/faculty ratio	10:1
% female faculty	24
% minority faculty	3
Hours of study per day	4.36

FINANCIAL FACTS

Tuition	$16,130
Cost of books	$500
Fees	$221
Room & board (on/off-campus)	$2,620
% first-year students receiving aid	90
% all students receiving aid	90
% aid that is merit-based	NR
% of all students receiving loans	88
% receiving scholarships	67
% of all students receiving assistantships	NR
Average grant	$5,500
Average graduation debt	$48,000

ADMISSIONS

# applications received	1,844
% applicants accepted	27
% acceptees attending	23
Average LSAT	165
Average undergrad GPA	3.51
Application fee	$40
Regular application	February 1
Regular notification	rolling
Rolling notification?	Yes
Early decision program?	No
Admission may be deferred?	Yes
Maximum length of deferment	Variable
Evening division offered?	No
Part-time accepted?	No
Gourman Report Rating	**3.21**

WASHINGTON UNIVERSITY
School of Law

The nearly 130 year-old Washington University School of Law is the oldest continuously operating private law school west of the Mississippi, located seven miles west of the river in suburban St. Louis, just ten minutes from downtown. This mid-size private law school is solidly Midwestern, drawing the majority of its students from, and sending a majority of its graduates to, the greater Midwest, where the school's long-established reputation for excellence is best known. The overall strength of the Washington J.D. program comes in large part from the law school's highly respected (read: highly published) faculty. The law school offers numerous opportunities for interdisciplinary study through the many excellent departments of the broader university. Co-curricular activities abound, and participation is extremely high in the law school's Advocacy and Litigation Program.

A faculty that is well-published does not always provide the best classroom instruction. This is definitely not the case at Washington University, as the students were quite unstinting in their praise of the professors. "It is unbelievable how they can find so many professors of different types and backgrounds who are all enjoyable to [have] for class," wrote one satisfied 3L. The school's proportion of female faculty, about 30 percent, is one of the highest among U.S. law schools. Another third-year student commented, "The faculty are extremely generous with their time and energy. They are fully committed to furthering the education of their students." The physical setting for this education has definitely changed for the better, according to students, thanks to the completion of a "great new law school building" in the words of one 2L. "The old building was hellish and awful," wrote a 1L, "but the new building is beautiful."

The curriculum administered within the new building is broad within traditional boundaries and is supplemented by a wealth of highly regarded clinical programs, including a D.C.-based Congressional Clinic, in which twenty-four third-year students participate annually. This clinic gives students the opportunity to work full-time for a member of Congress, a congressional committee, or an administrative agency. Unlike many law schools, Washington University offers clinical courses to students through-

Janet Laybold Bolin, Director of Admissions
1 Brookings Drive, Campus Box 1120
St. Louis, MO 63130
Tel: 314-935-4525 • Fax: 314-935-6493
Email: admiss@wulaw.wustl.edu
Internet: www.wulaw.wustl.edu

Washington University

out their three-year law school stay. The school also offers numerous joint-degree programs.

Now that the new building is in use, the main area of student dissatisfaction seems to be career services. A 2L observed that it "needs a bigger, better staff. They don't seem to have any pull on the West Coast and this doesn't seem to bother them." Some students observed that the location of the career services office in the new building appeared symbolic. "If Wash U. wants to be a great school, it must have great students. To get great students you must get your students great jobs. To get your students great jobs, you can't put Career Services in the basement," wrote one 2L. Other students suggested that the school take measures to improve its "underwhelming" national reputation. One 3L claimed, "Wash U. is in the predicament of being a regional school in a locale fearful of hiring its grads because the grads may attempt to leave the state." While expressing reservations and fears such as these, students were quick to note that they had a very positive experience at the law school.

ADMISSIONS

Prospective law students hoping to be among Washington University School of Law's entering class of approximately 200 should feel somewhat secure with the university's generous acceptance rate of over 50 percent. In terms of numerical standards, however, it is clear that only students with quite solid credentials are admitted.

ACADEMICS
Student/faculty ratio	5:1
% female faculty	29
% minority faculty	3
Hours of study per day	3.90

Academic specialties:
Civil Procedure, Commercial, Constitutional, Corporation Securities, Criminal, Environmental, Human Rights, International, Labor, Legal History, Legal Philosophy, Property, Taxation

FINANCIAL FACTS
Tuition	$21,475
Cost of books	$1,120
Fees	$40
Room & board (on/off-campus)	NR/$7,476
% first-year students receiving aid	82
% all students receiving aid	76
% aid that is merit-based	94
% of all students receiving loans	71
% receiving scholarships	38
% of all students receiving assistantships	0
Average grant	$9,260
Average graduation debt	$60,000

ADMISSIONS
# applications received	1,665
% applicants accepted	56
% acceptees attending	21
Average LSAT	160
Average undergrad GPA	3.30
Application fee	$50
Regular application	April 15
Regular notification	April 15
Rolling notification?	No
Early decision program?	Yes
Admission may be deferred?	Yes
Maximum length of deferment	1 year
Evening division offered?	No
Part-time accepted?	No
Gourman Report Rating	**4.17**

UNIVERSITY OF WASHINGTON
School of Law

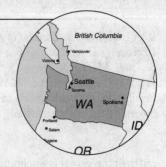

OVERVIEW

Type of school	public
Environment	metropolis
Scholastic calendar	quarter
Schedule	full-time only

STUDENTS

Enrollment of parent institution	20,448
Enrollment of law school	468
% male/female	56/44
% out-of-state	37
% part-time	NR
% minorities	40
% international (# of countries represented)	NR (NR)
Average age at entry	24

APPLICANTS ALSO LOOK AT

University of California, Berkeley
Georgetown University
Harvard University
Stanford University
University of Michigan

SURVEY SAYS...

HITS
Library staff
Sleeping
Academic reputation

MISSES
Not enough courses

Located just a few miles outside downtown Seattle, the University of Washington School of Law is one of the largest and best public universities in the West, and it has long enjoyed a regional reputation for excellence.

The law school is "a strong leader in Pacific Rim country law" and its students have access to the vast resources of the broader university. They can also pursue concurrent degrees in any of its ninety graduate departments. With more than thirty full-time professors and fewer than 500 students, UW has one of the most favorable student-faculty ratios in the nation. Students said there are "some stellar professors and a couple of dinosaurs" here. The entire faculty "truly maintains its open-door policy," though, and most "are well-respected, leading academics in their fields." The "autocratic and unresponsive" administration, on the other hand, "tends to pay students a lot of lip service. They encourage student participation on committees but then schedule meetings at times that students cannot attend."

The legal education available at UW is definitely a bargain. "We get a great education for the cost of a few lattes per day," quipped one student. "The professors, the administration and your fellow students foster a strong sense of community and take a very humanitarian approach to law school," said one satisfied student. "If they accept you they expect you to graduate, and they provide the support services necessary to accomplish this." Other students disagreed. Strongly. "Because our reputation is so inflated, professors feel no obligation to prepare good lawyers. There's no Socratic method, no skills training, just touchy-feely theory. Result: An average student here can't even get an interview with local firms."

While the clinical programs are good, the future attorneys at UW are not exactly ecstatic about their employment prospects. "UW would have more national recognition if more of its students would practice in other parts of the country." But as one student asked, "why would anyone want to leave Seattle anyway?" Exactly, argued a 2L: "The problem is the Northwest is so great, so everyone wants to stay here and everyone else wants to move here, too. As a result, it's very competitive." The way we heard it,

Shannon Dahill
Box 353200
Seattle, WA 98105
Tel: 206-543-4078

"job placement for the bottom 80 percent is alarmingly weak. Students not on Law Review better be prepared for universal rejection from downtown Seattle."

"Thanks to Bill Gates," a new building is in the hopper for the UW law school. "Ground should be broken in 1999." Until then, the current "windowless" facility "looks like a bomb shelter" and is "ugly and dysfunctional." "Sadly," lamented a 2L, "the proposed new building looks like a gas chamber," and may not be much of an improvement on its surface. In good news, "the library is unparalleled" but "should be opened until at least midnight," which it currently is not.

As for competition, a 1L beamed: "I have yet to find anyone who is not totally willing to help me in any way they can. Competition is literally non-existent. The 2Ls and 3Ls almost beg you to take their course outlines." For the most part, "the students are a delightful bunch," explained a 2L. "When the school voted (during Finals Week!) to change our grading system without consulting students, there was a general uprising. Students organized an Email list to distribute information (bypassing the official list, which requires the Dean's approval to use), plastered the school with fliers, contacted the local media, and forced the reversal of the decision. Now that's community."

ADMISSIONS

The strength of Washington's traditional curriculum, the cachet of it surroundings, and the attractiveness of its low tuition have combined to send application volume through the roof. Consequently, numerical admissions standards are very high, and the law school's overall acceptance rate is understandably low. Though few people yet mention its name in the same breath as some elite public law schools in, the University of Washington School of Law comes very close to equaling those giants in terms of admissions selectivity. Dizzying applicant demand has sent numerical standards sky-high, to the point that those applicants whose numbers fall even a bit short of stellar might do better investing their application fees in lottery tickets.

ACADEMICS

Student/faculty ratio	12:1
% female faculty	31
% minority faculty	8
Hours of study per day	3.33

FINANCIAL FACTS

Tuition (in/out-state)	$4,500/$11,500
Cost of books	$800
% first-year students receiving aid	NR
% all students receiving aid	NR
% aid that is merit-based	NR
% of all students receiving loans	NR
% receiving scholarships	NR
% of all students receiving assistantships	NR
Average grant	NR
Average graduation debt	NR

ADMISSIONS

# applications received	2,550
% applicants accepted	21
% acceptees attending	34
Average LSAT	162
Average undergrad GPA	3.55
Regular application	January 15
Regular notification	April 1
Rolling notification?	No
Early decision program?	NR
Admission may be deferred?	NR
Gourman Report Rating	4.41

WAYNE STATE UNIVERSITY
Law School

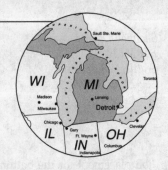

Residents of Michigan are as fortunate as any in the country when it comes to the availability of excellent, inexpensive institutions of higher education. When it comes to the availability of excellent, inexpensive law schools, however, their options are limited. For the lucky few, there is the University of Michigan Law School, a tremendously selective law school that enrolls a large proportion of nonresidents. Michiganians seeking a solid legal education at a bargain price have only one other option: Detroit's Wayne State University Law School, a law school with a very strong regional reputation and much lower admissions standards. Indeed, Wayne State is surely the finest law school in the state, dedicated primarily to educating Michigan residents and producing Michigan lawyers. State residents make up almost all of Wayne State's well-qualified student body of about 900, most of whom remain in the immediate region after completing their degrees.

The J.D. program at Wayne State is, by all reports, rigorous and comprehensive. After a traditional first-year curriculum that includes an especially intensive Legal Writing program, students chart their own courses of study, choosing from among the Law School's varied and extensive classroom offerings and a sizable number of clinical programs. Special programs at Wayne State include the Intellectual Property Institute, dedicated to research and teaching in the growing area of law for which it is named.

Students at Wayne State expressed a moderate level of satisfaction with their chosen school. On certain matters, (e.g., the "excellent education for half the price of comparable schools"), opinion among the students we heard from was unanimously positive. But overall student responses gave us the impression that the Law School meets students' needs without inspiring much in the way of enthusiasm. Still, many words of praise were heard from Wayne State students, particularly when describing the quality of their faculty. The responses we received paint a picture of professors that are "real people" who are genuinely "interested in teaching students." There was also a considerable amount of praise for the low student-to-faculty ratio and the range of evening class offerings, "making life easier for the majority of us who

Linda Fouder Sims, Assistant Dean for Recruitment and Admissions
468 Ferry Mall
Detroit, MI 48202
Tel: 313-577-3937 • Fax: 313-577-6000
Email: lsims@novell.law.wayne.edu
Internet: www.law.wayne.edu

Wayne State University

commute, maintain jobs, or have other alternative scheduling needs."

Prevailing opinion on the general atmosphere at the Law School was less forgiving. One 2L admitted, "Since virtually all students commute from the surrounding area, inter-student relations are limited." And although most would not go so far as to label their classmates as "cutthroat," a number of students described tense relations in a "highly competitive" environment. A subdued undercurrent of racial tension within the school was also reported, possibly arising from Detroit's own ignominious history of segregation. Finally, the facilities were a sore point with almost all the students. "If the school's resources were anywhere near the general quality of its faculty," a 2L student opined, "it might be better than a certain, highly regarded, Top Ten law school located about twenty-five miles west of it." However, a fellow classmate assured, "The school has made (and continues to make) a concerted effort to improve the physical facilities here as part of a campaign to become more competitive with other schools in the region-and it shows!" Hopefully, Wayne State will be able to keep tuition low as it implements the changes necessary to develop its resources and foster its intrinsically sound reputation.

ADMISSIONS

Michigan's "other" public law school may not measure up to the world-class school in Ann Arbor in terms of admissions selectivity, but the admissions process at the Wayne State University Law School is, in the grand scheme of things, a bit more competitive than average. In terms of the numerical standards to which it holds applicants, in fact, Wayne State ranks 62nd among all U.S. law schools.

ACADEMICS

Student/faculty ratio	19:1
% female faculty	35
% minority faculty	6
Hours of study per day	3.28

FINANCIAL FACTS

Tuition (in/out-state)	$6,834/$14,364
Cost of books	NR
Room & board (on/off-campus)	$8,645/$8,645
% first-year students receiving aid	NR
% all students receiving aid	80
% aid that is merit-based	NR
% of all students receiving loans	65
% receiving scholarships	50
% of all students receiving assistantships	NR
Average grant	$2,000
Average graduation debt	$27,000

ADMISSIONS

# applications received	1,137
% applicants accepted	43
% acceptees attending	46
Average LSAT	156
Average undergrad GPA	3.30
Application fee (in/out-state)	$20/$20
Regular application	rolling
Regular notification	NR
Rolling notification?	Yes
Early decision program?	No
Admission may be deferred?	No
Evening division offered?	Yes
Part-time accepted?	Yes
Gourman Report Rating	**3.66**

WEST VIRGINIA UNIVERSITY
College of Law

OVERVIEW

Type of school	public
Environment	suburban
Scholastic calendar	semester
Schedule	full-time or part-time

STUDENTS

Enrollment of parent institution	21,517
Enrollment of law school	428
% male/female	51/49
% out-of-state	15
% part-time	3
% minorities	5
% international (# of countries represented)	NR (2)
Average age at entry	26

APPLICANTS ALSO LOOK AT

Duquesne University
University of Pittsburgh
Washington and Lee University
Dickinson College Of Law
Ohio Northern University

SURVEY SAYS...

HITS
Legal writing

MISSES
Quality of teaching
Not enough courses

EMPLOYMENT PROFILE

Firms recruiting on campus	60
Job placement rate (%)	90
% grads employed immediately	65
% grads employed within six months	91
Average starting salary	$35,000

Grads employed by field (%):

Academia	2
Business/industry	10
Government	15
Judicial clerkships	3
Private practice	67
Public interest	3
Other	2

As the only law school in the state, the West Virginia University College of Law bears a heavy responsibility: It must import lawyers to meet the demand of its population for legal services. The school must also make itself as accessible as possible to all members of the state's populace, and it must provide its home state with lawyers competent to serve all segments of local society. On all counts, the law school succeeds, as it has for more than a century. Located at WVU's rural campus, just outside the northern West Virginia community of Morgantown, this very small public law school offers a solid, traditional J.D. program administered by a faculty that is large enough to ensure a relatively high degree of personal attention. And it charges very little to do it. At around $4,000, the annual tuition at West Virginia gives state residents little incentive to consider attending law school elsewhere. Nearly 90 percent of the law school's attendees are natives of West Virginia, and a similar—though slightly lower—proportion of them stay within the state after graduating.

Special programs at the law school include the standard array of clinical programs and co-curricular activities, including a trial-advocacy program of which the school is particularly proud. WVU is also the site of the Eastern Mineral Law Foundation, an institute dedicated to scholarship in an area of law that is of particular concern to this coal-producing state. Students extolled their school's commitment to public interest law and to the state's legal community. "Most classes emphasize West Virginia law, which is beneficial to those who intend on staying in the area," said a 1L. Although many students noted the school's commitment to the people of the state as impressive and inspiring, a few others feel the school needs to focus its attention elsewhere. "I think the law school must attempt to move itself to the national forefront of legal education rather than primarily serving the needs of this state," said a 1L.

However, students we surveyed often complained of the lack of clinical opportunities at the school as well as a generally "limited" curriculum. Some WVU students mentioned that the school needs to pay more attention to pragmatic instruction. One student, a 3L, gave us this list of needed improvements: "More clinical programs, class offerings for other subjects like sport and

Janet L. Armistead, Assistant Dean for Admissions
P.O. Box 6130
Morgantown, WV 26506-6103
Tel: 304-293-5304 • Fax: 304-293-6891
Email: devince@wvu.edu

West Virginia University

entertainment law, better professors that take a practical approach to teaching." A 3L suggested: "The law school needs to offer areas of concentration, so students can specialize in certain areas."

Students we spoke with at WVU are overall relatively pleased with their education and surroundings. They are quick to cite the affordable tuition as one the school's major strengths. "The best thing about WVU law school is the value. You get a good education at a great price," said one 2L, and added, "You may not be at Harvard, but you aren't paying anything close to Harvard prices."

The school also, reports students, maintains close ties to alumni, which comes in handy around job time. However, students who do not wish to reside in the state after graduation may have to do additional legwork in order to secure a job. Although a couple of students said the area needs "better restaurants," few complaints were heard on the geographic location of WVU. One vocal student who told us that WVU is "one of the finest schools in the country," also offered: "it's not the 'hillbilly-haven' everyone outside the state thinks it is."

The feelings of most WVU students were summed up well in this assessment by a 1L: "A student can get one of the most open, informative, and well-structured educations in the country here. WVU is certainly one of the finest schools in the country." This public law school offers a great deal to future lawyers, particularly those who are from the state and want to practice there after graduation.

ADMISSIONS

Although the West Virginia University College of Law's numerical standards are slightly below the national law school average, the school is relatively selective; WVU admits only about one third of those who apply, and very few students turn down an invitation to enroll.

ACADEMICS

Student/faculty ratio	10:1
% female faculty	27
% minority faculty	6
Hours of study per day	4.18

Academic specialties:
Civil Procedure, Commercial, Constitutional, Corporation Securities, Criminal, Environmental, Government Services, Human Rights, International, Labor, Legal History, Legal Philosophy, Property, Taxation

FINANCIAL FACTS

Tuition (in/out-state)	$3,696/$10,576
Cost of books	$600
Fees (in/out-state)	$592/$592
Room & board (on/off-campus)	NR/$8,690
% first-year students receiving aid	83
% all students receiving aid	81
% aid that is merit-based	1
% of all students receiving loans	78
% receiving scholarships	26
% of all students receiving assistantships	0
Average grant	$2,553
Average graduation debt	$30,890

ADMISSIONS

# applications received	554
% applicants accepted	53
% acceptees attending	49
Average LSAT	154
Average undergrad GPA	3.30
Application fee (in/out-state)	$45/$45
Regular application	rolling
Regular notification	rolling
Rolling notification?	Yes
Early decision program?	No
Admission may be deferred?	Yes
Maximum length of deferment	1 year
Evening division offered?	No
Part-time accepted?	Yes
Gourman Report Rating	**3.18**

WESTERN NEW ENGLAND COLLEGE
School of Law

OVERVIEW

Type of school	private
Environment	suburban
Scholastic calendar	semester
Schedule	full-time or part-time

STUDENTS

Enrollment of parent institution	1,673
Enrollment of law school	691
% male/female	52/48
% out-of-state	48
% part-time	39
% minorities	10
% international (# of countries represented)	NR (2)
Average age at entry	27

APPLICANTS ALSO LOOK AT

New England School of Law
University of Connecticut
Suffolk University
Quinnipiac College
Franklin Pierce

SURVEY SAYS...

HITS
Quality of teaching
Socratic method
Faculty-student relations

EMPLOYMENT PROFILE

Firms recruiting on campus	10
Job placement rate (%)	88
% grads employed immediately	47
% grads employed within six months	88
Average starting salary	$39,333

Grads employed by field (%):

Academia	1
Business/industry	31
Government	19
Judicial clerkships	5
Military	2
Private practice	39
Public interest	3
Other	6

Western New England School of Law offers some attractive features that several of its Boston rivals do not: a peaceful small-city location with a low cost of living, the flexibility of both day and evening programs, a close-knit faculty and student body, and a non-competitive atmosphere. Located off the beaten path in the western Massachusetts city of Springfield, roughly three quarters of the school's 800 students come from Massachusetts or nearby Connecticut. WNEC is a moderately priced private school with an evening division comprised of almost 300 part-time students.

Students were overwhelmingly satisfied with the quality of teaching and student/faculty relations at the school. "Here, students are more than a name or number on the seating chart," wrote one 2L. "The profs want to see you learn and to enjoy the Law School experience." Nearly everyone we heard from emphasized the faculty's accessibility to the students. Beyond the open-door policy, however, students stressed the comfortable familiarity they share with their educators. Listen to what one 3L had to say: "When you approach one of the faculty here or even the dean of the school, you feel like you are talking to an old friend." A classmate confided, "It's not unusual to find students hanging out with professors in relaxed social settings." The administration of the school is also highly regarded, and, according to one student, they focus "on the needs of the students, and not the economic outlook relevant to each decision that needs to be made."

WNEC students also gave high marks to their Legal Writing program and practical experience with the law-undoubtedly enhanced by the fact that nearly all the school's full- and part-time faculty are experienced practitioners. Moreover, the students felt their school "fosters a very strong sense of community and a desire for involvement." Although present, competition at the school is more of a personal struggle. Students told us they're constantly striving to better themselves, and waste little time trying to one-up their classmates. A 2L told a revealing story: "A law professor once said he would be 'shocked and appalled' if he heard of one student failing to give a fellow student help when it was requested." Cooperative, yes, but the students at WNEC are

Victoria J. LaFore, Assistant Dean
1215 Wilbraham Road
Springfield, MA 01119
Tel: 800-782-6665 • Fax: 413-796-2067
Email: lawadmis@wnec.edu
Internet: www.law.wnec.edu

Western New England
College

not necessarily a united front. Many pointed out that their classmates tend to be either liberal or conservative, with very few moderates to speak of. "What this creates," wrote a 3L, "is a fantastic adversarial analysis so that it is virtually impossible not to see every aspect of every issue discussed in class or outside of class . This school puts out lawyers who are not just able to argue a point, but who can make a better argument because they have developed a better understanding of the other side."

However, there is one issue where both liberals and conservatives agree: "The professors, administration, facilities, and overall quality of the education at WNEC Law are grossly underrated in the law community." Although "the school is well-known in New England," one student claimed that area employers pay more attention to WNEC because "they know this school puts out good, practical lawyers." Almost everyone we asked bemoaned their school's lack of a national reputation. A 2L voiced the worries of many when she wrote, "My concern is that no one outside of the immediate area has heard of this law school. Most people are unaware that this school exists and sometimes I'm questioned whether or not this school is accredited." While students at WNEC continue to push their school to develop a name within the tight legal job market, a last-year student offered this challenge: "Hire one of our graduates and you'll see. Believe me."

ADMISSIONS

With numerical standards ranking well below the national average for all U.S. law schools, Western New England College School of Law is one of the twenty least selective schools in the Northeast. This could be good news for prospective students who wish to attend law school in New England, but have only moderate credentials.

ACADEMICS	
Student/faculty ratio	19:1
% female faculty	24
% minority faculty	7
Hours of study per day	4.25

FINANCIAL FACTS	
Tuition	$16,750
Cost of books	$615
Fees	$616
Room & board (on/off-campus)	NR/$6,120
% first-year students receiving aid	84
% all students receiving aid	93
% aid that is merit-based	1
% of all students receiving loans	85
% receiving scholarships	14
% of all students receiving assistantships	1
Average grant	$2,101
Average graduation debt	$46,000

ADMISSIONS	
# applications received	1,406
% applicants accepted	63
% acceptees attending	24
Average LSAT	150
LSAT range	134-177
Average undergrad GPA	3.00
GPA range	1.87-3.92
Application fee	$45
Regular application	rolling
Regular notification	rolling
Rolling notification?	Yes
Early decision program?	No
Admission may be deferred?	Yes
Maximum length of deferment	1 year
Evening division offered?	Yes
Part-time accepted?	Yes
Gourman Report Rating	**2.75**

WHITTIER COLLEGE
School of Law

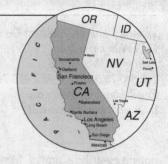

Just over sixty years ago, Whittier College produced its most famous graduate. He would go on to earn a law degree with honors from Duke and to become president of the United States, presiding over an administration that did more to sully the reputation of the legal profession than any ambulance-chaser ever did. It was not until 1975, three years after the Watergate scandal broke, however, that Richard Milhous Nixon's tiny alma mater established a law school of its own. The Whittier College School of Law is the youngest of California's sixteen fully accredited law schools. While the school has educated several thousand lawyers in its Tudor-style facility near downtown Los Angeles, Whittier has not had the time to develop an academic reputation on the level of its many neighboring schools. However, its large, well-educated faculty— of whom an admirably large percentage are women—and its rising admissions standards spell potential. The school may be taking its first huge step toward reaching that potential by relocating its base of operations from Los Angeles to Orange County. The move should be complete by the fall of 1997. By becoming the only accredited law school in Orange County, Whittier should be able to develop an even bigger niche for itself. The Law School's curriculum is traditional in scope, and while there is no in-house legal clinic, Whittier does sponsor numerous externship programs.

Not surprisingly, most students we heard from mentioned the "move south" to Orange County. As one student put it, "Whittier is in transition, moving from culturally diverse L.A. to homogenous, conservative Orange County." Students were uniformly optimistic about the move. "We are hoping that the move will bring greater opportunities for jobs and better resources for the students," wrote one 2L, "The L.A. market is a tough market in which to compete, and Orange County is virtually untapped." Another student agreed, noting that it should be easier to get internships and externships from the new location. One of the unfortunate by-products of the move has been a "split" campus, with first years attending classes at a temporary campus in Irvine. While first-year students seemed to be weathering the strange situation and the relative lack of facilities well, some felt, in the words of one student, like "second-class citizens." Another 1L summed up his classmates' feelings: "This has placed a strain on

Mary Davis Upton, Director of Admissions
5353 West Third Street
Los Angeles, CA 90020
Tel: 213-938-3621

Whittier College

everybody, but it is opening up a fantastic opportunity for all of us to get increased recognition for our Whittier education."

It remains to be seen whether the "move south" will have the desired effect. In the meantime, students seemed to be content with the quality of their education. Most gave the faculty rave reviews. "If rankings were only on quality of education, we would be Top Ten," enthused one 2L. A first-year student wrote, "The professors are extremely intelligent, and their use of the Socratic method is a breath of fresh air. For once, it is nice to actively participate and be creative." The Center for Children's Rights Program "where lawyers are specifically trained to be child advocates," was also singled out for recognition. Some students felt there was a need for more clinics.

While students were nearly unanimous in praising the quality of the professors, opinions were definitely mixed about the administration. A second-year student claimed, "Student success is not the administration's main goal." Others, though, agreed with the 3L who praised the "immediate access to the administration" and "the administration's support of student organizations." Some students also complained that the cost of a Whittier education was too high.

It is clear that Whittier is a school that is literally in transition. Students thinking about practicing in Orange County should definitely give the school serious consideration as it seems to have positioned itself perfectly. Those who are unsure of where they might want to practice could also be served well by Whittier, because the school offers more than just geographic convenience. In the words of one 3L, "I will leave here feeling as if I received a high quality education."

ADMISSIONS

In terms of the numerical standards to which it holds applicants, the Whittier College School of Law ranks as the least selective of California's sixteen law schools and, indeed, as one of the least selective in the nation. This should come as good news to those prospective students whose numerical credentials might otherwise keep them from pursuing a legal education. It should be noted, however, that Whittier is considerably less charitable to those whose performance falls short once enrolled at the law school.

ACADEMICS

Student/faculty ratio	45:1
% female faculty	21
% minority faculty	18
Hours of study per day	4.20

FINANCIAL FACTS

Tuition	$18,900
Cost of books	$250
% first-year students receiving aid	84
% all students receiving aid	90
% aid that is merit-based	3
% of all students receiving loans	81
% receiving scholarships	0
% of all students receiving assistantships	0
Average grant	$0
Average graduation debt	$65,000

ADMISSIONS

# applications received	2,339
% applicants accepted	45
% acceptees attending	23
Average LSAT	151
Average undergrad GPA	2.91
Application fee	$50
Regular application	March 15
Regular notification	rolling
Rolling notification?	Yes
Early decision program?	No
Admission may be deferred?	Yes
Maximum length of deferment	one semester
Evening division offered?	Yes
Part-time accepted?	Yes
Gourman Report Rating	**2.54**

WIDENER UNIVERSITY
School of Law

OVERVIEW

Type of school	private
Environment	metropolis
Scholastic calendar	semester
Schedule	full-time or part-time

STUDENTS

Enrollment of parent institution	2,209
Enrollment of law school	1,810
% male/female	57/43
% out-of-state	60
% part-time	33
% minorities	6
Average age at entry	26

APPLICANTS ALSO LOOK AT

Temple University
Villanova University
Rutgers University, Camden
Dickinson College Of Law
Seton Hall University

SURVEY SAYS...

HITS
Diverse faculty
Socratic method

MISSES
Library staff
Quality of teaching
Not enough courses

EMPLOYMENT PROFILE

Firms recruiting on campus	40
Job placement rate (%)	80
% grads employed immediately	45
% grads employed within six months	80
Average starting salary	$36,097

Grads employed by field (%):

Academia	2
Business/industry	21
Government	15
Judicial clerkships	18
Private practice	39
Public interest	1
Other	4

Delaware has always been a favorite state of trivia-mongers. Any self-respecting purveyor of useless factoids could tell you that this tiny mid-Atlantic state is the home of more U.S. corporations than any other state. But fewer people could tell you that Delaware is home to the largest law school in the country, the Widener University School of Law. Actually, Widener wins on a technicality, since it isn't really one law school. In 1989, this 20-year-old law school opened a branch campus in Harrisburg, Pennsylvania, at which about a third of Widener's more than 2,000 students study. Please note that both the Wilmington and Harrisburg campuses of Widener University have full, independent accreditation from the ABA. In the 1996 edition of The Best Law Schools, we mistakenly said that the Harrisburg campus was not yet fully accredited. In fact, it has been accredited since commencing operation in 1989. We were wrong, and we apologize.

The curricula at both campuses are complete; a student at Harrisburg need never see the Delaware campus in order to graduate. Emphasis on practical skills is one of the school's strengths. But the programs differ significantly. Widener has made its main campus, located in suburban Wilmington, the center for its programs in corporate and tax law. The Harrisburg branch emphasizes administrative and public law. Currently, prospective Widener students file a single application, at the top of which they designate their choice of campus. Admissions to both schools are only moderately competitive. About one-third of all applicants are accepted, and numerical standards are moderate.

The Pennsylvania students were decidedly more upbeat about their school than those who study at the older branch in Delaware. One Harrisburg student told us that Widener was "the best overall school of thirty I applied to." Students at both campuses admire and respect their professors, for the most part, but the Pennsylvania students enjoy more attention from professors thanks to the faculty's open-door policy. Over and over they made comments such as this 1L's: "I feel I have been fortunate to have extremely intelligent yet accessible professors." "The greatest strengths are the profs. They are excellent. They always have time for the students and are more than willing to help. The

Barbara Ayars, Assistant Dean for Admissions
P.O. Box 7474, 4601 Concord Pike
Wilmington, DE 19803
Tel: 302-477-2162 • Fax: 302-477-2224
Email: law.admissions@law.widener.edu
Internet: www.widener.edu/law/law.html

Widener University

community is also good. Everyone feels like a giant family. People really go out of their way for you," said a 2L. Delaware students appreciated the school, too, with a 1L listing the following reasons to attend Widener: "The two reviews on campus, the faculty, ITAP (Intense Trial Advocacy Program), moot court competition, the Widener Law Rugby Team, the Environmental Law Clinic (undefeated in litigation)" and the fact that it's a "young school, [with a] great faculty, great location, solid reputation in the Philadelphia region."

Many students however, worry that the school's reputation within and beyond Philadelphia is not strong enough. Consequently, competition and dissatisfaction with the grade deflation common at lower-ranking schools trying to inch their way up are present on both campuses. The faculty's warmth helps to offset this infighting, especially in Pennsylvania, but the lack of community spirit, thanks to a heavy commuter population, and splits between day and evening students in Delaware, plus limited social activities, means the lifestyle can leave something to be desired—unless you are on the rugby team, of course. One 2L summed up quite succinctly what Widener needed to improve on: "Recruiting, better computer systems, more up-to-date buildings (aesthetically pleasing), on campus housing!" Many also called for more practical skills training and legal writing attention. Another gave us his philosophic view of Widener, with all its good and bad qualities. He said it "fits the old cliché that 'it is what you make of it.' I have no doubt one can receive an above-average if not excellent education here if they really strive to."

ADMISSIONS

In terms of its numerical admissions standards, the Widener University School of Law ranks as one of the fifty least-selective law schools in the nation. The numerical credentials of the average Widener student are not all that far below the national average, but few law schools offer applicants with moderate-to-low grades and test scores such a good chance of admission.

ACADEMICS	
Student/faculty ratio	20:1
% female faculty	35
% minority faculty	6
Hours of study per day	3.77

Academic specialties:
Civil Procedure, Commercial, Constitutional, Corporation Securities, Criminal, Environmental, Government Services, Human Rights, International, Labor, Property

FINANCIAL FACTS	
Tuition	
Cost of books	$1,000
Room & board (on/off-campus)	$6,750/$6,750
% first-year students receiving aid	92
% all students receiving aid	87
% aid that is merit-based	7
% of all students receiving loans	91
% receiving scholarships	16
% of all students receiving assistantships	0
Average grant	$6,416
Average graduation debt	$45,910

ADMISSIONS	
# applications received	2,326
% applicants accepted	61
% acceptees attending	41
Average LSAT	150
LSAT range	141-170
Average undergrad GPA	2.90
GPA range	2.03-4.00
Application fee	$60
Regular application	rolling
Regular notification	rolling
Rolling notification?	Yes
Early decision program?	No
Admission may be deferred?	Yes
Maximum length of deferment	1 year
Evening division offered?	Yes
Part-time accepted?	Yes
Gourman Report Rating	**2.13**

WILLAMETTE UNIVERSITY
College of Law

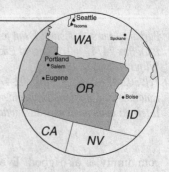

In the 1980s and early 1990s, tens of thousands of southern Californians (and numerous others as well) engaged in a mass exodus to the Pacific Northwest, transforming that region's largest cities, Seattle and Portland, in the process. But the thundering hordes left Salem, the quiet capital of Oregon and home of the Willamette University College of Law, relatively untouched. To be sure, Willamette, like the region's other law schools, has felt the impact of the burgeoning economies of these larger cities. The Pacific Northwest has become a major job market for law school graduates, a market that has absorbed its share of Willamette law grads.

Willamette (locals say wil-LAM-et, not wil-a-MET) University is located literally across the street from most of the offices of the Oregon state government, an arrangement that greatly benefits the students at its law school. The courts and other state offices employ many Willamette graduates full time, and many second- and third-year students as interns. Willamette's Law School is home to what was one of the nation's first centers for Alternative Dispute Resolution (ADR). The J.D. curriculum allows for formal specialization in this area, which explores alternatives to litigation.

Willamette College of Law has an enrollment of fewer than 500, and students are genuinely appreciative of the small-school environment. The atmosphere at the school was characterized as "great" and "cooperative," with a "family environment." In fact, some students joked that the friendly, relatively noncompetitive atmosphere had the potential to create problems. A 2L wrote, "Sometimes I think people get along too well. It can be a long process finding a quiet place in the library because everyone talks to everyone else; there is a sense of sincere camaraderie." Easy access to the professors helps to foster a positive atmosphere. "The professors here are open and accessible, so you get very intelligent, experienced professors who actually teach first-year classes and who are not too preoccupied with their own research...to take the time to speak to you," commented one 3L. A 2L touted the "kind and gentle Socratic method that most

Lawrence Seno Jr., Director of Admissions
245 Winter Street, SE
Salem, OR 97301-3922
Tel: 503-370-6282 • Fax: 503-370-6375
Email: law-admission@willamette.edu
Internet: www.willamette.edu

Willamette University

professors use, and the way all of the professors treat you as an intelligent professional."

Students also praised the facilities. "You pay a lot for tuition," a first-year student wrote, "but Willamette also spends a lot of money on their students' behalf. Classrooms and computer facilities are first-class." Other students echoed the praise for the facilities, but were decidedly unhappy with the tuition. "Nothing the school offers is worth the nearly $17,000 I pay each year," claimed one 2L. The lack of a loan forgiveness program and problems with financial aid were also noted.

By far the most common complaint among respondents, nearly all of whom were quite happy with their experience, was the lack of diversity at the Law School. "Willamette tends to reflect the somewhat homogenous culture of its surroundings," a 2L noted. "Have some diversity in the faculty," another suggested. Others recommended adding some younger faculty. It was clear that even for students who did point to shortcomings at the school, the positive aspects of going to this small school with a friendly environment, excellent faculty, and a good

ADMISSIONS

The Willamette University College of Law's numerical admissions standards rank well below the national average, and hopeful applicants' prospects are made even brighter by Willamette's overall acceptance rate of 47 percent—one of the most generous in the nation. Those applicants whose numbers equal or exceed Willamette's averages can consider admission virtually certain, and those whose numbers fall only slightly short also face very favorable odds.

ACADEMICS

Student/faculty ratio	19:1
% female faculty	28
% minority faculty	3
Hours of study per day	4.54

Academic specialties:
Government Services

FINANCIAL FACTS

Tuition	$16,350
Cost of books	$1,250
Fees	$50
Room & board (on/off-campus)	$10,820/$10,820
% first-year students receiving aid	93
% all students receiving aid	85
% aid that is merit-based	8
% of all students receiving loans	96
% receiving scholarships	28
% of all students receiving assistantships	NR
Average grant	$7,044
Average graduation debt	$64,100

ADMISSIONS

# applications received	1,037
% applicants accepted	53
% acceptees attending	24
Average LSAT	156
Average undergrad GPA	3.20
Application fee	$50
Regular application	March 15
Regular notification	February-June
Rolling notification?	No
Early decision program?	No
Admission may be deferred?	Yes
Maximum length of deferment	1 year
Evening division offered?	No
Part-time accepted?	Yes
Gourman Report Rating	**3.61**

WILLIAM AND MARY
School of Law

OVERVIEW

Type of school	public
Environment	town
Scholastic calendar	semester
Schedule	full-time only

STUDENTS

Enrollment of parent institution	5,326
Enrollment of law school	532
% male/female	56/44
% out-of-state	35
% minorities	17
% international (# of countries represented)	NR (6)
Average age at entry	25

APPLICANTS ALSO LOOK AT

University of Virginia
Washington and Lee University
George Washington University
University of Richmond
Georgetown University

SURVEY SAYS...

HITS
Practical lawyering skills
Legal writing
Students feel well prepared

MISSES
Not enough courses

EMPLOYMENT PROFILE

Firms recruiting on campus	143
Job placement rate (%)	95
% grads employed immediately	62
% grads employed within six months	95
Average starting salary	$48,324

Grads employed by field (%):

Academia	3
Business/industry	7
Government	9
Judicial clerkships	18
Military	1
Private practice	60
Public interest	3
Other	6

The College of William and Mary, established in 1693 by King William III and Queen Mary II of England, is the second oldest in the country. The law school in its current incarnation is a little over fifty years old, but the tradition of legal education at William and Mary dates back much further, to 1779, when, at the behest of Thomas Jefferson, the university established the first Chair of Law in the newly independent United States. A list of men who studied law at the university in this era reads like an American history textbook; the law chair's first occupant, Declaration of Independence signer George Wythe, and the legendary Chief Justice John Marshall, gave William and Mary's Law School its full name: The Marshall-Wythe School of Law.

With a student body of about 500, W&M is the smallest of Virginia's three outstanding public law schools, all of them excellent bargains. While numerical standards and recognition at the school are not as high as those at the better-known University of Virginia School of Law in Charlottesville, William and Mary enjoys a strong reputation that extends well beyond the surrounding region, and it attracts a highly qualified group of applicants.

The school has devised a curriculum that emphasizes practical-skills training, ensuring that its graduates are well prepared for practice. W&M's innovative Legal Skills Program, a nine-credit, two-year mandatory program, helps students master lawyering skills and ethical concepts. First-year students enter the program during a week of intensive instruction prior to the start of the semester. Each student then becomes part of a group of about fifteen who comprise a simulated law office. During the program's two-year life, students, representing simulated clients, are introduced to a wide range of skills: interviewing, counseling, negotiating, researching, writing opinion letters and briefs, and arguing cases.

It's no wonder that over 80 percent of current students rated the practical instruction at W&M as excellent. Not only did the students extol the faculty for accessibility, dedication to teaching, and genuine concern for their pupils, they also spoke highly of the

Faye F. Shealy, Associate Dean
Office of Admissions, P.O. Box 8795
Williamsburg, VA 23187-8795
Tel: 757-221-3785 • Fax: 757-221-3261
Email: lawadm@facstaff.wm.edu
Internet: www.wm.edu

William and Mary

school's focus on clinical settings. As a 1L put it, "If you want to learn skills that will make you an effective real-life lawyer, the Legal Skills Program here will make it happen."

Students extended their praise to many other aspects of their education at W&M. Despite an "extremely challenging academic environment," almost everyone we heard from made a point to mention the pervading sense of community among the student body, describing "a place where the students know each other and care about each other—a rare asset in a law school." A 2L credited the community-orientated mindset of W&M with the existence of a "student-initiated and run, non-profit corporation that raises over $40,000 to find summer public interest jobs." And if you're worried about finding a job after graduation, you might want to consider that students at W&M were uniformly positive about their career services office—rare praise as students nationwide feel the bite of a hostile job market. "The career planning staff, while not large, is extremely helpful and effective in generating interest among a broad range of employer," wrote one 2L. "I have often sought, and always received, individual advice."

Students offered much more elusive criticisms of W&M. Besides some minor gripes about unfriendly photocopiers and the decor in the student lounge, the only universal complaint was directed at the facilities. A lack of classroom space has restricted class sizes and many feel that William and Mary is "busting at the seams." However, the school is currently planning to break ground on a 20,000 square foot addition in the summer of 1998 that will effectively expand the law school and free up much needed space. Regardless of space constraints, students are extremely pleased with their school. According to one, "William and Mary is affordable and a respectable institution—a necessary combination in a market flooded by lawyers."

ADMISSIONS

Eighteen applicants vie annually for each place in William and Mary's Marshall-Wythe School of Law's entering class, making the law school one of the thirty most in-demand in the United States. If you want to be among the 170 students admitted to William and Mary, you had better be sure your numerical credentials are in shape.

ACADEMICS

Student/faculty ratio	13:1
% female faculty	26
% minority faculty	7
Hours of study per day	3.57

Academic specialties:
Civil Procedure, Commercial, Constitutional, Corporation Securities, Criminal, Environmental, Government Services, Human Rights, International, Labor, Legal History, Legal Philosophy, Property, Taxation

FINANCIAL FACTS

Tuition (in/out-state)	$7,758/$17,574
Cost of books	$800
% first-year students receiving aid	40
% all students receiving aid	40
% aid that is merit-based	12
% of all students receiving loans	75
% receiving scholarships	33
% of all students receiving assistantships	4
Average grant	$2,000
Average graduation debt	$50,000

ADMISSIONS

# applications received	2,681
% applicants accepted	28
% acceptees attending	26
Average LSAT	162
LSAT range	145-173
Average undergrad GPA	3.36
GPA range	2.27-3.96
Application fee (in/out-state)	$40/$40
Regular application	March 1
Regular notification	March 31
Rolling notification?	No
Early decision program?	No
Admission may be deferred?	Yes
Maximum length of deferment	1 year
Evening division offered?	No
Part-time accepted?	No
Gourman Report Rating	**3.44**

WILLIAM MITCHELL COLLEGE OF LAW

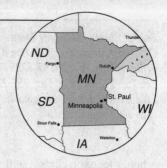

OVERVIEW

Type of school	private
Environment	metropolis
Scholastic calendar	semester
Schedule	full-time or part-time

STUDENTS

Enrollment of parent institution	NR
Enrollment of law school	1,052
% male/female	52/48
% out-of-state	17
% part-time	49
% minorities	11
% international (# of countries represented)	1 (8)
Average age at entry	26

APPLICANTS ALSO LOOK AT

Hamline University
University of Minnesota
Drake University
DePaul University
University of Wisconsin

SURVEY SAYS...

HITS
Practical lawyering skills
Legal writing

MISSES
Not enough courses

EMPLOYMENT PROFILE

Firms recruiting on campus	68
Job placement rate (%)	93
% grads employed immediately	63
% grads employed within six months	91
Average starting salary	$40,184

Grads employed by field (%):

Academia	2
Business/industry	27
Government	14
Judicial clerkships	10
Private practice	47
Public interest	1

William Mitchell College of Law traces its roots back more than 100 years. This large private institution evolved from six predecessor schools, the earliest of which was the St. Paul College of Law, founded in 1900, and is named after William Mitchell, an associate justice of the Minnesota Supreme Court. William Mitchell is far and away the state's largest law school, with large entering classes of around 340 students.

The school is best known for its commitment to making law school accessible to all people. As the only law school in the state offering a part-time option—and one of the only law schools in the nation to provide an on-campus daycare for students with children—William Mitchell gives thousands of future lawyers the opportunity to pursue a legal education. The school even offers special late-afternoon courses for added flexibility in addition to day and evening courses.

When asked to discuss their school's strengths, nearly every student surveyed discussed the practical bent of the Mitchell J.D. program. "William Mitchell would be an excellent choice for people who wish to excel in the practical aspects of the legal profession," said one 3L. The school's strong emphasis on practical skills is evident in course offerings, which include an increasing number of "lawyering" classes. William Mitchell also has very extensive clinical programs to help students integrate classroom instruction into practical lawyering early on in their academic careers. Students at William Mitchell praised their chosen school particularly for the most fundamental aspect of their law school experience: their training as lawyers. A 3L praised the school's "hands-on practicum programs and 'real-world' practice and preparation skills." Students also showed appreciation for the school's part-time option, as well as the general "flexibility of the curriculum" that includes over 100 elective course offerings.

While many students praised William Mitchell's curriculum and wide array of courses, a minority of the student body called for more variety of courses offered amid what it claims is a business-oriented curriculum. "[The school] is weak in offering diverse courses from many business-type courses," said a 2L.

Dr. James H. Brooks, Dean of Students
875 Summit Avenue
St. Paul, MN 55105
Tel: 888-962-5529
Email: admissions@wmitchell.edu
Internet: www.wmitchell.edu

William Mitchell College of Law

The vast majority of students surveyed rated the quality of teaching as excellent or very good, but we did hear some negative comments, particularly regarding adjunct professors. "The faculty is too unpredictable. [There are] too many inexperienced adjunct faculty, and too much concentration on Minnesota law," said one 3L. When it came to the legal writing program at William Mitchell, students were even more critical of their instruction. "The legal writing course is supposed to be extremely important but some of the adjunct faculty don't have the time to come to class or meet with students," wrote one 2L.

Students did indicate a need for racial, ethnic, and political diversity among the student body and faculty. One student, a 1L, noted: "Most students are from the Midwest. The school would do well to bring in some new blood." Another student, a 2L, was more specific, in calling for "more female and diverse faculty" at the school.

Many students at William Mitchell believe the school's biggest weakness is its lack of a national reputation. William Mitchell students are confident that their school is providing them with a solid, practical education with enough flexibility for many "non-traditional" students.

ADMISSIONS

William Mitchell College of Law is at the bottom third of all U.S. law schools in terms of its numerical standards and selectivity. The prospects of the hopeful William Mitchell applicant are made even brighter by the law school's overall acceptance rate of 53 percent—one of the most generous rates of admission in the nation.

ACADEMICS	
Student/faculty ratio	23:1
% female faculty	28
% minority faculty	37
Hours of study per day	3.74

FINANCIAL FACTS	
Tuition	$15,330
Cost of books	$610
Fees	$30
% first-year students receiving aid	85
% all students receiving aid	86
% aid that is merit-based	3
% of all students receiving loans	81
% receiving scholarships	24
% of all students receiving assistantships	8
Average grant	$3,100
Average graduation debt	$54,380

ADMISSIONS	
# applications received	1,200
% applicants accepted	67
% acceptees attending	37
Average LSAT	153
LSAT range	140-171
Average undergrad GPA	3.15
GPA range	2.00-4.00
Application fee	$45
Regular application	July 1
Regular notification	rolling
Rolling notification?	Yes
Early decision program?	No
Admission may be deferred?	Yes
Maximum length of deferment	1 year
Evening division offered?	Yes
Part-time accepted?	Yes
Gourman Report Rating	**2.90**

UNIVERSITY OF WISCONSIN
Law School

OVERVIEW

Type of school	public
Environment	city
Scholastic calendar	semester
Schedule	full-time or part-time

STUDENTS

Enrollment of parent institution	26,207
Enrollment of law school	904
% male/female	56/44
% out-of-state	27
% part-time	7
% minorities	20
% international (# of countries represented)	2 (17)
Average age at entry	25

APPLICANTS ALSO LOOK AT

Marquette University
University of Minnesota
George Washington University
University of California, Berkeley
University of Michigan

SURVEY SAYS...

HITS
Practical experience
Diverse faculty

MISSES
Library staff
Not enough courses

EMPLOYMENT PROFILE

Job placement rate (%)	88
% grads employed immediately	65
% grads employed within six months	88
Average starting salary	$46,000

The 125-year-old University of Wisconsin Law School is, simply stated, one of the most highly regarded public law schools in the country. Its long-standing reputation for excellence both derives from and contributes to its parent institution's widely acknowledged status as one of the finest universities in the hemisphere. Some combination of the vast resources of the broader university and the law school's own impressive strengths (e.g., its widely respected faculty) draws one of the most highly qualified groups of law students in the nation to Madison, Wisconsin.

In the eyes of those who run the law school, Wisconsin's success must be understood in terms of the philosophy to which the law school subscribes, an idea they call "Law in Action." As a guiding principle, this phrase is meant to convey a recognition on the part of the law school of the social context of the law, or "how the law relates to social change and to society as a whole." The tangible manifestations of this recognition are evident in the breadth of Wisconsin's classroom curriculum and in the size and variety of its clinical programs, which serve the dual purpose of providing law students the opportunity to gain and hone practical lawyering skills while also involving them extensively in the world outside the law school. Wisconsin is certainly not unique in its recognition of the importance of clinical education, but it is notable for its commitment to making participation in such programs possible for more than a small segment of its student body. The school's clinical programs and focus on practical skills garnered high praise from students. "Wisconsin is a hands-on place where students and faculty live and work as professionals," reported one 3L.

Despite the variety of course offerings, students called for a broader range of courses and an increase to the already substantial number of "hands-on" courses offered at UW. "The school is beginning to take a more practical approach but needs to do more. There must be a balance of practical experience with academics. There is still too much of an attempt of the latter," suggested a 3L. Most of the specific criticisms regarding the curriculum focused on Wisconsin's legal writing program. One student, a 2L, made this comment: "Improve the legal writing program! It consumes

James E. Thomas, Assistant Dean,
Dean of Admissions and Financial Aid
975 Bascom Mall
Madison, WI 53706
Tel: 608-262-8558

an exorbitant amount of time, but no one really learns the needed skills." Another student suggested: "If they really want us to write well, offer more instruction and support."

The well-respected faculty figured heavily in Wisconsin students' generally positive assessments of their chosen school. When asked to list the school's strengths, students made comments like "excellent faculty," "faculty that actually knows how to teach," and "professors listen to us!" One student gave us this run-down of Wisconsin's selling points: "Excellent reputation and credentials, especially for the low cost of in-state tuition, nationally-recognized faculty."

The terms most often used to describe the social climate at the law school were "laid-back," "liberal," and "friendly." One student, a 1L, made this observation: "The most surprising—and pleasant—thing about coming to UW Law was the amount of beer that is consumed for just about any reason. This helps create a very laid-back atmosphere. Also, in my first semester, three out of four of my professors invited groups of students to their homes for parties or out for pizza and beer." Although certainly not all Wisconsin law students are party animals, this is, for the most part, a non-competitive and relaxed group of students.

Students agree that new facilities dramatically improve and greatly enhance their school.

One cannot help but be impressed by the overall sense of well-being that most Wisconsin students conveyed, as summed up by this 1L: "Wisconsin is the best deal in the country! Great faculty, great students, great environment, great tuition. Now, with the new law library, the package will be complete."

ADMISSIONS

Students admitted to the University of Wisconsin Law School are some of the best and the brightest in the country. Numerical averages of those attending this public law school are very strong, and the admissions process is quite competitive.

ACADEMICS

Student/faculty ratio	20:1
% female faculty	20
% minority faculty	15
Hours of study per day	3.87

FINANCIAL FACTS

Tuition (in/out-state)	$5,211/$13,488
Cost of books	$1,620
% first-year students receiving aid	NR
% all students receiving aid	42
% aid that is merit-based	10
% of all students receiving loans	77
% receiving scholarships	56
% of all students receiving assistantships	1
Average grant	NR
Average graduation debt	$31,708

ADMISSIONS

# applications received	2,220
% applicants accepted	32
% acceptees attending	39
Average LSAT	158
Average undergrad GPA	3.35
Application fee (in/out-state)	$38
Regular application	February 1
Regular notification	rolling
Rolling notification?	Yes
Early decision program?	No
Admission may be deferred?	Yes
Maximum length of deferment	1 year
Evening division offered?	No
Part-time accepted?	No
Gourman Report Rating	**4.47**

UNIVERSITY OF WYOMING
College of Law

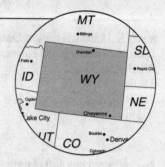

OVERVIEW

Type of school	public
Environment	town
Scholastic calendar	semester
Schedule	full-time only

STUDENTS

Enrollment of parent institution	11,000
Enrollment of law school	211
% male/female	56/44
% out-of-state	30
% part-time	NR
% minorities	6
% international (# of countries represented)	1 (2)
Average age at entry	24

APPLICANTS ALSO LOOK AT

University of Colorado
University of Denver
Arizona State University
Creighton University
University of Arizona

SURVEY SAYS...

HITS
Studying
Sense of community
Faculty-student relations

MISSES
Not enough courses
Quality of teaching

EMPLOYMENT PROFILE

Job placement rate (%)	85
% grads employed immediately	40
% grads employed within six months	80
Average starting salary	$33,000

Grads employed by field (%):

Business/industry	9
Government	11
Judicial clerkships	9
Private practice	65
Public interest	6

Until you have been to Wyoming, you have not seen the real face of the American West. The borders of the nation's forty-ninth least populous state encompass some of the world's most spectacular, least spoiled mountain wilderness and some of the nation's best ranch land. Wyoming's economy is dominated by agriculture and natural resources, and it may be the only state in the union that is home to more cowboys than law students. Indeed, the suitably small University of Wyoming School of Law is the state's only law school. If every state were to have only one law school, however, Wyoming's would serve as an ideal model. Situated on the handsome campus of its very well funded and highly respected parent institution, the UW law school is very small, very inexpensive and very solid. With sixteen full-time faculty members and a tiny student body, the law school offers favorable conditions for learning, conditions that are further enhanced by the significant resources of the broader university. Like any good public law school, Wyoming administers a J.D. program that clearly reflects the priorities of its home state. The curriculum is particularly strong, for example, in natural-resources law. Located in Laramie, a university and ranching town of about 35,000 set among the Rocky Mountains, UW is within easy reach of some of America's best spots for hiking, skiing, fishing, and, as the law school's admissions bulletin points out, big-game hunting. These activities are an important part of life in and around the law school, but no more so than is studying, for Wyoming's curriculum is traditional and rigorous. Applications volume at the law school is light, but the overall acceptance rate is kept low. Numerical admissions standards are moderate.

Distinctly immoderate, however, is the enthusiasm most Wyoming law students seem to feel for the quality of life at their chosen school. Though they criticized some important aspects of their program, students here sounded a clear and positive overall theme. In the words of one 3L, "If you want to go to a school where people leave bookmarks in casebooks to help you, where the mountains clear your head, where everybody is nice, and if you don't mind country music, then Wyoming is the place for you." To judge from this and other responses to our survey, the University of Wyoming College of Law succeeds in creating on campus

Debra J. Madsen, Associate Dean
P.O. Box 3035
Laramie, WY 82071
Tel: 307-766-6416
Email: candid@uwyo.edu
Internet: www.uwyo.edu

the kind of "family atmosphere" to which so many other schools merely pay lip service. "The small class size here fosters a great sense of community among the students," wrote one 2L, "and nearly all of them are willing to help one another." "It's a close-knit community based on trust and freedom," added one pleased 1L. "You can leave stuff anywhere in the school and not worry about it being gone when you return." Not surprisingly, most of the students we heard from pointed to the law school's manageable size and favorable student-faculty ratio in explaining their overall comfort and satisfaction. "Both small school size and long, cold winters help build a great community here," explained one 2L before going on to advise that "if you're not prepared for seven months of winter, don't even think about coming here."

Most Wyoming students we heard from tempered their enthusiasm with more substantive criticism. "It's great to be able to get personal attention," said one 2L, "but it would also be great if you could get any book you wanted in the library and access to a working computer." Many others had similar complaints concerning the inevitable limitations of such a tiny school. "Course selection is good in some areas but limited in most," wrote a 3L, "and the small faculty makes the poor teachers really stand out." Indeed, few here raved about the breadth of their curriculum or the overall quality of their instructors. But consider the words of one student who was as critical as any: "I will never regret my decision to come here. Wyoming has everything I want in a school and it is a tremendous value."

ADMISSIONS

In terms of numerical admissions standards, the University of Wyoming School of Law ranks as one of the most selective law schools in the West. This fact is particularly remarkable when one considers that only about 600 people apply annually to this tiny, inexpensive law school. Unhappily for the prospective Wyoming student, however, applicants are not admitted across a relatively broad range of grade-point averages and test scores.

ACADEMICS

Student/faculty ratio	15:1
% female faculty	39
% minority faculty	0
Hours of study per day	4.57

FINANCIAL FACTS

Tuition (in/out-state)	$4,234/$9,322
Cost of books	$600
Room & board (on/off-campus)	$6,800/$8,500
% first-year students receiving aid	75
% all students receiving aid	75
% aid that is merit-based	NR
% of all students receiving loans	75
% receiving scholarships	33
% of all students receiving assistantships	6
Average grant	NR
Average graduation debt	$30,000

ADMISSIONS

# applications received	548
% applicants accepted	47
% acceptees attending	3
Average LSAT	154
LSAT range	145-173
Average undergrad GPA	3.30
Application fee (in/out-state)	$35
Early application	February 15
Early notification	March 15
Regular application	April 1
Regular notification	May
Rolling notification?	No
Early decision program?	Yes
Admission may be deferred?	No
Evening division offered?	No
Part-time accepted?	No
Gourman Report Rating	**2.74**

YALE UNIVERSITY
Yale Law School

Yale students, situated as they unfortunately are in New Haven, do not consider their surroundings much of a plus. "The buildings are crappy. The computer room is too small. The social life could be more accommodating," complains a 1L. "The library is a Gothic chamber of terror without adequate lighting and with a labyrinthine dungeon five stories high which I'm afraid to research in after night fall, and increased enrollment is crowding the school," bellyaches another. "The paint is flaking, the toilets overflow, the carpet is ripped." Yeah, it must really suck attending arguably the most prestigious law school on the planet where there are no grades and a diploma virtually guarantees you pick of the legal job litter. It's Bill's and Hillary's alma mater for crying out loud. So what if the paint chips?

The Yale curriculum is innovative, flexible, and broad, not only in terms of traditional classroom offerings but also in terms of clinical programs. Essentially, though, "Constitutional Law is all that is taught here." Explain a 1L: "They don't bog us down in the details." The curriculum is also, believe it or not, "a breeze" According to a 2L, "Everyone passes first semester. In the past, a professor tried to fail a student but the Dean wouldn't allow it. Another professor responded to a crying student who claimed to have blanked on her exam by saying, 'Don't worry. The grades are already in.'" The "phenomenally knowledgeable and insightful" faculty is outrageously qualified and the "administration has an anything-is-possible attitude." With six journals, nearly a dozen clinical programs, and countless student organizations, Yale offers nothing if not options. The resources available to every student here "are tremendous. You really have the opportunity to do anything." A 3L elaborates: "With the school's money, connections, and willingness, combined with the amazingly enthusiastic and hard-working students, you can do just about anything. You can put together a comprehensive tutorial program for inner-city kids or host a major international feminist legal conference. The trick is to figure out who in the administration is authorized to make an actual decision about anything."

Yale is unique in its service law students who do not necessarily want the highest-paying jobs in the finest New York City firms. Not that they couldn't get them. But most Yale grads are more

Lauretta Tremblay, Associate Director of Admissions
P.O. Box 208329
New Haven, CT 06520-8215
Tel: 203-432-4995
Email: admissions@mail.law.yale.edu
Internet: www.law.yale.edu

Yale University

likely to begin their careers in judicial clerkships, or to pursue more non-traditional avenues of employment. "One of the advantages of Yale is that you needn't specialize," relates a 1L. "Most of us don't have set career plans, but will be able to seize whatever opportunities present themselves." A 3L agrees: "I had no problems finding a job and a clerkship coming from Yale. Rightly or wrongly, the reputation helps a great deal. The stress comes from having to choose between the numerous job offers you have, any one of which would satisfy you. It's amazing!" Yale has a great loan forgiveness program in the nation (covering all educational debt). "So if you want to work in government or public interest positions, Yale makes it financially possible."

The combined "intellectual firepower" among the "ultra-talented overachievers" here is mind-boggling. Students say "there are a lot of really wonderful, good-hearted people here. But there are a handful of truly arrogant and obnoxious people to balance things out and make your blood boil." It's a "low-stress atmosphere" because "there are, in all honesty, no real concerns about grades." Also, "Yale is teeny, which translates into smallish classes, faculty accessibility, and lots of fun hanging out in the dining hall." A 2L explains: "The environment is incestuous at times. From the same group of individuals, you must draw your friends, colleagues, and lovers. Sometimes I think we each wear too many hats. It's like someone giving you a tray of ingredients and saying, 'From these you must make your breakfast, lunch, and dinner.' But in general the benefits of being in a small academic and social community far outweigh the disadvantages. The social cohesion keeps you afloat when the academic drudgery weighs you down." Sticking with the food theme, "If Yale Law School were a food, it would be a Happy Meal. It's not very nutritious, but it tastes good and you get a prize at the end." And, as we hear Scott Turow recently said, "I wish I had gone to Yale."

ADMISSIONS

If you hope to have better than a one in ten chance of gaining admission to what may be the country's finest law school, you had better have an undergraduate GPA above 3.75 from a respected university and an LSAT score at or above 165 - the 94th percentile. Even applicants with those kinds of credentials are denied admission 75 percent of the time, and those whose numbers fall more than slightly lower are hoping for a miracle. Best of luck!

ACADEMICS

Student/faculty ratio	10:1
% female faculty	17
% minority faculty	7
Hours of study per day	3.42

FINANCIAL FACTS

Tuition	$21,692
Cost of books	$740
% first-year students receiving aid	70
% all students receiving aid	75
% aid that is merit-based	NR
% of all students receiving loans	70
% receiving scholarships	40
% of all students receiving assistantships	NR
Average grant	$9,000
Average graduation debt	$50,000

ADMISSIONS

# applications received	3,811
% applicants accepted	8
% acceptees attending	61
Average LSAT	171
Average undergrad GPA	3.83
GPA range	2.70-4.00
Application fee	$65
Regular application	February 15
Regular notification	rolling
Rolling notification?	Yes
Early decision program?	No
Admission may be deferred?	Yes
Evening division offered?	No
Part-time accepted?	No
Gourman Report Rating	**4.90**

YESHIVA UNIVERSITY
Benjamin N. Cardozo School of Law

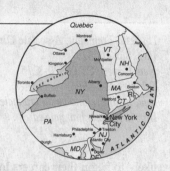

OVERVIEW

Type of school	private
Environment	metropolis
Scholastic calendar	semester
Schedule	full-time only

STUDENTS

Enrollment of parent institution	5,200
Enrollment of law school	950
% male/female	54/46
% out-of-state	40
% part-time	NR
% minorities	16
% international (# of countries represented)	NR (11)
Average age at entry	23

APPLICANTS ALSO LOOK AT

Brooklyn Law School
Fordham University
New York University
New York Law School
Columbia University

SURVEY SAYS...

HITS
Sleeping
Academic reputation
Grads expect big bucks

MISSES
Library staff
Practical lawyering skills
Not enough courses

EMPLOYMENT PROFILE

Firms recruiting on campus	85
Job placement rate (%)	92
% grads employed within six months	92
Average starting salary	$54,301

Grads employed by field (%):

Academia	3
Business/industry	12
Government	11
Judicial clerkships	7
Private practice	59
Public interest	4
Other	4

In the span of just two decades, Yeshiva University has built an astonishingly successful law school from the ground up, and while the intangible quality "prestige" is generally something that a law school either acquired or lost long before any of us were born, the Benjamin N. Cardozo School of Law enjoys, at the very least, tremendous respect.

To earn this respect, Cardozo has had to impress both applicants and employers, something it has done by assembling a highly accomplished faculty, the indispensable foundation of any good law school. Cardozo's academic strengths are nicely augmented by a heavy emphasis on practical preparation for the practice of law. The law school's own clinical programs are extensive, and external placement opportunities are as numerous and richly varied as one would expect in a city that is home to the country's largest legal community. Cardozo is one of the few law schools in the country that allows students to begin their studies in either September, January, or May. The flexible Accelerated Entry Plan also gives the approximately ninety students who enter in January or May the opportunity to complete their legal education in two and a half years as opposed to the traditional three. These strengths, along with the increasing success of Cardozo graduates in finding employment with prestigious firms, help explain the rising popularity of this law school. Moreover, thanks to the success of its graduates and to the ongoing efforts of its faculty and administration, this is a law school still very much on the rise.

Students at Cardozo told a remarkably consistent story when asked about the strengths of their school. "The faculty is well-regarded, well-written, and generally good at teaching," reported one typical student. And accessible, too, according to an excited classmate: "I learn more in office hours and in the bars with them than in class." Many students offered ringing endorsements of their program's overall strength as well: "So far in school," claimed a 1L, "I've learned more in three months than I did in four years of college." Try not to be intimidated, though, as a fellow student advised: "All of my first-year professors started off slowly so we could get the hang of it before picking up the pace." Clinical opportunities in New York abound and all of our

Robert L. Schwartz, Director of Admssions
55 Fifth Avenue
New York, NY 10003
Tel: 212-790-0274 • Fax: 212-790-0345
Email: lawinfo@ymail.yu.edu
Internet: www.yu.edu/csl/law

Yeshiva University

respondents felt that the internships and externships available bring a wealth of real-world experience to the classroom. Many described the atmosphere at the Cardozo as "quite competitive," but one student had some compelling insight into his classmates' need to achieve: "There is a strong feeling of commitment," he explained, "because the students know that the school is young and that their performance will dictate Cardozo's standing in the future."

Cardozo students were quick to answer when asked to name the areas in which their school could stand to improve. Most seemed pleased with their general location, but none could muster any enthusiasm for the physical plant. Complaints ranged from the lack of computers to the presence of obstructive poles in classrooms. One befuddled student mused, "Either the organization of the law or of the library is in a state of disarray. I'm not sure which." A lack of diversity and the effects of the law school's Jewish tradition on administrative policies—the closure of the library on Sabbath from Friday afternoon through Saturday—are both causes for division among students, and many feel the school should take a more active role in helping to resolve these issues. Although many adamantly denounced Cardozo's placement office for concentrating recruitment efforts on the top 10 percent of classes, employment statistics suggest that Cardozo students have less reason to be concerned about the tightening New York job market than many others. The overwhelming majority of those we heard from expressed a high degree of satisfaction with their decision to attend Cardozo.

ADMISSIONS

With more than eight applicants vying for each spot in its entering class of about 250, the Benjamin N. Cardozo School of Law is in a position to select its students carefully. Although Cardozo ranks fourth among Manhattan's five law schools in terms of the numerical standards to which it holds applicants, it ranks among the seventy most selective schools in the nation. For a law school with such high numerical standards, however, Cardozo has a relatively generous overall acceptance rate.

ACADEMICS

Student/faculty ratio	21:1
% female faculty	31
% minority faculty	4
Hours of study per day	3.27

Academic specialties:
Civil Procedure, Commercial, Constitutional, Corporation Securities, Criminal, Human Rights, International, Legal Philosophy, Property, Taxation

FINANCIAL FACTS

Tuition	$18,825
Cost of books	$220
Room & board (on/off-campus)	NR/$17,742
% first-year students receiving aid	64
% all students receiving aid	67
% aid that is merit-based	30
% of all students receiving loans	41
% receiving scholarships	55
% of all students receiving assistantships	6
Average grant	$2,193
Average graduation debt	$55,000

ADMISSIONS

# applications received	2,201
% applicants accepted	48
% acceptees attending	33
Average LSAT	157
LSAT range	147-174
Average undergrad GPA	3.34
Application fee	$60
Regular application	April 1
Regular notification	rolling
Rolling notification?	Yes
Early decision program?	No
Admission may be deferred?	Yes
Maximum length of deferment	1 year
Evening division offered?	No
Part-time accepted?	No
Gourman Report Rating	**3.82**

THE CBA SCHOOLS

INTRODUCTION

As of April 1997, there are fifty-seven law schools in the state of California. However, you're only going to find sixteen of them in any publication that is prepared in conjunction with the ABA. That's because there are forty-one law schools in California that are *not* approved by the ABA. Why not? Well, the ABA does have certain standards for accreditation—such as the number of volumes in the law school library, the school's bar pass rate, etc. But if your intention is to learn the law, there are many schools not approved by the ABA that do a fine job teaching the law.

Many states, such as Massachusetts, Florida, and Alabama have a few schools that are not ABA-approved. One such school, the University of Massachusetts School of Law, is continually at war with the ABA over its accreditation process (see the interview with University of Massachusetts School of Law Dean Lawrence Velvel on page tktk).

While it's nice to have options, many states do have restrictions on what graduates of these non-accredited law schools are allowed to do. Very few states will allow other states' non-ABA school graduates to sit for a bar exam. If you are interested in a non-ABA school in a specific state, it would be best to obtain documentation from, and have conversations with, that state's Board of Bar Examiners (every state has one). Some boards, such as California's, provide tons of excellent information on their web sites (California's is www.calbar.org).

Ah, California . . . land of hopes and dreams. Land of such law schools as the Larry H. Layton School of Law, in Acton. When you call the Layton School of Law, Larry Layton himself picks up the phone! Another school is rumored to be run out of someone's garage (hey—it's not so bad . . . there are some pretty large garages in the state of California). Actually, there are so many law schools in the state of California that the California Committee of Bar Examiners did something about it—they created their own accreditation process.

The State Bar of California lists fifty-seven law schools in their web site. There are five categories of accreditation—every school is in a category. Here are the California Bar's categories and the number of schools in each category:

CATEGORY NUMBER

Category	Number
Approved by the American Bar Association	16
Accredited by the California Committee of Bar Examiners	17
Unaccredited, but Preliminary Approved by the California Committee of Bar Examiners	0
Unaccredited	16
Correspondence Law Courses	8

TOTAL 57

In 1996, for instance, Southern California Institute of Law (with campuses in both Ventura and Santa Barbara) was listed under the "Unaccredited, but Preliminarily Approved by the California Committee of Bar Examiners" category. Subsequently, they received accreditation and are now listed under "Accredited by the California Committee of Bar Examiners." So, Southern California Institute of Law is now considered a "CBA" school.

What does it mean to be a CBA (California Bar Association) law school? It means that the State of California, for the purposes of licensing you as a lawyer, considers graduates from these schools to be equal to ABA-approved schools in California. If you graduate from a CBA-approved school, you don't have to jump through any extra hoops during the California Bar Exam and licensing processes. Here's a brief summary of the educational requirements needed to sit for the California Bar:

SUMMARY OF EDUCATIONAL REQUIREMENTS TO TAKE THE CALIFORNIA BAR EXAMINATION

Eligibility questions should be referred to the Office of Admissions, The State Bar of California, 1149 Hill Street, Los Angeles, California 90015-2299. To be eligible to take the California Bar Examination, one must have completed at least two years of college before entering law studies or passed specified College Level Equivalency Program (CLEP) examinations administered by the College Board and graduated from a law school approved by the American Bar Association or accredited by the Committee of Bar Examiners of The State Bar of California or completed four years of legal studies at an institution authorized to confer degrees.

Those studying at a law school not approved by the American Bar Association or accredited by the Committee of Bar Examiners of The State Bar of California must take and pass an examination upon completion of their first year of law study and before commencing their second year. Individuals may also qualify to take the California Bar Examination by four years of qualifying law office or correspondence study. They, too, must take and pass the First-Year Law Students' Examination before commencing their second year of law study.

As you can see from the italicized paragraph above, if you're going to a school in California that is not approved by either the ABA or the CBA, you've got some extra work on your hands. Students who attend "unaccredited" law schools in the state of California must pass an extra examination to receive "credit" for their first year of law school—an exam called the "First-Year Law Students' Examination" or, more commonly, the "Baby Bar."

The Baby Bar is pretty much exactly what you might think—a shorter version of California's brutal, interminable, three-day bar exam. The Baby Bar lasts one day—essays in the morning, and a 100-question multiple-choice test (on Contracts, Torts, and Constitutional Law) in the afternoon. You cannot take the California Bar Exam and be licensed in California as a lawyer if you went to an unaccredited California Law School and did not pass the Baby Bar. Seems like no problem, right? Well, here's a little chart on Baby Bar pass rates in the last few years:

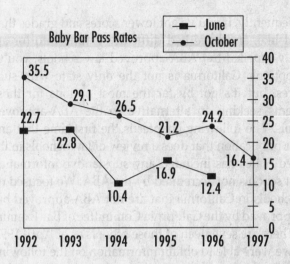

Baby Bar Pass Rates

Legend: June ■, October ●

Year	June	October
1992	22.7	35.5
1993	22.8	29.1
1994	10.4	26.5
1995	16.9	21.2
1996	12.4	24.2
1997		16.4

As you can see, the numbers are not too promising. Students take the Baby Bar again, and again, and again. And once they pass the Baby Bar and graduate from an unaccredited school, passing the California Bar is still far from simple. Here are the pass rates from the July 1995 California Bar Exam, by specific categories of students who where taking the Bar for both the first time and students who were repeating the exam:

LAW SCHOOL CATEGORY	1st TIME TAKERS PASS RATE	REPEATER PASS RATE
California Law Schools Accredited by the American Bar Association	83.1%	25.6%
California Law Schools Accredited by the Committee of the State Bar of California	48.2%	14.8%
California Law School Not Accredited by the ABA or the CBA	36.8%	5.3%
Correspondence by Law Schools	30.0%	11.1%
Overall California Pass Rate	**73.4%**	**N/A**

Source: The State Bar of California, "Bar Admissions."

As you can see, graduating from an ABA-approved school gives you a better chance of passing the California Bar the first time around. However, law school is not there specifically to teach you how to pass the bar exam. It is mind training and the teaching of the law in a very specific way. The bar exam is merely just another in a long line of moronic, pseudo-intellectual standardized tests that you'll take.

Consequently, if you've got lower scores and grades than you'd like, and have had difficulty getting into (or are merely repelled by) ABA-approved law schools, you've got options. California is not the only state with such choices, but it's got by far the most options for those students seeking an alternative to the ABA-approved schools. The following chapter is the first time that any major publication that does a review of law schools in the United States has included any substantive information about schools not accredited by the ABA. We focused on the schools in California that are not ABA-approved but are approved by the California Committee of Bar Examiners. There are seventeen of those schools as of April 1997, and we were able to obtain information on the following twelve.

Cal Northern

California Pacific

Glendale University

Humphrey's College

John F. Kennedy University

University of LaVerne

Lincoln Law School of San Jose

New College of California

San Francisco Law School

San Joaquin College of Law

University of West Los Angeles

Western State University

And now for the schools ...

CAL NORTHERN SCHOOL OF LAW

1395 Ridgewood Drive
Chico, CA 95928
Tel: 916-891-6900 • Fax: 916-891-3429
Email: info@calnorthern.edu
Internet: www.calnorthern.edu

Accredited by the State Bar of California in 1992, Cal Northern School of Law remains a relatively new addition to the legal community. Situated in Chico, Cal Northern was formed in response to the need for an evening law school in Northern California—some students faithfully commute two hours each night just to attend. The faculty, trial lawyers, and judges from the court systems of Butte, Sutter, and Shasta counties, also show unflagging determination to ensure that Cal Northern continues to provide quality legal education to its students. In addition to the traditional foundations of a J.D. degree, courses also cover relevant lawyering skills such as interviewing, fact gathering, research advocacy, negotiations, and even considerations for opening a solo practice.

According to almost every respondent, their school is more than just a great bargain. Praise for the faculty and administration was adamant, primarily for the sincere concern they display for the law students. The students were thrilled to be learning from actual practitioners, rather than law school academics. In addition to mentioning the "special effort to be approachable" made by the faculty, students at Cal Northern cited small class sizes as the major influence on commendable faculty-student relations as well as on a close bond between students.

Students who worried about the need for expanded resources at Cal Northern can look forward to the new facility and the construction of a new library about twice the size of the current one. Major complaints focused on the lack of clinical experience available, and the low number of elective course offerings that provide a more specialized legal education.

ADMISSIONS

The Cal Northern School of Law offers would-be law students a good opportunity to pursue a J.D. degree even if they lack some of the credentials to get into more exclusive institutions. Particularly encouraging is Cal Northern's interest in expanding enrollment at the institution. Traditionally enrolling about half of its applicants—already a promising statistic for anyone interested in attending—the school reassures that they actually accept a higher number, realizing that outside commitments usually prevent a number of accepted applicants from attending.

CALIFORNIA PACIFIC SCHOOL OF LAW

1600 Truxtun Avenue, Suite 100
Bakersfield, CA 93301
Tel: 805-322-5297 • Fax: 805-322-3409
Email: inquiry@calpaclaw.edu
Internet: www.calpaclaw.edu

The California Pacific School of Law (CPSL) is housed in the heart of downtown Bakersfield, the center of government of Kern County—California's third-largest county. The CPSL facilities are easily within walking distance of Kern County's Courts and its law library. Bakersfield offers all the amenities of an urban center and the most affordable housing on the West Coast and a friendly "hometown atmosphere."

The CPSL faculty is composed almost entirely of practicing attorneys and judges from the Bakersfield area who bring hands-on, cutting-edge instruction to the classroom as well as a unique perspective on local issues. According to one alum, "The faculty is as impressive, dedicated, and committed as anyone could hope to encounter in the study of law."

The program here "gives students who work full-time, or have a family or other obligations, the opportunity to earn their professional law degree and qualify to sit" for the California State Bar Exam. Students at CPSL come from a diverse range of backgrounds and many spent several years in non-legal careers before deciding to pursue a legal education.

You definitely won't be a number at Cal Pacific. Not only are prospective applicants and current students encouraged to communicate directly with the Dean and the faculty—the Dean's office handles almost all academic advising. In addition, group meetings are held frequently to address student concerns. The Dean and the faculty also assist 1Ls "to identify problem areas and solutions," and a unique Law School Survival Course offers tutoring from alumni and upper-class students.

Though CPSL does not have a formal placement service, many CPSL grads are able to secure clerk positions with local law firms and public agencies. The intimacy of the Bakersfield and Kern County law community can be a great help to students in their job search.

ADMISSIONS

Students may be admitted as either regular students or special students. Regular students need a B.A. from an accredited institution or, in some circumstances, an Associate of Arts degree. Special student admission requires minimum scores on a battery of College Level Examination Program (CLEP) tests and an LSAT score "in the upper 50th percentile."

OVERVIEW

Type of school	private
Environment	metropolis

FINANCIAL FACTS

Tuition	$5,200
Cost of books	$500
Fees	$150

ADMISSIONS

Application fee	$75
Regular application	June 1
Regular notification	rolling

GLENDALE UNIVERSITY COLLEGE OF LAW

220 North Glendale Avenue
Glendale, CA 91206
Tel: 818-247-0770 • Fax: 818-247-0872
Email: admissions@glendalelaw.edu
Internet: www.glendalelaw.edu

OVERVIEW

Type of school	private
Environment	town
Scholastic calendar	quarter
Schedule	part-time only

STUDENTS

Enrollment of law school	130
% male/female	60/40
% out-of-state	0
% part-time	100
% minorities	35
Average age at entry	36

ACADEMICS

Student/faculty ratio	23:1

FINANCIAL FACTS

Tuition	$9,057
Cost of books	$800
% first-year students receiving aid	90
% all students receiving aid	85
% aid that is merit-based	0
% of all students receiving loans	85
% receiving scholarships	no scholarships
Average grant	no grants

ADMISSIONS

# applications received	99
% applicants accepted	35
% acceptees attending	60
Regular application	rolling
Regular notification	rolling
Rolling notification	Yes
Early decision program?	Yes
Admission may be deferred?	Yes
Evening division offered?	Yes
Part-time accepted?	Yes

The Glendale University College of Law (GUCL) is conveniently nestled between the San Fernando and San Gabriel Valleys, a mere nine miles from downtown Los Angeles. GUCL bills itself as "an exceptional school for exceptional students;" it aims to attract those students who have "the desire and ability to study law," but are "foreclosed by their circumstances from attending traditional law schools."

The evening-only J.D. Program here is flexible and affordable; it requires a minimum of four years to complete. GUCL offers evening courses only and students attend classes from 6:30 p.m. to 9:30 p.m. Alternative programs allow students to take "fewer classes at one time (and attend school fewer nights each week) during the onerous first year."

The classes are small (between fifteen and thirty-five students), which allows a great deal of interaction among students and personal attention from instructors. The curriculum, although broad in many respects, is grounded very heavily in substantive law and practical training. The first three years emphasize legal research and legal writing as well as the development of a case "from initial client contact through all the steps and pleadings in a civil lawsuit." Students "write briefs and present oral arguments in appellate moot court." Finally, in the fourth year, all students "argue motions and conduct a trial."

Free tutoring is available year round for 1Ls who need extra help. Faculty members and administrators also commit their time to advise students, and GUCL maintains an "open door" policy to answer questions and assist students.

GUCL's facilities are excellent all-around, including a newly expanded computer lab—the library is noteworthy, as well. Also, Glendale is to be commended for emphasizing legal databases and "the many ways the electronic media can be used in the practice of law."

ADMISSIONS

Although most of the enrolled students at GUCL have at least a Bachelor's degree, students with an Associate's degree (or junior standing at an accredited university) may be considered for admission. On rare occasions, extremely promising candidates with fewer than two years of college credit may also be admitted.

HUMPHREYS COLLEGE SCHOOL OF LAW

6650 Inglewood Avenue
Stockton, CA 95207
Tel: 209-478-0800 • Fax: 209-478-8721

The Humphreys College School of Law was founded in 1951. Its campus is located in a residential area of Stockton, an easily accessible city about eighty miles east of the Bay Area and about fifty miles south of Sacramento, California's state capital. In addition to being convenient for commuters coming from every direction, Humphreys offers a limited number of on-campus student apartments. The city of Stockton also offers abundant, reasonably priced housing.

Classes here are small and faculty members prefer the casebook method of instruction. "Classroom presentations, library research, written exercises, and mock court practices are among the methods used" as well. The Humphreys academic calendar operates on a quarter system; each quarter is twelve weeks long. The course of study tends almost exclusively to the basic concepts of law and the topics that students need to know to pass the California State Bar Exam. The new law library provides access to WESTLAW services. Although Humphreys attracts many recent college graduates, it is also a popular destination for non-traditional students who are returning to pursue a legal education after several years away from the classroom. Many of the students here continue to hold full-time jobs while obtaining their law degrees in the evenings.

ADMISSIONS

According to the admissions staff, "The college prefers that candidates possess a bachelor's degree from an accredited college or university. However, Humphreys does admit students who meet certain other requirements." Humphreys accepts applications from two varieties of candidates: "regular" and "special." Regular applicants must present a bachelor's degree or a minimum of sixty semester hours from an accredited undergraduate college. Special applicants must achieve acceptable scores on three College Level Examination Program (CLEP) tests, submit three letters of recommendation, interview with the Dean of the law school, and pass the "Baby Bar" following the first year of study. All applicants must submit an LSAT score.

OVERVIEW

Type of school	private
Environment	city
Scholastic calendar	quarter
Schedule	part-time only

STUDENTS

Enrollment of law school	96
% male/female	52/48
% out-of-state	0
% part-time	100
% minorities	11
Average age at entry	30

ACADEMICS

Student/faculty ratio	8:1

FINANCIAL FACTS

Tuition	$5,874
Cost of books	$650

ADMISSIONS

# applications received	82
% applicants accepted	51
% acceptees attending	78
Regular application	June 1
Regular notification	rolling
Rolling notification?	Yes
Early decision program?	Yes
Admission may be deferred?	Yes
Evening division offered?	Yes
Part-time accepted?	Yes

JOHN F. KENNEDY UNIVERSITY SCHOOL OF LAW

547 Ygnacio Valley Road
Walnut Creek, CA 94596
Tel: 510-930-6040 • Fax: 510-254-6964
Email: law@jfku.edu
Internet: www.jfku.edu/law

OVERVIEW

Type of school	private
Environment	suburban
Scholastic calendar	semester
Schedule	part-time only

STUDENTS

Enrollment of law school	249
% male/female	50/50
% out-of-state	0
% part-time	100
% minorities	24
Average age at entry	36

ACADEMICS

Student/faculty ratio	30:1

FINANCIAL FACTS

Tuition	$7,823

ADMISSIONS

Regular application	May 30
Evening division offered?	Yes
Part-time accepted?	Yes

John F. Kennedy University School of Law is conveniently located in Walnut Creek, a rapidly growing suburban area about twenty-five miles east of San Francisco. JFKU is the only state-accredited law school between San Francisco and Sacramento that offers both day and evening classes.

JFKU is a great choice for prospective law students who seek to balance the demands of a legal education with family and employment responsibilities. Both the day and evening J.D. programs take four years to complete and first-year students may choose to enter in the fall or at "mid-year." Either way, the first class all students end up in is a preparative course called Introduction to Law. The rest of the required curriculum is relatively straightforward, integrating meat-and-potatoes law courses with various electives, legal writing and research, and jurisprudence. In addition, all students are required to complete hands-on trial and appellate advocacy training courses in order to graduate.

An array of moot court and clinical programs gives students a chance to gain practical experience. "Clinical opportunities are available with courts, government agencies, public interest organizations, and private practitioners," says the admissions staff. "For example, we currently offer a clinical placement at Contra Costa County Legal Services, Contra Costa County, Solano County, and Alameda district attorney and public defender offices."

Small, "dynamic" classes foster "close faculty-student interaction" and "individual participation," and JFKU claims to have assembled a "dedicated" and "eager" crack faculty composed of "some of the most outstanding practicing lawyers and judges in the San Francisco Bay Area" who "bring a wealth of practical experience and teaching ability to the classroom." A free tutoring program is also available six days of the week to 1Ls and 2Ls.

ADMISSIONS

Prospective students may apply for admission in the fall or in midyear. In addition to transcripts, an LSAT score, a fee, and the traditional articles required for consideration, all candidates "must also be interviewed by a designated administrative staff or faculty member." For applicants who are unable to show up in person, this interview can take place over the phone. Candidates with fewer than two years of college credit must meet special requirements in order to be admitted.

UNIVERSITY OF LA VERNE COLLEGE OF LAW

1950 Third Street
La Verne, CA 91750
Tel: 909-596-1848 • Fax: 909-392-2707

It's not often that one university has two law campuses. Such is the case, however, at the University of La Verne. The original campus in San Fernando Valley was established in 1962 under the auspices of the University of San Fernando Valley. It became part of ULV in 1983. The law school at the 26-acre central ULV campus, which is situated about thirty miles east of Los Angeles, became functional in 1970. La Verne has two separate law libraries as well. A shuttle service and electronic communication keep students conveniently connected to both of them.

Nobody said law school was easy, and the standards here are reportedly quite high, but ULV tries to maintain a "kinder, gentler" atmosphere. Classes are small and the faculty is extremely accessible; informal discussions concerning legal questions among professors and students are not uncommon. Legal writing is definitely stressed here, and required in numerous courses. "Courses such as Evidence and Criminal Procedure stress the practical application of legal rules. Trial practice, moot court, lawyering skills, and clinical education programs provide the opportunity for experience in counseling clients and the effective presentation of their varied legal positions." Case study and the Socratic method are also big here.

ADMISSIONS

Most ULV applicants are armed with a bachelor's degree, or its equivalent, from an accredited college or university. Applicants who have earned a minimum of 60 hours of "substantial" college-level credit will also be considered. According to ULV, "A very limited number of 'special students' who lack the [standard] prerequisites may be considered for admission each year. Special students are admitted after successfully passing a College Level Equivalency Program Examination and a score in at least the fiftieth percentile on the LSAT. All students admitted in this category are required by rules of the Committee of Bar Examiners of the State Bar of California to successfully pass a First Year Law Students' Examination before being able to continue beyond the first year of law school study."

OVERVIEW	
Type of school	private
Environment	suburban
Scholastic calendar	semester
Schedule	full-time or part-time

STUDENTS	
Enrollment of law school	400
% male/female	50/50
% part-time	50

ACADEMICS	
Student/faculty ratio	25:1

FINANCIAL FACTS	
Tuition	$12,030
% first-year students receiving aid	40

ADMISSIONS	
# applications received	147
% applicants accepted	60
% acceptees attending	60
Average LSAT	150
Application fee (in/out of state)	$30/$30
Regular application	August 1
Evening division offered?	Yes
Part-time accepted?	Yes
Admission may be deferred?	Yes
Maximum length of deferment	1 year

LINCOLN LAW SCHOOL OF SAN JOSE

2160 Lundy Avenue
San Jose, CA 95131-1852
Tel: 408-434-0727 • Fax: 408-434-0730

OVERVIEW

Type of school	private
Environment	suburban
Scholastic calendar	semester
Schedule	part-time

STUDENTS

Enrollment of law school	170
% male/female	60/40
% part-time	100
% minorities	30
Average age at entry	30

FINANCIAL FACTS

Tuition	5400
Cost of books	200
% of all students receiving loans	1

ADMISSIONS

# applications received	90
% applicants accepted	30
% acceptees attending	25
Early decision program?	No
Admission may be deferred?	No

Lincoln Law School is Silicon Valley's only state-accredited law school devoted exclusively to providing an evening J.D. program. Most of Lincoln's current students are slightly older "non-traditional law students" who have chosen to enter the legal profession after extensive experience in some other field. Students who enroll in the fall finish the program in four years; January enrollees take an additional semester because they are required to start with a "lighter course load" for their first year-and-a-half. Though Lincoln Law does not offer dormitory facilities, San Jose offers a multitude of local housing options. Ample free parking at and around the law school building is available for commuter students.

The "rigorous" first two years of the Lincoln Law program cover the basics: "Contracts, Torts, Civil Procedure, Real Property, Criminal Law, and Constitutional Law." During the second half of Lincoln's four-year program, students concentrate on sharpening their practical lawyering skills "through elective courses and legal internships." The law library contains over 20,000 volumes and a WESTLAW-equipped computer center. Since 1996, Lincoln has provided every student with software, which allows them to log on to Lincoln's WESTLAW program from their home computers.

Tuition scholarships in the amount of $1,000 are awarded to "the Editor-in-Chief of the Lincoln Law Review, the President of the Student Bar Association, and to student tutors in the Academic Support Program. Lincoln also offers $150 book scholarships to the student with the highest grade point average in each class.

ADMISSIONS

Accepted students at Lincoln Law School come in two varieties: Regular students and special students. Regular students must have at least sixty hours of college credit and submit LSAT scores, letters of recommendation, etc. Applicants with fewer than sixty hours of college credit, or no college credit at all, may still be admitted provided they submit acceptable scores on a battery of College Level Examination Program (CLEP) tests. At the end of their first year at Lincoln Law, and in order to continue in the program, special students must also pass the "Baby Bar," a special test of given by the California State Bar.

NEW COLLEGE OF CALIFORNIA SCHOOL OF LAW

50 Fell Street
San Francisco, CA 94102
Tel: 415-863-4111 • Fax: 415-626-5541
Email: lawinfo@infogate.newcollege.edu
Internet: www.newcollege.edu/pro/law/law.html

Since its inception in 1973, the New College of California School of Law has been a haven for leftists, a sort of utopia for liberals with a social-activist streak. The locally reputable and tremendously diverse faculty of this Bay Area law school is composed of attorneys and legal educators who share a strong commitment "to social and political change" and an equally strong desire to educate "socially responsible" public interest lawyers. Over forty percent of the faculty members here are female; one-third represent minority groups; and more than 15 percent are gay or lesbian.

Of the overall enrollment of 160 students, about 55 percent are women and more than 40 percent represent minority groups. A lesbian and gay student contingent is significant as well. And while the law school provides a "small, supportive environment," students are surrounded by the excitement and sophistication of San Francisco. Literally.

New College offers good research facilities and a choice of two programs: full-time (three-year) or part-time (four-year). The curriculum here includes the traditionally required substantive courses, trial advocacy and practical skills courses, and clinical programs both on and off campus. Substantive courses, though they cover the topics tested on the California Bar Exam, generally offer critical analysis on "the role of law in promoting or hindering social change" as well. Counseling, tutorials, and workshops are available to all students. The unique Apprenticeship Program "places advanced students in law offices and agencies to earn academic credit while learning about the practice of law." The on-campus Criminal Defense Program gives 3Ls the opportunity to provide direct legal represent clients directly.

ADMISSIONS

"New College School of Law seeks to attract socially concerned students from diverse backgrounds who intend to pursue careers in public interest law." Any candidate able to convey a passion for either, or preferably, both will have a decisive edge over other applicants. While most applicants hold a Bachelor's degree, New College doesn't rule out applicants "with less than four years of college and significant life experience."

OVERVIEW

Type of school	private
Environment	city
Scholastic calendar	semester
Schedule	full-time or part-time

STUDENTS

Enrollment of law school	160
% male/female	45/55
% part-time	25
% minorities	43

ACADEMICS

Student/faculty ratio	40:1

FINANCIAL FACTS

Tuition	$8,515

ADMISSIONS

# applications received	200
% applicants accepted	35
% acceptees attending	71
Application fee	$45
Regular application	March 1
Evening division offered?	No
Part-time accepted?	Yes

SAN FRANCISCO LAW SCHOOL

20 Haight Street
San Francisco, CA 94102
Tel: 415-626-5550 • Fax: 415-626-5584
Email: admin@sfls.edu
Internet: www.sfls.edu

OVERVIEW

Type of school	private
Environment	city
Scholastic calendar	semester
Schedule	part-time only

STUDENTS

Enrollment of law school	178
% male/female	60/40
% part-time	100
% minorities	31
Average age at entry	34

FINANCIAL FACTS

Tuition	$4,200
Cost of books	$200
Fees	$120

ADMISSIONS

Application fee	$50
Regular application	June 15
Admission may be deferred?	No
Evening division offered?	Yes
Part-time accepted?	Yes

San Francisco Law School (SFLS) is located in its own building near the corner of Haight and Market Streets, in a perennially happening Bay Area neighborhood. SFLS is closely affiliated with the nationally better-known Hastings School of Law. The two schools have considered merging in the past so that SFLS could become the evening division of Hastings, but nothing has ever come of these proposals. As a result, SFLS has been able "to follow its own tradition of offering a low cost, quality legal education to law students who, for various reasons, prefer not to attend a three-year, daytime law school." The regular four-year program and the extended four-and-a-half-year program here are specifically planned for students who are unable to commit to a full-time course of study.

SFLS was incorporated in 1909 and was one of the first law schools in California to implement an admissions policy of actively seeking out and enrolling both women and students from under represented minority groups. "Today," according to the SFLS administration, "the school's ongoing commitment to diversity is still unmistakable." The average student here is thirty-something years old and has spent a good chunk of time in another career-track profession. Many students have family responsibilities as well. About half of the students who begin studying law here go on to complete the program. Of those graduates, approximately 75 percent pass the California State Bar Examination.

The faculty at San Francisco Law School is composed of "about thirty prominent Bay Area judges and attorneys, most of whom practice in the subjects they teach." As the enrollment here is only 178, classes tend to be small. The curriculum is, for the most part, very traditional and straightforward. The law library is somewhat small, but students here are eligible to use the larger library at Hastings College of the Law.

ADMISSIONS

According to the folks at the admissions office, "San Francisco Law School admits students with demonstrated academic abilities and high potential for success in law school. Acceptance to the law school is determined by the admissions committee, which takes into account the LSAT score, undergraduate GPA, professional background, and personal history of each applicant.

San Joaquin College of Law

Joyce Morodomi, Admissions Officer
901 Fifth Street
Clovis, CA 93612-1312
Tel: 209-323-2100 • Fax: 209-323-5566

During its brief twenty-eight year history, approximately 90 percent of the graduates of San Joaquin College of Law (SJCL) have passed the California Bar Examination. Ninety percent. This rate is easily comparable with some of the most distinguished and prestigious law schools in the state, and the entire nation as well. Since its establishment in 1969, SJCL's success is evident. It is the center of legal study for both law students and practicing attorneys in the fast-growing, pleasant San Joaquin Valley. No comparable institution exists within 120 miles in any direction—this is especially true since San Joaquin just moved into a new facility in 1996.

A little over 200 students attend SJCL on a full- or part-time basis. In addition to offering a traditional three-year program, SJCL offers a flexible part-time law course of study, which can be completed in four or five years. The faculty is composed of six full-time members and over thirty adjunct faculty members, all of whom practice law in the Fresno area.

Clinical programs include a Regional Family Law and Mediation Center, through which students facilitate the non-adversarial resolution of real-world problems. In addition, SJCL maintains the Fresno County Small Claims Advisor's Office, which offers legal assistance to members of the Fresno community in their legal battles. SJCL also brags that its students consistently take some of (if not all of) the highest honors in national moot court competitions against big-time, ABA-accredited schools. The San Joaquin Agricultural Law Review is the only legal journal in the country devoted to issues of agricultural law. A very active placement office assists many students in securing clerking positions to supplement their law studies with practical experience working.

ADMISSIONS

The admissions process at San Joaquin School of Law is very similar to the process at the handful of schools in this book approved only for the California State Bar but not by the American Bar Association. Under nearly all circumstances, successful candidates for admission possess a Bachelor's degree, a decent LSAT score, a high level of maturity, and a solid motivation to learn the law.

OVERVIEW

Type of school	private
Environment	metropolis
Scholastic calendar	semester
Schedule	full-time or part-time

STUDENTS

Enrollment of law school	209
% male/female	54/46
% part-time	85
% minorities	20
Average age at entry	33

ACADEMICS

Academic specialties:
Commercial, Criminal, Environmental, International, Labor, Taxation, Other

FINANCIAL FACTS

% first-year students receiving aid	75
% all students receiving aid	75
% of all students receiving loans	75
% of all students receiving assistantships	0
Average graduation debt	$50,000

ADMISSIONS

# applications received	132
% applicants accepted	102
% acceptees attending	74
Average LSAT	49
LSAT range	139–168
Average undergrad GPA	3.0
GPA range	2.0–4.0
Application fee	$40
Early application	rolling
Early notification	rolling
Regular application	June 30
Regular notification	rolling
Rolling notification	Yes
Early decision program?	No
Admission may be deferred?	Yes
Maximum length of deferment	1 year
Evening division offered?	Yes
Part-time accepted?	Yes

University of West Los Angeles

1155 West Arbor Vitae Street
Inglewood, CA 90301-2902
Tel: 310-215-3339 • Fax: 310-342-5295

The Law School at the University of West Los Angeles was founded in 1966. The first entering class consisted of about 100 students, a handful of instructors, and a small facility in Culver City. Since then, "UWLA has grown to become a respected college with two schools, nearly 4,000 graduates, and over 700 students." A groundbreaking School of Paralegal Studies was added in 1971.

The law school's stated mission is to provide legal education programs to those who must study part-time. "UWLA's commitment is reflected in its "non-exclusive admissions policies, flexible and varied schedules, and reasonable tuition rates." The outstanding law library here contains over 34,000 bound volumes as well as thousands of microfiche. It provides access to WESTLAW and other searchable databases, and it's open to the public. UWLA also maintains a Legal Aid Clinic, which "offers legal advice to the community and assistance to people representing themselves in court," and allows students to gain a wealth of real world knowledge and practical training.

The Law School places a great deal of value on diversity, boasting a "high enrollment of minorities, women, and adult students." Many of the students here have chosen to pursue a legal education after extensive experience in a different profession, or after raising families. Also, most UWLA students "are eligible for assistance through the Federal Stafford Loan Program."

ADMISSIONS

You can enroll at UWLA as a "regular student" or as a "special student." Regular student status can be obtained by applicants who have successfully completed sixty or more semester hours of undergraduate study. If you haven't completed your Bachelor's degree, though, you'll need to score at or above the 31st percentile on the LSAT.

Applicants who do not qualify as regular students may still enroll if they are accepted as special students. In addition to scoring at or above the 31st percentile on the LSAT, candidates for special student status must achieve acceptable scores on a handful of College-Level Examination Program (CLEP) tests and successfully pass the "Baby Bar" at the end of their first year of legal study.

WESTERN STATE UNIVERSITY COLLEGE OF LAW

P.O. Box 4310
1111 North State College Boulevard
Fullerton, CA 92631
Tel: 714-738-1000 • Fax: 714-441-1748
Email: adminfo@wfulaw.edu
Internet: www.wfulaw.edu

The campus at Western State University College of Law inhabits four beautiful acres in the city of Fullerton, a thriving Orange County community of approximately 125,000 residents.

Western State offers both full-time and part-time courses of study and boasts one of the largest law student populations in the state of California, or anywhere else for that matter. About two-thirds of the over 1,000 students here are part-time, evening students with first careers already under their belts.

The curriculum here relies heavily on the Socratic method and aims to train capable attorneys with practical skills. As is the case at many larger law schools, once students at WSU complete their substantive requirements, several concentration areas and elective courses are offered. Externship opportunities in association with two Appeals courts are available. Also, WSU recently completed construction of a brand-new, 31,000 square-foot, state-of-the-art library.

WSU's career services office is solid all-around. In addition to job placement, it "provides seminars and workshops, career counseling, assistance in student resume writing and help in preparing students for employment interviews."

ADMISSIONS

Here's what the admissions office has to say: "Western State University College of Law examines each applicant's overall potential for success in law school by evaluating several factors in addition to numerical indicators. While undergraduate grade point averages and LSAT scores are very important, the admissions committee gives considerable weight to other factors such as maturity, oral expression, employment background, community involvement and motivation."

OVERVIEW

Type of school	private
Environment	suburban
Scholastic calendar	semester
Schedule	full-time or part-time

STUDENTS

Enrollment of law school	1,191
% male/female	43.2/56.8
% part-time	71.2
% minorities	34
Average age at entry	34

ACADEMICS

FINANCIAL FACTS

Tuition	$8,625
Cost of books	$500
% all students receiving aid	80

ADMISSIONS

# applications received	811
% applicants accepted	52
% acceptees attending	27
Application fee	$35
Regular application	rolling
Regular notification	rolling
Rolling notification	Yes
Early decision program?	No
Admission may be deferred?	No
Evening division offered?	Yes

SCHOOL INDEXES

ALPHABETICAL INDEX

ABA SCHOOLS

A

Akron, University of | 146
Alabama, University of | 148
American University | 150
Arizona State University | 152
Arizona, University of | 154
Arkansas at Little Rock,
University of | 156
Arkansas, Fayetteville,
University of | 158

B

Baltimore, University of | 160
Baylor University | 162
Boston College | 164
Boston University | 166
Brigham Young University | 168
Brooklyn Law School | 170

C

California Western | 172
California, Berkeley, University of | 174
California, Davis, University of | 176
California, Los Angeles,
University of | 178
California, University of | 180
Campbell University | 182
Capital University | 184
Case Western Reserve University | 186
Catholic America, University of | 188
Chicago, University of | 190
Chicago-Kent School of Law | 192
Cincinnati, University of | 194
City University of New York | 196
Cleveland State University | 198
Colorado, University of | 200
Columbia University | 202
Connecticut, University of | 204
Cornell University | 206
Creighton University | 208

D

Dayton, University of | 210
Denver, University of | 212
DePaul University | 214
Detroit College of Law | 216
Detroit Mercy, University of | 218

Dickinson School of Law | 220
Drake University | 222
Duke University | 224
Duquesne University | 226

E

Emory University | 228

F

Florida State University | 230
Florida, University of | 232
Fordham University | 234
Franklin Pierce Law Center | 236

G

George Mason University | 238
George Washington University | 240
Georgetown University | 242
Georgia State University | 244
Georgia, University of | 246
Golden Gate University | 248
Gonzaga University | 250

H

Hamline University | 252
Harvard University | 254
Hawaii, Manoa, University of | 256
Hofstra University | 258
Houston, University of | 260
Howard University | 262

I

Idaho, University of | 264
Illinois, University of | 266
Indiana University, Bloomington | 268
Indiana University, Indianapolis | 270
Iowa, University of | 272

J

John Marshall Law School | 274

K

Kansas, University of | 276
Kentucky, University of | 278

L

Lewis and Clark College | 280
Louisiana State University | 282

Louisville, University of | 284
Loyola Marymount University | 286
Loyola University, Chicago | 288
Loyola University, New Orleans | 290

M

Maine, University of | 292
Marquette University | 294
Maryland, University of | 296
Memphis, University of | 298
Mercer University | 300
Miami, University of | 302
Michigan, University of | 304
Minnesota, University of | 306
Mississippi College | 308
Mississippi, University of | 310
Missouri, Columbia, University of | 312
Missouri, Kansas City,
University of | 314
Montana, University of | 316

N

Nebraska, University of | 318
New England School of Law | 320
New Mexico, University of | 322
New York Law School | 324
New York University | 326
North Carolina Central University | 328
North Carolina, University of | 330
North Dakota, University of | 332
Northeastern University | 334
Northern Illinois University | 336
Northern Kentucky University | 338
Northwestern University | 340
Notre Dame, University of | 342
Nova Southeastern University | 344

O

Ohio Northern University | 346
Ohio State University | 348
Oklahoma City University | 350
Oklahoma, University of | 352
Oregon, University of | 354

P

Pace University | 356
Pacific, University of the | 358
Pennsylvania, University of | 360
Pepperdine University | 362
Pittsburgh, University of | 364

Q

Quinnipiac College   366

R

Richmond, University of   368
Rutgers University, Camden   370
Rutgers University, Newark   372

S

Samford University   374
San Diego, University of   376
San Francisco, University of   378
Santa Clara University   380
Seattle University   382
Seton Hall University   384
South Carolina, University of   386
South Dakota, University of   388
South Texas College of Law   390
Southern California,
    University of   392
Southern Illinois University   394
Southern Methodist University   396
Southern University   398
Southwestern University   400
St. John's University   402
St. Louis University   404
St. Mary's University   406
Stanford University   408
State University of New York
    at Buffalo   410
Stetson University   412
Suffolk University   414
Syracuse University   416

T

Temple University   418
Tennessee, University of   420
Texas Southern University   422
Texas Tech University   424
Texas, University of   426
Thomas Jefferson School of Law   428
Thomas M. Cooley Law School   430
Toledo, University of   432
Touro College   434
Tulane University   436
Tulsa, University of   438

U

Union University Albany
    Law School   440
Utah, University of   442

V

Valparaiso University   444

Vanderbilt University   446
Vermont Law School   448
Villanova University   450
Virginia, University of   452

W

Wake Forest University   454
Washburn University   456
Washington and Lee University   458
Washington University   460
Washington, University of   462
Wayne State University   464
West Virginia University   466
Western New England College   468
Whittier College   470
Widener University   472
Willamette University   474
William and Mary, College of   476
William Mitchell College of Law   478
Wisconsin, University of   480
Wyoming, University of   482

Y

Yale University   484
Yeshiva University   486

CBA SCHOOLS

C

Cal Northern   496
California Pacific   497

G

Glendale University
    College of Law   498

H

Humphreys College School of Law   499

J

John F. Kennedy University   500

L

La Verne, University of   501
Lincoln Law School of San Jose   502

N

New College of California   503

S

San Francisco Law School   504
San Joaquin College of Law   505

W

West Los Angeles, University of   506
Western State University   507

STATE INDEX

ALABAMA
Alabama, University of   148
Samford University   374

ARIZONA
Arizona State University   152
Arizona, University of   154

ARKANSAS
Arkansas at Little Rock,
    University of   156
Arkansas, Fayetteville,
    University of   158

CALIFORNIA
California Western   172
California, Berkeley, University of   174
California, Davis, University of   176
California, Los Angeles,
    University of   178
California, University of   180
Golden Gate University   248
Loyola Marymount University   286
Pacific, University of the   358
Pepperdine University   362
San Diego, University of   376
San Francisco, University of   378
Santa Clara University   380
Southern California, University of   392
Southwestern University   400
Stanford University   408
Thomas Jefferson School of Law   428
Whittier College   470
Cal Northern School of Law   496
California Pacific School of Law   497
Glendale University
    College of Law   498
Humphreys College
    School of Law   499
John F. Kennedy University   500
La Verne, University of   501
Lincoln Law School of San Jose   502
New College of California   503
San Francisco Law School   504
San Joaquin College of Law   505
West Los Angeles, University of   506
Western State University   507

COLORADO
Colorado, University of   200
Denver, University of   212

CONNECTICUT
Connecticut, University of   204
Quinnipiac College   366
Yale University   484

DELAWARE
Widener University   472

DISTRICT OF COLUMBIA
American University   150
Catholic America, University of   188
George Washington University   240
Georgetown University   242
Howard University   262

FLORIDA
Florida State University   230
Florida, University of   232
Miami, University of   302
Nova Southeastern University   344
Stetson University   412

GEORGIA
Emory University   228
Georgia State University   244
Georgia, University of   246
Mercer University   300

HAWAII
Hawaii, Manoa, University of   256

IDAHO
Idaho, University of   264

ILLINOIS
Chicago, University of   190
Chicago-Kent School of Law   192
DePaul University   214
Illinois, University of   266
John Marshall Law School   274
Loyola University, Chicago   288
Northern Illinois University   336
Northwestern University   340
Southern Illinois University   394

INDIANA
Indiana University, Bloomington   268
Indiana University, Indianapolis   270
Notre Dame, University of   342
Valparaiso University   444

IOWA
Drake University   222
Iowa, University of   272

KANSAS
Kansas, University of   276
Washburn University   456

KENTUCKY
Kentucky, University of   278
Louisville, University of   284
Northern Kentucky University   338

LOUISIANA
Louisiana State University   282
Loyola University, New Orleans   290
Southern University   398
Tulane University   436

MAINE
Maine, University of   292

MARYLAND
Baltimore, University of   160
Maryland, University of   296

MASSACHUSETTS
Boston College   164
Boston University   166
Harvard University   254
New England School of Law   320
Northeastern University   334
Suffolk University   414
Western New England College   468

MICHIGAN
Detroit College of Law   216
Detroit Mercy, University of   218
Michigan, University of   304
Thomas M. Cooley Law School   430
Wayne State University   464

MINNESOTA
Hamline University   252
Minnesota, University of   306
William Mitchell College of Law   478

MISSISSIPPI

Mississippi College	308
Mississippi, University of	310

MISSOURI

Missouri, Columbia, University of	312
Missouri, Kansas City, University of	314
St. Louis University	404
Washington University	460

MONTANA

Montana, University of	316

NEBRASKA

Creighton University	208
Nebraska, University of	318

NEW HAMPSHIRE

Franklin Pierce Law Center	236

NEW JERSEY

Rutgers University, Camden	370
Rutgers University, Newark	372
Seton Hall University	384

NEW MEXICO

New Mexico, University of	322

NEW YORK

Brooklyn Law School	170
City University of New York	196
Columbia University	202
Cornell University	206
Fordham University	234
Hofstra University	258
New York Law School	324
New York University	326
Pace University	356
St. John's University	402
State University of New York at Buffalo	410
Syracuse University	416
Touro College	434
Union University Albany Law School	440
Yeshiva University	486

NORTH CAROLINA

Campbell University	182
Duke University	224
North Carolina Central University	328
North Carolina, University of	330
Wake Forest University	454

NORTH DAKOTA

North Dakota, University of	332

OHIO

Akron, University of	146
Capital University	184
Case Western Reserve University	186
Cincinnati, University of	194
Cleveland State University	198
Dayton, University of	210
Ohio Northern University	346
Ohio State University	348
Toledo, University of	432

OKLAHOMA

Oklahoma City University	350
Oklahoma, University of	352
Tulsa, University of	438

OREGON

Lewis and Clark College	280
Oregon, University of	354
Willamette University	474

PENNSYLVANIA

Dickinson School of Law	220
Duquesne University	226
Pennsylvania, University of	360
Pittsburgh, University of	364
Temple University	418
Villanova University	450

SOUTH CAROLINA

South Carolina, University of	386

SOUTH DAKOTA

South Dakota, University of	388

TENNESSEE

Memphis, University of	298
Tennessee, University of	420
Vanderbilt University	446

TEXAS

Baylor University	162
Houston, University of	260
South Texas College of Law	390
Southern Methodist University	396
St. Mary's University	406
Texas Southern University	422
Texas Tech University	424
Texas, University of	426

UTAH

Brigham Young University	168
Utah, University of	442

VERMONT

Vermont Law School	448

VIRGINIA

George Mason University	238
Richmond, University of	368
Virginia, University of	452
Washington and Lee University	458
William and Mary	476

WASHINGTON (STATE)

Gonzaga University	250
Seattle University	382
Washington, University of	462

WEST VIRGINIA

West Virginia University	466

WISCONSIN

Marquette University	294
Wisconsin, University of	480

WYOMING

Wyoming, University of	482

BIBLIOGRAPHY

Chapter 5

1. A Review of Legal Education in the United States—Fall 1995, The American Bar Association, Chicago, IL, 1996.

2. *Women in Legal Education: A Comparison of the Law School Performance and the Law School Experiences of Women and Men*; Linda F. Wightman, LSAC Research Report Series; 1996; Law School Admissions Council, Inc. Newtown, PA.

3. "Diversity Dilemma," Christine Riedel, *The National Jurist*, April/May 1996, p.14-16.

4. Association of American Law Schools Statistical Report on Law School Faculty and Candidates for Law Faculty Positions 1995-96, www.aaals.org/stats 3, Table 2B.

5. "Affirmative Action: New Spin on an Old Trick," Monroe Freedman, New Jersey Law Journal, July 11, 1991.

6. *Still Unequal: The Shameful Truth About Women and Justice in America*, Lorraine Dusky; Crown Publishers, 1996, New York, NY.

7. *Critical Race Theory: The Key Writings that Formed the Movement*, Edited by Kimberle Crenshaw, Neil Gotonda, Gary Peller, Kendall Thomas; The New Press, New York, NY 1995.

8. "The Tower of Babel: Bridging the Divide Between Critical Race Theory and 'Mainstream' Civil Rights Scholarship," Eleanor Marie Brown, Student Note, The Yale Law Journal, Volume 105, p. 513 (1995).

9. The *Hopwood v. Texas*, 78 F. 3rd 932 (5th Cir. 1996), reh'g en banc den., 84 F. 3rd 720 (5th Cir. 1996) , cert. den., 116 S. Ct. 2581 (1996).

10. "High Court Refuses to Hear Appeal of Ruling That Barred Considering Race in Admissions," Douglas Lederman and Stephen Burd, *Chronicle of Higher Education*, July 12, 1996.

11. *DeFunis v. Odegaard*, 416 U.S. 312 (1974).

12. *Regents of The University of California v. Bakke*, 438 U.S. 265 (1978).

13. *Approved Law Schools: Statistical Information on American Bar Association Approved Law Schools*, 1988 Edition, Rick L. Morgan and Kurt Snyder, Esq., Editors, MacMillan, New York, 1997.

Chapter 6

14. *Women in Legal Education: A Comparison of the Law School Performance and Law School Experiences of Women and Men*; Linda F. Wightman, LSAC Research Report Series; Law School Admission Council, Inc., Newtown, PA, 1996.

15. Elusive Equality: The Experiences of Women in Legal Education; American Bar Association Commission on Women in the Profession; American Bar Association, Chicago, IL, January 1996.

16. Class of 1995 Employment Report and Salary Survey; National Association for Law Placement; NALP, Washington, DC, 1996.

17. "Law Schools Where Women Can Excel," Linda R. Hirshman; *Glamour*, pg. 122, September 1995.

18. "Is Law School Still a Man's World?" Shanie Latham; *The National Jurist*, pg. 22-29, Oct./Nov. 1995.

19. "The Legal Education of Twenty Women," Louise Melling and Catherine Weiss; Stanford Law Review, Vol. 40, #5, May 1988.

20. *Still Unequal: the Shameful Truth About Women and Justice in America*, Lorraine Dusky; Crown Publishers, New York, NY, 1996.

21. "Becoming Gentlemen: Women's Experiences at One Ivy League Law School," Lani Guinier, Michelle Fine, Jane Balin, Ann Bartow, and Deborah Lee Stachel; University of Pennsylvania Law Review, Nov. 1994.

22. Unfinished Business: Overcoming the Sisyphus Factor, American Bar Association Commission on Women in the Profession; American Bar Association, Chicago, IL, 1995.

23. Women in the Law: A Look at the Numbers, American Bar Association Commission on Women in the Profession; Dec. 1995, American Bar Association, Chicago, IL.

24. "Symposium: Is the Law Male," Linda R. Hirshman, Editor; Chicago-Kent Law Review, Vol. 69, #2, 1993.

25. "Strength in Diversity: Feminist Theoretical Approaches to Child Custody and Same-sex Relationships," Mary Becker; Stetson Law Review, Vol. 23, #3, Summer 1994.

26. "Gender Law," Katharine T. Bartlett; Duke Journal of Gender, Law, and Policy, Vol. 1, 1994.

UPCOMING READING

1. Becker, Mary. "Questions Women (and Men) Should Ask When Selecting a Law School," Wisconsin Women's Law Journal. Projected publication date: 1997.

2. Hirshman, Linda. *A Woman's Guide to Law Schools*. Projected publication date: 1998.

3. Sander, Richard. Professor Sander is currently at UCLA Law School and will be submitting a report to LSAC that is based on a representative national sample of 30 law schools.

ABOUT THE AUTHORS

David Adam Hollander and Rob Tallia, the co-authors of this book, have been running The Princeton Review Law Division, Worldwide for the past two years.

David wrote chapters 1, 4, 5 and, 7. Rob wrote chapters 2, 3, and 6. David and Rob wrote chapter 8 together.

NOTES

NOTES

NOTES

NOTES

Trust your future *to* snail mail?

This is your life we're talking about!
Send your law school applications with FedEx.®

Don't trust your law school applications to just anyone. Use FedEx. That way you'll know your applications were delivered promptly—you can even track your packages on-line at www.fedex.com. For a FREE FedEx Fast Apps Shipping Kit—including airbills,

envelopes, and everything you need—call us toll free at (888)321-3557. Every time you send a package with FedEx, you get a chance to win great stuff from Bose® and Panasonic.® It's all part of our Fast Apps Sweepstakes. You can ship for a chance to win through 3/30/98.

Call **(888)321-3557** for your FREE FedEx Fast Apps Shipping Kit today.

For details and alternate means of entry see official rules below. See current FedEx® Service Guide for terms and conditions of carriage.

FedEx.®
Federal Express

The Way The World Works.®

FIND US...

International

Hong Kong
4/F Sun Hung Kai Centre
30 Harbour Road, Wan Chai,
Hong Kong
Tel: (011)85-2-517-3016

Japan
Fuji Building 40, 15-14
Sakuragaokacho, Shibuya Ku,
Tokyo 150, Japan
Tel: (011)81-3-3463-1343

Korea
Tae Young Bldg, 944-24,
Daechi- Dong, Kangnam-Ku
The Princeton Review- ANC
Seoul, Korea 135-280,
South Korea
Tel: (011)82-2-554-7763

Mexico City
PR Mex S De RL De Cv
Guanajuato 228 Col. Roma
06700 Mexico D.F., Mexico
Tel: 525-564-9468

Montreal
666 Sherbrooke St.
West, Suite 202
Montreal, QC H3A 1E7 Canada
Tel: (514) 499-0870

Pakistan
1 Bawa Park - 90 Upper Mall
Lahore, Pakistan
Tel: (011)92-42-571-2315

Spain
Pza. Castilla, 3 - 5º A, 28046
Madrid, Spain
Tel: (011)341-323-4212

Taiwan
155 Chung Hsiao East Road
Section 4 - 4th Floor,
Taipei R.O.C., Taiwan
Tel: (011)886-2-751-1243

Thailand
Building One, 99 Wireless Road
Bangkok, Thailand 10330
Tel: (662) 256-7080

Toronto
1240 Bay Street, Suite 300
Toronto M5R 2A7 Canada
Tel: (800) 495-7737
Tel: (716) 839-4391

Vancouver
4212 University Way NE,
Suite 204
Seattle, WA 98105
Tel: (206) 548-1100

National (U.S.)

We have over 60 offices around the U.S. and
run courses in over 400 sites. For courses and
locations within the U.S. call **1 (800) 2/Review**
and you will be routed to the nearest office.

Look!

Did you know that The Microsoft Network gives you one free month?

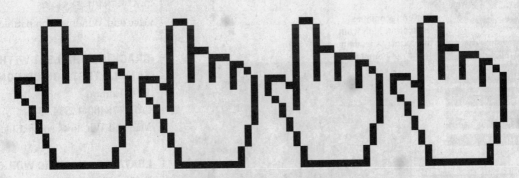

Not online? Call us at 1-800-FREE MSN. We'll send you a free CD to get you going. Then, you can explore the World Wide Web for one month, free. Exchange e-mail with your family and friends. Play games, book airline tickets, handle finances, go car shopping, explore old hobbies and discover new ones. The world online is fun. And for one month, it's free.

Some restrictions apply. Call 1-800-FREE MSN for details. Dept. 3197.

The Microsoft Network

MORE EXPERT ADVICE FROM THE PRINCETON REVIEW

If you want to give yourself the best chance for getting into the law school of your choice, we can help you get the highest test scores, make the most informed choices, and make the most of your experience once you get there. We can even help you make a career move that will let you use your skills and education to their best advantage.

CRACKING THE LSAT
1998 Edition
0-679-78402-0 $20.00

CRACKING THE LSAT WITH SAMPLE TESTS ON DISK
1998 Edition
0-679-78401-2 $34.95
Mac and Windows compatible

CRACKING THE LSAT WITH SAMPLE TESTS ON CD-ROM
1998 Edition
0-679-78400-4 $34.95
Mac and Windows compatible

LSAT/GRE ANALYTIC WORKOUT
0-679-77358-4 $16.00

THE BEST LAW SCHOOLS
The Buyer's Guide to Law Schools
1998 Edition
0-679-77781-4 $20.00

PRE-LAW SCHOOL COMPANION
0-679-77372-X $15.00

LAW SCHOOL COMPANION
0-679-76150-0 $15.00

ALTERNATIVE CAREERS FOR LAWYERS
0-679-77870-5 $15.00